KV-510-939

LIVERPOOL HOPE
UNIVERSITY COLLEGE

LIBRARY

PO BOX 95
LIVERPOOL

CLHBGC

Developing with Asymetrix ToolBook

Applied Programming Theory

Stephen F. Hustedde
Arizona State University

INTEGRATED MEDIA GROUP

An Imprint of Wadsworth Publishing Company

I(T)P® An International Thomson Publishing Company

Belmont • Albany • Bonn • Boston • Cincinnati • Detroit • London • Madrid • Melbourne
Mexico City • New York • Paris • San Francisco • Singapore • Tokyo • Toronto • Washington

New Media Publisher: Kathy Shields
Assistant Editor: Tamara Huggins
Production Services Coordinator: Gary Mcdonald
Production: Robin Lockwood & Associates
Print Buyer: Karen Hunt
Permissions Editor: Peggy Meehan
Copy Editor: Toni Murray
Cover: Craig Hanson
Printer: Malloy Lithographing, Inc.

Copyright © 1996 by Wadsworth Publishing Company
A Division of International Thomson Publishing Inc.

I(T)P   The ITP logo is a registered trademark under license.

Printed in the United States of America
1 2 3 4 5 6 7 8 9 10

For more information, contact Wadsworth Publishing Company:

Wadsworth Publishing Company
10 Davis Drive
Belmont, California 94002, USA

International Thomson Publishing Europe
Berkshire House 168-173
High Holborn
London, WC1V 7AA, England

Thomas Nelson Australia
102 Dodds Street
South Melbourne 3205
Victoria, Australia

Nelson Canada
1120 Birchmount Road
Scarborough, Ontario
Canada M1K 5G4

International Thomson Editores
Campos Eliseos 385, Piso 7
Col. Polanco
11560 México D.F. México

International Thomson Publishing GmbH
Königswinterer Strasse 418
53227 Bonn, Germany

International Thomson Publishing Asia
221 Henderson Road
#05-10 Henderson Building
Singapore 0315

International Thomson Publishing Japan
Hirakawacho Kyowa Building, 3F
2-2-1 Hirakawacho
Chiyoda-ku, Tokyo 102, Japan

All rights reserved. No part of this work covered by the copyright hereon may be reproduced or used in any form or by any means—graphic, electronic, or mechanical, including photocopying, recording, taping, or information storage and retrieval systems—without the written permission of the publisher.

Library of Congress Cataloging-in-Publication Data

Hustedde, Stephen F.
     Developing with Asymetrix ToolBook : applied programming theory /
  Stephen F. Hustedde
          p.   cm.
     Includes index.
     ISBN 0-534-26046-2
     1. Object-oriented programming (Computer science)   2. Computer
  software—Development.   3. ToolBook.   I. Title.
  QA76.64.H88   1996
  005.265—dc20
                                                95-20636

To my parents,
Louis and Regina Hustedde

Contents

Contents

Section III: Programming

13 Variables and Other Containers 173

14 Handling Events and Input/Output 187

15 Performing Mathematical Calculations 205

Section IV: Appendices

Preface and Acknowledgments

As a child, one of my favorite toys was an Erector Set, a toolbox filled with various metal objects, wheels, pulleys, motors, nuts, and bolts. With my Erector Set, I could create a variety of other toys from working cranes to vehicles. It was a toy to create other toys. Likewise, Asymetrix Toolbook is a software program used to create other programs. Like the Erector Set of my youth, Toolbook has become one of my favorite toys of adulthood.

As an instructional technologist at Arizona State University, I spend the majority of my day developing courseware. I believe technology and computers can play a pivotal role, in every curriculum, in enhancing the education of our students. That is one of the reasons for writing this book. I believe the computer can be a more valuable tool in the classroom than the chalkboard or the textbook. One hope for this book is that it will be a starting point for educators who wish to use the classroom computer as a tool to enhance both their teaching and the students' learning.

The average computer user thinks of programming and software development to be beyond reach. In truth that is not the case, and Toolbook puts that world within easy grasp. Although programming experience is helpful, this book assumes no such knowledge. It is possible to develop a ToolBook application without any programming, but for advanced applications programming with ToolBook's OpenScript language becomes essential. The emphasis of this text is on programming with OpenScript. This text is designed to teach the basic concepts of programming theory along with the syntax of OpenScript. Practical examples, illustrations, software tutorials accompanying each chapter, hands-on projects, and useful reference materials are features that I hope will help the reader become a proficient ToolBook developer.

This book has come to fruition through the contributions of many people. I thank Kathy Shields, Tamara Huggins, Stacy Steiner, and all the other people at Wadsworth who have had a part in the production of this text. A heartfelt thanks goes to Robin Lockwood and Toni Murray for their thorough and thoughtful editing of the manuscript. I especially thank Chris MacCrate who, in the four years I've worked for him, has always challenged my thinking and offered me incredible freedom to dream, experiment, be creative, and even fail. I thank Chris, as well as Larry Conrad, for his support of this project; Rick Birney for sharing with me his ToolBook expertise and for his encouragement; Nancy Tribbensee for her legal advice; and Dr. Larry North for helping stretch my ToolBook knowledge and creativity as we collaborated together on courseware, as well as for his encouragement and patience. I thank Wilhelmina Savenye, Peter Lafford, and Dan Brink for beta-testing the text and software in their classes. A note of appreciation goes to their students, and to Bill McBrayer, Nadia Hsiung, and Gary Sprunk for their suggestions and editing assistance. I'd also like to express my gratitude to Carole Statham and the folks at Asymetrix who have created a wonderful product backed up with solid technical support. I'd like to also thank the following reviewers: Phyllis J. Broughton, Pitt Community College; Donald L. Jordan, Lamar University; Ali Nazemi, Roanoke College; Brian Scarbeau, Beacon College; and Tim Sylvester, Glendale Community College. Finally, I thank Kari Chesney, Guy Mullins, Mark Ahn, Eric Pasternak, Jennifer Ramirez, Jeff Meade, Starr Swanson, Jeremy Rowe, George Watson, Jon Koehler, Les Satterthwaite, Louis and Regina Hustedde, Dr. Ronald J. Hustedde, Rick and Debbie Kelly, Kevin Crane, Beth Myers, and the many other colleagues, family, and friends who have encouraged and supported me throughout this project.

Section I
Browsing

LIVERPOOL HOPE ⎯⎯ ⎯LLEGE

Chapter 1

In the Beginning
What Is ToolBook?

Asymetrix ToolBook is a software development tool for creating Windows programs. It is not an application in the sense of a word processor or a spreadsheet package or a page layout program, for such software is focused on performing specific end-user tasks. Rather, ToolBook is a program for creating applications. To use an analogy, ToolBook is a creative medium, much like the potter's clay. In a sense, the objects of ToolBook can be molded, stretched, rolled, and massaged to create a variety of applications, utilities, presentations, and so on.

Applications and presentations created with ToolBook are known as **books**. ToolBook books are not compiled as self-executing, but require the ToolBook application (or at least its runtime version) to run. Think of the ToolBook application as a tool or platform for executing books created with it. Fortunately, the need to have ToolBook to run a book does not hinder distribution of created books, for Asymetrix provides developers with a runtime version of ToolBook that they may distribute royalty-free. (The runtime version allows playback of created applications but not the ability to create them.) Section I of this text begins by describing ToolBook's antecedents and telling how ToolBook developed from them. In addition the first section tells how to install and run the program and install the data files that accompany this text. The focus of Section I, however, is on defining what ToolBook-developed books are and telling how to use them. Using ToolBook books is termed **browsing** or **reading**.

If ToolBook were to be classified in the sense that WordPerfect is classified as a word processing package and Aldus PageMaker as desktop publishing software, ToolBook would be considered an authoring package. There are a variety of authoring tools on the market. Although their individual features vary widely, they all offer the ability to assemble, with little or no programming, an interactive hypertextual presentation or courseware with limited interactive capabilities. Compared to a programming language such as C or BASIC, authoring packages are easier to use and more graphic. The majority of authoring tools (including ToolBook) can incorporate sound, animation, video, and high-resolution graphics. Simple interactive presentations can be built in ToolBook without programming by utilizing the linking and script-recording features. Section II of this text focuses on authoring with ToolBook.

Programming languages offer some distinct advantages over authoring tools. Programming languages, especially those that are compiled, tend to execute faster. Languages offer greater flexibility and power; traditionally, authoring packages have limited options and features. ToolBook is different from the traditional authoring package because it offers the powerful OpenScript language, whose capabilities and syntax are similar to those of true programming environments such as BASIC and C. Through the use of OpenScript and a knowledge of programming theory, the ToolBook developer can create a whole range of applications, limited only by his or her imagination. Although OpenScript is very powerful, extensive, and usually more than sufficient, ToolBook is not limited to the functionality of its built-in language. Dynamic link libraries, or DLLs, may be written in C or C++ and accessed through the OpenScript language. This makes all Windows-related routines available to ToolBook. By combining an authoring environment and a true programming language, ToolBook enables developers to build applications much faster than is possible with traditional programming languages. Section III discusses the use and syntax of the OpenScript language, along with general programming theory.

There are two versions of ToolBook. ToolBook (or regular ToolBook) and Multimedia ToolBook differ in that Multimedia ToolBook has features for incorporating sound, video, and animation files. With the exception of Chapter 27, the information in this text applies to both versions. Chapter 27 explores the added features of Multimedia ToolBook. Later in Chapter 1, the section called ToolBook's Features and Capabilities will further highlight the differences between the two versions.

Where Did ToolBook Come From?

In August of 1987, Apple Computer introduced HyperCard. It was billed as "Programming for the rest of us" — a tool for the average computer user to develop applications and publish information on the Macintosh platform. HyperCard, developed by Bill Atkinson, owed its roots to other similar packages that preceded it. One was a software environment called Notecards, a product developed by Xerox but never brought to market. HyperCard was not the first authoring tool, but Apple's marketing strategy placed it above the rest and made the programming world take notice. Because Apple provided HyperCard free with every Macintosh sold, producing and marketing low-cost HyperCard applications became a cottage industry.

ToolBook's deepest roots are in HyperCard. The similarities between the two tools are unmistakable. Both are object-oriented, with buttons, fields, and graphics. The OpenScript language uses many of the same commands as HyperCard's HyperTalk language, and the syntax of the languages is similar. But ToolBook is not a mere clone of HyperCard. ToolBook's OpenScript language is more powerful and flexible than HyperTalk. Unlike HyperCard, ToolBook offers full color support. ToolBook's graphics are draw-oriented; HyperCard's are paint-oriented. Although paint-oriented (or bitmapped) graphics offer some advantages, the draw-type objects of ToolBook are easier to edit and scripts may be attached to them. Draw-type graphics lend themselves to animation better than do bitmapped graphics.

Asymetrix was founded by Paul Allen, who started Microsoft with Bill Gates. Allen left Microsoft in 1983, and launched Asymetrix in 1985. The Asymetrix crew spent 4 years doing research and development before releasing ToolBook in 1989. Although a runtime version and a calendar application was distributed with Windows 3.0, ToolBook did not become a success until the release of Multimedia ToolBook 1.5, coupled with the release of a much-improved version of Windows, Windows 3.1. ToolBook continues to gain attention, especially in the education arena, where HyperCard has long been the authoring king. The Macintosh-like, graphical user interface of Windows; the low price of Windows-based computers; and their popularity in the business sector have made the 386 and 486 personal computers common in educational institutions. And, given the popularity of HyperCard with teachers and students, ToolBook was a natural attraction.

ToolBook's Features and Capabilities

Some of the key features of both ToolBook 3.0 and Multimedia ToolBook 3.0 are

- The ability to create and run graphical user interface applications under Microsoft Windows. Multiple-windowed applications may be developed through the use of ToolBook features called viewers. Such windows include interactive dialog boxes, palettes, graphics displays, and progress boxes.

- Menus may be customized or even deleted. Cascading menus and comboboxes are also supported.
- Interactivity is driven by events, such as mouse movements, presses of the mouse button, keyboard entry, page changes, and the like.
- Text may be added by using fields and recordfields. The text may be editable or locked, and may be fully formatted by selecting font, style, spacing, and alignment.
- Hypertextual command is provided through the use of hotwords in fields and recordfields.
- Interactive buttons may be formatted in a variety of styles. Captions, bitmapped images, and/or icons may be attached to buttons.
- Vectored (object-oriented) images may be created with the built-in drawing tools. Both vectored and bitmapped images may be imported.
- Objects shared by several pages may be placed on the background, saving time and the need to re-create objects. Objects may also be copied from one application to another.
- Any object may be colored, including backgrounds. Colors may be either solid or dithered (composed of a pattern of two colors), and various patterns may be employed.
- Scripts (OpenScript code) may be attached to any object—including the page, background, or book—to handle user and system events.
- The OpenScript language may be extended through the use of DLLs, including the Windows API (Application Programming Interface).
- Objects may be grouped and are fully editable in the Author mode.
- Objects may be right-clicked in the Author mode to quickly access properties, scripts, and so on.

Additional Features of Multimedia ToolBook

In addition to the features listed previously, Multimedia ToolBook 3.0 also offers

- The ability to include multimedia clips in ToolBook applications and presentations. These clips might consist of .WAV digitized sound files, MIDI songs (synthesized musical scores), still graphics, digitized video, animations, or combinations of these imported from the Digital Video Producer application shipped with Multimedia ToolBook.
- The ability to add various effects to an imported visual media clip when opening or closing it.
- An additional object (the stage). A stage is used as a place holder and port through which visual media is played. Stages can have a fancy 3-D appearance.
- Multimedia ToolBook supports additional bitmap resource formats, including .TIF, .GIF, .WMF, and .PCX. Regular ToolBook supports .BMP and .DIB formats.
- A full-featured spelling checker for checking text in fields and recordfields.
- Adjustable audio volume.
- The ability to embed TrueType fonts in a book. For distributed books with unique fonts, the user need not have the required fonts installed on his or her system.

Installing ToolBook and the Data Files

ToolBook requires a 386SX processor operating at 20 megahertz or faster. (For multimedia applications, this author recommends a 386DX-33 or 486 processor as a minimum, with a 486-50 or better.) ToolBook needs between 8 and 36 megabytes of hard drive storage space, depending on the options installed, and at least 4 megabytes of RAM. Windows 3.1 or later is also required. ToolBook may be installed on a local hard drive or a network server. Installation of ToolBook and its associated files is completely menu driven from an installer application, as described in Hands-On Project A at the end of this chapter.

This text is accompanied by a compact disk containing sample books and chapter tutorials designed to enhance and illustrate the material presented here, along with the Multimedia ToolBook 3.0 runtime files. During their installation, a Program Manager group with the title "Developing with ToolBook" will be created for easy access (see Figure 1.1). Inside this group are icons representing the software included with this text. The steps for installing the accompanying data files are discussed in Hands-On Project B at the end of this chapter. (Note: the CD is not distributed with the academic version of this text. Rather, the files are distributed with the Instructor's Manual for this textbook. Please consult your instructor before loading any software on your school's computers and/or network.)

Figure 1.1
The installation program creates in the Program Manager a group with icons for the various tutorials and examples that accompany this text.

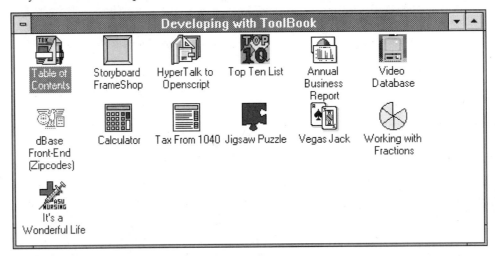

Running ToolBook

To start ToolBook from the Program Manager, open the "ToolBook" group (different from the "Developing with ToolBook" group) and double-click the ToolBook or Multimedia ToolBook icon (depending on which version you have). This runs the full version of ToolBook or Multimedia ToolBook.

To start the runtime version of Multimedia ToolBook and access the example files accompanying this text, double-click the "Table of Contents" icon shown in Figure 1.1. The examples were created with Multimedia ToolBook, and so the regular ToolBook application will not open them.

Where to Find Help

There are a variety of sources for assistance with ToolBook. The documentation that comes with ToolBook is the best starting point. This documentation includes *ToolBook User's Guide*, which gives general information about the program, its environment and use, and details regarding each of ToolBook's objects (buttons, fields, pages, backgrounds, and so on.) Also included is *OpenScript Reference Manual*, which details information about each of the commands, keywords, functions, and properties. *OpenScript Reference Manual* will prove to be a valuable reference in writing program code.

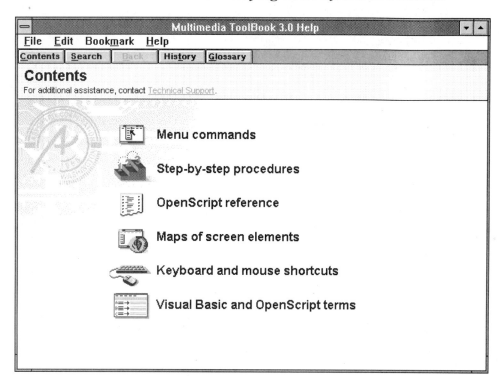

Figure 1.2
ToolBook's on-line help contains detailed information about menu options, step-by-step instructions to perform certain processes, and syntactical and usage examples of OpenScript commands.

The ToolBook package also includes a variety of electronic references. The on-line help makes the OpenScript reference material readily available on screen (see Figure 1.2). The on-line help also provides step-by-step instructions for many of the common procedures, and lists details about each of ToolBook's menu commands. Clicking the ToolBook Tutorial icon in the Asymetrix ToolBook 3.0 group (or the Multimedia ToolBook Tutorial icon in the Multimedia ToolBook 3.0 group) opens the "Learning ToolBook" book (or the "Learning Multimedia ToolBook" book). This book interactively teaches its user about the ToolBook environment and the basic concepts of development. It includes a basic course about OpenScript, ToolBook's programming language. Other specialized electronic references provide additional information and examples about special topics.

ToolBook user's groups can be found at many colleges and universities, as well as within larger computer clubs and organizations. User's groups meet regularly to share ideas and provide technical support to one another. Occasionally, highly experienced members mentor novices within the group.

Asymetrix offers technical support to registered owners of its products; the phone number of the technical support crew is 206-637-1600. Chances are, if they can't answer your question, few people can! Before you call, have your ToolBook serial number handy. The technician will want to know about the configuration of your system—what processor it has (486SX, for example), how much memory it has, and information about its video display (VGA or SVGA, and resolution). The technician will also want the exact wording of any error messages, a description of the problem, and how you've attempted to resolve it.

In-depth technical support is available from Asymetrix for those who subscribe to the Developer Services program. The benefits of membership (currently $795 per year; $695 for academic members) include additional development tools; assignment of a personal technician; top-priority phone access; rights to beta-test new versions; access to new versions before public release; and discounts on other services, such as the annual Developer's Conference. In addition, Asymetrix offers in-depth, hands-on training classes on ToolBook and Multimedia ToolBook at users' sites and at Asymetrix's Bellevue, Washington, facility. Other third-party corporations or

Figure 1.3
The main menu screen of the Asymetrix BBS provides access to a variety of resources. Callers may leave a question for the system operator (sysop) and receive a response within 48 hours.

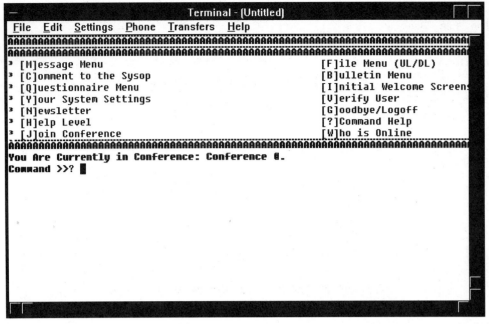

```
─                           Terminal - (Untitled)                        ┌┌
  File   Edit   Settings   Phone   Transfers   Help
ÄÄÄÄÄÄÄÄÄÄÄÄÄÄÄÄÄÄÄÄÄÄÄÄÄÄÄÄÄÄÄÄÄÄÄÄÄÄÄÄÄÄÄÄÄÄÄÄÄÄÄÄÄÄÄÄÄÄÄÄÄÄÄÄÄÄÄÄÄÄÄÄÄÄ
ÄÄÄÄÄÄÄÄÄÄÄÄÄÄÄÄÄÄÄÄÄÄÄÄÄÄÄÄÄÄÄÄÄÄÄÄÄÄÄÄÄÄÄÄÄÄÄÄÄÄÄÄÄÄÄÄÄÄÄÄÄÄÄÄÄÄÄÄÄÄÄÄÄÄ
³ [M]essage Menu                            [F]ile Menu (UL/DL)
³ [C]omment to the Sysop                    [B]ulletin Menu
³ [Q]uestionnaire Menu                      [I]nitial Welcome Screen
³ [Y]our System Settings                    [V]erify User
³ [N]ewsletter                              [G]oodbye/Logoff
³ [H]elp Level                              [?]Command Help
³ [J]oin Conference                         [W]ho is Online
ÄÄÄÄÄÄÄÄÄÄÄÄÄÄÄÄÄÄÄÄÄÄÄÄÄÄÄÄÄÄÄÄÄÄÄÄÄÄÄÄÄÄÄÄÄÄÄÄÄÄÄÄÄÄÄÄÄÄÄÄÄÄÄÄÄÄÄÄÄÄÄÄÄÄ
You Are Currently in Conference: Conference 0.
Command >>? █
```

institutions offer training and materials, such as IAT at North Carolina University.

The Asymetrix bulletin board service (BBS) may be reached at 206-451-1173 with a 1200- or 2400-baud modem; 206-451-8290 with a 9600- or 14400-baud modem. The bulletin board contains an archive of free downloadable files. These files include examples, multimedia samples, tutorials, and development tools. A conferencing area allows users to communicate with each other as well as the technical consultants. The menu screen of the Asymetrix BBS is presented in Figure 1.3. ToolBook archives and discussions can also be found on popular subscription service boards, such as CompuServ and America Online.

The Internet is a computer network connecting most universities and colleges, as well as government agencies and some commercial companies. Individuals may obtain dial-in access to the network through local Internet providers. Via anonymous FTP (file transfer protocol) format Internet users can access several archives that contain ToolBook files. Two popular archives available at this printing are ftp.cica.indiana.edu (access the /PUB/PC/WIN3/TOOLBOOK directory) and wuarchive.wustl.edu (access the MIRRORS2/WIN3/TOOLBOOK directory). Many of the Asymetrix bulletin board files are obtainable through Internet access at asymetrix.com, by logging on with the user ID anonymous and an e-mail address as the password. Electronic mail may be sent to the Asymetrix technical support staff at support@asymetrix.com or techsup@asymetrix.com. Internet listservs are open membership discussion groups. Electronic mail between members is publicly posted and archived. The popular listserv toolb-l@listserv.arizona.edu focuses on Tool-Book. The participants answer questions posted by other members. Listservs may be subscribed (you receive all the generated messages directly) or browsed in their archive formats. For more information on using the Internet, pick up one of the many popular books on the topic or consult your Internet provider.

Summary Questions

Answer the following true/false questions.

1. The capabilities of ToolBook's programming language are comparable to those of BASIC or C.
2. Multimedia ToolBook offers more features than regular ToolBook.
3. New applications may be created with just the runtime files of ToolBook.
4. OpenScript is extendable through the use of dynamic link libraries written in C.
5. ToolBook will run on an AT (286-based processor) computer.
6. ToolBook requires Microsoft Windows 3.1 or later to run.
7. ToolBook is the only authoring package on the market.
8. Draw-type graphics are more easily animated than bitmapped (paint-type) graphics.
9. ToolBook contains a very useful on-line help feature.
10. ToolBook discussion groups can be found on CompuServ and the Internet.

Complete the following statements by filling in the blanks.

11. ToolBook is best categorized as an _____ package.
12. ToolBook's built-in programming language is _____ .
13. _____ is the Macintosh-based package from which ToolBook was derived.
14. ToolBook applications and presentations are referred to as _____ .
15. Using a ToolBook book is referred to as _____ .
16. The company that developed and distributes ToolBook is _____ .
17. *ToolBook* _____ _____ , documentation accompanying the program, provides general information about ToolBook and its environment and gives details about its various objects.
18. ToolBook is an _____-driven program—in other words, it is driven by using the mouse to click an object, navigating to another page, and the like.
19. ToolBook is installed by running the _____ program from the Windows Program Manager.
20. Asymetrix was founded by one of the founders of _____ .

Hands-On Projects

A. The ToolBook and Multimedia ToolBook files are distributed on either several diskettes or compact disk. To install ToolBook onto the hard disk of your computer or network server, complete the next five steps.

1. Open Windows.
2. Insert Disk 1 into drive A or drive B. If installing ToolBook from a compact disk, insert the CD into the CD drive. (Note: These instructions are for installing the full version of ToolBook, not the files that are on the CD accompanying this text.)
3. From the Program Manager, choose "Run" from the File menu, and type "a:\setup" on the command line of the resulting dialog box. See Figure 1.4. Press the Enter key or click the "OK" button. (If installing from the B drive, type "b:\setup" instead. If installing from a compact disc, substitute the appropriate letter for the CD-ROM drive instead of "a" or "b".)
4. A dialog box will be displayed with options for performing a complete installation, setting

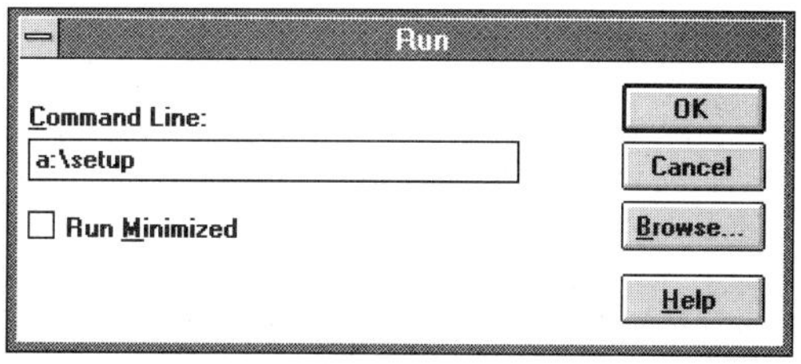

Figure 1.4
Use the "Run" option in the Program Manager to install ToolBook.

Figure 1.5
A dialog box is displayed by
the setup program from
which the user may choose
to install all or only part of
ToolBook / Multimedia
ToolBook.

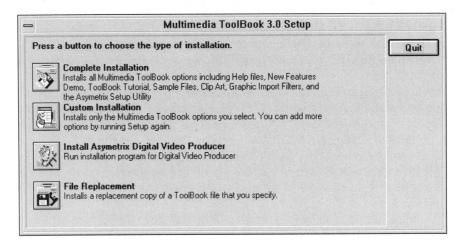

up a custom installation, or quitting (see Figure 1.5). A complete installation involves copying all files—including tutorials, sample files, and clipart—to the hard disk. The custom installation allows the user to choose what is copied and what is not copied. If enough storage space is available, a complete installation is suggested. Choose the appropriate selection by clicking your choice. Follow the instructions given on screen, inserting the appropriate diskettes as requested. The setup program will automatically create the group window with the various ToolBook items (see Figure 1.6), as well as make necessary changes to the AUTOEXEC.BAT and WIN.INI files.

5. After the installation is complete, restart Windows.

B. To install onto your hard disk the data files from the CD accompanying this book, complete the steps that follow. (Note: The data files and runtime ToolBook may be run from the accompanying CD by first running the SETUP.EXE application on the root drive of the compact disc. However, if space is available, it is

Figure 1.6
In the Program Manager,
the setup program creates a
group with icons for the
various applications,
utilities, and examples that
compose the ToolBook
package.

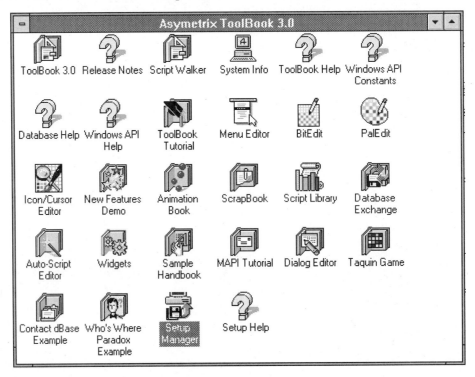

recommended that files be installed on the hard disk. This will increase performance as well as create a group for the needed files. The CD is not distributed with the academic version of this text; rather, the files are distributed to the instructor. For more information, see the README.WRI file on the CD.)

1. Open Windows.
2. Insert the accompanying CD into the CD-ROM drive.
3. From the Program Manager, choose "Run" from the File menu, and type "d:\install\setup.exe" on the command line of the resulting dialog box; press the Enter key or click the "OK" button. (If the CD is not drive D, change the letter in the command line to the letter appropriate for the CD drive.) If installing from floppy diskettes, insert Disk 1 and run "a:\setup" from the Program Manager.
4. A dialog box will be displayed that includes options for performing a complete installation, setting up a custom installation, or exiting (see Figure 1.7). A complete installation involves copying all files, including the Multimedia ToolBook runtime files, to the hard disk. (The Multimedia ToolBook runtime files are included for those readers without access to the full version of Multimedia ToolBook. The books distributed on this CD may be viewed with the runtime files, but books cannot be created or edited.) The custom installation allows the user to choose what is copied and what is not copied. If enough storage space is available, a complete installation is suggested. Choose the appropriate selection by clicking your choice. The installation program will copy the files to the hard disk and automatically create the group window with the various items. The group window is shown in Figure 1.1. If installing on a network, set to read only the file attributes of all .TBK files and the DEV_TOFC.EXE file. This will allow multiple users to access the files simultaneously. (To set the read-only attribute, select the file(s) in the Windows File Manager, choose "Change Attributes" from the File menu, and check the "Read Only" box in the resulting dialog box.)

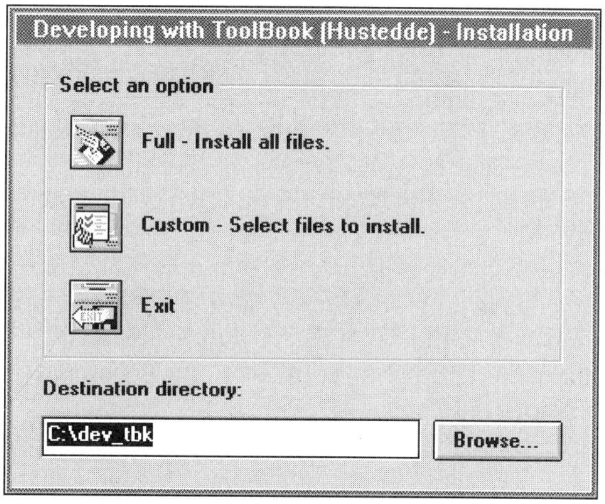

Figure 1.7
A dialog box is displayed by the setup program, from which the user may choose to install all or only part of the files distributed with this text.

C. CHAP01.TBK, distributed with this text, demonstrates some of the features of ToolBook and Multimedia ToolBook. (There are similar files for each chapter.) The file is accessed through DEV_TOFC.TBK, a file that provides a front-end menu. It is this menu file (see Figure 1.8) that is opened when the icon labeled Table of Contents (shown in Figure 1.1) is double-clicked. Examine CHAP01.TBK by completing the steps that follow.

1. Open Windows. In the Program Manager, open the "Developing with ToolBook" group window.
2. Open the "Main Menu" book by double-clicking the Table of Contents icon

Figure 1.8
The Main menu of the
DEV_TOFC.EXE file
serves as a front end to the
files associated with each
chapter of this text.
Clicking a volume in the
"bookcase" launches the file
for that chapter.

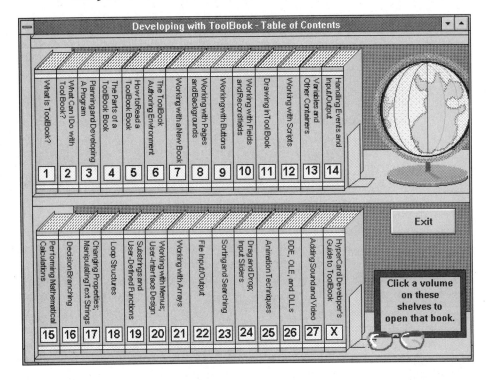

in the "Developing with ToolBook" group window.

3. The Main menu is a graphic of a bookcase with many volumes, one for each chapter of this text. Clicking a volume will launch the file associated with that chapter. Click the "Volume 1" graphic.

4. On the opening screen of the CHAP01.TBK file (What is ToolBook?), press the left mouse button to go to the next screen (note the on-screen instructions).

5. View the remainder of the book linearly by clicking the right-hand icon at the bottom right to move forward and the button at the bottom left to go back one page.

6. Click the "Exit" button (with the bookshelf icon) to return to the "Table of Contents" book (the Main menu).

7. To exit the "Main Menu" book, click the "Exit" button.

D. If you have access to the full version of ToolBook/Multimedia ToolBook, browse the "Learning ToolBook" book that accompanies it. The file is LEARN30.TBK, located in the TUTORIAL subdirectory of the ToolBook directory. It can be launched from the "ToolBook" group window by double-clicking the "ToolBook Tutorial" icon.

1. Open Windows. Open the "Toolbook" group.

2. Double-click the Toolbook Tutorial icon in the "ToolBook" group window. (Alternatively, the LEARN30.TBK file may be double-clicked in the File Manager.)

3. Upon opening the tutorial, you will see an animation of a book opening, revealing a table of contents. Click the right arrow, in the bottom right, to continue (see Figure 1.9).

4. On the next screen, you'll see a discussion about the XSAT application that you'll observe being built in this tutorial. Click the right arrow.

5. At the third screen, the user is given two options: (1) the full tutorial or (2) focusing only on the new features of version 3.0. Choose the full tutorial by clicking the appropriate choice. Click the right arrow to continue.

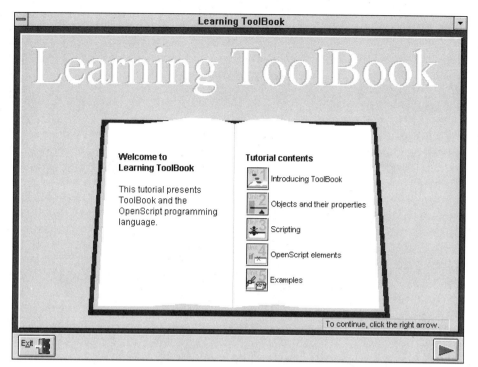

Figure 1.9
The opening screen of the
ToolBook tutorial that
accompanies ToolBook 3.0
and Multimedia ToolBook
3.0. Students using the
tutorial are walked through
the creation of a book,
including various aspects of
programming in
OpenScript.

6. The next page is the opening page of Unit 1 ("Introducing ToolBook"). Note the "Map" button at the bottom of the page. Click the "Map" button.
7. The Map screen (see Figure 1.10) lists the five units of the tutorial. Click an option to reveal an expanded list of the lessons for that unit. Any of the lessons may be accessed by clicking its listing. (This is handy for review later. You need not go through the entire tutorial to access a certain area.) Note: Unless you are familiar with ToolBook, you should go through the tutorial in a linear fashion and not jump ahead, at least the first time through, because each lesson builds upon preceding lessons. Return to the opening page of

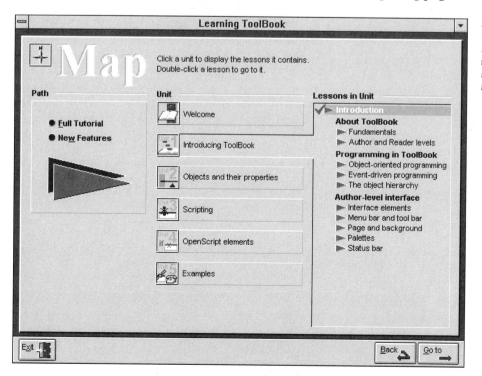

Figure 1.10
The Map screen of the
Learning ToolBook tutorial
serves as a menu that lists
the various lessons of the
tutorial.

Figure 1.11
*The Learning ToolBook
tutorial includes animated
demonstrations ("Show")
and interactive practice
("Try").*

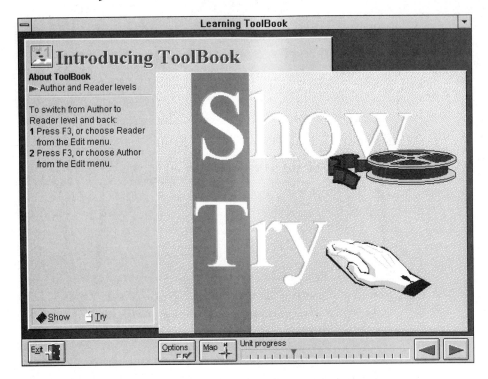

Unit 1 by clicking the "Back" button, at the bottom right, or by clicking "Introducing ToolBook" in the listing for Unit 1.

8. Work through Unit 1 by clicking the right arrow after reading each page. The unit progress bar, at the bottom, reveals the current position within the unit. Some pages (screens) are marked "Show - Try" (see Figure 1.11) and include an animated demonstration of the discussed process as well as an interactive opportunity to try the process yourself. To see the demo, click the "Show" button, the left button on the left half of the screen. To practice the lesson, click the "Try" button, the right button on the left half of the screen.

9. To exit the Learning ToolBook tutorial, click the "Exit" button, at the bottom left, at any time.

Chapter 2

Applications and Ideas

What Can I Do with ToolBook?

ToolBook can be used to create a variety of books (programs), limited by virtually only the creativity of the developer or team of developers. The types of books can be grouped into five distinct categories: presentations; database management; applications and utilities; entertainment (games); and training software or courseware. Some books may overlap categories. For instance, in designing instruction, I believe that the best courseware has an element of fun to it. Courseware, for instance, may be designed as a role-playing game. Such a product may be classified as a game with an instructional bent or as courseware with an entertainment slant, depending on how it is used.

Presentations

A picture says a thousand words, and studies show that audiences remember more of what they see and hear than what they just hear. With the increasing presence of computers in classrooms and boardrooms, portable notebook computers, and data projection devices, more and more presenters are using computer technology to get their points across. A variety of good commercial software packages are available for such presentations. Most have a major limitation: They are not interactive. In other words, depending on how the audience is responding or the amount of time left for the meeting, the presenter cannot choose whether to view slide 5 or jump to slide 12. ToolBook, with its interactive authoring, easily handles such a task. Also, video clips, animations, and sounds can be imported into Multimedia ToolBook to jazz up a presentation.

Presentations are the easiest type of book to create. They generally require little or no knowledge of the OpenScript programming language. Interactive links may be created by pointing and clicking. More complicated tasks, such as animating an object on the screen, may be performed through the use of the script recorder, a programming code generator for use by nonprogrammers (and programmers too).

Two sample presentations are included with the software accompanying this text. To access them, double-click the Table of Contents icon in the "Developing with ToolBook" group window (Figure 1.1). Click the "Chapter 2: What Can I Do with ToolBook?" selection. This will take you to a different book, which serves as a front-end menu for the various example books discussed in this chapter. Also it summarizes the types of books that are commonly developed with ToolBook.

- **"Top Ten List" (TOP10.TBK)** This book presents a 10-item list similar to that made popular by a famous nighttime talk-show host (see Figure 2.1). Such a presentation might be used as a humorous icebreaker or introduction for a presentation. The 10 items are revealed one by one in descending order by clicking the "Show" button in the upper right. Similarly, they may be hidden in reverse order by clicking the "Hide" button. All 10 items are automatically hidden upon exiting the book, so the presentation is ready for next time, with the items hidden to start. This presentation was designed for projection to a large group, thus the choice of a large, bold font. This book

Figure 2.1
*A top-10 list presentation
is made by clicking the
"Show" button to reveal
the items one by one in
descending order.*

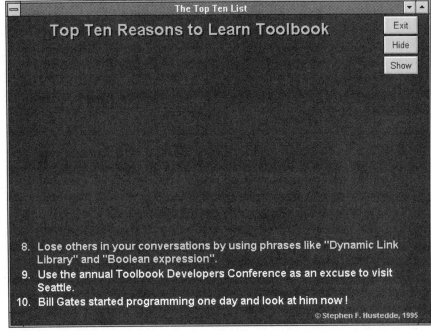

is adaptable for other presentations. The 10 items and the category title may
be altered by clicking the right mouse button an on item or the category title.
A dialog box will appear, requesting the new text. The new text for the
chosen item is entered and the "OK" button clicked. The existing text is
replaced with the new text. This procedure is repeated for the other items
and the title until all have been changed as desired. Each item may occupy
up to two lines of text.

- **"Annual Business Report" (BUSINESS.TBK)** This presentation might be
  used at an annual board meeting or stockholders' meeting, using a liquid
  crystal display (LCD) projection system attached to a computer, or mailed
  on diskette to stockholders or potential investors. It includes annual

Figure 2.2
*A presentation might
include both text and
graphs. Compare this
screen with that shown in
Figure 2.3 and note how
certain design elements are
repeated.*

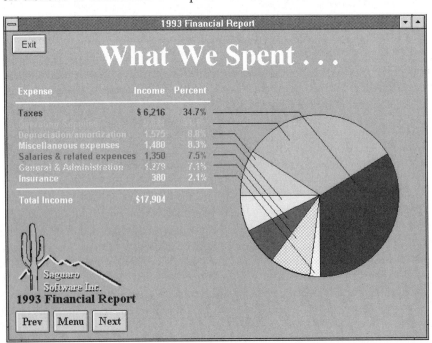

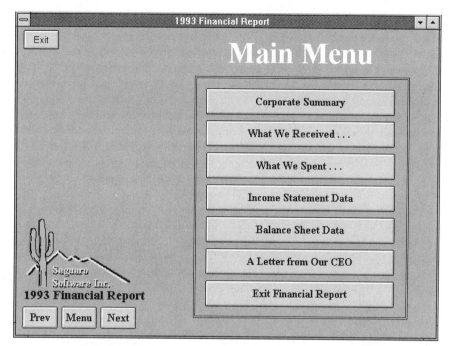

Figure 2.3
A presentation might include a main menu from which the presenter or viewer accesses certain portions of the presentation. This ability to jump around nonlinearly allows the presenter freedom to alter the presentation as needed.

summaries, a letter from the CEO, and financial information (see Figure 2.2). This book allows the presenter or viewer to skip around in the presentation via its main menu (see Figure 2.3). The presenter may return to the main menu from a page and then select the next topic to view. He or she may choose to skip a page, change the order of the presentation, or revisit a previously viewed screen. Many of the so-called sophisticated presentation packages do not have such interactive features, so viewing is linear only.

Even if the designer has not included an interactive menu or navigational buttons, the user can often access any page of the book by using the F12 key. F12 is a toggle switch that causes the statusbar to appear or not appear. The current page number is displayed at the right in the statusbar. Clicking the page number display prompts the user for a page number to go to. The user enters the page number and that page is then accessed.

An instructor might develop a presentation similar to this business presentation to accompany his or her lecture. The ability to go freely to any screen in the presentation is ideal for reviewing or answering questions about previously presented material, restructuring the flow of the content, and adjusting to the needs and desires of the audience.

Database Management

Next to word processing, the most popular use for computers is database management. Large amounts of data may be stored efficiently on disk and easily manipulated. A database user can find desired information quickly and sort the data in a variety of ways. Numerous database packages are available for managing large amounts of data. They are usually very fast, but most lack a graphical user interface (GUI). ToolBook, with its GUI, permits the incorporation of graphics with textual data (see Figure 2.4). The clipart book (CLIPART.TBK) included with Asymetrix ToolBook is a collection of clipart graphics that may be copied and pasted into other ToolBook books. With Multimedia ToolBook, collections of sounds (.WAV files, MIDI files, and so on) might be cataloged, accessed, and even played. Computer animation files (.FLI and .FLC files, for example) and digitized video files (such as

.AVI files or QuickTime movies) might also be cataloged or used to enhance the interface in some way.

Two sample database management books are provided with this text. The files that show sample database management books are accessible from the "Chapter 2" book just as the presentation examples discussed in the previous section were. The examples include

- **Video Database (VIDEO.TBK)** This database is an inventory of video-tapes. It might be used for a personal collection or in a video rental store. A graphic rendition of a television monitor and a videocassette recorder (VCR) surrounds the data (see Figure 2.4). Data is displayed on the "monitor" and the VCR provides the interface location and buttons for

Figure 2.4
Data may be presented in recordfields within a graphical interface. In this example, data about each movie occupies one page of the book.

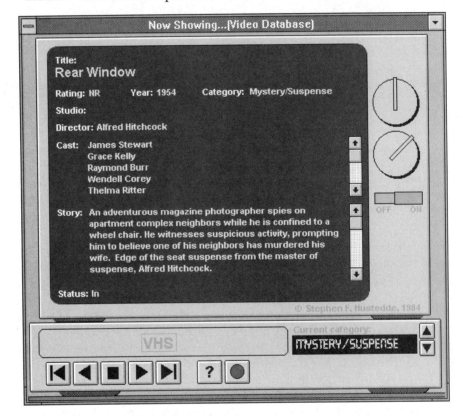

going to the first screen of data (in alphabetical order), the previous screen, the next screen, and the last screen. A search button (the button labeled with a question mark) takes the user to a search screen where he or she may enter a name or title to search for. The result of a search is a list of titles matching the criteria (see Figure 2.5). The Record button (the button labeled with the dot) is for administrative use. It prompts the user for a password. If the correct password is given, an edit box appears over the upper right of the monitor graphic. The edit box contains three buttons: one for adding a new video record to the database, one for deleting the currently displayed record, and one that is a toggle to control the ability to edit the data fields (that is, for locking and unlocking the fields). When the edit feature is on, the user may edit any of the text in the data fields. When new records have been added, an "Update Index" button appears to allow the user to sort all the video records alphabetically by title. For a public-access situation, the password protection restricts unauthorized users from making changes to the data.

Figure 2.5
A search engine built into a
data collection allows a user
to find desired information
quickly.

- **dBASE Front End (ZIPCODES.TBK)** The "Database Exchange" book that comes with ToolBook allows the user to import a dBASE III Plus or Paradox file and create either a ToolBook front end to access the data or a ToolBook book containing the same data. The zip codes database included with this text was created with the Database Exchange application. ZIPCODES.TBK is a front end file accessing the data of ZIPCODES.DBF, the dBASE file (see Figure 2.6). One record of the data file is accessed and written into the appropriate fields of the ToolBook front end, which in this case are the zip code, city, and state fields. The zip codes data file is organized by zip code.

Accessing the next record reveals the next zip code in numeric order. However, indexes (.NDX files) may be accessed (by choosing "Open Index" in the dBASE menu). Indexes provide a presorted structure for the records of the data file. An index (CITY_ST.NDX) is provided to sort the data by a combination of city and state. Upon opening an index, the user may search for a specific data record by using the index key (in this case, it is city and state). As you will see when you use the CITY_ST.NDX in Hands-On Projects, you will click the "Find Key" button and in the resulting dialog box type the name

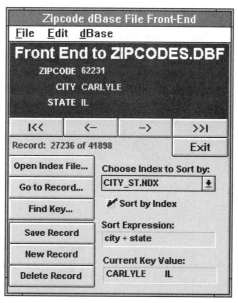

Figure 2.6
A ToolBook application
may serve as a front end to
data files developed with
other popular database
management applications.
Unlike the video database,
there is only one data page
in the book. Data is read
from the external file and
written in the appropriate
fields of this page.

of the city to search for. Click "OK" and the zip code for the requested city will appear. You will verify that it is the correct state. If not, you will click the Next-record button (the arrow pointing to the right). Using the index, the records are sorted alphabetically by city and state (for example, the code for Glendale, California, follows the one for Glendale, Arizona).

Records may be added to or deleted from an external database file by using the ToolBook front end, clicking the "New Record" or "Delete Record" button. However, be aware that removing or adding records will cause the index to be improperly sorted.

ZIPCODES.TBK uses dynamic link library functions to retrieve the records from the external file (Chapter 26). Other database files may be accessed through object linking and embedding (OLE) or dynamic data exchange (DDE), providing they support such functions (Chapter 26).

Applications and Utilities

ToolBook is interpretive, whereas most mainstream languages, such as C or Pascal, are compiled. **Compiled programs** are in a format that the computer can read and understand quickly; **interpreted programs** must be translated as they run. Interpretation takes extra time, so interpreted applications run slower than compiled applications. Therefore, in designing mainstream applications that will be heavily marketed, a developer would probably choose C or C++ over ToolBook. But ToolBook is easier and quicker, and is therefore ideal for prototyping applications. A **prototype** is a fully functional program usually used for personal purposes, as opposed to one that will be marketed to the masses. Prototypes are also valuable as working models of software that will be developed later with a higher-level language. A prototype might be used to achieve financing, build interest, and communicate to other programmers what the finished product will look like and how it will function.

Applications include useful and practical tools of productivity. Examples of popular applications include investment trackers, word processors, spreadsheets, communications packages, and graphic design programs. Applications are generally designed to meet a specific need or serve a particular purpose.

Utilities are similar to applications but may be used for multiple purposes and are usually used in conjunction with applications. A calculator, for instance, might prove useful with an investment tracker, a spreadsheet, and a point-of-sale cash-register application. An alarm clock and appointment reminder might run all day in the background of other applications. A utility is not so much a tool of specific productivity, but rather one of very general use.

Two sample application and utility books accompany this text:

- **Calculator (CALCUL8.TBK)** A standard-function calculator has the ability

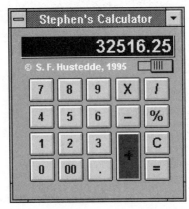

Figure 2.7
Utilities such as a calculator might be used in conjunction with other applications.

to multiply (*), divide (/), add (+), and subtract (-) two numbers. CALCUL8.TBK shows ToolBook's ability to perform mathematical calculations. The calculator page occupies only a small portion of the screen, so that this book can be opened on top of another book and used to solve problems the first book presents (see Figure 2.7). The calculator is presented as a separate book, though it might instead be designed into an application as a separate viewer.

- **Tax Form 1040 (1040.TBK)** This application presents electronically the 1993 federal tax form 1040 (see Figure 2.8). The user enters the appropriate data and the application automatically does the calculations. This book presents a scrollable page (the page is larger than the screen) and a menubar from which associated forms may be pulled up. Pop-up windows for providing instructions appear when the user clicks, using the right mouse button, on a field (such as line 7).

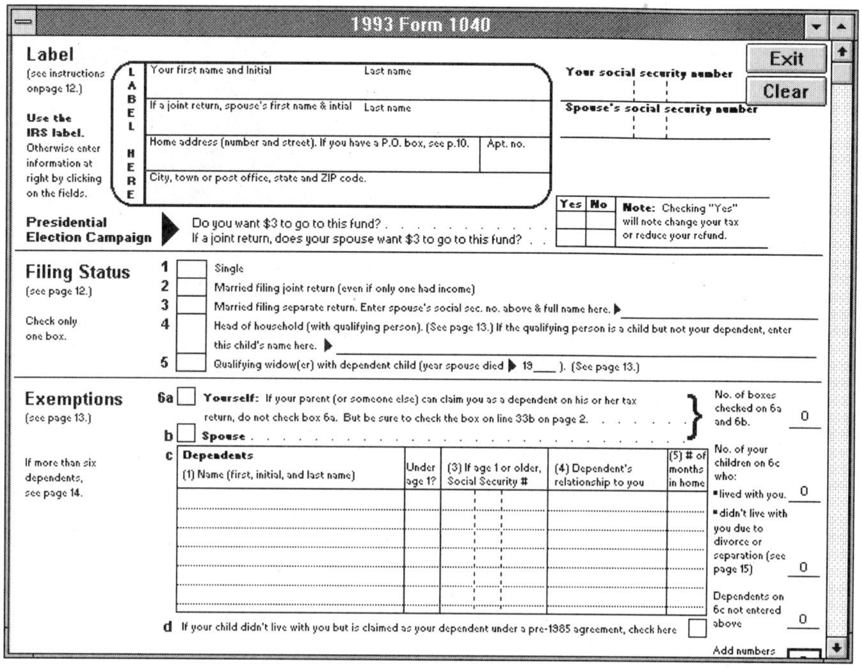

Figure 2.8
Tax Form 1040, an application, allows the user to enter requested data and have the computer perform all calculations. The user can view pop-up windows containing help and instructions about each line by using the right mouse button to click the line. Clicking the left mouse button causes the application to prompt the user for information. The program also verifies certain replies. For instance, the user can't file as a single person at one point and then try to take a deduction available only to a married couple.

Entertainment

Many people purchase a computer primarily to take advantage of the vast array of entertainment software on the market. High-resolution, multimedia-oriented games such as flight simulators, fantasy role-playing games, and sports arcades earn software publishers millions of dollars each year. Computerized games offer the ability to partake in competition when no human opponents are available. For instance, a computer can prove to be the most worthy opponent for a game of chess.

Designing computer games can be one of the most challenging experiences in programming. Programming the computer to approach a game scenario logically and strategically can be complicated. While many people find hours of enjoyment in playing computer games, I find more enjoyment and challenge in designing and programming them. After all, programming is a game of great strategy. It is a game of combat between the programmer and the computer. If you can get the computer to do what you want it to, you win!

The accompanying files devoted to entertainment include

- **Jigsaw Puzzle (JIGSAW.TBK)** The jigsaw puzzle demonstrates the graphical interactivity available in ToolBook applications. The puzzle consists of 49 small high-resolution bitmapped images. When placed in the appropriate places on a 7 by 7 grid, the images create a picture (see Figure 2.9). The pieces are randomly placed in their starting positions so that the user cannot memorize their locations. When all the pieces are placed in their correct locations, a dialog box congratulates the user for putting the puzzle together.

Figure 2.9
The pieces of the jigsaw puzzle are randomly placed outside the grid so the puzzle's initial state is never the same.

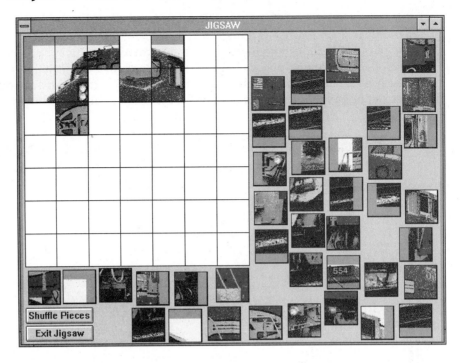

- **Vegas Jack (BLCKJACK.TBK)** This is a single player version of Blackjack, the popular gambling card game. The user competes against the computer, which serves as the dealer. The object is to draw cards to get as close to a value of 21 as possible without going over that number. BLCKJACK.TBK uses the standard Las Vegas rules, including the ability to double down, split a pair, and buy insurance against the dealer drawing Blackjack (an ace and a card of value 10) (see Figure 2.10). Four decks of 52 cards are used. Bets are placed prior to the deal by clicking the chips in the bottom right. The player starts with $500 in chips and the program keeps track of his or her balance and the amount won or lost during the session.

Figure 2.10
The graphical user interface of ToolBook is well suited to interactive games.

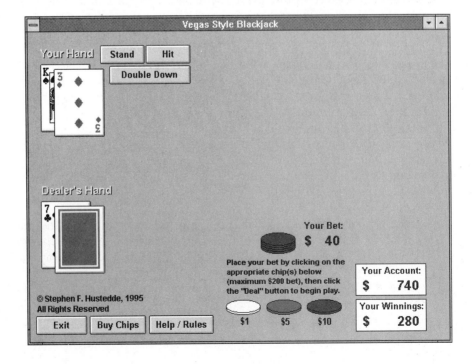

Courseware

Computer-assisted instruction (CAI) is gaining popularity not only in educational institutions, but also in corporate training centers. In 1987, when Apple's HyperCard hit the market, teachers and trainers found it to be an excellent tool for quickly developing educational applications, including simulations, drill-and-practice presentations, and information publishing. ToolBook follows in the footsteps of HyperCard, allowing easy program development for Windows-based machines.

The hypertextual capabilities of ToolBook allow students to access information in a nonlinear format. They can choose their own paths when finding information, weeding through the irrelevant to find the relevant. Hypertextual hotwords might be used to pop up a definition of an unknown word, give more details about a topic, or play an audio clip.

Information publishing and drill-and-practice exercises are the two most common educational formats and the easiest to produce, though not necessarily the most effective. **Information publishing** is nothing more than the dissemination of electronic textbooks. The one advantage to computerized delivery is that it allows students to access information nonlinearly, thus customizing their learning to their styles and needs. **Drill-and-practice software** teaches students by testing them interactively. Drill-and-practice applications usually include an element of information publishing (see Figure 2.11). A lesson is given and then the student is tested on his or her understanding. The application provides feedback and, if necessary, remedial instruction.

Simulations place students in a specific scenario and ask them to respond. A student in a desert-survival class, for instance, might be placed in a multimedia-simulated desert and asked to react to certain situations. The simulation might begin with packing the equipment, asking the student to decide what is necessary. They may have to decide the best way to deal with dehydration, how to ration their water, and what to do in a dust or lightning storm. A medical simulation may describe a patient with specific symptoms and the triage student must decide what measures will save the patient.

Role playing is another popular technique used by educational software. In a

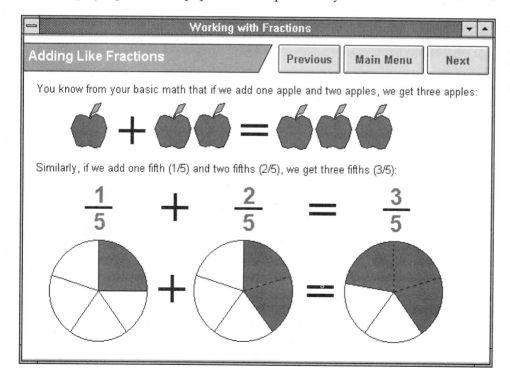

Figure 2.11
This drill-and-practice software presents a lesson and then questions that test the student's understanding of the lesson.

political science class, students might use courseware to role-play members of Congress. The computer presents biographical data on the members as well as information about certain issues. The students interact with various computer-controlled characters — lobbyists, the president, other members, constituents, and so on.

The files that show sample instructional books are

- **Working with Fractions (FRACTION.TBK)** This application is a drill-and-practice tutorial. Students are given instruction on various aspects of working with fractions (see Figure 2.11) and then the opportunity to test their understanding by solving randomly generated problems (see Figure 2.12). The computer provides immediate feedback on their answers and gives a cumulative score for each section.

Figure 2.12
ToolBook allows full interactivity, including the ability to generate questions randomly.

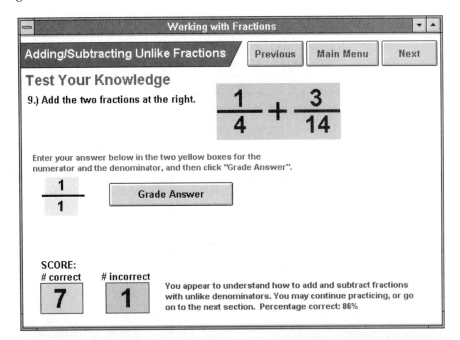

Figure 2.13
Courseware might include a role-playing situation where students make choices for a computerized character and see the ramifications of those choices. (Used with the permission of Dr. Larry North, Arizona State University.)

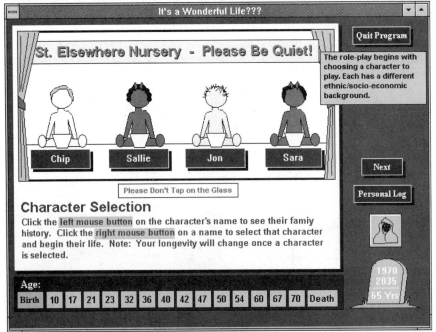

- **It's a Wonderful Life? (WONDLIFE.TBK)** It's a Wonderful Life? is a demonstration of a small piece of courseware developed for an introductory nursing class at Arizona State University. In this module students role-play a character from birth to death, making diet, exercise, and lifestyle choices (see Figure 2.13). Their choices affect the character's longevity, which is relayed to the student by the changing years on the headstone graphic at the bottom right. Upon completion, students are given an opportunity to evaluate their performance and to state what they would have done differently. In the full version of this software, there are over eight million different combinations of decisions that a student can make in playing the four different characters.

Summary Questions

Answer the following true/false questions.

1. ToolBook is very limited in the types of programs that can be created with it.
2. Creating interactive links between pages of a book requires an in-depth understanding of scripting with the OpenScript language.
3. Multimedia ToolBook presentations can incorporate animation and video clips.
4. By pressing the F12 key, a user may toggle the statusbar on and off.
5. Clicking the page number display of the statusbar allows users to enter a page number to access.
6. One of the advantages of ToolBook over many popular database management packages is its ability to work with graphical data.
7. A limitation of ToolBook is that it cannot be used as a front end to data files from other database applications.
8. Interpreted programs generally run faster than compiled programs.
9. In presenting information, electronic publishing offers an advantage over print-based texts: Users of electronic text can more easily access information nonlinearly.
10. Entertainment software, such as interactive games, cannot be developed with ToolBook.

Complete the following statements by filling in the blanks.

11. A _____ is the easiest type of book to create.
12. GUI is an acronym for _____ _____ _____ .
13. A _____ is a program developed for personal use (as opposed to one developed for distribution).
14. _____ educational software tests students on their understanding of presented material.
15. _____ place students in a specific scenario and ask them to respond.
16. _____ publishing is nothing more than the dissemination of electronic textbooks.
17. Courseware often employs the technique called _____ , in which a student takes the part of a character.
18. The _____ recorder can generate program code.
19. _____ may be used for multiple purposes, often in conjunction with applications.
20. _____ programs are translated as they run, as opposed to programs that are translated when compiled.

Hands-On Projects

A. Examine the software that accompanies this chapter. Open the "Table of Contents" book by double clicking its icon in the "Developing with ToolBook" group window in the Windows Program Manager. Inside the "Table of Contents", click the book representing Chapter 2. On the resulting menu screen (What Can I Do with ToolBook?), click the buttons on the right to access the various examples (see Figure 2.14).

Figure 2.14
The What Can I Do with ToolBook? menu screen serves as a front end to the various program examples discussed in this chapter.

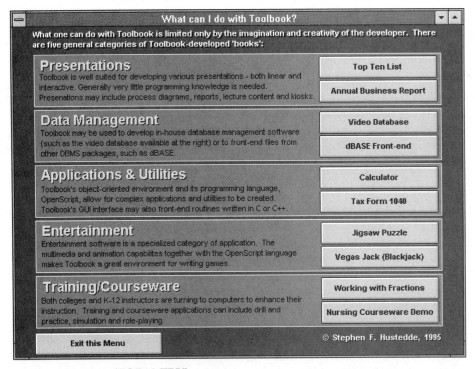

1. Top Ten List (TOP10.TBK)
   a. Click the "Top Ten List" button.
   b. Display each of the 10 items by clicking the "Show" button.
   c. Hide the items by clicking the "Hide" button.
   d. Show all items again. Create your own presentation by clicking, with the right mouse button, each of the items and the title. In the resulting dialog boxes, enter new text for each item and the title.
   e. Choose "Save As..." from the File menu, giving the revised list a different name (such as MYTOP10.TBK) and specifying the desired path.
   f. To exit and go back to the What Can I Do with ToolBook? menu, click the "Exit" button, located in the upper right.
2. Annual Business Report (BUSINESS.TBK)
   a. Open the Annual Business Report from the What Can I Do with ToolBook? menu screen. On the title screen, click the "Go to Main Menu" button.
   b. Explore the presentation. From the Main menu, you can choose to visit any section, such as "What We Spent...", by clicking the appropriate button at the right. The presentation may also be viewed linearly by clicking the "Next" button (in the lower left) to move forward or the "Prev" button to move backward. The "Menu" button on each screen will return you to the Main menu.
   c. To exit and go back to the What Can I Do with ToolBook? menu, click the "Exit" button, in the upper left.

3. Video Database (VIDEO.TBK)
   a. Open the video database by clicking the "Video Database" button in the What Can I Do with ToolBook? menu.
   b. From the title screen, click the power switch on the monitor graphic to access the data.
   c. Use the right arrow button and the left arrow button to browse through the data. (Figure 2.15 shows the different buttons.) Note that the records cycle in a circular fashion — going forward at the last record brings up the first record, and going backward at the first record brings up the last record.
   d. The current category may be set by clicking the up or down arrow next to the current category field in the VCR graphic. The program will present the various category choices. Once a current category is selected, the user will then see videos in that category only. Choosing the category "All Videos" allows the user to browse videos from any category. Browse through the videos of a specific category by choosing a category selection and then using one of the navigational buttons discussed in step c.
   e. Perform a query by clicking the button labeled with a question mark. On the query screen, enter a word of a title to look up. For instance, type "train" and click the "Title Search" button. All videos containing the string train within their titles will be shown in the results field. Searching for train, for instance, results in the display of the titles Planes, Trains, and Automobiles and Strangers on a Train. To see the full records of one of these two videos, click its title. A director search or actor/actress search may be conducted in the same way. Typing "Grace Kelly" and clicking the "Actor/Actress Search" button would bring up the titles of the films in the database in which Grace Kelly starred. In this case, Rear Window and To Catch a Thief appear in the results field. Perform a director search on Alfred Hitchcock.
   f. Click the Record button (see Figure 2.15). (Note: You must be viewing a data record, not the query screen.) Enter the authorization code, "sfh", (lowercase), when prompted. A box containing three buttons appears in the upper right corner of the screen. The buttons are "New Video," "Delete Video," and "Edit On" or "Edit Off."

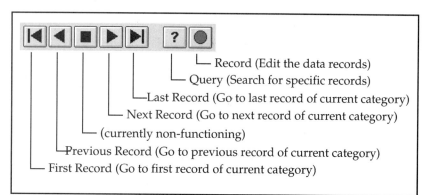

Figure 2.15
The buttons at the bottom of the video database program are used as navigational controls.

   g. Click the "New Video" button to create a new blank data record. Click each field and enter the appropriate text. Repeat this step for each new video to be added.
   h. The "Done — Update Index" button, which appears, will sort the new records alphabetically into the existing database. Click this button when you are finished adding new records.

i.   Turn off the editing controls by clicking the Record button again. Browse the database or conduct a query to ensure that your new records are in the database.

j.   Display the editing controls again, as you did in step f. Try clicking a data field to edit its text and you'll notice that it can't be changed. Click the "Edit On" button. This will unlock the recordfields so that existing data may be altered. When the records are unlocked, the name of the "Edit On" button will change to "Edit Off." Clicking the "Edit Off" button will lock the data so that it cannot be edited. Edit one of the data records you created in step g.

k.   View another one of the records you added in step g. Click the "Delete Video" button to remove the current record from the database. A dialog box will prompt you to verify this action, guarding against accidental clicking of the "Delete Video" button.

l.   Exit the database by clicking the off/on switch of the monitor graphic; the title screen reappears. From the title screen, click the "Quit" button to return to the What Can I Do with ToolBook? menu screen.

4.   dBASE Front End (ZIPCODES.TBK)

a.   Open the zip codes database front end by clicking the "dBASE Front End" button from the What Can I Do with Toolbook? menu screen.

b.   Browse a few records by clicking the Next Record button (right arrow). Note that the records are in numeric order by zip code.

c.   Click the "Open Index File" button and choose "city_st.ndx" in the resulting file dialog box. (Note: This is a very large index and may take several minutes to load. Be patient!) CITY_ST.NDX will appear in the "Choose Indexes to Sort by:" combo box and "city + state" will appear in the "Sort Expression" field.

d.   Browse the records as in step b. The records are now sorted primarily by city and secondarily by state.

e.   Click the "Find Key" button and type "Carlyle" in the resulting dialog box. The zip code for Carlyle, Illinois, should be shown (62231).

f.   Find the zip code of the following towns and cities:
1) Grass Valley, California
2) Ajo, Arizona
3) Dallas, Texas (There are several.)
4) Moscow, Idaho

g.   Choose "Exit" from the File menu to close the book and return to the What Can I Do with ToolBook? menu screen.

5.   Calculator (CALCUL8.TBK)

a.   Open the calculator by clicking the "Calculator" button from the What Can I Do with ToolBook? menu screen.

b.   Perform several math calculations by clicking the number keys of the first number, then the desired operator (*, /, + or -) followed by the second number. Clicking the button displaying the equals sign will generate the answer to the entered procedure. Manually verify that the results are correct.

c.   Close the calculator by clicking the power switch graphic of the calculator.

6.   Tax Form 1040 (1040.TBK)

a.   Open the tax form by clicking the "Tax Form 1040" button on the What Can I Do with ToolBook? menu screen.

b.   Enter either imaginary data or, if handy, enter your 1993 tax return data to verify accuracy of your filed return. To enter data into a field (yellow box), click the field and enter the data in the resulting dialog box. Checkboxes may be checked by clicking them. Use the scrollbar to move up or down the page. Note: There are two pages; remember to fill out both. Buttons to go from page to page are located at the bottom of page 1 and the top of page 2.

c.   Use the right mouse button to click the field for line 7. The IRS instructions accompanying this item appear. (Note: Only lines 7 through 15 have been thus programmed.)

d.   All the data may be cleared by clicking the "Clear" button at the top of page 1.

e.   Click the "Exit" button at the top of page 1 to return to the What Can I Do with ToolBook? menu screen.

7. Jigsaw Puzzle (JIGSAW.TBK)

a.   Open the jigsaw puzzle application by clicking the appropriate button on the What Can I Do with ToolBook? menu screen.

b.   Read the instructions given on the title page.

c.   Click the "Go to Puzzle" button and solve the puzzle, dragging the pieces to the grid to form a picture. When you've successfully completed the puzzle, a dialog box will appear to congratulate you.

d.   Click the "Exit Jigsaw" button to close the book and return to the What Can I Do with ToolBook? menu screen.

8. Vegas Jack (BLCKJACK.TBK)

a.   Open this game by clicking the "Vegas Jack (Blackjack)" button on the What Can I Do with ToolBook? menu screen.

b.   At the title screen, click the "Let's Play" button.

c.   If you are unfamiliar with Las Vegas style Blackjack, click the "Help / Rules" button to view the rules. This program supports the standard rules for doubling down, splitting a pair, and buying insurance.

d.   A game begins with an account of $500. Place a bet by clicking the white, red, and blue chips as desired. The value of the current bet is displayed and updated as chips are clicked.

e.   A "Deal" button appears to the right when a bet is placed. Click the "Deal" button. Two cards are dealt to the player's hand along with two cards to the dealer's hand.

f.   Click the appropriate button to hit (take a card), stand (take no more cards), or double down (take only a third card and then stand, while doubling your bet). If the dealer draws an ace as the up card, you may also choose to place an insurance bet. A "Split" button will appear if a pair is dealt to you, giving you the option to split the pair into two separate hands. When you have hit 21, gone over 21, or decided to stand, the computer will play the dealer's hand, determine the winner and adjust your account.

g.   Repeat steps d through f to play additional hands.

h.   Click the "Exit" button to return to the What Can I Do with ToolBook? menu screen.

9. Working with Fractions (FRACTION.TBK)

a.   Open the tutorial by clicking the "Working with Fractions" button on the What Can I Do with ToolBook? menu screen.

b.   Browse through this instructional program by clicking the different section buttons from its main menu screen. The first section is Fractions and Their Parts. Each section consists of one or more lesson pages followed by an interactive, randomly generated drill-and-practice test. You might wish to use the "Next" button to access all the material in a linear fashion.

c.   To close the application, click the "Exit this Program" button on the main menu screen.

    10. It's a Wonderful Life? (WONDLIFE.TBK)
       a. Access the educational role-playing example by clicking the "Nursing Courseware Demo" button on the What Can I Do with ToolBook? menu screen.
       b. Follow the instructions presented on screen.
       c. Upon exiting the file, you will be returned to the What Can I Do with ToolBook? menu screen.

B. Look at each of the example books presented in this chapter (as discussed in Hands-On Project A). From a user's perspective, write a paragraph about each example telling what you liked or disliked about the interface and layout and your opinion of the value of each. How might each program be improved?

C. Develop a list of ideas for each of the five categories: presentations, databases, applications/utilities, entertainment, and courseware that might be developed with ToolBook.

Chapter 3

Back to the Drawing Board

Planning and Developing a Program

Contrary to popular belief, computers are dumb objects. They do not think. They possess neither intelligence nor knowledge. A computer does not act on its own, but obediently follows the instructions it has been given. A computer may appear to be intelligent in that it performs certain actions faster and more accurately than a human could, providing the instructions it has been given for these tasks are correct and efficient. Inaccurate results obtained in a procedure or calculation are virtually always the result of bad instructions or incorrect data. The set of instructions the computer follows to perform a task are what we call a **program**. Determining these instructions and communicating them to the computer is **programming**.

Programming a computer might be compared to writing a list of instructions about how to perform some task, such as how to change a tire, build a birdhouse, or calculate the sum of two fractions. In each case there is a step-by-step procedure to be followed, the order of which is often crucial. Trying to remove a flat tire before jacking up the car is difficult at best and dangerous at worst. So is driving the car with the new tire installed but the lug nuts not tightened. Likewise, in building a birdhouse, one would not nail the boards together before they have been cut to the proper dimensions. The mathematician knows well that if numerators are added before finding the least common denominator and converting the fractions, the answer will be incorrect. If the driver, carpenter, or mathematician omits a step, the results will also be less than desired.

The job of the computer programmer is to carefully determine the necessary steps to solve a problem. Omitting a step may result in incorrect output, just as inserting an unnecessary or wrong step might, or ordering the instructions in an erroneous sequence. The primary task of the programmer is to develop a solution (called an algorithm) that produces error-free results and communicate that solution to the computer via a programming language so that it carries out the task accurately.

For a given problem, there may be a variety of solutions, methods, and approaches. No two programmers would code a complex program the exact same way. The bottom line is does the program successfully, consistently, and accurately perform the task for which it was designed? One approach may be just as good as another—providing, of course, it always produces correct output.

However, a secondary goal of the programmer is to produce an efficient solution. Generally speaking, the faster a program solves a problem, the better. A program that takes 2 hours to alphabetize 300 names is not as useful as a program that performs the same task in 2 seconds. Although both programs produce correct results, the faster program is clearly more advantageous and economical.

Given the graphical user interfaces (GUIs) of today's computers and the competitiveness within the software industry, the programmer must also be concerned with the aesthetics of a program. End-users prefer flashy screen designs, intuitive interfaces, and bells and whistles, but there is often a trade-off between aesthetics and efficiency. Incorporating multimedia (sound, animation, video) into a program may enhance the interface but deflate the efficiency—screen refresh rates diminish; sound files must be loaded into memory, taking extra time; and the size of the program increases. The programmer must base aesthetic choices on the objectives and purposes of the application. Interface choices may affect the marketability of the software, as well as profitability, productivity, and cost. The more complex the interface is, the more time the programmer requires to design and produce the code. However, as hardware technology improves and becomes more accessible to a broader audience, the trade-offs between efficiency and aesthetics diminish, though the profitability of the project may remain at stake.

Developing an application from start to finish requires several steps. First the program must be planned, then produced, and finally packaged. The complexity of the final product will determine the complexity of each of these steps. This chapter will examine each programming phase in detail.

The Planning Stage of Program Development
Conceptualization

First the idea for the software is conceived. The idea is generally based on some perceived or presented need. A problem exists for which a computerized solution is desired or necessary. Perhaps a software solution already exists, but the goal is a better solution—one that is more efficient, has a better interface, or implements more bells and whistles. In this stage, the programmer or the development team analyzes the problem, examines the input data and the desired output, and contemplates the user interface.

The problem must be properly defined. The goal of managing automotive expenses, for example, is not a properly defined problem. One should ask what tasks must be performed by this software? Should it calculate the miles-per-gallon efficiency? Should it track repair expenses? Should the application provide a reminder of routine maintenance schedules? Will it track only one vehicle or a fleet? Are printed reports needed? How about charts and graphs? Is monthly or annual analysis of expenditures needed? Should it calculate depreciation? The purpose of the program must be examined in detail. The needs and wants of the client and/or the end-user should be researched.

The type of data to be input is examined. The format of the data (numeric or alphabetic, for example) is considered as well as its source. Will the user enter it from the keyboard? Will the data be retrieved from a file on disk? Will it be acquired via the communications port, as in the case of downloading data from a host computer with a modem?

Given the data input and what the program is meant to do, the next step is to determine output. What format will the output take and what will be the mode of display—monitor, printer, file, audio speaker?

The user interface is also decided upon in the planning stage. How will the user interact with the computer to input the needed data? Will the user have any options to choose in working with the data? Should the screen be graphical or textual? Are animations needed to get a point across? How about video or audio? What approach will the interface take—will the tone be all business, whimsical, or technical? The screen designs might be sketched out using a storyboard.

Storyboarding

The storyboard is a design tool borrowed from the television and motion-picture industry. In that context, producers, directors, and writers work with storyboard artists to chart the visual flow of a project. They consider such aspects as props, camera angles, and the direction of the action. These resulting sketches, produced with paper and pencil, are used to explain the story to actors, investors, prop and stage designers, and the production crew. In the world of programming, the increasing popularity and marketability of highly graphical interfaces have made storyboarding necessary as a design tool. Advancements in multimedia and computer animation have made software development as artistic as it is technical. This is especially evident in entertainment software. Full-motion video, CD-quality sound, and high-resolution animation provide realistic gaming experiences for the MTV generation.

Storyboards are helpful for visual problem-solving. Software storyboards for ToolBook-developed applications would show general screen design and graphics, define object locations and attributes, and describe actions and links of controls. Because video games, animations, and simulation courseware often present a story to the user, a programmer uses a storyboard in the planning stage to depict its feel and flow. A development team might use a storyboard to maintain consistency, divide the labor, keep everyone on track, or tell a graphic artist what to produce to be imported into the application. In addition to aiding in the design process,

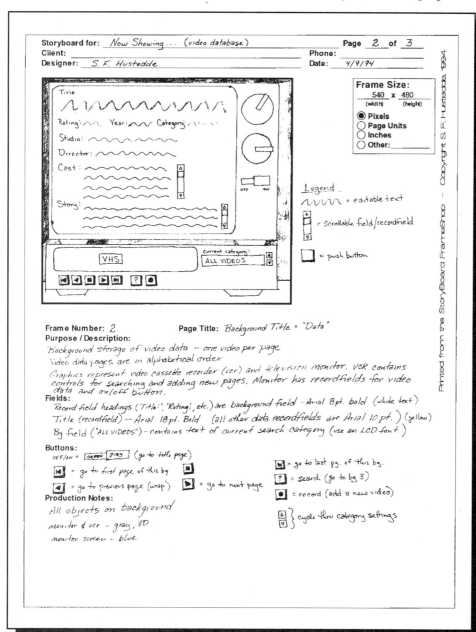

Figure 3.1
A sample storyboard frame. The focus of the storyboard is the sketch of the screen design. Specifications and descriptions of features, explanations of purpose, and production notes assist in the design and development of the project.

storyboards convey information to financial investors, supervisors, and others. In the team approach to development, storyboards can promote brainstorming. Figure 3.1 shows a storyboard frame for the video database presented in the previous chapter.

Brainstorming

Creating modern applications requires a variety of skills: graphic design, video editing, music composing, sound engineering, technical programming, content expertise, and script writing, to name a few. By necessity, software development has become a team project. Large applications, even those that are not multimedia-enhanced, are too complex and time-consuming for one person to develop in a timely manner. A project such as a major commercial word processor may involve hundreds of programmers, designers, and other team members. For entertainment and instructional applications, creativity and thoroughness are best developed through group brainstorming. **Brainstorming** is a problem-solving technique that involves the spontaneous contribution of ideas from members of a group. In the case of program development, the group of brainstormers can be strikingly diverse.

Algorithm Development

The set of procedures used to solve a problem or perform a particular task is called an **algorithm.** If the algorithm is written in a human language, such as English (rather than a programming language), it is called **pseudocode**. Algorithms specify a precise list of procedures that guarantee a correct answer and may involve mathematical analysis, exploratory reasoning, or the simple formulation of linear steps. The number of algorithms to be specified depends on the scope and purpose of the application. Designing a simple program that receives a list of ten numbers and calculates their mean might require only one algorithm; the development of a desktop publishing package would require thousands, one for each task.

The algorithm must be complete. Missed steps or steps performed out of sequence result in inaccurate output or program-halting errors. The algorithm must be accurate and leave no room for ambiguity or misinterpretation. It should also take into account all possible data values, having a strategy for each different scenario. Suppose your algorithm divides one number by another. What if the second number (the divisor) is zero? Dividing by zero results in an error, so the programmer may want to validate that the divisor is not zero before having the computer attempt the calculation. How about negative numbers? A good algorithm also anticipates possible user errors and handles them.

To determine that an algorithm is complete, accurate, and unambiguous, the programmer must design test data. He or she runs this data manually through the algorithm, playing the role of the computer. Such testing is performed for all the various scenarios. A listing of the test data and the results of running it should be maintained for use in testing the produced software.

Flowcharting

The primary tool used by programmers in algorithm development is the flowchart. A **flowchart** is a graphic representation of the steps a computer must perform. Most flowcharts utilize five basic graphical symbols, each containing a text description of the process they represent. A rectangle is used to represent an internal process, such as a mathematical calculation. A parallelogram indicates input and output functions, and a diamond is used for branching questions, where more than one path is possible. A cigar shape indicates the beginning and termination of a process; a small circle is used to connect procedures and link multiple pages (see Figure 3.2). The symbols are connected by vertical and horizontal lines (called flow lines) and arrows that depict the flow from one step to another. The flow is generally represented as moving from top to bottom, with branched steps drawn left to right. A sample problem, with its algorithm solution and flowchart, is illustrated in Figure 3.3.

Flowcharts serve as blueprints for the programmer when he or she goes to

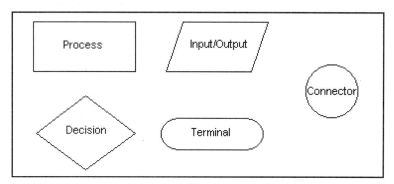

Figure 3.2
The five basic flowcharting symbols.

Figure 3.3
A sample problem, with a possible algorithm and its representative flowchart. The programmer translates the flowchart into code.

Problem: Given any two positive integers, determine the greatest common factor (g.c.f) that they share.

Algorithm: Find the g.c.f by dividing the larger integer by the smaller. If the remainder is zero, the smaller number is the g.c.f. If the remainder is not zero, substitute the smaller number for the larger and the remainder for the smaller number and repeat this process until a remainder of zero is reached and, therefore, the g.c.f. is discovered. To summarize these steps:
1. Get the two integers and assign to variables a and b.
2. If b is greater than a, then exchange them.
3. Divide a by b, assign remainder to variable r.
4. If r = 0, go to step 8.
5. Replace a with b.
6. Replace b with r.
7. Go to step 3.
8. Report the value of b as the g.c.f. End.

Test Data:
Find g.c.f. of 96 and 76.

a	b	r
96	76	20
76	20	16
20	16	4
16	4	0

The g.c.f is 4.

Flowchart:
The flowchart at the right is a graphic representation of the algorithm steps listed above.

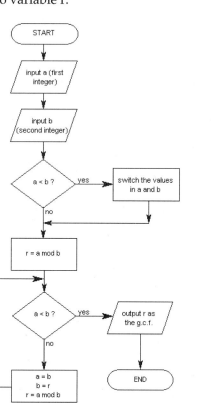

develop the code. They visually depict the logic and process structure of an algorithm and are thus easily translated into programming language code. As the flowchart is developed, the details of the problem may become more apparent, showing unforeseen pitfalls as well as solutions and alternative methods. The symbols employed in flowcharting are used worldwide. Flowcharts are not language specific; the processes they describe could be coded in any of numerous computer languages.

Flowcharting facilitates algorithm testing, because the programmer can run test data through the logic flow. The flowchart also aids in the debugging process because the graphic layout points to logic flaws, unterminated processes, and the like.

Because the symbols and their uses are standardized, flowcharts are an excellent tool for communicating ideas and processes to other programmers. They can be helpful in discussing proposed solutions and brainstorming ideas. In the team approach to software development, flowcharts aid in the division of labor. After the flowcharts are completed, the systems analyst or project manager might distribute the various flowcharts to assign different processes to different programmers.

Flowcharts provide essential technical documentation months or years later, when the original programmers or their successors must modify, update, or expand the code. Without a flowchart, the logic expressed by the code might be hard to understand. The process of flowcharting is described in detail later in this chapter.

The Production Stage of Program Development
Coding

The algorithm developed, the programmer sets out to instruct the computer. He or she translates the steps of the algorithm into the commands of a computer language. Human languages are comprised of words and grammatical rules. Likewise, computer languages have vocabulary—composed of commands, keywords, properties, parameters, and function names—and grammatical rules or **syntax.** OpenScript, like all computer languages, has vocabulary and syntax.

Humans can generally break the grammatical rules of their language and still understand each other. They can even use an unknown word but still get the point across via contextual meaning. One can watch a foreign film and understand the story line because of the actions of the actors. Such contextual understanding is not available in communicating with computers. Computers are exact, very structured beasts. They can't think or feel or guess at what you mean. The programmer learns quickly that the code entered into the computer must be precise, follow the syntax rules, and utilize only the clearly defined commands of the computer language. The computer cannot be told to "obtain the text of field lastname" when it only understands "get the text of field lastname." *Get* and *obtain* may mean the same thing to us humans, but the computer's vocabulary is quite limited. In fact, ToolBook's OpenScript language only has 96 commands, the majority of which are rarely employed. In some human languages—Greek, for example—the order of the words in the sentence is not important. But once again, a computer language is exact and the order of the parameters and options following commands and keywords is essential.

Some programmers write the code on paper and then enter the finished code into the computer. Others write the code directly into the computer, using the editor to make changes as necessary. Whichever method you choose, remember that the code must be exact. An extra comma here or a misspelled variable name there will likely result in an error or erroneous output.

Testing

After entering the code into the computer, the programmer tests it by running the program. It is necessary to confirm that the result is error-free and the desired performance is achieved. With an authoring package like ToolBook and its object-oriented environment, the entire application need not be completed before testing. One of the advantages of ToolBook is that most object processes are small and stand alone. Each script may be developed, executed, tested, and debugged without regard for unrelated sections of code or the other processes. The author often codes parts of an application before even designing other portions.

After the programmer has tested the application and deemed it sound, others may be invited to use and test it. Such field tests (sometimes referred to as beta testing) often turn up unforeseen problems and errors. One reason for unforeseen problems is that different computers have different capabilities. Different users constitute another reason. Users may click something, press some keyboard key, enter some piece of data, or perform some other action that was not considered in the planning stage. Remember that the objective in algorithm design was to consider all the bases? Field tests often point out bases unknown. Field tests also allow end-users to provide feedback about what features they like or dislike, what capabilities are missing, and how easily they interacted with the interface. The more types of computers and configurations the application is tested on and the more end-users who put the program through its paces, the more stable and error-free it will be when finally distributed.

Debugging

Back in the early days of computing, a repairman was called to a computer site because a gigantic room-sized computer was not functioning properly. The problem, the repairman determined, was a dead moth inside the computer's housing. The repairman removed the moth, and proclaimed the computer "debugged." The term stuck and is used today to refer to locating and fixing errors in a program. The errors may be rooted in the logic of the algorithm or be as simple (but just as fatal) as a typographical error in the code. The programmer returns to the algorithm or coding stages as required. This process is repeated until the code functions properly, efficiently, and 100% consistently.

The Packaging Stage of Program Development

Documentation

How many times have you heard someone exclaim "This software manual is horrible! I can't understand anything it's telling me to do." Documentation is too often the forgotten or hurried step of program development. This is not without reason. The documentation, in particular the user's manual, is usually not written until the program is complete and bug-free. What this means for a software manufacturer is that, while the manual is being written, the finished product is sitting on the warehouse shelves, waiting to be shipped. Needless to say there is great pressure to complete the documentation quickly and get the product to market, not only to generate income but to also get a jump on the competition. Hence, inferior documentation. Fortunately, this problem is diminishing. The documentation in-cluded with ToolBook is thoughtfully organized and relatively well written. As a student of ToolBook, you are encouraged to become familiar with both the written and on-line documentation provided by Asymetrix. It will prove invaluable when you begin writing code—particularly the *OpenScript Reference Manual*, which lists important syntactical information as well as examples.

Accurate, thorough, and understandable documentation must be provided for the user. Documentation should explain the interface and each control and option. Documentation must be nontechnical, describing the purpose of the program as well as its use. The user should be clearly informed as to what data must be provided and in what format. Interpretation of the output and potential error messages may need to be covered. Documentation may be in print, provided as an on-line help feature, attached as a separate "read-me" file, or a combination of these. Installation instructions should be provided in printed documentation or in a read-me file.

There is one other document that the wise developer will produce. This is technical information for him- or herself or perhaps other programmers who someday may need to modify, expand, update, or debug the code. As mentioned, no two programmers think alike or code alike. Trying to read someone else's code without guiding comments is like reading a map without knowing which direction is north. This is even true of reading one's own code a year or two later. A programmer's techniques change as experience deepens. Technical documentation should explain logic, identify variables (and the values they contain), and list user-defined properties or functions. Flowcharts should be included or maintained. Like the user's manual, technical documentation may be written separately or included on line in the form of comments sprinkled amongst the working code. Commented code is ignored by the computer in running the application. It is there for the human's benefit, not the computer's. In OpenScript, any line of code that starts with two hyphens (--) is regarded as a comment and ignored. Figure 3.4 shows an example of OpenScript code (called a script) with embedded comments. Commented scripts are easy to understand; therefore they are easier to edit or debug.

Figure 3.4
An example of OpenScript code containing comments. This is the program script of the algorithm presented in Figure 3.3. Note the indented format, which enhances reading the code and following its logic.

```
to handle buttonup
    --get the two integers and assign to variables a and b
    ask "Enter the first positive integer:"
    put it into a
    ask "Enter the second positive integer:"
    put it into b
    if a < b then --if the first integer is the smaller
        --next 3 lines switch values of a and b
        put a into c
        put b into a
        put c into b
    end if
    put a mod b into r
    -- (a mod b) is the remainder of a divided by b
    while r<>0 --repeat this section until remainder = 0
        -- replace a with b, b with r, and find remainder.
        put b into a
        put r into b
        put a mod b into r
    end while
    --output the answer
    request "The greatest common factor is " & r & "."
end buttonup
```

Distribution

Few programs are actually distributed; most applications are developed for personal use. But, for those that are shared with others, the programmer must consider how the application will be distributed and marketed. Commercial applications are marketed through retail stores. While commercial applications may have printed documentation, applications distributed as shareware will likely require on-line help for the user. Public domain and shareware programs are most often uploaded to electronic bulletin boards or provided to distributors of such packages. Before distribution, one must consider copyright and legal issues. Does your package contain audio clips, digitized video, text or scanned artwork or photos that are copyrighted? If so, the copyright holder must give permission for the use of the copyrighted elements. Another issue to be addressed in the distribution stage is support. Who will end-users contact for technical assistance and how will they do it? Will they use e-mail, phone, or mail, for example?

Design Issues

As the program is being designed, the developer must look at its objectives. Who are the intended users? What are their ages and computer skills? In designing an educational program for preschool children, the interface needs to be entirely graphical. Likewise, if it is a phonetic tutorial for illiterate adults. If the user is likely to be computer illiterate, a tutorial on how to use a mouse may need to be included.

What hardware will be needed to run the application? Dependence on a sound card will reduce the size of the potential audience—only those with sound capabilities in their machines will be able to use the program. The same holds true when utilizing high-resolution color graphics. Those without such video capabilities will not be able to appreciate the programmer's efforts. Large multimedia applications may only be useful to those with CD-ROM drives.

Production considerations can also affect program design. Is there a time frame for completion? Are there budget constraints? In designing a kiosk for a local convention, the program is of little use if it is not completed until after the convention dates have passed. What are your distribution medium constraints? Digitized video might assist in showing a novice how to use a mouse, but the large file the technology requires might make the application suitable for CD-ROM distribution only.

The user interface is a key design consideration. What type of navigational tools are needed? Should the navigational buttons be on the pages of the book or in a movable palette floating on top? Navigational buttons on the pages should be presented consistently, in the same location on each page. Can the user explore the book randomly, or must the material be presented linearly? In this day of multimedia and high-resolution graphics, aesthetic issues must be addressed.

Content needs are determined before the project is designed. Should a map be included? How about an index, a table of contents, or graphics? If graphics are to be included how will they be obtained? Will they be drawn with ToolBook, designed with another software package, or scanned? Perhaps the best course is to use commercial clipart. Is multimedia needed? Sound might be important for a phonetic tutorial but inappropriate for a financial management program. Is feedback required on choices the user will make? For instructional courseware, should the user be able to provide feedback to the instructor on line?

Attention to legal issues, such as copyright considerations, is necessary to keep you out of court. Copyright laws apply when including digitized audio and video, scanned photographs, or even copyrighted fonts. Code and functions borrowed from other ToolBook books may also be copyright-protected and entitle the copyright holder to a portion of your bank account.

What about security? Does the application store sensitive information such as payroll data, security passwords, or unlisted phone numbers? An on-line exam graded by the computer may need to have the answers in an encrypted format, hidden from the curious eyes of the computer hacker. Do you care if users with ToolBook authoring knowledge have access to your code? If so, scripts may need to be removed or a password protection scheme built in.

The Process of Flowcharting

Flowcharts have traditionally been drawn with paper and pencil, and a plastic template available at graphic art or computer stores. Today, like graphics in general, they are increasingly being generated electronically. There are numerous flowcharting packages on the market. The advantage of drawing on the computer is the ease with which the symbols may be rearranged and modified.

Flowcharts consist of standardized symbols, each shape representing a particular type of task. Flowcharts are drawn in such a way that they generally flow from top to bottom or left to right. The symbols are connected by flow lines (horizontal and vertical), which traditionally have arrows at one end to show the flow direction. The flow lines may meet but should not cross. Descriptions written inside the symbols briefly but precisely outline the procedure the symbol represents. Typically each description starts with a verb, such as *get*, *print*, or *calculate*. Complicated flowcharts can take many pages.

Flowcharts begin with the cigar-shaped **terminal symbol** with the word "Start" written in it (see Figure 3.5). This standardized start symbol provides assistance in locating the beginning point; it doesn't necessarily correlate to a programming language command. The terminal symbol is used to depict the beginning of a procedure as well as the end or ends of the procedure. In signifying an end point, the word "End" is written inside the symbol rather than "Start."

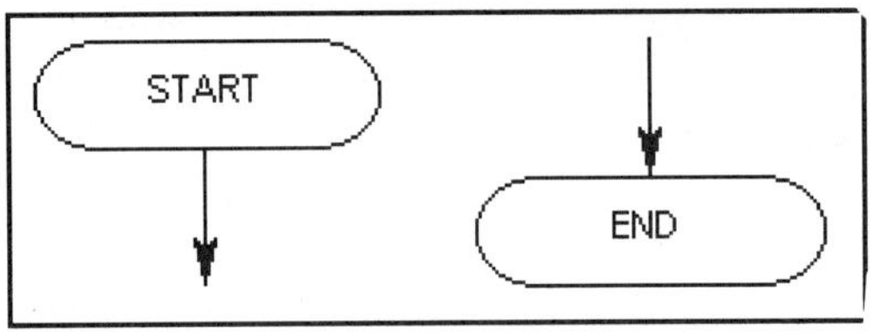

Figure 3.5
The terminal symbol is used to mark the start of a process as well as an end point of the process.

Each process must have only one starting point and at least one ending point. For a procedure with multiple paths (called **branches**), there may be multiple end points. There should be only one flow line coming out of the starting terminal symbol, and only one flow line going into the ending symbol.

The **input/output symbol** (often abbreviated **I/O symbol**) is a parallelogram used to represent data entering the computer (see Figure 3.6). The source of this data might be the user pressing a mouse button or typing on the keyboard. Or it might be information stored in a file on a diskette that is sought by the program. In the case of a communications task, the data may come from the computer's serial port, to which is connected a modem receiving downloaded information from an electronic bulletin board service.

Figure 3.6
The input/output symbol represents steps involving the acquisition of data and the displaying or storage of data.

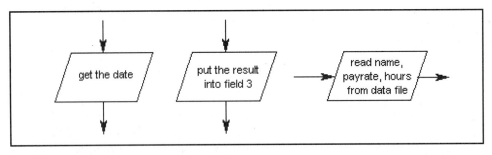

The input/output symbol is also used to represent information being output from the program. This would include data being displayed on the monitor screen, written to a file on diskette, printed to a printer, or sent to a serial port or sound being played on the computer's internal speaker or sound card.

A description of the input being gathered or the output being generated is written inside the symbol, in the same manner that "Start" or "End" was written in the terminal symbol. The I/O symbol should always have one flow line in and another flow line out.

Operations performed internally, by the computer, are represented by the rectangular **process symbol** (see Figure 3.7). Mathematical calculations, alphabetical sorting of a list of names, parsing of an alphanumeric string, the declaration of a constant value, or the dimensioning of an array are just a few examples of internal processes. As with the input/output symbol, the process symbol always has one flow line coming in and another flow line coming out.

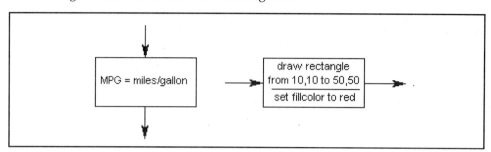

Figure 3.7
The process symbol represents an internal process performed by the computer. Such processes include mathematical calculations, animations and drawing routines, and built-in functions.

Oftentimes there is a need for the application to evaluate whether some condition exists and perform different processes depending on the evaluation. For instance, the computer might evaluate whether one value is larger or smaller than another. If it is larger, the program subtracts the second from the first, but if it is smaller, the first is subtracted from the second. Each of the two different processes is called a branch, and the point at which the decision is made is a condition. It is this condition that is represented by the diamond-shaped **decision symbol** (see Figure 3.8).

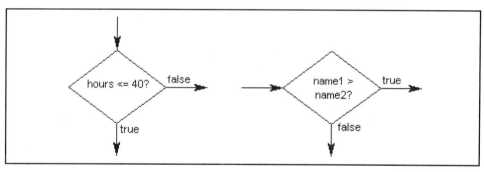

Figure 3.8
The decision symbol shows that the program is evaluating a situation and branching to one of two different paths, depending on the result (true or false).

The description in the decision symbol is a question that can be answered yes or no (or true or false). One line comes to the decision symbol at one of its points. Two lines go away from the symbol, each from another point. The lines leaving the symbol go to two different branches. These two lines are labeled Yes and No, or True and False (or sometime abbreviated as Y and N, or T and F).

The **connector symbol**, a small circle, is used to connect intersecting flow lines to mark an exit from or an entry to another part of the flowchart (see Figure 3.9). In the case of two branches coming together (where two flow lines turn into one) the connector symbol might be used. (Some programmers just intersect the flow lines without the connector symbol, using arrows to clarify the flow.) In some branches control may jump to a later position in the flowchart. Two connector symbols are used to indicate such a broken flow line. A letter or number is written inside each circle. Others reading the flowchart match the identically labeled connectors and regard them as if they were connected by flow line.

Algorithms can be complex, requiring the flowchart to extend across several pages. The connector symbol is used to connect the flow between pages. Some programmers use

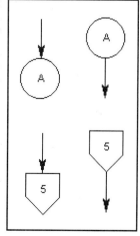

Figure 3.9
The connector (top) and the off-page connector (bottom) are used to connect remote pieces of a flowchart symbolically.

the specialized **off-page connector symbol,** resembling the home plate of a baseball field or an upside-down house, for connecting processes across pages. In either case, there should be one line in or one line out of the connector symbol.

A flowchart template or a flowcharting software application will contain symbols in addition to those discussed here. Many, carried over from mainframe development, represent input/output devices such as punched cards or magnetic tape. Others represent specialized processes, such as sorting or collating, and are rarely used.

Summary Questions

Answer the following true/false questions.

1. Computers are very intelligent and can easily decide what process must be performed to accomplish a specific task.
2. Programming is essentially determining the steps to solve a problem and writing these steps in a language and format the computer can understand.
3. The flowchart symbol that represents an input of data is a rectangle.
4. The connector symbol is used to mark a remote entrance to or a remote exit from a flowchart.
5. There is always one line in and one line out of a process symbol.
6. In OpenScript, a line of code beginning with two hyphens (--) is considered a comment and is ignored by the computer during the execution of the script.
7. The OpenScript language consists of over two thousand commands.
8. Using, without permission, a digitized video segment of a recent movie in a computer application is likely to be a violation of copyright laws.
9. There are generally several approaches to handling a programming task.
10. Programming languages are very exact and require the programmer to adhere to rules of syntax .

Complete the following statements by filling in the blanks.

11. The set of steps used to solve a problem is an _____.
12. A diagram of an algorithm is a _____.
13. In flowcharting, a mathematical calculation is represented by the _____ symbol.
14. A diamond-shaped flowchart symbol is called the _____ symbol.
15. A _____ consists of sketches of screen designs and addresses the flow and linking of the various screens.
16. Finding the errors in a program is known as _____.
17. I/O is an abbreviation for _____.
18. Terminal symbols contain the word _____ or _____.
19. _____ in the code assists debugging and modification.
20. Algorithm steps written in English are referred to as _____.

Hands-On Projects

A. Examine the software that accompanies this chapter. Open the "Table of Contents" book by double-clicking its icon in the "Developing with ToolBook" group window in the Windows Program Manager. Inside the "Table of Contents", click the book representing Chapter 3. Work your way through the tutorial as a means of enforcing and enriching the information presented in this chapter (see Figure 3.10).

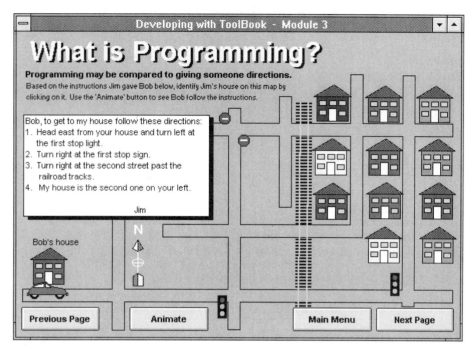

Figure 3.10
The software tutorial for this chapter interactively enforces and enriches the material presented in the text.

B. The Storyboard FrameShop is a utility application supplied with this text. It is used to print a blank storyboard frame. The frame size can be adjusted by clicking the width and height fields at the right of the frame. From the menu, choose Print Storyboard. (If you do not have access to a printer, create your own form with paper and pen.) Create a storyboard for one of the following three projects. Each storyboard should contain frames for each significant screen of the proposed project—a title, or opening, screen; a data screen; and so on.

1. Design a program that will teach kindergarten students the letters of the alphabet. You might consider a screen that shows a letter, such as *A*, and words and pictures that start with the letter *A*. You might consider an interactive game requiring the student to click on a requested letter. As the developer, you decide the approach and design the screens. (Storyboards need not contain every screen but should represent each particular design. For instance, if there is one screen for each letter of the alphabet and the screens are all similar, choose one letter and show the format for that screen. If there are other significantly different screens, sketch those as well. In developing courseware, a question screen, a feedback screen, and a remedial-instruction screen might be appropriate.)

2. Choose a popular board game or card game and design a storyboard for a computerized version. Consider what changes might need to be made for the electronic version.

3. Design a book containing information about various wild animals in your state, creating a storyboard of sample screens. Think through the type of information that should be included about each species.

C. Study the flowchart shown in Figure 3.11 which deals with changing a flat tire. Choose one of the following everyday processes and draw a similar flowchart, showing the steps and decisions involved.

1. Building a snowman
2. Changing a baby's diaper
3. Filling your car's gas tank (include the steps of paying for it)
4. Getting from your home to work or school

Figure 3.11
A flowchart showing the steps in changing a tire. Note the use of connector symbols (A matches A and B matches B) and the two terminal ends. The flowchart flows from top to bottom and from left to right.

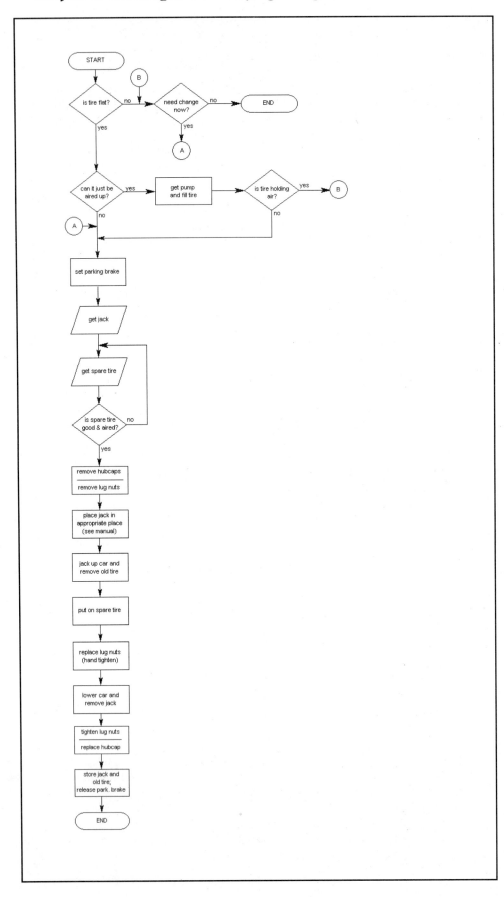

Chapter 4

Dissection of a Book

The Parts of a ToolBook Application

A ToolBook application can be compared to a stage production. Both the ToolBook book and the play are media for presenting information and ideas. Just as the ToolBook book presents information one screen or page at a time, the play is organized into various acts and scenes. A ToolBook application presents information through textual fields; these might be comparable to the actors and actresses on the stage. The book itself is presented inside the fixed area of a window, often with a titlebar, menubar, and scrollbars. Likewise, the action of the play is confined to the space of the stage, with its curtain, spotlights, and other features. In ToolBook, collective pages might share the same background, which contains various objects. Collective scenes of the play might share the same backdrop. Various graphical objects dress up the ToolBook screens; props enhance the action on the stage. The actions of ToolBook objects are determined by their underlying scripts, written in OpenScript, the programming language of ToolBook. The action and words on the stage are dictated by the playwright's script.

Books

Files created with ToolBook are called **books**. These files usually have a .TBK extension, though some specialized books called system books can have an extension of .SBK. Books may be saved as executable files; in that case they should be given the .EXE filename extension. Although most often consisting of one book, ToolBook applications may be made up of several books that are linked. The software designed for Chapter 2 of this text, for instance, was composed of several different books. There was the What Can I Do with ToolBook? menu screen, which was one book. This book served as a front end to other books, such as the top-10 list, the calculator, the video database, and the fraction tutorial. Each of these was called by clicking a button on the menu screen and returned to the menu screen when closed. A programmer designing an accounting-inventory application might use one book for the inventory, another as a customer database, a third as a current billing database, and a fourth as a point-of-sales application. All of these may be interconnected and share data.

Viewers

On the computer monitor, books are presented inside a window or within several windows. In ToolBook terminology, such windows are defined as **viewers**. The programmer determines the viewer's size and position; whether it will have a titlebar; and, if so, what its caption will be; whether it will have scrollbars; and if the viewer can be minimized or maximized. Every book has at least one viewer, often referred to as the main window. Viewers are set up by making selections in a properties dialog box called "Viewer Properties" (see Figure 4.1). Therefore, defining a viewer requires little or no programming on the part of the author. Besides defining the main window of the book, viewers are also used to present progress boxes,

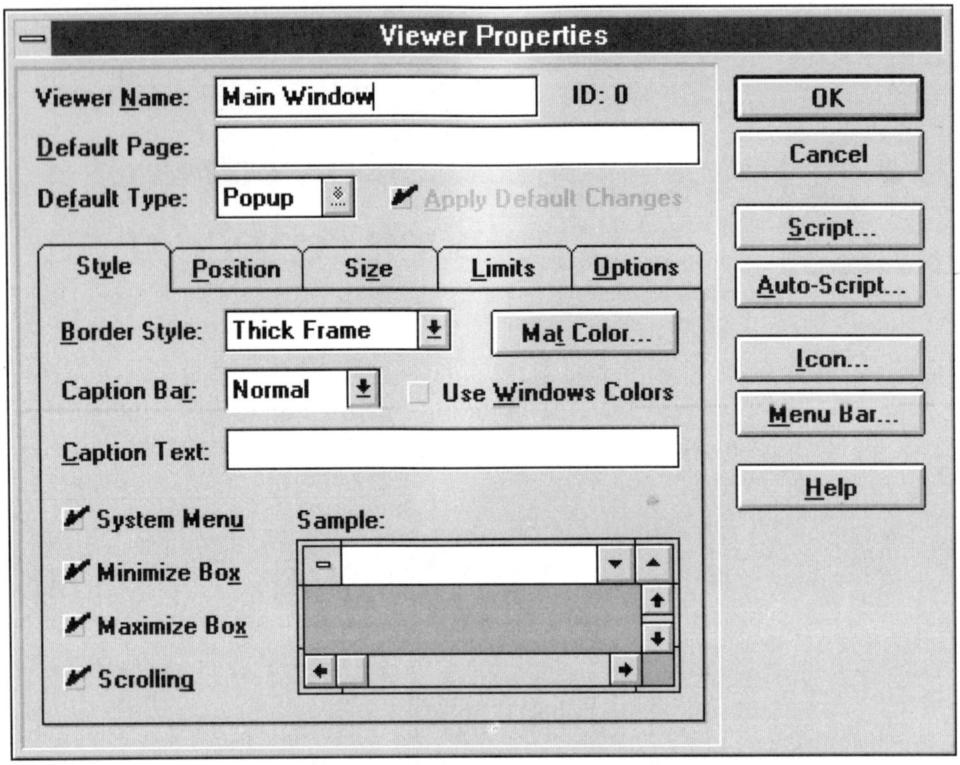

Figure 4.1
The attributes of a viewer
are set up in the "Viewer
Properties" dialog box,
which eliminates
complicated programming.

dialogs, palettes, and pop-up information windows. Viewers are briefly discussed in Chapter 7.

Pages

Every book is made up of one or more **pages**. Pages are also referred to as screens. Some books have only one page. The calculator presented in Chapter 2 has only one page, for only one page was necessary. The information on the page may change, as does the display at the top of the calculator. Objects on a page may even appear, disappear, and move as in an animation. Other books might be composed of many pages. In the video database introduced in Chapter 2, each video was represented by one page and the user could flip through the pages or seek certain pages. The search screen where the user enters a name or title to search for is a separate page as well. The number of pages in a book is determined by the author, based on how the information is best organized.

The page size of a book is variable and best determined by the amount of information, the book's purpose, and aesthetic issues. The page size of the calculator application was very small. Its interactive buttons and the display field fit into a small area. The calculator might be utilized in conjunction with another book; by keeping its page size and viewer size small, information in another book can be viewed simultaneously. In developing courseware, there is often large amounts of information to be presented, requiring a large page and viewer size. A full-screen viewer and page are often desired to eliminate other visible applications, such as the Program Manager. The tax form application of Chapter 2 utilizes a full-screen (640- by 480-pixel) viewer. The page size is even larger than the viewer, conforming to the dimensions and size of the paper-based tax form it represents, and permitting all of the same information to be presented and requested. Although the viewer and page size are often correlated, the tax form application shows that they need not be the same.

Backgrounds

Every page has two layers on which information can be attached: a page or foreground layer, and a **background** layer. Since every page has a background and every book has at least one page, every book then has at least one background. The number of backgrounds in a book varies from one to the number of pages in a book. A 20-page book, for instance, may have one background or 20 backgrounds or any number in between. The reason for this is that, though every page has a background, several pages can share the same background. Back to the analogy between ToolBook and a play: This is like several scenes or acts of a play sharing the same backdrop and props.

Backgrounds are positioned behind the pages (see Figure 4.2). Pages are transparent in that all objects on a background are visible, unless there are objects on the page layer hiding them. If a background is colored, all pages that share it are the same color. Backgrounds are also used to maintain objects that are common to two or more pages. For instance, consider a 20-page book where the author wants one button to take the user to the previous page and another to navigate to the next page. The buttons should appear on every page of the book. The author can create 2 such buttons on every page of the book for a total of 40 buttons. An alternative (and better)

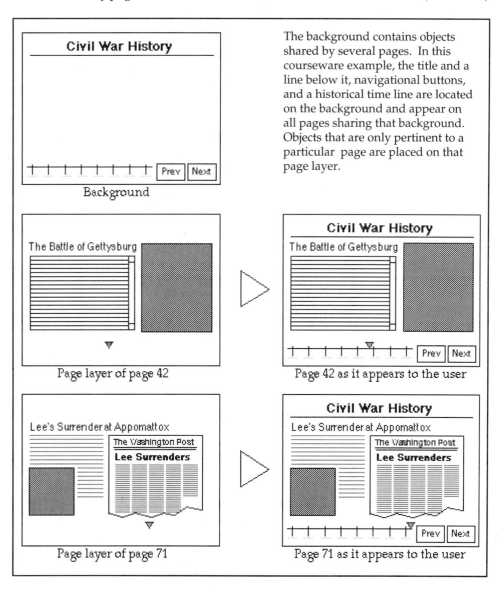

The background contains objects shared by several pages. In this courseware example, the title and a line below it, navigational buttons, and a historical time line are located on the background and appear on all pages sharing that background. Objects that are only pertinent to a particular page are placed on that page layer.

Figure 4.2
The page layer is transparent, revealing the underlying background. The objects on both layers are visible to the user.

approach would be to place the two buttons on a background shared by the 20 pages. Since the background objects are visible through the pages, each page would still have the 2 buttons, but instead of creating 40 buttons the author would create only 2. Think of the memory and time savings! If the author did not want a "previous page" button on the 1st page nor a "next page" button on the 20th page, he or she could cover the undesired button on those two pages with a rectangle the same color as the background, or with some other object.

Objects

The primary functionality of a ToolBook book derives from the **objects** on its pages and backgrounds. The pages and backgrounds of a book merely provide a framework or foundation upon which the book is built. But it is the various objects and their scripts that define the book's purpose, usefulness, interface, and aesthetics. There are several types or classes of objects in ToolBook—buttons, fields and recordfields, and graphics—and each class of objects has many styles and formats.

Buttons are the primary interactive object of a book. Buttons are most commonly used as the controls of the user interface. A user clicks a button to advance to the next page, toggle an option on or off, make a selection, start an animation, and so on. Buttons can take on a range of attributes (see Figure 4.3). Buttons may be animated (as in the case of the push-button style), contain captions, be highlighted when clicked, and even contain an icon or bitmap. Buttons may perform various functions, depending on the user activity. Clicking a button may result in one action; a double-click or a right-button click may result in a completely different action. Creating buttons is covered in detail in Chapter 9.

Fields and **recordfields** are containers for textual information. There are a variety of styles (see Figure 4.4), and the font and paragraph characteristics of their text is fully alterable. Specific words or phrases of the text may be selected and defined as **hotwords**—textual buttons within the text of the field that perform some action when acted upon by the user. Typical actions include showing a definition or navigating to a different page containing related information. Like buttons, fields may be placed on either the background or the page. Text in a background field

Figure 4.3
Buttons come in a variety of sizes and styles, including push buttons, radio buttons, checkboxes, and shadowed buttons.

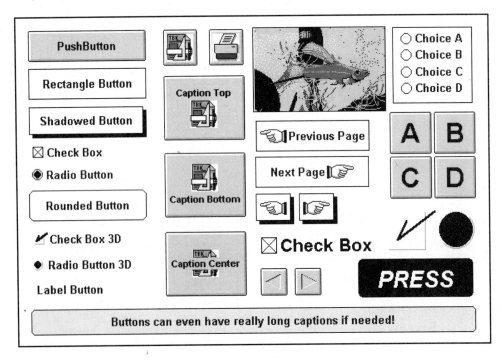

Text fields come in a variety of sizes and styles. This is a rectangle style field.

This is a scrolling style field. These are used to hold more text than is viewable in the size of the field.

This is a shadowed style field.

This is a raised style field.

This is an inset style field.

The text in a field can utilize different fonts such as Arial, Times, Bordeaux, or Marquee. The text can also be different sizes:

8 9 10 12 16 18 24

Fields can even include bitmap images:

𝔉𝔦𝔢𝔩𝔡𝔰 𝔡𝔬𝔫'𝔱 𝔥𝔞𝔳𝔢
𝔱𝔬 𝔥𝔞𝔳𝔢 𝔞 𝔟𝔬𝔯𝔡𝔢𝔯!

Wherever you see text, there is probably a field or recordfield.

1 2 3 4 5 6 7 8 9 10 11

Figure 4.4
Like buttons, fields may have a variety of styles, including inset, scrolling, shadowed, and combo boxes.

Figure 4.5
The ToolBook Tool palette (in the upper left) includes several tools for creating draw-type graphics such as those pictured here.

appears on each page sharing that background. Recordfields are like background fields, except that while placed on the background they allow different text to appear on each page. Fields, recordfields, and hotwords are further discussed in Chapter 10.

The ToolBook authoring environment has several different tools for creating **graphical objects,** such as rectangles, ellipses, lines, and polygons (see Figure 4.5). These objects are draw-type (also referred to as vector-oriented or object-oriented), meaning that their shape, size, and position are defined by mathematical formulas. Such graphics may be easily resized, moved, and even reshaped. This is in contrast to paint-oriented, or bitmapped graphics, which are defined as a collection of pixels, or dots. Paint-type graphics are not easily resized or reshaped without distortion or loss. There are advantages and disadvantages to each type, but draw-type graphics provide greater flexibility and superior printing and are better utilized in animations. Although only draw-type graphics may be created within ToolBook, both draw-type and bitmapped graphics can be imported from other graphics packages. Chapter 11 discusses creating graphics in ToolBook and importing images.

Scripts

Buttons, fields, and graphics have no functionality when they are created. The author defines the action of each by writing a script attached to the desired object. **Scripts** are short programs written in OpenScript, ToolBook's programming language (see Figure 4.6). Each script has a handler that defines the event triggering the action. The most common handler is **to handle buttonUp**, which, when the user clicks the object, executes the code between itself and the **end buttonUp** statement. It is the scripts that perform the work of the application. Although it is possible to develop simple interactive applications by using the hyperlink, autoscript, and script recorder functions, the power of ToolBook cannot be unleashed without a good understanding of OpenScript and how to write effective, efficient scripts. Chapters 12 through 29 focus on scripting and the programming theory behind writing code in OpenScript or other programming languages.

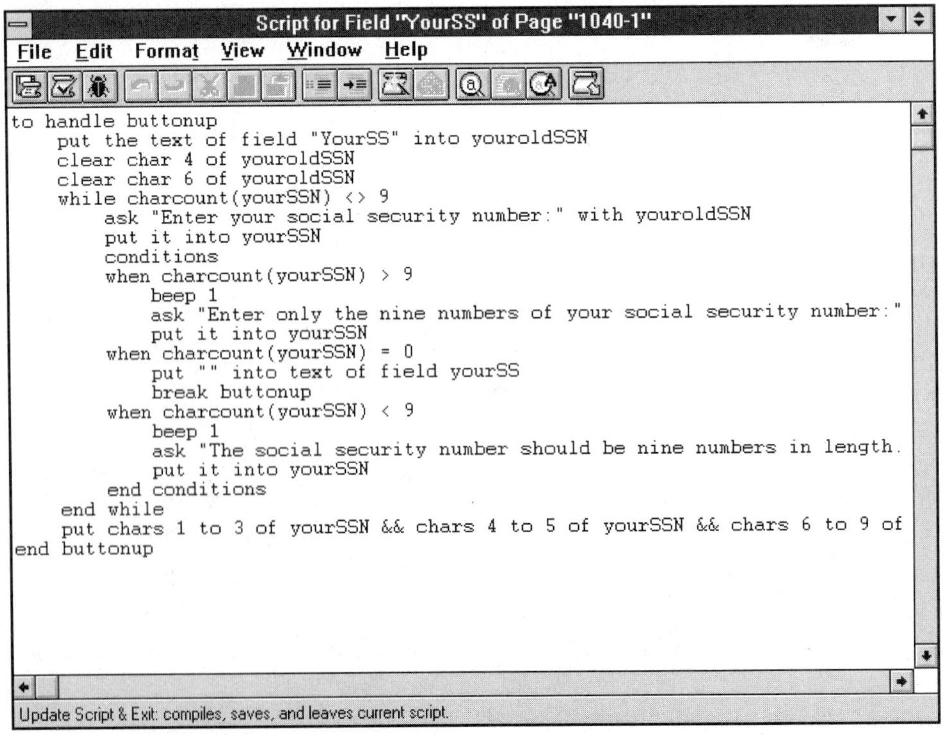

Figure 4.6
Scripts are written in the script editor, a word processor-like window. Scripts contain handlers defining the events; handlers trigger the code's action. In this example the event being handled is the release of the left mouse button.

```
to handle buttonup
    put the text of field "YourSS" into youroldSSN
    clear char 4 of youroldSSN
    clear char 6 of youroldSSN
    while charcount(yourSSN) <> 9
        ask "Enter your social security number:" with youroldSSN
        put it into yourSSN
        conditions
        when charcount(yourSSN) > 9
            beep 1
            ask "Enter only the nine numbers of your social security number:"
            put it into yourSSN
        when charcount(yourSSN) = 0
            put "" into text of field yourSS
            break buttonup
        when charcount(yourSSN) < 9
            beep 1
            ask "The social security number should be nine numbers in length."
            put it into yourSSN
        end conditions
    end while
    put chars 1 to 3 of yourSSN && chars 4 to 5 of yourSSN && chars 6 to 9 of
end buttonup
```

Script for Field "YourSS" of Page "1040-1"

File Edit Format View Window Help

Update Script & Exit: compiles, saves, and leaves current script.

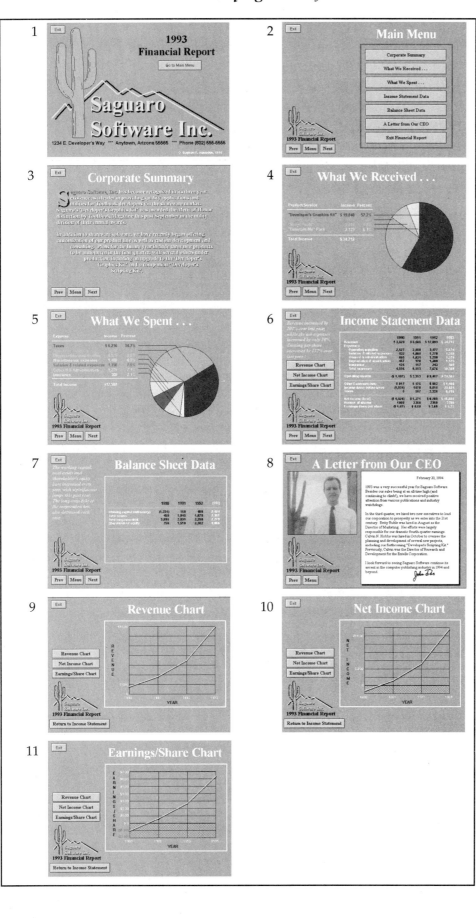

Figure 4.7
Books are made up of pages. Each page is a separate screen. The business report presented in Chapter 2 consists of the 11 pages shown here. The user navigates through the pages by clicking interactive buttons such as "Prev" or "Next" or the buttons on the menu screen (page 2).

Dissection of a Book

In this section, the business report application presented in Chapter 2 is examined to show the various objects that make up the presentation. The application consists of one file (book) named BUSINESS.TBK. The book consists of the 11 pages shown in Figure 4.7, which are navigated by the user.

Page 1 (Title Screen)

Page 1 is the presentation's title screen and is composed of various objects, as illustrated in Figure 4.8. The gray color of the page is set up on the background. All other objects (the text, graphics, buttons) are located on the foreground page layer. The title, "1993 Financial Report," is a field with its character attributes set up as Times New Roman, 24 point. The company name, "Saguaro Software Inc.," is created with two overlapping fields to create the shadowed effect. The text of the bottom-layered field is black; the top-layered field is yellow. Likewise, the mountain image (the logo) was created with two separate graphics, a black line and an overlapping yellow line. The address text is a fourth field of black text and a smaller font, and the copyright notice is a fifth field with its text set to white. The saguaro cactus is a clipart image drawn in another graphics package and imported into this book. There are two buttons on this page. The "Exit" button closes this presentation; the "Go to Main Menu" button takes the user to the "Main Menu" screen (page 2) when clicked. Scripts attached to each of the buttons define these actions.

Figure 4.8
The objects of page 1 of the business report application include fields, graphics, and buttons.

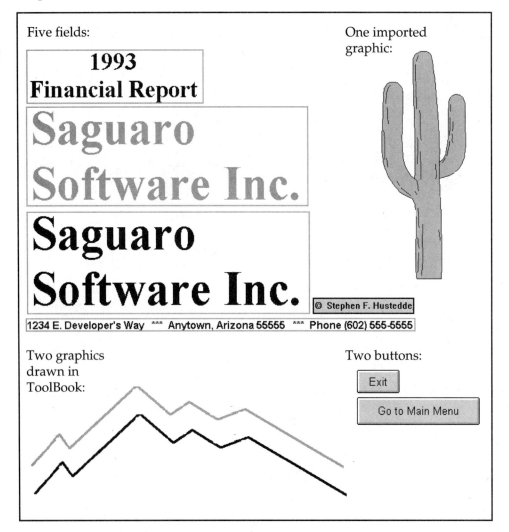

Background 2

Pages 2 through 11 all share a second background. The page color of this background is the same shade of gray as the background of the first page. On this background are several objects. A smaller version of the logo of page 1 was created with a background field, two lines for the mountain image, and the same cactus clipart, but smaller. Towards the top of the background is a recordfield that serves as a place holder for the title text of each page with this background. Recordfields are specialized background fields that allow different text on each page. There are four buttons on the background. The "Exit" button closes the presentation. The "Prev" button navigates to the previous page (for example, clicking the "Prev" button on page 6 brings up page 5). In the same manner, the "Next" button navigates to the next page of the book. Clicking the "Menu" button brings up the "Main Menu" screen (page 2). Each of these buttons has a script attached that determines the reaction to the user's click. For example, the "Menu" button's script is activated when the mouse button is released on the "Menu" button. A click generates three event messages: a buttonDown (the mouse button is pressed down); a buttonUp (the mouse button is released); and finally, a buttonClick. Note that the word *button* is used here in discussing two different things: an interactive object in ToolBook and the physical button on the mouse. The following is the script attached to the "Menu" button.

```
to handle buttonUp
    go to page "Main Menu"
end buttonUp
```

The following is the script of the "Prev" button.

```
to handle buttonUp
    go to previous page
end buttonUp
```

Page 2 (Main Menu)

The objects of background 2 are active and visible through page 2. Figure 4.9 shows how page 2 is constructed of background 2 and the foreground (page) layer of page 2. The text "Main Menu" is entered on the page layer into the background's recordfield. Additional objects on the page layer include seven push buttons linking to several other pages of the book and a rectangular graphic surrounding the buttons. The graphic is used here as a visual aid to tie all the buttons together.

Page 3 (Corporate Summary)

Besides the objects of background 2, page 3 contains four fields. The body text of this page is duplicated in two overlapping fields to provide a shadowed effect, the same effect used with the company name on page 1. The drop cap (the "S" starting the body text) was created with two additional overlapping fields. The title, "Corporate Summary," is contained in the background recordfield.

Page 4 (What We Received...)

In addition to the background objects, page 4 consists of four separate pie graphics creating the pie chart; a field for the page title; a field for the labels; a field for the column of income data; another for the column of percentages; and six lines, four used as links to the pie chart wedges and two separating the data from other table elements.

Figure 4.9
Page 2: What the user sees
on a screen is composed of
objects on the background
as well as objects on the
page.

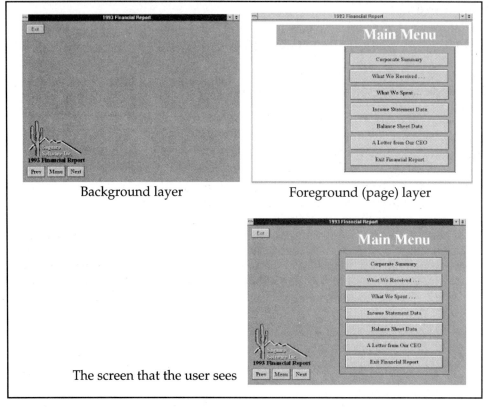

Background layer   Foreground (page) layer

The screen that the user sees

Page 5 (What We Spent...)

Page 5 consists of objects similar to those of page 4. The pie chart is composed of seven pie graphics, each filled with a different color.

Page 6 (Income Statement Data)

The text of income statement data was created with five fields (one for the labels and one for each of the four years of data). A rectangular graphic serves as a visual boundary for the data and three white lines separate the sections of the data. Another field is utilized for the information at the left side of the page. Three push buttons on the page layer link to the three charts presented on pages 9, 10, and 11 of the book. The page title is entered into the background recordfield.

Page 7 (Balance Sheet Data)

The "Balance Sheet Data" page is very similar to the "Income Statement Data" page. There is not as much data and there are no additional push buttons. In creating page 7, the author copied and pasted the objects of page 6 and then altered them for the purposes of this page.

Page 8 (A Letter from Our CEO)

Page 8 consists of the same background as that of the previous six pages. The objects on this page are a field containing the CEO's letter and two scanned images (the photograph and the signature) imported as .BMP files. A shadow style was selected for the letter field. The signature bitmap is on top of the letter field. Figure 4.10 illustrates the anatomy of this page.

Page 9 (Revenue Chart)

The line chart on this page was created with several rectangles composing the chart background, a couple lines showing the data, and several fields for the chart's labels.

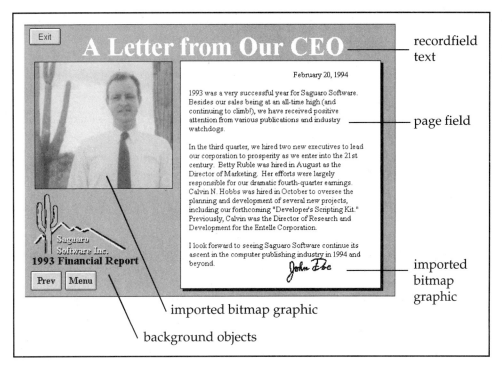

recordfield
text

page field

imported
bitmap
graphic

imported bitmap graphic

background objects

Figure 4.10
The objects of page 8 of the
business report
presentation.

This page utilizes background 2 as well, but the "Prev," "Menu," and "Next" buttons are hidden by the "Return to Income Statement" button of the foreground. Those background buttons are not accessible on this page, because the "Return" button receives the user's click in those areas. Buttons are also provided on the page for accessing the three different charts of pages 9, 10, and 11. Clicking the "Revenue

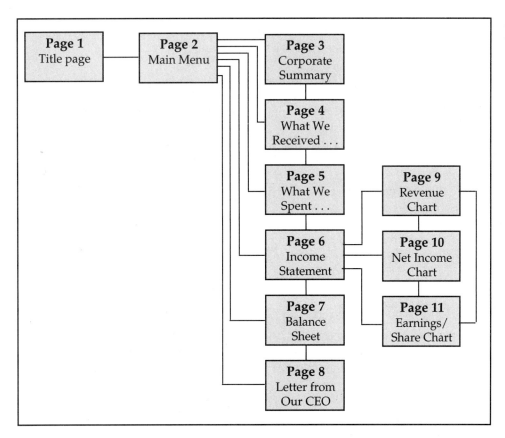

Figure 4.11
A map of how the pages of the
business report are linked.

Chart" button on this page results in no visible action, since the user is already at the revenue chart. The button is included here to provide visual consistency among the last three pages. As with the other pages of this book, the title is given at the top of the page, in a text field.

Pages 10 (Net Income Chart)

Page 10 is similar to page 9. The "Net Income Chart" button is visually inactive on this page, since it links back to this page.

Page 11 (Earnings/Share Chart)

Page 11 is similar to pages 9 and 10. Like the inactive buttons on the previous two pages, clicking the "Earnings/Share Chart" button has no effect on this page.

A Map of the Book's Links

The push buttons on the pages and backgrounds of the business report application focus on interpage navigation. A map of the links between the pages is provided in Figure 4.11. Note that nonlinear access is provided from page 2 (the Main Menu) to pages 3 through 8. Linear access is provided for the first eight pages, primarily through the background "Prev" and "Next" buttons. Page 6 provides nonlinear access to pages 9 through 11, with additional nonlinear access between those pages.

Summary Questions

Answer the following true/false questions.

1. ToolBook-developed applications always consist of just one file or book.
2. Viewers can be generated by choosing selections in a dialog box.
3. All ToolBook books consists of at least three pages.
4. Page sizes vary from book to book.
5. The size of a page can be larger than the size of the viewer it is displayed in.
6. The number of backgrounds in a book is equivalent to the number of pages in the book.
7. Buttons may contain an icon or bitmap image in addition to their captions.
8. Graphics created with ToolBook's drawing tools are paint-type (bitmap) images.
9. A book may have just one background, regardless of the number of pages in the book.
10. *Draw-type*, *object-oriented*, and *vector-oriented* are synonymous terms referring to graphics defined by underlying mathematical formulas.

Complete the following statements by filling in the blanks.

11. ToolBook books usually have a filename with the extension of _____.
12. ToolBook windows are called _____.
13. Objects shared by several pages can be placed on a common _____.
14. The primary object of interactivity in a book is the _____.
15. Background fields that hold different text on each page are called _____.
16. Specific text elements of a field set up to perform some action when clicked by the user are referred to as _____.
17. Program code attached to an object is called a _____.
18. An object for holding text is called a _____.
19. The _____ of a script defines the event triggering the script's action.
20. ToolBook scripts are written in the language _____.

Hands-On Projects

A. Examine the software that accompanies this chapter. Open the "Table of Contents" book by double clicking its icon in the "Developing with ToolBook" group window in the Windows Program Manager. Inside the "Table of Contents," click the book representing Chapter 4. Work your way through the tutorial as a means of enforcing and enriching the information presented in this chapter.

B. Examine other applications (for example, those discussed in Chapter 2, the sample applications shipped with ToolBook, applications obtained through Internet archives, and so on.) Can you determine what the various objects are? Which items do you think are on the background(s)?

C. Using the storyboards you created in Hands-On Project B of Chapter 3, determine what different objects are required for each screen. Which might be placed on the background? Will the book require more than one background?

Chapter 5

Just Browsing

How to Read a
ToolBook Book

One of the most important aspects of program development is the design of the interface. The end-user must find the program easy to use and understand. ToolBook books, in general, conform to Windows interface standards. By default, the main window viewer of a book has a titlebar, system menu box with standard menu choices, a menubar with default item choices, a minimize box and a maximize box, and a window frame, though the author may choose to eliminate any of these.

Within ToolBook applications, there are several popular interface methods, and this chapter examines their use. Books may be navigated by interfacing with buttons, menus, or keyboard input. Buttons may be interacted with in different ways, resulting in different actions being performed based on the attached scripts. Hotwords, interactive text information, may take on distinct appearances, alerting the user to their existence. ToolBook users should be made aware of the appearance of any hotwords. Likewise, information displayed in fields and recordfields may be set up as editable text, and the user should understand how to enter, edit, and format this text. Dialog boxes, which display or receive information, are a popular means of interacting with a user. There are some options available via the default File menu to print pages and reports. Finally, this chapter examines navigating from the Author to Reader mode and back.

Navigating a Book

There are many ways in which to navigate the pages of a book. The author or developer of a book usually places navigational buttons on the book's pages and/or backgrounds. Navigational buttons to page forward or backward are most common. Traditionally these buttons are labeled "Previous" or "Next" (or have synonymous captions) and/or contain an icon, such as an arrow or hand pointing to the left or right (see Figure 5.1). Many authors utilize a menu screen interface. Often such interface menus occupy a page designated for such a purpose and contain buttons that link to specific pages. The business report application presented in Chapters 2 and 4 contains such a menu screen (refer back to Figure 2.3). In some cases, the menu's buttons might link to pages of another book. The interface menu, "What Can I Do with ToolBook?" (see Figure 2.14) has buttons that link to other books, such as the calculator utility and the fractions tutorial.

For such menu screens to be used effectively, the other pages of the book should have a means of returning to the menu screen. Thus the user can navigate to another menu-linked page in two easy steps: returning to

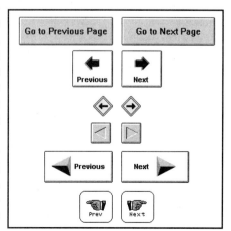

Figure 5.1
Navigational buttons to go to the previous or next page are commonly labeled "Previous" or "Next" or contain an icon pointing to the left or right.

the menu and then navigating to the desired page from the menu interface. To return to the menu screen, authors traditionally include on the book's pages or backgrounds a button linked to the menu screen. As with the "Previous" and "Next" buttons, this might be labeled with the caption "Menu" or incorporate a suitable icon.

By default, ToolBook applications have a menubar with a Page menu, (see Figure 5.2). Items in the Page menu include "Previous" (to linearly navigate to the previous page in the book); "Next" (to go to the next page); "First" (to go to the first page of

Figure 5.2
The Page menu contains options for navigating the pages of a book.

Page	
Next	Alt+Right
Previous	Alt+Left
First	Alt+Up
Last	Alt+Down
Back	Shift+F2
History...	Ctrl+F2
New Page	Ctrl+N

the book); "Last" (to go the last page of the current book); "Back" (to go to the previously viewed page, not necessarily the previous linear page); and "History" (to show a record listing of the pages visited during a session, any of which may be clicked to navigate to). Choosing any of these commands from the menu will result in the navigation being performed.

Many menu commands may be performed from the keyboard. In Figure 5.2, keyboard shortcuts are listed next to the menu item. Navigating to the previous page, for instance, may be performed from the keyboard by holding down the Alt key and pressing the left arrow key. Likewise, the next page may be viewed by holding down the Alt key and pressing the right arrow key.

ToolBook windows may have a statusbar at the bottom. The statusbar is primarily used in authoring (discussed further in Chapter 6), but developers often make the statusbar available to the end-user to display information for the reader. The current page number is displayed at the right-hand side of the statusbar. The reader can click on this page number and be prompted for the number of the page to display (see Figure 5.3). The reader enters a page number and presses Enter or clicks the checkbox next to the page number prompt to display the specified page. To cancel the operation, the reader may click the box labeled "X" or press the Esc key.

Figure 5.3
The statusbar at the bottom of many books may be used for navigating. Clicking the page number changes the right-hand side of the statusbar, prompting for a new page number to display.

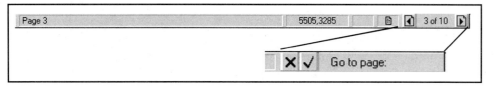

Mouse Operations

There are several different operations that may be performed with a computer mouse or trackball. The user positions the pointer (cursor) over an object on the monitor screen by moving the mouse or rolling the trackball. This process is referred to as **pointing**. The pointer is a small graphical object (traditionally an arrow, though the programmer may give it any shape) whose movements correspond to the physical movements of the mouse. The most common mouse operation that causes a script to execute is that of **clicking** an object. Clicking actually involves two separate mouse events—the mouse button being pushed down and the mouse button being released so that it returns to its normal "up" position. In OpenScript terms these two events are referred to as buttonDown and buttonUp respectively, and the entire operation may be referred to as buttonClick. (These terms will become important when programming in OpenScript is discussed later in the book.)

Another mouse operation is double-clicking an object by pressing the left mouse with two rapid presses. The author of a book can set up an object to respond differently to specific mouse operations performed by the user. For instance, when the user clicks an on-screen button, it might change colors, but when he or she double-clicks the button, an audible sound might be played by the computer. The same button might be set up to perform a third action (such as change its caption) if the user presses the right mouse button instead of the left.

Dragging is a mouse operation performed by pointing to an object (placing the tip of the mouse pointer over it), pressing the mouse button down, and holding it down while moving the mouse. This operation was utilized in interfacing with the jigsaw puzzle application presented in Chapter 2.

The Options of the Reader-Mode Menus

Menus are often available to readers of a book. The default menubar allows access to the File, Edit, Text, Page, and Help menus. Each menu offers several choices or options, which this section will describe. It is important to note that not all choices are available at all times. When a menu option is unavailable, its listing will be in gray text instead of black. This means that the task it represents cannot currently be performed. For example, when nothing is selected, the user cannot cut or copy.

File Menu Options

The File menu contains options associated with file management, including opening and closing files, printing books and reports, and importing and exporting data to and from text files (see Figure 5.4).

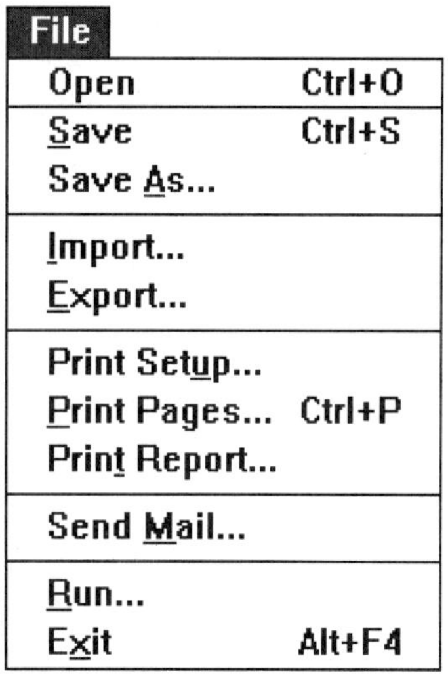

- **"Open"**: Prompts the user for a name and path of another book to open. In opening another book, the current book is closed.
- **"Save"**: Saves any changes in the current book. If the book has never been saved, the "Save As" option is executed.
- **"Save As"**: Saves the current book after prompting the user for a name and path. This command may be used initially to save a book or to save a copy of the book under a new name or path, leaving the older version intact.
- **"Import"**: Imports data from a fixed-field or delimited-field ASCII file or the pages of another book.
- **"Export"**: Exports recordfields of a background to a delimited-field text file.
- **"Print Setup"**: Brings up a dialog box from which the user can choose a printer and the printer's port assignment.
- **"Print Pages"**: Allows the user to specify a range of pages of the current book to print in a specified arrangement.
- **"Print Report"**: Prints, in the specified format, a report of the information contained in the book's recordfields.
- **"Send Mail"**: Provides a link to Microsoft Mail software if available.
- **"Run"**: Brings up a dialog box from which the user can specify an application to execute or another book to open. This option differs from the "Open" option in that the current book is not closed, but rather the new book is opened in a new window.
- **"Exit"**: Quits the current instance of ToolBook and closes the active book.

Figure 5.4
The File menu houses options for managing and printing files.

Figure 5.5
Options related to making
changes in a book are in the
Edit menu.

Edit	
Undo	
Cut	Ctrl+X
Copy	Ctrl+C
Paste	Ctrl+V
Clear	Del
Select All	Shift+F9
Select Page	Shift+F12
Size to Page	F11
Find...	F5
Replace...	
Author	F3

Edit Menu Options

The Edit menu contains options related to making changes in a book (see Figure 5.5).

- **"Undo":** Undoes the last action performed, if the last action is reversible.
- **"Cut":** Deletes the selected object or text, but places a copy of it on the Windows clipboard. The copy can then be pasted elsewhere. The current content of the clipboard is replaced with the new selection.
- **"Copy":** Performs like the "Cut" option except the selection is not deleted. Instead, a copy of the selection is placed on the Windows clipboard. The copy may then be pasted elsewhere. The current content of the clipboard is replaced with the new selection.
- **"Paste":** Copies the current contents of the clipboard to the current book. In the case of text, a field must be active (contain the flashing insertion point). The text on the clipboard is inserted in the location of the flashing insertion point.
- **"Clear":** Performs like the "Cut" option except the selection is not copied to the clipboard. In essence, choosing "Clear" is the same as selecting text or an object and pressing the Delete key.
- **"Select All":** Selects all the objects of a book or all the text of a field or recordfield if the field is active (that is, contains the flashing insertion point).
- **"Select Page":** Selects the current page with all its objects, script, and so on.
- **"Size to Page":** Resizes the main window to fit the dimensions of the page. If necessary, scrollbars are added to allow the user to view the undisplayed areas of a page.
- **"Find":** Brings up a dialog box from which the user can seek specified text within the current book.
- **"Replace":** Brings up a dialog box from which the user can specify text to seek within a book and replace any found text with specified new text.
- **"Author":** Switches to the Author mode of ToolBook (discussed later in this chapter).

Text Menu Options

The Text menu offers options for formatting the text of fields and recordfields (see Figure 5.6). These may be applied to existing text by first selecting the text to be formatted and then choosing the menu option to be applied to the selected text.

- **"Character":** Displays a dialog box from which the user can select a font (for example, Arial, Times, or MS Serif), a font size (measured in points), and font styles (bold, italic, and so on).
- **"Paragraph":** Brings up a dialog box from which the text of the active field or recordfield may be formatted. Formatting consists of alignment (left, right, centered, justified), indentations, tab measurements, and line spacing.
- **"Regular":** Formats the selected text in a "plain" style (that is bold, italic, underlining, and the like are turned off).
- **"Bold":** Toggles the bold style on or off for the selected text.
- **"Italic":** Toggles the italic style on or off for the selected text.
- **"Underline":** Toggles the underline style on or off for the selected text.

- **"Strikeout"**: Toggles the strikeout style on or off for the selected text.
- **"Superscript/Subscript"**: Displays a pop-up menu from which the user can format the selected text as a subscript, as a superscript, or as text whose baseline aligns normally.
- **"Show Hotwords"**: Allows hotwords to be set up to be displayed in a distinct color, in a different style, or with

Text	
Character...	F6
Paragraph...	F7
Regular	Ctrl+Space
√ Bold	Ctrl+B
Italic	Ctrl+I
Underline	Ctrl+U
Strikeout	Ctrl+K
Superscript/Subscript	▶
√ Show Hotwords	F9

Figure 5.6
Options for formatting text are housed in the Text menu.

a rectangle surrounding them. This option toggles these displays on or off. Hotwords are discussed later in this chapter.

Page Menu Options

The Page menu houses choices for navigating a book (see Figure 5.2). In addition to the options discussed in the section called Navigating a Book, earlier in this chapter, the option "New Page" is available in the Page menu in ToolBook's Reader mode.

- **"New Page"**: Selecting "New Page" inserts, after the current page, a new page into the book. The new page shares the current background.

Help Menu Options

The Help menu houses options for finding additional information that might benefit the user (see Figure 5.7).

- **"Contents"**: Provides a link to ToolBook's on-line help system (see Figure 1.5).
- **"Status Bar"**: Toggles, on or off, the display of the statusbar at the bottom of the window (see Figure 5.3).

Help	
Contents	F1
Status Bar	F12

Figure 5.7
The Help menu contains options for obtaining additional information or assistance.

Utilizing Hotwords

ToolBook, along with its predecessor, HyperCard, grew out of a textual linking concept known as hypertext. Hypertext allows a user to navigate amongst textual information by clicking specific words or phrases that are linked to other sections of the text. This allows the user to browse, or read, the text in a nonlinear fashion, customizing the reading according to his or her own interests. In ToolBook applications, these hypertextual links are called **hotwords**. These links, specified

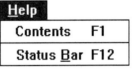

ToolBook is an authoring / software development package for creating Windows-based applications. **ToolBook** requires a 386 computer or better with at lease 4 MB of RAM. Developers use ToolBook to create educational tutorials, databases, information presentations, utilities, and applications of all kinds. There are two versions of ToolBook: the regular version and a multimedia version that includes additional features for adding sound, video, and animation clips into ToolBook books.

Even if the ToolBook developer chooses not to format hotwords differently, they can be distinguished in that the mouse pointer turns into a hand when placed over an active hotword.

Figure 5.8
Hotwords in a text field may take on various appearances: bold, italicized, a different color, or surrounded by a rectangle. The word "ToolBook" is a hotword in each occurrence of the text at the left. Note that the last distinguishing treatment is apparent only when the mouse pointer is positioned over the hotword (the pointer changes into a hand).

words or phrases within text fields and recordfields, may be set up by the author to perform some action when clicked by the user. Hotwords may take on a distinct appearance amidst the nonlinked text; they may be a different color (perhaps all the hotwords are red), a different style (hotwords may be bold or italicized), or outlined with a rectangle (see Figure 5.8). Common actions performed by clicking a hotword include navigating to other text or pages, and popping up a window containing more information or a definition of the term.

Editing Text

Text inside a field or recordfield may be set up as editable, allowing the user to enter, edit, and even format it. If a field is editable, the pointer (cursor) changes to an I-beam when positioned over the field or recordfield. The text of the field is edited by first making the field active (a process also referred to as giving it the focus). This is done by clicking the field, resulting in a flashing insertion bar in the text where the field was clicked (or at the end of the existing text if the click location was below the text). Text entered from the keyboard will be inserted at the location of the flashing insertion bar. Likewise, text may be deleted by placing the insertion bar behind the text to be eliminated and pressing the Backspace key the appropriate number of times to delete the preceding characters.

Editable text may be selected (highlighted) by placing the mouse pointer I-beam at the beginning of the chosen text and dragging to the end of the desired text. The selected text will be highlighted (for example, instead of black letters on a white background, selected text will be white on black, also referred to as reverse video). Highlighted text may be replaced with new text by entering the new data from the keyboard, or deleted by pressing the Delete key.

Responding to Dialog Boxes

Dialog boxes are a popular means of interfacing with the user. Dialog boxes require the user to respond before continuing to browse or interact with the book. Two forms of dialogs ToolBook developers use to get input from the user are the request dialog and the ask dialog. The **request dialog** presents a prompt statement or question with one to three buttons (see Figure 5.9). The user must click one of these buttons before

Figure 5.9
Request dialogs ask the user a question or provide a statement with one, two, or three buttons for input from the user.

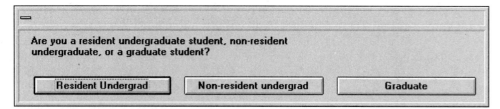

he or she can do anything else. Such dialogs are used to present output to the user, pausing the execution of a script until the user clicks the "OK" button or makes one of two or three choices. The request dialog might confirm that a user wants to perform some action. For example, when the reader clicks an "Exit" button, the computer might verify that he or she actually wants to quit and didn't just accidentally click the button; the computer asks "Do you really want to exit?" and provides two response buttons, "Yes" and "Cancel." If the user clicks "Yes," the program is exited but, if the user clicks "Cancel," the program continues to run.

The **ask dialog** is similar to the request dialog, but instead of allowing one to three responses, it requires the reader to enter an alphanumeric string (see Figure 5.10). Such dialogs are used to receive input for a script, verify passwords, or edit existing text in a locked (uneditable) field. By default, two buttons are utilized in the ask dialog along with a one-line text field in which the user enters his or her response. After entering a response, the user can click the "OK" button to send the response to the computer or "Cancel" to send no response.

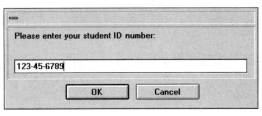

Figure 5.10
Ask dialogs ask a question of the user and provide space for the user to enter a response from the keyboard.

There are numerous other types of dialog boxes. ToolBook includes a dialog editor utility that allows developers to create their own dialogs quickly and easily. It provides the ability to specify numerous styles of buttons, fields, comboboxes, icons, and so on. Viewers can be used to create dialogs as well. Many options—such as "Save As...," "Find...," and "History..."—produce dialog boxes in which the user must respond. Conforming to Windows interface standards, menu options with three periods following the name indicate that a dialog box is associated with the option.

Printing Techniques

ToolBook provides means of printing the pages of a book or a report of data contained in the recordfields of the current background. Selecting "Print Pages" from the File menu results in the "Print Pages" dialog (see Figure 5.11). An arrangement of the pages may be chosen from the horizontally scrolling display of thumbnail sketches at the top. Arrangements range from one page per printout to 32 pages of the book positioned in miniature form in an 8 by 4 grid on each printout. The user can choose to print a range of pages, all pages, the pages of the current background, or the current page only. Headers and/or footers may be added by clicking the buttons at the right and specifying the information for the header or footer.

The "Print Report" option in the File menu allows the user to print a report consisting of the data contained in recordfields of a background. Database users are the typical users of this ability. The "Print Report" option is available only when the current page has recordfields on its background. In the resulting dialog, a field name or ID is selected in the "Available Record Fields" listing at the top left (see Figure 5.12). Clicking the "Add>>" button moves the field identification to the "Print These Record Fields" listing. The process is repeated until all desired recordfields are listed in the "Print These . . ." listing. The recordfields will be listed and printed in the order in which they are selected.

Reports may be printed in either a column or group format. Column formats are useful for printing directories, inventories, and financial statements; group formats are most often used for mailing labels. Figure 5.13 reveals the differences between these formats. As when printing pages, a range of pages to be included may be specified, headers and footers added, and the printout previewed.

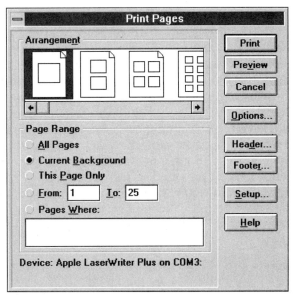

Figure 5.11
Choosing the "Print Pages" option from the File menu brings up this dialog box from which the user can choose an arrangement of the pages on the printout and specify which pages to print.

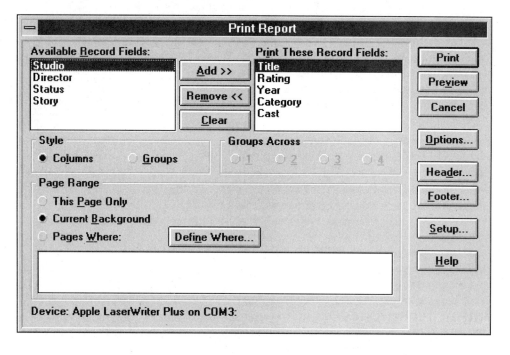

Figure 5.12
In the "Print Report"
dialog, data in recordfields
may be selected to be
included in the report and a
range of pages may be
specified.

Figure 5.13
Reports may be printed in
either a column format or a
group format.

Column Format

Name	Address	City, ST Zip
John Doe	123 E. Main	Wadsworth, CA 55555
M. M. Toolbook	4567 N. Oak	Asymetrix, WA 54321
Johnny B. Good	987 Western Sunset	Phoenix, AZ 85008

Group Format

John Doe	M. M. Toolbook	Johnny B. Good
123 E. Main	4567 N. Oak	987 Western Sunset
Wadsworth, CA 55555	Asymetrix, WA 54321	Phoenix, AZ 85008

Changing from Author and Reader Modes

Thus far, this text has focused on ToolBook applications as viewed by an end-user. Books are used in the **Reader mode** of ToolBook. But the development of a book is done in the **Author mode**. The Author mode is available only in the full versions of ToolBook and Multimedia ToolBook, not in the runtime versions of these programs. The user changes the mode by choosing the "Author" or "Reader" option from the Edit menu. (The "Author" option shown in Figure 5.5 changes to "Reader" when ToolBook is in the Author mode.) The same keyboard shortcut, the F3 key, is used for both commands. Pressing the F3 key is the most popular way of toggling between the two modes. Though the remainder of this text focuses on the Author mode of ToolBook, the Reader mode is heavily utilized in running and testing scripts, since scripts generally do not execute in the Author mode. The next section of this text, Chapters 6 through 12, focuses on using the Author mode and its tools to create a ToolBook book.

Summary Questions

Answer the following true/false questions.

1. The pages of a book are often navigated by clicking "Previous" and "Next" buttons located on its pages and/or backgrounds.
2. The statusbar can be used to navigate to other pages in some books.
3. An object can only be scripted to respond to one type of mouse operation.
4. The "Save" option allows the current book to be saved under a new name.
5. The "Copy" option deletes the selection and places a copy of it on the clipboard; from there it may be pasted elsewhere.
6. Options for formatting the contents of a field or recordfield are found in the default Text menu.
7. Hotwords always appear as bold text in a field or recordfield.
8. Ask dialogs provide information to the user but receive no input from the user.
9. Pages of a book may be printed in different arrangements with regard to the number of pages on a printout.
10. The user may choose which recordfields to include in a report.

Complete the following statements by filling in the blanks.

11. Positioning the mouse pointer over an object is called _____.
12. The _____ option in the Page menu takes the user to the next page in a book.
13. Two rapid presses of the mouse button is known as a _____ _____.
14. Making a field active so its text can be edited is referred to as giving it the _____.
15. Options related to making changes in a book are found in the default _____ menu.
16. _____ dialogs provide one to three buttons for the user to provide input regarding a question.
17. Inventory reports are usually best printed in a _____ format.
18. Mailing label reports are best printed in a _____ format.
19. Books are created in the _____ mode of ToolBook.
20. The _____ key is used to toggle between the Author and Reader modes of ToolBook.

Hands-On Projects

A. Examine the software that accompanies this chapter. Open the "Table of Contents" book by double-clicking its icon in the "Developing with ToolBook" group window in the Windows Program Manager. Inside the "Table of Contents," click the book representing Chapter 5. Work your way through the tutorial as a means of enforcing and enriching the information presented in this chapter.

B. ToolBook includes an icon and cursor editor. The editor application is ICONEDIT.EXE, which may be run directly from the Program Manager or File Manager or executed via the "Run" option under ToolBook's File menu. The editor (see Figure 5.14) is a typical paint package, only its "canvas" is limited to a 32- by 32-pixel area (the maximum size of an icon). Graphics created with the editor may be saved as a separate file with the .ICO extension (such files can later be imported into a book's resources) or exported directly into a book. The graphical tools at the left-hand side are used for drawing the image, and the toolbar at the top provides quick access to common menu options. The color palette, at the bottom, is used to associate specific colors with either the left or right mouse button; the user clicks the desired color by pressing the appropriate mouse button. Experiment with the different tools. Then use the editor to create icons that would be appropriate for attaching to "Previous," "Next," and "Menu" buttons. Be creative!

Figure 5.14
Custom icons may be created with the icon and cursor editor (ICONEDIT.EXE) which accompanies ToolBook.

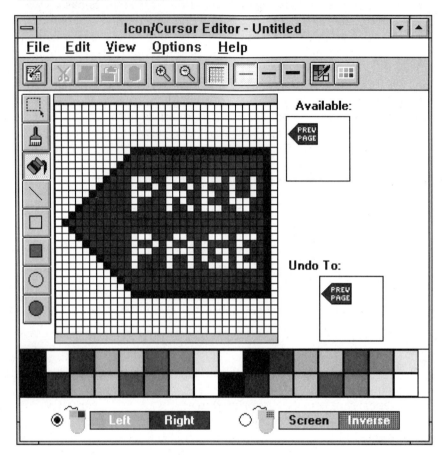

Section II
Authoring

Chapter

6

The ToolBook Authoring Environment

Authoring packages allow developers to create applications without having to write program code. Although the full power of ToolBook is realized only through programming in OpenScript, impressive interactive applications can be developed without writing code. Screens are laid out through ToolBook's graphical interface, which resembles that of popular drawing programs. Scripts may be generated and attached to objects through the hyperlinking, autoscript, and script recorder functions. Authoring is a prerequisite to programming in ToolBook, because objects must first be created before programming code (scripts) can be attached to them. Both authoring and programming are performed in the Author mode of ToolBook. This section (Chapters 6 through 12) focuses on authoring—creating books, pages, backgrounds, buttons, fields, and graphics. It provides an introduction to object-oriented programming and how scripts work, preparing the way for the look at OpenScript programming presented in Section III.

The Author mode of ToolBook provides an environment for creating new books, designing pages and backgrounds, and writing scripts. Tools, menus, and palettes are provided that make the development process simpler than it would be in a traditional programming language such as C or Pascal. The ToolBook authoring environment resembles that of graphical drawing programs.

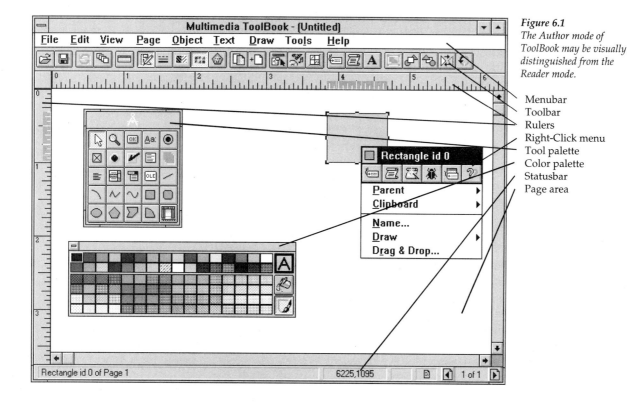

Figure 6.1
The Author mode of ToolBook may be visually distinguished from the Reader mode.

Menubar
Toolbar
Rulers
Right-Click menu
Tool palette
Color palette
Statusbar
Page area

Author Mode

When ToolBook or Multimedia ToolBook is launched directly from the Program Manager or File Manager (without specifying a book), the program opens in the Author mode by default. If a book is open, choosing "New" from the File menu will close the existing book and open up a new book in Author mode. A current book running in Reader mode may be switched to Author mode by choosing "Author" from the Edit menu or pressing the F3 function key. Figure 6.1 shows a new book as viewed in Author mode, revealing ToolBook's authoring environment.

The Author mode is visually distinguishable from the Reader mode. In the Author mode the page area, where the pages and backgrounds are displayed and created, is in the center. Scrollbars, perhaps unnecessary in Reader mode, may appear by default so that the entire page may be accessed. The default menubar and associated menus are different from those displayed in Reader mode; Author mode contains several additional menus: View, Object, and Draw. A toolbar containing icons associated with often-used menu choices usually appears at the top of the window, though it may be positioned elsewhere. The tool palette contains tools used to create the various objects of a book. Other palettes may be displayed in the Author mode, including the Color palette, Line palette, Line Ends palette, Polygon palette, and Pattern palette. Optionally, the user may display rulers, along the top and left of the page area, and a variable-sized grid to assist him or her in the development process. The statusbar, at the bottom of the window, reveals information about menus, toolbar selections or toolbox choices, the location of the mouse pointer, and the page number and navigation buttons. The "Command" window, in which OpenScript commands may be executed, may also be displayed.

The Page Area

The **page area** reveals the pages and backgrounds as they would be viewed in the Reader mode and is the area in which objects are drawn and edited as the book is developed. This area is also referred to as the "Client" window. If the page is bigger than the "Client" window, scrollbars will be displayed at the bottom and right—these allow the user to access all areas of the page. These scrollbars may be hidden by entering and executing the "hide scrollbar" option in the "Command" window. The page area can be used to display both the foreground (page) layer and the background layer together while working with objects on the foreground, or to display only the background layer and work with only its objects. Switching from the page-and-background view to the background-only view is accomplished by choosing the "Background" option in the View menu or pressing the F4 function key. When viewing only the background, the page number display in the statusbar will state "Background" instead of "__ of __" (see Figure 6.2).

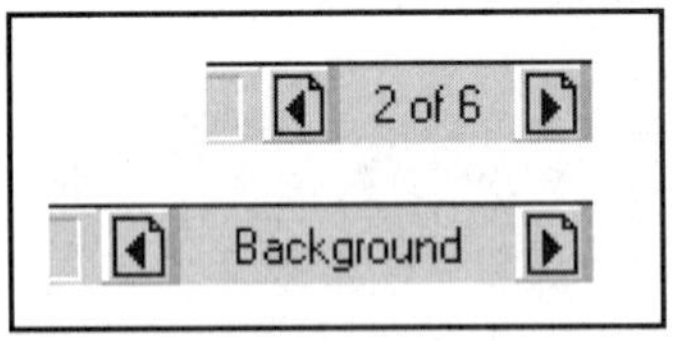

Figure 6.2
At the right-hand side of the statusbar, the current page number is displayed as well as the total number of pages in the book (top). If the view is of the background only, the statusbar displays the word "Background" instead of the page number (bottom).

The Options of the Author-Mode Menus

As the menubar changes from Reader mode to the Author mode, additional commands appear in the File, Edit, Text, Page, and Help menus, and three new menus (View, Object, and Draw) are added. A fourth new menu, Tools, may be added by an optional system book, TOOLS30.SBK, if it is active. As with the menus in the Reader mode, not all options are available at all times, with non-applicable choices being "grayed out." The availability of any menu choice is based on the current state of the authoring mode. For instance, one cannot choose to see the "Object Properties..." if no object is selected.

The File Menu

The File menu in the Author mode (see Figure 6.3) contains the same options as in the Reader mode, with the following additions:

- **"New"**: Creates a new untitled book with one blank page of default size and a blank accompanying background.
- **"Save As EXE..."**: Allows books to be saved as executable .EXE files, making the books easier to execute from the Program Manager or the File Manager. The ToolBook software or the ToolBook runtime files still need to be available for the book to be opened.
- **Names of last four opened files:** Lists the names of the last four files used. The names appear at the bottom of the File menu. Any of the files may be opened by clicking its name.

```
┌─ File ──────────────────────────┐
│ New                             │
│ Open...                  Ctrl+O │
│ Save                     Ctrl+S │
│ Save As...                      │
│ Save As EXE...                  │
├─────────────────────────────────┤
│ Import Graphic...               │
│ Import...                       │
│ Export...                       │
├─────────────────────────────────┤
│ Print Setup...                  │
│ Print Pages...           Ctrl+P │
│ Print Report...                 │
├─────────────────────────────────┤
│ Send Mail...                    │
├─────────────────────────────────┤
│ Run...                          │
│ Exit                     Alt+F4 │
├─────────────────────────────────┤
│ 1 E:\DEV_TBK\DEV_TOFC.TBK       │
│ 2 E:\DEV_TBK\CHAP04.TBK         │
│ 3 B:\GRAPHIC1.TBK               │
│ 4 E:\MTB30EA\GRAPHIC1.TBK       │
└─────────────────────────────────┘
```

Figure 6.3
The File menu contains options related to working with files.

The Edit Menu

The Edit menu houses the same options in Author mode (see Figure 6.4) as in Reader mode, with several additions:

- **"Spelling..."**: Brings up the spelling checker dialog from which the user may check the spelling of text in the current book's fields and recordfields. This option is only available in Multimedia ToolBook.
- **"Insert OLE Object..."**: Allows ToolBook to insert graphics and data from other applications capable of object linking and embedding (OLE). This option inserts an OLE object onto the current page or background.
- **"OLE Links..."**: Edits the links between an OLE object and the application from which it was imported.
- **"OLE Action..."**: Starts the application in which an OLE object was created, activating the link. This menu choice changes to reflect the object's source application.
- **"Reader"**: Replaces the "Author" option found in the Reader mode. The "Reader" option switches the current ToolBook book to the Reader mode.
- **"Start Recording"**: Begins recording the author's actions until the "Stop Recording" choice is selected. (The menu's name changes to "Stop Recording" when the recorder is active.) The actions are translated into OpenScript code, which may then be pasted into a script.

```
┌─ Edit ──────────────────────────┐
│ Undo                            │
├─────────────────────────────────┤
│ Cut                      Ctrl+X │
│ Copy                     Ctrl+C │
│ Paste                    Ctrl+V │
│ Paste Special...                │
│ Duplicate                Ctrl+D │
│ Clear                       Del │
├─────────────────────────────────┤
│ Select All              Shift+F9│
│ Select Page            Shift+F12│
├─────────────────────────────────┤
│ Find...                      F5 │
│ Replace...                      │
│ Spelling...                     │
├─────────────────────────────────┤
│ Insert OLE Object...            │
│ OLE Links...                    │
│ OLE Action...                   │
├─────────────────────────────────┤
│ Reader                       F3 │
│ Start Recording              F8 │
└─────────────────────────────────┘
```

Figure 6.4
The Edit menu includes options for editing objects.

The View Menu

The View menu (see Figure 6.5) is only encountered in the Author mode. The menu contains options related to the authoring environment and interface.

- **"Background"**: Serves as a toggle for going from the page-and-background' view to the background-only view. When in the background-only

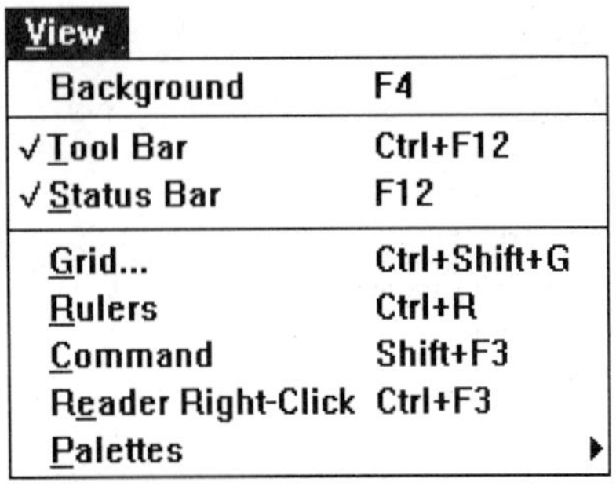

Figure 6.5
The View menu contains
options related to the
authoring environment.

View

Background	F4
√ Tool Bar	Ctrl+F12
√ Status Bar	F12
Grid...	Ctrl+Shift+G
Rulers	Ctrl+R
Command	Shift+F3
Reader Right-Click	Ctrl+F3
Palettes	▶

view, a check mark will appear to the left of the option name.

- **"Tool Bar":** Toggles the toolbar (discussed later in this chapter) on and off. When the toolbar is visible, a check mark appears next to the option name.

 "Status Bar": Toggles the statusbar (discussed later in this chapter) on and off. When the statusbar is visible, a check mark appears next to the option name.

- **"Grid...":** Displays a dialog box that asks for the grid measurement, whether the grid should be displayed, and whether objects should snap to the grid.
- **"Rulers":** Toggles the rulers (discussed later in this chapter) on and off. When the rulers are visible, a check mark appears next to the option name.
- **"Command":** Toggles the "Command" window (discussed later in this chapter) on and off. The "Command" window is used for executing OpenScript commands. When the "Command" window is visible, a check mark appears next to the option name.
- **"Reader Right-Click":** Allows an author to choose whether a reader should be able to display an object-specific Right-Click menu in the Reader mode. Right-Click menus are generally only available in the Author mode. Right-Click menus allow properties of an object to be viewed and set and are explained later in this chapter.
- **"Palettes":** Brings up a submenu from which the different palettes may be toggled on or off. There are six palettes (Tool, Color, Line, Line Ends, Pattern, and Polygon), and each is discussed later in this chapter.

The Page Menu

The Page menu (see Figure 6.6) lists, for the most part, the same options found in the Reader mode. (The "New Page" option in this menu in the Reader mode is moved to the Object menu in the Author mode.) Two additional options appear in the Page menu in the Author mode:

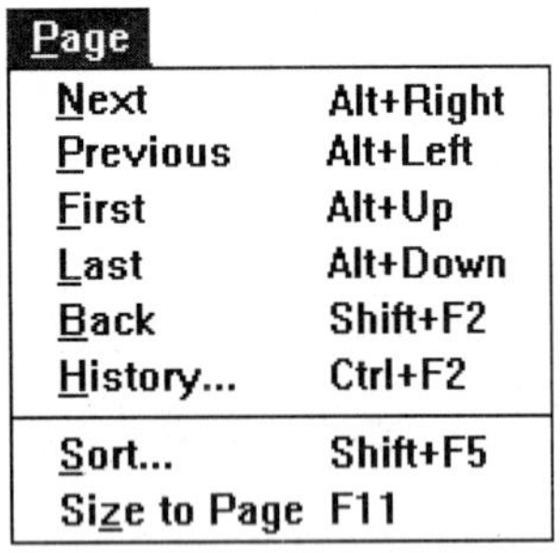

Figure 6.6
The Page menu lists options
for navigating the pages of
a book.

Page

Next	Alt+Right
Previous	Alt+Left
First	Alt+Up
Last	Alt+Down
Back	Shift+F2
History...	Ctrl+F2
Sort...	Shift+F5
Size to Page	F11

- **"Sort...":** Brings up a dialog box from which the author can sort the pages of the current book based on the text of one or more record-fields.
- **"Size to Page":** Adjusts the size of the viewer to match that of the page size. If the page is larger than the viewer, scrollbars are added to the display.

The Object Menu

The Object menu (see Figure 6.7) is only available in the Author mode and contains options related to the various objects of a ToolBook book.

- **"Object Properties...":** Brings up a dialog from which the properties of the current selected object may be viewed and changed. This menu option changes its name according to the type of object currently selected. For instance, if a button is selected, the option will be listed as "Button Properties..." in the menu.
- **"Page Properties...":** Brings up a dialog box from which the properties of the current page may be viewed and changed. The "Page Properties" dialog

is examined in depth in Chapter 8.

- **"Background Properties..."**: Brings up a dialog box from which the properties of the current background may be viewed and modified. The "Background Properties" dialog is examined in depth in Chapter 8.

- **"Book Properties..."**: Brings up a dialog box from which the properties of the current book may be viewed and changed. The "Book Properties" dialog is examined in depth in Chapter 7.

```
┌─────────────────────────────────────────┐
│ Object                                    │
├─────────────────────────────────────────┤
│ Object Properties...        Shift+F6      │
│ Page Properties...          Shift+F7      │
│ Background Properties...    Ctrl+F7       │
│ Book Properties...          Shift+F8      │
├─────────────────────────────────────────┤
│ Viewers...                  Shift+F10     │
│ Resources...                Ctrl+F10      │
│ Media Clips...                            │
├─────────────────────────────────────────┤
│ New Page                    Ctrl+N        │
│ New Background              Ctrl+M        │
│ New Viewer                            ▶   │
├─────────────────────────────────────────┤
│ Group                       Ctrl+G        │
└─────────────────────────────────────────┘
```

Figure 6.7
The Object menu contains options related to working with the various objects of a book.

- **"Viewers..."**: Brings up a dialog box from which viewers may be created, deleted, and modified.

- **"Resources..."**: Brings up a dialog from which various resources (icons, bitmaps, fonts, cursors, menus) may be imported, exported, and edited. Resources are discussed in Chapter 7.

- **"Media Clips..."**: Brings up a dialog from which sound, movie, and picture clips may be imported into a book, edited, and played. This command is only available in Multimedia ToolBook. Media clips are discussed in Chapter 27.

- **"New Page"**: Inserts a new blank page after the current page. Both pages share the same background. This option is the same as the "New Page" option in the Page menu in the Reader mode.

- **"New Background"**: Inserts a new blank page after the current page. The new background is blank.

- **"New Viewer"**: Brings up a submenu from which a new viewer may be created. Six different viewer styles are available: Dialog Box, Palette, Tool Bar, Status Bar, Read-Only Popup, and Thick Frame.

- **"Group"**: Groups two or more selected objects into a single group. Grouped objects may also be ungrouped. (The option name changes to "Ungroup" if a group object is selected.)

The Text Menu

The Text menu (see Figure 6.8) is the same as the Text menu found in the Reader mode, with two additional commands:

```
┌─────────────────────────────────────────┐
│ Text                                      │
├─────────────────────────────────────────┤
│ Character...                F6            │
│ Paragraph...                F7            │
├─────────────────────────────────────────┤
│ Insert Graphic...                         │
├─────────────────────────────────────────┤
│ Regular                     Ctrl+Space    │
│ √ Bold                      Ctrl+B        │
│ Italic                      Ctrl+I        │
│ Underline                   Ctrl+U        │
│ Strikeout                   Ctrl+K        │
│ Superscript/Subscript                 ▶   │
├─────────────────────────────────────────┤
│ Create Hotword              Ctrl+H        │
│ √ Show Hotwords             F9            │
└─────────────────────────────────────────┘
```

Figure 6.8
The Text menu contains options related to working with text of fields and recordfields.

- **"Insert Graphic..."**: Brings up the "Insert Resources" dialog from which a resource (bitmap, icon, and the like) may be selected and inserted at the active insertion point in a field or recordfield.

- **"Create Hotword"**: Defines the selected text (word or phrase) of a field as a hotword to which a script may be attached. When an already-defined hotword is selected, this option name changes to "Remove Hotword," allowing the hotword definition to be deleted. Hotwords are discussed in detail in Chapter 10.

The Draw Menu

The Draw menu (see Figure 6.9) is only available in the Author mode, and lists options associated with the drawing and displaying of objects. Drawing objects with the ToolBook tools is the topic of Chapter 11.

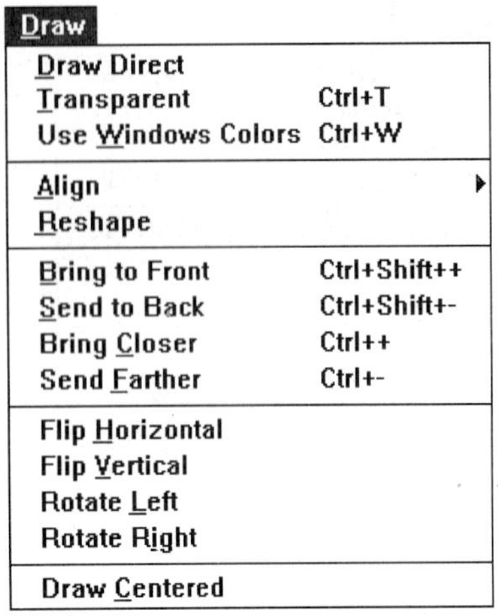

Figure 6.9
The Draw menu lists
options related to drawing
and editing objects in
ToolBook.

```
┌─────────────────────────────────────┐
│ Draw                                 │
├─────────────────────────────────────┤
│ Draw Direct                          │
│ Transparent          Ctrl+T          │
│ Use Windows Colors   Ctrl+W          │
├─────────────────────────────────────┤
│ Align                            ▶   │
│ Reshape                              │
├─────────────────────────────────────┤
│ Bring to Front       Ctrl+Shift++    │
│ Send to Back         Ctrl+Shift+-    │
│ Bring Closer         Ctrl++          │
│ Send Farther         Ctrl+-          │
├─────────────────────────────────────┤
│ Flip Horizontal                      │
│ Flip Vertical                        │
│ Rotate Left                          │
│ Rotate Right                         │
├─────────────────────────────────────┤
│ Draw Centered                        │
└─────────────────────────────────────┘
```

- **"Draw Direct":** Toggles the drawDirect property of the selected object(s) to true or false. When the drawDirect property is true, a check mark appears next to the option, and the object is drawn directly on screen. When drawDirect is false, the object is first drawn in an offscreen area and then displayed on the screen. Objects drawn directly to the screen draw faster, but the user sees them being formed. Objects not drawn directly tend to be better in animation. If no objects are selected, the draw-direct state is chosen for subsequently created objects.

- **"Transparent":** Toggles the transparent property of the selected object(s) to true or false. When it is true, a check mark appears next to the option, and objects behind the selected object(s) are visible through the selected object(s). If false, the selected object is opaque. If no objects are selected, subsequently created objects will be transparent.

- **"Use Windows Colors":** Specifies whether a background or object should use the colors specified in the Windows Control Panel. This choice overrides any fill and stroke colors established for the selected object. When this option is chosen, a check mark will appear next to the option name.

- **"Align":** Brings up a submenu from which two or more selected objects may be aligned on the left, right, top, or bottom or centered vertically or horizontally.

- **"Reshape":** Allows a selected polygon, irregular polygon, or pie graphic to be reshaped. The option name changes to reflect the type of object currently selected. The name might be "Reshape Polygon," for example.

- **"Bring to Front":** Brings the selected object(s) to the front of the page or background, with the exception that all objects whose drawDirect property is true are displayed on top of any objects whose drawDirect property is false.

- **"Send to Back":** Sends the selected object(s) to the back of the page or background, with the exception that all objects whose drawDirect property is true are displayed on top of any objects whose drawDirect property is false.

- **"Bring Closer":** Brings the selected object(s) forward by one layer on the page or background.

- **"Send Farther":** Sends the selected object(s) back by one layer on the page or background.

- **"Flip Horizontal":** Flips the selected object(s) along the horizontal axis.

- **"Flip Vertical":** Flips the selected object(s) along the vertical axis.

- **"Rotate Left":** Rotates the selected object(s) 90 degrees counterclockwise. Text of fields and recordfields cannot be rotated, nor can a bitmap graphic image, though its boundaries may be.

- **"Rotate Right":** Rotates the selected object(s) 90 degrees clockwise.

- **"Draw Centered":** Determines whether an object will be drawn from its center or from its edge. When the drawCenter property is true, a check mark appears next to the option name and subsequently created objects are drawn from their center out.

The Help Menu

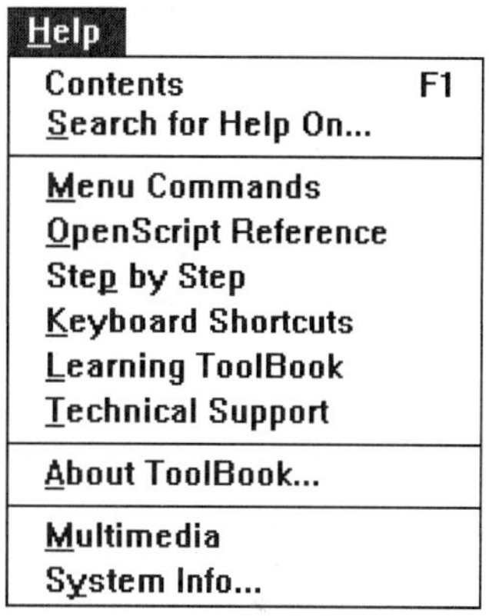

The Help menu in the Author mode (see Figure 6.10) is an expanded version of the Help menu found in the Reader mode. The statusbar switch found in the Reader mode is gone (the statusbar is displayed by default in the Author mode), but several additional items appear in the Author mode:

- **"Search for Help On..."**: Brings up a dialog from which commands and topics discussed in the on-line help may be sought.
- **"Menu Commands"**: Displays on-line help regarding each of the menu choices.
- **"OpenScript Reference"**: Displays on-line help regarding each of the commands, functions, properties, and keywords encountered in writing OpenScript code. These terms are listed alphabetically and include syntax rules and usage examples.
- **"Step by Step"**: Displays on-line help specifying step-by-step instructions for performing many popular routines and procedures in ToolBook, such as how to create a hotword or how to declare an array in OpenScript code.
- **"Keyboard Shortcuts"**: Displays a listing of keyboard and mouse shortcuts, by topic.
- **"Learning ToolBook"**: Opens the on-line tutorial, Learning ToolBook, discussed in Chapter 1.
- **"Technical Support"**: Displays information about accessing the technical support staff at Asymetrix.
- **"About ToolBook..."**: Displays release date and version, licensing information, and information about system resources.
- **"Multimedia"**: Displays the Multimedia ToolBook Encyclopedia, which discusses functions available in the Multimedia version of ToolBook. This option is not available in the regular version of ToolBook.

Figure 6.10
The Help menu lists options for accessing the on-line help features.

The Toolbar

The **toolbar** is a palette of buttons for quick access to popular menu options. Instead of choosing a menu option, an author may simply click the appropriate button on the toolbar. By default, the toolbar is positioned at the top of the window, just below the menubar. It may, however, be pulled away from that location and resized by dragging it with the mouse pointer (see Figure 6.11). As the pointer is placed over a button on the toolbar, a description of the option associated with that button is revealed in the left frame of the statusbar. A secondary toolbar may be displayed by holding down the Ctrl key (some of the icons change to reflect different associated options). Figure 6.12 reveals the options associated with each of the buttons. Right-clicking the toolbar reveals its Right-Click menu. From this menu, the toolbar may be hidden (and reshown via the View menu) and the author can specify whether the buttons should be wrapped to form more than one row if they do not fit the width of the window and which of three different formats—graphics only, text only, or both text and graphics—should be used. Figure 6.13 shows the statusbar's Right-Click menu and the three display formats of the toolbar.

The Tool Palette

There are six palettes provided in the Author mode of ToolBook for creating and modifying objects. The primary palette is the Tool palette (not to be confused with

Figure 6.11
Although the toolbar is normally displayed horizontally along the top of the page area, the bar may be moved and rearranged by using the mouse pointer to drag its frame.

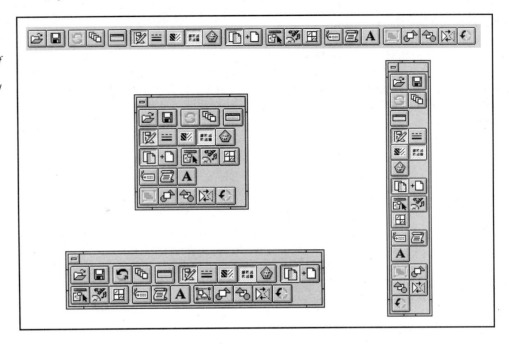

the toolbar). The Tool palette contains buttons for accessing various tools for creating various styles of buttons, fields, text fields, comboboxes, OLE objects, and graphic images (rectangles, ellipses, lines, and the like). A tool is selected from the palette by clicking the appropriate button of the palette. The currently selected tool button appears recessed on the palette. Figure 6.14 shows the function of each tool. The Tool palette may be repositioned on the screen by pointing to its titlebar and dragging it to a new location. Like the toolbar, the Tool palette may be reshaped by dragging its frame.

Figure 6.12
The options associated with each of the buttons on the toolbar are listed at the left. Pressing the Ctrl key results in the toolbar on the right.

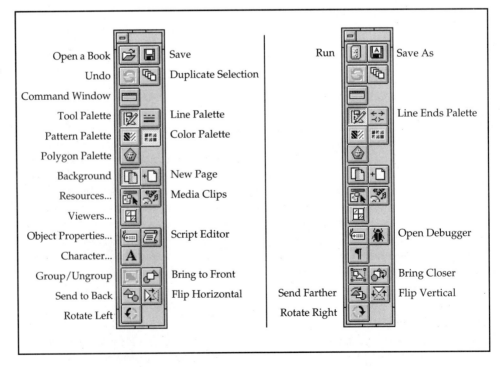

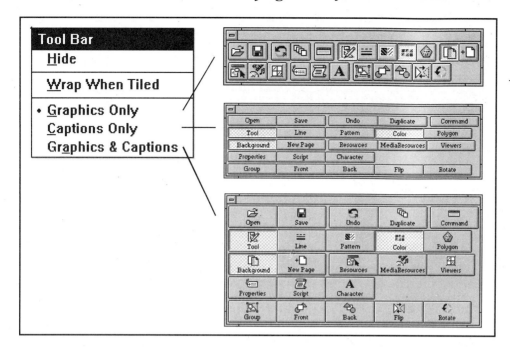

Figure 6.13
The Right-Click menu of the toolbar allows the author to choose a format for the toolbar's display.

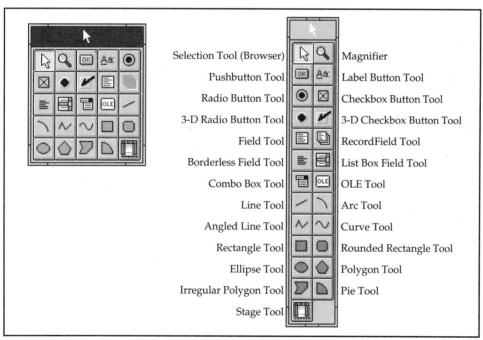

Figure 6.14
The Tool palette may be moved and resized on the screen by dragging its frame. The view on the right identifies the various tools of the Tool palette.

The Color Palette

The Color tray (see Figure 6.15) is used for choosing the fill color and stroke color of objects and is displayed by choosing "Palettes" from the View menu and selecting "Color" from the submenu, or clicking the Color tray icon in the toolbar. The **stroke color** is the color of text and borders of objects; the **fill color** is the interior shade of enclosed objects. The palette consists of 96 displayed shades of color and three large icons at the right-hand side. The top icon displays the current color selections. The "A" and the surrounding frame are the chosen stroke color and the inside of the icon is the chosen fill color. The middle icon (with the paint bucket) is for selecting the fill color. It is a button, appearing recessed when selected and active. When active, the

Figure 6.15
The Color palette is used to assign fill and stroke colors to objects.

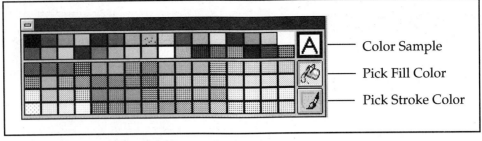

Color Sample
Pick Fill Color
Pick Stroke Color

Figure 6.16
Double-clicking one of the lower 64 shades of the Color palette allows the author to edit the chosen color.

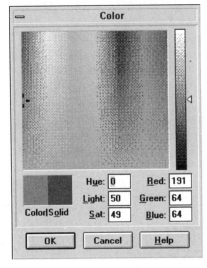

current fill color is outlined with a white frame. A different fill color may be chosen by clicking the desired shade. The icon at the bottom right (with the paintbrush) is a button for selecting the stroke color. It works like the middle button. The stroke and fill colors of a created object may be altered by selecting the object and then picking new shades from the palette. A color in the palette may be customized by double-clicking the color. Figure 6.16 shows a dialog from which a new color may be chosen or new values entered for hue, light, and saturation or for the proportion of red, green, and blue.

The Line Palette

The width of the outside line of an object may be changed by selecting a line width from the Line palette (see Figure 6.17). The Line palette is toggled on or off by choosing the "Palettes" option from the View menu or by clicking the Line icon on the toolbar. Like the color and pattern choices, the chosen line width is applied to any selected graphic objects or to any subsequently created graphics if none are selected.

Figure 6.17
The Line palette (left) is used for assigning a line width to an object. The Line Ends palette (right) allows arrows and other line ends to be assigned to line objects.

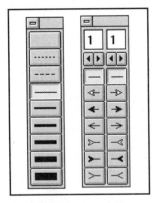

The Line Ends Palette

The Line Ends palette (see Figure 6.17) affects the starting and ending points of a drawn line by creating arrows and other shapes. The choices made on this palette affect any selected lines or any subsequently drawn lines if no lines are selected. The Line Ends palette is toggled on or off by choosing the "Palettes" menu option or by clicking the Line Ends icon on the toolbar. (Hold the Ctrl key down to change the toolbar so that the Line icon changes to the Line Ends icon.)

The Pattern Palette

In addition to fill and stroke colors, a fill pattern may be applied to an object. The Pattern palette (see Figure 6.18) may be displayed by choosing "Palettes" from the View menu and selecting "Pattern" from the submenu, or clicking the Pattern icon in the toolbar. The Pattern palette displays 128 different patterns that may be applied to a filled object. The patterns are displayed on pages of 32 patterns, and the different pages may be displayed by clicking the arrow buttons above the patterns. Above the arrow buttons are four icons, which may also be clicked to apply a pattern to an object. The top button fills the object with the current fill color. The second button fills the object with the current stroke color and the third fills the object with no fill pattern (the fill of the object is transparent). The fourth button fills the object with the pattern chosen from the display below it. The pattern is a combination of the current stroke and fill colors. Like the Tool and Color palettes, the Pattern palette may be toggled on or off and moved around the screen by dragging its titlebar.

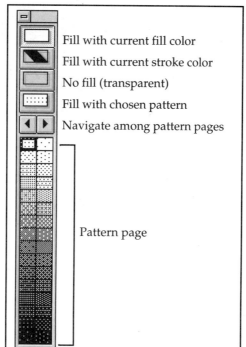

Figure 6.18
The Pattern palette is used for applying a fill pattern to an object.

The Polygon Palette

The Polygon palette (see Figure 6.19) is associated with the Polygon tool on the Tool palette. The Polygon palette is used to dictate the number of sides a polygon drawn with the Polygon tool should have. Choices range from three (the polygon is a triangle) to eight (the polygon is an octagon), or the user may click an arrow to specify a different number (for example, 12), or enter a number in the top. Like the other palettes, the Polygon palette may be moved by dragging its titlebar and toggled on or off via the Palettes menu option or the Polygon icon on the toolbar.

Figure 6.19
In the Polygon palette, an author may specify the number of sides a regular polygon should have.

Rulers and Grids

Rulers may toggled on or off by choosing "Rulers" from the View menu. The rulers may be displayed in either inches or centimeters and are actual size. Moving lines on the rulers correspond to the mouse's location, and the position of a selected object appears on the rulers as a gray rectangle. To change the rulers' units of measure, choose "Book Properties..." from the Objects menu, click the "Page Size" button in the resulting dialog, and then choose the appropriate unit of measure (inches or centimeters) at the bottom left of the "Page Size" dialog.

A grid is available to assist in designing pages and backgrounds. The author displays or hides it by choosing "Grids" from the View menu. A dialog box is displayed (see Figure 6.20) in which the grid size may be specified. The dialog box also allows the author to specify whether to display the grid and if objects should snap to the grid as they are created and moved. Objects that snap to the grid are attracted like a magnet to the grid dots. Figure 6.21 shows a window with the rulers and grid displayed.

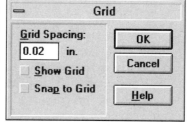

Figure 6.20
The "Grid" option in the View menu brings up a dialog box in which the grid spacing may be specified. The dialog also allows the author to display the grid and specify whether objects should snap to it.

Figure 6.21
The authoring environment
with the rulers and grid
made visible.

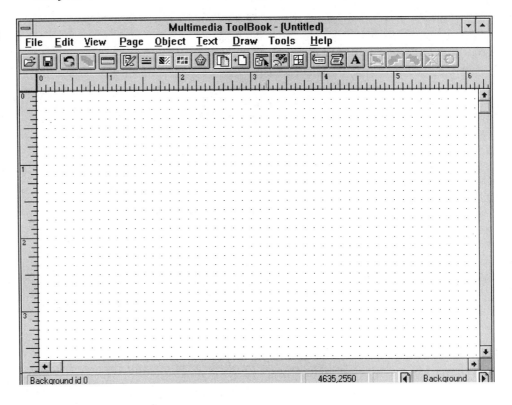

The Statusbar

A statusbar is displayed at the bottom of the window. It presents three distinct pieces of information (see Figure 6.22). At the left is the caption area, in which explanations regarding menu, toolbar and palette selections (context-sensitive help) is given. In the center is given the location of the mouse pointer, in page units as measured from the top left corner of the page. (There are 1440 page units per inch.) On the right, the page number is displayed along with navigational buttons for going to the previous and next pages. As in Reader mode, clicking the page number results in a prompt that asks for the number of the page the user wants to see.

Figure 6.22
The statusbar displays
context-sensitive help about
menus and tool selections,
the current location of the
mouse pointer, and the
current page number.

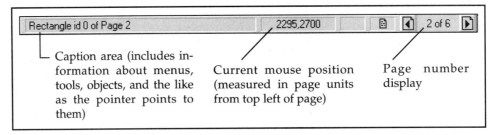

The "Command" Window

The **"Command" window** (see Figure 6.23) is a line editor from which an OpenScript command can be executed. It is toggled on or off via the "Command Window" choice in the View menu, by clicking the Command Window icon on the toolbar, or by pressing the Shift-F3. A command is entered into the window below the split bar and is executed when the Enter key is pressed. Multiple commands (an entire script, for example) may be entered by using a semicolon to separate the commands or by pressing Ctrl-Enter after each statement. The script is executed by pressing Enter.

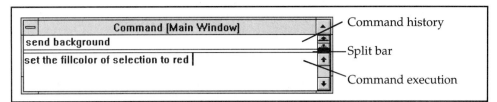

Figure 6.23
The "Command" window
is used to execute
OpenScript commands
when designing a book or to
test commands and scripts.
A history of executed
commands is located in the
top portion of the window;
commands are entered in
the bottom portion.

The last 20 commands executed in the "Command" window are listed in the top portion of the "Command" window and may be re-entered by clicking them. The "Command" window is utilized for executing commands in designing a book or to test a command or script.

Right-Click Menus

In the Author mode, objects may be clicked, using the right mouse button, to reveal a pop-up menu window that allows quick access to properties associated with the object. The Right-Click menu differs, depending on the type of object clicked. A **Right-Click menu** for the current background is displayed by clicking the right mouse button while pressing Ctrl; the book's Right-Click menu is displayed by clicking the right mouse button while holding down Shift. The viewer's Right-Click menu is displayed by pressing the right mouse button while pressing Shift-Ctrl. Figure 6.24 shows different Right-Click menus. Right-Click menus contain a titlebar with a caption showing the object's name or ID. Below the titlebar is a toolbar with icon buttons for viewing the "Properties" dialog, the script recorder, the "Auto-Script" dialog, the debugger, the complete properties editor, and on-line help. Below the toolbar is a menu listing for accessing various property dialogs and toggling certain properties off and on.

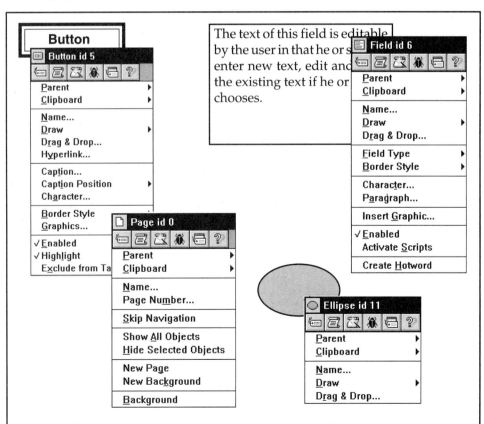

Figure 6.24
Right-clicking an object in
the Author mode reveals a
pop-up menu in which
properties of that object
may be accessed and edited.
Since each object type has
different properties, the
Right-Click menus vary
with the object chosen.

Summary Questions

Answer the following true/false questions.

1. The Author mode is visually identical to the Reader mode.
2. ToolBook books may be saved as executable .EXE files.
3. The options for showing and hiding the rulers and grid are in the View menu.
4. Options for rotating graphic objects, sending an object to the back, and making an object transparent are in the Draw menu.
5. The toolbar is permanently positioned at the top of the "Client" window in Author mode.
6. The Tool palette contains tools for creating buttons, fields, and graphics.
7. The colors of the Color palette may not be edited.
8. In addition to a fill color, an object may be filled with a particular pattern.
9. The spacing of the layout grid is always a half inch.
10. The option for creating a hotword is in the Text menu.

Complete the following statements by filling in the blanks.

11. Laying out the pages of a book and entering the scripts of objects (programming) are done in the _____ mode.
12. Authors may switch between the page-and-background view and the background-only view by pressing the _____ key.
13. The_____ menu contains options for viewing and setting the properties of objects, page, background, and book.
14. The _____ is a graphical interface menu containing buttons that allow quick access to popular menu options.
15. A second set of toolbar options is displayed by pressing the _____ key.
16. The Color palette allows the author to set the _____ and _____ colors of an object.
17. The coordinates of the current mouse pointer position may be found in the _____ .
18. The _____ _____ is a line editor from which an OpenScript command may be executed in Author mode.
19. The _____ palette is used to apply arrows to a selected line.
20. A _____ menu gives quick access to the properties associated with an object. It pops up when the author clicks the object by using the right mouse button.

Hands-On Projects

A. Examine the software that accompanies this chapter. Open the "Table of Contents" book by double-clicking its icon in the "Developing with ToolBook" group window in the Windows Program Manager. Inside the "Table of Contents," click the book representing Chapter 6. Work your way through the tutorial as a means of reinforcing and enriching the information presented in this chapter.

B. Open ToolBook. In the author mode:
   1. Switch from Author to Reader mode, and back.
   2. Hide and show the Tool palette by clicking the Tool palette icon in the toolbar.
   3. Move the Tool palette around on the screen by dragging its titlebar.
   4. Reshape the Tool palette by dragging its frame.
   5. Grab the toolbar and pull it down from the top of the window so that it becomes a palette. Reshape it by dragging its frame. Drag it back to the top;

It will reattach itself to the window frame. You can also attach it to the window frame on the left, right, or bottom by dragging it to those locations.

6. Show the Color palette by clicking its icon in the toolbar. Reposition the Color palette on the screen by dragging its titlebar. Hide it by clicking its icon in the tool bar. Show and hide it again by using the "Palettes" option in the View menu.

7. Show the line palette by clicking its icon in the toolbar. Move the palette around the screen by dragging its titlebar. Hide it in the same way. Show and hide it again, using the "Palettes" option in the View menu.

8. Show the Pattern palette by clicking its icon in the toolbar. Reposition the Pattern palette in the window. Hide the Pattern palette by using the toolbar. Show and hide it again, using the "Palettes" option in the View menu.

9. Show the Line Ends palette by pressing the Ctrl key and clicking its icon in the toolbar. Reposition the Line Ends palette in the window. Hide the palette by clicking its icon in the toolbar. Show and hide it again, using the "Palettes" option in the View menu.

10. Show the Polygon palette by clicking its icon in the toolbar. Reposition the Polygon palette in the window. Hide the palette by clicking its icon in the toolbar. Show and hide it again, using the "Palettes" option in the View menu.

11. Right-click the toolbar. In the resulting Right-Click menu, change the display of the toolbar so it reads "Captions Only." Note the new display. Change the display again, to "Graphics & Captions." Note the new display. Change the display back to "Graphics Only."

12. Point at the different icons on the toolbar and the tool palette. Note how context-sensitive help captions are displayed in the left frame of the statusbar. Information is given about the function of each button. Note how mouse pointer location information is displayed in the statusbar as the pointer is moved around in the page.

13. Turn the rulers on by clicking the "Rulers" option in the View menu. Turn the grid on by choosing "Grid" in the View menu. In the "Grid" dialog box, set the grid spacing to 0.5 inch. Be sure to check the "Show Grid" option to display the grid. Turn the rulers off by reselecting the "Rulers" option in the View menu. Hide the grid.

14. Display the book's Right-Click menu by pressing Shift and clicking the page area by pressing the right mouse button. Click outside the menu, using the left mouse button, to hide the Right-Click menu.

15. Call up the Right-Click menu for the current page by clicking the page area by pressing the right mouse button. To hide the menu, press the left mouse button to click the page.

16. Display the Right-Click menu for the current background by holding down the Ctrl key and using the right mouse button to click the page area. Hide the background Right-Click menu by pressing the left mouse button when the pointer is outside the menu.

Chapter
7

Laying the Foundation

Working with a New Book

In developing a book, the first step is to create a new blank book. This new book is then developed by adding new pages and backgrounds as needed and adding fields, buttons, and graphic objects to the pages and backgrounds. Various properties of the book are set up at the book level, including the page size, titlebar caption, and colors. A book is displayed within the page area of the associated main window viewer for that book. Certain viewer properties may need to be set for the book to be displayed as the author desires. Resources such as icons, bitmaps, cursors, and TrueType fonts may be embedded into a book and made accessible to the book's buttons, fields, and so on.

Creating a New Book

A new blank book can be created using two different methods. The first is simply to start ToolBook without specifying a book to open, such as by double-clicking the ToolBook icon in the Program Manager (see Figure 7.1) or running the TB30.EXE (or MTB30.EXE) file from the File Manager. ToolBook will launch and open a new empty book, untitled and unsaved. If ToolBook is already open, a new book may be created by choosing, in Author mode, the "New" option in the File menu.

Figure 7.1
The Multimedia ToolBook icon as it appears in the Program Manager.

Changing the Page Size Property of a Book

When a new book is created, its page size is 6 inches wide and 4 inches high by default. This is the size property of the book. ToolBook objects, including pages, have **properties** that define such things as their size, color, shape, position, and so on. Each property of an object is defined by at least one value and this value may be changed by the author. Often, changing the value results in a change in the object's appearance. When an author moves an object on the screen by dragging it with the mouse pointer, what he or she is actually doing is changing the position property of that object. Many properties are set by interfacing with the object, but properties may also be set through a "Properties" dialog box associated with the particular type of object. Figure 7.2 shows the "Book Properties" dialog box, which may be opened by choosing "Book Properties" in the Object menu or by using the keyboard shortcut, Shift-F8. Several different book properties may be set through this dialog. To adjust the size of the book's pages, click the "Page Size" button in the middle right of the "Book Properties" dialog. The "Page Size" dialog appears (see Figure 7.3). The "Page Size" dialog lists several size options (9 x 6, 8 x 5, 6 x 4, and 5 x 3 inches), as well as the opportunity to specify other measurements. Select one of the size options by clicking the radio button in front of the listing so that it is highlighted (filled). Specify a nonlisted size by clicking the "Other" radio button and entering a width and height in the two areas provided. The maximum width and height are each 14 inches. The default, the 6- by 4-inch page size, results in a book that is slightly smaller than the

Figure 7.2
The "Book Properties"
dialog box is opened from
the Object menu and allows
the author to change such
properties as page size,
whether to save a book on
closing, and what type of
style should be applied to
hotwords.

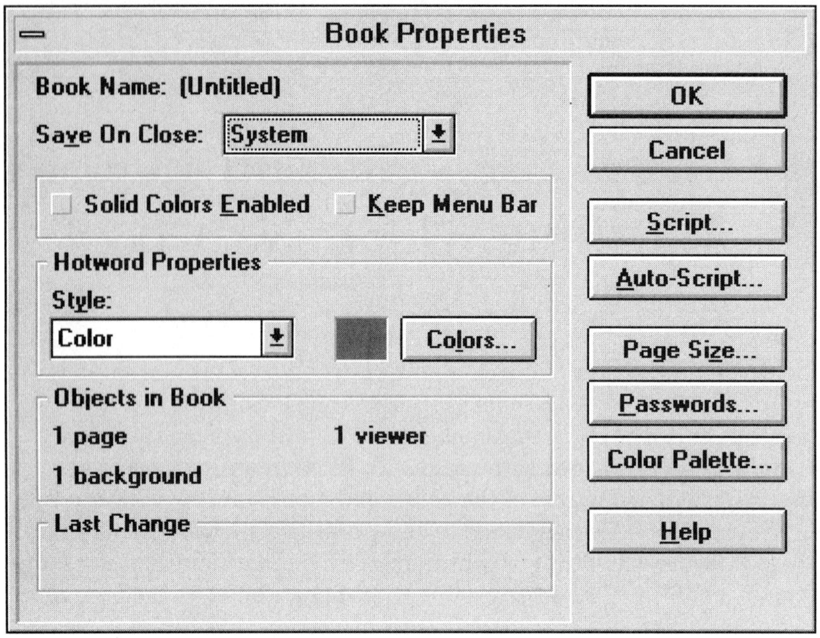

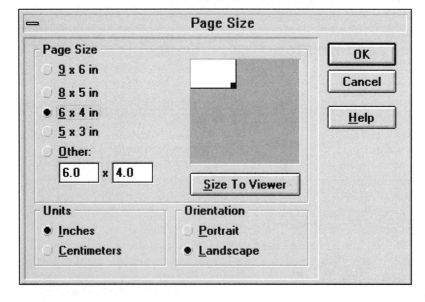

standard 640- by 480-pixel monitor. For a full screen (640 by 480) display, a custom page size of 6.6 by 4.5 inches is recommended for a book with a Reader mode menubar and titlebar; 6.6 by 4.7 inches is recommended if the menubar is to be hidden in the Reader mode.

Measurements are in inches by default, but if centimeters are preferred, the measurement system may be changed by clicking the "Centimeters" radio button in the "Units" field. The orientation of the page may be changed from landscape (the default) to portrait. Objects with **landscape orientations** have a greater width than height; those with **portrait orientations** have a greater height than width.

Figure 7.3
Clicking the "Page Size"
button in the "Book
Properties" dialog opens
this dialog, from which a
standard page size may be
chosen or a custom size
specified.

Other Book Properties

As seen in the "Book Properties" dialog box, there are several different properties associated with a book. Each property has a specific OpenScript term associated with it. The page size property in OpenScript terms is known as the **size** of the book. Other book properties include saveOnClose (which determines when and how a book should be saved), solidColorsEnabled (whether to use a dithered-, or patterned-color, palette or a solid-color palette), keepMenuBar (whether to retain the current book's menu when it calls a different book), hotwordStyle (determines the default style—such as underlined, framed, a specific color, and so on—of hotwords in the book), and hotwordColor (what the color of hotwords should be if "Color" was chosen as the hotword default style). Note that property terms are one word, though they may be made up of several words without spaces between them.) The "Book Properties" dialog also allows the author to set passwords for the book. This allows the author to restrict certain activities by a user and to choose for a book a palette other than the default palette.

Choosing the "Save on Close" option displays four settings for determining if the book should be saved when closed: "System," "Yes," "No," and "Ask." The value chosen is assigned to the book's saveOnClose property. If "System" is chosen (the default), the value of another property belonging to the system (sysChangesDB) determines whether the book is saved when closing. (If sysChangesDB is true, the "Save Changes" dialog box (see Figure 7.4) is displayed, giving the user the option of saving any changes or not. If sysChangesDB is false, the book closes without asking or saving the changes.) Setting the value of saveOnClose by choosing "Yes" guarantees that any changes will be saved automatically, without asking when the book is closed; choosing "No" allows the book to be closed without asking the user if he or she wants to save the changes. If the value of the saveOnClose property is determined by choosing "Ask," the "Save Changes?" dialog appears regardless of the value of sysChangesDB.

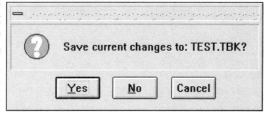

Save current changes to: TEST.TBK?

Yes   No   Cancel

Figure 7.4
If the "Save On Close" option is defined as "System" or "Ask," the user will be prompted by this screen, the "Save Changes?" dialog.

The "Solid Colors Enabled" checkbox sets the solidColorsEnabled property to either true (checked) or false (unchecked). When solidColorsEnabled is false (the default value), the Color palette consists of the 16 colors used by Windows, plus 8 shades created by dithered patterns of those 16 colors. Enabling the solid colors by checking the box in the "Properties" dialog, or otherwise setting the solidColorsEnabled property to true, produces a Color palette of 96 solid colors of which 64 are customizable. This solid-colors palette is for systems whose display supports 256 colors or more (SVGA).

The keepMenuBar property specifies whether the book's menubar should be retained in the main window even when navigating to a different book. This property is for multiple book applications, when a custom menu is being utilized in each of the same linked books. This property would be set in a book that front-ends the other books of the application, saving the author the time and storage space of including the menubar resource in the other books.

As discussed in Chapter 5, hotwords may utilize one of several possible styles. The author may determine which style should be applied by default when a hotword is created. The style may include color, frame, underlining, or none of these. Each individual hotword also has a hotwordStyle property, which is initially set to the hotwordStyle property of the book. Thus the style may be adjusted for any specific hotword, or a different style may be applied to the chosen text by manually formatting the text, to make it bold, italic, or a different font, for example.

If the value of the hotwordStyle property is color, the specific color utilized for displaying hotword text is set up by clicking the "Color..." button next to the hotword properties style designation and choosing a stroke color in the resulting Color palette. The selection is assigned to the book's hotwordColor property and appears in the on-

Figure 7.5
*In this screen the script
editor displays a book script
for hiding the menubar and
scrollbars in the Reader
mode and making them
visible in the Author mode.*

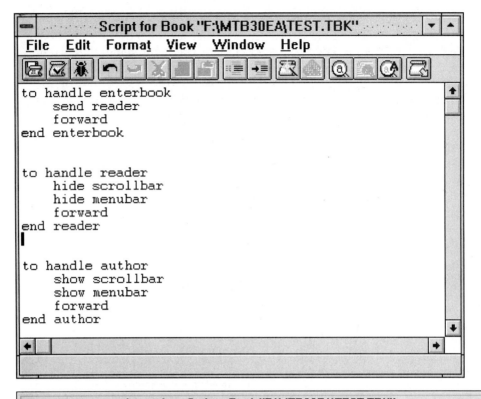

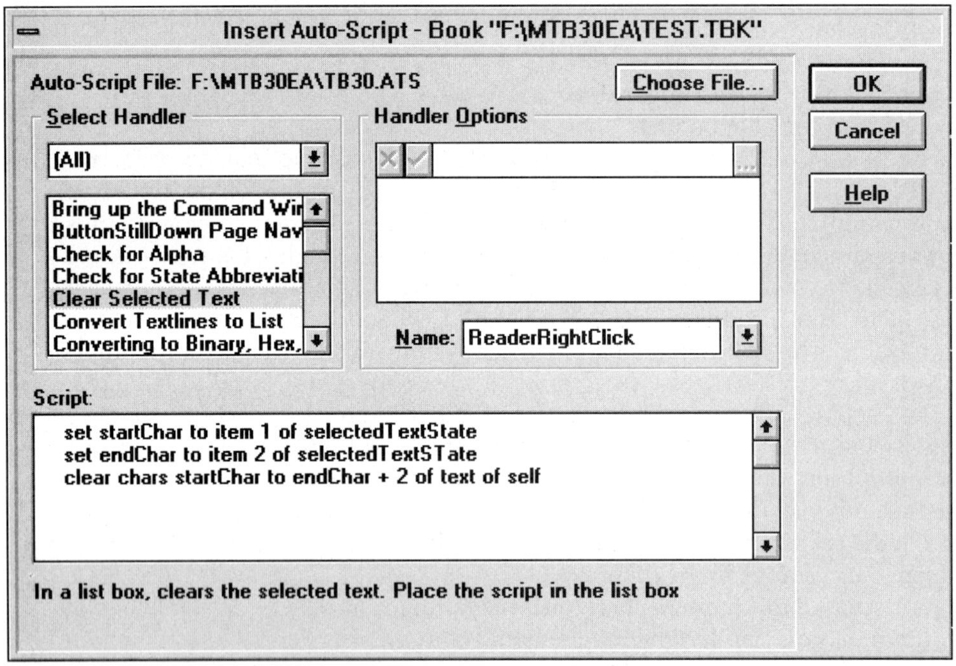

Figure 7.6
*The "Insert Auto-Script"
dialog allows the author to
import predefined scripts
into the book script or the
scripts of any other object.*

screen sample next to the "Color..." button.

The "Script..." button displays the script editor and the script attached to the
book. The book script is used to handle events that have a bookwide scope—in other
words, when the script might be called from any page in the book, or handle events
that occur at the book level (such as entering the book). Figure 7.5 shows the script
editor and a book script commonly used by this author to hide the menubar and
scrollbars in Reader mode but show them in the Author mode.

The "Auto-Script..." button of the "Book Properties" dialog brings up the "Insert

Auto-Script" dialog (see Figure 7.6). In this dialog, the author may choose from a list of predefined handlers to include in the book's script. The auto-script feature as well as the script editor are examined in Chapter 12.

The "Passwords..." button displays the "Passwords" dialog box, in which the author may password-protect certain activities (see Figure 7.7). A password may be specified in the "Password to Switch to Author Level" field. The password is re-entered in the "Retype Password to Confirm" field to help verify that the password was not entered incorrectly, since the display of the password's characters are hidden (plus signs are displayed instead). If a password is entered here, it will need to be entered anytime the current book is switched to Author mode. This helps keep end-users from making modifications to a book, accessing hidden information, or seeing the scripts of a book and its objects. In addition, passwords may also be specified for allowing the book to be saved under the same name (the user can save the book but only under a different name, unless supplying the required password). This is useful in situations where a master copy of a book exists on a computer or network and the master copy should never be changed. Users, however, may save altered versions under a new name or path. Such a situation may include an educational application where the student's progress and data are maintained in a book owned by the individual student, with that book being a copy of a master file. Finally, input of a password attached to a book may be required before the book may be opened. Password protection is useful for books that contain sensitive or private information.

The "Help" button of the "Book Properties" dialog accesses on-line information about each of the options contained in the dialog. The dialog also shows information about the book, including the number of pages, backgrounds, and viewers it contains.

Figure 7.7
Passwords may be attached to a book, restricting accessibility to the Author mode, saving the book, or even opening the book itself.

Choosing a Palette and Importing Resources

Resources are Windows system elements that can be embedded into a book and then utilized within the book's objects, scripts, properties, and so on. Resources include icons, cursors, bitmap images, menubars and color palettes. In addition, TrueType fonts may also be embedded in books created with Multimedia ToolBook. From the "Book Properties" dialog, the "Choose Palette" dialog (see Figure 7.8) may be displayed by clicking the "Color Palette" button. Palettes consist of files in palette (.PAL) format. Palette files may be created or edited with the PalEdit application that accompanies ToolBook (see Figure 7.9). For more information about creating and editing palette resources with PalEdit, refer to *ToolBook User Manual* or access the on-line help within the PalEdit application. Palettes are embedded into the book by clicking the "Import..." button and specifying the .PAL file to import in the resulting dialog box. Embedded palettes are shown in the "Resource List" of the "Choose Palette" dialog and may be selected (highlighted) by clicking their listing. The "New"

Figure 7.8
*The "Choose Palette"
dialog allows palette format
(.PAL) files to be imported
and applied to a book and
its objects.*

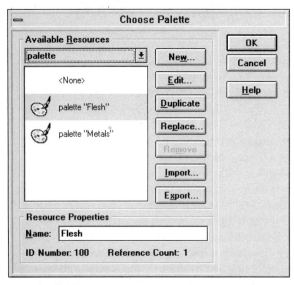

Figure 7.9
*The ToolBook package
includes PalEdit, a utility
for creating and editing
custom palettes.*

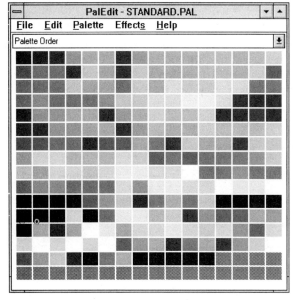

Figure 7.10
*The Resource Manager is
an expanded version of the
"Choose Palette" dialog
(see Figure 7.8). Besides
palettes, other resources —
such as cursors, icons,
bitmap images and custom
menubars—may be
imported.*

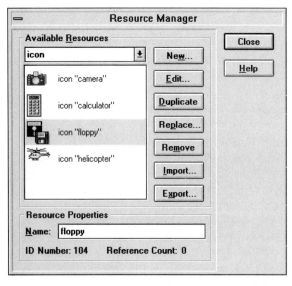

button opens the PalEdit application, as does the "Edit" button. (The "Edit" button also loads the selected palette into PalEdit for alteration. The "Duplicate" button duplicates the selected palette so that a copy may be edited and the original left intact.) Clicking the "Replace" button deletes the selected palette and allows a new palette to be imported in its place. The "Export" button permits the selected palette to be exported to disk as a .PAL file. A palette may also be selected and assigned a name such as "Flesh Tones" or "Pastels." Its assigned ID number and the number of times it is used within the book will be shown within the "Resource Properties" section at the bottom of the dialog.

The palette resources of the book may also be accessed through the Resource Manager (see Figure 7.10). The resource editor is opened by clicking the Resource Manager icon on the toolbar, choosing "Resources..." in the Object menu, or pressing Ctrl-F10 on the keyboard. The Resource Manager works exactly like the "Choose Palette" dialog, except that any of the various types of resources may be accessed. The "Available Resources" list box shows the different types (bitmaps, cursors, icons, and so on). Select the desired resource type and the embedded resources of that type are then listed below it. The buttons discussed for the "Choose Palette" dialog function the same for each of the specified resource types.

Bitmaps are in .BMP or .DIB format and may be attached to a button or embedded in the text of a field or recordfield. Bitmaps may be created and edited with BitEdit, an application accompanying ToolBook, or other Windows graphic applications such as PaintBrush. Cursors and icons are small graphics (their maximum size is 32 pixels by 32 pixels). Cursors are assigned to represent the mouse pointer; icons may be attached to a button, embedded in the text of a field, assigned to drag and drop images, or assigned as cursors. Cursors and icons may be created and edited with the icon- and cursor-editing application discussed in Chapter 5 (see Figure 5.14) or Windows icon- and cursor-editing applications. Menubar resources contain menus such as File or Page and their associated menu items. Menubar resources define the appearance of the menubar (for example, which items are included, whether a menu item has a toggle check mark displayed next to it, or whether associated keyboard shortcuts, and the like are listed) but not the actual workings of the menu items. The actions of the menu items are usually defined in the book script or viewer script. Menubar resources may be created and edited with the menu bar editor, MENUEDIT.EXE. Creating and defining menus is addressed in Chapter 20.

Other Ways of Accessing a Book's Properties

The properties of a book may also be accessed through the book's Right-Click menu in the Author mode (see Figure 7.11). The Right-Click menu for the book is displayed by holding down the Shift key while pressing the right mouse button while the mouse pointer is in the window's page area. Each of the properties discussed in relation to the "Book Properties" dialog may be accessed and set by clicking the appropriate listing. The buttons at the top, respectively from left to right, display the "Book Properties" dialog; display the script editor with the book's script; invoke the "Insert Auto-Script" dialog; invoke the script debugger; bring up the property browser (see Figure 7.12), in which all the properties associated with the book object may be accessed and changed; and access the on-line help topics related to books.

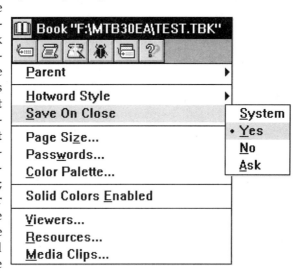

Figure 7.11
Book properties may be conveniently accessed through the book's Right-Click menu The menu is displayed by pressing Shift and the right mouse button simultaneously.

The "Command" window may also be used to get and set the book's properties by using OpenScript commands. The "Command" window is shown and hidden, in Author mode, by pressing Shift-F3. Commands are typed into the "Command" window, after clicking it to make it active, and executed by pressing the Enter key. To display the current value of a book property, the command structure put the <property> of this book is entered. The appropriate property term is substituted for <property>. For instance, to get the current hotword style, the command put the hotwordStyle of this book is typed into the "Command" window (see Figure 7.13). The Enter key is pressed and the

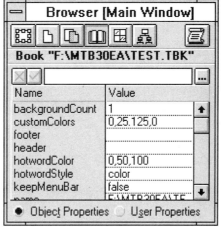

Figure 7.12
The property browser may be accessed from the book's Right-Click menu. The browser lists all the properties of the book, and their values, in the scroll field.

Figure 7.13
Property values may be
displayed or set by entering
OpenScript commands in
the "Command" window.

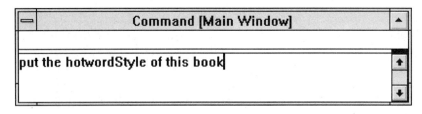

hotword style is displayed in the "Command" window. Likewise, a book property may be set by entering set the <property> of this book to <value> into the "Command" window, substituting the appropriate property term and value, and pressing the Enter key to execute the command. For instance, executing set the hotwordStyle of this book to frame sets up the frame style as the default hotword style. An alternative command structure is <property> of this book = <value>. The command hotwordStyle of this book = frame has the same effect as set the hotwordStyle of this book to frame.

Saving a Book

In the file menu are three options for saving a book. The "Save" option saves any changes to a previously saved book under the same filename and path. If the book is new and has not yet been saved, the "Save" option invokes the "Save As..." option. The "Save As..." option displays the "Save As" dialog (see Figure 7.14) in which a filename and path are specified according to Windows standards. The "Save As..." option may be specified directly, and invoking it for a previously saved book allows the altered book to be saved under a new name or path while the original file remains unchanged. Books may also be saved as executable (.EXE) files by invoking the "Save As EXE..." menu item. Books saved as .EXE files contain instructions for launching ToolBook and thus still require the ToolBook application or its runtime module to be opened and executed. The sole advantage to saving a book as an executable file is that it simplifies the process of opening or running the book, as long as the directory containing the ToolBook application is listed in the computer's path statement.

Figure 7.14
The "Save As" dialog
permits a book to be saved
under a specified filename
and in a specified directory.

A Word About Viewers

It is necessary to say a few things about the main window viewer, since the viewer is closely related to the display of the book. Since books are displayed within their associated main window viewer, they may not display appropriately if the viewer is not sized appropriately. This requires setting several properties of the main window viewer, and this is done in the "Viewer Properties" dialog (see Figure 7.15). This dialog is accessed by choosing the "Viewers..." option, selecting the "Main window" listing in the resulting dialog, and then clicking the "Properties..." button. There are five different settings pages in the "Viewer Properties" dialog: "Style," "Position," "Size," "Limits," and "Options." Each is represented by a label designed to look like a tab on a file folder. Each "tab" may be clicked to go to the associated page. Adjustments may need to be made to the viewer properties for the book's pages to be fully displayed, especially if a size other than 6 by 4 inches was chosen. For example to have the viewer conform to a full 640- by 480-pixel screen and fit a page size of 6.6 by 4.5 inches, complete the following steps:

1. Choose "Viewers..." in the Object menu. Highlight the "Main window" listing in the resulting dialog box; click the "Properties..." button.
2. In the "Viewer Properties" dialog, click the "Position" tab to access the "Position Properties" page. Click the "Custom" radio button and type "0" for both the x and y values. (This will position the main window in the upper left of the screen when the "Viewer Properties" dialog is closed.)
3. Click the "Size" tab. Uncheck the "Auto Size" box. In the "Units" field, specify pixels. Click the "Custom" radio button. Type "640" to specify the width and type "480" to specify the height.
4. Click the "Limits" tab. Choose pixels as the units of measure. Uncheck the "None" button in the "Maximum Size" field and type "640" and "480 as the width and height values. Do the same for the "Minimum Size" field (see Figure 7.15).
5. Click the "Options" tab. Set the default state to normal or maximized.
6. Click the "OK" button to return to the "Viewer Properties" dialog.
7. Click the "Done" button to close the "Viewer Properties" dialog. The main window should now fill the screen.

(Note: If using a different page size, you can still use these procedures; just type size values different from those cited in steps 3 and 4.)

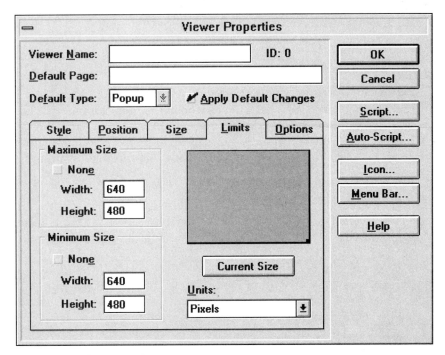

Figure 7.15
The size, position, and behavior of the main window viewer is set up in the "Viewers Properties" dialog.

Summary Questions

Answer the following true/false questions.

1. When ToolBook is launched from the Program Manager without specifying a book to open, a new book is created by default.
2. The booksize property determines the size of the pages of a book.
3. The default 6- by 4-inch page size fills a 640- by 480-pixel monitor.
4. The palette of solid colors is designed for systems that can display 256 colors in Windows (SVGA).
5. Portrait orientations have a greater width than height.
6. The hotwordColor property determines whether hotwords are displayed as a different color, underlined, or framed.
7. Setting the saveOnClose property by choosing "System" causes the book to always be saved when it is closed.
8. A password may be set up that must be provided by the user before a book can be opened.
9. Icons are small graphics with a maximum size of 64 by 64 pixels.
10. To execute a book saved as an .EXE, or executable, file does not require ToolBook nor the runtime ToolBook modules.

Complete the following statements by filling in the blanks.

11. _____ contain values that define an object's appearance and behavior.
12. The standard monitor measures _____ by _____ pixels.
13. To ensure that all changes to a book are saved when it is closed, its saveOnClose property should be set by selecting _____.
14. When a page is wider than it is high, it is said to have a _____ orientation.
15. The Right-Click menu for the book is displayed by clicking the page area by using the right mouse button, while pressing the _____ key.
16. Scripts are entered and edited in the _____ _____.
17. Windows palette resource files have the extension _____.
18. Book properties may be set and retrieved by entering OpenScript commands in the _____ window.
19. Books are generally displayed in the _____ _____ viewer.
20. The _____ _____ option allows a user to specify a filename and path to which the current book is saved.

Hands-On Projects

A. Examine the software that accompanies this chapter. Open the "Table of Contents" book by double-clicking its icon in the "Developing with ToolBook" group window in the Windows Program Manager. Inside the "Table of Contents," click the book representing Chapter 7. Work your way through the tutorial as a means of reinforcing and enriching the information presented in this chapter.

B. Business Report Presentation (Part I) At the end of Chapters 7 through 11, you will build part of the business report presentation shown in Chapters 2 and 4. By the end of Chapter 11, you will have created a duplicate presentation from scratch.
   1. Create a new book by launching ToolBook. Or if ToolBook is already running, choose, in Author mode, "New" from the File menu.
   2. Open the "Book Properties" dialog from the Object menu. Click the "Page Size" button and select "Custom" in the resulting dialog. Type "6.6" as the width and "4.7" as the height. Click "OK" to return to the "Book Properties" dialog.

3. Open the script editor by clicking the "Script" button. Type the script shown in Figure 7.5. (Be careful not to make any typographical errors!) Indented lines are created with the Tab key. When finished, choose "Update Script & Exit" from the File menu or click the first icon on the script editor's toolbar. (If an error warning appears, click "Cancel" and check your typing. Look for misspelled words, omissions, and the like. ToolBook will usually highlight offending commands, parameters, and so on. When the mistake is found, choose "Update Script & Edit" again to close the editor.)
4. Change the position, size, maximum size, minimum size, and default state of the main window viewer by completing the seven steps listed earlier in this chapter.
5. Save the book under the name BIZRPT1.TBK. (If working on a community computer, save it to a floppy disk.)

C. Complete the following steps to use the on-line help to gather more information about working with books.
1. Open ToolBook. Access the step-by-step procedures in ToolBook's on-line help.
2. Click "Working with Objects."
3. Click "Book" to choose the topic. Access each of the items listed about books—for example, "Adding a book caption to the title bar." (Use the "Back" button to return to the listing of step-by-step procedures. Access the next topic.)
4. Do the same for the "Using Resources" topic, clicking "Palettes" and reading the "Overview: Color Palettes" selection.
5. Use the search function to look up the following entries: book properties, windows, size, hotwordStyle, saveOnClose, and solidColorsEnabled.

Chapter
8

Laying Out the Book
Working with Pages and Backgrounds

Pages and backgrounds are the blocks upon which a book is built. Most ToolBook applications consist of multiple pages, and the author must carefully consider how the pages and their backgrounds relate. Designing a book so that pages, via the background, can share many objects can greatly reduce the size of the book, not to mention save production time. How the pages are linked and navigated is of great importance, and the wise developer will carefully plan the book's layout—if not on paper, at least in his or her mind—prior to producing it. A visual map (such as Figure 4.11) as well as a storyboard, may be helpful.

When a new book is initially created, it has one page and one background. Any number of pages and backgrounds may be added. Pages and backgrounds can also be deleted or rearranged. As with the book itself, both pages and backgrounds have various properties associated with them. These properties are set by the author to determine their appearance, behavior, and status.

Defining Pages and Backgrounds

In review, there are two primary object layers of a ToolBook screen: the screen, often referred to as a page, consists of the transparent foreground layer (or page layer) and the underlying background layer. Note that the term "page" is used here to mean two different things—the foreground layer, as well as the screen made up by the foreground and the background. There may be any number of pages in a book and, though each page has a background, multiple pages may share the same background, incorporating the background objects into their displays (see Figures 4.2 and 4.9). Since every page has an accompanying background but a background can be shared by several pages, a book may have just one background, as many backgrounds as there are pages (if each page has its own background—such a book is probably not well designed), or any number in between. Generally, the fewer number of backgrounds, the better.

Adding New Pages and Backgrounds

To add a new page sharing the background of the current page, choose "New Page" from the Object menu, use the equivalent keyboard shortcut Ctrl-N, or click the New Page icon in the toolbar. A new blank page is inserted after the current page that utilizes the background of the current page.

To add a new page with a new background, choose "New Background" from the Object menu or use the equivalent keyboard shortcut Ctrl-M. A new blank page and a new blank background are inserted after the current page.

Navigating from Pages and Backgrounds

Pages of a book may be navigated by using the "Next," "Previous," "First," "Last," and "History" options of the Page menu, their keyboard shortcuts, or the navigational abilities of the statusbar (see Chapter 6). The author may display just the background and work with its objects by selecting the "Background" option from the View menu or utilizing the keyboard shortcut F4. The page number display in the statusbar changes to the word "Background" when in the background view. The author can return to the page view (foreground layer with the underlying background) by selecting the "Foreground" option from the View menu or pressing the F4 key.

Removing Pages and Backgrounds

To remove a page, navigate to the unwanted page. Choose the "Select Page" option from the Edit menu to select the page and all its objects. Choose "Clear" or "Cut" from the Edit menu. Both clearing and cutting the page removes it, but cutting the page places a copy of the page and its objects on the clipboard, allowing it to be pasted back into the current book or another book. Click the "OK" button in the resulting warning dialog. All objects may be removed from a page, leaving the page blank, by choosing the "Select All" item from the Edit Menu and then choosing either "Cut" or "Clear." Likewise, all the objects on a background may be deleted by navigating to the background by pressing the F4 key, or choosing "Background" from the View menu then selecting all the objects and either cutting or clearing them. A background is deleted when the only page using the background is deleted.

Coloring the Background

Pages are colored by setting the fillColor property of the background. The background fill color is visible through the transparent foreground layer. To set the fillColor property, choose the "Background Properties" option in the Object menu. The "Background Properties" dialog (see Figure 8.1) provides an interface for viewing and setting properties of the current background. To set the fillColor property of the background, click the "Colors..." button. The Color palette will appear. Click the "Fill Bucket" icon on the right to activate the fillColor selector and

Figure 8.1
The "Background Properties" dialog allows the author to set various properties of the current background, such as the background's name and color.

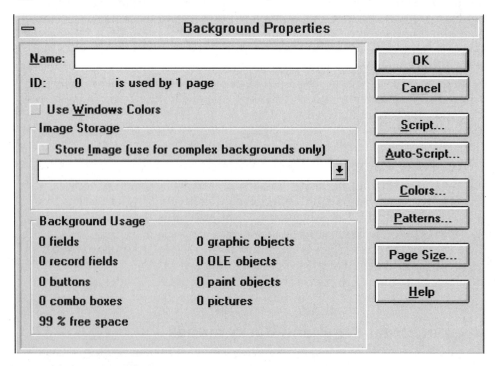

then click a color in the palette. The background will be shaded with the chosen color. A stroke color may be chosen in the same manner for the background, making the strokeColor selector active by clicking the Paintbrush icon of the Color palette and then choosing a color. The background stroke color is used if a pattern is applied to the background, since patterns are made up of both the fill color and stroke color. Patterns are applied by clicking the "Patterns..." button in the "Background Properties" dialog. The Pattern palette is displayed and the clicked pattern is applied to the current background. After the selections are made, the Pattern palette and the Color palette may be closed by clicking the close box, in the upper left.

Other Background Properties

Backgrounds may be named by entering a string of up to 32 characters in the "Name" field of the "Background Properties" dialog. Examples of background names are Game Board and The First Background. The name may be more than one word. Backgrounds may be referred to by their names in OpenScript commands (for example, set the fillColor of background "Game Board" to red) or by the id assigned them by ToolBook, such as id 0 (set the fillColor of background id 0 to red). The id property of the background is set by the ToolBook system and cannot be changed. (Many properties of objects can only be retrieved and not set by the author or reader.)

The author may also choose to utilize the color scheme set up in the Control Panel of the Windows environment, by checking the box in front of "Use Windows Colors." This sets the useWindowsColors property of the current background to true, using the color specified as the Windows background for the fill color and the color specified as the application workspace color as the background's stroke color. This feature might be used in developing a utility that would be integrated into the Windows environment, giving it the appearance of being part of Windows.

A bitmapped image of the background may be stored and displayed before the background can be drawn. An image can be stored by checking the "Store Image" box. This should only be done for very complex backgrounds that contain many objects and that do not change shape, position, and so on (in other words, in cases where no animation occurs on the background) and as a last step in the book's production. Stored images are device-dependent, based on the computer's display. Problems may occur if the image was saved on a VGA display and the program runs on a system with an SVGA display, and vice versa. For more information on storing images, consult the *ToolBook User Manual* and the on-line help.

The number of objects—fields, recordfields, buttons, comboboxes, graphic objects (rectangles, ellipses, polygons, and the like), OLE objects, paint objects, and pictures—on the background is displayed in the "Background Usage" section of the "Background Properties" dialog. Keeping track of the number of objects is helpful because, as objects are added to a background, they take up space in memory. A maximum of 64 kilobytes is reserved in memory for a background; thus, there is a limit to the number of objects that may be placed there. The percentage of free space available for a background is shown in the usage area as well.

Backgrounds may have scripts attached to them. The "Script..." button of the "Background Properties" dialog displays the script editor and the script of the current background. Handlers that have pertinence to all pages of a background, but not the entire book, should be placed in the background script. The "Auto-Script" button allows a predefined script to be inserted into the background script.

Backgrounds may have page sizes different from those set up for the book. Clicking the "Page Size" button brings up the "Page Size" dialog at the book level. The size property of the book is shown as the selected size. This may be changed for the pages of the current background by specifying a new size.

Page Properties

Each page of a book has certain properties associated with it, just as the book and its backgrounds do. Many of the current page's properties may be viewed and changed via the "Page Properties" dialog (see Figure 8.2). This dialog is made visible by selecting "Page Properties," in the Object menu, or executing the keyboard shortcut Shift-F7. As with the background, the author may give a name—such as "Main Menu" or "Title Page"—to the page. The name can contain up to 32 characters. The page may be referred to in OpenScript commands by its name, number, or the ID assigned by the system. The pageNumber property reflects its ordinal position in the book. The first page of a book is page 1, the second page of the book is page 2, and so on. The ordinal position of a page may be changed by entering a new page number in the "Page Properties" dialog. Assigning the page number 1 to a page moves it to the front of the book. Thus the pages of a book may be shuffled at any time, as needed.

Certain pages may contain hidden or sensitive data, provide behind-the-scenes support for a book, or be otherwise reserved for the author's use. These pages should be removed from the navigation cycle. For example, assume that the fifth page of a book contains sensitive data that the reader should not see (perhaps answers to an on-line quiz). When the user selects "Next Page" on the fourth page, the author wishes that the user would next see page 6 and not page 5. Likewise, the reader should go to page 4 when choosing "Previous" from page 6. This is performed by checking the "Skip Navigation" box in the "Page Properties" dialog, eliminating the page from normal navigation at the reader level.

As with the background, a bitmap image of a complex page may be stored and displayed. The number of objects on a page's foreground layer are listed in the "Page Usage" section of the "Page Properties" dialog, and so is the percentage of free memory space available to the page. Scripts may be attached to the page. Most often such scripts contain handlers pertaining to events associated with the page, such as entering or leaving it, or handlers for routines that are only performed on the particular page, such as a specific calculation. Predefined scripts may be inserted by using the auto-script feature.

Figure 8.2
The "Page Properties" dialog provides an interface for the author to view and edit properties of the current page, including the page's name, number (ordinal position in the book), and whether the reader may navigate to it.

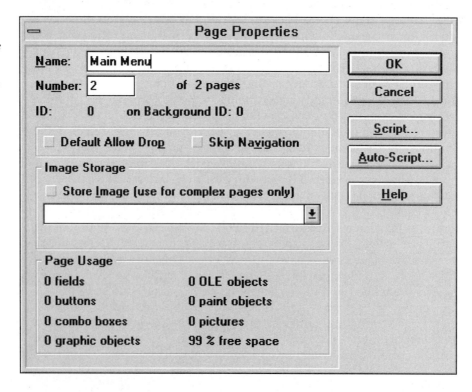

Using Right-Click Menus to Access Properties

As with the book properties, Right-Click menus provide quick access to both page and background properties. Clicking, with the right mouse button, on any blank area of a page (that is, where no foreground object exists) displays the Right-Click Page menu (see Figure 8.3). The Right-Click menu for the background (see Figure 8.4) is displayed by pressing the Ctrl key while pressing the right mouse button while the mouse pointer is anywhere on the page. From the Right-Click menus, the property browser (see Figure 8.5) may be called. It lists all the properties of the page or background. Specific properties may be edited in the browser by clicking the current value and changing it either in the combobox or by clicking the "..." button next to the top listing (the button is not visible in Figure 8.5).

Figure 8.3
Page properties may also be accessed through the Right-Click menu for the page.

Figure 8.4
The Right-Click menu for the current background is displayed by pressing Ctrl while pressing the right mouse button.

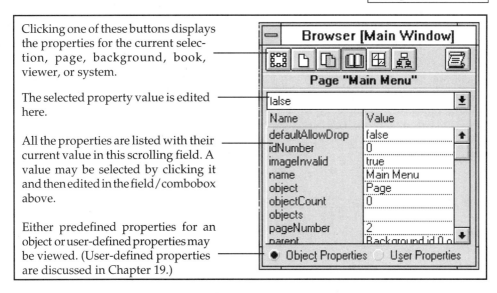

Clicking one of these buttons displays the properties for the current selection, page, background, book, viewer, or system.

The selected property value is edited here.

All the properties are listed with their current value in this scrolling field. A value may be selected by clicking it and then edited in the field/combobox above.

Either predefined properties for an object or user-defined properties may be viewed. (User-defined properties are discussed in Chapter 19.)

Figure 8.5
The property browser is accessible from the Right-Click menus. When accessed from the Page Right-Click menu, the page properties are listed. When accessed from the Background Right-Click menu, the background properties are shown.

Summary Questions

Answer the following true/false questions.

1. There is a unique background for every page in a book.
2. When a new book is created, it initially has one page and one background.
3. Pages and backgrounds have properties associated with them.
4. Pages in a book can only be reordered by cutting and pasting them.
5. A page in ToolBook is composed of both a foreground layer and a background layer.

6. A book may not have more backgrounds than it does pages.
7. Choosing the "New Background" option results in both a new background and a new page.
8. Both a fill color and a pattern may be applied to a background.
9. Backgrounds and their pages must use the page size set up in the "Book Properties" dialog.
10. Specific pages in a book may be excluded from the normal navigation methods.

Complete the following statements by filling in the blanks.
11. Objects shared by pages are best placed on the _____ layer.
12. To insert a new blank page after the current page but assign the same background to the new page, an author may choose the _____ _____ option from the Object menu.
13. The keyboard shortcut for switching back and forth from background and foreground views is _____ .
14. To delete a page, it must first be _____ and then either cut or cleared.
15. Pages are colored by setting the _____ property of the background.
16. Checking the box in front of the "Use Windows Colors" item of the "Background Properties" dialog causes the color scheme set up in the _____ _____ of Windows to be used.
17. A background is allotted a maximum of _____ kilobytes memory for it and its objects.
18. The _____ property of a page reflects its ordinal position in a book.
19. Handlers that might be used by any page of a background should be located in the _____ script.
20. The Background Right-Click menu is displayed by pressing the right mouse button while pressing the _____ key.

Hands-On Projects

A. Examine the software that accompanies this chapter. Open the "Table of Contents" book by double-clicking its icon in the "Developing with ToolBook" group window in the Windows Program Manager. Inside the "Table of Contents," click the book representing Chapter 8. The software provides visual aids to enhance the material presented in this text.

B. Business Report Project (Part II)
   1. Launch ToolBook and open BIZRPT1.TBK, which you created in the Hands-On Project B of Chapter 7.
   2. Name the first page of the book "Title", excluding the quotation marks.
   3. Open the "Background Properties" dialog for the background of page 1 and click the "Colors..." button. Set the fill color to dark gray (the eighth color from the left on the top row of the Color palette).
   4. Review Figures 4.7 and 4.9. These illustrations reveal the layout of the presentation. There are two backgrounds to the book, the first is used only by page 1 (the title page) and the second is shared by pages 2 through 11. Create the new background (and page 2) by selecting the "New Background" option from the Object menu.
   5. On the new page (page 2), display the "Background Properties" dialog and set the fill color of this second background so it is the same as the first, dark gray.
   6. Set the name of the second page to "Main Menu".
   7. Create a third page by choosing the "New Page" option. Name this third page "Summary".

8. Repeat step 7 eight times to create a total of 11 pages in the book. Name the pages as follows:

Page 4: "Received"	Page 8: "CEO"
Page 5: "Spent"	Page 9: "Revenue"
Page 6: "Income Statement"	Page 10: "Net Income"
Page 7: "Balance Sheet"	Page 11: "Earnings/Share"

9. Choose the "Save As" command from the File menu, saving the file under a new name, BIZRPT2.TBK.

10. Exit ToolBook.

C. Use the on-line help to gather more information about working with pages and backgrounds.

1. Access the step-by-step procedures for books and pages by clicking the page and background topics inside the "Working with Objects" topic.

2. Use the search function to look up the following entries: page properties, background properties, pageNumber, skipNavigation.

Chapter

9

Button, Button Who's Got the Button?

Working with Buttons

Buttons are interactive objects that generally perform some task when acted upon by a specific event, such as a click, a double click, or the mouse pointer entering their boundaries. Buttons come in a variety of sizes and styles and—like books, pages, and backgrounds—their appearance and behavior are defined by their various properties. Buttons are commonly used as controls by which the user interfaces with the program. Clicking a button might toggle a feature on or off, prompt the user for input, initialize an animation, or navigate to a different page. The script of the button determines the action. Using the hyperlinking feature of ToolBook, functioning navigational buttons may be set up without the author having to write any code.

Button Styles

There are several styles of buttons available in ToolBook (see Figure 9.1). The borderstyle property of the button determines the appearance of the button. The **push-button style** is perhaps the most popular, consisting of a raised three-dimensional appearance. When clicked, a push button gives the visual impression of being pushed in.

The **checkbox style button** has a checkbox in front of its caption. In the box, an X may be toggled on and off by clicking the button. When the X is visible, the button is said to be highlighted (its checked property is true). Its checked property is false when the X is not visible. Checkbox buttons are often used as interface controls in which the user may toggle certain features on and off, or in electronic forms where data items may be selected by checking them.

A **radio button** is very similar to a checkbox-style button, but a radio button has a circle, or "bubble," instead of a checkbox square. The bubble is filled when the button is highlighted and empty when its checked property is false. Like checkbox buttons, radio buttons are often used as interface controls, or as answer choices in electronic true/false or multiple-choice exams.

A **rectangle button** has a rectangular line border. A **shadowed button** looks like a rectangle button but with a drop shadow behind it. **Rounded buttons** have a borderstyle property of rounded and are rectangle buttons with rounded corners. Buttons with the styles discussed so far are highlighted briefly in reverse (inverted) video when clicked if their highlight property is set to true. These buttons are used for general purposes and navigation. Different developers prefer different designs. The choice of which button styles to employ is largely an aesthetic one.

Buttons whose borderStyle property are set to either checkBox3D or radioButton3D—**3-D checkbox buttons**

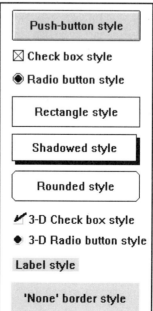

Figure 9.1
Buttons come in a variety of styles. The style of a button is dictated by the value of its borderStyle *property.*

or **3-D radio buttons**—are like checkbox and radio buttons, but with a three-dimensional appearance. The 3-D checkboxes display a check mark graphic instead of an X, and this is toggled on or off by clicking the button. The 3-D radio buttons behave similarly to radio buttons, with the 3-D bubble being filled when its checked property is true.

The **label-style buttons** are used to label diagrams or to list a group of options. They have no border surrounding them, but rather the emphasis is on their caption. It may be impossible to distinguish between a label button and a small text field used as a label. Since scripts may be attached to any object, both may be used for the same purposes, providing interactivity when clicked by the reader.

Finally, a button with its borderStyle to none, a **none-style button**, looks like a label button if it has a caption. None-style buttons, however, are most commonly used as transparent overlays on top of other objects. When fillColor and strokeColor are both set to white and the transparent property is true, they cannot be distinguished by the user. Thus they may overlay part of an imported bitmap. They provide an interactive response when a particular location of the bitmap is clicked.

The borderStyle property of a button may be changed at any time through the button's Right-Click menu or "Object Properties" dialog box. Thus a push button may be changed into a 3-D checkbox at any time the author so desires.

Creating a Button

In the Tool palette there are six tools for the purpose of creating buttons. Each of the six is used to create buttons with a different border style, including push buttons, label buttons, radio and checkbox buttons, and 3-D radio and checkbox buttons (see Figure 9.2). To create a button, select the appropriate tool from the Tool palette. The mouse pointer will become a crosshair. Position the crosshair at one corner of the desired button location, hold down the left mouse button, drag to the diagonally opposite corner, and release the button. A button with the selected border style is drawn, its boundaries defined by the mouse drag. To create a button with one of the other border styles (rectangle, shadowed, rounded, none), create a button of any style (a pushbutton, for example) and then change the borderStyle property via the "Object Properties" dialog or the button's Right-Click menu.

Figure 9.2
There are six different tools for creating buttons with different border styles. The borderStyle *property of any button created may always be changed.*

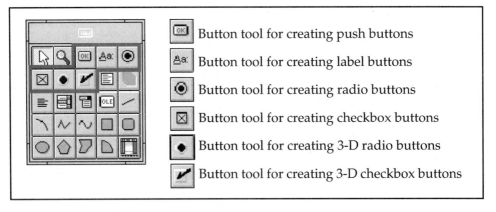

Button tool for creating push buttons

Button tool for creating label buttons

Button tool for creating radio buttons

Button tool for creating checkbox buttons

Button tool for creating 3-D radio buttons

Button tool for creating 3-D checkbox buttons

A button may be created on the background so that it is available on all pages sharing the background. To create a button on the background, access the background-only view by choosing the "Background" option from the View menu. Then create the button as you would create a button for a page.

Using the "Button Properties" Dialog

As with all ToolBook objects, buttons have several properties that define their appearance and behavior. The borderStyle, highlight, and checked properties have already been mentioned. Like books, pages, and backgrounds, properties may be viewed and edited via the "Object Properties" dialog. To access a button's properties, you must **select** it by left-clicking it with the Selection tool so that the eight selection "handles" (small squares) surround it. Selected objects have handles at each corner of its rectangular boundary and in the center of each boundary line (see Figure 9.3). These squares are filled solid if the selected object's drawDirect property is true and hollow if the drawDi-

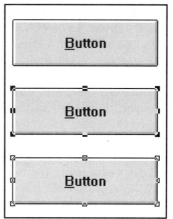

Figure 9.3
Objects are selected by clicking them, using the left mouse button, in the Author mode. Selected objects have eight "handles" (small squares) surrounding their borders. The handles of selected objects whose drawDirect property is false appear solid (see the middle button); objects whose drawDirect property is true have hollow handles (bottom button).

rect property is false. Objects whose drawDirect property is true are drawn directly to the screen when the page is drawn or updated. The user sees the page being formed. If the drawDirect property is false, objects are drawn in an off-screen buffer and, when complete, shown on the monitor. Objects drawn off screen provide a smoother screen transition, though there is a pause as the objects are drawn. The more objects drawn off screen, the longer the pause. In some instances, the user may feel the program is slow in responding.

To change the properties of a button, select the button and choose "Button Properties..." from the Object menu. The "Button Properties" dialog appears and the properties of the selected button may be accessed and changed (see Figure 9.4).

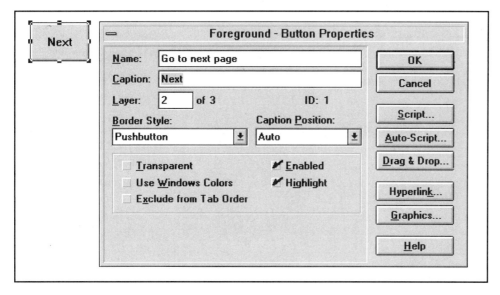

Figure 9.4
The "Button Properties" dialog for a specific button is accessed by selecting the button and choosing "Button Properties..." from the Object menu.

At the top of the dialog is a field for assigning a name to the button. Sample names are "myButton," "Next," and "Go to Main Menu". Names may be up to 32 characters and can be more than one word. The name is used internally by the author in referring to the button and is not visible to the user. Buttons may be referred to in OpenScript code by their names; their IDs (which are assigned by the system and uneditable); or less preferably by their number (layer).

A field for entering a caption to be displayed with the button is located below the "Name" field. The caption is what the user sees and can be up to 255 characters. The default caption is "&Button." The "&" in the caption defines the character following it as a mnemonic access character. The mnemonic access character will be displayed with a line under it. The reader may move the focus to the button by pressing the Alt key while pressing the letter that serves as the mnemonic access character. A button having the focus can be executed by pressing the Enter key in lieu of clicking it. If, for instance, an author wishes a "Next" button to be given the focus by pressing Alt-X, then he or she would define the caption of the button by typing "Ne&xt" (without the quotation marks). Buttons are not required to have a caption, nor must the caption have a mnemonic access character. Captions do not wrap and can only occupy one line of text. If more than one line is desired, a field may be used instead and a script attached to it to perform the desired action.

The layer property of a button defines its location in terms of being in front of or behind other objects. The smaller the layer number, the farther back an object. Objects, including buttons, may be brought closer to the front or sent farther back by editing the layer number. The layer number is also used in determining the tab order of objects in receiving the focus.

The borderStyle is changed by clicking the down arrow next to the field displaying its current value and selecting the new value from the resulting list. The captionPosition property is changed in the same way. The caption may be positioned on the button in various locations in relation to an attached graphic (for example, an icon or bitmap) or to the checkbox or radio bubble. Caption positions include top, bottom, left, right, center and auto. In this case "auto" stands for automatic. Automatic caption positioning for a push button with an attached graphic places the caption underneath the graphic. If the push button does not have a graphic, the caption is centered. Automatic caption positioning for a radio button or checkbox button places the caption to the left of the circle or checkbox. Figure 9.5 shows the various positions for a radio button and a push button with an icon.

Figure 9.5
Button captions may be positioned differently in relation to an icon or the radio bubble or checkbox by changing the value of the button's captionPosition *property.*

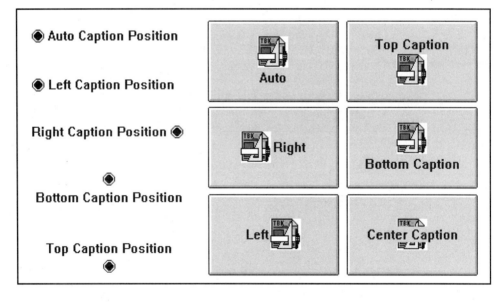

Figure 9.6
The transparent *property of a button determines if the button's colors and the colors of any objects behind it are blended together. Buttons whose* transparent *property is* false *are opaque (top button).*

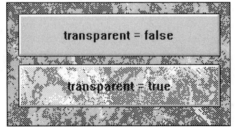

Buttons may be either opaque or transparent. Checking the "Transparent" option in the "Button Properties" dialog sets the button's transparent property to true. When an object is transparent, its colors are blended with the colors of any objects visible behind it. Figure 9.6 shows an opaque button and a transparent button set against a marble graphic.

A fill color and stroke color may be applied to a button by selecting the button and then using the Color palette. Choosing "Use Windows Colors" uses the color scheme set up in the Control Panel of Windows, applying the Windows button face and text colors for push-button, rectangle, shadowed, rounded, and none-style buttons. For radio and checkbox buttons, the Windows background color is utilized as the fill color while the Windows text color is used as the stroke color.

The Tab key may be used by the reader to determine which object has the focus. The focus cycle is an order determined by the layer order of the objects. On entering a page the focus defaults to the object at the lowest layer that can receive the focus. Only buttons, fields, recordfields, and comboboxes may receive it. When a button has the focus, a dotted line frames its caption (see Figure 9.7). When the user presses the Tab key, the focus switches to the next layered object that can receive the focus. The script of a button that has the focus may be executed by the reader when he or she presses the Enter key. A button may be excluded from receiving the focus by checking the "Exclude from Tab Order" option in the "Button Properties" dialog. This sets the button's excludeTab property to true. Buttons marked as such will be passed over when the reader uses the Tab key to cycle through the focus-receivable objects.

Figure 9.7
When a button has the focus, its caption is surrounded by a dotted line.

The "Enabled" switch in the "Button Properties" dialog controls whether a button may receive mouse or keyboard messages. A **disabled button** is one whose enabled property is false—that is, the "Enabled" option is unchecked. A disabled button with a script set to run when the button is clicked will ignore the click and not execute its script. Disabled buttons cannot receive the focus and are automatically excluded from the tabbing order.

Buttons whose highlight property is set to true react visually to a click. The video of push buttons with highlight values set to true reverse momentarily when clicked, giving the impression that the button has been recessed and released. Rectangle, shadowed, rounded, and none-style buttons flash briefly when clicked if their highlight property is true. The borders of checkboxes and radio bubbles darken momentarily before hiding or showing their check marks; the three-dimensional versions of the buttons appear to recess momentarily. The highlight property is unavailable for label buttons, which have no associated visual reaction.

Attaching a Graphic to a Button

Bitmap graphics and icons can be attached to a button along with a caption or in lieu of a caption. Icons and graphics are used to identify buttons visually or for aesthetic purposes. In developing educational programs for young children, controls should be graphical and for non-readers. To attach a graphic or icon, click the "Graphic..." button in the "Button Properties" dialog. In the resulting "Button Graphics" dialog (see Figure 9.8), a combobox is provided for choosing the state with which the button is associated. Different icons and graphics may be assigned for different situations— normal (when nothing is happening), inverted (when the button is briefly high-lighted), disabled (when the enable property is false) and checked (for radio and checkbox buttons). Click the "Choose..." button to access the "Choose Button Graphic" dialog (see Figure 9.9). This is actually the same dialog as the "Resource Manager" presented in Chapter 7 (see Figure 7.10).

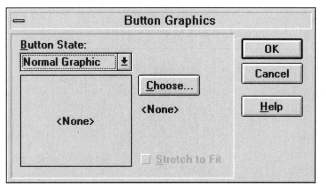

Figure 9.8
The "Button Graphics" dialog allows a bitmap or icon to be attached to a button. Different graphics may be displayed, depending on the state of the button (that is, whether it is normal, shown in reverse video, checked, or the like).

Figure 9.9
*The "Choose Button
Graphic" dialog actually
uses the Resource Manager
to a select a graphic to be
attached to a button.*

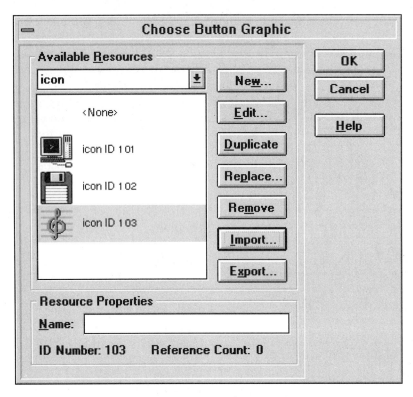

The type of resource (icon or cursor, for example) to attach to the button is chosen from the combobox at the top left, and the resources of that type embedded in the book are listed in the scrolling field below it. The resource is selected (highlighted) from the list by clicking it. Resource files may also be imported from disk by using this dialog and selecting the files. The "OK" button is selected to return to the "Button Graphics" dialog and the "OK" button of that dialog is clicked to attach the chosen graphic to the button. To remove an attached graphic from a button, follow these procedures but choose "None" from the resource list.

Attaching a Script to a Button

A script must be attached to a button before it will perform any actions. Scripts contain **handlers** declaring the event that triggers the execution of a collection of code statements. The code may consist of one statement or several thousand statements. The author may enter scripts into the script editor from the keyboard. Clicking the "Script..." button in the "Button Properties" dialog box brings up the script editor with the button's attached script. Scripts from the collection of autoscripts may also be inserted by clicking the "Auto-Script..." button. Simple navigation scripts may be automatically generated for a button by using ToolBook's hyperlink feature, which is described in the next section.

Hyperlinking a Button

Hyperlinked buttons are used for navigating to other pages. Their scripts are generated by specifying a link between the button and the page to be navigated to. This link is created by clicking the "Hyperlink..." button in the "Button Properties" dialog for the selected button. A dialog is displayed in which two types of links may be chosen: one way or two way (see Figure 9.10). Choosing the "One-Way Link" button adds the to handle buttonClick handler and code to the selected button's script for navigating to a specified page. The "Two-Way Link" button performs the same function but also creates a button on the target page that is linked back to the page with the selected button. In either case, after the link type is selected, the author navigates to the target page by using the cursor arrows, statusbar, or menus, and then clicks

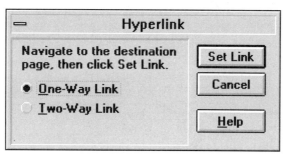

Figure 9.10
A one-way link to navigate to another page may be set up through the hyperlink feature. A two-way link (with an additional button created on the target page to return to the current page) may also be created.

the "Set Link" button in the Hyperlink dialog. The script is added to the button. The return button is created on the target page with a script if the "Two-Way Link" button was chosen. The button is then functional in the Reader mode. The script generated by the hyperlink feature will resemble the following:

```
to handle buttonClick
    go to page id 5
end
```

Cutting, Copying, Pasting, Moving, and Resizing

Buttons, like any ToolBook object, may be cut, copied, and pasted. A button on one page or background may easily be transferred to another page or background by selecting it and either cutting or copying it (cutting it will remove it from the current page or background) and then navigating to the other page or background and pasting the button from the clipboard. Buttons may thus be transferred to and from the pages and backgrounds of different books. The attached script and associated properties are copied and pasted with the button. A new button may also be created by copying an existing button and then pasting the copy back to the page or background. It will be pasted in the position of the original and can be moved to a new location by dragging it. Copying and pasting buttons and other objects can be a great time-saver.

A selected button may be moved by dragging it with the mouse pointer. It may be resized by grabbing and dragging any of its selection handles. Dragging one of the corner handles allows the button to be resized in two directions simultaneously; dragging one of the center handles restricts resizing to only one direction (note the arrow directions of the mouse pointer when a handle is grabbed).

Using the Right-Click Menu

Right-Click menus may be accessed for a button by right-clicking it in Author mode. The Right-Click menu for a button provides access to many of the button's properties, its script, and so on (see Figure 9.11). It functions exactly as the Right-Click menus for books, pages, backgrounds, and other objects.

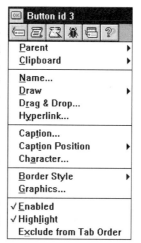

Figure 9.11
A button's Right-Click menu provides access to viewing and changing the button's properties.

Grouping Buttons and Creating Mutually Exclusive Radio Buttons

Multiple objects may be selected on a page or background by holding down the Shift key and clicking each of the desired

Figure 9.12
Multiple objects, including buttons, may be selected and then combined into one group object by using the "Group" option of the Object menu.

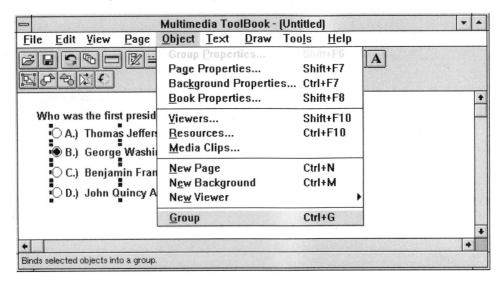

objects with the selection tool so that each is highlighted (their handles are visible) (see Figure 9.12). Multiple selected objects may be moved simultaneously by dragging; they can also be cut, copied, and pasted together. Multiple selected objects may also be **grouped**, which means they are treated as one object. To group two or more selected objects, choose "Group" from the Object menu. The objects will then appear as one group with one set of handles. Group objects are treated as any other object. They may be moved, resized, cut, copied, pasted, and so on. Groups have properties associated with them and these may be accessed by selecting the group and choosing "Group Properties..." to view the "Group Properties" dialog box (see Figure 9.13).

Groups, like other ToolBook objects, can be named and have scripts attached to them. In Figure 9.13, the group named "First President Answers" consists of the four radio buttons shown in Figure 9.12. The checkbox option "Auto-Radio Buttons" allows all the members of the group to be specified as **mutually exclusive radio buttons.** When a mutually exclusive radio button is selected by the user (checked), the other radio buttons become deselected. In the example shown in Figure 9.12, the group consists of four mutually exclusive radio buttons: "Thomas Jefferson," "George Washington," "Benjamin Franklin," and "John Quincy Adams." The user selects an answer to the question "Who was the first president of the United States?" by clicking the appropriate radio button. He or she might select "John Quincy Adams" by clicking that choice. The bubble in front of the fourth choice is filled in. But upon further reflection, suppose the reader changes the answer to "George Washington" by clicking the second response. Since the grouped buttons are set up as auto-radio buttons, the bubble in front of "George Washington" is filled and the bubble in front of "John Quincy Adams" is deselected.

Figure 9.13
Groups are treated as a single object and as such have properties. One of these is controlled by the "Auto-Radio Buttons" option. Choose this option and all the radio buttons will be mutually exclusive.

Summary Questions

Answer the following true/false questions.

1. A push-button style button has a three-dimensional appearance.
2. Buttons created on a background are only visible on the current page.
3. The name of a button may be displayed in different positions by changing the captionDisplay property.
4. Buttons have an ID number assigned to them by the system and by which they may be referred to in an OpenScript command.
5. A selected button with hollow handles has a drawDirect property of true.
6. An icon or bitmap graphic may be displayed on a button.
7. The action performed by a clicked button is determined by its script.
8. Unlike pages and backgrounds, there is no Right-Click menu associated with a button.
9. Different graphics may be displayed in a button, depending on its state (whether it is checked, in reverse video, or the like).
10. There is a specific tool in the Tool palette for creating shadowed buttons.

Complete the following statements by filling in the blanks.

11. A button with a borderStyle of _____ commonly has a bubble, or circle, in front of it. The bubble is filled when the button is checked.
12. The _____ style is most often used for labeling interactive diagrams.
13. Selected buttons have eight _____ surrounding their borders.
14. A mnemonic access character for a button is specified by placing an _____ character in the button's caption, in front of the mnemonic character.
15. The _____ property controls whether or not a button is opaque.
16. A dotted line surrounding a button's caption means the button has the _____ .
17. The _____ property of a button defines its location in terms of being in front of or behind other objects.
18. Multiple objects may be selected and combined together into one _____ object.
19. The script of a selected button may be disabled by unchecking the _____ option in the "Button Properties" dialog.
20. The _____ feature of ToolBook allows an author to create functional navigation buttons without writing code, by specifying the target page of the button.

Hands-On Projects

A. Examine the software that accompanies this chapter. From the "Table of Contents" book, click the book representing Chapter 9. Work your way through the tutorial to reinforce your understanding of the information presented in this chapter.

B. Business Report Project (Part III)
   1. Launch ToolBook and open BIZRPT2.TBK, created in Hands-On Project B of Chapter 8.
   2. On the first page, create a small push button in the upper left; it should look like the one in the upper left of Figure 9.14. (Use the rulers as an aid in placing and sizing it.) Access the button's properties by selecting the button and choosing "Button Properties..." (or by holding Shift and double-clicking it). In the "Button Properties" dialog, assign the new button the caption "Exit". Verify that the "Enabled" and "Highlight" options are marked with a check.

Figure 9.14
You will create two push
buttons on the first page of
the business report, one for
exiting the report and the
other for navigating to the
main menu (page 2).

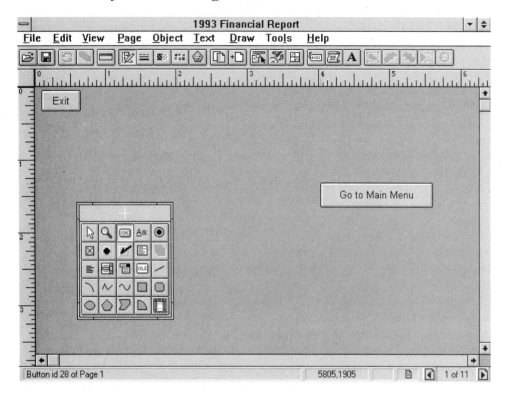

3. Access the button's script by clicking the "Script..." button in the "Button Properties" dialog. Enter the following script into the script editor:

```
to handle buttonClick
    request "Do you really want to exit?" with "Yes" or "Cancel"
    if it is "Yes" then
        send exit
    end if
end buttonClick
```

(The preceding script results in a request dialog being displayed when the reader clicks the button. The dialog prompts the user to verify that he or she actually wants to exit. If the reader responds by clicking the "Yes" button, the book closes and ToolBook is exited. If the reader responds by clicking "Cancel," nothing happens; he or she may continue browsing the book.) Choose "Update Script & Exit" from the File menu of the script editor or click the equivalent icon on the editor's toolbar (the first one on the left). Click the "OK" button in the "Button Properties" dialog to exit the dialog.

4. Create another push button about 4 inches from the left of the page and about 1.25 inches below the top (see Figure 9.14). For this button set the caption to "Go to Main Menu". In the "Button Properties" dialog for this button, click the "Hyperlink..." button. In the resulting "Hyperlink" dialog, click the "One-Way Link" radio button. Navigate to page 2 by choosing "Next" from the Page menu or by using the statusbar. On page 2, click the "Set Link" button in the "Hyperlink" dialog. The script to navigate to the second page will automatically be generated for the button. Test the button by switching to the Reader mode and clicking the button. It should take you to the second page of the presentation.

5. Switch back to the Author mode. Go to page 1 and select the "Exit" button by clicking it and making its handles visible. Choose "Copy" from the Edit

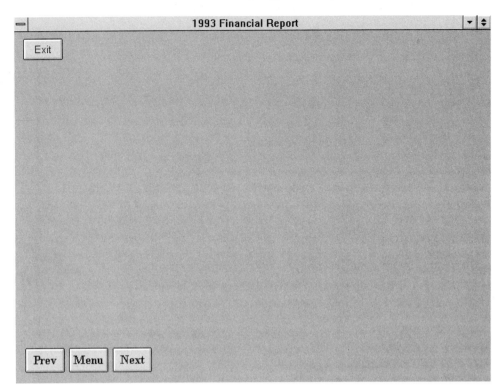

Figure 9.15
*The background of pages 2
through 11 of the business
report presentation
contains four buttons.
These four buttons are
accessible from the pages
sharing this background.*

menu to place a copy of the button on the Windows clipboard. Navigate to
the second page and view the background by choosing "Background" from
the View menu. Choose "Paste" from the Edit menu to move the button from
the clipboard and paste it onto the background.

6. While still on the background of page 2, scroll down to the bottom left of the
   page and create the three push buttons ("Prev," "Menu," and "Next") as
   shown in Figure 9.15. One way of ensuring that all three buttons are the same
   size is to create one and then copy it, paste it, and move it to create the second.
   Paste it again and move it to the location of the third button. Caption the three
   buttons as shown in the figure.

   (Note: There are three ways of creating a script. An autoscript may be
   generated and inserted, the button may be hyperlinked, or a script may be
   entered by the author by using the script editor. Each script for the three
   buttons created here will be generated using one of the different methods.
   The "Prev" button will utilize an autoscript, the "Menu" button will be
   hyperlinked to page 2, and a script will be entered for the "Next" button
   using the script editor.)

   Select the "Prev" button and view its "Button Properties" dialog. Click the
   "Auto-Script..." button to access the "Insert Auto-Script" dialog (see Figure
   9.16). In the "Insert Auto-Script" dialog, scroll through the field in the "Select
   Handler" section until the "Go to previous page" listing is found. Highlight
   it by clicking it. (The phrase "go previous page" should appear in the "Script"
   section at the bottom right of the dialog). In the "Handler Options" section
   of the dialog, click the arrow of the "Name" combobox and scroll through
   the alphabetical list until the "ButtonClick" listing is found. Click the
   "ButtonClick" listing so that it appears in the "Name" field, as shown in
   Figure 9.16. Click the "OK" button of the dialog. A handler to go to the
   previous page when the button is clicked is inserted into the button's script.
   You can verify this by clicking the "Script..." button in the "Button Properties" dialog. You should see the following script for the button:

Figure 9.16
The script for the "Prev" button may be generated using the autoscript feature. A handler is chosen from the list of prescripted handlers and a handler name identified. (The name is derived from the event triggering the handler's execution.) In this case the handler is ButtonClick. After the "OK" button is clicked, a complete handler is generated and inserted into the script of the button.

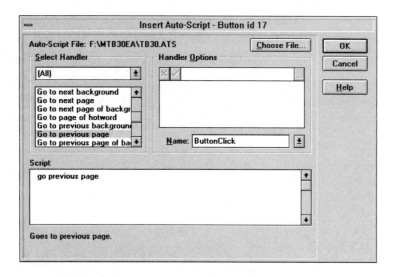

```
TO HANDLE ButtonClick
  --{Go to previous page}
  go previous page
END
```

Exit the script editor or "Button Properties" dialog for the "Prev" button.

7. Navigate to page 2, if not already there, and view the background. Select the "Menu" button on the background and open its "Button Properties" dialog. Click the "Hyperlink..." button. In the "Hyperlink" dialog, choose the "One-Way Link" option. Since the menu page is page 2, and it should already be your current page, return to the foreground view (press the F4 key) and click the "Set Link" button of the "Hyperlink" dialog.

Check the script for the "Menu" button by clicking the "Script..." button in its "Button Properties" dialog. The following script should have been attached through the hyperlink feature:

```
to handle buttonClick
    go to Page "Main Menu"
end
```

(Note: The above go to command may read go to page id 2 if the page is not named.) Close the script editor and the "Button Properties" dialog.

8. Access the script editor for the "Next" background button. Enter the following script:

```
to handle buttonClick
    go next page
end buttonClick
```

Choose "Update Script & Exit."

9. On page 2, create the seven push buttons shown in Figure 9.17.

10. For the "Exit Financial Report" button, enter the script as used for the "Exit" button in step 3. You may access the script of the "Exit" button of page 1 or the "Exit" button of the current background. Select the script by highlighting it (dragging through it with the mouse pointer) and copying it. The script may then be pasted into the script editor for the "Exit Financial Report" button.

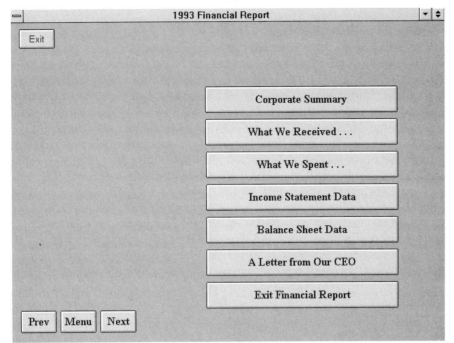

Figure 9.17
In addition to the four buttons on the background, page 2 has seven navigational buttons linked to the other pages of the book.

11. Access the button properties for the button labeled "Corporate Summary." Click the "Hyperlink..." button, choose the "One-Way Link" option, and navigate to page 3. Click "Set Link" to create the navigational script. Link the five buttons as follows:

a. Link the "What We Received..." button to page 4.

b. Link the "What We Spent..." button to page 5.

c. Link the "Income Statement Data" button to page 6.

d. Link the "Balance Sheet Data" button to page 7.

e. Link the "A Letter from Our CEO" button to page 8.

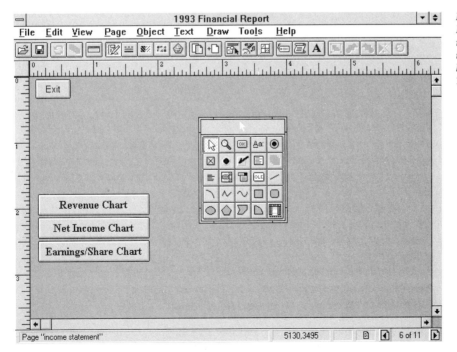

Figure 9.18
Page 6 of the business report presentation has three navigational buttons linked to pages 9, 10, and 11.

12. Go to page 6. Page 6 provides access to pages 9, 10, and 11. (See Figure 4.11 for a map of how the pages are linked.) Create three push buttons at the center left of page 6, as illustrated in Figure 9.18. Provide the captions "Revenue Chart," "Net Income Chart," and "Earnings/Share Chart" as illustrated. Link the "Revenue Chart" button to page 9, the "Net Income Chart" button to page 10, and the "Earnings/Share Chart" button to page 11.

13. On page 6, select all three buttons created in step 12 by holding down the Shift key while clicking each of the buttons. Selection handles should be visible for all three. With the three buttons selected, choose "Copy" from the Edit menu to copy all three buttons to the clipboard.

14. Navigate to page 9. Choose "Paste" from the Edit menu to paste the three buttons from the clipboard to the page.

15. Create, at the bottom of page 9, a push button that covers the three navigational buttons of the background (see Figure 9.19). This button hides the background buttons and also receives the user's button click, rendering the background buttons inoperative on page 9. Assign to the new button the caption "Return to Income Statement." Hyperlink the button to page 6.

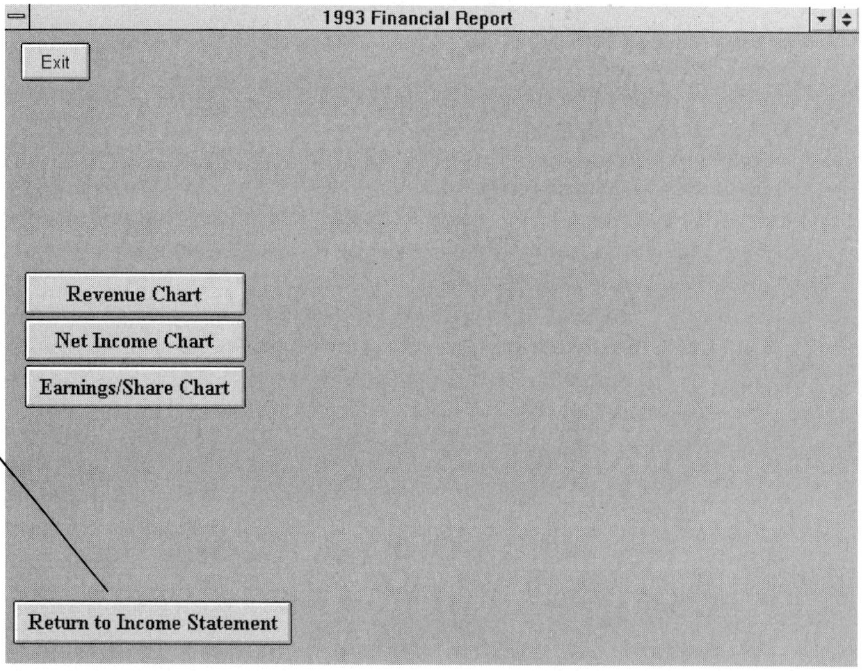

Figure 9.19
Pages 9, 10, and 11 of the business report presentation have a button hiding the "Prev," "Menu," and "Next" buttons of the background.

16. Hold down the Shift key while clicking each of the four buttons created in steps 14 and 15 to select them together. Copy all four buttons to the clipboard by choosing "Copy" from the Edit menu. Navigate to page 10. To place the buttons on the page, choose "Paste" from the Edit menu. The copy of the button created in step 15 (labeled "Return to Income Statement") should cover the three navigational background buttons.

17. Navigate to page 11. Choose "Paste" from the Edit menu. The four buttons, still on the clipboard, will be pasted onto the page as in step 16.

18. Save the file as BIZRPT3.TBK.

19. Go to the Reader mode and test the various buttons to make sure they work properly.

20. Exit ToolBook.

C. Open ToolBook and access the Author mode. In the on-line help, look up the "step-by-step" instructions for the following topics:

    a. Attaching a graphic to a button
    b. Creating a button
    c. Creating a label button
    d. Formatting text in a button caption
    e. Removing a graphic from a button
    f. Using buttons or hotwords to navigate

D. Use the on-line help glossary or search feature to look up the following terms:
    a. borderStyle
    b. checked
    c. drawDirect
    d. excludeTab
    e. focus

Chapter 10

Working with Fields and Recordfields

Information and ideas are most commonly communicated through verbal language, including written text. ToolBook provides **field** and **recordfield** objects to hold and display textual information. They may present information to or gather information from a user. An author and/or reader enters information into a field or recordfield by using the keyboard; information can also be imported from external fields. Words or phrases of the text may be selected and formatted as hotwords to perform some action when the user clicks them.

As with buttons, various styles of fields and recordfields are available to match the design and functionality of the book. Properties define the appearance and behavior of fields and recordfields. The text may be formatted with different fonts, font sizes, font styles (bold or italic, for example), colors, and alignment (left, centered, or justified, for example). Words and phrases of the text may be selected and formatted as hotwords to perform some action when clicked by the user. Figure 10.1 shows the different border styles that can delineate a field or recordfield. Either object may have a simple rectangular border, a shadowed border, or a border that gives the appearance of the field being raised or inset. A scrolling field permits the user to click a scrollbar to see additional text. A field or recordfield with a none-style border has no visible border. Such a field usually contains static text that the user cannot edit and appears to have been typed on the page rather than into an object. The border of a field is defined by its borderStyle property.

Fields Versus Recordfields

Fields may exist on either the foreground or background layer of a page; recordfields are only placed on the backgrounds. Both may contain up to 32,000 characters. Fields placed on a page (foreground), exist only on that page; while fields placed on a background are available to all pages of a book sharing that background. The text of a page field may or may not be editable in the Reader mode by an end-user, depending on the value of its activated property. The text of a background field is the same on all the pages and can only be entered and edited while in the background

view in the Author mode. The text of background fields may not be edited in Reader mode.

A recordfield is a special form of background field. Recordfields allow different text to be entered into its boundaries on each page sharing the background. Although recordfields are created on the background, the text they contain is entered and edited from the foreground view. The text may or may not be editable

Figure 10.1
There are six different styles available for fields and recordfields.

in Reader mode by the end-user, depending on the value of the recordfield's **activated** property. Recordfields are most commonly used in creating database applications, where each page contains prescribed information, such as a client's name, address, and phone number. Recordfields are also utilized for displaying titles and other information that appear in the same location on each page of a background.

Another significant difference between fields and recordfields is that the text in a recordfield may be printed in a report, while text of a field may not. Field text may be printed indirectly by printing the card, although nonvisible text (such as text not currently displayed in a scrolling field) will not print. To print the text of a field in a report, the text must first be copied to a recordfield, then printed.

Types of Fields and Recordfields

In addition to the various border styles, fields and recordfields may be of different types in terms of how the contained text behaves. The type determines how the text wraps and how a reader may select text. The type of a selected field or recordfield is defined by its **fieldType** property. The field type of a selected field may be specified in the "Field Properties" dialog (see Figure 10.2). The most widely used type is the

Figure 10.2
There are five types of fields and recordfields. The type determines various behaviors including whether or not the contained text wraps and whether the reader may select more than one item from a list.

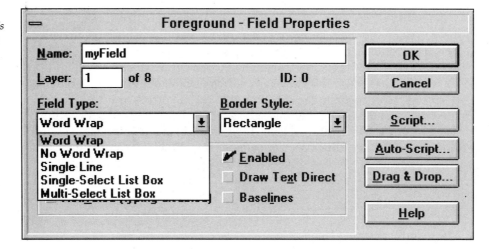

Word Wrap type (**fieldType** property = **wordWrap**), in which text automatically wraps to the next line of the field. The No Word Wrap type (**fieldType** = **noWordWrap**) does not allow text to wrap to the next line. A carriage return-linefeed, generated by the Return or Enter key, results in a new line, but text longer than that which can be displayed in the width of a field is truncated at the field's right border. The Single Line type (**fieldType** = **singleLineWrap**) limits the text to a single line, disallowing word wrapping and ignoring any linefeeds. The Single-Select List Box type (**fieldType** = **singleSelect**) is like the No Word Wrap type, but it allows the user to select and highlight a line of text by clicking or using the cursor keys. Fields and recordfields of the Multi-Select List Box type, (**fieldType** = **multiSelect**) appear and behave like fields of the Single-Select List Box type, but they allow the user to select or deselect multiple lines by clicking. Figure 10.3 shows a word wrap field, single-line field, single-select list box, and a multi-select list box. There is no visible difference between a word-wrap field and a no word-wrap field. List boxes, both single and multi-select, have their **activated** property set to **true** by default; therefore, their text is not editable in Reader mode.

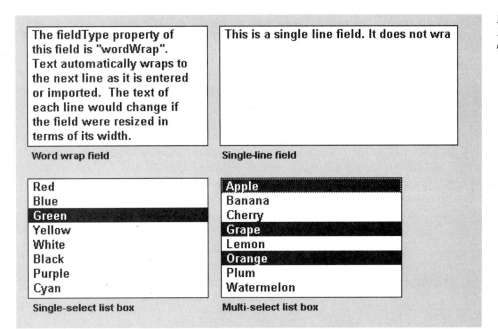

Figure 10.3
Examples of different field and recordfield types.

Creating Fields and Recordfields

There are three tools in the Tool palette for creating fields and one for creating recordfields (see Figure 10.4). The three field tools are used for creating rectangle fields, borderless fields (borderStyle = none) and single-select list boxes. Other styles and types are created by changing the appropriate properties of a field. In addition, there is one tool for creating recordfields, and this tool can only be chosen when in background view.

Figure 10.4
There are three tools for creating fields, one for recordfields, and one for combo boxes:
    Single-select list tool
    Borderless field tool
    Recordfield tool
    Rectangle field tool
    Combo box tool

Different border styles and types of recordfields are created by changing the properties of a selected recordfield. There is also a tool for creating combo boxes (discussed later in this chapter).

Creating a field, recordfield, or combo box is the same process as creating a button. After the appropriate tool is selected, the field or recordfield is created by using the mouse to drag the desired boundary, starting in one corner and dragging diagonally to the opposite corner.

Fields and recordfields may be copied or cut from other pages or backgrounds of the current book or other books and then pasted onto a page or background. Recordfields and background fields pasted onto the foreground layer of a page become page fields and exist only on that page. To paste a field or recordfield onto the background, go to the background view before pasting. Text contained in a field is copied and pasted with the field, but text contained in a recordfield is not copied and pasted with the recordfield.

Other Field and Recordfield Properties

Besides the fieldType and borderStyle properties, fields and recordfields have several other properties controlling their appearance and behavior. Like buttons, they have fillColor, strokeColor, name, idNumber, layer, transparent, and drawDirect properties. The strokeColor controls the border and default text color and the fillColor determines the interior shade of the field. The Color palette is used to set the fill color and stroke color for a selected field or recordfield. A name may be assigned to a field or

---

recordfield and it is that name to which a script refers. A field or recordfield may also be referred to by its ID number, which is assigned to it by the idNumber property. The ID number is assigned by the system and cannot be changed. Fields and recordfields may also be referred to by their layers. The layer property determines the position of the field in terms of being in front of or behind other objects on the page or background. The layer may be changed in the "Field Properties" dialog (see Figure 10.5). Fields may be either transparent or opaque, depending on the field's transparent property. A value of true (set in the "Field Properties" dialog) means the field or recordfield is transparent; false (unchecked) dictates an opaque field. Fields with a borderStyle of none are usually set up as transparent to give the appearance of the text being part of the page. The drawDirect property determines whether the field is drawn on the screen or drawn in an off-screen buffer area. As with buttons, hollow handles around a selected field indicate that its drawDirect property is true; solid filled handles indicate it is false.

Figure 10.5
The "Field Properties" dialog box allows the author to access and edit the properties of a field. The "Recordfield Properties" dialog box is identical.

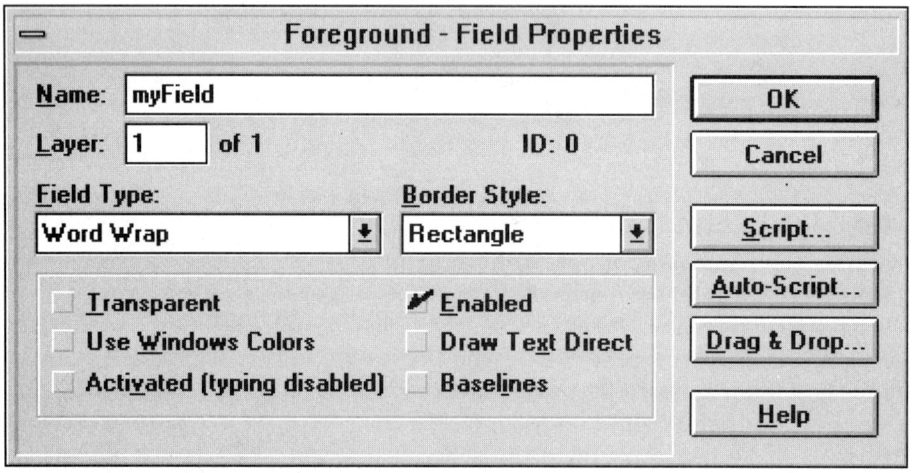

Foreground - Field Properties

Name: myField   OK

Layer: 1   of 1   ID: 0   Cancel

Field Type: Word Wrap   Border Style: Rectangle   Script...

☐ Transparent   ☑ Enabled   Auto-Script...
☐ Use Windows Colors   ☐ Draw Text Direct   Drag & Drop...
☐ Activated (typing disabled)   ☐ Baselines   Help

The enabled property determines whether the field or recordfield may receive the focus; the activated property dictates whether the text of the field is locked in Reader mode and its script activated, or if it is unlocked, allowing the user to make editing changes in Reader mode. The baselines property, when set to true, shows baselines of each text line of the field (see Figure 10.6)

Figure 10.6
When set to true, the baselines *property gives to a field the appearance of a ruled piece of paper.*

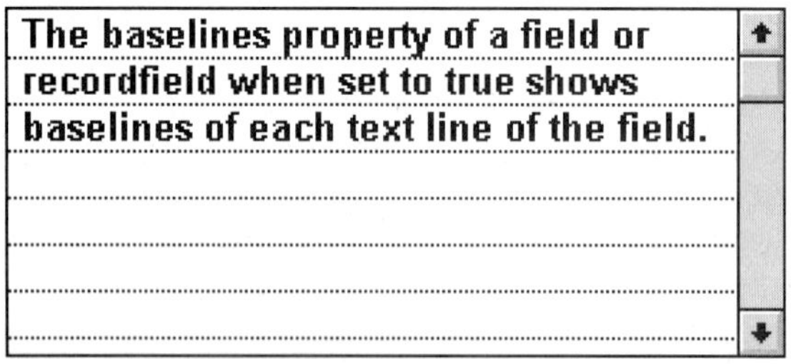

The baselines property of a field or recordfield when set to true shows baselines of each text line of the field.

Perhaps the most significant properties of a field are those that affect the text. The fontFace, fontSize, and fontStyle properties are set in the "Character " dialog (see Figure 10.7) by selecting the field and then choosing the "Character..." option from the Text menu or clicking the equivalent icon on the toolbar. The fontFace property determines the character design of the text. The font might be Arial, Times, Symbol, and so on. The fontSize is specified in a points measurement (there are 72 points in an inch). Choosing 10- or 12-point text is standard. The fontStyle property is used to specify whether text should be italic or bold, for example.

Likewise, the "Paragraph" dialog may be opened by selecting the "Paragraph..." option from the Edit menu. The textAlignment, spacing, and indents properties are set for a selected field. The text of a field may be aligned as left, right, centered, or justified (see Figure 10.8) by clicking the appropriate radio button in the dialog. Likewise, linespacing of the field's text may be single spacing, a line and a half, or

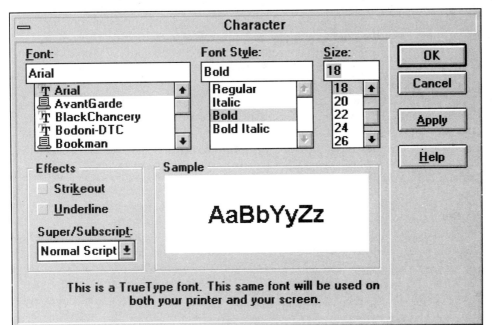

Figure 10.7
The "Character" dialog box
allows the author to set the
typeface, size, and style of
text in a selected field.
Selected text may consist of
a word, phrase, paragraph,
or paragaphs.

Figure 10.8
The "Paragraph" dialog allows
to format paragraphs in the
selected field or recordfield. The
user can specify alignment,
indentations, and linespacing.

double spacing. Indents for the first line of a paragraph, the left margin, and the right margin may be specified by entering measurements in the appropriate fields of the dialog.

Entering, Editing, and Importing Text

Text is entered into a field or recordfield in Author mode, by choosing the Selection tool (browser) and double-clicking the field or recordfield. The insertion cursor will flash at the location clicked or at the end of the existing text if clicked below or to the right of it. Text is entered and edited in the same manner as it is entered and edited in Reader mode (see Chapter 5). Text may only be entered in a background field while in the background view; text is entered into a recordfield from the foreground view. A reader can enter text into page fields and recordfields, but only if the field or recordfield is editable—that is, if its activated property is false.

Text may be imported from other applications. Text in another open Windows application, such as Microsoft Word or PageMaker, may be selected and copied to the clipboard. It may then be pasted into the active field or recordfield at the insertion point. Likewise, text may be copied from one field or recordfield in a book by dragging through it with the mouse pointer to select it, and then choosing "Copy." A field may be made active and the clipboard contents then pasted.

Most word processing applications can save formatted text in a rich text format

(.RTF). An .RTF file may be placed in a field or recordfield by choosing the "Import Text..." option from the Tools menu, if the Tools menu is available. There must be an active insertion point in a field or recordfield. An .RTF file or ASCII text file may be selected in the "Import File" dialog. The text of the file is imported into the active field or recordfield.

The "Import..." option in the File menu allows recordfield data to be imported into a book, with each record or paragraph of the data file dumped to a different page. Additional pages are created as needed. For more information about importing data records, see the on-line help regarding the "Import" option. Chapter 22 of this text discusses the use of OpenScript commands to access data from external files.

Inserting a Graphic into a Field

Graphic resources such as bitmaps, icons, and cursors may be inserted into the text of a field or recordfield (see Figure 10.9). The resource must first be imported into

Figure 10.9
Graphics such as icons and bitmap images may be placed as characters in the text of a field or recordfield.

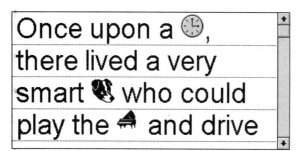

the book through the Resource Manager. Place the insertion point in the field or recordfield and select the "Insert Graphic..." option from the Text menu. A dialog box similar to the Resource Manager is presented, from which a resource may be chosen. Clicking "OK" inserts the graphic into the field at the insertion point.

Formatting Text

Individual words, phrases, paragraphs, and so on may be formatted differently from the default format of the field or recordfield. Text may be selected by dragging through it with the mouse pointer; the fontFace, fontStyle, and fontSize properties for the selected text can be changed using the "Character" option of the Text menu. Individual words and phrases, for example, might be emphasized in the text by making them italic or bold. Likewise, the strokeColor property of selected text may be changed using the Color palette, so that certain words, paragraphs, or even individual characters appear in a different color to provide dramatic effect or emphasis.

Creating Hotwords

Individual words and phrases may also be highlighted and specified as hotword objects. Hotwords may have scripts attached to them to perform some action when clicked by the user. Such actions include displaying additional information or navigating to a different page. To create a hotword, select the text and then choose "Create Hotword" from the Text menu. The hotword will be formatted in the default style specified in the "Book Properties" dialog—it will be framed, colored, underlined, or whatever. Hotwords have properties, one of which is the hotwordStyle, which may be different from the default style of the book. Hotword properties are changed via the "Hotword Properties" dialog, which is opened from the Object menu (see Figure 10.10). Other hotword properties include invert, highlight, and name. When the invert property is true (set in the "Hotword Properties" dialog), the hotword appears highlighted in the text. Checking "Highlight," and therefore setting the highlight property to true, causes the hotword to flash briefly when clicked. As with other ToolBook objects, hotwords may be assigned a name by which they may be referred in OpenScript commands.

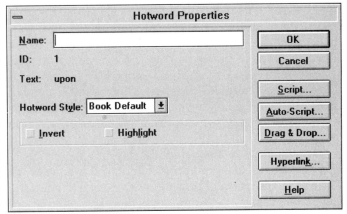

Figure 10.10
Properties control the appearance and behavior of hotwords.

In essence, hotwords are textual buttons. As such, their response to a user's action is determined by their scripts. The same handlers and scripts attached to a button can be utilized with a hotword. Hotwords may be hyperlinked to other pages, just like buttons, allowing navigational scripts to be automatically generated. This is accomplished in the same way as with buttons, by clicking the "Hyperlink..." button in the "Hotword Properties" dialog.

Combo Boxes

Combo boxes are a specialized form of single-select list box. A combo box is a single-line field with a downward arrow icon at its right edge. When the icon is clicked, a drop-down menu appears below the field. From the menu a value may be selected by clicking or by using the up or down cursor arrows to move the highlight to the desired choice; the user presses the Enter key to select the highlighted choice (see Figure 10.11). Combo boxes are created by choosing the combo box tool (see Figure 10.4) and dragging a shallow horizontal rectangular boundary diagonally from one corner to the opposite corner. The downward arrow may be clicked in the Author mode, revealing the drop-down menu. The user can use the keyboard to enter choices into the drop down menu area.

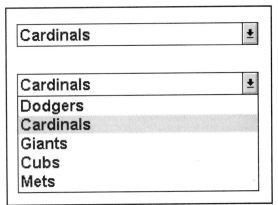

Figure 10.11
A combo box appears as a single-line field with a downward arrow icon (top) that, when clicked, reveals a drop-down menu (bottom). When the user clicks a choice, the drop-down menu disappears and the selection appears in the always-visible single line.

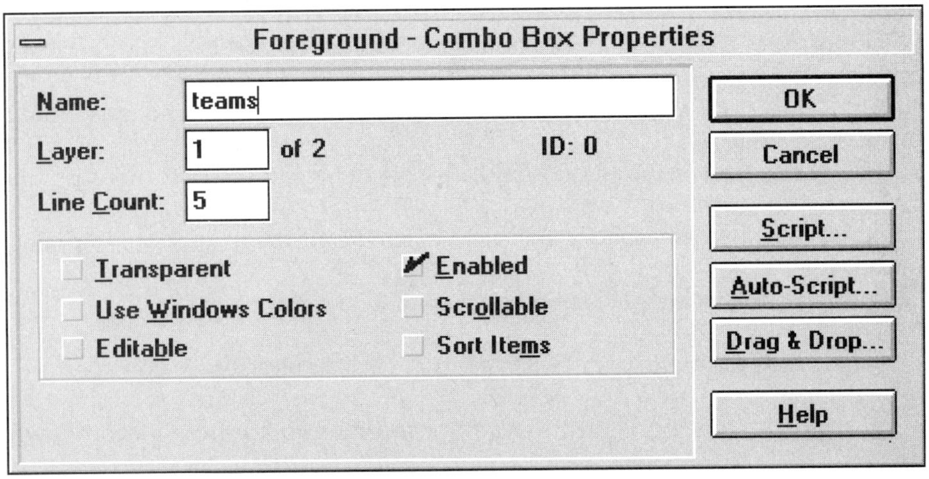

Figure 10.12
Combo box properties affect the ability of the user to edit his or her selections, have a scrollable drop-down menu list, and alphabetically sort list items automatically.

Combo boxes are used for dialog boxes, electronic forms, and databases where a choice is to be made from a list of preset options. The advantage of a combo box over a single-select list box is the reduced amount of space required.

Like fields and recordfields, combo boxes have properties associated with them. With the combo box selected, the "Combo Box Properties" dialog is accessed from the Object menu. The dialog is shown in Figure 10.12. Combo boxes may be assigned a name, and their layer on the page or background may be changed. Like fields and recordfields, combo boxes may be transparent, use the Windows color scheme, or be assigned a fill color and stroke color from the Color palette. Combo boxes may also be made editable in the Reader mode, meaning that the user can edit the text of the combo box's top field—that is, the field that shows what was selected in the drop-down menu. The menu choices themselves may not be edited in the Reader mode. The **enabled** property determines whether the combo box is active or whether it is inactive and grayed out. When not enabled, the combo box does not respond to any user actions. The combo box menu displays five options by default. If it is to have more than five, it is wise to make the combo box scrollable. This attaches a scrollbar to the drop-down menu so the user can access all the options. Checking the "Sort Items" option of the "Combo Box Properties" dialog causes the drop-down menu options to be listed in alphabetical order.

Summary Questions
Answer the following true/false questions.
1. Recordfields may be created on either the foreground (page) or background layer.
2. Fields and recordfields may be scrollable.
3. The author may dictate whether the text of a field should wrap or not.
4. The text of a field whose activated property is true cannot be edited in Reader mode.
5. To create a scrolling text field, one uses the Scrolling Field tool.
6. Fields may have different fill colors, but their text is always black.
7. Fields may be assigned a name to which they may be referred in a script.
8. Icons and cursors may be inserted into a field's text.
9. Text can only be entered into a recordfield when in the background view.
10. Hotwords can only use the hotword style set up in the "Book Properties" dialog.

Complete the following statements by filling in the blanks.
11. _____ contain different text on each page sharing a background.
12. A field's_____property defines whether a field is scrollable, shadowed, or inset.
13. Fields of the_____type allow the user to select more than one item from its list.
14. The _____ property defines whether a field may be edited or is locked in Reader mode.
15. The font face and font size of a field's text may be specified by choosing the _____ option.
16. Text alignment and linespacing for a field is specified in the_____dialog box.
17. Icons and bitmaps are placed in the text of a field by using the _____ _____ option.
18. In a field or recordfield, _____ are words or phrases set up to perform some action when clicked by the user.
19. _____ are specialized fields for selecting a choice from a drop-down menu.

20. Fields without a border have a borderStyle of _____ .

Hands-On Projects

A. Examine the software that accompanies this chapter. Open the "Table of Contents" book by double-clicking its icon in the "Developing with ToolBook" group window in the Windows Program Manager. Inside the "Table of Contents," click the book representing Chapter 10. Work your way through the tutorial as a means of enriching your understanding of fields and recordfields.

B. Business Report Presentation (Part IV)
   1. Open BIZRPT3.TBK (created in Hands-On Project B of Chapter 9).
   2. a. On page 1, in the upper-right, create a borderless field about an inch high and 3.5 inches wide, just above the "Go to Main Menu" button.
      b. If the field is not selected (that is, its handles are not visible) click it with the Selection tool. Access the "Character" dialog by choosing "Character..." from the Text menu or by clicking the "Character" button on the toolbar. Set the font of the field to "Times New Roman," the font style to "Bold," and the size to 28 point. Click "OK" to close the "Character" dialog.
      c. With the field still selected, choose "Paragraph..." from the Text menu (or click the "Paragraph" button on the toolbar by using the Ctrl key to access the alternative toolbar). Set the alignment so the text will be centered. Close the dialog by clicking the "OK" button.
      d. With the selection tool (browser), double-click the field; an insertion cursor appears. Type "1993" and press Enter. Then type "Financial Report" and click the Selection tool again in the Tool palette to release the focus from the field.
      e. The fill color of the field should be white and the stroke color black. Change the colors of the field if necessary, using the Color palette.
      f. Access the field's "Field Properties" dialog. Check the "Transparent" and "Activated" options. Close the "Field Properties" dialog. The field

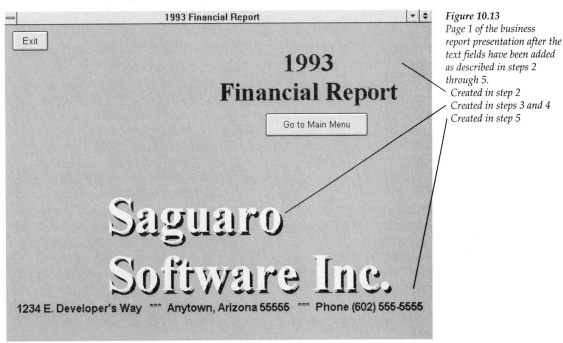

Figure 10.13
Page 1 of the business report presentation after the text fields have been added as described in steps 2 through 5.
Created in step 2
Created in steps 3 and 4
Created in step 5

should now look like one of the fields in Figure 10.13. (In steps 3 and 4 you will create the two fields that say "Saguaro Software Inc.")

3. a. Select the field created in step 2 and copy it. Paste it back onto the page (it will paste on top of the original). Drag it down and to the left and resize it by grabbing one of its corner handles. Using the rulers, the left-hand side of the field should start at the 1.5-inch mark and extend to the 6-inch mark. Its top should be about 2.5 inches from the top of the page and extend to the 4.5-inch mark on the vertical ruler.

    b. Double-click in the text field to get a cursor. Select the text of the field by dragging the mouse pointer through it so the text is highlighted. From the keyboard, type "Saguaro" and press Enter. Then type "Software Inc." The existing highlighted text should be replaced with this new text.

    c. Select the field and access the "Character" dialog box. Type "56" into the size field. (The typeface should still be Times New Roman.) Close the dialog.

    d. In the "Paragraph" dialog, set the text to align left. Close the dialog.

4. a. Copy the field selected in step 3 and paste it. It will paste directly on top of the original. By pressing the up arrow key five times, nudge the selected field up 5 pixels. Nudge the field to the left 4 pixels by pressing the left arrow key four times.

    b. With the field still selected, use the Color palette to change its stroke color to yellow.

5. Create a borderless field along the bottom of the page. Define text in the field to set 12-point Arial bold. Type "1234 E. Developer's Way *** Anytown, Arizona 55555 **** Phone (602) 555-5555." The fill color of the field should be white and the stroke color black. Make the field transparent. Page 1 should now look like Figure 10.13.

6. a. Go to page 2. View the background. Create a recordfield near the top, about 0.75 inch high and extending across the page. Text in this recordfield should be set 32-point Times New Roman bold and should be centered. Both the fill color and stroke color of the recordfield should

Figure 10.14
The title "Main Menu," on the second page of the presentation, is contained in a recordfield.

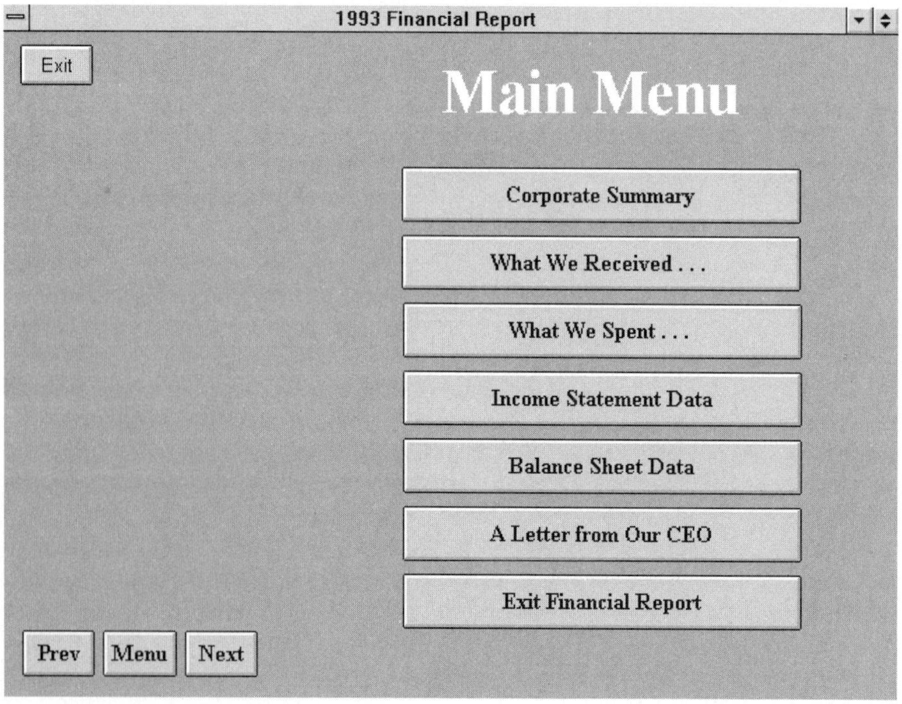

be white. In the "Recordfield Properties" dialog, give it a none-style border and the name "Title". Make it both transparent and activated.

b. Go to the foreground view. Type "Main Menu" as the text of the recordfield. Place the insertion cursor in front of the text and press the space bar until the text is centered over the group of seven buttons on the right. Figure 10.14 shows page 2 after step 6 has been completed.

7. a. Go to page 3. In the recordfield created in step 6, type "Corporate Summary".

b. Create fields for the summary text shown in Figure 10.15. The summary text consists of four fields:

1) A borderless field for all the text except the initial "S." The text sets 14-point Times New Roman bold. In the field, the stroke color is black and the fill color is white. The field is transparent and activated. Use Ctrl-Tab to indent the first three lines 0.5 inch. Indent the lower lines as shown in Figure 10.15 to leave room for the company logo in the lower left corner. (You will add the logo in the next chapter.)

2) The second field is a pasted copy of the first, nudged to the left and up 1 pixel in each direction. Make the stroke color of the field white. Select the first three words, "aguaro Software Inc." Set the stroke color green.

3) The third field, also borderless, contains the letter "S" and is transparent and activated. Its fill color is white and its stroke color is black. The text is 48-point Times New Roman bold.

4) The fourth field is a copy of the third, offset 5 pixels to the left and 5 pixels up. Its stroke color is green.

8. On page 4, type "What We Received . . ." into the title recordfield. Create the remaining text with three side-by-side fields and type the three columns of data shown in Figure 10.16. Use 10-point Arial bold. Make the first line of the table (that is, all the text and data referring to the "Developer's Graphic Kit") blue. Make the second line green; the third cyan; and the fourth, yellow.

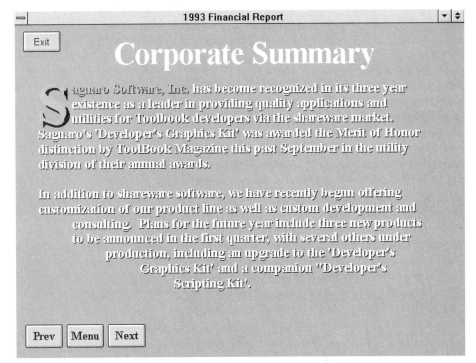

Figure 10.15
The text of the corporate summary is actually made up of four different fields: one for the inital drop cap, another for its shadow, a third for the other body text, and a fourth for its shadow.

Figure 10.16
The table of the "What We Received..." page is created with three fields, one for each column.

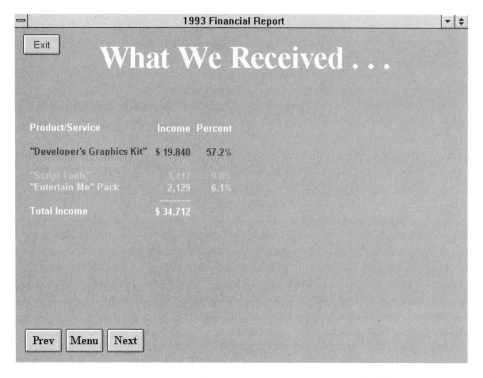

9. Use Figure 10.17 to create the text for page 5 of the presentation. The upper left field is 12-point Times New Roman bold italic. The table data (created with different fields for each column, as in step 8) is 8-point Arial bold.
10. Use Figure 10.18 to create the text of page 6. Fonts and sizes are the same as those in step 9.
11. Use Figure 10.19 to create the text shown for the "Balance Sheet Data" page. Font selections are the same as in steps 9 and 10.
12. Type "A Letter from Our CEO" in the title recordfield on page 8 of the

Figure 10.17
The table on page 5 of the presentation consists of three fields, one for each column. The title, "What We Spent...," is contained in a recordfield.

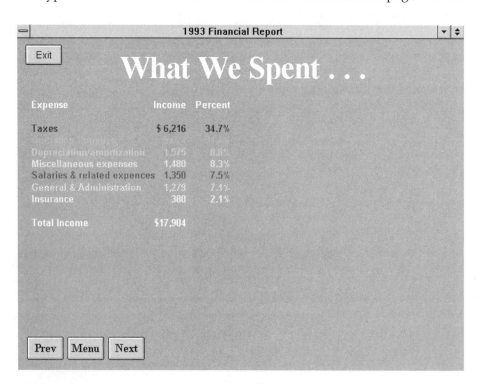

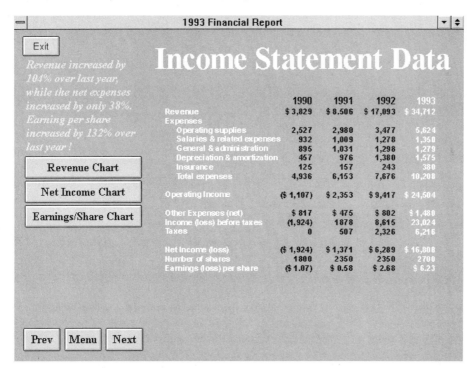

Figure 10.18
As with pages 4 and 5, each column of the table on page 6 of the presentation is a separate field.

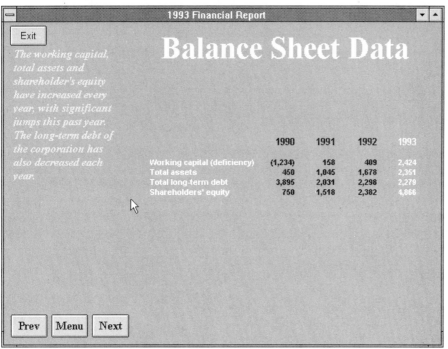

Figure 10.19
Five fields were used to create the table on the "Balance Sheet Data" page.

presentation. Create the letter as a shadowed field with a word-wrap field type. The text is 10-point Times New Roman regular. In the "Paragraph" dialog, set the indent of the first line and left and right margins to 0.15 inch. The field should be activated but not transparent. Adjust the size of the field as necessary to resemble that shown in Figure 10.20.

13. On pages 9, 10, and 11, type text into the title recordfield. The text should be "Revenue Chart", "Net Income Chart", and "Earnings/Share Chart". The text used in the charts will be added after the charts are drawn in the next chapter.

14. Save the file as BIZRPT4.TBK.

Figure 10.20
The letter from the CEO is
a shadowed field with left
and right indents set to
form margins.

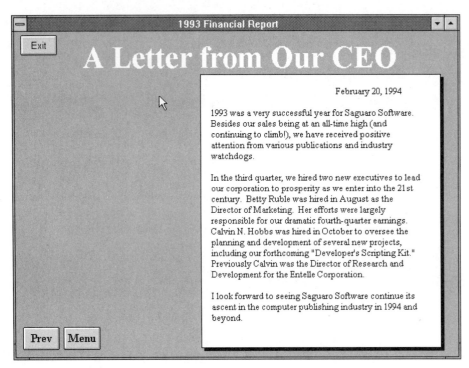

C. In the "Working with Objects" section of the on-line help, look up the step-by-step procedures for working with text, fields, and recordfields.

D. In project B, you created table columns that contained different fields. Tables can also be created with one field, using the Tab key. Use the on-line help to search for topics related to tabs, —tabStyle, and tabSetting, for example. Tabs can be set in the "Paragraph" dialog box for a field. By default they are spaced at 0.5-inch intervals and are left-justified.

E. Create a database to serve as an address book. The page size of the book might be small; recordfields should hold name, address, city, state, zip, and phone information. Each page of the book should hold one address, with background buttons allowing the user to navigate forward or backward through the book.

F. Create an electronic research paper. It might be the biography of a famous person, a report about a country, or a discussion of space exploration or the Civil War. Use a different page to hold textual information about each area of discussion (the person's childhood, accomplishments, family, and so on; the country's population, exports, climate, and the like). Use a main menu page like the one in Figure 10.14 to access the different areas. Provide buttons on the background of the pages to move forward and backward through the book or to return to the main menu page. Use hyperlinked hotwords where necessary.

G. Create a yearly calendar book consisting of 365 pages (one page for each day). Recordfields on the background should contain the date and an appointment schedule. To make the date input easier, create 12 backgrounds with a background field on each for the month name and a recordfield for the day of the month. Background buttons can be used to navigate forward or backward, as can 12 buttons that link to the first day of the appropriate month. In each month's background, there could be 28 to 31 buttons that navigate to the different pages of the month's days. (True, all this hyperlinking is rather time-consuming! Once you learn how to script, in Section III, you will see some easy shortcuts to do this.)

Chapter 11

Art 101

Drawing in ToolBook

The old adage "A picture's worth a thousand words" holds true for ToolBook presentations and applications. Books with just buttons and text fields tend to be uninteresting. Graphics go a long way in presenting information; providing reader interest; and setting the mood, or tone. ToolBook is highly graphical in nature, having several tools for creating vectored graphics, as well as the ability to import both bitmap and vector images from other paint and draw packages. Graphics, both those drawn in ToolBook and images imported from elsewhere, are objects in ToolBook and as such, have properties that control their appearance and may have scripts attached to define their behavior.

Draw Images Versus Paint Images

There are two types of computer graphics. **Vectored images**—also known as **draw images**, **draw-type images**, or **object-oriented images**—are defined by mathematical formulas. A rectangle that is a draw image, for instance, is defined as a rectangle with its upper left corner at a certain location (coordinates) and its lower right corner at a second set of coordinates. Likewise, a draw-image line is defined by the location of its endpoints. A numeric value defines the line's width in points. A draw-image circle might be defined by its center point at a set of coordinates and a radius of a specified length. Based on the user's input, the development software takes care of writing the correct mathematical formulas to the file. The mathematics are not visible to the user.

What is apparent to the user is the ease of editing vectored graphics and the lack of distortion. A draw-image rectangle may be resized at any time or the width of its line may be changed. A fill pattern for a draw-image ellipse may be changed or its colors altered. An object may be selected and deleted. Layered draw-type objects may be brought forward or sent backward. These changes are easily made, since all the software must do is alter the underlying mathematical definitions. When the user moves a draw-type object, for example, the software changes the defining coordinates to reflect its new position; the monitor screen is redrawn.

Vectored images are created with drawing software. In contrast, **bitmap images**—also called **bitmapped images**, **paint images**, or **paint-type images**—are created with paint software. Bitmap images are simply a collection of different-colored pixels that in their entirety form an image. Rather than using mathematical formulas, bitmaps are defined by their pixels, with the color of each pixel defined by the software. A square may be drawn in a paint program and then one of its sides erased by changing the color of the pixels on that side. In a draw package, part of an object cannot be erased. Instead, it is hidden by another object to achieve the same effect. Paint programs generally have several special-effects tools that draw packages lack. There are, however, many drawbacks to paint images. Bitmaps are not easily resized without distortion or loss. Objects cannot be sent back or brought forward, only painted over. Likewise, fill patterns and line widths are not as easily changed.

A further difference between draw and paint images is evident when they are printed. Vectored graphics generally print at the resolution of the printer, be it a 72-dpi (dots per inch) dot matrix printer, a 300-dpi laser, or a 1270-dpi Linotronic. If the printer is capable of printing a clear, sharp image, the draw graphic is clear and sharp. Bitmaps, on the other hand, are generally drawn for the screen resolution of 72-dpi and print at 72-dpi, even on a high-resolution laser printer. Bitmap images may print rastered (that is, have a jagged appearance), especially if the image is curved. Figure 11.1 shows two printed images, one created with a paint program and the other with a draw program. On the monitor, at 72-dpi, the two images would be hard to tell apart.

Graphics created in ToolBook are of the vectored type. There are tools for drawing lines, rectangles, ellipses, arcs, regular polygons, and irregular polygons. The images may be resized, moved, flipped horizontally or vertically, and reshaped. Their fill and stroke colors may be changed at any time, as can their fill patterns and line widths. The layer an object appears on may be changed, so you can bring an object forward or send it back. Complex images may be drawn with multiple objects and grouped together into one object.

Accompanying ToolBook is BitEdit, a paint utility for editing and creating bitmapped images. Bitmaps may be embedded into a book as a bitmap resource or saved as an external file that can be imported onto a page or background as a paint object.

Figure 11.1
There are two types of computer graphics: bitmap, or paint, images and vectored, or draw, images. Bitmaps are a collection of dots; vectored images are mathematically defined. The images may be indistinguishable on the screen, but, of the two, vectored images print the better on a high-resolution output device.

Bitmap (Paint) image   Vectored (Draw) image

Using ToolBook's Drawing Tools

Within the Tool palette are several tools for drawing objects of various shapes (see Figure 11.2). These tools are used in the same way as the button and field tools are used. After selecting the desired shape, the object is drawn by dragging the mouse

Figure 11.2
There are 10 different tools for objects of various shapes.

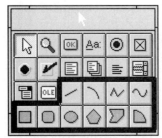

pointer or, in the case of drawing irregular polygons or angled lines, by clicking the mouse button when the pointer is at the desired vertices of the object. Options in the Draw menu are utilized in working with the drawn objects. Properties may be set for selected objects by using the "Object Properties" dialog boxes accessed from the Object menu.

Drawing Rectangles and Squares

Rectangles are drawn in the same manner that buttons and fields are created. The Rectangle tool is selected, then the mouse pointer is positioned at one corner of the rectangle's desired position and dragged diagonally to the opposite corner. The mouse button is released and the rectangle is drawn with the default fill color, stroke color, line width, and fill pattern.

To set a fill color or stroke color as a default, choose fill and stroke colors from the Color palette with no objects selected (no handles are showing). Any objects created henceforth will be drawn with the selected fill and stroke colors. In the same manner a default line width and fill pattern may be selected by choosing new settings from the Line Width and Pattern palettes while no objects are selected. To change these settings for an object that has already been created, select the object so its handles are showing and then set the desired option from the appropriate palette. For instance, to change the fill color of a rectangle, use the Selection tool to click the rectangle so its handles are visible and then choose a new fill color from the Color palette. The rectangle will change to display the chosen color.

Perfect squares are created by holding down the Ctrl key as the rectangle is drawn. Figure 11.3 shows rectangles and squares drawn in ToolBook with the Rectangle tool.

At the bottom of the Draw menu is the "Draw Centered" option. This option acts

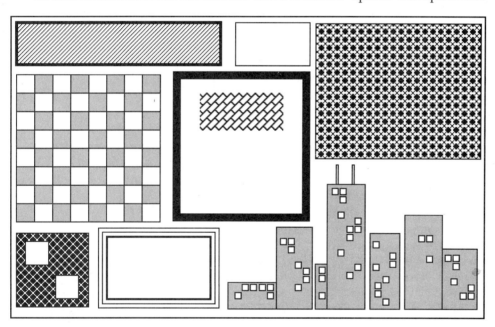

Figure 11.3
Rectangles and squares may be drawn in ToolBook and assigned different line widths, colors, and fill patterns.

as a toggle; a check mark precedes it if it is currently active. When "Draw Centered" is active, rectangles and squares are drawn by dragging from their desired center coordinate to one of their corners, instead of dragging from corner to corner. The checked "Draw Centered" option is toggled off by choosing it from the Draw menu.

Drawing Rectangles and Squares with Rounded Corners

Rounded rectangle and squares, as pictured in Figure 11.4, are drawn with the Rounded-Rectangle tool, which is next to or below the Rectangle Tool in the tool palette. Rounded rectangles are created using the same method as that for drawing rectangles. The Rounded-Rectangle tool is chosen, and the mouse pointer is dragged diagonally from one corner to the opposite corner. In the same manner, rounded squares may be created by holding down the Ctrl key while dragging. If the "Draw

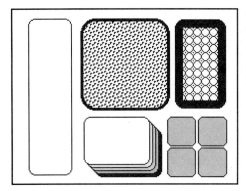

Centered" option is active, rounded rectangles and squares are drawn from the center out. Rounded rectangles and squares are drawn with the default fill and stroke colors, line width, and so on. The defaults may be changed by using the appropriate palettes.

Drawing Ellipses and Circles

The Ellipse tool is used to draw ellipses. The mouse pointer is dragged from the corner of an imaginary rectangle surrounding the desired ellipse to its diagonally opposite corner (see Figure 11.5). If the "Draw Centered" option is active, the ellipse is drawn from its center out. If the Ctrl key is held down while drawing the ellipse, a perfect circle is formed. As with rectangles, the default color, patterns, and so on are applied to a created ellipse and may be changed by selecting the ellipse and using the appropriate palettes.

Figure 11.5
Ellipses and circles are drawn with the Ellipse tool. Perfect circles are created by dragging the mouse pointer while holding down the Ctrl key.

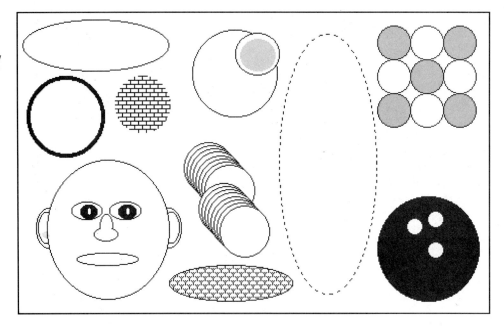

Drawing Lines

If the Line tool is selected in the Tool palette, a line may be drawn by dragging the mouse pointer from one endpoint of the desired line to the other. The default stroke color, line width, and line ends (arrows, for example) apply. These may be changed by selecting the drawn line and selecting a new value in the appropriate palette. If "Draw Centered" is active, the line is drawn from its center to an endpoint. Perfectly horizontal, vertical, or 45-degree lines may be created by holding down the Ctrl key while creating the line. Figure 11.6 shows sample lines.

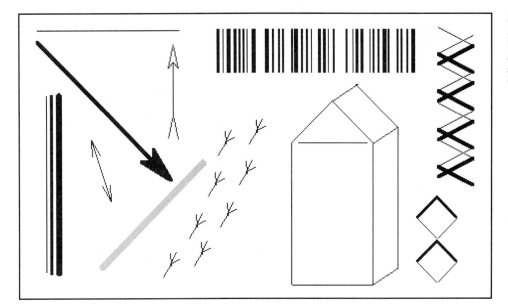

Figure 11.6
Lines drawn with ToolBook's Line tool may have arrows or other end styles and may be of various widths.

Drawing Regular Polygons

Regular polygons are multisided, closed objects in which each side is the same length and each interior angle contains the same number of degrees. An equilateral triangle is a three-sided regular polygon, a square is a four-sided regular polygon, a pentagon is a five-sided regular polygon, and so forth. The number of sides that a regular polygon will have when created is determined by the current selection in the Polygon palette (refer back to Figure 6.19). The Polygon palette provides buttons for 3, 4, 5, 6, or 8 sides, but any number from 3 to 99 may be entered into the field at the top of the palette. Regular polygons are always created by dragging the mouse pointer from the center to one of the vertices, despite the state of the "Draw Centered" option. Regular polygons may be drawn at any angle and rotated while dragging them in the creation process. The current fill and stroke colors, line width, and pattern are applied to a regular polygon when it is created and may be changed for a selected polygon. Figure 11.7 shows various regular polygons created in ToolBook.

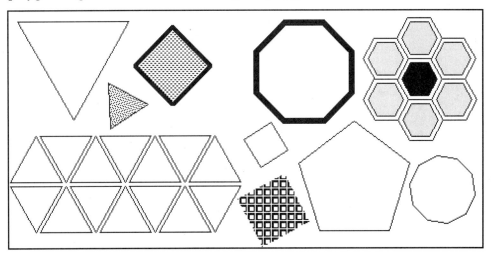

Figure 11.7
Regular polygons are multisided objects in which every side is the same length and every angle measurement is equal.

Drawing Irregular Polygons

Irregular polygons are multisided closed objects. The sides may be any length and the angles, any number of degrees. Irregular polygons are created by choosing the

Figure 11.8
This picture was created
using only the Irregular
Polygon tool of ToolBook.

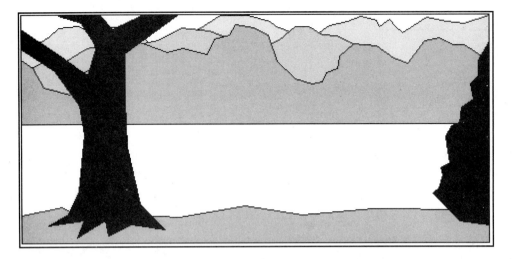

Irregular-polygon tool and clicking each desired vertex, but the last. The last vertex is double-clicked, signifying the completion of the polygon and the mouse pointer is released. The default colors, line width, and pattern apply to the polygon. The picture in Figure 11.8 was drawn with just the Irregular-polygon tool. The status of the "Draw Centered" option has no bearing on the use of the tool.

Drawing Pie Wedges

Figure 11.9
Pie wedges are created as
quarter ellipses or circles.

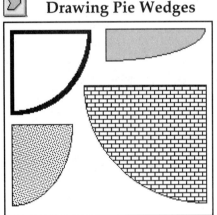

Pie wedges, like those pictured in Figure 11.9, are drawn with the Pie tool. The author drags the mouse pointer from one point on the pie's arc to the other to define the pie's boundary. If the "Draw Centered" option is active, then the pie is drawn from the center point (where the wedge's two lines meet) to the arc. Pie wedges are quarter ellipses. If the Ctrl key is held down while drawing, a quarter circle is drawn. The colors, line width, and pattern specified at the time of the drawing apply to the wedges.

Figure 11.10
Using the "Reshape Pie"
option in the Draw menu,
pies may be reshaped to
contain an angle greater
than, less than, or equal to
90 degrees.

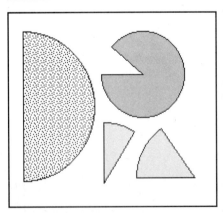

Pies are quarter ellipses. The angle formed by the two lines in a pie may be altered to create smaller or larger angles, as seen in Figure 11.10. This is done by selecting the pie and choosing "Reshape Pie" from the Draw menu. Two crosshair handles appear at the two endpoints of the arc. These may be grabbed with the mouse pointer and moved, on the arc, from 1 degree to 359 degrees. (A clear protractor may be held up to the monitor to get a precise angle.) A quarter circle is drawn, and reshaped to conform to the new measurement. To form other needed wedges, the first may be copied and pasted. Its arc points are altered with the "Reshape Pie" option, and the second wedge fits next to the first wedge. This process is repeated until the circle is complete with the necessary wedges. Each wedge can be colored differently and given a label.

Drawing Arcs

Arcs are drawn with the Arc tool and in the same manner as pie wedges. The mouse pointer is dragged from one point on the arc to the other point. The resulting arc is a quarter ellipse or, if the Ctrl key is held down, a quarter circle. If the "Draw Centered" option is invoked, the arc is drawn from the center point of its ellipse or circle. Arcs are drawn with the default stroke color, line width, and line end. Like a pie graphic, an arc may be selected and reshaped to form less or more than a quarter ellipse or circle. Figure 11.11 shows sample arcs drawn in ToolBook.

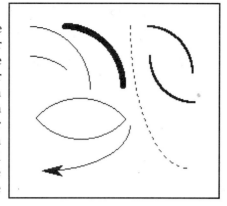

Figure 11.11
Arcs are created as quarter ellipse or circle lines, but they may be reshaped to be greater than or less than a 90-degree arc.

 ## Drawing Angled Lines

ToolBook's Angled-line tool is used to draw a series of connected lines, in a sense forming an open, unfilled irregular polygon. Examples of angled-line graphics are seen in Figure 11.12. Angled lines are drawn in the same way as irregular polygons—the author clicks each vertex of the graphic and double-clicks the last endpoint. Angled lines are drawn with the current stroke color, line width, and line ends. Like all the graphic objects, an angled line may be selected and its properties changed by selecting new values from the palettes.

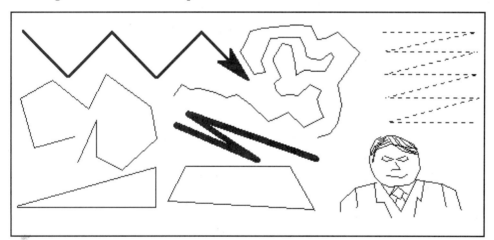

Figure 11.12
Angled lines are created in the same way as irregular polygons. The Angled-line tool is chosen and each vertex of the angled line is clicked. The final endpoint is double-clicked.

 ## Drawing Curves

Drawing curves is much like drawing angled lines. The Curve tool is selected and the first endpoint is clicked. Then the location where the first curve begins is clicked. The process is continued, with a click at each location of a new curve. Finally, the second endpoint is double-clicked. Figure 11.13 shows various curves drawn with the Curve tool in Tool-Book. The default stroke color, line width, and line ends are applied to the curve when it is drawn, but these may be changed by selecting the curve and choosing new values from the appropriate palettes.

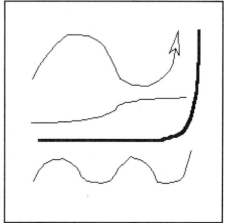

Figure 11.13
Curves are drawn by clicking the point on the line where each curve should begin. The second endpoint is double-clicked.

Graphic Properties

As with other ToolBook objects, graphics have properties and may contain scripts. The "Graphic Properties" dialog (see Figure 11.14) is accessed through the "Graphic Properties..." option of the Object menu. Graphic objects may be assigned a name in the "Graphic Properties" dialog by which they may be referred in a script. The system also assigns each object an ID number, which cannot be changed, and by which the object may also be referred. The layer dictates what objects are behind and in front of the graphic and may be changed in the "Graphic Properties" dialog. Objects may be made transparent, so that objects behind them show through (see Figure 11.15), or assigned the color scheme of the Windows system. As mentioned, each graphic object has a strokeColor and a lineStyle (line width) property, assigned through the Color and Line palettes. Some objects have fillColor, lineEndStyle, lineEndSize, and pattern properties, also assigned through the appropriate palettes. The position and bounds properties dictate the location and size of the objects.

Figure 11.14
Graphic objects drawn with ToolBook have properties that control their appearance. Scripts may also be attached to graphic objects.

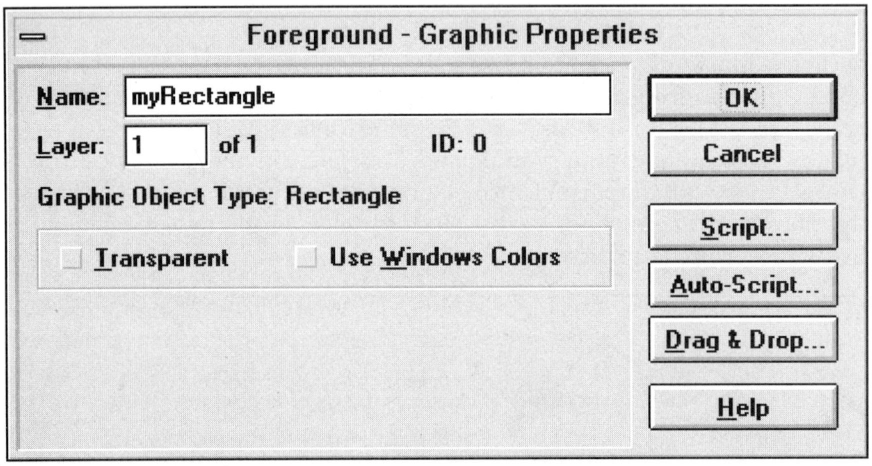

Foreground - Graphic Properties

Name: myRectangle

Layer: 1 of 1   ID: 0

Graphic Object Type: Rectangle

☐ Transparent   ☐ Use Windows Colors

OK | Cancel | Script... | Auto-Script... | Drag & Drop... | Help

Figure 11.15
Graphic objects can be transparent or opaque. Both circles pictured here are in front of the rectangles. The transparent property of the top circle is false, making the circle opaque. The bottom circle's transparent property is true, allowing the rectangle to show through the circle.

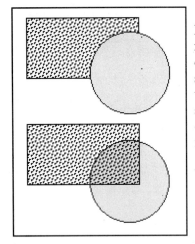

Properties may also be set through the object's Right-Click menus as well as the Draw menu on the menubar. The drawDirect property of a selected object may be set using the Draw menu option of the same name. When checked, the object's drawDirect value is true and the object is drawn directly to the screen. When unchecked, the value is false and the object is drawn in an off-screen buffer and then moved to its on-screen position. The advantage of drawing directly is that the objects are drawn faster. The advantage of drawing off screen is that the user does not see the image being drawn. Animated objects drawn off screen move more smoothly than those drawn on screen. This author recommends using objects whose drawDirect property is false.

Graphic objects may have scripts attached to them. A circle, for instance, might function as a round button. In creating interactive courseware, the author may simulate a working environment such as an office desk. On the desk might be a calculator, a "To Do" list, and a notebook. Clicking the calculator results in the display of a pop-up window with a calculator similar to that presented in Chapter 2. The user would navigate to the To Do list page or the "Notebook" book by clicking the appropriate graphics on the desk image. Other graphic objects might be clicked by a user to perform some animation. A red ball, for instance, might bounce up and down when clicked.

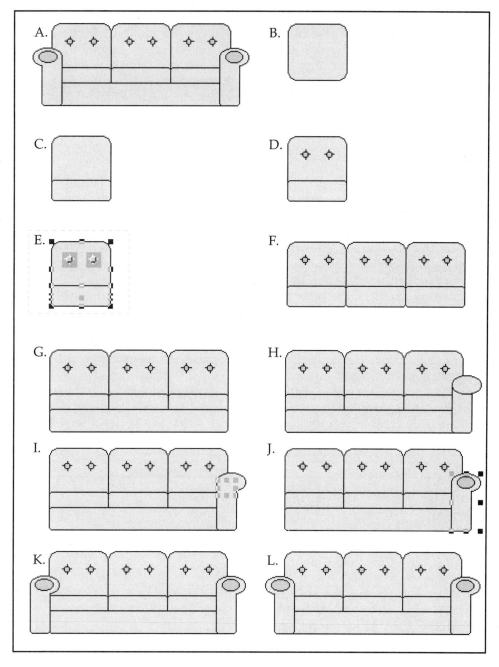

Figure 11.16
Complex graphics are drawn by combining several objects together. This figure illustrates how the couch pictured in A is drawn.

B. A rounded rectangle is drawn with a selected fill color.

C. A smaller rounded rectangle is drawn so that it overlaps the bottom of the first rounded rectangle.

D. Two small perpendicular lines are drawn with a small circle on top of them. This forms a button. A second set is drawn to the right of the the first, so that each cushion back has two buttons.

E. Using the Selection tool, a rectangular area is dragged, selecting all the objects inside the area. (The objects must be fully inside the area to be selected.)

F. The objects selected in E are grouped, copied, and pasted twice, each time being moved to the right to form the three seat cushions and back of the sofa.

G. Another rounded rectangle is drawn as the base.

H. A vertical rounded rectangle and an ellipse are drawn to form the arm.

I. The intersection of the two objects drawn in H, for the arm, is hidden with a rectangle whose fill and stroke colors match the fill color of the rectangle and ellipse.

J. A smaller ellipse is drawn inside the other and shaded darker. The four objects created in steps H-J are selected, grouped, and copied.

K. The copied arm is pasted and moved into position on the left.

L. The pasted arm is flipped horizontally, completing the couch graphic.

Layering and Grouping of Objects

In drawing complex vectored graphics, the concept of layering is important. Objects reside in front of and behind other objects. Parts of objects may be hidden by the objects in front of them. The layer of any objects may be changed as needed using the "Send to Back," "Bring to Front," "Send Farther," and "Bring Closer" options of the Draw menu. Figure 11.16 shows the creation of complex graphic composed of several layered objects.

Multiple objects may be selected by holding down Shift while clicking, or by dragging the Selection tool over an area as if creating a rectangle that surrounds the objects to be selected. Selected objects may then be grouped together into one group object by choosing the "Group" option of the Object menu. Groups are ToolBook objects, and as such have properties and may have an associated script. By grouping objects that form a complex graphic, the graphic may be moved, resized, and so on. In the desk simulation, the images of the calculator, notebook, and To Do list would likely be complex vectored images composed of several objects. By grouping the objects, the script may be attached to the group. Thus it would not matter which object of the group the user clicks to get the script to execute.

Objects of a group may be edited, moved, resized, and the like by double-clicking them with the Selection tool. Clicking an object in the group by pressing the right mouse button brings up the Right-Click menu for the individual object, not the group.

Importing Graphics

Both vectored and bitmap images may be imported from external files and placed on the page or background. ToolBook supports numerous file formats (see Figure 11.17). External graphic files are placed using the "Import Graphic" option in the File menu. A dialog box (Figure 11.18) is presented from which the file format is chosen and then the file is selected. The path and filename are specified in the appropriate areas of the dialog. The image may be previewed before it is imported.

Imported graphics are either of the picture object type or paintObject object type, depending on the format of the imported file. Vectored images are of the picture type. Bitmap images are of the paintObject type. Picture objects may be resized by selecting and dragging their handles. The paintObject objects cannot be resized. Dragging the handles of a paintObject object crops the image. A paintObject object displays faster than a picture object. A picture object may be converted to a paintObject object by accessing the "Picture Properties" dialog for the selected picture and choosing the "Convert" button. Imported graphics are treated as a single object in ToolBook. They have properties and may have scripts associated with them. The border around the graphic may be changed using the Line palette.

Figure 11.17
ToolBook can import files of various formats, both vectored and bitmapped.

Vector-file formats that can be imported into ToolBook:

Extension	Format
.AI	Adobe Encapsulated PostScript/Adobe Illustrator file
.CDR	CorelDraw file
.CGM	Computer Graphics metafile
.CHT	Harvard Graphics 2.3 chart file
.CH3	Harvard Graphics 3.0 chart file
.DRW	Micrografx Draw file
.DXF	Autodesk AutoCad file
.EPS	Encapsulated PostScript file
.SYM	Harvard Graphics 2.3 symbol file
.SY3	Harvard Graphics 3.0 symbol file
.PCT	Macintosh QuickDraw PICT file
.PIC	Lotus 1-2-3 chart file
.WMF	Windows metafile

Bitmap-file formats that can be imported into ToolBook:

Extension	Format
.BMP	Windows bitmap file
.DIB	Device-independent bitmap file
.GIF	Graphic interchange format file
.PCX	ZSoft PC Paintbrush file
.TIF	Tagged image file format file

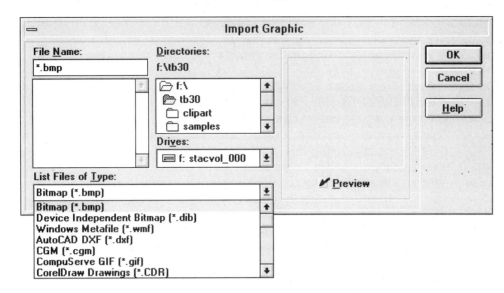

Figure 11.18
External graphics are imported onto a page or background by choosing "Import Graphic..." from the File menu and choosing the appropriate format type, directory path, and filename.

Summary Questions

Answer the following true/false questions.
1. Bitmap images are defined by mathematical formulas.
2. ToolBook's graphic tools are used to create bitmap images.
3. ToolBook can import both vectored and bitmap images.
4. Vectored images print at a higher resolution than bitmapped images.
5. Bitmaps are easier to resize without distortion than vectored images.
6. The stroke color of a rectangle controls the color of its border.
7. Circles are drawn by holding down the Alt key while dragging the Ellipse tool.
8. Regular polygons are closed images whose sides are all the same length and whose angles are all equivalent.
9. Scripts may be attached to a graphic object.
10. Graphic objects are layered and may be brought forward or sent farther back.

Complete the following statements by filling in the blanks.
11. Vectored images are created with _____ software.
12. Squares are drawn by holding down the _____ key while dragging the Rectangle tool.
13. Circles are drawn with the _____ tool.
14. Circles are drawn from the center out when the _____ _____ option is invoked.
15. Objects may show through an object if its _____ property is true.
16. Imported graphics are either of the _____ object type or the paintObject object type.
17. Irregular polygons are drawn by clicking each desired _____ .
18. Quarter-circle wedges are drawn with the _____ tool.
19. Multiple objects may be selected using the _____ key while clicking each object.
20. Regular polygons may have up to _____ sides.

Hands-On Projects

A. Examine the software that accompanies this chapter. Open the "Table of Contents" book by double-clicking its icon in the "Developing with ToolBook" group window in the Windows Program Manager. Inside the "Table of Contents," click the book representing Chapter 11. Work your way through the tutorial as a means of reviewing the information presented in this chapter.

B. Business Report Presentation (Part V)
1. Open the BIZRPT4.TBK file created in Hands-On Project B of Chapter 10.
2. a. On page 1, select "Import Graphic" from the File menu and set the file type to Windows Metafile (.WMF). Select the CACTUS.WMF file from the files accompanying this disk. Resize and position the picture as shown in Figure 11.19. Select the graphic, view the Line palette, and choose "none" to remove the border from the graphic.
    b. Use the Angled-line tool to create an angled line for the mountain graphic. The line should be 3 pixels wide and have a black stroke color.
    c. Copy the line created in step b and paste it back on top of the original. Give it a yellow stroke color. Use the left arrow key to move the line 15 pixels to the left.
    d. Select the two lines created in b and c and send them to the back (the black line should be behind the yellow line).
3. a. Select the two lines and the imported cactus image from step 2. Group these together and copy the group object.
    b. Go to page 2 and view the background. Paste the group object copied in the previous step. Change the line width of the two lines to 2 pixels each by double-clicking them to select them within the group. Click the Selection tool again to deselect the lines, and then click the group to select it. Hold down the Ctrl key and drag the group's lower right handle to shrink the image to a width of about 1.75 inches. Position the group above the buttons as shown in Figure 11.20. Create a background field for "Saguaro Software Inc." and another for its shadow. The font for both is 12-point Times New Roman bold. Add another field for the "1993 Financial Report" text. Use 14-point Times New Roman bold.
4. Go to the foreground view of page 2. Create a rectangle with a white stroke and a gray fill (matching the background color) that covers the seven buttons

Figure 11.19
The saguaro image of page 1 of the business report is an external clipart graphic imported into ToolBook. The mountain lines were created with the Angled-line tool.

Figure 11.20
The background used by pages 2 through 11 contains a resized group of the logo graphic created on the first page.

on the right. Send it to the back so that it provides a border that visually ties the seven buttons together (see Figure 11.21)

5. a. Go to page 4. Create the pie chart shown in Figure 11.22. The chart is created with four pie wedges, that are reshaped accordingly and positioned together to create a complete circle. Color the wedges to match the text labels of the accompanying table (for example, the largest wedge [57.2%] is filled blue to match the "Developer's Graphics Kit" text).

   b. Draw lines from the text labels to the appropriate wedges of the chart.

   c. Draw two white lines, each 2 pixels wide, to separate the headings and totals of the table on the left from the four product listings. Your screen should look like Figure 11.22.

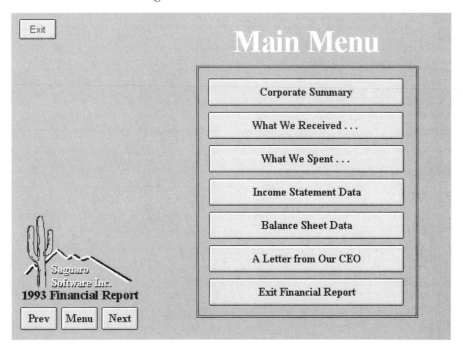

Figure 11.21
The border surrounding the seven buttons is a rectangle with a white stroke (line) color and a fill color matching the background. The rectangle is positioned behind the buttons.

Figure 11.22
The pie chart was created with four pie wedges, reshaped to conform to the appropriate percentages and placed to form a circle.

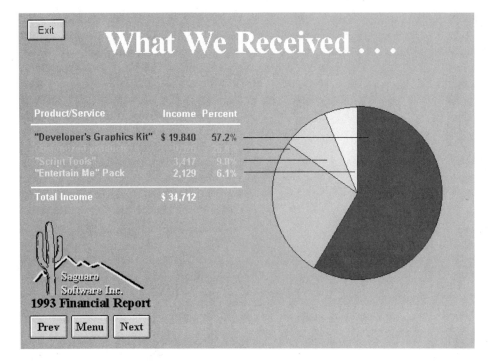

6. Go to page 5. Create the chart shown in Figure 11.23, using the same methods employed in step 5. Connect the wedges with lines to the appropriate text of the table. Color the wedges accordingly. Add white lines to the table to separate the headings and totals from the other text of the table.
7. Add a border to the table of page 6 by creating a rectangle that covers the table. Give it a white border and a gray fill. Send the rectangle to the back. Add white lines to the table. The finished page is shown in Figure 11.24.
8. Copy the border rectangle of step 7. Go to page 7, paste it, and send it behind the table text. Add white lines to the table as shown in Figure 11.25.
9. Import the CEOPHOTO.BMP file that accompanies this textbook. Position

Figure 11.23
The pie chart on page 5 is created in the same manner as that of page 4, using reshaped pie wedges.

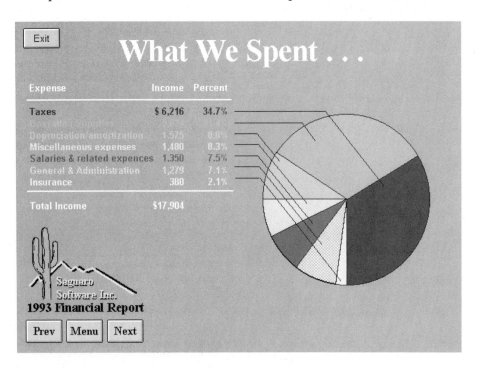

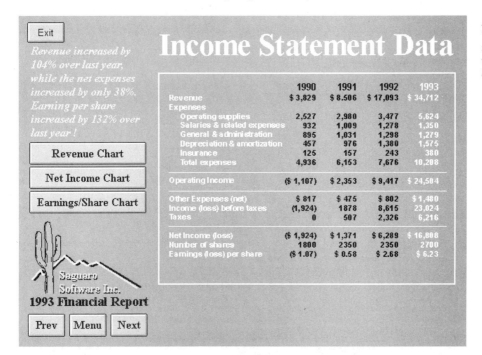

Figure 11.24
The border around the table is created by placing a white-lined rectangle behind it.

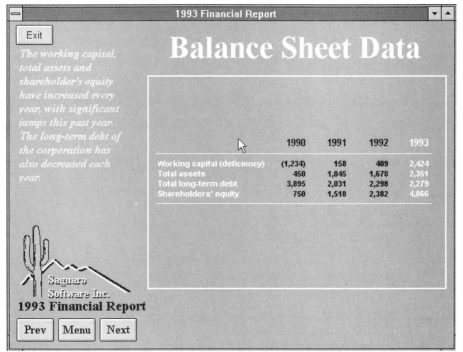

Figure 11.25
The rectangle border of the table on page 7 is a pasted copy of the table border from page 6 of the presentation. The rectangle is sent behind the table text.

it so that its top is aligned with the top of the letter field. The photo is a bit too long. Crop the bottom by dragging up the handle in the middle of hte bottom side of the photo. Your screen should look like Figure 11.26.

10. Import the CEOSIG.BMP file that accompanies this textbook. This is the scanned image of the CEO's signature and should be placed atop the letter field near the bottom, as shown in Figure 11.26. Give it a none-style line to remove its default border.

11. Go to page 9. Create the chart shown in Figure 11.27, using rectangles, lines, and fields. Tip: The chart grid was created with one rectangle that was copied and pasted to form one column, and the column then copied and

Figure 11.26
The scanned photo of the CEO and the scanned signature are both external graphic files that were imported into the ToolBook presentation.

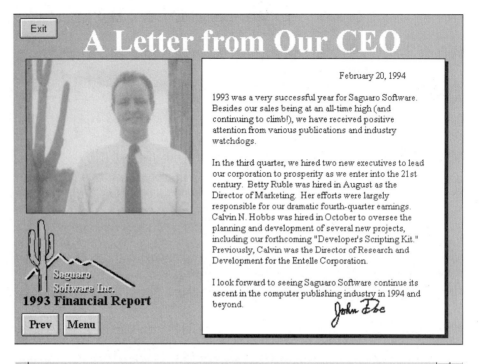

Figure 11.27
The chart on page 9 was created with rectangles, lines, and fields. The chart grid was creaed with one small rectangle that was copied and pasted to ensure that the grid was consistently spaced.

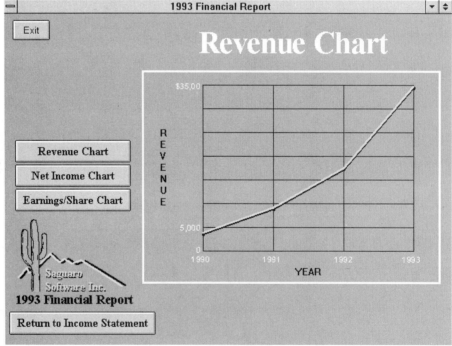

pasted to form the other columns. This creates a uniform grid. The area below the 0 line is filled with a light red to depict a loss.

12. Go to page 10. Create the chart shown in Figure 11.28, using rectangles, lines, and fields. The area of the chart below the 0 line is filled with light red to depict a loss.

13. Go to page 11. Create the chart shown in Figure 11.29 in the same manner as the charts of steps 11 and 12.

C. Create an information kiosk about your campus, town, state, or the like. Use a scanner to digitize photographs and import the images. Use the ToolBook

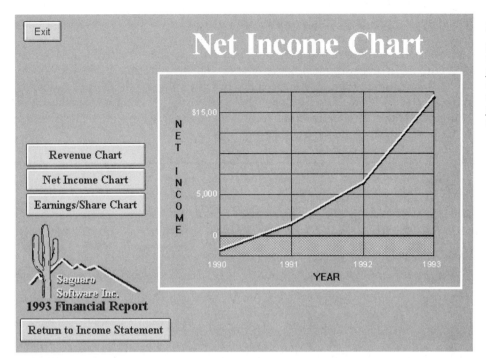

Figure 11.28
The chart on page 10 of the presentation was created with rectangles, lines, and fields. The rectangles composing the grid below the 0 line of the chart are filled with a light red color to depict financial loss.

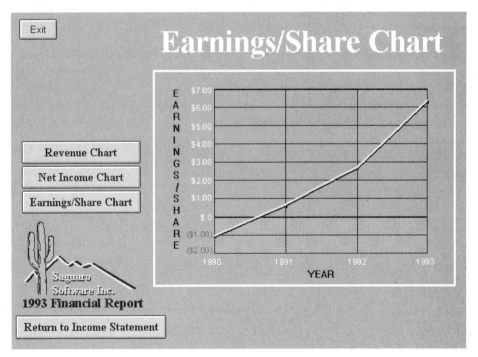

Figure 11.29
The chart of page 11 of the business report is created with rectangles, lines, and fields.

drawing tools to create maps and such.

D. Create an information kiosk for a small shopping mall. (You design the mall!) One page should be a drawing or floor plan of the mall, showing the individual stores. The user can click a store graphic to go to a page providing more detail about that store, including name, hours, phone, and graphics of some of its merchandise (scanned images, clipart, drawn with ToolBook, and so on). If a restaurant is located in the mall, you might include its menu with a nice graphic border, photos of the food, and the like.

E. The graphics in Figure 11.30 were all drawn with ToolBook's tools, as were the images in Figure 4.5. Try duplicating them. Group each image, and save the book for future use of the images as clipart. You might also re-create the sofa image of Figure 11.16. Create some images of your own design as well. Think through what objects compose an image, as well as how they should be layered and what parts of objects need to be hidden. The apple in Figure 11.30, for instance, is composed of four circles and four irregular polygons, one of which is only used to hide lines of the other objects.

Figure 11.30
Each of the images pictured here is composed of various objects drawn with ToolBook's drawing tools.

Chapter

12

Introduction to Programming
Working with Scripts

As seen in the previous chapters, any ToolBook object (field, button, page, rectangle, and so on) may have a script attached to it that defines some action. The action is triggered by a message that is sent as a result of some event, such as a mouse click. ToolBook searches objects in a hierarchical order, looking in their scripts for handlers associated with the specific message. If the specified handler is found, then the OpenScript code associated with that handler is executed. If no handler is found, nothing happens. Scripts are written using the OpenScript language and attached to an object by opening the script editor via the object's "Properties" dialog box and entering the script. The script editor is a word processor-like tool specialized for script writing.

There are various ways to generate scripts besides writing them. Hyperlinking navigational buttons to a specific page was examined in Chapter 9. Prewritten scripts may be imported from a script library by using the autoscript feature. Scripts may be copied from an object and pasted into the script for another object. ToolBook also has a script recorder that, when turned on, translates the author's actions into OpenScript code, which may be imported into an object's script.

It is the job of the programmer to produce accurate, error-free code. Errors are not uncommon in writing code, but they must be addressed and corrected before the program is ready for use. Errors may be discovered by ToolBook in compiling and saving the code, discovered by the programmer carefully examining the code for typographical and logic errors, or by using the debugger to examine what is happening when the code is executed.

Events and Messages

ToolBook applications are event driven. Events occur when the user performs some action such as entering information from the keyboard, moving the mouse or pressing one of its buttons, or navigating to a different page or book. Other events are caused by the system itself. ToolBook, for instance, considers an "idle" event as occurring when nothing else is happening. Events, therefore, are always occurring.

When an event takes place, one or more messages are sent by the system to a specified object. This specified object is known as the **target**. Which object is the target depends on the type of message being sent. When the user presses the left mouse button, several messages are sent to the object that was clicked. These messages include buttonDown, buttonUp, and buttonClick. If the mouse pointer is positioned over a button when it is clicked, the target is the button. If the mouse pointer is positioned over a field or over a rectangle, the field or the rectangle is the target. When the user navigates to a different page, a leavePage message is generated and its target is the current page. An enterPage is subsequently generated and its target is the page being navigated to. Figure 12.1 shows common events in ToolBook, the message(s) generated by the event, and the target of each message.

Figure 12.1
This table shows the
messages and target objects
asociated with common
events in ToolBook.

Event	Message	Target
An object is clicked	buttonDown	the object
	buttonUp	the object
	buttonClick	the object
Mouse button held down while mouse pointer is on an object	buttonDown	the object
	buttonStillDown	the object
	(multiple buttonStillDown messages are sent until the mouse button is released)	
	buttonStillDown	the object
	buttonUp	the object
	buttonClick	the object
Navigating to a different page	leavePage	current page
	enterPage	page navigated to
Navigating to a different page on a different background	leavePage	current page
	leaveBackground	current background
	enterBackground	background of page being navigated to
	enterPage	page navigated to
Navigating to a different page in a different book	leavePage	current page
	leaveBackground	current background
	leaveBook	current book
	enterBook	book navigated to
	enterBackground	background of page being navigated to
	enterPage	page being navigated to
Entering a character from the keyboard	keyDown	object having the focus
	keyUp	object having the focus
	keyChar	object having the focus

Why so many messages? Suppose the mouse pointer is on an on-screen button. There may be times when you want the button to do one thing when the mouse button is pressed and something else when the mouse button is released. In the case of navigating to a different page, perhaps certain things must happen when a page is exited regardless of what page is navigated to. The message leavePage allows this to take place. Different pages may have different scripts associated with their enterPage code sections. More messages are sent than are used by the application, but the variety of messages provides greater flexibility in designing the application.

Handlers

Messages are received by an object and acted upon if that object has a corresponding handler. The **handler** of a script dictates what event causes its code to executed. The **to handle** statement marks the beginning of a handler. Figure 12.2 shows the syntax of the to handle statement and several examples of it use. Every handler contains at least two lines of code. The top line consists of to handle *message* and the bottom line consists of **end** or **end** *message*. In between these two handler statements are the lines of code that are executed when the object receives the message. Consider the following handler of a navigational button:

Figure 12.2
The to handle *statement is used to mark the beginning of a handler for a specific event message.*

The to handle keyword

Syntax: **to handle *message* [*parameter list*]**

Purpose: Defines a handler for responding to a specified message. When an object receives a message, ToolBook checks the object's script for the appropriate handler and, if found, executes it until it encounters an end *message*, break *message*, or return *value* statement. The handler started with the to handle statement is always completed with the end *message* statement.

Examples: to handle buttonClick

            to handle buttonClick loc, shiftState, controlState

            to handle keychar key

            to handle myRoutineMessage

```
to handle buttonClick
    go to page "Main Menu"
end buttonClick
```

The handler handles the buttonClick message. If the button receives a buttonClick message (that is, if the left mouse button was clicked when the mouse pointer was on the button), the line of code between the to handle buttonClick and the end buttonClick statements is executed, and the "Main Menu" page is navigated to. The **end statement** marks the end of a handler for a specific event message. Figure 12.3 shows the syntax of the end statement and examples of its use. The message name is optional in the end statement. However, it is a good habit to include the message name. This makes scripts easier to read when they contain multiple handlers or are very long. A script may have several handlers. Consider the page pictured in Figure 12.4, which presents a question and six buttons with six different answers, of which only one is correct. The page's script might have three handlers:

```
to handle enterPage
    put "0" into the attempts of this page
end enterPage

to handle buttonClick
    beep 1
    request "Click on one of the answer buttons." with "OK"
end buttonClick

to handle leavePage
    request "It took you" && attempts of this page &&
                        "to answer the question." with "OK"
end leavePage
```

The page keeps track of how many attempts the user takes to correctly answer the question. Upon entering the page, it sets the number of attempts to zero. When the user leaves the page (which happens when he or she clicks the correct answer), the user is told how many attempts it took to get the correct answer. If on the page the user clicks something other than one of the six answer buttons, a message the user

Figure 12.3
The end *statement is used to mark the ending of a handler for a specific event message.*

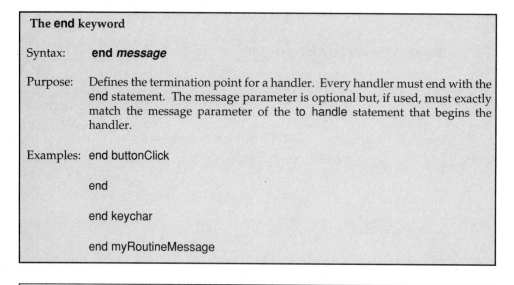

The **end** keyword

Syntax: **end** *message*

Purpose: Defines the termination point for a handler. Every handler must end with the end statement. The message parameter is optional but, if used, must exactly match the message parameter of the to handle statement that begins the handler.

Examples: end buttonClick

                 end

                 end keychar

                 end myRoutineMessage

Figure 12.4
The script of this page contains three handlers, one each for enterPage, leavePage, *and* buttonClick *messages.*

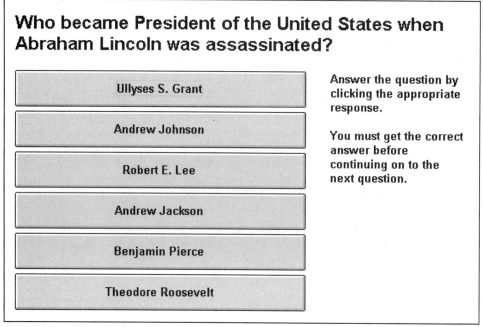

Who became President of the United States when Abraham Lincoln was assassinated?

Ullyses S. Grant

Andrew Johnson

Robert E. Lee

Andrew Jackson

Benjamin Pierce

Theodore Roosevelt

Answer the question by clicking the appropriate response.

You must get the correct answer before continuing on to the next question.

to click an answer button. Thus three different actions are performed based on the event that is currently happening. (At this point, don't get hung up on the lines between the to handle and end statements. You will understand them as you read subsequent chapters.)

Who Receives the Message?

As already mentioned, a message is sent to a specified target, whether it be a button, a page, a background, a graphic, or any other ToolBook object. A button does not necessarily have a script handler associated with the message. For instance, when a user clicks a button, it sends a buttonClick message to the button. But what if the author did not include a to handle buttonClick handler in the script for that button? If a target does not include a handler for a message, the message is forwarded up the object hierarchy. Figure 12.5 shows a table that demonstrates the hierarchy of objects receiving a message. For instance, if the target is an object (field, button, ellipse, or the like) but it contains no handler for the message, the message is forwarded to the next higher object in the hierarchical chain, an object referred to as the target's **parent**.

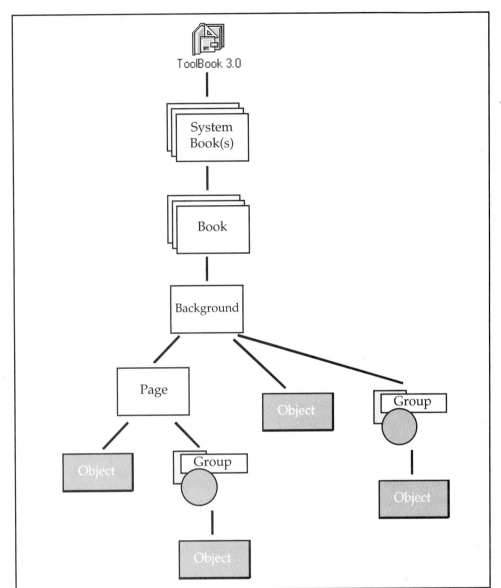

Figure 12.5
The hierarchy of objects in which ToolBook looks for a handler when a message is sent. If the target is an object on the page and that object does not have the message handler in its script, ToolBook then checks the group (if the object is part of a group) and then the page, background, book, system book(s), and finally the ToolBook system until the sought-after handler is found. If the target is an object or group on the background, the page script is not checked.

If the object is a member of a group object, the group's script is checked for a handler for the particular message. If none is found in the group script or if the target is not part of a group, the page script is checked. If the page script does not contain the appropriate handler, the message is forwarded to the background. If the background does not contain the handler, the message is forwarded to the book. In advanced applications, the message would be forwarded to any system books and finally to the ToolBook system itself. There are a couple variations on this theme. If the original target of the message is a background object, the page script is not checked. And if a checked group is, in turn, a member of a larger group, the script of the larger group is checked before the page or background scripts are. If the larger group is a member of another group, this third group is also checked before the message is forwarded to the page or background, and so on.

Forwarding Messages

Once a handler is found, the message is no longer forwarded up the hierarchical ladder unless the forward statement is encountered in the first object's script. The

Figure 12.6
The forward *statement*
sends the message up the
object hierarchy in search of
other handlers to execute.

The forward command

Syntax: **forward [*message*] [*parameter list*]**

Purpose: Forwards a message to the next higher object on the object hierarchy. If no
             message is specified (and it rarely is), the message and parameter list of the **to
             handle** statement is forwarded.

Examples: forward

             forward buttonClick loc, shiftState, controlState

             forward buttonClick

forward statement sends the message up the object hierarchy in search of other
handlers to execute. Figure 12.6 shows the syntax of the forward statement and
examples of its use. For instance, consider the scripts that follow:

Button Script:
```
to handle buttonClick
    beep 1
    forward
end buttonClick
```

Parent Page's Script:
```
to handle buttonClick
    beep 1
end buttonClick
```

In this example, when the user clicks the button, the buttonClick message is received
by the button's to handle buttonClick handler and the computer beeps once. However, the next line of code forwards the buttonClick message up the hierarchical
ladder, where it finds a to handle buttonClick handler in the page script. This
handler's code is executed and the computer beeps again as dictated by the beep 1
line (the 1 telling it how many times to beep).

When ToolBook encounters the forward statement in a handler's code, it
immediately forwards the message up the hierarchical ladder and performs any
scripts encountered there. Any subsequent lines in the lower object's script after the
forward statement are executed only after the scripts of the higher-ordered objects are
executed. For instance, suppose we change the preceding scripts so they appear as
shown.

Button Script:
```
to handle buttonClick
    beep 1
    forward
    request "I just beeped twice."
end buttonClick
```

Parent Page's Script:
```
to handle buttonClick
    beep 1
end buttonClick
```

The button script's handler is executed and the computer beeps once. The **buttonClick** message is forwarded to the page script, where its handler causes the computer to beep a second time. Once the page script handler is finished executing, the subsequent lines of the button script handler are executed and the user sees a request dialog box stating "I just beeped twice."

Where Should a Handler Be Placed?
The author must consider the hierarchical order of objects when deciding where to place a handler and its code. First, the author considers what event should trigger the execution of the code and chooses a handler that corresponds to a message sent by that event. If the action is to be triggered by the user's interaction with a particular object, then the handler should be entered into the script for that object. If the action is to be triggered by interacting with the page, such as when first opening the page, the handler and its code should be attached to the page's script. If it applies to all the pages sharing a background, the background script is a more likely suitable site. Of course, the handler could be attached to every page script, but entering it once in the background script is quicker, easier, and takes less storage space than entering it 10 times in the scripts of the 10 different pages sharing that background. If the author desires to have something happen each time the user presses the F2 function key, he or she would place the necessary handler for this action in the book's script.

Entering and Editing Scripts
Scripts are written and modified in ToolBook's built-in script editor (Figure 12.7). Using the script editor is like using a word processor. The script editor is opened in

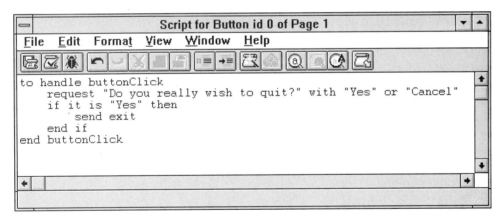

Figure 12.7
The script editor is used for entering and editing the scripts of objects.

Figure 12.8
The script editor may be accessed from the keyboard by clicking any ToolBook object and pressing the appropriate key.

Object	Keyboard shortcut for accessing the script editor
Objects (fields, buttons, graphics, and so on)	Hold down the Ctrl key and double-click the object
Current page	Hold down the Ctrl key and click the page number on the status bar
Current background	Hold down both the Ctrl key and the Alt key and click the page number on the statusbar
Current book	Hold down the Alt key and click the page number on the statusbar

relation to a specific object and accessed through an object's "Properties" dialog or Right-Click menu, or by selecting an object and then clicking the "Script Editor" button on the toolbar. The table presented in Figure 12.8 reveals other keyboard shortcuts for opening the script editor for certain objects.

Scripts are entered from the keyboard, with one command placed on each line; imported from the "Auto-Script" dialog or the script recorder; or pasted from the Windows clipboard, having been copied from another script. The lines between the handler statements are indented slightly by the editor. Other indentations are provided by the author to make the script easier to read, but such indentations are optional. Additional blank lines or blank spaces may be added to assist reading of the script. These are ignored by the system in executing the code. In addition, it is wise to embed comments in the code as described later in this chapter.

When finished entering the script, the author chooses the "Update Script & Exit" option from the editor's File menu. This compiles and saves the script and exits the editor, returning to the book. **Compiling** means the system takes the English-like code and translates it into a machine language that the computer understands. When saving and exiting the script, the script editor automatically checks the syntax of the script. If it locates a syntax error, the request dialog pictured in Figure 12.9 is displayed. Choosing "Cancel" closes the dialog and returns to the editor, where the offending statement or word is highlighted by reverse video. The programmer may then make the necessary changes. Such syntax errors are caused by misspelled commands, incomplete scripts (a missing **end** statement, for example), excessive or omitted parameters, and the like. If no syntax errors are found, the script will not necessarily execute correctly. There may still be logic errors that result in incorrect results, failed routines, and the like. Code that adds two numbers when it should have subtracted them is an example of a logic error. The code is syntactically correct, but the programmer issued the wrong directions.

The script editor has a menubar with choices that access the File, Edit, Format, View, Window, and Help menus. In the File menu, the author may choose to print the script; check its syntax; or exit the editor, with or without saving the script. In the Edit menu, the author may choose options to cut or copy a selected section of code, paste code from the clipboard, search for specific text, replace specified text with new specified text, import an autoscript, or paste code recorded with ToolBook's script recorder. The Format menu houses options for adding comments to selected lines of code (or removing comments, or uncommenting) and indenting selected lines of code. The View menu contains options for toggling the display of the toolbar and the statusbar of the editor as well as an option for changing the font of the code displayed. The Window menu provides a listing of other objects whose scripts may be viewed by selecting them from the list. Finally, on-line help about the script editor as well as about the OpenScript language is accessed through the Help menu.

The statusbar of the script editor reveals information about each of the buttons of the editor's toolbar when the mouse pointer is placed over them. The statusbar also displays information about each menu item as it is highlighted.

Figure 12.9
When saving a script, the compiler checks the code for errors. If errors such as illegal commands and improper parameters are discovered, this warning dialog is displayed.

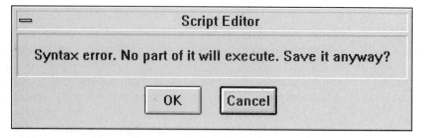

Commenting Code

The wise programmer places comments in his or her code. The comments explain the logic process of the code, reference the values contained by variables in the script, and so on. No two programmers approach a problem in the exact same way, and a programmer may approach the same problem differently at different points in his or her career. In a corporate setting, it is not unusual for a programmer to edit or update the programs written a year or several years earlier by another programmer or even by him- or herself. Comments in the code help the programmer understand another's perspective and logic or refresh his or her memory about a now-outgrown approach.

In OpenScript, comments are preceded with two hyphens. On a line, any text following two hyphens is ignored when the script is compiled. Consider the following script:

```
to handle buttonClick
        -- This script adds two inputted numbers together
        -- and outputs the answer in a request dialog.
        ask "Enter the first number:"
        put it into a
        ask "Enter the second number:"
        put it into b
        put a + b into c
        request "The answer is" && c &"." with "OK"
end buttonClick
```

The first two lines of code following the to handle statement are comments. They are for the programmer's use only and are ignored by ToolBook when the script is compiled and executed. The comments in the preceding example define the purpose of the script: This script adds two inputted numbers together and outputs the answer in a request dialog. The two hyphens may be entered from the keyboard or the programmer may highlight the two lines and choose the "Comment" option from the Format menu. A comment may also be placed on the same line as code, providing it follows the executable code. Consider the following additions to the preceding script (the new lines have been italicized for emphasis):

```
to handle buttonClick
        -- This script adds two inputted numbers together
        -- and outputs the answer in a request dialog.
        ask "Enter the first number:"
        put it into a  --variable a contains the 1st number
        ask "Enter the second number:"
        put it into b  --variable b contains the 2nd number
        put a + b into c  --variable c contains the sum of a and b
        request "The answer is" && c &"." with "OK"
end buttonClick
```

Comments have been added after the code statements they explain. Everything after the two hyphens is ignored, but the statements preceding the hyphens are executed. This script performs the exact same function as does the previous script, but the additional comments may make it easier to understand months or years down the road. The more complex the script, the more essential comments are to maintaining understandability. The preceding scripts are relatively short and easy to understand without the comments. However, in a script of 200 lines of code, comments may greatly aid in understanding the code and the logic behind it.

Hyperlinking

ToolBook provides several ways to attach a script to an object, without having to write the scripts. In Chapter 9, hyperlinking was explained as a means of linking a navigational button to a specified page so that, when the user clicks the button, he or she is taken to the page. In using the hyperlink feature, ToolBook in actuality created a handler and code defining the navigational action and attached it to the button's script. If you were to go back and look at the script of the button created in step 4 of Hands-On project B of Chapter 9, which was used for navigating to the "Main Menu" page, you would see something like this:

```
to handle buttonClick
    go to Page id 2
end
```

The hyperlink feature created this script for the "Go to Main Menu" button. When the button receives a buttonClick message (when the user clicks the left mouse button when the mouse pointer is on the on-screen button), the program navigates to the page whose ID is 2, which in this case is the "Main Menu" page.

Using Prewritten Autoscripts

In Chapter 9's Hands-On Project B, step 6, you used ToolBook's autoscript feature to import a coded handler into the button for navigating to the previous page. The "Insert Auto-Script" dialog (see Figure 12.10) contains precoded handlers used for common tasks. The "Insert Auto-Script" dialog may be accessed by clicking the "Auto-Script" button in an object's "Properties" dialog box, through an object's Right-Click menu; by choosing the "Insert Auto-Script" option from the script editor's Edit menu; or by clicking the button equivalent to "Insert Auto-Script" on the editor's toolbar.

The author may choose which file containing autoscript definitions he or she would like to use. The ToolBook package includes TB30.ATS, but it is likely that Asymetrix or third-party companies will distribute other autoscript files. The Asymetrix Bulletin Board will be a likely place to find such files. (Autoscript action

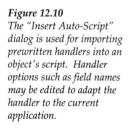

Figure 12.10
The "Insert Auto-Script" dialog is used for importing prewritten handlers into an object's script. Handler options such as field names may be edited to adapt the handler to the current application.

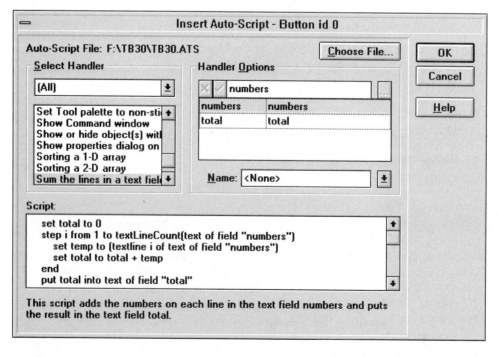

files [*.ATS] are text files containing information for the "Insert Auto-Script" dialog and as such may be created with Windows Write or some other word processor. In the box at the upper left in Figure 12.10, a combo box presents the names of different categories of scripts. A list of the scripts in the chosen category appears in the scrolling field below it. By default, "All" appears in the combo box and all scripts are listed. But if one wanted only the scripts associated with mathematical operations, the "Math" category would be chosen and only those scripts associated with math would be listed.

Some prewritten scripts have references to fields, pages, or other information that must be supplied in order for the script to work properly. For instance, in Figure 12.10, the "Sum the lines of a text field" handler has been chosen. In the box at the upper right are listed two handler options: "numbers" and "total." The "numbers" option contains the name of the field that holds the number to be summed. This is defined at the bottom of the dialog. Likewise, the "total" option is the name of the field that will contain the total. The value of these options is changed by clicking the option name in the list box and then changing its value in the field above the name. Enter the new definition and click the check mark button in front of it. The script listed at the bottom will change accordingly. Change all options as necessary. The message triggering the handler, such as buttonClick, can be changed by selecting a value in the "Name" combo box. To import the autoscript into the object's script, click the "OK" button.

Borrowing Scripts

Another way of incorporating scripts without writing them is to borrow them from other objects and applications. When an object is copied from another page or another application, its script is copied with it and pasted into your application along with the object. Scripts of other objects, books, and so on may be opened in the Author mode and copied by selecting their text in the script editor. The copied script may then be pasted into a different object. (Note: In some cases the author has stripped the scripts from his or her application, making them invisible; therefore they cannot be copied. Or he or she has password-protected the book with regard to accessing the Author mode.) In borrowing scripts from another object, use the script editor to carefully examine the script. Look for specific references to objects, user-defined properties (discussed in Chapter 13), and other things that must be altered for the script to function properly in its new setting. Borrowing scripts is not necessarily a way to avoid learning to program in OpenScript; view borrowing as a time-saving process.

Recording Scripts

Actions performed by an author in developing a book may be recorded as a handler and pasted into the script of an object. The **script recorder** may be used to create scripts that mirror menu options (such as a script for adding a new page), create new objects, animate objects on a page, or print reports. The script recorder, however does not record text entered from the keyboard; display or hide the toolbar, statusbar, or palettes; or record mouse movements.

To record a script, choose the "Start Recording" option from the Edit menu (or press the F8 function key). When the recorder is turned on, the recording indicator will be shown in the statusbar and will be highlighted (see Figure 12.11). Perform the actions you wish to capture. When finished, choose the "Stop Recording" option from the Edit menu (or press the F8 function key again). The steps performed are translated into OpenScript code and contained in the script recorder buffer, which

Figure 12.11
When the script recorder is
running, the recording
indicator appears on the
statusbar and is
highlighted.

is similar to the Windows clipboard. When the recorder is stopped, the recording indicator on the statusbar is no longer highlighted. The unhighlighted indicator remains and indicates the presence of code in the recording buffer. Open the script editor for the object to which the recording is to be imported, and choose "Paste Recording" from the editor's Edit menu. (If you wish the recording to be pasted below existing handlers, place an insertion point by clicking the appropriate location in the editor's text before pasting the recording.) In some cases, the script may need to be edited. You may need to change the handler message name (from buttonClick to enterPage, for example). Update and save the script. Test the script in the Reader mode. Recorded scripts remain in the recording buffer until a new recording is made or the ToolBook session is closed. Therefore, a recording may be pasted into multiple scripts. The following list presents steps for using the script recorder to attach a script to a button to insert a new page into a book.

1. Create a background button with the caption "Insert New Page".
2. Start the recorder by choosing "Start Recording" from the Edit menu.
3. Choose "New Page" from the Object menu.
4. Stop the recorder by choosing "Stop Recording" from the Edit menu.
5. Open the script editor for the "Insert New Page" background button.
6. Choose "Paste Recording" from the editor's Edit menu. The following handler is pasted:
   ```
   to handle buttonClick
       send NewPage
   end buttonClick
   ```
7. Choose "Update Script & Exit" from the editor's File menu.
8. Go to the Reader mode and test the button to verify that it inserts a new page.

Debugging Scripts

Debugging refers to finding errors in a script that does not execute properly. There are several ways of debugging scripts, including manually checking the code; using ToolBook's debugger; or inserting commands that display values, cause beeps at certain points, and so on. Figure 12.12 lists the most common errors in scripts.

Figure 12.12
This list cites the most
common errors in scripting.

Common scripting errors
- Making typographical errors that result in misspelled command or variable names
- Referring to an object by the wrong name or failing to assign to the object the name by which it is referred
- Using OpenScript commands or keywords as variable names
- Making logic errors (subtracting two values when they should have been added, for example)
- Referring to a system variable without declaring it (discussed in the next chapter)
- Trying an illegal operation (such as trying to take the square root of a negative number or dividing by zero)
- Specifying too many or too few parameters for a command or function
- Specifying the wrong type of data for an operation (for example, adding two variables together when one of them contains text data instead of numeric data)

The compiler checks for obvious errors—such as illegal commands, improper parameters, or incomplete code—and will display the warning dialog shown earlier, in Figure 12.9. The offending text is highlighted in the editor if the author responds by choosing "Cancel." In most cases, such a compilation error should be attended to immediately by means of the script editor. The wise programmer will not leave the script editor until his or her script compiles without error.

Errors can often be discovered in the script editor by visually checking the code for misspelling or logic errors. Spelling is of the utmost importance, since OpenScript is a very exact language. Typing to handle buttonClik instead of to handle buttonClick will assure that the handler will never execute. Such an error will go unnoticed by the compiler.

In a non-functioning script, some authors like to include statements that help them discover what is happening and find logic errors. The put command can be used to place a value in the "Command" window. The command put a places the value of the variable a in the "Command" window, allowing the author to verify that a has the correct value at a given point in his or her script. (The put command is examined at length in the next chapter.) To verify that a portion of a script is executing, that author may place a beep 1 command in the script. When the script is executed, a single beep should be heard. Such tell-tale commands are removed from the script once the problem has been diagnosed.

In running a script, ToolBook may display the "Execution Suspended" dialog (see Figure 12.13) if it encounters a runtime error. Runtime errors are encountered, for instance, when an inappropriate value is encountered for a variable (for example, when the variable contains text when the system needs a number to perform addition) or when an object is referred to

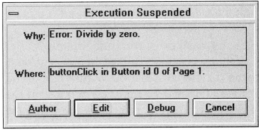

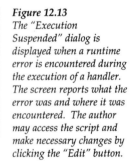

Figure 12.13
The "Execution Suspended" dialog is displayed when a runtime error is encountered during the execution of a handler. The screen reports what the error was and where it was encountered. The author may access the script and make necessary changes by clicking the "Edit" button.

that does not exist. Details about the runtime error are given in the "Why" and "Where" fields of the "Execution Suspended" dialog. The "Why" field explains the error encountered. The "Where" field lists the object containing the offending handler and the handler name. If running the book with the full version of ToolBook or Multimedia ToolBook (as opposed to using the runtime modules), the script may be accessed and edited in the script editor by clicking the "Edit" button in the

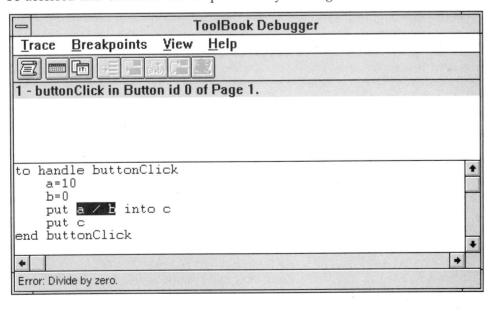

Figure 12.14
The debugger highlights the operation that suspended the handler's execution. It allows the programmer to change values of variables and execute the script one line at a time.

"Execution Suspended" dialog. The offending statement or word is highlighted in the script editor.

ToolBook includes a debugger, a utility for locating problems in a script. The debugger (see Figure 12.14) includes options for viewing and altering the value of a variable, setting breakpoints to temporarily halt execution of a script (to check the status of variables, properties, and objects), and executing the script one statement at a time. Appendix G examines the use of the debugger in more detail.

Using the "Command" Window to Test or Debug

Figure 12.15
The "Command" window may be used to test OpenScript statements.

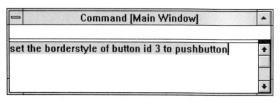

As discussed in Chapter 7, the "Command" window (see Figure 12.15) may be used to execute a statement or series of statements in either Author or Reader mode. The "Command" window may be utilized in the authoring process to set or get a property of an object or group of objects. For example, several objects may be selected and their fill colors collectively set by issuing the following command in the "Command" window:

    set the fillColor of selection to red

Statements may be test run immediately in the "Command" window to check their syntax or observe the results of their execution. Several lines of code may be executed from the "Command" window, thus the full code of a handler could be executed and evaluated. (Since pressing the Enter key in the "Command" window executes the statement(s) contained within it, press Ctrl-Enter to separate lines of code. Lines may also be separated with semicolons.)

Within scripts, the value of a variable or other container may be displayed in the "Command" window using the put statement. The syntax is

    put *container*

For example, the statement

    put myVariable

displays the value of the variable named myVariable in the "Command" window.

Summary Questions
Answer the following true/false questions.
 1. Events are always occurring, whether the user is doing something or not.
 2. One event, such as a click, can result in several different messages being sent.
 3. The "target" of a message is always the object that currently has the focus.
 4. The various messages sent by one event, such as navigating to a different page, may have various targets.
 5. Every handler is completed with an end statement.
 6. A script may contain only one handler.
 7. If the target does not have the appropriate handler, nothing happens.
 8. Comments in OpenScript code are preceded by two asterisks (**).
 9. Comments may be placed after executable statements, on the same line.

10. A script that compiles without error will run without error.

Complete the following statements by filling in the blanks.

11. _____ occur when the user performs some action such as clicking an object or pressing a key on the keyboard.
12. The specific object that first receives a message is known as the _____ .
13. Scripts contain one or more _____ that intercept a specific message.
14. If the appropriate handler is not found in the target's script, the message is forwarded to the object's _____ .
15. The _____ statement in a handler causes a message to continue up the object hierarchy.
16. Handlers that pertain to every page of a book are probably best placed in the _____ script.
17. When the system translates the code into a language the computer understands, the script is _____ .
18. _____ are prewritten handlers that may be inserted into an object's script.
19. The _____ _____ translates an author's actions into Open-Script code.
20. The _____ allows an author to examine what is happening as a script is executed and therefore find and correct logic errors.

Hands-On Projects

A. Examine the software that accompanies this chapter. Open the "Table of Contents" book by doubling clicking its icon in the "Developing with ToolBook" group window in the Windows Program Manager. Inside the "Table of Contents," click the book representing Chapter 12. Work your way through the tutorial as a means of increasing your understanding of the information presented in this chapter.

B. 1. Open the script editor for an object. Examine the on-line help about the script editor (see Figure 12.16). Use the on-line help to learn more about each of the menu and toolbar options by clicking them in the on-line help.
2. Explore the OpenScript Reference in the on-line help and look up the following

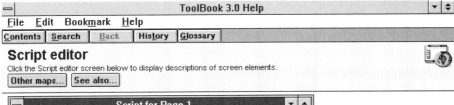
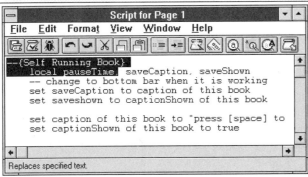

Figure 12.16
The on-line help provides information about the script editor. To access the on-line help, open the script editor and choose "Script Editor" from the Help menu.

terms in its glossary:

forward	buttonUp	buttonClick	leavePage
handler	buttonDown	enterPage	beep

C. Create a new book with one page as shown in Figure 12.17. The page consists of two fields: a scrolling field named "numbers" and a smaller rectangle field below it named "sum". The page also contains a push button with a caption "Sum list." Open the script editor for the push button.

    1. Choose "Insert Auto-Script" from the Edit menu.

    2. Select "Sum the lines in a text field" as in Figure 12.10

    3. The script assumes the total field is named "total", but here it is named "sum". Click the "total" option in the "Handler options" box. Change "total" to "sum" in the edit field and click the check mark button to change every occurrence of the field named "total" to "sum".

    4. Click the "OK" button to insert the handler into the script of the button.

    5. Choose "Update Script & Exit" from the script editor's File menu.

    6. Go to the Reader mode. Enter several values into the numbers field (one value per line). Click the "Sum list" button to test its script.

Figure 12.17
A prewritten autoscript is utilized for the "Sum list" button. The script tells the system to add the numbers in the larger scrolling field and place the result in the lower rectangle field.

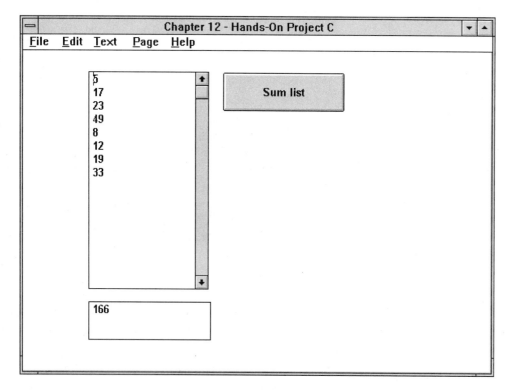

Section III
Programming

Data Storage Units
Variables and Other Containers

ToolBook's authoring environment makes it easy to design an application, but the power and flexibility of ToolBook is not evident until you begin programming with OpenScript. Section III, Chapters 13 through 27, focuses on programming theory and writing OpenScript code. You will learn how to store and manipulate data, perform mathematical calculations, make branching decisions, manipulate objects, design interface menus, work with external files, sort and search data, perform animations, utilize multimedia, and much more.

In general, programming involves devising an algorithm that takes input data and acts upon it to generate some desired output. The data may be different each time the program runs and may or may not change during the execution of the program. The data is stored, therefore, in containers so that it can be referenced, regardless of its value. Containers in which values may be stored and recalled include variables, fields, recordfields, and properties.

Data is most commonly stored in **variables**. The data stored in variables may be of three general types: integers, floating-point decimals, and alphanumeric strings. The scope of a variable may be **local** in that the variable ceases to exist after the particular handler has executed, or **global**, in which the variable retains its value even after the handler has been executed.

Data may also be stored in fields and recordfields. Text in fields and recordfields may be set or retrieved through OpenScript code.

Additional object properties may be defined by the author for the purpose of storing data. The values of these user-defined properties may be set or retrieved through OpenScript commands. User-defined properties retain their value even after the application has been exited.

The Value of Containers

Data used in a program can be numeric or text, and of various lengths. Data may consist of a single-digit integer, but it may also be several paragraphs of text or a list of a thousand numbers. Given the size of such data, it is usually impractical to refer to it literally in a script. Referring to data literally also defeats the purpose of developing an algorithm that works with various values of input data. Therefore, data values are stored in a container and the container is referenced in the script instead. In executing the handler, ToolBook substitutes the value of the container in place of the container reference.

Variables

The most common container used in scripting is the **variable**. Variables are so named because the values they contain may change during the execution of the program. Variables are actually addresses to memory locations where data is stored. To simplify their use and to make the address references meaningful, the variables are named with alphanumeric titles such as x, total, payRate, lastName, and record1.

Naming Variables

The author assigns variables a name by which the values they contain are referenced. The variable name must remain the same throughout a handler, although the names are not case sensitive. In other words, uppercase and lowercase characters are treated the same; for example, myVariable, myvariable, and MYVARIABLE are all the same variable. (In some languages, such as C and C++, variable names are case sensitive and these three names would represent three distinct values, but not so in ToolBook or OpenScript.) An author must follow several rules in naming variables:

1. Variable names must begin with a letter (A-Z, a-z), an underscore (_), or the at symbol (@). Thus, the following are legal variable names:

hoursWorked	lastname	X1
xyz	a	_a
_payment	@fillColor	TheSubject

   The following are illegal names and would result in compiler errors:

1a	#hours	12345
-myValue	%percent	!total
+cost	*xyz	?payment

2. Variable names may only include alphanumeric characters (0-9, A-Z, a-z) or underscores (_). Special characters such as -, *, ?, /, and . are not allowed and neither are spaces. (The symbol @ may only be used as the first character.) Thus, the following are legal variable names:

the_last_name	x1y1	_total_payment
vWeight_1	@fillColor1	_12345
not_funny	number5	number_5

   The following are illegal names and would result in compiler errors:

the last name	theLastName!	_$cost
payment$	percent%	hours-worked
person'sLastName	pay.rate	total*

3. OpenScript commands, keywords, or properties may not be used as variable names. They may, however, be part of a larger variable name. Thus, the following are legal variable names:

xbutton	fieldText	myFillColor
theRectangle	theMenuBar	text1
circle_bounds	vrequest	@step

   The following are illegal names and would result in compiler errors:

button	field	fillColor
rectangle	menubar	text
bounds	request	step

To make variable names easier to read and understand, follow these optional suggestions:

1. Use meaningful names for variables, such as hoursWorked or lastName, rather than meaningless names such as x, a1, or qwerty.
2. Begin the variable name with a lowercase letter, underscore, or @ symbol instead of an uppercase letter.
3. Capitalize the first letter of subsequent words in variable names that consist of multiple words: lastName or hoursWorked.
4. Some authors like to start all variable names with a lowercase v to provide a visual clue that the term is a variable: vCost, vHoursWorked, and so on.
5. Begin the names of system (global) variables (discussed later in this chapter) with sv, g, or sys: svCost, gCost, or sysCost. The prefix distinguishes them as being system variables.

Variable Types and Declarations

Variables may contain various **data types**, including **integers** (1, 2, 3 and so on), **floating point values** (1.23), or alphanumeric **strings** (The dog is brown). In many languages, such as C, the programmer must **declare** each variable—that is, the programmer must state what type of data each variable will contain. Declared variables can only contain data of the type declared. If an alphanumeric string is assigned to a variable that has been declared as an integer-type variable, an error is encountered. OpenScript does not require that variables be declared. An undeclared OpenScript variable may be assigned text data at one point and numeric data later in the handler. OpenScript variables may, however, be declared if the author so wishes. Why declare variables? Declaring variables prevents data of the wrong type from being assigned to a variable. Declared variables use less memory and often result in the handler being executed faster. Variables are declared in handlers before they are referenced. **Local variables** (those that exist only during the execution of the handler) are declared by specifying local along with the data type, followed by the variable name.

```
local INT quantitySold
local STRING productName
local DATE saleDate
```

In the preceding examples, the variable named quantitySold is declared as a local variable of type INT (that is, containing integer data). The variable named productName is a local variable of type STRING (containing text string data) and the variable named saleDate is declared as a local variable of type DATE (containing date information). Multiple variables of the same type may be declared together on the same line. For instance:

```
to handle buttonClick
    local INT num1, num2, num3
    . . .
    . . .
end buttonClick
```

The preceding handler declares three variables—num1, num2 and num3—as type INT. (The ellipses, or three dots, indicate an undetermined number of statements missing from the handler.) Figure 13.1 shows the syntax of a **local statement** and presents several more examples of its use. Figure 13.2 presents a table of the data types that variables may be declared. In declaring variables, the author must carefully consider all possible data that might be contained within the variable. Assigning data to a variable outside the range of its type will result in an error. For instance, assigning the value 40000 to a variable of type INT brings about an error because the value is outside of its range of 32,767. Performing mathematical calculations on a variable's contents can also bring its value outside the range. Assigning 20000 to an INT value is acceptable, but later multiplying that value by 2 and attempting to store the product in the same INT variable would result in an error. At the same time, declaring a variable type that is too big (for example, declaring a variable as type LONG when it will only handle integers between 1 and 100) uses up more of the computer's memory than is necessary.

Local Versus Global Variables

Variables declared locally or not declared exist only during the execution of a handler. When the handler is finished, the variables and the values they contain are

Figure 13.1
The local *command is used to declare local variables of a specific data type. Data types are listed in the table in Figure 13.2.*

The local command

Syntax: **local [*type*] *variable*(*s*)**

Purpose: Declares a variable as having a local scope (it exists only until the handler is finished executing). The variable may be declared as containing a specific data type (see the table in Figure 13.2). Multiple variables may be declared with one local statement; however, they all must be of the same type. (Local variables do not need to be declared if they are not defined as a specific data type.)

Examples: local INT counter   --variable named counter is declared as holding integers

            local STRING lastName, firstName, Address, City, State, Zip
            --six variables are declared as string containers in the above statement

            local myVariable --myVariable is declared as an untyped local variable

            local REAL hoursWorked, payrate, netPay, grossPay

Figure 13.2
ToolBook and OpenScript support several different types of variables. Declaring the type of a variable is optional in OpenScript.

OpenScript's Declared Variable Types

Data type	Value description/range
INT	Integers in the range of -32,768 to 32,767
WORD	Integers in the range of 0 to 65,535
LONG	Integers in the range of -2,147,983,648 to 2,147,983,647
DWORD	Integers in the range of 0 to 4,294,967,295
REAL	Floating-point numbers (decimals)
STRING	Text character string (e.g., The cat has fleas.)
LOGICAL	Boolean value (true or false)
POINT	Coordinate value consisting of two integers (x,y)
COLOR	Color value consisting of three numbers (hue,light,saturation) or (red,green,blue)
STACK	List of comma-separated items
DATE	Date in system format
TIME	Time in system format
BOOK	Unique book path name reference
BACKGROUND	Unique background name reference
PAGE	Unique page name reference
LAYER	Reference to specific page or background layer
OBJECT	Unique reference to an object (book, page, field, button, etc.)
FIELD	Unique reference to a field, recordfield, or comb box.
GRAPHIC	Unique reference to a graphic object (page or background)

cleared from memory. Sometimes, however, it is necessary to maintain the value of a variable for future reference. In writing courseware, an author may wish to store the names of the pages that the student has examined. Perhaps he or she will visually depict this information by clicking check marks on a main menu page in front of the choices the reader has already examined. In writing a business application, such as the 1040 tax form demonstrated in Chapter 2, the author might use a variable to store how many deductions the user is declaring. This variable should maintain its value because it might be used in several different calculations on the form. Variables that retain their value even after the handler is executed are called **global variables**. ToolBook and OpenScript refer to global variables as **system variables.** Since local variables are the default, system (global) variables must be declared as such. This is done similarly to declaring local variables. The syntax for doing so includes the word system followed by the data type and then the variable name (or several variable names separated by commas). For instance:

```
system INT productQuantity
system STRING customerName, customerAddress, CustomerCity
system  LOGICAL credit
```

In the first example, productQuantity is declared as a system variable containing an integer value. In the second example, there are three variables (customerName, customerAddress, and customerCity) all declared as system variables containing character strings. In the third example, credit is a system variable declared as containing a logical value (either true or false). System variables may use the same data types as local variables; Figure 13.2 listed the data types. System variables do not have to be typed, but still must be declared as system variables. The syntax is the same as that used in the preceding examples but without the type declaration. For instance:

```
system cost
system andy, barney, opie, thelmaLou
```

In these examples, cost, andy, barney, opie, and thelmaLou are all variable names declared as system variables. System variables retain their values until the current instance of ToolBook is exited (that is, the book and any other books opened from that book are closed). Figure 13.3 summarizes the syntax of the **system statement** and presents more examples of its use.

One important rule for system variables: System variables must be declared in each handler in which they are referenced and before they are referenced. Most programmers declare all their variables at the beginning of their handlers, and some languages require this. For example:

```
to handle buttonUp
      system LOGICAL flag1, flag2, flag3
      local STRING customer, address, city, state, zip
      local INT customerNumber
```

Figure 13.3
The system *command is used to declare global variables of a specific data type.*

The system command

Syntax: **system [*type*] *variable(s)***

Purpose: Declares a variable as having a global (system) scope (it continues to exist even after the handler is finished executing and until the current session of ToolBook is closed). The variables may be declared as containing a specific data type (see the table in Figure 13.2). Multiple variables may be declared with one system statement; however, they all must be of the same type. (System variables do not need to be declared, if they are not defined as a specific data type.)

Examples: system INT custNum --system variable custNum is declared as holding integers

           system STRING lastName, firstName, Address, City, State, Zip
           --six variables are declared as global string containers

           system myVariable --myVariable is declared as an untyped system variable

```
    . . .
    . . .
end buttonUp
```

It is also wise to comment on the use or values of variables that have unclear names. For example:

```
to handle buttonUp
      system LOGICAL flag1, flag2, flag3
      -- flag1 contains whether or not the order has been delivered
      -- flag2 contains whether or not the customer has been previously billed
      -- flag3 contains whether or not the customer has a balance due
      local STRING customer, address, city, state, zip
      local INT customerNumber
      . . .
end buttonUp
```

Assigning Values to Variables

Values are assigned to variables through OpenScript references to the variables. This may be done in several different ways. A variable may be assigned a value in an **equation statement,** which uses the equals sign as an operator. Figure 13.4 presents the syntax of an equation statement and several examples of its use. The syntax of an equation statement is

> *variable = value*

For example:

```
cost = 123.45
customerName = "Fred Flintstone"
customerCity = "Bedrock"
```

The value, 123.45, is assigned to the cost variable, while the strings Fred Flintstone

Figure 13.4
The equals sign is used as an assignment operator to place a value into a container.

The = operator

Syntax: ***container = value***

Purpose: The equals sign is used to assign a value to a variable or other container. The value may be a straightforward value, such as 20, or an expression such as 5 + 15. Values may also be strings, such as My dog has fleas., or contain other variables already assigned a value.

Examples: customerName = "John Doe" --value "John Doe" is assigned to variable

            hoursWorked = 35.5

            cost = 105.79 + 23.10 -- puts 128.89 into the variable named cost

            the text of field id 0 = 10

            netPay = grossPay - payments

---

and Bedrock are assigned to the customerName and customerCity variables, respectively. The value may also be an expression that can be evaluated. For example:

```
cost = 10 + 5 + 3
myAnswer = 25 - 10
```

In these two examples, cost is assigned the value of 18 (the sum of 10 + 5 + 3) and myAnswer is assigned the value of 15 (the result of 25 - 10). Other variables may be used in the assignment of a value, providing those variables have already been assigned a value.

The commands of an OpenScript handler are read from the top down. Consider the following handler:

```
to handle buttonClick
    system INT a, b, c
    a = 10
    b = 7
    c = a + b
end buttonClick
```

After the handler is executed, the value of system variable c is 17, since c is the sum of variables a and b, which previously had been assigned the values of 10 and 7. Mathematical expressions will be discussed in more detail in Chapter 15.

Text strings assigned to a variable should always be surrounded by quotation marks. (Quotation marks are optional if the value consists of only one word, but mandatory if the string consists of multiple words. Therefore, always putting quotation marks around a string is a good habit to get into. In addition, the marks visually identify even the single word as a literal string rather than another variable name.) For example:

```
productName = "Crest Toothpaste"
```

is the proper way to assign the string, Crest Toothpaste, to variable productName. The value of the variable does not contain the quotation marks, but only the text between the marks. The form

```
productName = Crest Toothpaste
```

would result in a compiler error. The statement

```
productName = Crest
```

would assign the value, Crest, to the productName variable, but the handler

```
crest = "toothpaste"
productName = crest
```

would assign the value, toothpaste, to the variable productName, since the compiler would recognize crest as a variable, having already been defined. Therefore, it would substitute the crest variable's value in assigning a value to the productName variable.

Versions of ToolBook before version 3.0 did not support the use of equation statements to assign values to a variable. Instead, values were assigned using the **put command**, which is still supported (see Figure 13.5). The syntax for assigning values with the put statement is:

```
put value into container
```

or, more specifically, since a variable is one type of container:

```
put value into variable
```

Thus, the equation statements cited previously may be written with the put statement:

```
put 123.45 into cost
put "Fred Flintstone" into customerName
put "Bedrock" into customerCity
```

Note that literal strings are treated the same way in a put statement as in an equation statement. The strings must be in quotation marks. Formulas may also be used for the value in a put statement. Thus, the buttonClick handler written above with equations may be rewritten with put statements:

```
to handle buttonClick
    system INT a, b, c
    put 10 into a
    put 7 into b
    put a + b into c
end buttonClick
```

Once again, after this handler is executed the value of c is 17.

Using Fields as Containers

The text of a field or recordfield may also be used as a container for data that can be accessed and manipulated from within an OpenScript handler. The text of a field is a property of the field and thus may be retrieved, changed, or cleared (set to a null value). Text is assigned to a field by using the put statement in the handler, as demonstrated previously in regard to variables. Remember the general syntax of the put statement:

Figure 13.5
The put command is used to assign a value to a container.

The put command	
Syntax:	**put *value* into *container***
Purpose:	The put command is used to assign a value to a variable or some other container. The value may be a straightforward value such as 20, an expression such as 5 + 15, a string such as My dog has fleas., or reference other variables that already have assigned values.
Examples:	put "John Doe" into customerName
	put 35.5 into hoursWorked
	put 105.79 + 23.10 into cost
	put 10 into the text of field id 0
	put grossPay - payments into netPay

```
put value into container
```

The text of a field is a container; therefore, the syntax for entering data into a field is

```
put value into text of field
```

The field must be specified by its name, ID, or layer. For example:

```
put "123.45" into text of field "cost"
put "123.45" into text of field id 1
put 123.45 into text of field 2
```

Assuming that field id 1 is named cost, is layer 2 of the page, the preceding statements would be three different ways of saying the same thing. Data in a field is not typed, but rather is always treated as a character string, although mathematical operations may be performed on numeric data in a field. The value being assigned as a field's text should be in quotation marks, although the marks are not necessary if the value is a single number or word and is not an OpenScript keyword or command, or a variable name. (Be careful in referring to fields and other objects in a handler by their layer numbers. Layer numbers may change as objects are brought forward or sent back. It is best to refer to objects by their name or ID. The name only changes when the author specifies a new name. A name remains constant even if the object is copied from another page and pasted. The ID of an object never changes on the current page or background, though if copied and pasted onto a different page, the ID of the pasted object may be different.)

In the same manner, values may be assigned to the text of a recordfield by its name, ID, or layer:

```
put "Charlie Brown" into text of recordfield "customer"
put "Charlie Brown" into text of recordfield id 4
put "Charlie Brown" into text of recordfield 3
```

Likewise, the text of background fields may be assigned a value by specifying that the field is on the background:

```
put "Bugs Bunny" into text of field "cartoonCharacter" of this background
put "Bugs Bunny" into text of field id 17 of background id 0
put "Bugs Bunny" into text of field 3 of background "Cartoons"
```

In the preceding examples, not only may the field be referenced differently, but the background may be referred to in various ways. The code this background refers to the background of the current page. The background may also be referred to by name or ID. The statement

```
put "Bugs Bunny" into text of field "cartoonCharacter" of this background
```

may seem lengthy and not conforming to the

```
put value into container
```

syntax, but it actually does. Of course, Bugs Bunny is the value and text of field "cartoonCharacter" of this background is the container. The words of this background are essential. Without these or some other reference that the field exists on the background, ToolBook would look for the field on the foreground (page) layer, and thus would not find it.

In working with variables, it was demonstrated that referring to the variable in an OpenScript handler was the same as referring to the data contained within the variable. Thus the handler

```
to handle buttonClick
    put 5 into x
    put x into y
end buttonClick
```

is the same as

```
to handle buttonClick
    put 5 into x
    put 5 into y
end buttonClick
```

Likewise, the value contained in the text of a field or recordfield may be referenced by referring to the container itself. For example:

```
put the text of field id 1 into the text of field id 2
put the text of recordfield "customer" into vCustomer
-- in the above, vCustomer is a variable
put text of field "socialSecurity" of page 1 into text of recordfield id 3
```

The data contained in fields and recordfields may be used in a formula for the value:

```
to handle buttonClick
    put "10" into the text of field id 1
    put "7" into the text of field id 2
    put text of field id 1 + text of field id 2 into text of field id 3
end buttonClick
```

After this handler is executed, the text of field id 3 contains the number 17. Values may also be assigned to field text by using the equation statement:

```
to handle buttonClick
    text of field id 1 = 10
    the text of field id 2 = 7
    text of field id 3 = text of field id 1 + text of field id 2
end buttonClick
```

Hidden Fields

Fields and recordfields may be hidden from the user's view to store data that the user should not or need not see. This may be accomplished by issuing a **hide statement** from the "Command" window or executing one from within a handler. As Figure 13.6 shows, the syntax of the hide statement is:

```
hide object
```

where the object is referenced by name, ID, or layer. For example:

The hide command

Syntax: **hide *object***

Purpose: The hide command is used to set the visible property of an object to false, thus
                 hiding the object from view. Hidden objects may be displayed with the show
                 command. Objects may be referred to by ID, name, or layer.

Examples: hide field id 0

                 hide button "Next" of this background

                 hide group "race car"

Figure 13.6
*The hide command is used
to hide an object from view.*

hide field "tempData"
hide field id 4
hide recordfield field 2

The text of a hidden field or recordfield may be assigned or retrieved even though
the field is not visible. Hidden objects may be made visible by using the **show
command** (see Figure 13.7). The syntax of a show statement is

show *object*

For example:

show field "tempData"
show field id 4
show recordfield field 2

The show command

Syntax: **show *object***

Purpose: The show command is used to set the visible property of an object to true, the
                 result being that a hidden object is displayed. Objects may be hidden with the
                 hide command. Objects may be referred to by ID, name, or layer.

Examples: show field id 0

                 show button "Next" of this background

                 show group "race car"

Figure 13.7
*The show command is
used to display a hidden
object.*

Creating and Storing Data in User-Defined Properties

Storing data in the text of a field is nothing more than setting the value of an object's
property. The text property of a field or recordfields is well suited for such a task since
its value is not limited to certain choices. As seen in previous chapters, every object
in a book (including the book itself) has many properties. New properties may be
created for any object and assigned a value through the put command. User-defined

properties are actually containers for whatever values are assigned. In referencing a property in OpenScript, the property must be named, as must the object to which it belongs. The syntax for referencing a property is

    put *value* into the *property* of *object*

The word the in the preceding statement is optional. (In the discussion of placing values in the text of fields and recordfields, you may have noticed that reference was made to the text of field or just text of field.) The only advantage to using the word the is that it provides a visual clue to the fact that the next word is a property name. The word the only appears before property names. Placing the before a variable name would result in an error. Consider the following examples of the preceding syntax:

    put "Bugs Bunny" into the cartoonCharacter of this book
    put "False" into the correct12 of this page
    put 1995 into the yearDate of page "Data"
    put the text of field "name" into student of this background

In the examples, cartoonCharacter is a property of the book, correct12 is a property of the current page, yearDate is a property of page Data, and student is a property of the background. None of these is a default system property of the object, but is created by the author. In assigning values to a property, the property is automatically created when the handler is executed if it does not already exist. If the property already exists, any data it contains is replaced with the new value.

The equals sign (also referred to as the assignment operator) may be used to assign a value to a property. For example:

    cartoonCharacter of this book = "Bugs Bunny"
    the correct12 of this page = "False"
    yearData of page "Data" = 1995
    the student of this background = the text of field "name"

Properties retain their value even when the book is closed and the computer is turned off, providing the book is saved before exiting. User-defined properties, therefore, are useful for saving work in progress, tracking usage statistics, and the like.

Should You Use a Variable, Field, or Property?

With three different types of containers for storing data, which should you use? It depends on the scope of the data, whether it should be displayed to the user, and memory management needs. Variables are best used for temporary data that need not be stored when the book is exited and does not need to be displayed for the user. Text of fields and recordfields may be used for both temporary and long-term storage when there is a need for the data to be displayed. Hidden fields and recordfields may be used to store data that need not or should not be visible to the user. Like fields, user-defined properties retain their value in a saved book even when the user exits the application. User-defined properties take less storage space and memory. So, compared to fields and recordfields, user-defined properties are better in cases involving long-term storage of undisplayed data.

Summary Questions

Complete the following statements by filling in the blanks.

1. Variables, properties, and fields can all be used as _____ .
2. In declaring a variable, the variable is specified as containing data of a specific _____ .
3. My dog is hungry is an example of the _____ data type.
4. If a variable is to contain integer values ranging from 100 to 50,000, it should be declared as type _____ .
5. Values are assigned to a variable by using the assignment operator (=) or the _____ command.
6. Global variables are declared using the _____ command.
7. The scope (life) of _____ variables is limited to the duration of the execution of the handler containing them.
8. Objects may be hidden with the _____ command.
9. A value that should be retained even when the computer is turned off should be stored in the text of a field or recordfield or assigned to a user-defined _____ .
10. String values should be enclosed in _____ _____ .

Identify the variable names in 11 through 20 as being valid or invalid. If a name is invalid, why is it illegal?

11. cost	15. COST	19. 1put
12. cost$	16. put	20. put_cost
13. @cost	17. %put	
14. _cost	18. put1	

Hands-On Projects

A. Examine the software that accompanies this chapter. Open the "Table of Contents" book by double-clicking its icon in the "Developing with ToolBook" group window in the Windows Program Manager. Inside the "Table of Contents," click the book representing Chapter 12. Work your way through the tutorial as a means of increasing your understanding of the information presented in this chapter.

B. Create a book with the three display fields and two buttons shown in Figure 13.8. The two fields on the left are editable by the user, who enters a different number into each field. The third field is locked (activated). Clicking the "Add" button sums the two numbers and displays the result in the third field; also, a plus sign appears between the two numbers (see Figure 13.8). Clicking the "Subtract" button results in the second number being subtracted from the first. The answer is displayed in the third field and the plus sign between the two left fields changes to a minus sign (see Figure 13.9). (The plus sign, minus sign, and equals sign are line graphics. The plus sign and minus sign are switched by hiding or showing the vertical line of the plus sign.)

Figure 13.8
Clicking the "Add" button sums the two numbers and displays the result. An addition sign is displayed between the two numbers.

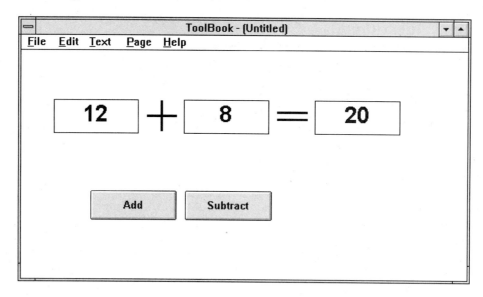

Figure 13.9
Clicking the "Subtract" button subtracts the second number from the first and displays the result. The addition sign changes to a subtraction sign.

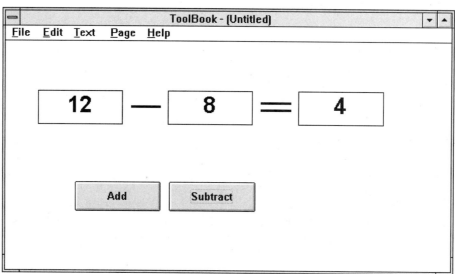

Chapter 14

"I/O, I/O, Off to Work We Go"
Handling Events and Input/Output

Computer programming generally involves taking some input; performing some action, such as the manipulation of data; and generating some prescribed output. In Chapter 12, the concepts of events and messages were introduced, along with the basic mouse event messages buttonDown, buttonUp, and buttonClick. These messages are trapped by the handlers of an object's script, resulting in some action and output. They are also basic input—the mouse messages being generated by the interaction of the end-user with the computer and the application. Additional messages caused by mouse events include mouseEnter and mouseLeave, buttonDoubleClick, rightButtonDown, rightButtonUp, and rightButtonDoubleClick.

The mouse is only one input device among many. The keyboard is another essential input device and, like the mouse, its use by an end-user constitutes an event and generates various messages. Computers are binary devices. In computer science, everything—including characters—is represented by numbers composed of a series of ones and zeroes. In some tasks it is easier to work with the number representing a character than the character itself. OpenScript includes functions for converting a character to its numeric representation and vice versa..

Dialog boxes are popular Windows devices for getting input and displaying output. OpenScript's request and ask commands are useful for getting user input. The request command can also be used for displaying output. Likewise, fields and recordfields are used for both receiving input and displaying output.

Mouse Event Messages

Messages generated from the event of pressing the left mouse button were introduced in Chapter 12 and included buttonDown, buttonUp, and buttonClick. The buttonDown message is generated when the mouse button is pressed, a buttonUp message when it is released, followed by a buttonClick upon the completion of the event.

If the left mouse button is pressed twice, quickly, a sequence of five messages is generated: buttondown, buttonUp, buttonClick, buttonDoubleClick, and buttonUp. If the right button is pressed, a rightButtonDown message is generated followed by a rightButtonUp message. The software tutorial for this chapter contains a page for using the mouse to interact with a button. This will show what messages are generated (see Figure 14.1). The table in Figure 14.2 lists the different types of mouse event messages that ToolBook can handle.

Each of these messages may be trapped with a handler using the to handle *message* statement. The result is that the statements between the to handle *message* statement and the end *message* statement of the handler are executed. Each of the handlers mentioned so far in this chapter has optional parameters available, except the mouseEnter and mouseLeave statements. **Parameters** are variables associated with a message, command, or function and contain additional information. The others have three parameters that contain system data regarding the location of the

Figure 14.1
The software tutorial for
this chapter contains a page
for seeing the messages
generated by using the
mouse to interact with a
button.

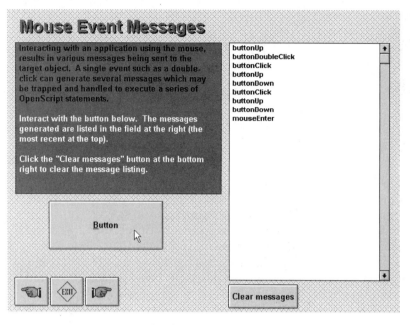

Figure 14.2
A variety of event messages
are generated by the
reader's interaction with
the mouse.

Message	Event trigger
mouseEnter	Mouse pointer enters bounds of object
mouseLeave	Mouse pointer leaves bounds of object
buttonDown	Left mouse button is pressed
buttonUp	Left mouse button is released
buttonClick	Left mouse button has been pressed and released
buttonStillDown	Left mouse button is being held down
buttonDoubleClick	Left mouse button is pressed and released twice quickly
rightButtonDown	Right mouse button is pressed
rightButtonUp	Right mouse button is released
rightButtonDoubleClick	Right mouse button is quickly pressed and released twice

mouse pointer, the state of the Shift key, and the state of the Ctrl key. The format for including the parameters is to list three variable names after the message in the to handle *message* statement:

```
to handle buttonClick mouseLoc, shiftState, ctrlState
```

The first parameter contains the location of the mouse pointer in x,y coordinates as measured from the top left of the page in page units (an inch contains 1440 page units). The second parameter contains the value false if the Shift key is not pressed and true if it is. Likewise, the third parameter contains the value false if the Ctrl key is not pressed and true if it is. If these values are not needed, the parameters need not be included in the to handle statement. If only the mouse location is needed, only the first parameter must be included. If both the mouse location and the status of the Shift key are needed, or just the status of the Shift key is needed, then only the first two parameters need to be present. If the status of the Ctrl key is needed, with or without the other two values, all three parameters must be listed. The values contained by the parameters may be referenced in the OpenScript code. For example:

```
to handle buttonClick loc
     -- loc is the coordinates of the mouse pointer
     if item 2 of loc is < =4800 then     -- item 2 is y coordinate
          request "You clicked in the top half of the page."
     else
          request "You clicked in the bottom half of the page."
     end if
end buttonClick
```

or

```
to handle rightButtonUp mouseLoc, isShift, isCtrl
     if isShift = true and isCtrl = true
          send selectPage
          send cut
     end if
end rightButtonUp
```

The first of the two preceding handlers examines the *y* coordinate of the mouse pointer location, which is contained in the variable (parameter) loc. If the value of the second item of loc is less than or equal to 4800, the handler places a dialog box on the screen. The box informs the user that he or she clicked the top half. Otherwise, if it is greater than 4800, a dialog box pops up to inform the user that he or she clicked the bottom half of the page. The if, else, and end if statements seen in the handlers discussed in this chapter will be explained in detail in Chapter 16.

In the second handler, the page is cut if the user presses the right mouse button while holding down the Shift and Ctrl keys. This eliminates the possibility of the handler's code being executed with an accidental or inadvertent click. Notice that the mouseLoc parameter is not utilized, but it is included because the Shift-state parameter is always the second parameter and the Ctrl-state parameter is always third.

As the user moves the mouse pointer on the screen, it passes over various objects. Messages are sent as the pointer enters or exits the boundaries of an object. A mouseEnter message is sent to an object as the mouse pointer enters its boundaries. A mouseLeave message is generated as the pointer exits its boundaries. Authors use these two messages to display additional information to the user about an object as he or she points to it. For instance, when the mouse enters a button, information about its purpose is displayed in a field by using a mouseEnter handler. When the mouse leaves the boundaries of the button, the text of the field is set to null (or a blank string) by using a mouseLeave handler. The scripts that follow illustrate this.

```
to handle mouseEnter
     put "This button displays the next page." into text of field "info"
end mouseEnter
```

```
to handle mouseLeave
     put "" into text of field "info"
end mouseLeave
```

Bits, Bytes, and Binary Representation of Characters

The computer is an electronic device that operates entirely on electronic signals through circuits that are either on or off. The state of any given circuit may be represented by either the number 1 or 0. A circuit that is off is assigned a value of

Figure 14.3
Computers operate on
electronic signals consist-
ing of high and low
voltages.

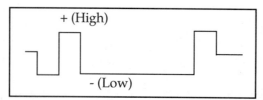

0; a circuit that is on is assigned a value of 1. Likewise, the electronic signals a computer uses to communicate between its different components may be thought of in terms of a series of high and low voltages in a square wave (see Figure 14.3). High voltages are assigned a 1 and low voltages are assigned a 0. A single 1 or 0 of this binary mathematical system is called a **binary digit**, or **bit** for short. A series of 8 bits is referred to as a **byte**. A byte is the basic building block of computer communications. Each character typed in a word-processed letter, for example, is formed by a byte and requires a byte of storage space when the letter is saved. There are 256 possible patterns of bits in a byte. The value of a byte consists of a specific pattern of bits equivalent to a number between 0 and 255. The numeric value of the byte is determined by the value of each bit and its place in the byte. In our decimal mathematical system, the number 345 is equivalent to five 1s, four 10s and three 100s. The places of the eight digits in a binary mathematical system are the number of 1s, 2s, 4s, 8s, 16s, 32s, 64s, and 128s. The byte 01000001 is equivalent to decimal 65. It has one 1, no 2s, no 4s, no 8s, no 16s, no 32s, one 64 and no 128s (see Figure 14.4). In other words, 1 plus 64 equals 65.

Figure 14.4
The byte 01000001 is the
binary equivalent of the
number 65. The character
displayed by 65 is an
uppercase A.

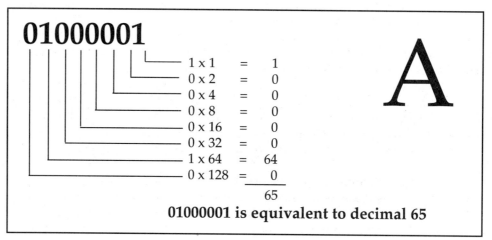

Each character entered from the keyboard, displayed on the monitor, or included in an alphanumeric string is represented by a byte. Since each byte is equivalent to a numeric value, each character has an equivalent numeric value. The numeric value of a character is referred to as its ANSI value (ANSI is an acronym for the American National Standards Institute) or ASCII value (ASCII is an acronym for American Standard Code for Information Interchange). The table in Appendix E lists the characters represented in the Arial font and their numeric equivalents.

OpenScript provides two functions for translating characters to their ANSI numeric equivalents, and vice versa. The ansiToChar statement (see Figure 14.5) converts a number to its character equivalent; the charToAnsi statement (see Figure 14.6) takes a character and returns the decimal equivalent.

How might these functions be used? OpenScript is not case sensitive. An uppercase C and a lowercase c are treated the same when compared. Consider the following script:

```
to handle buttonClick
    if the text of field id 1 = "A" then
        beep 3
```

Figure 14.5
The ansiToChar *function converts an integer between 0 and 255 to its character equivalent.*

The ansiToChar function

Syntax: **ansiToChar(*number*)**

Purpose: Converts a decimal number between 0 and 255 to the character represented by that number. This function might be used with a put statement to place a character into a variable or the text of a field, or with an assignment operator.

Examples: put ansiToChar(65) into the text of field id 3
            --places an A in the text of field id 3

            myVariable = ansiToChar(100)
            -- assigns a lowercase d to the value of the variable named "myVariable"

Figure 14.6
The charToAnsi *function converts a character to its ANSI decimal equivalent.*

The charToAnsi function

Syntax: **charToAnsi(*character*)**

Purpose: Converts a character to its decimal equivalent. This function might be used with a put statement to assign the value of a character to a variable.

Examples: put charToAnsi(A) into xyz
            -- assigns 65 to the value of variable xyz

            put charToAnsi(the first char of text of field id 4) into xyz

---

```
        end if
    end buttonClick
```

This handler looks at the text of a field and, if it is the letter A, then the computer beeps three times. Since OpenScript is not case sensitive, it does not distinguish between an uppercase A and a lowercase a and the computer will beep if the text of field id 1 is either A or a. But suppose an author only wants the computer to beep if it is an uppercase A and disregard it if it is a lowercase a. An uppercase A has an ANSI value of 65 while a lowercase a has an ANSI value of 97. The above handler can be rewritten to check for the numeric value of the character of text of field id 1.

```
    to handle buttonClick
        if charToAnsi(text of field id 1) = 65 then
            beep 3
        end if
    end buttonClick
```

Now the computer will only beep if the text of field id 1 is equal to an uppercase A. Another use of the ansiToChar function is to place special characters and nonprinting characters into a text string. The ANSI value of the copyright symbol, ©, is 169. Using the ansiToChar function, the copyright symbol may be placed in the text of a field or assigned to a variable.

```
    put ansiToChar(169) into the text of field id 4

    copyright = ansiToChar(169)   --copyright is a variable
```

Tabs can be placed in a field's text as well. The ANSI value of a tab is 9.

```
to handle buttonClick
     put "Fred" into text of field id 3
     put ansiToChar(9) after text of field id 3
     put "Flintstone" after text of field id 3
end buttonClick
```

The preceding handler places Fred   Flintstone into the text of field id 3. The first name and the last name are separated by a tab character.

Handling Keyboard Input

Along with the mouse, the keyboard is an extremely important input device. Information sent from the keyboard should be able to trigger an action in the same way that a press of the left mouse button does. Pressing the F2 function key in a courseware application might cause a pop-up dialog to appear for a student to enter a comment or suggestion to the designer or instructor. Keyboard messages are sent to the object that has the focus or to the page if no object has the focus. Keyboard messages are most often handled in a field or recordfield script but can be placed in a page, background, or book script for more global uses. The handler to trap for the F2 key in the scenario involving the pop-up dialog would probably be best placed in the book script, so that this functionality would be available from any page in the book.

Just as there were messages associated with mouse events, there are also messages associated with keyboard events. And like the mouse messages, keyboard messages may be trapped by a handler to trigger some action. Pressing a key on the keyboard generates a sequence of messages: keyDown, keyChar, and keyUp. Each of these messages also generates parameters that designate the key that was pressed, the state of the Shift key, and the state of the Ctrl key. As with button messages, there

Figure 14.7
The software tutorial for this chapter contains a page that shows the messages generated when the user interacts with a field by using the keyboard.

Keyboard Event Messages

Interacting with an application using the keyboard also results in various messages being sent to the target object.

Enter text in the field below. As you do so you will see the keyboard messages generated shown at the right. Keyboard messages are in the form:
message key shiftState ctrlState
where key is the keyboard key pressed, shiftState and ctrlState are with "true" or "false" depending on whether the shift and control keys are up (false) or down (true)

Click the "Clear messages" button at the bottom right to clear the message listing.

```
keyup 67 false false
keychar 99 false false
keydown 67 false false
keyup 66 false false
keychar 98 false false
keydown 66 false false
keyup 65 false false
keychar 97 false false
keydown 65 false false
```

abc

Clear messages and text

is a page in the accompanying software for this chapter that interactively demonstrates the messages generated from keyboard input (see Figure 14.7).

The keyDown message is generated as a key is pressed. Its **key parameter** relates to a keyboard constant as Figure 14.8 shows. The constant is not necessarily the same as the ANSI value of the key. An uppercase **A** and an lowercase **a** entered from the keyboard both assign a value of 65 to the **key** parameter. The difference would be in the value of the second parameter, that of the Shift key's state. If the value is an uppercase **A**, the shiftState parameter would equal **true**. If the value is a lowercase **a**, the shiftState parameter would be equal to **false**. Either the key value or the equivalent key constant may be used in referring to the value of the key parameter in an OpenScript command. For example, the statement

```
if key = 65 then
```

and the statement

```
if key = keyA then
```

are the same.

The **keyDown** message is followed by a **keyChar** message if the key pressed

Key constant	Value	Key constant	Value	Key constant	Value
keyLeftButton	1	keyE	69	keySeparator	108
keyRightButton	2	keyF	70	keySubtract	109
keyBack	8	keyG	71	keyDecimal	110
keyTab	9	keyH	72	keyDivide	111
keyClear	12	keyI	73	keyF1	112
keyEnter	13	keyJ	74	keyF2	113
keyShift	16	keyK	75	keyF3	114
keyControl	17	keyL	76	keyF4	115
KeyMenu	18	keyM	77	keyF5	116
keyEscape	27	keyN	78	keyF6	117
keySpace	32	keyO	79	keyF7	118
keyEnd	35	keyP	80	keyF8	119
keyHome	36	keyQ	81	keyF9	120
keyLeftArrow	37	keyR	82	keyF10	121
keyUpArrow	38	keyS	83	keyF11	122
keyRightArrow	39	keyT	84	keyF12	123
keyDownArrow	40	keyU	85	keyF13	124
keyPrint	42	keyV	86	keyF14	125
keyInsert	45	keyW	87	keyF15	126
keyDelete	46	keyX	88	keyF16	127
key0	48	keyY	89	keyNumLock	144
key1	49	keyZ	90	keyScrollLock	145
key2	50	keyNumpad0	96	keyQuote	186
key3	51	keyNumpad1	97	keyEqual	187
key4	52	keyNumpad2	98	keyComma	188
key5	53	keyNumpad3	99	keyDash	189
key6	54	keyNumpad4	100	keyPoint	190
key7	55	keyNumpad5	101	keySlash	191
key8	56	keyNumpad6	102	keyBackQuote	192
key9	57	keyNumpad7	103	keyLeftBracket	219
keyA	65	keyNumpad8	104	keyBackSlash	220
keyB	66	keyNumpad9	105	keyRightBracket	221
keyC	67	keyMultiply	106	keySemicolon	222
keyD	68	keyAdd	107		

Figure 14.8
This table lists the key constants and key values used by the keyDown *and* keyUp *messages.*

generates a displayable character and is not a keyboard shortcut for a menu item (such a shortcut is called an accelerator key). Ctrl-N, for example, is the keyboard shortcut for creating a new page. The keyChar message has the same parameters as the keyDown message, except that the key parameter relates to the ANSI value of the character generated. Entering an a (lowercase) generates the message keyChar 97 false false while pressing the Shift key with the A key (an uppercase A) generates the message keyChar 65 true false. The key value for the keyChar message can be looked up in the ANSI chart of Appendix E.

A popular use of the keyChar message is to alter the effect of the Enter or Tab keys. In designing a database application, there may be several single-line fields. Suppose the desire is to move the cursor from field id 1 to field id 2 when the reader presses the Enter key while the cursor is in field id 1. The following handler is placed in the script of field id 1:

```
to handle keyChar key
    if key = 13 then
        set the focus to field id 2
    else
        forward
    end if
end keyChar
```

In the preceding script, if the reader presses the Enter key, the focus is moved to field id 2. Otherwise, the keyChar message is forwarded up the object hierarchy. The forwarding of keyboard messages is often essential for proper handling. For instance, failing to forward the message if the key is not the value being trapped results in all other keys being ignored. This concept, however, leads to another use of handling the keyChar message. The keyChar message may be used to restrict only certain characters from being typed into a field. The following handler placed in a field's script allows only numeric data to be entered into its text from the keyboard.

```
to handle keyChar key, shiftState, ctrlState
    if key >= 48 and key <= 57  and shiftState = false then
        forward
    else
        beep 1
    end if
end keyChar
```

If the user types a numeric character, the preceding handler allows it to be placed in the field's script by virtue of the message being forwarded. If the user presses any other character, the computer beeps. (This is demonstrated in the accompanying software tutorial for this chapter, on the page titled "Trapping Keyboard Messages—Examples.")

When a key is released, a keyUp message is generated. The KeyUp message is identical to the keyDown message. The keyUp message uses the same key parameter as the keyDown message and also translates the Shift and Ctrl key states in the second and third parameters, respectively.

```
to handle keyUp a, b, c
    -- a is the key
    -- b is the shift key state
    -- c is the control key state
    if a = keyPrint then  -- Print Screen key was pressed
```

```
            send printReport
        end if
    end keyUp
```

Note that the names assigned to the parameters of a to handle *message* statement are arbitrary. For keyboard messages, the terms key, shiftState, and ctrlState do not have to be used. In the preceding script, the names a, b, and c were used instead. Parameter names follow the same rules as variable names.

The **enter** and **leave** Messages

There are numerous other events and messages besides those that are generated by the user's interaction with the mouse and keyboard. There are a variety of **enter** and **leave** messages similar to the mouseEnter and mouseLeave. When a book is opened, an enterBook message is sent to the book script. This message might be handled to perform some opening action. A popular use of enterBook is to assign values to global (system) variables. For instance:

```
    to handle enterBook
        system bookmark, enterTime
        put 1 into bookmark
        put the sysTime into enterTime
    end enterBook
```

Similarly, when the book is exited, a leaveBook message is sent to the book script. A leaveBook handler might clear data entered by the user during this session, so that a particular field is empty for the next session or user. It might also write data to an external text file. The script that follows empties the text of particular field when the book is exited.

```
    to handle leaveBook
        put "" into text of field "score" of page id 12
    end leaveBook
```

The enterPage and leavePage messages are sent to a page when it is opened and exited, respectively. These messages are often handled to reset an animation, clear a field, or hide an object. Hiding a pop-up field upon exiting a page ensures that the page will be ready for the next session or user, with the pop-up field hidden. Such a script might look like this:

```
    to handle leavePage
        hide field "moreInfo"
    end leavePage
```

Likewise, an enterBackground message is sent when a user navigates to a page with a background different from the current background. A leaveBackground message is generated when the user leaves the current background for a new one.

The enterField and leaveField messages are sent to a field when it receives or loses the focus, respectively. These messages may be handled to change the color of the fields, so that the field with the focus is distinguished from the others by color. The following handlers might appear in the scripts of each editable field of a page:

```
    to handle enterField
```

```
        set the fillColor of self to yellow
    end enterField

    to handle leaveField
        set the fillColor of self to white
    end leaveField
```

When the field receives the focus, fillColor is set to yellow. The fillColor is reset to white when the field loses the focus. The enterRecordField, enterButton, enterComboBox, leaveRecordField, leaveButton, and leaveComboBox messages work the same way as recordfields, buttons, or combo boxes receive or lose the focus. There are other less common enter and leave messages. These are listed in the table in Figure 14.9. For specific information about their use, the messages may be looked up in ToolBook's on-line help.

Figure 14.9
There are several enter *and* leave *type messages that are generated by ToolBook. Many are infrequently used and not addressed further in this book. For further information, consult Tool-Book's on-line OpenScript help.*

enter and **leave** Messages		
activateInstance	enterMenu	leaveComboBox
enterApplication	enterPage	leaveDrop
enterBackground	enterRecordField	leaveDropDown
enterBook	enterSystem	leaveField
enterButton	enterWindow	leavePage
enterComboBox	leaveApplication	leaveSystem
enterDrop	leaveBackground	leaveWindow
enterDropDown	leaveBook	
enterField	leaveButton	

The **idle** Message

Even when the user is not interacting with the ToolBook book, messages are being generated. ToolBook sends an idle message when there is no other activity. An **idle message** is first sent to the page script and are then forwarded to the background and book scripts if not handled. By handling the idle message, an author can script some action to occur when the application is sitting idle, with no interaction from the user. Often idle messages are handled to perform some animation. In the following script, a rectangle changes colors when nothing else is occurring.

```
to handle idle
    put item 1 of the fillColor of rectangle "chameleon" into x
    put x + 3 into x  -- increments x by 3
    if x > 360 then
        put 0 into x
    end if
    set item 1 of fillColor of rectangle "chameleon" to x
end idle
```

Also idle messages are used to control timers and display clocks. An idle message can calculate if the computer has been inactive for a specified length of time and then perform some action. This is how most screen savers work. The following idle message displays the current system time in the text of a field.

```
    to handle idle
```

```
    set sysTimeFormat to "hh:min:sec AMPM"
    -- time format example: 04:23:55 PM
    put the sysTime into text of field "clock"
end idle
```

(Both of these scripts are demonstrated on the "The Idle Message" page of the software tutorial for this chapter.)

Using the **notifyBefore** and **notifyAfter** Handlers

As mentioned earlier, idle messages are sent to the page as a target. Looking at the object hierarchy of Figure 12.5, it is apparent that an object on the page could not handle an idle message because the object would never receive the message. Beginning with version 3.0, ToolBook includes notifyBefore and notifyAfter handler structures. These are alternatives to the to handle structure discussed thus far. The notifyBefore and notifyAfter handlers can be placed in an object's script to receive a message sent to the page (or background, if the object resides on the background). The **notifyBefore handler** executes before the message is sent to the page; the **notifyAfter handler** executes after the message is sent to the page. The syntax for using notifyBefore and notifyAfter is shown in Figures 14.10 and 14.11.

Reconsider the clock example in the preceding section. A notifyBefore handler could be placed in the script of the field displaying the time:

```
notifyBefore idle
    set sysTimeFormat to "hh:min:sec AMPM"
    put the sysTime into the text of self
end idle
```

The primary advantage to using notifyBefore over handling the idle message in the page script, as discussed earlier, is that the clock field becomes a self-contained object. It may be copied and pasted into another application without having to re-enter the

---

The **notifyBefore** handler structure
Syntax: **notifyBefore *message***
Purpose: Allows a page object to intercept a message targeted for the page before it is sent to the page. An end message must terminate the handler.

Example: notifyBefore enterPage
          set the text of self to null
      end enterPage

Figure 14.10
The notifyBefore *handler structure allows messages targeted for the page to be received by objects on the page before the message has been sent to the page.*

The **notifyAfter** handler structure
Syntax: **notifyAfter *message***
Purpose: Allows a page object to intercept a message targeted for the page after it is sent to the page. An end message must terminate the handler.

Example: notifyAfter idle
          set the text of self to the sysTime
      end idle

Figure 14.11
The notifyAfter *handler structure allows messages targeted for the page to be received by objects on the page after the message has been sent to the page.*

script or copy and paste the script as well. The field's script is copied and pasted with the object itself.

Consider a background button that navigates to the previous page in a database application. You want to hide the button on the first page. But the pages may be shuffled as records are added or deleted, or as the database is sorted. The result is that the page of the book that is presented first changes. Therefore, it is not a solution to hide the background button with another object, such as a rectangle on the page layer of the first page. To solve this problem, a notifyBefore handler can be added to the script of the "Previous" button to hide the button itself on the first page.

```
to handle enterPage
    if pageNumber of this page = 1 then
        hide self
    else
        show self
    end if
end enterPage
```

The preceding handler examines the page number of the page when it is opened. If it is the first page of the book, it hides the button. If it is not the first page, it makes sure that the button is visible. A similar script could be written to instruct a "Next" button to hide itself on the last page of a book.

Getting Input with Ask and Request Dialogs

Figure 14.12
This request dialog box contains a prompt string and up to three response buttons for user input.

Figure 14.13
This ask dialog box contains a prompt string and a field for receiving user input.

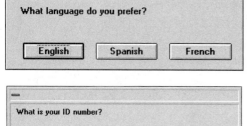

A popular device for interacting with a user is the dialog box. OpenScript provides two commands for creating simple dialogs. The **request command** displays a dialog with a prompt string and up to three response buttons (see Figure 14.12). The **ask command** displays a dialog with a prompt string and a single-line field for entering textual information (see Figure 14.13).

The request command is used to gather input from the user. The syntax of the request command is:

request "*prompt string*" with "*caption1*" or "*caption2*" or "*caption3*"

where the prompt string is the textual information presented to the user in the dialog box. The caption1, caption2, and caption3 strings are the captions that appear on the three buttons in the dialog box, as well as the value placed in the variable named it when the user clicks the button. For instance, the statement

request "What language do you prefer?" with "English" or "Spanish" or "French"

produces the dialog box displayed in Figure 14.12. If the user clicks the "English" button, English is automatically placed in a variable named it. If the user clicks the button labeled "Spanish," the value of variable it becomes Spanish, and if he or she clicks "French," the value French is placed in the variable it. The value of the variable it may then be assigned to another variable. Several command use it to temporarily hold a value; thus, its value is subject to change. (The variable it is a reserved, or special, variable. It should not be declared.) Chapter 16 will examine performing different tasks based on certain conditions—that is, tasks involving branching. The request statement is often used in conjunction with such branching commands. For example, text in the book might be displayed in English, Spanish, or French, depending on the user's selection in the request dialog.

```
to handle enterpage
    system STRING gLanguage
    request "What language do you prefer?" with "English" or "Spanish" or
"French"
    put it into gLanguage
    if gLanguage = "English" then
        hide field "Spanish"
        hide field "French"
        show field "English"
    end if
    if gLanguage = "Spanish" then
        hide field "English"
        hide field "French"
        show field "Spanish"
    end if
    if gLanguage = "French" then
        hide field "English"
        hide field "Spanish"
        show field "French"
    end if
end enterpage
```

The request statement may be used to produce a dialog with two button choices, by eliminating the or "caption3" section. For example, the statement

request "What is your sex?" with "Male" or "Female"

produces the dialog shown in Figure 14.14. In Figures 14.14 and 14.12, notice that the leftmost button has a darker border. This is the default button. The user may press the Enter key to select that option. He or she may use the Tab key to move the default selection to one of the

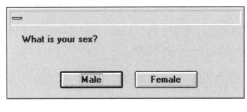

Figure 14.14
A request dialog may be limited to two response buttons, if desired.

other buttons and then press Enter to select the desired choice instead of using the mouse. The first choice is always the default option to start.

Request dialogs can also be used to display information to the user. In this case only one button is required (since the user isn't making a choice). This is accomplished by eliminating the or "caption2" section as well as the or "caption3" section from the request statement. The statement

request "Welcome!" with "Thank you"

displays the dialog pictured in Figure 14.15. The next request statement

Figure 14.15
Request dialogs can also have just one response button.

request "This application developed with ToolBook."

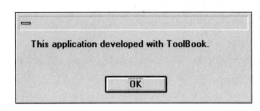

Figure 14.16
If no response buttons are specified in the **request** *statement, ToolBook adds an "OK" button by default.*

has an "OK" button added by default, as pictured in Figure 14.16.

The execution of the OpenScript statements in the handler subsequent to the **request** statement is delayed until the user responds to the dialog. A **request** statement can be used, therefore, to pause a script until the user clicks the "OK" button or presses the Enter key. For instance, the statement

request "Click the 'OK' button to continue..."

pauses the script at the point of the **request** statement until the reader responds to the dialog.

The **ask** statement is similar to the **request** statement. The difference is that, rather than allowing the user to choose from three options, the **ask** dialog provides a field for user input. Default text may be specified, which the user may accept or change. The syntax for the **ask** statement is:

ask "*prompt string*" with "*default response*"

where **prompt string** is the message displayed to the user in the dialog and **default response** is the default text displayed in the response field. For instance, the statement

ask "What is your ID number?" with "123-45-6789"

displays the ask dialog shown in Figure 14.13. The user may accept the ID number ·provided by clicking the "OK" button or edit the response, in the field, and then click the "OK" button. The string in the response field is assigned to the variable named it. If the user clicks the "Cancel" button (or presses the Esc key, or closes the dialog box from the Control menu, in its upper left corner), the variable it is set to null (a blank string).

Variables and functions may be used in place of the default response string. For instance, the statement

ask "What is the date?" with sysDate

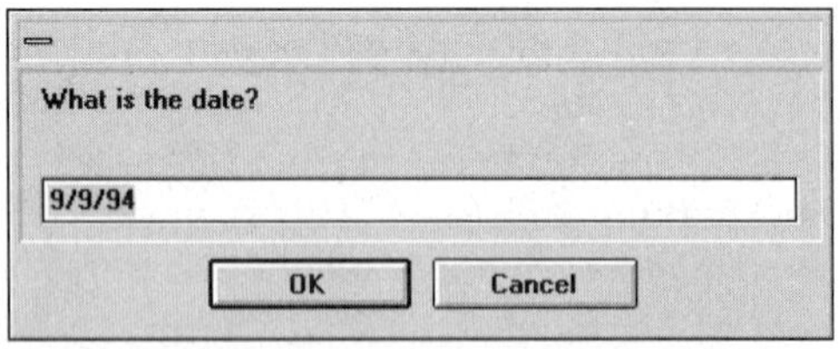

Figure 14.17
The default response in the ask dialog may be generated by a variable, such as the current system date of the computer.

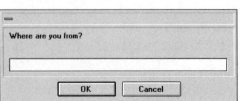

produces the dialog shown in Figure 14.17. The **sysDate** variable is a Tool-Book-reserved system variable that contains the current date as stored by the computer. The default response string is optional and, if not included, produces an ask dialog box without a default response. For instance:

ask "Where are you from?"

Figure 14.18
If a default response is not provided, the response field is blank.

displays the dialog shown in Figure 14.18. As with the **request** statement, the handler is paused until the user responds to the ask dialog. After the user responds, the handler continues executing, proceeding with the statement following the **ask** statement.

Summary Questions

Complete the following statements by filling in the blanks.

1. When the right mouse button is pressed, it generates a _____ message.
2. An eight-digit binary number is referred to as a _____ .
3. The binary number represented by 01010101 is equivalent to the decimal value
   _____ .
4. Variables and values passed with a message are called _____ .
5. The _____ function returns the numeric equivalent of a character.
6. When nothing is happening, ToolBook sends an _____ message to the current page.
7. The _____ handler structure can be used to allow a button to receive an **enterPage** message before it is sent to the page.
8. The _____ command displays a dialog box with a field for user input.
9. The _____ command displays a dialog box with up to three captioned buttons for user input.
10. The value entered in an ask dialog by the user or clicked in a request dialog is assigned to a variable named _____ .

Identify the statement that produces the dialog box pictured.

11.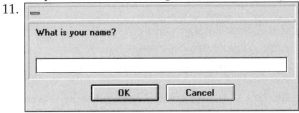

    a. request "What is your name?"
    b. request "What is your name?" with "OK" or "Cancel"
    c. ask "What is your name?"
    d. ask "What is your name?" with "OK" or "Cancel"

12.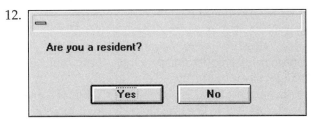

    a. request "Are you a resident?" with "Yes" and "No"
    b. ask "Are you a resident?"
    c. request "Are you a resident?" with "No" or "Yes"
    d. request "Are you a resident?" with "Yes" or "No"

13.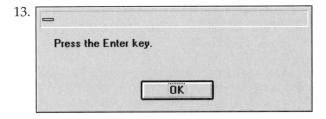

    a. ask "Press the Enter key."
    b. request "Press the Enter key."
    c. request "Press the Enter key." with "True" or "False"
    d. ask "Press the Enter key." with "OK"

14.

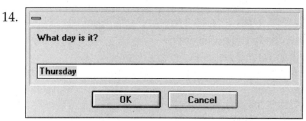

    a. ask "What day is it?" with "Thursday" and "OK" or "Cancel"
    b. ask "Enter the day of the week:" with "Thursday"
    c. request "What day is it?"
    d. ask "What day is it?" with "Thursday"

15.

    a. ask "Choose a color:" with "Red" or "White" or "Blue"
    b. request "Choose a color:" with "Red" or "White" or "Blue"
    c. request "Choose a color:" with "Blue" or "White" or "Red"
    d. request "Choose a color:" with "Red" and "White" and "Blue"

Each of the next five statements produces a compiler error. Identify the problem.
16. to handle buttonClick loc shiftState ctrlState
17. to notifyBefore enterPage
18. request "What is 4 x 5?" with "15" or "20" or "25" or "45"
19. ask 'What is the your name?'
20. request "What's the capitol of Arizona?" with "Ajo" and "Phoenix" and "Tucson"

Hands-On Projects

A. Examine the tutorial that accompanies this chapter. Open the "Table of Contents" book by double-clicking its icon in the "Developing with ToolBook" group window in the Windows Program Manager. Inside the "Table of Contents," click the book representing Chapter 14. The tutorial provides interactive instruction regarding messages sent when interacting with the mouse or keyboard. It also includes an interactive lesson on binary numbers and what characters they represent. Experiment with the controls on these pages to get a better understanding of the material presented in this chapter.

B. Create a book with one page that gathers information from the user by using request or ask dialog boxes and displays the information in the fields as illustrated in Figure 14.19.
      salutation (Mr., Ms., or Dr.?)
      last name
      first name
      address

city
state
zip code
phone number
sex
own home or rent?

Activate the fields so that they can only be edited through the dialog boxes. Attach a handler to each field to display the appropriate dialog box when clicked. Include a button that prompts for input for all the fields.

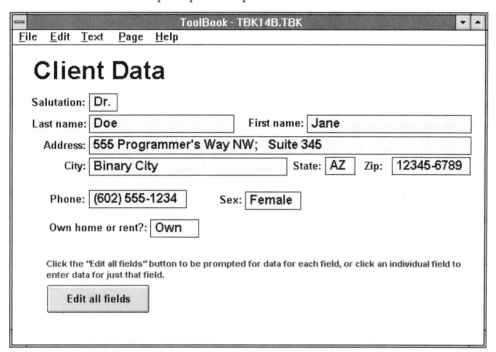

Figure 14.19
Request and ask dialogs
may be used to prompt the
user for information to
complete a data entry
screen.

C. Create a book with one 3- by 2-inch page that has five fields, each large enough to display one character (consider the width of characters—a W is the widest). The first field is editable, the other four are not. On idle, the text of the first field should be examined and the next four characters in the ANSI table displayed in the other four fields. The finished book should look like Figure 14.20.

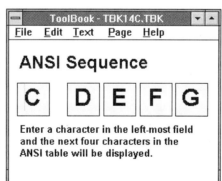

Figure 14.20
In Hands-On Project C, an
application is created in
which the user enters a
character and is shown the
next four ANSI characters.

Chapter 15

Performing Mathematical Calculations

As learned in the previous chapter, computers operate on all data in terms of binary numeric data. The capital "A "seen on the monitor by the user, is seen by the computer as a byte with the binary value of 01000001. It should come as no surprise, then, that computers excel at mathematical operations. In reality, all a computer can do internally is mathematical operations and comparisons. OpenScript provides operators, commands, and functions for performing simple and complex mathematical functions. Math is required for many programming operations. Performing math with OpenScript is very similar to using a scientific calculator.

OpenScript operators for mathematical formulas include +, −, /, *, ^, div, and mod. These operators can be mixed in complex formulas, but there is an order of precedence in which the operations are carried out. The use of parentheses can override the default order in which a formula is solved. The increment and decrement commands can also be used to add or subtract a variable or other container.

There are numerous functions built into OpenScript for returning arithmetic, trigonometric, logarithmic, financial, and statistical values. These include functions for finding the square root of a number, rounding a number, truncating a decimal, finding the average value of a list of numbers, determining the smallest value in a list of numbers, finding the tangent of an angle, and calculating the periodic payment for a loan.

Data output as part of an algorithm may need to be formatted so that it is accurate, visually appealing, and readable. The number 123456789 is probably easier to read when displayed as 123,456,789. It might be more pertinent to display it as 123,456,789.00 in a financial application, or as 1.234E8 in a scientific application. OpenScript's format command and the sysNumberFormat, sysDateFormat, and sysTimeFormat properties may be used to format numeric, date, and time data as it is displayed in a field or recordfield.

Arithmetic Expressions
Adding and Subtracting
In the discussion on assigning values to variables, in Chapter 13, it was seen that the value could be composed of a mathematical expression. When encountered in a statement, ToolBook always evaluates the expression immediately. For example, in an assignment statement, the expression is evaluated and the result is assigned to the specified variable or container. The expression can include constant values, other variables, or a combination of constants and variables.

```
hours = 30 + 5
hours = regHours + overtimeHours
hours = regHours + 5
```

In the first statement, the value 35 would be placed in the variable named hours. In the second statement, the value of the variable regHours and the value of the variable overtimeHours are added together and the result is assigned to the variable hours. If, for instance, the value of regHours were 40 and the value of overtimeHours was 13, hours would contain 53. In the third statement, the sum of the value of variable regHours and 5 are assigned to the variable hours.

As one would expect, the plus sign, +, is used to add two or more values together. The plus sign is referred to as an operator. The expression may consist of many values:

```
totalPay = regPay + overtimePay + commissionPay + bonusPay
```

Subtraction is performed in an expression by using the minus sign.

```
abc = 100 – 25
netPay = grossPay – deductions
put balanceDue – amountPaid into text of field id 3
myVariable = 2000 – 100 – 700 – 300
```

In the first statement, 75 is placed in the variable abc. The value of variable grossPay less the value of variable deductions is assigned to the variable netPay in the second statement. If, for instance, the value of grossPay were 520.75 and the value of deductions were 205.50, netPay would contain a value of 315.25. In the third statement, the value of variable balanceDue less the value of variable amountPaid is placed in the text of field id 3. In the fourth statement, myVariable is assigned the value 900.

Multiplication and Division

Multiplication operations are performed in an expression by using an asterisk, *, operator between the values being multiplied.

```
i = 5 * 6
totalCost = productCost * units
put productCost * units into totalCost
put 10 * 3.75 into text of field "velocity"
```

In the first statement, the variable i is assigned the value 30. The second and third statement produce the same result, assigning the product of variables productCost and units to the variable totalCost. If, for instance, the value of productCost were 5.25 and the value of units were 3, totalCost would contain the value 15.75. In the fourth statement, 37.5 would be placed in the field named velocity.

The division operator is the slash, /. (Be careful to not use the backslash, \.) The division operator is placed between the dividend and the divisor.

```
j = 20 / 5
put 300 / 6 into the text of field id 16
put casePrice / units into unitPrice
unitPrice = casePrice / units
```

The value 4 is assigned to j when the first statement is executed. The value 50 is placed in field id 16 in the second statement. The third and fourth statements perform the same function, assigning the quotient of the value of variable casePrice divided by the value of variable units to the value of variable unitPrice. For example, if casePrice were 30 and units were 24, the value 1.25 would be assigned to the variable unitPrice.

Integer and Remainder Division

Division expressions evaluate to a decimal value. The expression 18 / 10 evaluates to 1.8. But what if one only wants the integer of the division and decides to drop any remainder? Such an operation is performed using the integer division operator, div, between the dividend and the divisor instead of the division operator, /. The result of a div operation is always an integer. For instance:

```
abc = 25 div 3
put 45 div 12 into y
put pointsScored div 25 into bonusPoints
put x div y into text of field id 5
```

In the first statement, the variable abc is assigned the value 8 (3 goes into 25 eight times with a remainder of 1). In the second statement, y is equal to 3 (45 divided by 12 is 3 with a remainder of 9). If pointsScored is equivalent to 140, then bonusPoints would be assigned the value 5 in the third statement (25 goes into 140 five times with a remainder of 15).

A popular use of integer division is to ensure that a number input by a user is an integer. By dividing the value input by 1 in an integer division operation, the program drops any decimal portion of the original number:

```
ask "Enter an integer:"
put it div 1 into x
```

If the user enters 4.6 as an integer value in the preceding ask statement, the second statement drops the decimal portion of the value and assigns 4 as the value of variable x.

Occasionally, an algorithm may require knowing the remainder of an integer division. The modulo operation is performed in OpenScript by using the mod operator. The mod operator returns the remainder of an integer division operation. Consider the following:

```
x = 15 mod 6
put 7 mod 2 into y
z = 6 mod 3
```

In the first statement, y is assigned the value 3 (6 goes into 15 twice, with a remainder of 3). In the second statement, a 1 is placed into y because 2 divides into 7 three times with a remainder of 1. In the third statement, the value of z becomes 0 (there is no remainder when 6 is divided by 3).

The mod operator might be used to evaluate whether a particular number is odd or even by using a divisor of 2. If the remainder is 1, the dividend is odd. If the remainder is 0, the dividend is even. The code for such a task might look like this:

```
to handle buttonClick
    ask "Enter an integer:"
    x = it mod 2
    if x = 1 then
        request "The number you entered was odd." with "OK"
    else
        request "The number you entered was even." with "OK"
    end if
end buttonClick
```

In the preceding handler, the reader is asked to input an integer in a dialog box. The value entered is assigned to the variable it by the system. It is then divided by 2, with the remainder of the integer division being assigned to the variable x. If the value of x is 1, a dialog box is displayed to inform the reader that the number he or she entered was odd. Otherwise (if the value is 0), a dialog is displayed stating the number entered was even.

Exponentiation

The last arithmetic operator is the caret, ^. The ^ (created by pressing Shift–6) is used to exponentiate a number to a certain power. It is placed between the number being raised and the exponent:

```
x = 5 ^ 2
put 2 ^ 3 into the text of field id 4
```

In the first example, x is assigned the value 25 (5 raised to the power of 2). In the second statement, 8 is placed in the text of field id 4 (2 raised to the power of 3 [equivalent to 2 * 2 * 2]). By raising a number to a power of one–half (0.5), the square root of the number is returned. The statement

```
y = 16 ^ .5
```

puts 4 into y (4 is the square root of 16).

The table in Figure 15.1 summarizes the seven different arithmetic operators available in OpenScript expressions.

Figure 15.1
There are seven basic mathematical operations performed by ToolBook.

OpenScript Operators

Operation	Operator	Example	Value of x
Addition	+	x = 5 + 3	8
Subtraction	–	x = 5 - 3	2
Multiplication	*	x = 5 * 3	15
Division	/	x = 5 / 3	1.66667
Integer division	div	x = 5 div 3	1
Remainder division	mod	x = 5 mod 3	2
Exponentiation	^	x = 5 ^ 3	125

Mixed Expressions and the Order of Precedence

Complex expressions of multiple operations may be evaluated in an OpenScript statement and the resulting value assigned to a container:

```
x = 5 * 7 + 3 / 2 – 2 ^ 2
pay = payrate * regHours + payrate * 1.5 * overtimeHours – deductions
put 2 ^ 7 – 3 ^ 3 * 2 into the text of field "result"
```

In writing complex expressions, the most important aspect to take into account is the order of precedence in which mathematical operations are performed in an expression. In evaluating an expression, ToolBook first looks for any exponentiation operations and performs those in order from right to left. Next it looks for any multiplication, division, integer division, or modulo (*, /, div, mod) operations and

---

Order of Precedence for Basic Mathematical Operators

Order	Operator	Comments
1	( )	Operations inside parentheses performed inside out
2	^	Exponentiation performed right to left
3	*, /, div, mod	Performed left to right
4	+, −	Performed left to right

---

performs these in order from left to right. Finally, any addition or subtraction operations are performed in order from left to right. Note that all operations are performed from the left to the right except for exponential operations, which are performed from right to left. The table in Figure 15.2 summarizes the order of precedence for mathematical operations. For example, when the statement

$$x = 3 + 4 * 2$$

is executed, x is assigned the value of 11. The multiplication operation is performed before the addition operation so, x is equal to 3 plus 8, which equals 11. Likewise, the statement

$$y = 5 * 2 \wedge 2 + 12 / 2 \wedge 2 - 13 \bmod 7$$

places 17 in the variable y. The exponentiation is performed first from the right to the left; then the multiplication, division, and modulo operations from the left to the right; and finally the addition and subtraction operations are performed from left to right. Figure 15.3 shows step-by-step how ToolBook calculates the expression in the preceding statement.

Figure 15.2
Expressions are evaluated in a prescribed format. Expressions enclosed within parentheses are evaluated first, starting with the innermost set and working out. Exponential operations are performed before multiplication and division operations, which are performed before addition and subtraction operations.

The Evaluation of an Expression

Statement: $y = 5 * 2 \wedge 2 + 12 / 2 \wedge 2 - 13 \bmod 7$

Step 1:   There are no parentheses in the expression. The rightmost exponentiation is performed first:
            $y = 5 * 2 \wedge 2 + 12 / \mathbf{2 \wedge 2} - 13 \bmod 7$

Step 2:   Next exponentiation is performed:
            $y = 5 * \mathbf{2 \wedge 2} + 12 / 4 - 13 \bmod 7$

Step 3:   Leftmost multiplication, division, integer division, or remainder division operation is performed:
            $y = \mathbf{5 * 4} + 12 / 4 - 13 \bmod 7$

Step 4:   Leftmost multiplication, division, integer division, or remainder division operation is performed:
            $y = 20 + \mathbf{12 / 4} - 13 \bmod 7$

Step 5:   Leftmost multiplication, division, integer division, or remainder division operation is performed:
            $y = 20 + 3 - \mathbf{13 \bmod 7}$

Step 6:   Leftmost addition or subtraction operation is performed:
            $y = \mathbf{20 + 3} - 6$

Step 7:   Leftmost addition or subtraction operation is performed:
            $y = \mathbf{23 - 6}$

Step 8:   The expression is complete and the value is assigned to the variable:
            $\mathbf{y = 17}$

Figure 15.3
ToolBook evaluates a mathematical expression in a prescribed and consistent method.

The order of precedence may be overridden with the use of parentheses. Operations within pairs of parentheses are performed before any other operations. Operations within the parentheses are performed using the standard order of precedence. Consider the preceding expression rewritten with a set of parentheses:

y = (5 * 2 ^ 2 + 12) / 2 ^ 2 − 13 mod 7

Instead of placing the value of 17 into y, the value of 250 is assigned to y. The expression inside the parentheses is evaluated first. It is quite obvious that a misplaced parenthesis can make a great difference in the evaluation of an expression. Care must be taken by the programmer in writing complex equations to ensure that the desired results are achieved.

If an expression contains a pair of parentheses within a pair of parentheses, the operations are performed from the inner pair of parentheses out to the outside pair, with the operation within each pair following the order of precedence. The statement

x = (4 + ((3 + 1) * 2)) ^ 2

assigns the value 144 to variable x. The evaluation begins with the innermost set of parentheses, that surrounding 3 + 1. The statement, therefore, is equivalent to x = (4 + (4 * 2)) ^ 2 . The operation within the next inner set of parentheses is 4 * 2, which evaluates to 8. At this stage, the statement is equivalent to x = (4 + 8) ^ 2 . The operation within the remaining pair of parentheses is performed, namely adding 4 and 8, which is equivalent to 12. The statement then is equivalent to x = 12 ^ 2, or 144. The value 144 is placed in x.

Built-In Numeric Functions

Commands perform some action, but **functions** return some value after performing a calculation. Functions appear within a statement, such as a put statement, and perform their task when the statement is executed. Functions generally contain, following the function's name, one or more arguments within a set of parentheses. For instance, in the statement

put sqrt(25) into x

the function is sqrt( ), which returns the square root of the argument, 25. The square root of 25 is 5, so the value 5 is placed in variable x. The **argument** or arguments are the value or values acted upon by the function. Arguments may be variable references as well as constant values. For instance:

y = 25
put sqrt(y) into x

performs the same action as the previous statement, putting 5 into the variable x. Some functions require multiple arguments. The hypotenuse( ) function finds the length of the hypotenuse of a right triangle when given the length of the other two sides. It takes two arguments, the lengths of the two sides:

put 6 into a
put 8 into b
put hypotenuse(a,b) into c

A right triangle with the two shorter sides measuring 6 units and 8 units would have a hypotenuse of 10 units (see Figure 15.4). The preceding code segment puts 10 into the variable c.

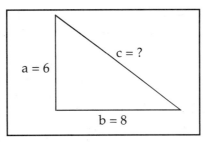

Figure 15.4
The length of the hypotenuse of a right triangle can be calculated using OpenScript's hypotenuse( ) *function if the lengths of the two shorter sides are known.*

The financial function, pmt( ), calculates the payment for a loan or annuity at a specified interest rate, for a certain number of payment periods. The function requires three arguments and may contain two optional ones. They syntax is

pmt(*rate*, *numberOfPeriods*, *startingValue*, [*endingValue*], [*beginningOrEnd?*])

The order of the arguments listed within the parentheses is essential. Failure to follow the order would result in erroneous computations. Specifying too few or too many arguments would result in a compiler error. In the pmt( ) function, the first argument is the percentage rate expressed as a decimal (for example, .085 for 8.5%). The second argument is the number of periods for which the annuity is calculated (monthly for 20 years would be 240 payments, which may be expressed as 12 * 20). The third argument is the beginning principal (for example, an $80,000 loan would be expressed as 80000 in the argument). The fourth argument is the ending balance at the end of the last period. Normally this would be 0, and if so, this argument does not need to listed. The fifth argument tells when the payments are due. If it is true, the payments are due at the beginning of the period and if false, the payments are due at the end of the period. If this argument is omitted, it is assumed to be false (the default value). If the fifth argument is specified, the fourth one must be specified as well. The following code calculates the payment for a 30-year $100,000 loan at 9% interest.

```
put pmt(.09/12, 12 * 30, 100000) into payment
```

or

```
put pmt(.09/12, 360, 100000, 0, false) into payment
```

OpenScript has many built-in functions for calculating arithmetic, statistical, trigonometric, financial, and logarithmic values. **Arithmetic functions** return the absolute value of a number; the ceiling of a number (the smallest integer greater than or equal to the number), or the floor of a number (the largest integer less than or equal to the number); pick a random integer between 1 and a specified integer; round a number; return the square root of a value; or truncate the decimal portion of a floating-point value. The table in Figure 15.5 shows the syntax for the built-in arithmetic functions.

Statistical functions in OpenScript return the average of a list of values; the maximum or minimum value of a list of numbers; or the sum of a list of numbers. The lists of values are comma-delimited. For instance:

```
x = sum(12, 5, 9, 11, 6)
```

puts 43 into the value of x. This is the same as

```
x = 12 + 5 + 9 + 11 + 6
```

Such a function has great value where a user enters a list of numbers into a field, and

Figure 15.5
OpenScript contains many
built-in functions for
returning values from
arithmetic operations.

Arithmetic functions

abs( ) Returns the absolute value of a number
            Syntax: abs(*number*)
            Example: x = abs(-5)   -- puts 5 into x

ceiling( ) Returns the smallest integer greater than or equal to the number specified
            Syntax: ceiling(*number*)
            Example: x = ceiling(17.89)   -- puts 18 into x

floor( ) Returns the largest integer less than or equal to the number specified
            Syntax: floor(*number*)
            Example: x = floor(17.89)   -- puts 17 into x

random( ) Returns an integer between 1 and the number specified (inclusive)
            Syntax: random(*number*)
            Example: x = random(100)   -- puts integer btween 1 and 100 into x

round( ) Returns the number rounded to the nearest integer
            Syntax: round(*number*)
            Example: x = round(4.6)   -- puts 5 into x

sqrt( ) Returns the square root of a number
            Syntax: sqrt(*number*)
            Example: x = sqrt(49)   -- puts 7 into x

truncate( ) Returns the integer value of a number, truncating any decimal portion
            Syntax: truncate(*number*)
            Example: x = truncate(4.6)   -- puts 4 into x

Figure 15.6
OpenScript includes
functions for basic
statistical procedures.

Statistical functions

average( ) Returns the average value of a list of numbers
            Syntax: average(*list*)
            Example: x = average(3, 9, 10, 6)   - puts 7 into x

max( ) Returns the largest value in a list of numbers
            Syntax: max(*list*)
            Example: x = max(3, 9, 10, 6)   -- puts 10 into x

min( ) Returns the smallest value in a list of numbers
            Syntax: min(*list*)
            Example: x = min(3, 9, 10, 6)   -- puts 3 into x

sum( ) Returns the sum of a list of numbers
            Syntax: sum(*list*)
            Example: x = sum(3, 9, 10, 6)   -- puts 28 into x

the algorithm requires the sum of the numbers entered. For instance:

    put sum(text of field id 1) into x

Figure 15.6 reveals the syntax and use of OpenScript's statistical functions.
        OpenScript's **trigonometric functions** can be used to calculate the sine, cosine, or tangent of an angle; the arccosine, arcsine, or arctangent of a number between −1 and 1; the hyperbolic cosine, sine, or tangent of an angle; and the hypotenuse of

Figure 15.7
OpenScript has several built-in functions for calculating trigonometric values.

Trigonometric functions

acos( ) Returns the arccosine of a number between –1 and 1 (inclusive) in radians
    Syntax: acos(*number*)
    Example: x = acos(1)   -- puts 0 into x

asin( ) Returns the arcsine of a number between –1 and 1 (inclusive) in radians
    Syntax: asin(*number*)
    Example: x = sin(1)   -- puts 1.570796326794897 (pi/2) into x

atan( ) Returns the arctangent of a number in radians.
    Syntax: atan(*number*)
    Example: x = atan(60)   -- puts 1.554131203080956 into x

cos( ) Returns the cosine of an angle measured in radians (radians = degrees * (pi/180))
    Syntax: cos(*angle*)
    Example: x = cos(60 * (pi/180))   -- puts .5 into x

cosh( ) Returns the hyperbolic cosine of an angle measured in radians
    Syntax: cosh(*angle*)
    Example: x = cosh(60 * (pi/180)) -- puts 1.600286857702386 into x

hypotenuse( ) Returns the hypotenuse of a right triangle given the length of the sides
    Syntax: hypotenuse(*side1, side2*)
    Example: x = hypotenuse(3,4)   -- puts 5 into x

sin( ) Returns the sine of an angle measured in radians
    Syntax: sin(*angle*)
    Example: x = sin(60 * (pi/180))   -- puts 0.8660254037844386 into x

sinh( ) Returns the hyperbolic sine of an angle measured in radians
    Syntax: sinh(*angle*)
    Example: x = sinh(60 * (pi/180))   -- puts 1.249367050523975 into x

tan( ) Returns the tangent of an angle measured in radians
    Syntax: tan(*angle*)
    Example: x = tan(60 * (pi/180))   -- returns tangent of a 60 degree angle

tanh( ) Returns the hyperbolic tangent of an angle measured in radians
    Syntax: tanh(*angle*)
    Example: x = tanh(60 * (pi/180))   -- puts 0.7807144353592677 into x

a right angle, given the lengths of the other two sides. The table in Figure 15.7 shows the syntax for the trigonometric functions.

The **financial functions** OpenScript offers are used to calculate the payment due for an annuity; the interest rate; the present value of an annuity; the depreciation of an asset; the amount of interest paid on an investment or loan; and other less frequently used functions. The table in Figure 15.8 lists the financial functions available in OpenScript.

The **logarithmic functions**, which include an exponential function complete the list of built-in numeric functions. Primarily used in scientific applications, these logarithmic functions are described in further detail in Figure 15.9.

The **increment** and **decrement** Commands

A variable may be assigned a value in which the evaluated expression contains a reference to itself. Consider the following:

Figure 15.8
OpenScript has many
functions for performing
financial calculations.

Financial Functions

annuityFactor( ) Returns factor of present value of an ordinary annuity to the payment
Syntax: annuityFactor(*rate, periods*)
Example: x = annuityFactor(.075, 12)   - - for 12-month loan at 7.5%

compoundFactor( ) Returns future value of interest-bearing account
Syntax: compoundFactor(*rate, periods*)
Example: x = compoundFactor(.075/12, 12)

ddb( ) Returns depreciation of an asset for a specified period of time
Syntax: ddb(*cost, salvage, life, period, rate*)
Example: x = ddb(20000,6000, 36, 12, 2)   -- x = depreciation of a
--$20,000 car at 18 months which will have a salvage value
-- of $6000 after 36 months at the end of the first year.

fv( ) Returns the future value of an investment
Syntax: fv(*rate, periods, payment, currentValue, beginningOrEnd?*)
Example: x = fv(.12/12, 36, 380, 0, false)

ipmt( ) Returns amount of interest on an investment or loan
Syntax: ipmt(*rate, period, totalPeriods, presValue, futureValue, type*)
Example: x = ipmt(.065/12, 1, 48, 16000, 0, false)

irr( ) Returns the interest rate or return for a series of cash flow amounts
Syntax: irr(*valueList, expectedRate*)
Example: x = irr("12000, 9500, 3000, 2300, 750, -1200, -4800",)

nper( ) Returns number of periods required for an investment or loan to reach a value
Syntax: nper(*rate, payment, presentValue, futureValue, type*)
Example: x = nper(.10/12, 200, 12000, 0 , false)

npv( ) Returns present value of investment based on cash-flow values
Syntax: npv(*rate, cashFlowValues, type*)
Example: x = npv(.09/12, "12000, 10000, 6500, 1000,-2500", true)

pmt( ) Returns the periodic payment of an annuity
Syntax: pmt(*rate, totalPeriods, principal, futureValue, type*)
Example: x = pmt(.125/12, 240, 95000, 0, false)
--Calculates the payment of a 20-year loan of $95,000 at
an interest rate of 12.5%.

ppmt( ) Returns the payment on the principal for an investmentor loan
Syntax: ppmt(*rate, period, totalPeriods, principal, futureValue, type*)
Example: x = ppmt(.10/12, 180, 240, 120000, 0, false)

pv( ) Returns the present value of an investment or loans
Syntax: pv(*rate, totalPeriods, payment, futureValue, type*)
Example: x = pv(.12/12, 360, 650, 0, false)

rate( ) Returns the interest rate per period for an investment or loan
Syntax: rate(*totalPeriods, payment, presVal, futVal, type, expectRate*)
Example: x = rate(240, 450, 75000, 0, false, 0.1)

syd( ) Returns the depreciation of an asset using an accelerated depreciation method
Syntax: syd(*cost, salvage, life, period*)
Example: x = syd(15000, 4500, 60, 24)   --Calculates the
-- depreciation after 24 months on $15,000 piece of
-- equipment with a life expectancy of 5 years (60
-- months) and a salvage estimation of $4,500.

Logarithmic Functions

exp( ) Returns value of *e* (2.7182818) raised to a specified power
  Syntax: exp(*power*)
  Example: x = exp(2)   - - puts 7.38905609893065 into x

ln( ) Returns the natural logarithm (base *e* log) of a number
  Syntax: ln(*number*)
  Example: x = ln(7.38905609893065)   - - puts 2 into x

log( ) Returns the logarithm of a value in a specified base
  Syntax: log(*number, base*)
  Example: x = log(125,3)   - - puts 4.394920562153781 into x

---

Figure 15.9
For scientific applications, OpenScript contains functions for finding the exponential, logarithms, and natural logarithms of values.

```
to handle buttonClick
    a = 5
    b = 3
    a = a + b
    b = a + b
    put a into the text of field id 1
    put b into the text of field id 2
end buttonClick
```

After this handler is executed, 8 is placed into the text of field id 1 and the contents of field id 2 is 11. In the second and third lines of the code, a is assigned the value 5 and b the value 3. In the fourth line, a is assigned the value a + b, which is equivalent to 5 + 3 or 8. (Expressions are evaluated before the assignment is made.) The value of a is now equal to 8. In the fifth line, b is assigned the value of a + b, which is now equivalent to 8 + 3, or 11. The value of b becomes 11. The sixth line places the value of a, which is 8, into the text of field id 1. The seventh line places the value of b, which is 11, into the text of field id 2.

The procedures in the fourth and fifth lines could also be performed using OpenScript's **increment** command:

```
to handle buttonClick
    a = 5
    b = 3
    increment a by b
    increment b by a
    put a into the text of field id 1
    put b into the text of field id 2
end buttonClick
```

The syntax of the increment command is specified in Figure 15.10. Likewise, a command such as:

```
x = x − 4
```

which subtracts 4 from the value of x, can also be performed with the **decrement command**:

```
decrement x by 4
```

The syntax of the decrement command is explained in Figure 15.11.

Figure 15.10
OpenScript's increment
command is used to increase
the value held by a variable
or other container.

The increment command

Syntax:　　**increment** *container* **by** *value*

Purpose:　Adds the specified value to the value of the container.

Examples:　increment x by 1

　　　　　　increment the text of field id 5 by newVal

Figure 15.11
OpenScript's decrement
command is used to
decrease the value
contained in a container,
such as a variable.

The decrement command

Syntax:　　**decrement** *container* **by** *value*

Purpose:　subtracts the specified value from the value of the container

Examples:　decrement counter by 1

　　　　　　decrement the text of field "countdown" by 1

Formatting Numeric Data

In managing and presenting data, it is often desirable to have the data conform to a certain format. Financial data might be displayed in a format that has two decimal places and a leading dollar sign, such as $567.89. Scientific data might be formatted in a scientific notation format, such as 5.1234E8. Commas in a large number, such as 725,901,338, make it more readable than 725901338.

The **format command** is used to convert numbers in a field or variable to a specific format. The syntax for converting numeric data is

　　format [number] *container* as *newFormat* [from *oldFormat*]

The word "number" is optional for numeric data and is used to distinguish numeric data from date and time data (discussed later in this chapter). The existing format may also be optionally specified. For numeric data, the formats are specified as strings (enclosed in quotation marks) using certain symbols. A zero (0) is used as a place holder for a digit and a 0 is displayed if there are fewer digits than place holders. Likewise, the pound sign (#) may be used as a digit place holder with spaces substituted for fewer digits than the number of place holders specified. If the number 56.3 were formatted as 000.00, the number 056.30 is displayed. If formatted as ###.##, the number 56.3 is displayed. If there are more digits to the left of the decimal in the number than specified in the format string, the digits are displayed. If there are more digits to the right of the decimal than specified in the format string, the decimal is rounded to the last place holder specified. For instance, if the number 123.4567 is formatted as 0.00, the number 123.46 is displayed.

A decimal may be specified as shown in the examples in the previous paragraph. Commas may specified in the format string as well. When 12345.67 is formatted as #,###.#, 12,345.7 is displayed. Other literal characters may be specified: $, (,), spaces, and %. When 12345.67 is formatted as $ 0,000.00, $ 12,345.67 is displayed.

Scientific notation format is specified using the E+ or E− symbol in the format string. An E+ places either a positive or negative sign in front of the exponent; an E− symbol places a minus in front of the exponent if it is negative and nothing if it is positive. Formatting 12,345 as 0.0000E+0 displays the number as 1.2345E+4; formatting it as 0.0000E–0 displays 1.2345E4. Formatting the number .012345 in either 0.0000E+0 or 0.0000E–0 formats produces a display of 1.2345E–2.

A null format strips out leading and trailing spaces, commas, dollar signs, and percentage symbols, primarily for calculation purposes. (Other literal characters are not removed, however.) Data containing nonnumeric characters, such as a dollar sign or comma, cannot be used in mathematical expressions.

Decimal, hexadecimal (base 16), octal (base 8), and binary (base 2) formats may be specfed using the @d, @h, @o, and @b symbols respectively. 65 formatted as @b00000000 is displayed as 01000001. In the same way, a field containing the binary number 01000001 can be converted to a decimal 65 by using the command

```
format number field id 1 as "@d0" from "@b0"
```

Figure 15.12 lists the various symbols used in the formatting strings for numeric data. The software tutorial for this chapter contains several pages that interactively demonstrate the results of various format commands (see Figure 15.13).

Symbols Used in Formatting Numeric Data	
Symbol	**Use**
0	Used as digit place holder. Zeroes are displayed if the data takes fewer places than specified in a formatting string.
#	Used as a digit place holder. Spaces are displayed if the data takes fewer places than specified in a formatting string.
E-	The number is displayed in scientific notation. A negative or positive sign is displayed in front of the exponent.
E+	The number is displayed in scientific notation. A negative sign is displayed in front of the exponent if negative.
@b	Displays the number in a binary (base 2) format.
@d	Displays the number in a decimal (base 10) format.
@h	Displays the number in a hexadecimal (base 16) format.
@o	Displays the number in an octal (base 8) format.
null	Strips spaces, commas, and dollar signs for calculation purposes.

Figure 15.12
Symbols are used to designate place holders for digits and the appearance of data in the formatting string for numeric data.

Formatting Dates and Times

The format command is also used to format date and time data. To format a date or time, the general syntax of the command is the same as for numeric data, with the exception that the word date or time is substituted for the word number.

```
format date container as newFormat [from oldFormat]
```

```
format time container as newFormat [from oldFormat]
```

Figure 15.13
The software that accompanies this chapter includes an interactive page demonstrating the effects of various format strings.

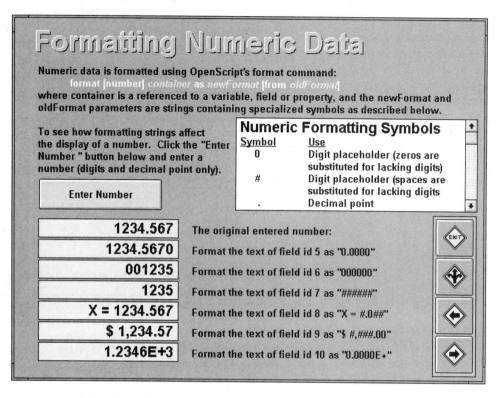

Figure 15.14
As with numeric data, time and date data may be formatted using special symbols in the format string.

Symbols Used in Formatting Date and Time Data

Symbol	Use
M	Month's name (e.g., January)
MMM	Three-letter abbreviation of the month (e.g., Jan)
m	The number of the month (e.g., 1)
mm	Number of the month in two digits (e.g., 01)
d	Number of the day (e.g., 5)
dd	Number of the day in two digits (e.g., 05)
y	Number of the year (e.g., 1994)
yy	Last two digits of the year (e.g., 94)
h	Number of the hour (12-hour clock) (e.g., 3)
hh	Number of the hour (12-hour clock) in two digits (e.g., 03)
h24	Number of the hour (24-hour clock) (e.g., 15)
hh24	Number of the hour (24-hour clock) in two digits (e.g., 03)
min	Number of minutes in two digits (e.g., 00)
sec	Number of seconds in two digits (e.g., 00)
seconds	The number of seconds since midnight (for time data) or the number of seconds since midnight of 1/1/94 (for date data)
AMPM	Displays either AM or PM.
Literal characters	Literal characters, such as a colon to separate time segments, may be included. For example: hh:min:sec AMPM

The strings used in specifying the format for date and time include the symbols listed in the table of Figure 15.14. The date 9/6/94, formatted as M d, y, is displayed as September 6, 1994. The same date formatted as MMM dd is displayed as Sep 06. A time of 1:15 PM, formatted as h24:min:sec, would be displayed as 13:15:00.

Two system properties, sysDate and sysTime, contain the current date and time according to the computer's internal clock. The date and time are in the current format as set in ToolBook's sysDateFormat and sysTimeFormat properties. The following handler puts the number of seconds since midnight into a system variable named timeCheck.

```
to handle buttonClick
    system timeCheck
    put the sysTime into timeCheck
    format timeCheck as "seconds"
end buttonClick
```

Figure 15.15 summarizes the syntax of OpenScript's format command.

```
The format command

Syntax:     format [number] container as newFormat [from oldFormat]
            format date container as newFormat [from oldFormat]
            format time container as newFormat [from oldFormat]

Purpose:    Converts data to a specified format

Examples:   format itemCost as "$ 0.00"

            format date text of field id 3 as "mm/dd/yy"

            format time startTime as "seconds" from "hh:min:sec"
```

Figure 15.15
The format *command is used to convert the format of numeric, date, and time data.*

Generating Random Numbers

As shown in Figure 15.5, OpenScript has a function that returns a "random" integer from 1 through a specified integer. For example, the statement

```
put random(100) into chance
```

puts a random integer between 1 and 100 (inclusive) into chance. The random( ) function is very useful in designing games (for instance, simulating the roll of a dice) and interactive courseware. The fractions tutorial presented with Chapter 2 makes use of the random( ) function in generating the quizzes at the end of each section. The random( ) function can be used as part of an expression. For instance, to generate a random number from 100 through 200, the following statement might be employed.

```
put random(101) + 99 into randomNumber
```

The random number is generated from a stored value (called a **seed**) by using an algorithm that produces numbers without a pattern. The numbers, therefore, appear to be random. The seed, however, produces a fixed list of numbers each time it is used. One problem with the random( ) function, then, is that it generates the same sequence of numbers each time the application runs. The solution to this problem is to alter the value of the seed number, and OpenScript provides a **seed** command for this very purpose (see Figure 15.16). The **seed** command is placed before the statement using the random( ) function. The seed can be any integer between 0 and 32,767. Each seed generates a particular sequence of numbers. The statements

```
seed 5000
put random(25) into y
```

would generate the same numbers each time the application runs. The key to successful random-number generation is to somehow vary the seed number. The most common method is to use the system clock of the computer. OpenScript provides a sysTime property that contains the current time of the computer's clock.

```
to handle buttonClick
    put the sysTime into x
    format time x as "seconds"
    -- x will be between 0 and 86400
    x = x div 3    -- the seed must be less than 32767
    seed x
    put the random(1000) into y
end buttonClick
```

Figure 15.16
The seed *command is used to change the numbers generated with the* random *statement.*

The seed command

Syntax: **seed *number***
            The number must be an integer between 1 and 32,767.

Purpose: Provides a base number for the algorithm used in generating "random" numbers

Example: seed 4567

            put sysTime into seedTime
            put seedTime div 5 into seedTime
            seed seedTime

Summary Questions

For each statement below, determine the value of **x** after the statement is executed **(a = 2; b = 3; c = 4).**

1. x = 34 * 2 - 7 * 3
2. x = a ^ b * c
3. x = (6 + a) * b + c
4. x = a * b mod c
5. x = 20 div 3
6. x = 18 mod 6 * 2
7. x = 18 mod (6 * 2)
8. x = (4 + 2) ^ (3 - 1) + 4
9. x = (9 - c) * (b + 3) / (a * 2)
10. x = 70 - b ^ a ^ a

If **text of field id 1** contains **12345.6789,** determine the value displayed after each of the following format statements is executed.

11. format text of field id 1 as "0.00"
12. format text of field id 1 as "0.00000"
13. format number text of field id 1 as "$ #,###.00"
14. format number text of field id 1 as "###"
15. format text of field id 1 as "0.00000E+"

If **text of field id 1** contains **12/06/61** and **text of field id 2** contains **01:30:00** (1:30 A.M.), determine the value displayed after each of the following format statements is executed. (Note: The statements should be considered individually; they do not build on each other.)

16. format date text of field id 1 as "M dd, y" from "mm/dd/yy"
17. format date text of field id 1 as "m/d/yy" from "mm/dd/yy"
18. format date text of field id 1 as "d M y" from "mm/dd/yy"
19. format time text of field id 1 as "h:min" form "hh:min:sec"
20. format time text of field id 1 as "seconds"

Hands-On Projects

A. Examine the software that accompanies this chapter. Open the "Table of Contents" book by double-clicking its icon in the "Developing with ToolBook" group window in the Windows Program Manager. Inside the "Table of Contents," click the book representing Chapter 15. Use the tutorial as a tool for better understanding the material presented in this chapter.

B. Create a book that will calculate the miles per gallon (MPG) that a vehicle achieved on a trip and keep a total of the gallons used, miles traveled, and MPG achieved to date this year. The user should only have to input the number of gallons used on the current trip and the ending odometer reading and then click a single button to calculate (1) the miles traveled this trip, (2) the MPG achieved this trip, (3) the total miles traveled to date this year, (4) the total gallons used this year to date, and (5) the average MPG achieved for the year. A sample design for the book is shown in Figure 15.17, but you are encouraged to create your own design. A "Reset" button should be available to clear the data from the fields. Format the year-to-date and MPG figures for this trip for two decimal places.

The text of all fields should be locked (activated) except those that the user will manually enter data into (that is, fields pertaining to the gallons this trip and the ending odometer reading). The fields should be single-line style. The ending odometer reading must be stored in a field (could be hidden) or assigned to a property so that it can be used as the starting odometer reading of the next trip and used to calculate the number of miles traveled. The MPG is calculated using the following formula:

MPG = (ending odometer – starting odometer) / gallons used

Test data: To verify that the script works, try entering the three sets of boldface figures shown in Figure 15.18 consecutively to get the results displayed in the table.

C. Create a book for calculating the area and volume of solid geometric shapes (boxes, cylinders, cones and spheres), by using dimensions input by the user. For a box, the reader would input the width (w), height (h), and depth (d) of the box. The surface area and volume are calculated using these formulas:

Figure 15.17
A sample design for Hands-On Project B. A good design includes an easy-to-read, attractive screen and instructions to help the user.

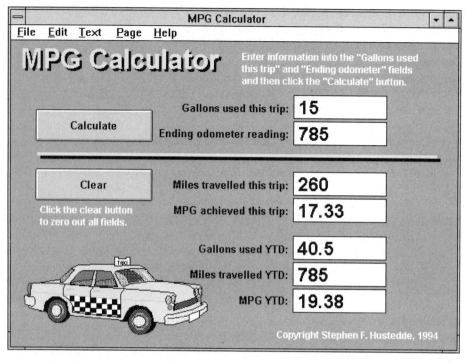

Figure 15.18
Test data for Hands-On Project B.

Test Data

	Trip 1	Trip 2	Trip 3
Gallons used this trip	13.5	12	15
Ending odometer this trip	270	525	785
Starting odometer (displayed?)	0	270	525
Miles traveled this trip	270	255	260
MPG this trip	20.00	21.25	17.33
Gallons YTD	13.5	25.5	40.5
Miles YTD	270	525	785
MPG YTD	20.00	20.59	19.38

$$\text{area} = 2wh + 2wd + 2hd$$
$$\text{volume} = whd$$

For a cylinder, the reader would enter the radius (r) of the base and the height (h) of the cylinder. Cylinder area and volume are found using these formulas:

$$\text{area} = 2\pi r^2 + 2\pi rh$$
$$\text{volume} = \pi r^2 h$$

(Note: In OpenScript π is represented by the constant pi. For instance, to find the circumference of a circle ($2\pi r$), the following statement might be utilized.

```
put (2 * pi * r) into circumference
```

For a cone, the reader would enter the radius (r) of the base and the height (h) of the cone. The cone's area and volume are calculated using

$$\text{area} = 2\pi r^2 + \pi rh$$

$$\text{volume} = \frac{\pi r^2 h}{3}$$

For a sphere, the user would simply enter the sphere's radius, and the area and volume would be calculated according to the following formulas.

$$\text{area} = 4\pi r^2$$

$$\text{volume} = \frac{4\pi r^3}{3}$$

The area and volume figures for each geometric solid should be formatted to three decimal places. One possible design for the book includes an opening page menu (see Figure 15.19) on which the user clicks the desired shape to navigate to the page for calculating the area and volume of that shape (see Figure 15.20). The book, therefore, would consist of five pages. Buttons on the pages navigate to the menu page and previous and next pages of the book. (Graphical objects were drawn with ToolBook's tools.)

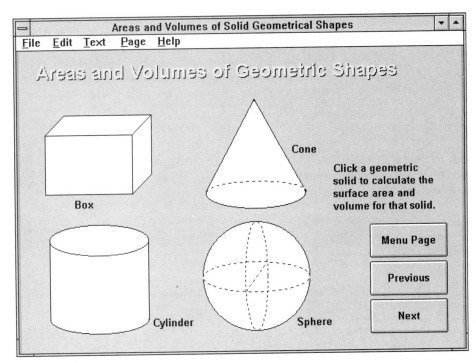

Figure 15.19
A design solution for Hands-On Project C might include an opening menu page that links to the other four pages for calculating area and volume for specific geometric solids.

Use the following to verify that your scripts calculate the area and volume correctly:

Box: w = 10; d = 5; h = 7	area = 310.000; volume = 350.000
Cylinder: r = 5; h = 10	area = 471.239; volume = 785.398
Cone: r = 5; h = 10	area = 314.159; volume = 261.799
Sphere: r = 5	area = 314.159; volume = 523.599

D. Create a one-page book that converts from Fahrenheit degrees to Celcius degrees and vice versa. The conversion formulas are

$$F = (C \times \frac{9}{5}) + 32$$

Figure 15.20
A possible design solution
for Hands-On Project C
might include a graphic
showing the measurement
to be input by the user.

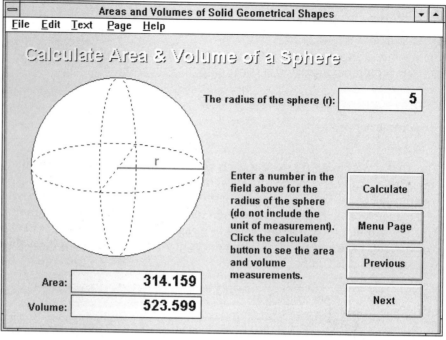

$$C = (F - 32) \times \frac{5}{9}$$

E.   Create a book for calculating the monthly loan payment for a car loan and the total amount that will be paid (monthly amount times the number of months). The calculations would be based on a principal, number of months for the loan (for example, 48 or 60), and the interest rate input by the user. (Use the pmt( ) function to calculate the solution.)

Sample data: A 60-month loan of $15,000 at 9.5% interest would have a monthly payment of $315.03. The total payments would equal $18,901.80 (see Figure 15.21).

Figure 15.21
In Hands-On Project E, a
loan calculator is designed
to calculate the monthly
payment for a loan at a
user-specified rate and
duration, as well as the
total payment amounts.

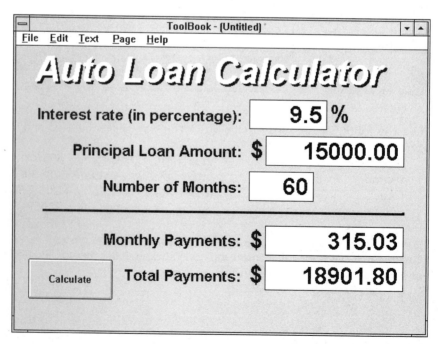

Chapter 16

On One Condition
Decision Branching

As we go about our daily tasks, we are constantly making simple decisions. If the milk for our breakfast cereal smells sour, we pour it down the drain and go to the store to buy a new carton. While driving to the store, if the traffic light is red, we stop. At the store, if our purchases total $7.85, we choose to give the cashier enough money to cover the charges, whether it be a 10- or 20-dollar bill or a 5- and three 1-dollar bills. The amount of change returned by the cashier depends on the amount originally given to him or her. We go through our day making such choices, the course of our day often decided by the choices we make. For a computer program to carry out many of our tasks and make our work easier, it too must be able to make decisions and perform different actions based on those decisions.

Thus far we have written OpenScript handlers that perform a list of commands in a linear fashion. To handle more complex algorithms, the handler must be able to determine whether a specific condition is met and perform a series of commands based on the determination. In programming theory, this process is called **branching**. Branching occurs when the computer reaches a conditional statement, which is comparable to a car reaching a fork in the road. The car's driver examines a road map and decides whether to take the right fork or the left fork; the computer examines whether a certain condition is true. It asks, for example, if the system clock is between midnight and noon—true or false? Then it performs the statements of the right branch or the statements of the left branch, depending on if the condition is true or false.

OpenScript has two conditional structures for branching. One is the if...then...end if structure (including its if...then...else...end if variant) and the other is the conditions...when...else structure. Both utilize Boolean expressions to decide which branch to perform, but each has its own purpose and circumstances for use.

Boolean Expressions

Boolean expressions (which use **relational operators**, or **logical operators**) consist of an equation that is evaluated as being either true or false. For instance,

$$3 + 2 = 5$$

is a Boolean expression that evaluates to true, but

$$3 \wedge 2 = 10$$

evaluates to false. Boolean expressions consist of two values compared. The expression may be an equality, like the preceding expressions, or may utilize one of many different comparison operators: <>, <, >, <=, >=, is, is not, contains, is in, and is not in. The table in Figure 16.1 examines the different operators in more detail. The following Boolean expressions are true.

Figure 16.1
OpenScript utilizes a
variety of Boolean (logical)
operators.

OpenScript BooleanOperators		
Operator	**Description**	**Example**
=	Tests true if both values are equal	x = 9
is	Same as =	x is 9
<>	Tests true if the values are unequal	x <> y + z
is not	Same as <>	x is not y + z
<	Tests true if left value is less than right value	x < 50
<=	Tests true if left value is equal to or less than right value	x <= 49
>	Tests true if left value is greater than right value	x > 0
>=	Tests true if left value is equal to greater than right value	x >= y
contains	Tests true if right expression appears in left value	"abc" contains "b"
is in	Tests true if left expression appears in right value	x is in "Yy"
is not in	Tests true if left expression does not appear in right value	x is not in "Yy"
and	Tests true if both Boolean expressions are true	x < 8 and y > 5
or	Tests true if either or both Boolean expressions are true	x < 8 or y > 5
not	Converts false expression to true and vice versa	not(x is in "Yy")

```
12 > 15 – 10
5 ^ 2 < 5 ^ 3
6 * 3 <> 8 * 2
3 + 4 + 5 is 12
```

The following expressions are false.

```
6 <= 2 * 2
90 <> 10 * (3 ^ 2)
25 = 8 * 3
"cd" is in "abc"
```

Note in the last expression, that text may be evaluated in addition to numeric values. Boolean expressions may also utilize the values of containers such as variables, properties, and the text of fields and recordfields. For example:

```
x > = y + z
cost < 500
"Yy" contains userAnswer
the text of field id 1 = "Yes"
the fillColor of rectangle id 15 is "red"
the name of this page = "Menu"
```

Assignment Verses Boolean Expressions

Wait a minute! What is the difference between an assignment expression, such as

```
x = 5 + 7
```

which places the value of 12 into x (even if x already has a value) and the Boolean expression

    x = 5 + 7

which would be evaluated as true or false, depending on the value of x? The difference is determined by the context—that is, how the expression is used. Standing alone, the expression is treated as an assignment operator. Boolean expressions, however, are always used as part of another statement. If we use the expression in the put statement:

    put (x = 5 + 7) into y

y would have a value of either true or false, depending on the value of x. Boolean expressions are primarily used in control structures such as if...then and conditions...when, which are discussed later in this chapter.

Complex Boolean Expressions (and, or, and not)

Two or more Boolean expressions may be evaluated together by using the and or or operator. An **and operator** placed between two Boolean expressions requires that both expressions be true for the entire expression to be true. For example, the expression

    5 < 7 and 9 > 3

is true because 5 is less than 7 *and* 9 is greater than 3. Both expressions are true; therefore, the entire expression evaluates to true. On the contrary, the expression

    5 < 7 and 9 < 3

evaluates to false because both parts of the expression are not true. The first part, 5 < 7, is true, but the second expression is false: 9 is not less than 3. Both halves of an and expression must be true. If one or the other is false, the entire expression evaluates to false. Likewise, if both halves of an and expression are false, the entire expression is false. The expression

    5 > 7 and 9 < 3

is false, since 5 is not greater than 7, nor is 9 less than 3.

The **or operator** is used in the same manner as the and operator, but evaluates to true if either of the expressions it separates is true, as well as if both are true. The following expressions, then, are true.

    5 < 7 or 9 > 3
    5 < 7 or 9 < 3
    5 > 7 or 9 > 3

The expression

    5 > 7 or 9 < 3

is false, since both expressions are false. The table in Figure 16.2 summarizes the results of the and and or operators.

Figure 16.2
The value of a Boolean expression containing an and *or* or *operator is dependent on the values of the two expressions linked by the operator.*

Results of the and and or operators

Results of the and operator

Value of left expression	and	Value of right expression	Result
true		true	true
true		false	false
false		true	false
false		false	false

Results of the or operator

Value of left expression	or	Value of right expression	Result
true		true	true
true		false	true
false		true	true
false		false	false

The **not operator** is infrequently used. It results in the expression to its right being reversed. If the expression is true, the not operator results in the expression being rendered false. Likewise, if the expression is false, the not operator results in the expression being considered true. The following expressions, then, are considered true.

```
not (5 = 2 + 4)
not (4 ^ 2 <> 16)
not (9 < 3)
```

The expressions

```
not (7 = 3 + 4)
not (20 < 30)
not (6 > 3 or 4 < 2)
```

are false, since the expressions to the right of the not operator evaluate to true.

Expressions may be even more complex with multiple and, or, and not operators. Boolean expressions such as

5 > 3 and 18 < 20 and 7 > 9 or 6 < 10 and 3 > 2

are evaluated in the following order: First, all not expressions are evaluated from left to right, then all and expressions are evaluated from left to right, and finally all or expressions are evaluated from left to right. The preceding expression, then, is evaluated like this:

```
5 > 3  and  18 > 20  and 7 < 9 or 6 < 10 and 3 > 2
true  and  false   and true or true  and  true
      false          and true or true  and  true
              false          or true and  true
              false              or    true
                          true
```

The final result is that the expression is true. As with the order of precedence in evaluating numeric operations, parentheses override the usual order of evaluation in Boolean expressions. Parentheses placed in the preceding expression could dictate the order in which the expressions are evaluated.

```
5 > 3 and 18 > 20 and (7 < 9 or 6 < 10  and 3 > 2)
true   and   false   and ( true   or   true   and true )
true   and   false   and ( true   or        true        )
true   and   false   and (        true        )
        false           and              true
                       false
```

As in writing numeric expressions, in writing Boolean expressions take care to obtain the desired results.

The if...then...end if Structure

The **if...then...end if structure** is used to perform a statement or set of statements if a certain condition (Boolean expression) is true. If the condition is not met (the Boolean expression is false), the statements are ignored. The general syntax of the if...then...end if structure is

```
if BooleanExpression [then]
    statement(s) to be executed if BooleanExpression is true
end [if]
```

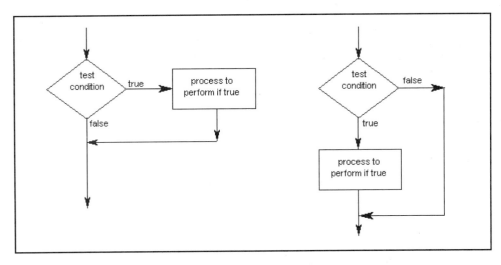

Figure 16.3
In a flowchart, if...then ...end if *structures may be represented in two different ways.*

Figure 16.3 shows the general flowcharting of an if...then...end if control structure. To make the code easier to read, it is advisable to indent the statements occurring between the if...then and end if statements. The following buttonClick handler for a field allows the user to enter text into it only if he or she has held the Shift key down while clicking the field.

```
to handle buttonClick location, shiftState
    if the shiftState is true then
        ask "Enter a title for this page:"
        put it into the text of self
    end if
end buttonClick
```

If the Shift key was down, the **shiftState** parameter would be **true** and the statements between the if...then and **end if** statements would be executed—that is, the user would be asked to type text into an ask dialog and then assign the entry to the text of the field. If the Shift key was not down, the **shiftState** parameter would be **false** and the user would not perceive any change after clicking the field.

The if...then...end if structure is often used with **request** and **ask** statements to allow the user to determine the direction the algorithm will take, to verify the user's desires, or to provide feedback about a choice. For an "Exit" button, it is often wise to verify that the user truly desires to exit the program and didn't accidentally click the button. The following handler might reside in the script of an "Exit" button.

```
to handle buttonClick
    request "Do you really wish to exit?" with "Yes" or "Cancel"
    if it is "Yes" then
        send exit
    end if
end buttonClick
```

The handler prompts the user to respond, in a request dialog box, that he or she intended to exit the program. If the "Yes" button is clicked, **yes** is assigned to the value of variable it and the **exit** command is sent to the system, which causes the book to close. If the user did not click "Yes," the **send exit** command between the if...then and **end if** statements is ignored and nothing happens.

The following handler presents a trivia question to the reader in an ask dialog box: "In what city was the first skyscraper built?" The reader enters the response and feedback is provided. If the answer includes "Chicago," then a request dialog box congratulates the user and a system variable containing the number of questions answered correctly is increased by one (assuming this question is one of several presented and a score is being maintained for the entire quiz). If the answer does not include "Chicago," then the reader is given feedback on the correct answer and a system variable used for tracking the number of incorrect answers is increased by one.

```
to handle buttonClick
    system gCorrect, gIncorrect
    ask "In what city was the first skyscraper built?"
    if it contains "Chicago" then
        request "Very good.  Chicago is the correct answer." with "OK"
        increment gCorrect by 1
    end if
    if "Chicago" is not in it then
        request "Sorry. The first skyscraper was built in Chicago in 1885."
        increment gIncorrect by 1
    end if
end buttonClick
```

The **if...then...else...end if** Structure

In the preceding handler, the answer cannot both contain Chicago and not contain Chicago. Therefore, only one of the if...then...end if structures is executed. Open-Script provides a variant of the if...then...end if structure to make the handler easier to read. The **if...then...else...end if structure** contains two sets of executable statements: one set for use if the Boolean expression is **true** and another for use if the Boolean expression is **false**. Figure 16.4 illustrates the flowcharting of an

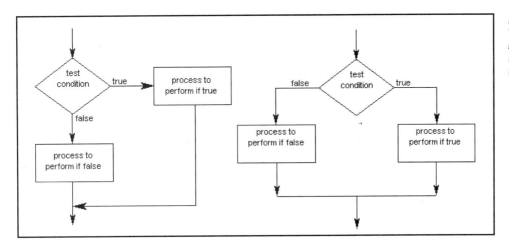

Figure 16.4
The if...then...else...end if
structure is commonly
represented in a flowchart
in one of two ways.

if...then...else...end if structure. The if...then...else...end if structure uses the following syntax.

```
if BooleanExpression [then]
        statement(s) to be executed if BooleanExpression is true
else
        statement(s) to be executed if BooleanExpression is false
end [if]
```

The trivia question discussed in the previous section could be written using the if...then...else...end if control structure:

```
to handle buttonClick
        system gCorrect, gIncorrect
        ask "In what city was the first skyscraper built?"
        if it contains "Chicago" then
                request "Very good.  Chicago is the correct answer." with "OK"
                increment gCorrect by 1
        else
                request "Sorry. The first skyscraper was built in Chicago in 1885."
                increment gIncorrect by 1
        end if
end buttonClick
```

The following handler is attached to an object so that it changes from red to blue, or vice versa, when clicked.

```
to handle buttonClick
        if the fillColor of self is "red" then
                set the fillColor of self to "blue"
        else
                set the fillColor of self to "red"
        end if
end buttonClick
```

In the preceding handler, if the fill color of the object that was clicked (self) is red, it sets the fill color of the object to blue, otherwise (including if it is blue), its fillColor property is set to red. Figure 16.5 summarizes the syntax of the if...then...end if and if...then...else...end if structures.

Figure 16.5
The if...then...else...end if
*structure is used to branch
to one or two optional sets
of statements.*

The if...then...end if and if...then...else...end if structures

Syntax: if *BooleanExpression* [then]
                                statement(s) to be executed if BooleanExpression is true
              [else
                                statement(s) to be executed if BooleanExpression is false]
              end [if]

Purpose: Executes one or more statements if a condition represented by a Boolean
              expression is true. Ignores those statements if it is false and executes an optional
              second set of statements.

Examples: if theKey is in "Yy" then
                                forward
              end if

              if x/2 = x div 2 then
                                request "You entered an even number." with "OK"
              else
                                request "You entered an odd number." with "OK"
              end if

Nested **if...then...else...end if** Structures

At times there may be more than one condition to be evaluated within another
condition. As the next program segment shows, the message sent by the F2 function
key might be used in a keyUp handler. An if...then...else...end if structure is utilized
to perform an action if the F2 function key is pressed; the keyUp message is forwarded
up the object hierarchy ladder if any other key is pressed. (The key code for the F2
key is 113.)

```
to handle keyUp key
    if key = 113 then
        <perform some action>
    else
        forward
    end if
end keyUp
```

If the F2 function key is pressed, the computer either hides or displays an imported
paint-type object, depending on whether the object is currently hidden or shown. The
<perform some action> in the handler is replaced with an if...then...end if or
if...then...else...end if structure.

```
to handle keyUp key
    if key = 113 then
        if the visible of paintObject "shuttleLaunch" is true
            hide paintObject "shuttleLaunch"
        else
            show paintObject "shuttleLaunch"
        end
    else
        forward
    end if
end keyUp
```

This handler contains an if...then...else...end if structure within an if...then...else...end if structure. This format is referred to as a **nested if...then structure**. The flowchart for the handler is illustrated in Figure 16.6.

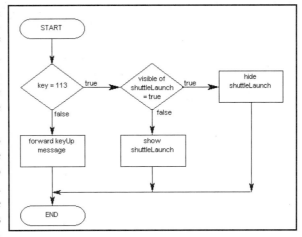

Figure 16.6
This flowchart illustrates an algorithm for hiding and showing a paint-type object named shuttleLaunch *when the F2 key is pressed and forwarding the* keyUp *message when any other key is pressed.*

Nested if...then statements might also be used in a case where there are more than two possible branches. Consider a number-guessing game. The computer randomly generates a number between 1 and 100 on entering the page and places the value in a system variable called gNum. It also sets a system variable named gGuesses to zero. The variable gGuesses will be used to keep track of how many guesses a user has made.

```
to handle enterPage
     system gNum, gGuesses
     put random(100) into gNum
     put 0 into gGuesses
end enterPage
```

The user clicks a button labeled "Guess," which prompts for an integer to be entered. The computer then displays a dialog box stating if the guess is correct, too high, or too low—three different paths. On each guess, the system variable, gGuesses is increased. If the user answers correctly, the total number of guesses is displayed in a request dialog and the user is asked whether he or she wishes to play again. If so, another random number is generated and the gGuesses variable is reset to zero.

```
to handle buttonClick
     system gNum, gGuesses
     increment gGuesses by 1
     ask "Enter your guess (an integer between 1 and 100):"
     if it = gNum   --a correct guess has been made
          request "Correct! Number of guesses:" with gGuesses
          request "Would you like to play again?" with "Yes" or "No"
          if it is "Yes" then
               put random(100) into gNum
               put 0 into gGuesses
          end if
     else
          if it < gNum then
               request "Your guess is too low." with "OK"
          else
               request "Your guess is too high." with "OK"
          end if
     end if
end buttonClick
```

In the preceding handler there are three if...then...end if or if...then...else...end if structures—one nested in each of the two branches of the first. Pay careful attention to the indentations used. These make the script easier to read and help make the if...then structures stand out. The three different branches are handled in the first if... clause and the if...then...else...end if structure nested in its else clause. The other if...then structure nested in the first if... clause is merely a routine carried out if the first condition is met. Figure 16.7 shows the flowchart of the preceding handler.

Figure 16.7
This flowchart illustrates an algorithm that includes several conditional branches. Coding such an algorithm in OpenScript requires nested if...then *structures.*

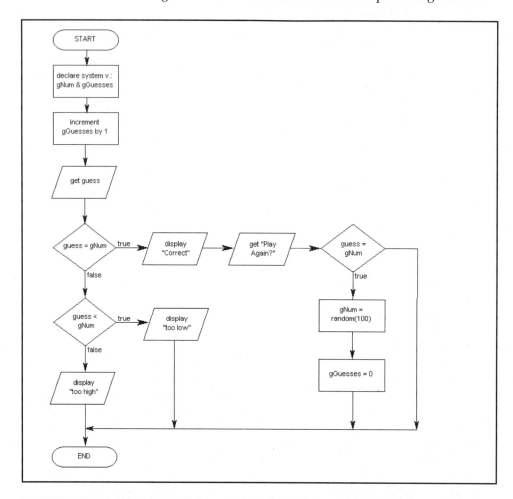

Figure 16.8
A menu page like this allows a user to navigate to another page by pressing a particular letter on the keyboard. The handler for such a process might utilize nested if...then *structures or a* conditions...when *structure.*

A menu page such as that pictured in Figure 16.8 might use a key press to determine which page to navigate to. If the user presses the A key, he or she would navigate to the page ID 2; if he or she presses the B key, the book would turn to page ID 3. If the user presses the C or D key, he or she would navigate to page ID 7 or 9, respectively. The following **keyChar** handler would be placed in the page script of the menu page.

```
to handle keyChar key
    if ansiToChar(key) is in "Aa" then
        go to page id 2
    else
        if ansiToChar(key) is in "Bb" then
            go to page id 3
        else
            if ansiToChar(key) is in "Cc" then
                go to page id 7
            else
                if ansiToChar(key) is in "Dd" then
                    go to page id 9
                else
                    forward
                end if
            end if
        end if
    end if
end keyChar
```

The **is in** operator can make use of both uppercase and lowercase input. If any other keys are pressed, the message is forwarded up the object hierarchy chain. The flowchart for this handler is shown in Figure 16.9.

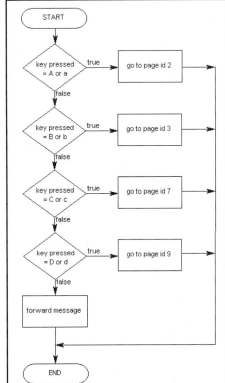

Figure 16.9
A flowchart of a four-branch nested if...then *structure.*

The **conditions...when...else** Structure

The format of nested if...then statements utilized for four branches in the preceding handler might be expanded to handle 5, 6, 20, or more branches. However, even at four branches the coding can become messy and hard to read. Many languages utilize a **case structure**, which allows multiple branching. A generic case structure flowchart for four branches is shown in Figure 16.10. In OpenScript, case structures are performed by using the conditions, when, else, and end conditions statements. The generic case structure, in OpenScript terms, is also referred to as a **conditions...when....else** structure. Figure 16.11 summarizes the syntax of the conditions...when...else structure. The keyChar menu handler shown previously can be rewritten using the conditions...when...else structure.

Figure 16.10
Flowcharting a conditions...when...else *case structure involves showing the branches listed from left to right in the order in which they would be evaluated.*

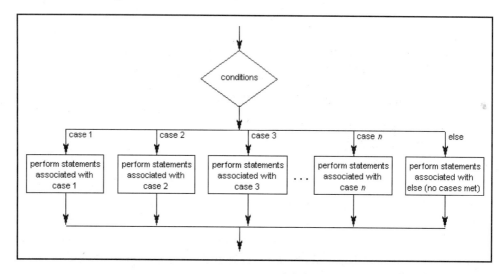

Figure 16.11
The conditions...when *structure is used when multiple branches occur in an algorithm.*

The conditions...when...else structure

Syntax: **conditions**
                when *BooleanExpression1*
                        statement(s) to be executed if BooleanExpression1 is true
                when *BooleanExpression2*
                        statement(s) to be executed if BooleanExpression2 is true
                    . . .
                when *BooleanExpressionN*
                        statement(s) to be executed if BooleanExpressionN is true
                [else
                        statement(s) to be executed if none of the above is true]
            end [conditions]

Purpose: Executes one or more statements of a branch if a condition represented by a Boolean expression is true. Only one of multiple branches is executed.

Example: conditions
                when x < 0
                        request "The number is negative." with "OK"
                when x = 0
                        request "The number is zero." with "OK"
                when x > 0
                        request "The number is positive." with "OK"
                else
                        request "An error occurred." with "OK"
            end conditions

```
to handle keyChar key
    conditions
        when ansiToChar(key) is in "Aa"
            go to page id 2
        when ansiToChar(key) is in "Bb"
            go to page id 3
        when ansiToChar(key) is in "Cc"
            go to page id 7
        when ansiToChar(key) is in "Dd"
            go to page id 9
        else
            forward
    end conditions
end keyChar
```

In executing a conditions...when...else structure, the first case (when...) is examined. If the Boolean expression is true, the statements between the first when statement and the next when statement are executed. All subsequent cases are ignored (even if they evaluate to true). If the Boolean expression evaluates to false, the next case (when...) is evaluated and handled in the same manner. If none of the cases is true, the statements between the else and end conditions statements are executed. Once a case is executed, the program continues by executing the statement following the end conditions statement. Compare the preceding handler with the nested if...then handler for the same function and it should be apparent that the case structure is easier to read and follow. The difference would be even more obvious if the code included more than four branches.

The else clause of the conditions...when...else structure is optional if there are no statements to be executed because none of the when cases are true. Execution continues with the statement after the end conditions statement if none of the when cases are true and there is no else case. For example:

```
to handle buttonClick
    conditions
        when the fillColor of self is "red"
            set the fillColor of self to "blue"
        when the fillColor of self is "blue"
            set the fillColor of self to "white"
        when the fillColor of self is "white"
            set the fillColor of self to "green"
        when the fillColor of self is "green"
            set the fillColor of self to "yellow"
        when the fillColor of self is "yellow"
            set the fillColor of self to "red"
    end conditions
end buttonClick
```

The preceding handler changes the fill color of an object when the object is clicked. The new color depends on the current fill color of the object. For instance, if the fill color of the clicked object is white, the fillColor property of the object is set to display green. If however, the fill color is magenta or cyan, nothing happens because there is no else clause and none of the when cases evaluates to true.

Like the if...then structures, the conditions structure may utilize complex Boolean expressions. The following handler displays a dialog that states which quadrant of a page the user clicked (see Figure 16.12). A 6- by 4-inch page is equivalent to 8640 page units by 5760 page units, since there are 1440 page units to an inch. To determine which quadrant the user clicks, the loc parameter of buttonClick is examined. The loc parameter consists of the location of the mouse pointer when clicked in a format of two comma-separated integers, the *x* coordinate and the *y* coordinate.

```
to handle buttonClick loc
    conditions
        when item 1 of loc < 4320 and item 2 of loc <=2880
            request "You clicked in the upper left quadrant."
        when item 1 of loc < 4320 and item 2 of loc >2880
            request "You clicked in the lower left quadrant."
        when item 1 of loc >=4320 and item 2 of loc <=2880
            request "You clicked in the upper right quadrant."
        else
            request "You clicked in the lower right quadrant."
    end conditions
end buttonClick
```

Can conditions...when...else structures be nested? Yes, the preceding handler could be rewritten using conditions structures nested within the cases of another structure.

```
to handle buttonClick loc
    conditions
        when item 1 of loc < 4320
            conditions
                when item 2 of loc <=2880
                    request "You clicked in the upper left quadrant."
                else
                    request "You clicked in the lower left quadrant."
            end conditions
        else
            conditions
                when item 2 of loc <=2880
                    request "You clicked in the upper right quadrant."
                else
                    request "You clicked in the lower right quadrant."
            end conditions
    end conditions
end buttonClick
```

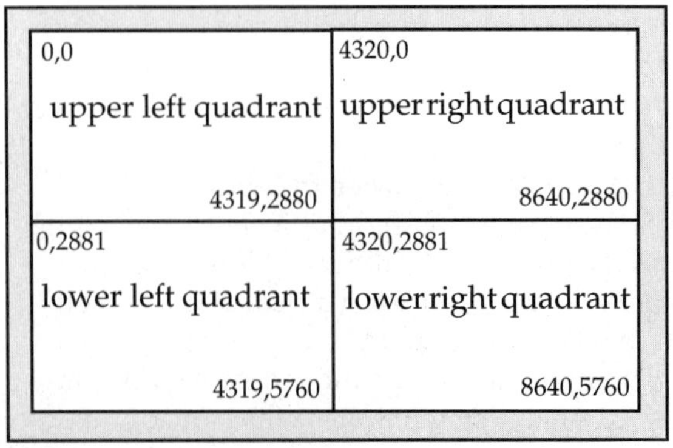

Figure 16.12
A 6- by 4-inch page is divided into four quadrants as measured in page units. By using the case structure, conditions... when, *the handler tells the reader which quadrant he or she clicked.*

0,0 upper left quadrant 4319,2880	4320,0 upper right quadrant 8640,2880
0,2881 lower left quadrant 4319,5760	4320,2881 lower right quadrant 8640,5760

Summary Questions

Given that variable **x = 5**, **y = 10**, and **z = 3**, evaluate each of the following expressions as either **true** or **false**.

1. x >= 10
2. y < 25
3. z < y − x
4. x * z > y
5. x < 10 and y > 5

6.   x < 10 and z > 5
7.   x < 5 and y = 10 or z > 5
8.   x < 5 or z < 5
9.   x < 5 or y > 10
10. (y > 5 or z < 10) and x < 4

Use the following handler in answering questions 11 through 13.

```
to handle buttonClick
    system a, x, y
    if x>5 and y<=5 then
        put y * z into a
    else
        put  x * 3 into a
    end if
end buttonClick
```

11. If x = 3 and y = 5, what is the value of a after the above handler is executed?
12. If x = 7 and y = 2, what is the value of a after the above handler is executed?
13. If x = 7 and y = 6, what is the value of a after the above handler is executed?

Use the following handler in answering questions 14 through 16.

```
to handle buttonClick
    system a, x, y
    if x>5 or y<=5 then
        put y * z into a
    else
        put  x * 3 into a
    end if
end buttonClick
```

14. If x = 3 and y = 5, what is the value of a after the above handler is executed?
15. If x = 7 and y = 6, what is the value of a after the above handler is executed?
16. If x = 3 and y = 6, what is the value of a after the above handler is executed?

Use the following handler in answering questions 17 through 20.

```
to handle buttonClick
    system a, x, y, z
    conditions
        when x >= 5
            put 1 into a
        when y <= 10
            put 2 into a
        when z >= 5
            put 3 into a
        when x * y > 30
            put 4 into a
        else
            put  5 into a
    end conditions
end buttonClick
```

17. If x = 3, y = 12, and z = 10, what is the value of a after the above handler is executed?
18. If x = 3, y = 12, and z = 5, what is the value of a after the above handler is executed?
19. If x = 5, y = 8, and z = 8, what is the value of a after the above handler is executed?
20. If x = 1, y = 12, and z = 3, what is the value of a after the above handler is executed?

Hands-On Projects

A. Examine the software that accompanies this chapter. Open the "Table of Contents" book by double-clicking its icon in the "Developing with ToolBook" group window in the Windows Program Manager. Inside the "Table of Contents," click the book representing volume 16. Examine the contents of this tutorial as a means of strengthening your understanding of the material presented in this chapter.

B. Create a book that quizzes the reader on the material presented in this chapter. The quiz should consist of 10 questions, with one question presented on each page. Feedback should be provided after each question has been answered. After the reader has taken the quiz, he or she should be presented with a score.

C. Create a book that simulates the rolling of a pair of dice when the user clicks a button. Use the random() function to calculate the value each time, and seed the random-number generator by using the sysClock property upon entering the page. The images of the dice can be drawn using ToolBook's drawing tools, grouped and hidden or shown, depending on the value of the two random numbers generated (one for each die). (See Figure 16.13.)

Figure 16.13
Conditional statements can be used to show grouped objects representing dice.

D. Workers in the XYZ Widgets Factory are paid according to the number of widgets they assemble in a week. The pay rate per piece varies depending on how many widgets each successfully assembles. The pay rate is based on the following schedule.

Number of assembled widgets	Price per widget
1–299	$1.25
300–349	$1.40
350–399	$1.55
400+	$1.70

For instance, a worker who assembles 200 widgets would earn $250 for the week ($1.25 * 200), while a worker who assembles 300 widgets would earn $420 ($1.40 * 300). Create a book with a button that asks for the number of widgets assembled by a worker and then displays the wages earned by that worker.

E. In the fictitious country of Xambu, a worker's annual income tax is calculated so that the taxable income is equal to total income minus $3000 for each dependent claimed. The first $20,000 of the taxable income is taxed at 15%, the next $20,000 is taxed at 20%, and any taxable income over $40,000 is taxed at 25%.

For example, a worker earns $65,000 a year and has four dependents. His taxable income is $65,000 – (4 * $3000) which equals $53,000. The income tax is then calculated as follows.

$$15\% \text{ of } \$20,000 = \$3,000$$
$$20\% \text{ of } \$20,000 = \$4,000$$
$$25\% \text{ of } \$13,000 = \$3,250$$
$$\text{Income tax due} = \$10,250$$

Create a book like that pictured in Figure 16.14, in which the user enters the annual income and the number of dependents, clicks the "Calculate" button, and sees the income tax due. The tax is calculated according to the preceding instructions. The tax due should be formatted as $#,0.00. Use the sample data that follows.

Income	Dependents	Tax due
34500	3	$ 4,100.00
150000	5	$30,750.00
8000	3	$ 0.00

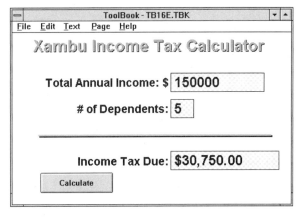

Figure 16.14
Hands-On Project E utilizes a conditions *structure nested within an* if...then...else *structure.*

19000	1	$ 2,400.00

F. Create a page that tests a grade school student's ability to add two-digit numbers (see Figure 16.15). The screen should display a pair of two-digit numbers (that is, values between 10 and 99) randomly when the user enters the page. Instruct the student to enter the sum of the two numbers in a field provided and click the "Grade my answer" button for feedback. If the answer is incorrect, the screen should display the correct answer. Display a new question automatically, after the feedback is given and the answer field cleared. (Bonus: Display an ongoing score for the student.)

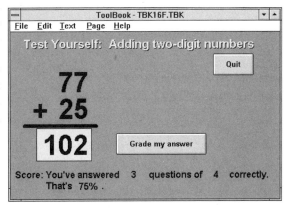

Figure 16.15
Hands-On Project F utilizes an if...then...else *structure to provide appropriate feedback to the student.*

Chapter 17

Changing Properties and Manipulating Text Strings

In the second section of this textbook, various properties of objects were set that defined the appearance and behavior of objects. These properties were set through dialog boxes, such as a "Button Properties" dialog; from Right-Click menus; or from the menus. In previous chapters, certain properties have been set through statements in a handler, such as the text of a field. In reality, almost any property of an object can be set. The value of a property can also be "checked" by a handler and an action taken based on the value of the property. For instance, the action of a handler might be based on whether a radio button has been checked, the caption of a button is on or off, or the fill color of a circle is red or green. By Using OpenScript to set the property of an object, a program can change the font of a field, the color of an object, and the position or size of an object. System properties include the cursor style and the ability to lock the screen so that the user does not see the process of the screen being altered as a script is executed.

String type data in a container may be manipulated in much the same manner as numeric data. Multiple strings may be concatenated to form one string. Parts of a string may also be extracted. OpenScript also includes functions for returning the size of a string (how many characters it contains), counting the number of text lines, and converting between upper- and lowercase.

Getting the Properties of an Object

The status of an object property or system property may be accessed by an OpenScript command. Chapter 13 discussed properties in terms of being a container much like a variable. The value of a container may be referenced in a statement and this includes the value of a property. The fillColor property value of a rectangle might be referenced in an assignment operator, put statement, or Boolean expression just as a variable would be:

    myColor = the fillColor of rectangle id 3

    put the fillColor of rectangle id 3 into myColor

    if the fillColor of rectangle id 3 is green then

The general syntax for working with object properties is to state the property and the object to which it belongs:

    [the] *property* of *objectReference*

The word the is optional. The object may be referred to by ID number, layer, or name:

    the strokeColor of field id 3

caption of button 4

the transparent of group "video monitor"

Since the object's layer may change when an object is brought forward, sent backward, or deleted, the wise OpenScript programmer will refer to an object by name or ID, and not by layer. (The use of the layer reference should be limited to special situations, such as in an animation where the layer of an object is being changed.)

In addition to referencing a property in an assignment operator statement, put statement or Boolean expression, the get command can be used to place the value of a container in the variable name it. The syntax of the get command is shown in Figure 17.1.

get the bounds of button id 5

get fontSize of recordfield "page title"

The get command is rarely used. It is generally an unnecessary step, since the value of a container may be referenced directly in a statement. For instance, the handler

```
to handle buttonClick
    get the fillColor of self
    if it is red then
        request "The object you clicked is colored red."
    else
        request "The object you clicked is NOT colored red."
    end if
end buttonClick
```

can be written in one less step without the get command:

```
to handle buttonClick
    if the fillColor of self is red then
        request "The object you clicked is colored red."
    else
        request "The object you clicked is NOT colored red."
    end if
end buttonClick
```

Figure 17.1
The get *command places the value of an expression —such as a property, variable, or calculation— into the variable* it.

The get command

Syntax: **get *expression***

Purpose: Evaluates an expression, assigning the value to the variable it.

Examples: get x + y - z

            get the text of field id 12

            get the fillColor of ellipse "red ball"

self, my, and target

In the preceding script, a value of a property belonging to self is checked. In OpenScript, the **self keyword** refers to the object in whose script it is referenced. If the preceding handler is in the script of ellipse id 5, the statement

```
if the fillColor of self is red then
```

would be the same as saying

```
if the fillColor of ellipse id 5 is red then
```

The advantage of using self in referring to an object in its script relates primarily to reusability, an important concept in object-oriented programming. If ellipse id 5 were copied and pasted onto another page or book, or even onto the same page, it may no longer be ellipse id 5, but rather ellipse id 8, ellipse id 75, or some other ID number. Referring to the object as self in its script allows the object to be pasted and have its script function without error (assuming it doesn't reference other necessary objects or external containers). Likewise, if the name is referenced instead of the ID number, there may already be an object by that name that might receive the action designated for itself.

The property of an object may also be referenced in its own script by using the **my keyword**. The syntax is simply

```
my property
```

instead of

```
the property of self
```

The handler you saw earlier might also be written as

```
to handle buttonClick
    if my fillColor is red then
        request "The object you clicked is colored red."
    else
        request "The object you clicked is NOT colored red."
    end if
end buttonClick
```

A third keyword that might be used in referencing a property is **target**, which refers to the object originally receiving a message. Although target and self often refer to the same object, this is not always the case. When a user clicks a group object for instance, an object that makes up part of the group object receives the original buttonClick message. If the object has no buttonClick handler, the message is forwarded to the group object. A reference to the target in the group's buttonClick handler would not refer to the group as a whole (as the self reference would), but to the object of the group that was clicked. The following handler in a group's script would hide the entire group momentarily:

```
to handle buttonClick
    hide self
    pause 2 seconds
    show self
end buttonClick
```

but if **self** were changed to **target**, like so:

```
to handle buttonClick
    hide target
    pause 2 seconds
    show target
end buttonClick
```

only the object of the group that was clicked would be hidden for 2 seconds. The other objects composing the group would not disappear. The **target** reference to an object, then, is used in scripts that may be higher up the object hierarchy than where the message originated but that get or set a property of the object originally receiving the message.

Setting the Properties of an Object

Previously, properties of an object have been set using the assignment operator or the **put** command:

```
fillColor of self = green
```

```
fillColor of self = "120,50,100"  -- Hue, lightness and saturation of 'green'
```

```
put green into the fillColor of self
```

Another common way of setting a property of an object is to use the **set command**:

```
set the fillColor of self to "green"
```

The syntax and use of the **set** command is shown in Figure 17.2. Not all properties can be set. Some, such as the **idNumber** of an object, are only obtainable. The **idNumber** of an object is set by the system upon creation and may not be set in an OpenScript command. User-defined properties, as explained in Chapter 13, may also be gotten and set using the methods discussed in this chapter. Appendix B lists the various built-in properties of ToolBook objects. Additional information about each property may be found in Toolbook's on-line help or the OpenScript manual that accompanies ToolBook.

Setting the property of an object allows a handler to change the appearance of an object or group of objects. The following handler in an object's script causes the object to randomly change colors when nothing else is happening.

Figure 17.2
The set *command can be used to assign a value to a property or other container.*

The set command

Syntax: **set *container* to *value***

Purpose: Assigns a value to a container (generally used for properties). The value may be a literal constant, an expression, or a reference to another container.

Examples: set the text of field id 4 to "Hello world!"

            set the strokeColor of rectangle "box" to "red"

            set the text of field id 3 to the script of field id 4

```
notifyBefore idle
    set the rgbFill of self to random(255),random(255),random(255)
    pause 30 ticks
end idle
```

The rgbFill is similar to the fillColor property of an object. The fillColor and strokeColor properties of an object use three numbers separated by commas to reference a particular number or a color constant such as red, green, or white. The three numbers in the fillColor or strokeColor property refer to the HLS (hue, lightness, and saturation) values of an object. The hue is a number between 0 and 360; the lightness and saturation values are numbers between 0 and 100. Any shade may be referenced by its hue, lightness, and saturation values. Color shades may also be referenced by their RGB (red, green, blue) values as well. These three values are integers between 0 and 255, representing a color's red, green, and blue intensities. OpenScript allows programmers to use either scheme. When the rgbFill property of an object is set, ToolBook also adjusts the value of the object's fillColor property and vice versa. The **pause command** is used to pause the execution of a handler for a specified amount of time. A **tick** is approximately 1/100 second, so 30 ticks would be roughly 1/3 second. Figure 17.3 further explains the syntax of the pause command.

Figure 17.3
The pause *command temporarily halts the execution of a handler for a certain length of time.*

The pause command

Syntax:　　**pause *duration***

Purpose:　　Pauses the execution of a handler for a specified period of time. The duration may be specified in the number of seconds or the number of ticks (a tick is approximately 1/100 second).

Examples:　pause 5 seconds

　　　　　　pause 1 seconds

　　　　　　pause 50 ticks　　--approximately a half second

Using Properties with Conditional Structures

The value of a property is often sought in a handler and then used in an if...then...else...end if structure or conditions...when...else structure to direct the action of the handler. Consider the page shown in Figure 17.4. The four radio buttons are grouped and the "Auto-Radio Buttons" option is checked in the group's properties dialog so that, when one button in the group is clicked, its checked property is set to true and the other radio buttons are unchecked. The following handler in the group's script changes the fill color of the square to reflect the color chosen by the user.

```
to handle buttonClick
    conditions
        when the checked of button id 0 is true  -- red button
            set the fillColor of rectangle "mySquare" to red
        when the checked of button id 2 is true  -- blue button
            set the fillColor of rectangle "mySquare" to blue
        when the checked of button id 3 is true  -- yellow button
```

```
        set the fillColor of rectangle "mySquare" to yellow
    when the checked of button id 4 is true  -- magenta button
        set the fillColor of rectangle "mySquare" to magenta
    else
        set the fillColor of rectangle "mySquare" to white
  end conditions
end buttonClick
```

Figure 17.4
The checked *properties of the radio buttons reflect the color of the square.*

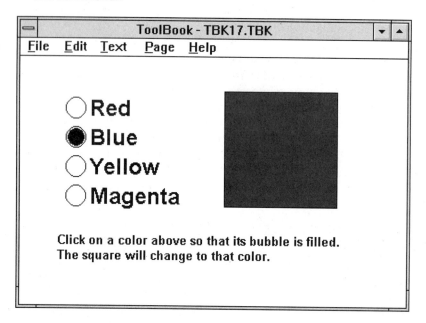

System Properties

Besides objects having properties, the ToolBook system also has certain properties. **System properties** control the appearance and behavior of the ToolBook application and affect such items as the shape of the mouse pointer; the ability to lock the screen temporarily; the date and time; whether to show runtime error messages; default formatting strings; default font face, size, and style values; and default drawing attributes. In general, system properties are easily identified because they start with sys such as sysCursor, sysDate, sysLockScreen, and sysFontSize, though there are a few rarely used exceptions. The keywords target and self are actually system properties that change as events occur. System properties are referenced merely by their name. No object is defined, since they belong to no particular object. A few commonly used system properties are discussed here, but all the system properties are listed in Appendix B, with the object properties. For additional information, consult the OpenScript on-line help in ToolBook.

If handlers are long, it might be wise to visually inform the user that the computer is processing. A popular means of achieving this is to change the cursor from the traditional arrow to an hourglass while the handler is executing. The system cursor is changed by setting the sysCursor property to an integer between 1 and 44, using the set command or assignment operator. Each integer corresponds to a different cursor symbol as shown in Figure 17.5. To switch the cursor to an hourglass image, the sysCursor is set to 4. This is usually done at the beginning of the handler. To reset the cursor to the default arrow, the sysCursor is set to 1, usually at the end of the script. For example:

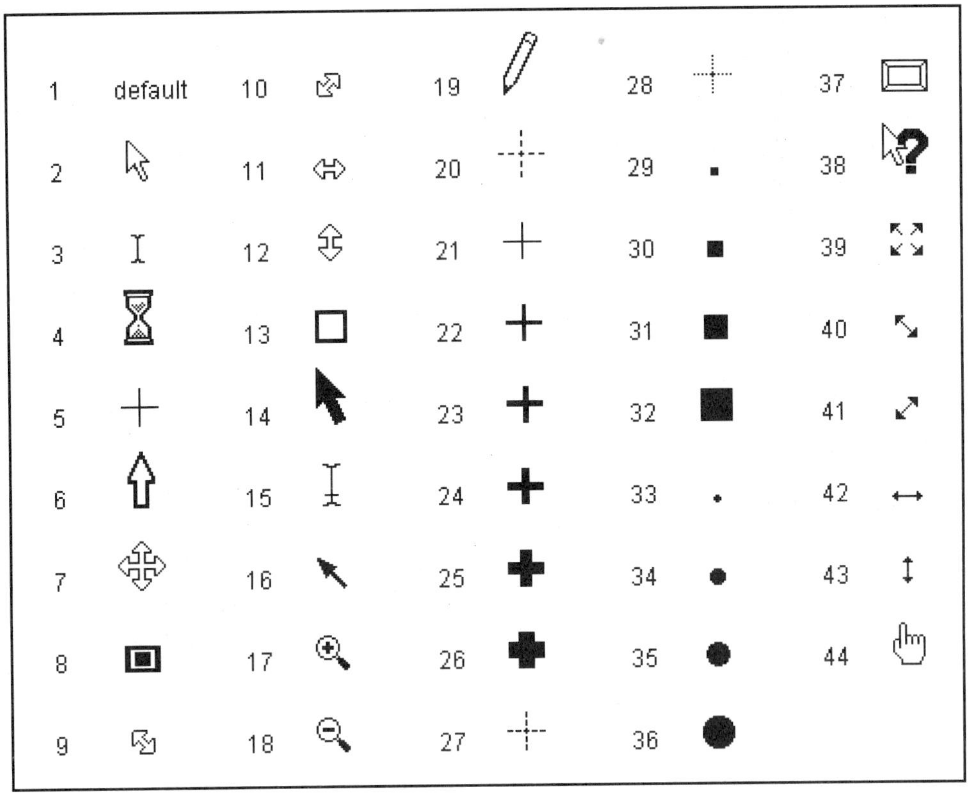

1	default	10		19		28		37	
2		11		20		29		38	
3		12		21		30		39	
4		13		22		31		40	
5		14		23		32		41	
6		15		24		33		42	
7		16		25		34		43	
8		17		26		35		44	
9		18		27		36			

Figure 17.5
There are 44 built-in values for the sysCursor *property. The integers 1 to 44 each correspond to a different cursor appearance.*

```
to handle buttonClick
    set sysCursor to 4

    . . .
    < additional statements go here>
    . . .
    set sysCursor to 1
end buttonClick
```

Cursor images besides the 44 built into ToolBook may be used by importing a cursor image as a resource and then referring to the resource in the set sysCursor statement. For instance:

```
set sysCursor to cursor id 105

sysCursor = cursor id 105
```

For handlers that make several visual changes to the screen, a programmer may wish to keep the viewer from seeing the changes occur until the handler is finished executing. To accomplish this, the sysLockScreen property may be set to true, which keeps the screen form refreshing until the sysLockScreen property is set to false or the handler finishes executing. Locking the screen is useful when several objects are being shown, hidden, or moved. In the following handler, the user does not see each object appear individually. Instead the screen is locked; the show commands are executed; and then the screen is unlocked, revealing the newly shown objects all at once.

```
to handle buttonClick
    set sysLockScreen to true
    show rectangle id 5
```

```
            show field "myText"
            show button "Hide objects"
            show ellipse id 8
            show rectangle id 9
            show irregularPolygon id 12
            set sysLockScreen to false
        end buttonClick
```

The last statement, set sysLockScreen to false, is not necessary, since this is the last statement and setting to false occurs automatically when the script is finished executing.

Setting system properties is often useful in the design process. An author might use the "Command" window to set system properties that control the attributes of newly created objects. Executing the command

```
        set sysFontSize to 18
```

from the "Command" window would cause all fields and recordfields created thenceforth to have 18-point text. In the same manner, the font and style could be set from the "Command" window to affect all future created fields and recordfields:

```
        set sysFontFace to "Times"
        set sysFontStyle to "Bold"
```

Likewise, to draw objects from the center out rather than from corner to corner, the author might issue the command

```
        set sysCentered to true
```

in the "Command" window. Objects created from that point would be drawn from the center out until the sysCentered property were changed to false or the "Draw Centered" option were unchecked in the Draw menu.

Strings: The Need for Quotation Marks

Perhaps the most-used property of any object is the text property of fields and recordfields. The text of a field or recordfield may contain numeric data as well as alphanumeric strings. When a string is assigned to a container, including the text of a field or recordfield, the string should be surrounded by quotation marks. The marks must be used if the string consists of more than one word, is a keyword or OpenScript command, or is the same as a variable name.

```
        put "My dog ate your cat." into the text of field id 2
```

```
        the text of recordfield "student" = "Linus Van Pelt"
```

```
        x = "Phoenix Suns"
```


Concatenating Strings

Separate alphanumeric strings may be combined in assigning them to a container by using after or before with the put command, instead of into. The following handler puts the string My dog has fleas. into the text of a field:

```
to handle buttonClick
    put "dog" into the text of field id 1
    put " has" after the text of field id 1
    put " fleas." after the text of field id 1
    put "My " before the text of field id 1
end buttonClick
```

The following script generates a random number and then displays the number in a request dialog as part of the prompt string (see Figure 17.6).

```
to handle buttonClick
    put random(100) into randNum
    put "The random number is " into prompt
    put randNum after prompt
    request prompt with "OK"
end buttonClick
```

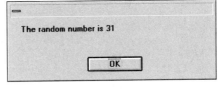

Figure 17.6
This dialog box is generated by a script that includes a variable as the prompt.

The preceding handler uses a variable named prompt as the prompt string in a request dialog box.

OpenScript has two **concatenation operators** for adding multiple strings together in an assignment, or put statement. A single ampersand, &, concatenates two strings together. The statement

```
put "Phoenix" & "Suns" into x
```

places the value PhoenixSuns into x. Note that there is no space between the two words because no space was included in the either of the strings. If a space is desired, the statement could be rewritten in one of two ways:

```
put "Phoenix " & "Suns" into x
```

```
put "Phoenix" & " Suns" into x
```

The value of variable x after either of these statements is executed is Phoenix Suns. OpenScript also has a double ampersand operator, &&, which functions in the same way as the & operator, but inserts a space between the two concatenated strings. The statement

```
put "Phoenix" && "Suns" into x
```

assigns the value Phoenix Suns to variable x. Note that neither string has a space, but a space is inserted by the && operator. The two handlers listed earlier, the ones that use the put...after and put...before commands to assemble strings, can be rewritten using concatenation operators:

```
to handle buttonClick
    put "My" && "dog" && "has" && "fleas." into the text of field id 1
end buttonClick
```

```
to handle buttonClick
    put random(100) into randNum
    request "The random number is " & randNum with "OK"
end buttonClick
```

In the first handler, the string **My dog has fleas.** is assigned to the **text of field id 1**. In the second, a request dialog similar to the one shown in Figure 17.6 is displayed, and the number displayed is randomly generated. Values returned by a function can also be used in a concatenation operation. Therefore, the preceding script can be further simplified:

```
to handle buttonClick
    request "The random number is " & random(100) with "OK"
end buttonClick
```

Character Constants

Carriage return-linefeeds, spaces, and tabs may be specified in a string concatenation by using the **crlf**, **space**, and **tab** constants.

```
put "Phoenix" & crlf & "Suns" into the text of field id 1
```

assigns the two phrases to two lines of the field's text, as seen in Figure 17.7. Note the carriage return-linefeed after the **Phoenix** phrase. The handler

```
to handle enterPage
    put "Name" & tab & "Score" into text of field id 5
    put crlf & "Jenny" & tab & "89" after the text of field id 5
    put crlf & "Bobby" & tab & "82" after the text of field id 5
    put crlf & "James" & tab & "94" after the text of field id 5
    put crlf & "Sarah" & tab & "78" after the text of field id 5
end enterPage
```

writes text to **field id 5**, as shown in Figure 17.8. The statement

```
myTeam = "St. Louis" & space & "Cardinals"
```

assigns the value, St. Louis Cardinals to the variable **myTeam**.

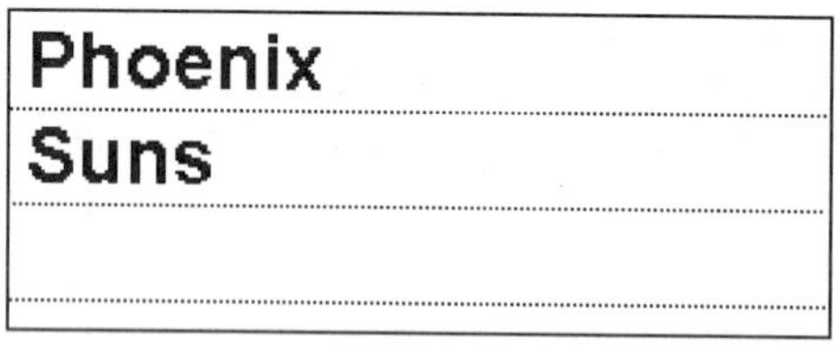

Figure 17.7
The crlf constant is used to place a carriage return-linefeed between text, placing the text on separate lines.

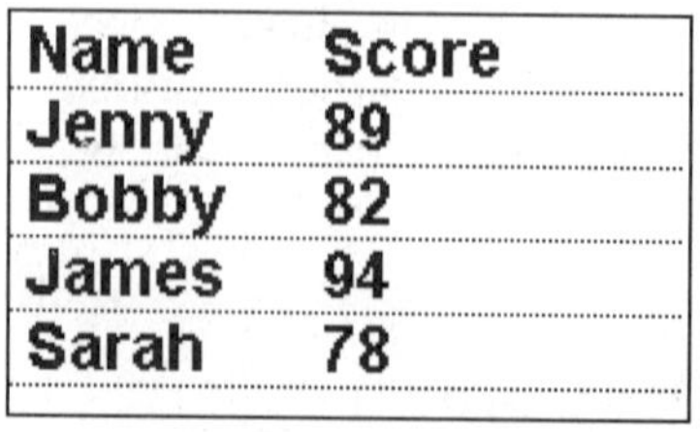

Phoenix
Suns

Figure 17.8
The tab constant can be concatenated into a string to produce a table.

Name	Score
Jenny	89
Bobby	82
James	94
Sarah	78

Extracting Parts of Strings

OpenScript has the ability to extract information from strings by specifying certain elements of a string. Characters, words, text lines, and items may all be extracted. A single character of a string may be isolated by using the expression

    character n of string

    char n of string

where *n* is the number of the character in the string and *string* is a reference to a container holding some value or to a literal string. For example:

    character 5 of text of recordfield "title"

    character 8 of x

    character 6 of "The Three Little Pigs"

Suppose, for instance that a handler asks a user if he or she wishes to exit in an ask dialog box. The user might answer by typing "yes" or "y", so the programmer designs the algorithm to examine just the first character of the user's response. If it is "y", then the box is exited; otherwise, nothing happens. The programmer's code looks like this:

```
to handle buttonClick
    ask "Do you wish to exit?"
    if char 1 of it is "y" then
        send exit
    end if
end buttonClick
```

The handler

```
to handle buttonClick
    x = "toolbook"
    a = char 5 of x
    b = char 2 of x
    c = char 1 of x
    text of field id 1 = a & b & b & c
end buttonClick
```

writes the word boot to the text of field id 1, since the character b is substituted for variable a in the last line, the value of variable b is the character o, and the value of variable c is t. A range of characters in a string may be extracted using the expressions

    characters x to y of string

    chars x to y of string

where x is the number of the first character to include and y is the number of the last character of the range to include. For example:

```
to handle enterPage
    system STRING x, y
    put "I like ToolBook" into x
    put chars 8 to 15 of x into y
end enterPage
```

assigns the value ToolBook to y since the eighth character of x is the T and the fifteenth character is the k. In the same manner, a specific word or range of words may be extracted from a string by using the general expressions

```
word x of string
```

```
words x to y of string
```

When the handler

```
to handle buttonClick
    put "Arizona Cardinals" into myTeam
    request "I live in " & word 1 of myTeam & "." with "OK"
end buttonClick
```

is executed, the request dialog shown in Figure 17.9 is displayed, with the word Arizona being the value of word 1 of myTeam in the request statement.

Figure 17.9
String operators such as
word 1 of... *may be used in*
a request *statement to form*
the prompt string of a
dialog.

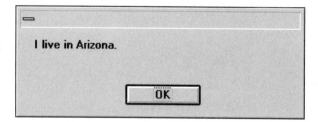

Figure 17.10 shows a field with several lines of text. A line of text in a container may be extracted using the textline operator. A range of text lines may be extracted using the textlines operator. The general syntax for these expressions is

```
textline x of container
```

```
textlines x to y of container
```

Assuming that field id 1 is that pictured in Figure 17.10, the following handler places the value New York Giants into variable x:

```
to handle buttonClick
    put textline 3 of field id 1 into x
end buttonClick
```

Figure 17.10
The text of a field may
consist of many lines.

```
Arizona Cardinals
Dallas Cowboys
New York Giants
Philadelphia Eagles
Washington Redskins
```

The next handler assigns the third and fourth lines of field id 1 to variable x and includes a carriage return-linefeed to separate them.

```
to handle buttonClick
     put textlines 3 to 4 of field id 1 into x
end buttonClick
```

Items in a comma-delimited list can be extracted using the item or items operators:

```
to handle buttonClick
     put "dog,cat,bird,fish,snake,monkey" into myList
     put item 3 of myList into animal
end buttonClick
```

```
to handle buttonClick
     put "dog,cat,bird,fish,snake,monkey" into myList
     put items 2 to 4 of myList into animal
end buttonClick
```

The first of the preceding handlers assigns the value bird to the variable animal; the second handler assigns the string cat,bird,fish to the variable animal.

The text operators can be used in conjunction with each other. For instance, the handler

```
to handle buttonClick
     put "dog,cat,bird,fish,snake,monkey" into myList
     put chars 2 to 3 of item 3 of myList into animal
end buttonClick
```

assigns the string ir to the variable named animal, since these are the second and third letters of the third item of the value in the myList variable. Likewise, using Figure 17.10 as field id 1, the handler

```
to handle buttonClick
     system STRING team
     put word 2 of textline 2 of the text of field id 1 into team
end buttonClick
```

Operators for Extracting String Data

Operator	Example
character	put character 1 of text of field id 1 into x
char	put char 1 of lastname into x
characters	put characters 4 to 7 of text of field id 1 into x
chars	put chars 2 to 5 of text of recordfield id 3 into x
word	put word 1 of text of field id 1 into x
words	put words 1 to 3 of text of field id 1 into x
item	put item 1 of myList into x
items	put items 3 to 5 of myList into x
textline	put textline 3 of text of field id 5 into x
textlines	put textlines 1 to 4 of x into y

Figure 17.11
There are several operators for extracting string data from a field or some other container.

puts the string Cowboys into the system variable named team. Figure 17.11 summarizes the operators available for extracting data from a string. The value and uses of these string operators and functions will become more apparent in the next chapter on loop structures. The number of text lines or items might be used to control the number of times that a loop is executed. The string operators can also be used in assigning text to a container. Again referring to Figure 17.10 as field id 1, the following handler would change the second line from Dallas Cowboys to Texas Cowboys and the first line from Arizona Cardinals to Atlanta Falcons.

```
to handle buttonClick
     put "Texas" into word 1 of textline 2 of the text of field id 1
     textline 1 of text of field id 1 = "Atlanta Falcons"
end buttonClick
```

String Data Functions

Just as OpenScript has several built-in functions for manipulating numeric data, OpenScript has several functions for returning information about string data. The ansiToChar( ) and charToAnsi( ) functions to convert a character to its ANSI number equivalent and vice versa were presented in Chapter 14. OpenScript has functions for determining the number of characters, words, text lines and items in a container, as well as finding the starting character of a string inside a container and converting the characters of a string from upper- and lowercase and vice versa.

The charCount( ) function returns the number of characters in a specified string or container. Its syntax is

```
charCount(string)
```

and it might be used in a put statement, with an assignment operator, or in a control structure as part of a Boolean expression.

```
to handle buttonUp
     system gNameLength
     ask "Enter your full name:"
     put the charCount(it) into gNameLength
     request "Your name consists of" && charCount(it) && "letters." with "OK"
end buttonUp
```

The preceding handler uses the charCount( ) function to determine the length of a text string entered by the user, assigning the count to a system variable and displaying the value in a request dialog box within a concatenated prompt string. The text of a field or recordfield can only contain 30,000 characters. Consider an application where a student is entering a long essay into a field or using a field to record notes about material presented in a courseware application. A handler in the field might periodically (perhaps each time the Enter key is pressed) check the number of characters in the text of a field and warn the user if he or she is approaching the limit.

```
to handle keyChar key
     if key = 13 then
          if the charCount(text of self) > 28,000 then
               request "You are nearing the 30,000 character limit for this field."
          end if
     end if
     forward
end keyChar
```

The syntax and usage of the wordCount( ), textlineCount( ) and itemCount( ) functions are similar.

```
to handle buttonClick
     put charCount(text of field id 1) && "characters" into prompt
     put crlf & wordCount(text of field id 1) && "words" after prompt
     put crlf & textLineCount(text of field id 1) && "textlines" after prompt
     put crlf & itemCount(text of field id 1) && "items" after prompt
     request "Information about Field id 1:" & crlf & prompt with "OK"
end buttonClick
```

If field id 1 in the preceding handler is the field shown in Figure 17.10, the handler displays the request dialog shown in Figure 17.12. In executing the handler, first the character count is placed into the variable named prompt. Then the word count is placed on the second line of the variable named prompt by virtue of inserting a carriage return-linefeed (crlf) before the word count. The next two lines place the text line and item counts on the third and fourth lines of variable prompt respectively. The request command uses a concatenated string to display the information consisting of a line of text (Information about Field id 1:) followed by a carriage return-linefeed and then followed by the value of variable prompt, which consists of the four lines with the counts.

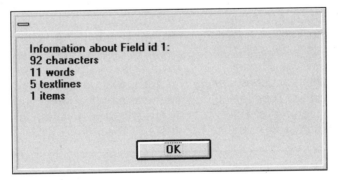

Figure 17.12
The string extraction operators might be used to define the prompt of a request dialog to display information about a field.

The offset( ) function returns the character number of a source string where a specified substring begins. In the string My dog has fleas., the substring dog begins at the fourth character. The syntax of the offset( ) function is

offset(*subString,sourceString*)

Therefore, its use in the command

put offset("dog", "My dog has fleas.") into x

would put the value of 4 into x. If Figure 17.10 is field id 1 the command

put offset("Cowboys", text of field id 1) into x

puts the value 27 into x because the carriage return-linefeed separating the first and second lines consists of two characters: an ANSI 13 (carriage return) and an ANSI 10 (line feed).

The uppercase( ) and lowercase( ) functions are used to convert a string to all uppercase or all lowercase, respectively. The syntax for each is uppercase(*string*)

lowercase(*string*)

The following handler puts the value MY DOG HAS FLEAS. into the system variable sUpper and the string my dog has fleas. into the system variable sLower.

```
to handle enterBook
    system STRING sMixed, sUpper, sLower
    put "My dog has fleas." into sMixed
    put uppercase(sMixed) into sUpper
    put lowercase(sMixed) into sLower
end enterBook
```

The uppercase( ) and lowercase( ) functions have obvious uses in an English grammar courseware application for teaching capitalization. Figure 17.13 summarizes the various string functions available in OpenScript.

Figure 17.13
OpenScript has several built-in functions for manipulating textual string data.

String Functions

Function	Use
ansiToChar(*integer*)	Converts ANSI integer to its character equivalent
charCount(*string*)	Returns number of characters in string
charToAnsi(*character*)	Converts a character to its ANSI equivalent
itemCount(*string*)	Returns number of items in a string
lowercase(*string*)	Converts string to all lowercase
offset(*subString,source*)	Returns char position number of substring in source
textLineCount(*string*)	Returns number of text lines in a string
uppercase(*string*)	Converts string to all uppercase
wordCount(*string*)	Returns the number of words in a string

Summary Questions

Given that **x = "A big brown bear ate my homework"**, evaluate each of the following expressions.

1. charCount(x)
2. wordCount(x)
3. chars 7 to 11 of x
4. word 4 of x
5. itemCount(x)
6. charCount(word 7 of x)
7. textLineCount(x)
8. words 1 to 4 of x
9. char 5 of x & word 5 of x
10. chars 2 to 3 of word 5 of x & char 1 of word 5 of x & char 21 of x

Which property would you set to change the item cited?

11. The color of text in a field
12. The appearance of the cursor
13. The contents of a recordfield

14. The date according to the computer's clock
15. The time according to the computer's clock

What is the value of x after each of the following handlers is executed?

16. to handle buttonClick
        put "mango,apple,banana,grape,strawberry" into y
        x = item 3 of y
    end buttonClick

17. to handle enterPage
        put "Hello world!" into myText
        put uppercase(myText) into y
        put char 11 of y & char 5 of y & chars 2 to 3 of y into x
    end enterPage

18. to handle buttonClick
        put "The boy caught a fish." into y
        put offset("boy:,y) into x
    end buttonClick

19. to handle leaveField
        put "touch" into y
        put "DOWN" into z
        x = uppercase(y) & lowercase(z)
    end buttonClick

20. to handle buttonClick
        put "My" & crlf & "dog" & crlf & "has" & crlf & "fleas." into text of field id 3
        put chars 2 to 5 of textline 4 of text of field id 3 into z
        put char 1 of textline 3 of text of field id 3 into y
        put textline 1 of text of field id 3 && word 2 of text of field id 3 into w
        put space & textline 3 of text of field id 3 into v
        put char 2 of textline 3 of text of field id 3 into k
        put w & v && k && y & z & char 6 of textline 4 of text of field id 3 into x
    end buttonClick

Hands-On Projects

A. Examine the software that accompanies this chapter. Open the "Table of Contents" book by double-clicking its icon in the "Developing with ToolBook" group window in the Windows Program Manager. Inside the "Table of Contents," click the book representing Chapter 17. The tutorial provides hands-on demonstration of the concepts and particulars presented in this chapter.

B. Create a page with a rectangle whose fill color changes as the user changes the values in three fields for the red, green, and blue values of the fill color. The acceptable values for each field are integers between 0 and 255 (inclusive). The color should change either when the user presses the Enter key in any of the fields or when the system is idle (choose one). As an option, use control structures to verify that the values are within the acceptable ranges and warn the user if they are not, substituting either 0 or 255 for the improper value. Also, make sure that the values are integers. A second option would be to provide buttons next to each field with buttonStillDown handlers for using the mouse to increment or decrement the values of the fields (see Figure 17.14).

Figure 17.14
In Hands-On Project B, a page is created with a square that changes colors as the user alters the values of the red, green, and blue intensities.

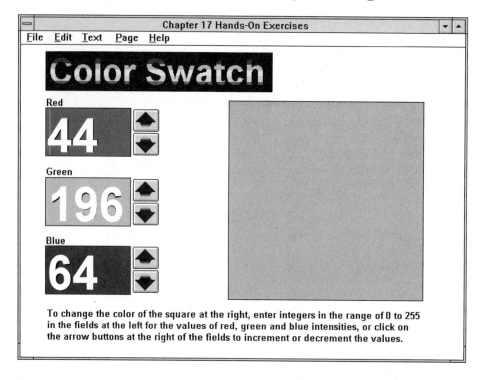

C. Create a page that has sample text in a field and groups of radio buttons for selecting fonts, sizes, and styles that apply the user's selections to the sample text (Figure 17.15).

Figure 17.15
In Hands-On Project C, a page is created in which the user changes the properties of a text field by selecting choices from groups of radio buttons.

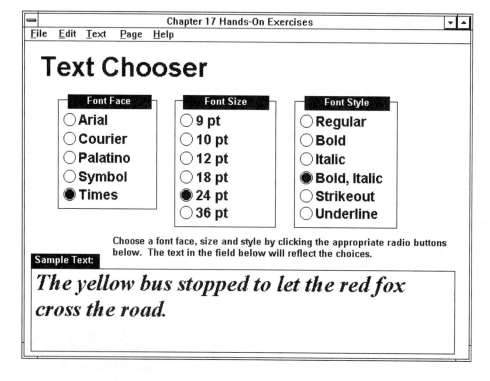

D. Write a button script in which the user is asked to enter his or her full name (first, middle, and last). The entry is extracted with the first and last names being placed in separate system variables and the three names displayed on separate lines in a dialog box, as shown in Figure 17.16.

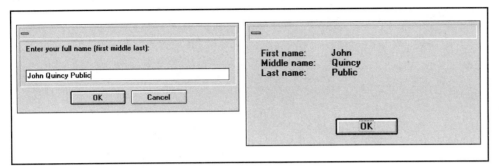

Figure 17.16
In Hands-On Project D, a
handler is written that asks
a user to enter a full name
(first, middle, and last) as
seen at the left. The handler
extracts the three names
from the inputted string
and redisplays them on
separate lines in a dialog
box (shown at the right).

E. Create a book in which prompts such as "Enter the name of an animal:", "Enter a verb:" or "Enter an occupation:" ask the user to input several words and phrases. The screen should then display a field with a story that inserts into a story line the words or phrases entered by the user. For example, the user is asked to enter the name of a place and he or she types "the moon"; the user types "palm tree" when asked to input an object. After several such entries, a field appears with a story that begins: "Once upon a time, a little boy went to the moon to buy a palm tree, when suddenly there appeared a . . ."

F. Create a page in which the user clicks a button and a nonsense sentence is formed by randomly pulling parts of speech from various containers. The page could have several hidden fields: one with a list of adjectives, one with nouns, one with verbs, another with adverbs, and one with prepositional phrases. The user clicks a button and the handler randomly chooses one text line from each and assembles the pieces in the format The <adjective> <noun> <verb> <adverb> <prepositional phrase>. Randomly generated, the nonsense sentence might read

The green hippopotamus ran slowly in the computer store.

Chapter

18

Could You Repeat That?
Loop Structures

Oftentimes, there arises the need to repeat a command or series of commands. A **loop** is a sequence of statements that consecutively executes more than once. The duration of such a routine may be for a specific number of repetitions; if so, the routine is called a **fixed-iteration loop**. If the routine continues until some condition is met, it is referred to as a **conditional loop**. OpenScript provides the step...end step control structure for performing fixed-iteration loops, and the while...end while and do...until control structures for performing conditional loops. In using conditional loops, the programmer must be careful to avoid endless loops. The continue and break statements may be used as loop-controlling devices to skip statements or terminate a loop prematurely.

Fixed-Iteration Loops

Suppose that a programmer wished to print the phrase "I will not chew gum in class." 10 times in a field, as shown in Figure 18.1. Using the commands learned previously in this text, this problem could be coded as follows.

```
to handle buttonClick
    put "I will not chew gum in class." into the text of field id 1
    put crlf & "I will not chew gum in class." after the text of field id 1
    put crlf & "I will not chew gum in class." after the text of field id 1
    put crlf & "I will not chew gum in class." after the text of field id 1
    put crlf & "I will not chew gum in class." after the text of field id 1
    put crlf & "I will not chew gum in class." after the text of field id 1
    put crlf & "I will not chew gum in class." after the text of field id 1
    put crlf & "I will not chew gum in class." after the text of field id 1
    put crlf & "I will not chew gum in class." after the text of field id 1
    put crlf & "I will not chew gum in class." after the text of field id 1
end buttonClick
```

Figure 18.1
Repetitive tasks are easily handled with loop structures.

In the preceding example, the statement

    put crlf & "I will not chew gum in class." after the text of field id 1

is repeated nine times. What if the phrase should be printed 100 or 1000 times? The preceding approach becomes less efficient as the number of repetitions increases. A structure represented by the flowchart in Figure 18.2 significantly reduces the number of statements and therefore increases the efficiency. OpenScript permits such a structure by providing the **step** and **end step** commands, which serve as "bookends" for the statement or sequence of statements being repeated.

    step *counter* from *startingValue* to *endingValue* [by *incrementValue*]
        statement(s) to be repeated
    end step

Figure 18.2
A loop is represented in a flowchart with a decision symbol and a branch that returns to the entry into the decision symbol.

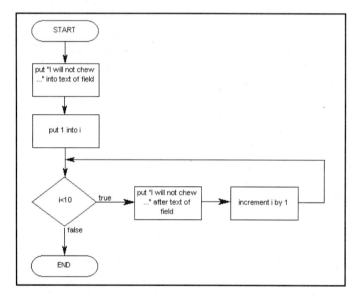

The **step** command defines the counter variable being used; starting and ending values for the counter; and, optionally the amount by which the counter is incremented for each repetition. If an increment amount is not specified, a value of 1 is assumed. Examples of valid **step** statements include

    step i from 1 to 10

    step x from 1 to 100 by 10

    step myCounter from 10 to 1 by –1

    step myCounter from x to y by z

In the second example, x is incremented from 1 to 100 by increments of 10, but in the third example the variable x is incremented by steps of –1, in essence counting backwards from 10 to 1. In each of the first three examples, the loop is repeated 10 times. In the last statement, the starting and ending values for the counter and the incremental value are specified by variables. This is a valid and useful statement. However, if x, y, and z have not been defined or are not integer values, a runtime error will be encountered. The handler given earlier for writing "I will not chew gum in class." 10 times can be rewritten using a step...end step structure:

```
to handle buttonClick
    put "I will not chew gum in class." into the text of field id 1
    step i from 1 to 9
        put crlf & "I will not chew gum in class." after the text of field id 1
    end step
end buttonClick
```

The loop is only repeated nine times, since the first put statement writes the text into the text of the field and the repeated put statement adds a carriage return-linefeed and places the text after the existing text of the field. To write the sentence 100 times instead of 10, the 9 in the step statement need only be changed to a 99. An alternative would be to ask the user to specify how many times the sentence should be written to the field, and use the entry in the step statement:

```
to handle buttonClick
    ask "How many times would you like to write the sentence (2 to 100)?"
    put it into repeat
    put "I will not chew gum in class." into the text of field id 1
    step i from 2 to repeat
        put crlf & "I will not chew gum in class." after the text of field id 1
    end step
end buttonClick
```

The variable used as the counter is assigned a value each time the loop is executed, beginning with the specified starting value the first time the loop is executed. The value is incremented by the specified value each time the loop is repeated. When the counter variable is greater than the specified ending value, the loop is exited and execution continues with the statement following the end step statement. The counter variable may be referenced (and even manipulated) within the statements to be executed inside the loop. The following handler writes the integers 1 through 10 down the text of a field.

```
to handle buttonClick
    put "" into text of field id 1
    step counter from 1 to 10
        put counter & crlf after the text of field id 1
    end step
    clear textline 11 of text of field id 1
end buttonClick
```

In the preceding handler, the text of the field is first cleared (in case there is pre-existing text in it) by writing a null string to it. Next the loop is encountered and the variable named counter increases by 1 with each iteration of the loop and writes the value and a carriage return-linefeed to the field each time. Because the 10th iteration adds a carriage return-linefeed after the number 10, an unneeded 11th text line is created. The final statement of the handler uses the clear command to remove this 11th line. If the step statement were changed to

```
step counter from 1 to 10 by 2
```

the text of field id 1 would contain

```
1
3
5
7
9
```

If it were changed to

    step counter from 2 to 10 by 2

the text of field id 1 would contain

```
2
4
6
8
10
```

A fixed-iteration loop might be used to convert the text of a field separated by carriage return-linefeeds into a comma-delimited list (see Figure 18.3). The number of text lines is determined and used as the ending value for a **step...end step** loop:

```
to handle buttonClick
    put the textlineCount(text of field id 1) into x
    put "" into text of field id 2
    step i from 1 to x
        put textline i of text of field id 1 & "," after text of field id 2
    end step
    clear the last char of text of field id 2
end buttonClick
```

Figure 18.3
A loop might be used to convert crlf-separated text (top field) into a comma-delimited list (bottom field).

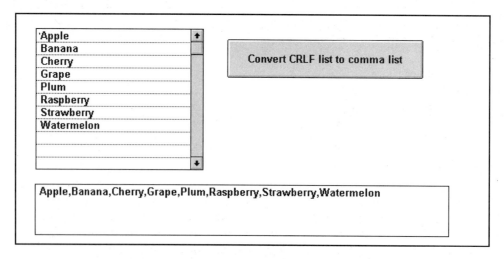

The preceding handler first determines how many text lines there are in the field id 1, placing this value into variable x. Next, any existing text in field id 2 (the target field) is cleared by writing an empty, or null, string to that field. A fixed-iteration loop is utilized from 1 to x (the number of text lines in field id 1). Within the loop, the loop counter, variable i, is used to select a line of text from field id 1 and write it to field id 2 with a comma concatenated behind it. The first time through the loop, the text of the first line of field id 1 is placed after the existing text of field id 2. In reference to the illustration in Figure 18.3, this would be Apple. A comma is also added behind it. In the second iteration of the loop, i would be equal to 2, and so textline 2 of field id 1's text along with a comma is written after the text of field id 2. The text of field id 2 at this point is Apple,Banana,. This procedure continues until i is equivalent to x, when the last text line of field id 1 is put after the text of field id 2. Having completed the specified number of iterations, the loop terminates and the handler continues with the statement following the end step statement. This statement simply removes the last comma after the text of field id 2, since it is unnecessary and would cause an incorrect value if an itemCount( ) function were encountered (there would appear to be one more item than there really is). A similar handler could be written to convert comma-delimited text in a field to a crlf-delimited listing. Again referring to the fields in Figure 18.3, the following script would do the trick.

```
to handle buttonClick
    put the itemCount(text of field id 2) into x
    put "" into text of field id 1
    step i from 1 to x
        put item i of text of field id 2 & crlf after text of field id 1
    end step
    clear the last textline of text of field id 2
end buttonClick
```

This is actually the same structure as before. The references to the fields have been reversed and, instead of using text lines in the loop, items are referenced. Instead of writing a comma after the text, a carriage return-linefeed is written, and the last text line is cleared instead of the last character. Figure 18.4 summarizes the syntax and use of the step...end step structure.

Conditional Loop Structures

The statements inside a conditional loop are reiterated as long as some condition is true or until some condition is met. OpenScript includes structures for both cases. The **while...end while structure** is utilized when the algorithm requires a loop to be

---

The step...end step structure

Syntax: **step *variable* from *startingValue* to *endingValue* [by *stepValue*]**
         statement(s) to be executed within the loop
         end step

Purpose: Repeats a statement or set of statements a specified number of times, using variable as a counter with an intial value (startingValue) that is incremented by the stepValue amount with each repetition of the loop until the variable is greater than the specified endingValue.

Examples: step x from 1 to 10
           . . . . .
           end step

           step i from 1 to 100 by 2
           . . . . .
           end step

           step counter from 100 to 1 by -1
           . . . . .
           end step

Figure 18.4
The *step...end step* structure is used for fixed-iteration loops, where statements are repeatedly executed for a specified number of times.

executed as long as a specified condition is true. The **do...until structure** is utilized when the algorithm calls for a statement or sequence of statements to be executed until some condition is met. One major difference between the two structures is that the do...until structure guarantees that the loop will be executed at least once, but the statements inside the while...end while structure are never executed if the condition is false the first time through. Figure 18.5 shows general flowchart representations of the two conditional loop structures.

Figure 18.5
Flowchart representations of the do...until *and* while...end while *structures demonstrate two major differences. The* do...until *structure repeats while the Boolean test expression is* false *and the* while *structure repeats when it is* true. *The process within the* do...until *loop is always performed at least once. The process within the* while...end while *structure may never be executed if the Boolean expression is initially* false.

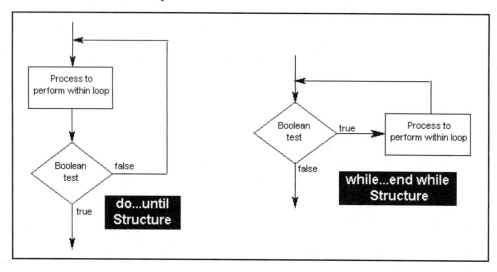

The while...end while Loop

The while...end while loop executes a statement or series of statements as long as the Boolean expression in the while... statement is true. The loop is repeated until the Boolean expression is false. When the expression is false, execution of the handler continues with the statement following the end while statement of the loop. The general syntax of the while...end while structure is shown in Figure 18.6.

The following handler asks the user to enter an integer between 1 and 100. The computer then randomly guesses within a loop until it finds the input integer. A running count is kept of the number of attempts to guess the number. The count is displayed after the loop is exited.

Figure 18.6
The while...end while *structure is used to repeat a process as long as a certain condition is* true.

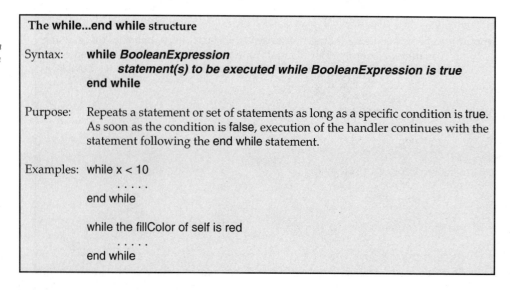

The while...end while structure

Syntax: while *BooleanExpression*
                       statement(s) to be executed while BooleanExpression is true
               end while

Purpose: Repeats a statement or set of statements as long as a specific condition is true. As soon as the condition is false, execution of the handler continues with the statement following the end while statement.

Examples: while x < 10
                  . . . . .
               end while

               while the fillColor of self is red
                  . . . . .
               end while

```
to handle buttonClick
    --seed the random number generator
    put the sysTime into seedNum
    format time seedNum as "seconds"
    seed (seedNum div 3)
    -- get user's number
    ask "Enter an integer between 1 and 100:"
    put it into userNumber
    -- initialize variables
    put 0 into attempts
    put 101 into guess    -- outside of range
    while guess <> userNumber
        increment attempts by 1
        put random(100) into guess
    end while
    request "It took the computer" && attempts && "tries to guess your number."
end buttonClick
```

The while...end while structure might also be used to verify that the user has input data in a specified range. The following handler asks the user to input an integer in the range of 1 to 100. A while...end while is used to verify that the user's entry is within the range. If it is not, the user is asked to re-enter the number. This process is repeated until the user enters an integer between 1 and 100.

```
to handle buttonClick
    system INT xyz
    ask "Enter an integer between 1 and 100:"
    put (it div 1) into xyz
    while xyz < 1 or xyz > 100
        ask "Input is outside range of 1 to 100.  Please re-enter:"
        put (it div 1) into xyz
    end while
end buttonClick
```

The original value entered is "integer divided by 1" as it is assigned to the system variable xyz. This ensures that, if it is not an integer, the decimal portion of the number is eliminated. If the value is between 1 and 100, the while...end while structure is ignored, since the Boolean expression in the while statement would evaluate to false. However, if the value of xyz is less than 1 or greater than 100, then the statements inside the while...end while structure are executed and the user is asked to re-enter a number between 1 and 100. The new value is forced into an integer format and assigned to xyz. The while loop is repeated and the number is again verified to be within the specified range. The statements within the while...end while loop are executed indefinitely as long as the user's entry is outside the range.

The do...until Loop

The do...until loop functions in the same way as the while...end while loop, with the exception that the Boolean logic test is performed after the statements inside the loop have been executed. This ensures that the statements inside the loop are executed at least once. Figure 18.7 summarizes the general syntax of the do...until loop structure. With a little thought and planning, the do...until and while...end while structures are interchangeable with few modifications. Individual programmers will generally favor using one structure or the other. Reconsider the handler used

Figure 18.7
The do...until *structure is*
used to repeat a process
until a certain condition is
met.

The do...until structure

Syntax: **do**

            statement(s) to be initally and repeated within loop if false
            until ***BooleanExpression***

Purpose: Executes a statement or set of statements and repeats the process as long as a
            specified condition is false. Once the condition evaluates to true, execution of
            the handler continues with the statement following the until statement.

Examples: do

            . . . . .
            until x >= 10

            do

            . . . .
            until the charCount(my text) >1000

previously to verify that a user's input is within the range of 1 to 100. It could be
rewritten using a do..until structure instead of a while...end while loop.

```
to handle buttonClick
    system INT xyz
    do
        ask "Enter an integer between 1 and 100:"
        put (it div 1) into xyz
    until xyz >= 1 and xyz <= 100
end buttonClick
```

The system variable xyz is initialized as an integer variable. The statements inside the
do...until loop are executed and the user is asked to enter an integer between 1 and
100. The input value is "integer divided by 1" to ensure that it indeed is an integer
value and the value assigned to variable xyz. The until statement verifies that the
value is within the range of 1 to 100. If it is, execution continues with the statement
following the until statement, which in this case is the termination of the handler. If
the value is outside the range (that is, if the Boolean expression xyz >= 1 and xyz <=
100 is false) the statements within the do...until structure are repeated until the
Boolean expression in the until statement evaluates to true.

A do...until structure might be used to perform some continuous loop until the
user holds the mouse button down. In the following handler, the fill color of a
rectangle randomly changes until the right mouse button is held down.

```
to handle buttonClick
    do
        put random(256) - 1 into r
        put random(256) - 1 into g
        put random(256) - 1 into b
        set the RGBFill of rectangle "Test Color" to r,g,b
    until keystate(keyRightButton) is "Down"
end buttonClick
```

Nested Loops

Just as if...then...else....end if structures could be nested within each other, loop structures can be nested within each other. The next handler creates the multiplication table shown in Figure 18.8. It resides in the script of the "Create Table" button. (The numbers preceding the statements are for the purpose of referring to statements in this discussion and would not be part of the handler entered in the script editor.) Statement 2 places the phrase MULTIPLICATION TABLE into the first line of the field named table. Statements 3 to 6 are a step...end step loop that creates the next two lines of the table, the column headings (consisting of numbers 1 through 9) with an "underscore" underneath each. Statements 7 through 12 constitute another fixed-iteration loop. This loop has a step...end step loop nested within it, in statements 9 through 11. In executing the outer loop (statements 7–12), a row heading is created each time through the loop, writing the loop counter (the value of x) and a vertical bar. The inner loop (statements 9–11) is executed a total of nine times, each time the outer loop is executed. The inner loop writes the product of the row heading and each column heading at the appropriate intersection (using the tab character to accomplish this). The outer loop then is iterated a total of 9 times, but the inner loop is iterated 81 times (9 times for each outer loop iteration).

```
1   to handle buttonClick
2       put "MULTIPLICATION TABLE" into text of field "table"
3       step i from 1 to 9
4           put tab & i after textline 2 of text of field "table"
5           put tab & "—" after textline 3 of text of field "table"
6       end step
7       step x from 1 to 9
8       put x && "|" into textline (x + 3) of text of field "table"
9           step y from 1 to 9
10              put tab & (x * y) after textline (x + 3) of text of field table
11          end step
12      end step
13  end buttonClick
```

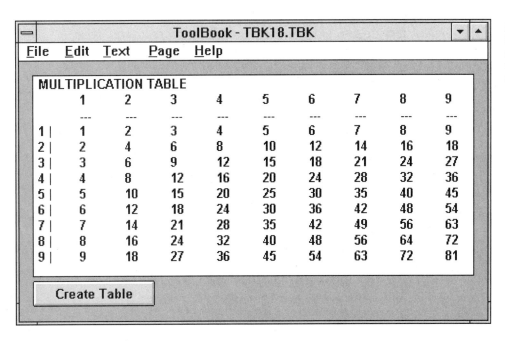

Figure 18.8
Using nested loops, the contents of a multiplication table can be created with a short handler.

Figure 18.9
The nested loops of an algorithm for creating a multiplication table are seen in the algorithm's flowchart.

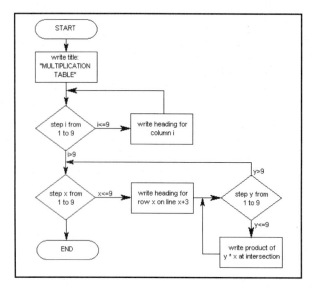

A flowchart for the preceding handler is shown in Figure 18.9.

Likewise, while...end while and do...until structures can be nested using the following general syntax:

```
while BooleanExpression1
    [statement(s) to execute while BooleanExpression1 is true]
    while BooleanExpression2
        [statements to execute while both Boolean expressions are true]
    end while
    [statement(s) to execute while BooleanExpression1 is true]
end while
```

and

```
do
    [statement(s) to execute while BooleanExpression1 is false]
    do
        [statements to execute while both Boolean expressions are false]
    until BooleanExpression2
    [statement(s) to execute while BooleanExpression1 is false]
until BooleanExpression1
```

Different types of structures may be nested within other types of structures. A step...end step fixed-iteration loop might be nested inside an if...then...else...end if conditional structure. A while...end while loop can be placed within a do...until loop, both of which might be inside a conditions...when control structure. The following handler is similar to the data-verification handlers already presented in this chapter. It uses a while...end while loop within a do...until loop to verify that the data entered is both an integer and within the specified range. Whereas the previous handlers changed a noninteger entry to an integer number, this handler forces the user to re-enter the number if it is not an integer.

```
to handle buttonClick
    system xyz
    do
        put 0 into xyz
```

```
        while xyz < 1 or xyz > 100
            ask "Enter an integer between 1 and 100:"
            put it into xyz
        end while
    until xyz = xyz div 1
end buttonClick
```

Danger! Beware Endless Loops

Conditional loops, such as those represented by the while...end while and do...until structures, repeat indefinitely until the condition evaluates to false in the while...end while structure or true in the do...until loop. But what if the condition is never met? For instance:

```
to handle buttonClick
    put 0 into x
    while x <> 1 then
        beep 1
    end while
end buttonClick
```

In the preceding handler, control never exits the while...end while loop; the computer would beep forever. Such a condition is known as an **endless loop**. A programmer must be careful to avoid such problems! But should it happen, pressing both Shift keys simultaneously will terminate the current handler's execution and open the script in the debugger.

Loop Control Statements

OpenScript includes two statements for exiting a loop prematurely and for skipping statements in a loop. The break statement can be used to exit a specific structure, including a handler. The syntax of the break statement is given in Figure 18.10. The break statement causes execution to jump to the statement after the end... statement of the specified structure. In the next handler, the user is asked to input a series of names and to type "Quit" when finished. With each repetition of the loop, the user enters a name and this name is added to a field. If he or she types "Quit", the loop terminates and the handler continues executing with the statement after the end while.

```
to handle buttonClick
    put "" into text of field names
    while 2 > 1   --creates an endless loop which the user may exit
        ask "Enter a name ('Quit' to exit):"
        if it = "Quit" then
            break while
        else
            put it & crlf after text of field names
        end if
    end while
    clear last textline of text of field names
end buttonClick
```

The continue statement allows statements within a loop to be bypassed while the loop

Figure 18.10
The break *command is used to prematurely exit a control structure or handler.*

The **break** command

Syntax: **break [step|while|do|conditions|*handleMessage*]**

Purpose: Exits a control structure or handler prematurely.

Examples: break

break do

break while

break step

break buttonClick

Figure 18.11
The continue *command is used to prematurely exit a control structure or handler.*

The **continue** command

Syntax: **continue [do|while|step [*value*]]**

Purpose: Skips the remaining statements within a loop and repeats the loop from the top, using the next value of the counter if it is a step loop unless a new value is specified.

Examples: continue

continue do

continue step

continue step 6

continues repeating. The syntax of the continue statement is provided in Figure 18.11. In the following handler, the contents of a field are displayed line by line in a loop. The user is asked whether to keep the line or not. If he or she chooses "Yes" when asked to retain the line, nothing happens. If the answer is not "Yes", then the line is deleted.

```
to handle buttonClick
    put textLineCount(text of field id 1) into x
    step i from x to 1 by -1
        request "Keep" && quote & textline i of text of field id 1 & quote & "?" \
        with "Yes" or "No"
        if it is "Yes" then
            continue
        end if
        clear textline i of text of field id 1
    end step
end buttonClick
```

The same process of course could be achieved by using this code:

```
if it is "No" then
    clear textline i of text of field id 1
end if
```

Both the break and continue commands are used infrequently.

The pause command is often used in a loop to slow its execution, most commonly in performing some animation. The next handler below writes text to a field to make it appear that it is being typed. About five characters of the sentence are added within each second. There are approximately 100 ticks in a second.

```
to handle buttonClick
    put "" into text of field id 1
    put "Now is the time for all good men to come to the aid of their country." into phrase
    step i from 1 to charCount(phrase)
        put char i of phrase after text of field id 1
        pause 20 ticks
    end step
end buttonClick
```

The push and pop Commands

Two commands, push and pop, are often used in conjunction with loops. The push command places a value onto an itemized (comma-delimited) list specified in the command. The list is also referred to as a **stack**. Items are pushed so that the last pushed value is the first item in the list. In contrast, the pop command retrieves the first item on a list. When an item is popped, it is removed from the stack. Used in conjunction with each other, push and pop operate on a principle known as LIFO (last in, first out). The last item pushed onto a stack is the first item that is popped from the stack. The syntax of the push and pop commands is given in Figures 18.12 and 18.13, respectively.

Given a field with separate items on each text line, such as the field shown on the left in Figure 18.14, the following handler pushes each text line of the field onto a stack. It clears the text from the field and then pops each item from the stack back into

---

The push command

Syntax: **push *value* onto *stack***

Purpose: Places a value as an item in front of a comma-delimited list (stack).

Examples: push 12345 onto myStack

push textline x of field id 4 onto castOfCharacters

push the fillcolor of rectangle id 15 onto xyz

Figure 18.12
The push command is used to add a value to the beginning of a stack container (usually a variable, but it could be the text of a field or other property).

The pop command

Syntax: **pop *stack* into|after|before *container***

Purpose: Places the first item of a specified stack into, after, or before the value of a container.

Examples: pop myStack into text of field id 1

pop castOfCharacters into starOfTheShow

pop xyz into my fillColor

Figure 18.13
The pop command is used to move the first item in a stack to a container.

separate text lines of the field. Operating on the LIFO principle, the result is the new listing is in reverse order of the original field, as seen in the field pictured on the right in Figure 18.14.

```
to handle buttonClick
     put the textLineCount(text of field id 0) into x
     step i from 1 to x
          push textline i of text of field id 0 onto myStack
     end step
     put "" into text of field id 1
     step i from 1 to x
          pop myStack into textline i of text of field id 1
     end step
end buttonClick
```

The stack is simply a container and, if it must retain its value after the handler has executed, it should be declared as a system variable, placed into the text of another field or recordfield, or assigned to a user-defined property. Popping items is faster than referring to them as "item *n* of . . .," but trying to pop an item from an empty, or null, container will result in an error. Therefore, in popping items from a global container, it is a good idea to first test that the container has a value by using the itemCount( ) in a Boolean expression. For instance:

```
if itemCount(myStack) <> 0 then
     pop myStack into myVariable
end if
```

Figure 18.14
The push *and* pop *commands might be used together to reverse the text listing in a field.*

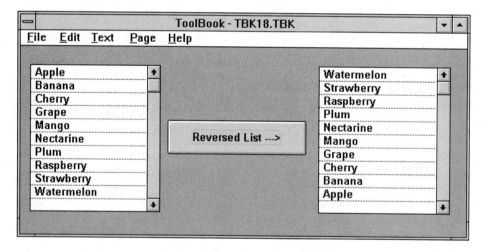

Summary Questions

Complete the following statements by filling in the blanks.

1. A _____ loop executes a specified number of times and is not dependent on some condition being met.
2. A _____ loop executes an unspecified number of times until some condition is met.
3. The _____ command is used to exit a structure prematurely.
4. The _____ structure is OpenScript's form of a fixed-iteration loop.
5. The _____ command is used to skip statements within a loop.
6. The statements within a _____ loop are executed at least once.

7. Tempo within a loop might be achieved with the _____ command.
8. When a loop never terminates it is referred to as an _____ loop.
9. Loops that never terminate may be stopped by pressing both _____ keys.
10. The statements within a while...end while structure are executed as long as the Boolean expression in the while statement evaluates to _____ .

What is the value of the variable x after each of the following loops is executed?

11.
```
put 2 into x
step i from 1 to 5
    put x + i into x
end step
```

12.
```
put 1 into x
step i from 10 to 1 by -1
    x = i
end step
```

13.
```
put 5 into x
step i from 1 to 10 by 2
    put x + i into x
end step
```

14.
```
put 2 into x
while x < 10
    put x * 2 into x
end while
```

15.
```
put 2 into x
do
    put x ^ 2 into x
until x < 10
```

16.
```
put 10 into x
do
    increment x by 1
    put 1 into y
    while y < 3
        put y * x into x
        increment y by 1
    end while
until x > 100
```

17.
```
put 5 into x
while x + 10 < 50
    x = x * 2
end while
```

18.
```
put 2 into x
step i from 1 to 5
    step j from 5 to 1 by -1
        put j * i into x
    end step
end step
```

19.  ```
     put 2 into x
     while x < 2
         step i from 1 to 10
             x = x + i
         end step
     end while
     ```

20.  ```
     put 1 into x
     step i from 1 to 5
         do
             put x + i into x
         until x > 10
     end step
     ```

Hands-On Projects

A. Examine the software that accompanies this chapter. Open the "Table of Contents" book by double-clicking its icon in the "Developing with ToolBook" group window in the Windows Program Manager. Inside the "Table of Contents," click the book representing Chapter 18. The tutorial provides hands-on demonstration of the concepts and particulars presented in this chapter.

B. Create an application for generating lottery numbers. It should include a button that randomly generates five integers between 1 and 43, with no two being the same. A sample design is shown in Figure 18.15.

Figure 18.15
In Hands-On Project B, an application is created for randomly generating five lottery numbers.

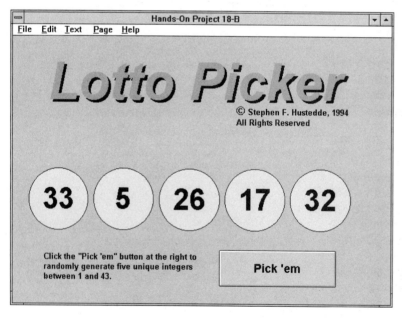

C. Create an application for randomly calling Bingo numbers, one at a time, when a button is pushed. (Bingo numbers fall into five columns labeled B, I, N, G, and O. Numbers in the B column range from 1 to 15, in the I column from 16 to 30, in the N column 31 to 45, 46 to 60 in the G column, and 61 to 75 in the O column.) The application should show the letter (for example, "I") and the number (for example, "27") for each pick. Numbers should not be repeated until a new game is started, and a "called numbers board" should indicate which numbers have been called in the current game. The application should also include a display of the quantity of numbers called. An additional button should clear the display, put 0 into the quantity field, and clear the called numbers board. Figure 18.16

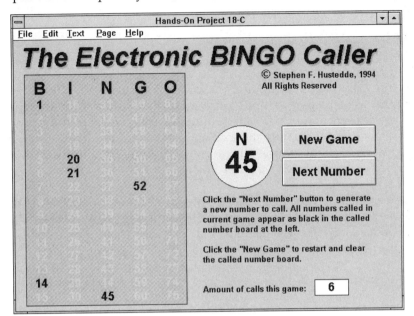

Figure 18.16
An application for picking Bingo numbers might be programmed using fixed-iteration and conditional loops.

shows a sample design for this project.

D. Create an application to generate a Bingo card randomly when the user clicks a button. Figure 18.17 shows a sample application. The numbers in each column, B through O, should be randomly generated and not repeated on the same card. Ranges for the numbers in each column are discussed in Project C. The center

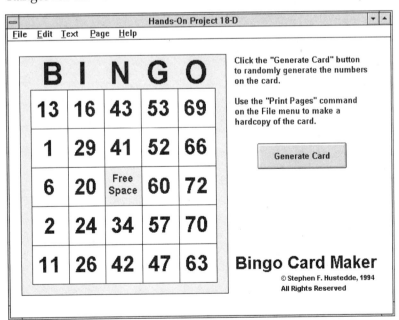

Figure 18.17
Nested loops are used in programming a button to randomly generate the numbers of a Bingo card.

square (in Column N) has no number but is considered a "Free" space.

E. Palindromes are words, phrases, sentences, or numbers that read the same backwards as forwards. Examples include

Bob

Able was I ere I saw Ebla.

1991

Dennis sinned.

mom

123,454,321

Madam, I'm Adam

He lived as a devil, eh?

As seen in the examples, spacing and punctuation are ignored. Create an application that asks the user to input a string and then displays whether the phrase is a palindrome or not. (Hint: In testing the string, use a fixed-iteration loop to first remove all punctuation and spacing, and then another loop to rewrite the resulting string to another variable in reverse order. Finally compare the two strings—if they're the same, it's a palindrome!)

F.   Create a button whose script asks the user to enter two integers, one smaller than the other. Use a loop to calculate the sum of all the integers between these two, inclusive. For instance, if the user enters a 2 and an 8, the handler would display the sum of the integers between these two as 35 (2 + 3 + 4 + 5 + 6 + 7 + 8).

The Structured Approach to Programming

Subroutines and User-Defined Functions

Thus far we have used a top-down approach to programming, in which individual handlers are self-contained and execute in a linear fashion. As the processes performed by handlers become more complex and their code becomes longer, the task of writing clear, easily understood handlers becomes more difficult. Today's **object-oriented** and **modular programming environments**, however, allow a programmer to take a large algorithm and break it up into smaller routines. Modularizing an algorithm allows individual code segments to be smaller and, therefore, more easily written, understood, and debugged. Another advantage is that a small module of one task might be applied as part of another algorithm. The ability to access a routine from several handlers allows the amount of needed code to be reduced, saving significant time. Individual routines may even be copied and pasted into other applications or made available in a system book for multiple applications to access.

In OpenScript programming, the individual tasks are written as separate handlers that may be called from within another handler. There are two broad categories of modular tasks. **Subroutines** perform particular tasks such as changing the color of an object, performing an animation, printing a report, creating a new page in the book, or the like. **User-defined functions** perform some operation and return a value or values to the calling handler. A user-defined function might calculate the number of days between two specified dates, convert a metric measurement into its U.S. equivalent, sort a list of names or numbers, or calculate the factorial of an integer.

Subroutines and user-defined functions can be in the same script as the handler from which they are referenced or in the script in the object hierarchy. Placing a user-defined function in the page script allows any object on that page to access the routine; placing it in the book script provides access to the routine from any handler in the book. Both a buttonClick handler in a button script on page 1 and an enterPage handler in the script of page 12 could access a user-defined function in the book's script for getting the system time and converting to the number of seconds. ToolBook also allows handlers (subroutines and user-defined functions) to be placed in other books and accessed as part of the object hierarchy. These books are referred to as **system books**.

Creating and Calling Subroutines

Complex processes may be broken up into smaller tasks, each being coded as separate handlers and referenced within another handler. These individual handlers are generally given names other than those of standard ToolBook messages. A subroutine handler begins like this:

    to handle printMyReport

The process defined within this handler is executed by calling the printMyReport handler from within another handler by using the **send** command:

```
to handle buttonClick
    . . .
    send printMyReport
    . . .
end buttonClick
```

The ellipses, . . . , represent statements to be executed before and after the process defined by the printMyReport handler is executed. The send command is used to send a message to a particular object or to the script of the same object if no other is specified. The message is routed up the object hierarchy if not handled by the target object's script. Figure 19.1 summarizes the syntax and use of the send command.

Figure 19.1

The send *command is used to send a message to an object.*

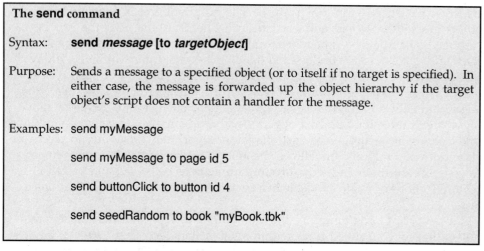

The **send** command

Syntax: **send *message* [to *targetObject*]**

Purpose: Sends a message to a specified object (or to itself if no target is specified). In either case, the message is forwarded up the object hierarchy if the target object's script does not contain a handler for the message.

Examples: send myMessage

            send myMessage to page id 5

            send buttonClick to button id 4

            send seedRandom to book "myBook.tbk"

Figure 19.2 shows a generic algorithm that consists of three distinct processes, called A, B, and C. Assume that each process is several lines long. Note that process B is performed at two different points in the algorithm, once after process A and also after process C. A loop is not easily used here since the repetition of process B is not consecutive. The following handler would perform the algorithm, using a top-down approach:

Figure 19.2

An algorithm may be broken down into a collection of processes. Each process may be coded separately as a subroutine and called from a parent script.

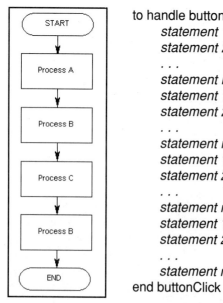

```
to handle buttonClick
    statement 1 of process A
    statement 2 of process A
    . . .
    statement n of process A
    statement 1 of process B
    statement 2 of process B
    . . .
    statement n of process B
    statement 1 of process C
    statement 2 of process C
    . . .
    statement n of process C
    statement 1 of process B
    statement 2 of process B
    . . .
    statement n of process B
end buttonClick
```

In a modular, or structured, approach to coding the algorithm, the processes are

defined as separate handlers and referenced within the calling handler (the calling
handler is buttonClick in the following example).

```
to handle processA
    statement 1 of process A
    statement 2 of process A

    . . .
    statement n of process A
end processA

to handle processB
    statement 1 of process B
    statement 2 of process B

    . . .
    statement n of process B
end processB

to handle processC
    statement 1 of process C
    statement 2 of process C

    . . .
    statement n of process C
end processC

to handle buttonClick
    send processA
    send processB
    send processC
    send processB
end buttonClick
```

In the preceding script, when the user presses the left mouse button, the buttonClick
handler is executed. In its execution, the message processA is sent to the current

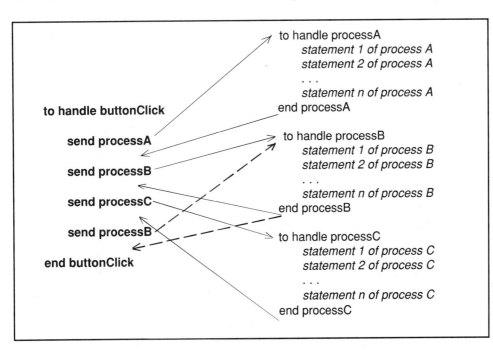

Figure 19.3
*Execution of the main
handler (*buttonClick*) is
suspended temporarily
while the subroutine is
executed.*

script (and up the object hierarchy as necessary). The message is intercepted by the processA handler and the statements within that handler are executed. When the processA handler is finished, execution of the buttonClick handler continues with the statement following the send processA statement. In the same manner, the processes defined by the processB and processC handlers are executed when called. Figure 19.3 illustrates the order in which the statements of the four handlers are carried out.

Container Values and Subroutines

Variables with the same name referenced in two different handlers are treated as separate and distinct variables. The values do not extend beyond the confines of the individual handler unless the variables are defined as global (system) variables. For instance, in the following handlers, the second is called by the first, and both reference a variable named xyz. The value of xyz in the first handler is distinct from the value of xyz in the second handler, since both are treated as local variables.

```
to handle buttonClick
    put 5 into xyz
    send multiplyXyz
    put xyz into the text of field id 3
end buttonClick

to handle multiplyXyz
    put 2 * xyz into xyz
end multiplyXyz
```

The value placed into the text of field id 3 is 5. In executing the buttonClick handler, 5 is assigned to xyz, then the multiplyXyz handler is called. Within the multiplyXyz handler, xyz is doubled in value. However, because xyz is local to the handler, the initial value of xyz in the multiplyXyz handler is 0 (not 5). When control goes back to the buttonClick handler, after the multiplyXyz handler is finished, the value 5 is placed in the text of field id 3. The value of the local variable is retained in the handler until the handler is completely finished executing, even while the handler is suspended as a subroutine executes.

One method of sharing the value of xyz between the two handlers is to declare xyz as a system variable in each:

```
to handle buttonClick
    system xyz
    put 5 into xyz
    send multiplyXyz
    put xyz into the text of field id 3
end buttonClick

to handle multiplyXyz
    system xyz
    put 2 * xyz into xyz
end multiplyXyz
```

Now when the buttonClick handler is executed, the value 10 is written to the text of field id 3. This is because the value of xyz is established as 5 in the buttonClick handler and, since xyz is treated globally in both handlers, that value is used in the multiplyXyz handler. When the multiplyXyz handler is finished executing, the value of the system variable xyz is 10 and this value is used in executing the remainder of the buttonClick handler.

Of course, to achieve the same goal, user-defined properties or the text of a field or recordfield may be used instead of system variables. For example:

```
to handle buttonClick
    put 5 into the text of field id 3
    send multiplyXyz
end buttonClick


to handle multiplyXyz
    put 2 * the text of field id 3 into the text of field id 3
end multiplyXyz
```

The preferable method of working with variables and subroutines is to pass the value of the variable in the calling routine to a variable in the subroutine. The two variables need not be named the same. For example, consider what happens when the following handlers are executed.

```
to handle buttonClick
    put 6 into x
    send double x
end buttonClick


to handle double y
    put 2 * y into the text of field id 3
end double
```

The value 12 is placed in the text of field id 3. In the buttonClick handler, variable x is assigned the value 6. This value is passed to the double handler. The value of x in the buttonClick handler is assigned to the value of y in the double handler. To pass values, **arguments** (references to container values) are specified in the send statement after the handler name. Corresponding **parameters** (variables receiving the passed values) are specified after the handler name in the called subroutine handler. Multiple arguments may be passed to a handler, but there must be an equivalent number of parameters. Multiple arguments and parameters are separated by commas. Consider the following handlers.

```
to handle buttonClick
    put 6 into x
    put 3 into y
    put 4 into z
    send multiplyVals x,y,z
end buttonClick


to handle multiplyVals  param1, param2, param3
    put param1 * param2 * param3 into the text of field id 3
end multiplyVals
```

Three arguments (the values of x, y and z) are passed to the values of three parameters (param1, param2, and param3). The value of param1 would be 6, the value of param2 would be 3, and the value of param3 would be 4. A value of 72 (that is, 6 * 3 * 4) is written to the text of field id 3.

Parameters and arguments may include references to objects, property values, and so on. The following handler accepts two parameters: one is a reference to an object, such as a circle or rectangle, and the other is a reference to a color constant.

```
to handle changeColor objectRef, colorRef
    set the fillColor of objectRef to colorRef
end changeColor
```

This handler might be placed in the book script and could therefore be accessed by handlers in other objects. The subroutine might be called by

```
to handle buttonClick
    send changeColor ellipse id 3, blue
end buttonClick
```

or

```
to handle enterPage
    send changeColor rectangle "mySquare", "0,50,100"
end enterPage
```

In the first example, ellipse id 3 is filled with the color blue. In the second example, the rectangle named mySquare is filled with the color represented by a hue, light, saturation value of 0,50,100 (which is red).

The **to set** Handler

OpenScript includes a subroutine structure for setting the value of a user-defined property. The syntax of the **to set** handler structure is given in Figure 19.4. The **to set** handler uses the setting of a user-defined property and allows the programmer to define the procedure for setting the property's value. This structure is most useful when a set of processes are to be executed when one property is set. For example, setting a user-defined property for an object might result in several built-in object properties being altered. The following handler is used to set a user-defined property named **binary** for the page pictured in Figure 19.5.

```
to set binary to zeroOrOne
    conditions
        when zeroOrOne = 0
            put "0" into text of target
            set fillColor of target to yellow
        when zeroOrOne = 1
            put "1" into text of target
```

Figure 19.4
The **to set** *handler structure is used to specify a routine for setting the value of a user-defined property.*

The **to set** handler structure	
Syntax:	**to set** *property* **[***parameters***] to** *value*
Purpose:	An alternative to the **to handle** handler structure, this structure is used for setting the value of a user-defined property. The *value* represents the expression or value to which the parameter is being set.

Example:	```to set myFill to x
	        if item 1 of x is >50 then
	                decrement item 1 of x by 50
	        end if
	end myFill```

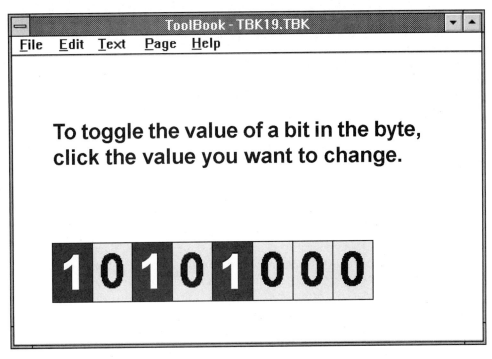

Figure 19.5
A to set handler might be used to change the text and color of a field representing 1 bit of a byte. A click activates the handler.

```
            set fillColor of target  to blue
        else
      end conditions
      forward
  end binary
```

The page pictured in Figure 19.5 contains eight fields. By clicking each field, the binary property is set to either 0 or 1 by using the following handler:

```
to handle buttonClick
    if the binary of self = "0" then
        set the binary of self to 1
    else
        set the binary of self to 0
    end if
end buttonClick
```

In setting the property, the to set binary handler in the page script is executed and both the text and the fill color of the field are altered. The same effect can be achieved using a to handle subroutine in the page script.

```
to handle changeBinary
    if the text of target = "0" then
        put "1" into the text of target
        set the fillColor of target to blue
        set the binary of target to 1
    else
        put "0" into the text of target
        set the fillColor of target to yellow
        set the binary of target to 0
    else
end changeBinary
```

The preceding code could be used in conjunction with each of the field scripts containing the following handler:

```
to handle buttonClick
     send changeBinary
end buttonClick
```

The to set handler, therefore, is used infrequently. Most authors simply use to handle handlers for their subroutines.

User-Defined Functions

As you have already learned, user-defined functions are subroutines that return a value to the calling handler, generally after performing a calculation or some other operation. The ability to create functions beyond those built into OpenScript greatly enhances algorithm development. Operations performed multiple times need only be coded once in a user-defined function and then called from within other handlers. Functions are defined using the to get handler structure. The general syntax of the to get handler is listed in Figure 19.6. User-defined functions are called as built-in functions. They specify the function name, which is followed by a set of parentheses. User-defined functions are called from within another statement (such as put), within an assignment operator, or within a Boolean expression of a control structure. A user-defined function must contain a return statement for each termination point. The return statement includes the value to be passed back to the calling handler and is

Figure 19.6
The to get *handler is used to define the action of a user-defined function.*

The **to get** handler structure	
Syntax:	**to get *functionName* [*parameters*]**
Purpose:	Defines a user-defined function. Statements within the to get handler determine the value returned to the calling statement. The structure must include a return statement for every terminating branch.

Example:	`to get cube x`
	`     return x ^ 3`
	`end cube`

Figure 19.7
The return *statement returns a value to the calling statement.*

The **return** statement	
Syntax:	**return *value***
Purpose:	Returns a value to the calling statement from a user-defined function. There must be a return statement for each termination point of the handler. The *value* may be a constant or a variable expression.

Example:	`to get lightOrDark color`
	`     if item 2 of color >50 then`
	`               return "Light"`
	`     else`
	`               return "Dark"`
	`     end if`
	`end lightOrDark`

summarized in Figure 19.7. The following user-defined function returns the number of seconds between midnight and the current system time.

```
to get timeInSeconds
    put the sysTime into nowTime
    format time nowTime as "seconds"
    return nowTime
end timeInSeconds
```

The user-defined function, timeInSeconds, might be called from within the following statements.

```
put timeInSeconds( ) into startTime
```

```
x = timeInSeconds( )
```

```
if startTime < timeInSeconds( ) + 3600 then   -- more than an hour has passed
```

There are a few rules to consider in writing functions. As with subroutines, the handler for the user-defined function must be in the script of the calling handler or in one of its parent's scripts (in other words, higher on the object hierarchy chain). Secondly, each terminating branch must have a return statement. The following function handler contains a conditions...when structure. Each branch contains a return statement.

```
to get AMorPM
    put the sysTime into nowTime
    format time nowTime as "seconds"
    conditions
        when nowTime = 0
            return "Midnight"
        when nowTime = 43200
            return "Noon"
        when nowTime < 43200
            return "AM"
        else  -- after 12:00 Noon
            return "PM"
    end conditions
end AMorPM
```

A return statement is encountered at each terminating branch. The handler may be rewritten as

```
to get AMorPM
    put the sysTime into nowTime
    format time nowTime as "seconds"
    conditions
        when nowTime = 0
            put "Midnight" into x
        when nowTime = 43200
            put  "Noon" into x
        when nowTime < 43200
            put "AM" into x
        else  -- after 12:00 Noon
```

```
            put "PM" into x
        end conditions
        return x
    end AMorPM
```

In the rewrite, the handler still reaches a return statement before terminating, regardless of which branch of the conditions...when structure was executed. The following handler, however, would result in a compiler error because, if the else branch were executed, no value would be returned to the calling handler.

```
    to get AMorPM
        put the sysTime into nowTime
        format time nowTime as "seconds"
        conditions
            when nowTime = 0
                return "Midnight"
            when nowTime = 43200
                return "Noon"
            when nowTime < 43200
                return "AM"
            else  -- after 12:00 Noon
        end conditions
    end AMorPM
```

One other rule in writing functions is that, once a return statement is encountered, the function terminates any further execution of itself and passes the specified value back to the calling handler. In the following handler, the value 0 is passed to the calling routine if the system time is before noon. The return command following the end if statement is ignored in that case, since the handler terminates after the first return command. If the system time is noon or later, the return statement inside the if...then conditional structure is not executed (because the Boolean expression is false) and the return command following the end if statement is executed and a value of 1 is passed to the calling routine.

```
    to get AMFlag
        put the sysTime into z
        format time z as "seconds"
        if it < 43200 then
            return 0
        end if
        return 1
    end AMFlag
```

Passing Arguments to a User-Defined Function

Arguments may be passed to a user-defined function in much the same way as they can be passed to subroutines. Arguments are listed inside the parentheses in the calling statement and separated with commas if there is more than one argument. In the following statements the values of variables x, y and/or z are passed to a user-defined function.

```
    get myFunction(x, y, z)

    if flagActive(z) is true then
```

put direction(x, y) into possession

The parameters of the user-defined function to which the argument values are passed are listed in the **to get** handler, after the function name and separated with commas if more than one parameter is used. The following **to get** handler statements use parameters named **a**, **b**, and/or **c**. Used in conjunction with the calling statements given previously, the value of **x** would go into **a**, the value of **y** would be assigned to **b**, and **z**'s value would be assigned to **c**.

```
to get myFunction a, b, c

to get flagActive c

to get direction a, b
```

In the following script, the **buttonClick** handler calls the user-defined function named **acreage**. Two values, representing the width and depth of a rectangular area of land, are passed to the function. The variables in the **buttonClick** handler are named **width** and **depth** and these are respectively passed to the parameters named **x** and **y**, which are in the **acreage( )** function.

```
to handle buttonClick
     -- measurements are in feet
     put 5000 into length
     put 3500 into depth
     put acreage(length, depth) into acres
     request "There are "&acres&" acres in a plot of land "&length \
     &" ft. by "&depth&" ft."
end buttonClick

to get acreage x, y
     put (x * y) / 43560 into z
     format z as "0.00"
     return z
end acreage
```

When a **buttonClick** message is encountered, the values of 5000 and 3500 are placed in the variables **length** and **depth**. These two values are passed to the **acreage( )** function. In the **acreage( )** function, the two values are multiplied and divided by the 43560, since there are 43,560 square feet in an acre. The result is formatted with two decimal places and returned to the calling statement. Back in the **buttonClick** handler, the returned value is assigned to a variable named **acres**. The values of variables **acres**, **length**, and **depth** are all used in a concatenated prompt string to display the request dialog shown in Figure 19.8.

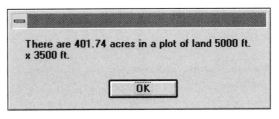

Figure 19.8
The value obtained from a function may be concatenated into a request or ask dialog prompt.

Danger! Beware of Excessive Recursion

Recursive subroutines and functions that call themselves result in a condition resembling endless loops. The following button script results in the error shown in Figure 19.9. The user-defined function named myFunction( ) calls itself in a never-ending fashion:

```
to handle buttonClick
    put 1 into x
    put myFunction(x) into y
    request y
end buttonClick

to get myFunction i
    put  i + 1 into i
    put myFunction(i) into i
    return i
end myFunction
```

Figure 19.9
Functions and subroutines that call themselves or each other repeatedly will result in a runtime error.

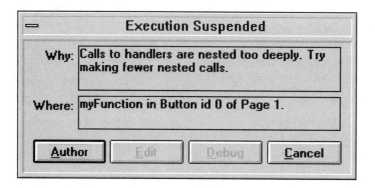

A similar condition can occur if two different subroutines or functions call each other in a circular fashion, as in the following code.

```
to handle buttonClick
    send mySub
end ButtonClick

to handle mySub
    put 5 into x
    put myFunction(x) into y
end mySub

to get myFunction i
    send mySub
    return (i * 2)
end myFunction
```

In this situation, the mySub handler calls the myFunction function, which in turn calls the mySub handler. The mySub handler then calls the myFunction function again, and so the cycle continues until ToolBook recognizes that the routines are nested too deeply and displays the error dialog shown in Figure 19.9. Care must be taken by the programmer in writing handlers that call other handlers or functions so that a recursive situation is not created.

Using System Books to Store Subroutines

In searching for a handler, ToolBook begins with the target object and then begins looking up the object hierarchy (see Figure 12.5). If the handler is not found after looking in the book script, the scripts of any system books are searched for the handler. System books are created as any other ToolBook book. They generally only have book-level scripts that contain handlers of commonly used subroutines and user-defined functions. When saved they are usually assigned a filename with an extension of .SBK instead of the normal .TBK, though this is not a requirement. Which system books are examined is specified in the value of the system property sysBooks. A book may be added to the sysBooks property through a handler, most often in an enterBook handler. For example:

```
to handle enterBook
    if "DATETIME.SBK" is not in sysBooks then
        push "C:\TB30\DATETIME.SBK" onto sysBooks
    end if
end enterBook
```

The preceding script adds a book to the sysBooks property. The following script replaces any listed books in the current sysBooks property with those specified in the statement.

```
to handle enterBook
    sysBooks = "c:\tb30\sysbook.sbk, c:\myapps\mybook.sbk"
end enterbook
```

Any handlers in the DATETIME.SBK system book may be utilized after the book is specified in the sysBooks property. The handler of a system book not listed in the sysBooks property or any other book may be accessed by specifying the location of the handler in the calling statement:

```
send mySubroutine to book "DATETIME.SBK"

get myFunction(x) of book "MYBOOK.SBK"

put theSeconds( ) of page id 4 of book "sample.tbk" into x
```

A system book may be removed from the sysBooks property in a handler by using a conditional loop:

```
to handle leaveBook
    step i from itemCount(sysBooks) to 1 by -1
        if item i of sysBook contains "DATETIME.SBK" then
            clear item i of sysBooks
        end if
    end step
end leaveBook
```

Summary Questions
Complete the following statements by filling in the blanks.
1. Handlers called by another handler to perform some specific task are called _____ .

2. External handlers that return a value or values are called _____ .

3. Subroutines are called by using the _____ command.
4. Values are passed to a subroutine by listing _____ in the calling statement.
5. Variables accepting passed values in a subroutine are listed in the **to handle** statement and are referred to as _____ .
6. A _____ handler structure is used to define the routine for setting a user-defined property.
7. User-defined functions are defined using the _____ handler structure.
8. Every terminating branch of a user-defined function must have a _____ statement.
9. The condition of a subroutine or function calling itself is termed _____ .
10. _____ books contain scripts that are searched if a message is not handled in the current book.

Using the functions that follow, determine the final value of system variable correctAnswer after each of the following buttonClick handlers is executed.

```
to get addTwo x,y
    return x + y
end addTwo
```

```
to get calculate x, y, z
    put x * y − z into q
    return q
end calculate
```

11.
```
to handle buttonClick
    system correctAnswer
    put 5 into a
    put 1 into b
    put addTwo(a,b) into correctAnswer
end buttonClick
```

12.
```
to handle buttonClick
    system correctAnswer
    put 5 into a
    put 1 into b
    put 3 into c
    put calculate(a,b,c) into correctAnswer
end buttonClick
```

13.
```
to handle buttonClick
    system correctAnswer
    put 5 into a
    put 4 into b
    put 3 into c
    put calculate(a,b,7) into correctAnswer
end buttonClick
```

14.   to handle buttonClick
          system correctAnswer
          put 12 into a
          put 5 into b
          put calculate(a,b,addTwo(a,b)) into correctAnswer
      end buttonClick

15.   to handle buttonClick
          system correctAnswer
          put 5 into a
          put 1 into b
          put 3 into c
          put calculate(a,b,c) into correctAnswer
      end buttonClick

16.   to handle integerCheck x,y
          system correctAnswer
          put x div y into correctAnswer
          increment correctAnswer by x mod y
      end integerCheck

      to handle buttonClick
          system correctAnswer
          a = addTwo(3,2)
          b = addTwo(5,a)
          c = addTwo(a,b)
          put calculate(a,b,c) into correctAnswer
          send integerCheck correctAnswer, 5
      end buttonClick

17.   to handle integerCheck x,y
          system correctAnswer
          put x div y into correctAnswer
          increment correctAnswer by x mod y
      end integerCheck

      to handle buttonClick
          system correctAnswer
          send integerCheck(17,3)
          increment correctAnswer by addTwo(2,1)
      end buttonClick

Each of the following handlers results in an error condition. Identify what the problem is.

18.   to get checkIt x, y
          system correctAnswer
          put x * y + y into correctAnswer
      end checkit

19.   to get myValue x, y
          put x * y into z
          put myValue(x,z) into w
          return w
      end checkit

20.   to get yeeHaw x, y
              system abc
              send yippee x,abc
              return (abc * y)
        end yeeHaw

        to handle yippee
              system abc
              increment abc by yeeHaw(1,2)
        end yippee

Hands-On Projects

A. Examine the software that accompanies this chapter. Open the "Table of Contents" book by double-clicking its icon in the "Developing with ToolBook" group window in the Windows Program Manager. Inside the "Table of Contents," click the book representing Chapter 19. The tutorial provides hands-on demonstration of the concepts and particulars presented in this chapter.

B. OpenScript lacks a function for returning the day of the week for a given date. Write a user-defined function that will return the day of the week, (Sunday, Monday, Tuesday, and so on) when called with an argument of a specific date, such as:

        get dayOfWeek(sysDate)
        put dayOfWeek("10/20/1989") into xyz
        put dayOfWeek(x) into theDay

The argument should be a date formatted as m/d/y. The formula for calculating the day of the week is

        w = (d + ((2.6 * m − 0.20) div 1) − (2 * c) + n + (n div 4) + (c/4)) mod 7

where:
  d is day (1 to 31)
  m is month with 1 = March, . . . , 10 = December, 11 = January, 12 = February
  c is the century (for example, for 1994, c = 19)
  n is last two digits of year (for example, for 1994, n = 94)
  (Note: Subtract 1 from year for January or February. For example, for January '94, n = 93.)
  w is day of week (0 = Sunday, 1 = Monday, . . . , 6 = Saturday)

Create a page with a button that asks the user to enter a date in the 1/1/1995 format and calls the preceding function to return the day of the week and display it in a dialog box.

C. Use the function created in project B to create a calendar maker. The user should be prompted for a month and year; a full-page calendar would be created with the "1" in the correct day of the week. The calendar might include small fields in each day's square to record appointments, "To Do" lists, notes, and so on. A sample screen is shown in Figure 19.10. Hints: Write a function to return the number of days in a specified month and use it in creating the calendar. January, March, May, July, August, October, and December all have 31 days. March, April, June, September, and November have 30 days. February has 28 unless the year is evenly divisible by 4. The exception is a year that is evenly divisible by 100 (for example, 1900). In such years, February has 28 days, unless the year is evenly divisible by 400 (for example, 2000), in which case February has 29 days.

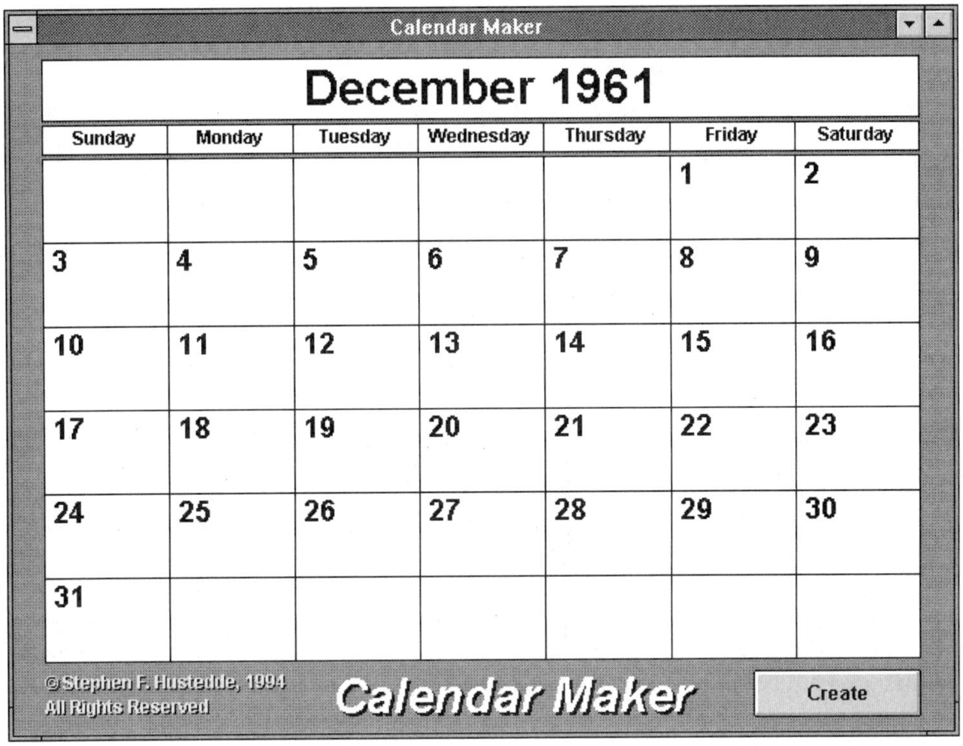

© Stephen F. Hustedde, 1994
All Rights Reserved

Figure 19.10
An application for creating
a calendar might utilize
user-defined functions to
return the number of days
in the month and which day
of the week the first day of
the month falls on.

D. Create a system book file named CONVRSN.SBK that contains the following functions. With each function is a statement of its purpose and any formula you need to create the book.
   1. inchesToMillimeters( )
       given a measurement in inches returns the millimeters equivalent
           number of inches * 25 = number of millimeters
   2. millimetersToInches( )
       given a measurement in millimeters returns the inches equivalent
           number of millimeters * 0.04 = number of inches
   3. yardsToMeters( )
       given a measurement in yards returns the meters equivalent
           number of yards * 0.9 = number of meters
   4. metersToYards( )
       given a measurement in meters returns the yards equivalent
           number of meters * 1.1 = number of yards
   5. milesToKilometers( )
       given a measurement in miles returns the kilometers equivalent
           number of miles * 1.6 = number of kilometers
   6. kilometersToMiles( )
       given a measurement in kilometers returns the miles equivalent
           number of kilometers * 0.62 = number of miles
   7. feetToCentimeters( )
       given a measurement in feet returns the centimeters equivalent
           number of feet * 30 = number of centimeters
   8. centimetersToInches( )
       given a measurement in centimeters returns the inch equivalent
           number of centimeters * 0.4 = number of inches

Create an application for converting from U.S. measurements to metric measure-

ments and vice versa by accessing the routines in the system book file
CONVRSN.SBK.

E. Create a database with a screen like the one pictured in Figure 19.11, which is
used for tracking charge accounts for a small business. All objects should be on
the background, with the white data fields being recordfields. Each button
should access a subroutine and/or user-defined function located in the background script. For instance the "Perform Billing" button might have this handler:

```
to handle buttonClick
    send billing
end buttonClick
```

The to handle billing subroutine handler is located in the background script.

The "Move Balance" button places the new balance amount in the field for
the old balance, to begin a new month's billing, and sets the other fields to 0.

The "Add Purchase" and "Add Payment" buttons each ask the user to enter
an amount that is added to the appropriate recordfield. For example, a customer
might make three purchases in a month, and each time the purchase amount can
be added to the "New Purchases" recordfield.

The "Perform Billing" button takes the old balance and deducts the payments made during the month. A finance charge is calculated on the remaining
amount. The finance charge is calculated according to the following:

If the amount is $0 or less, the finance charge is $0.

If the amount is $1,000 or less, the finance charge is 12% of the amount.

If the amount is $5,000 or less, the finance charge is 14.5% of the amount.

If the amount is $10,000 or less, the finance charge is 16% of the amount.

If the amount is greater than $10,000, the finance charge is 20% of the amount.
The remaining amount is incremented by the finance charge amount and the
amount of new purchases. The result is placed in the "New Balance" recordfield.

The "New Account" button creates a new page.

Figure 19.11
A database for tracking
charge accounts is created in
Project E. It utilizes
subroutines and
user-defined functions.

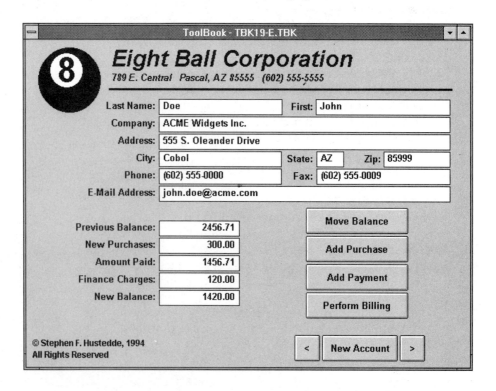

The "<" and ">" buttons navigate to the previous and next page, respectively.

The "Old Balance," "Add Purchase," "Add Payment," "Finance Charge," and "New Balance" recordfields should all be activated to keep the user from accidentally changing their text. A 0.00 format should be applied to the text of these recordfields whenever their values are changed.

F. 1. Create the calculator presented in Chapter 2. Design the screen shown in Figure 19.12. The screen is composed of a field for the numeric display whose text is right-justified. There are 19 buttons for the number entries, decimal point, and operators. The captions of the buttons should be as shown in Figure 19.12. The power button is created with two rectangles and four lines with a transparent button overlaying it.

The book utilizes a system variable as a flag to determine whether the decimal point is active. For instance, when entering a number, the handler checks the value of the flag, system variable decimalFlag. If the value of decimalFlag is 0 (the decimal point is not active), the value in the display field is multiplied by 10 and the number pressed is added to it. If the value of decimalFlag is not 0 (the decimal point is active), the target is divided by the value of decimalFlag. System variable decimalFlag is a multiple of 10, depending on how many decimal places have been entered. When the decimal point is clicked on the calculator, a value of 10 is put in the value of decimalFlag. Each time a decimal number is clicked, the value of decimalFlag is multiplied by 10.

Another flag, system variable sEquals, is used to determine whether the current value displayed is the result of an operation or not. If it is, the value of sEquals is true and the displayed is set to 0 when a number or the decimal is clicked. After a number or the decimal has been clicked, the value of sEquals is set to false.

2. Enter the following handlers into the book script:

```
to handle enterbook
    send reader
    system decimalFlag
    put 0 into decimalFlag
    put "0" into the text of field "display"
    set sysChangesDB to false
end enterbook

to handle reader
    hide menubar
    forward
end reader

to handle author
    show menubar
    forward
end author
```

3. Group the buttons labeled "1" through "9." In the group's script, enter the following handler:

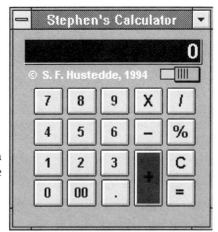

Figure 19.12
The calculator application uses system variables as flags and user-defined functions to process the mathematical operations.

```
to handle buttonup
    system decimalFlag,sEquals
    if the text of field "display" = "ERROR" then
        put 0 into text of field "display"
    end if
    if sEquals = "true" then
        put false into sEquals
        put 0 into text of field display
    end if
    if decimalFlag > 0 then  --decimal point is active
        increment the text of field "display" by \
        (the caption of target / decimalFlag)
        put decimalFlag * 10 into decimalFlag
    else   -- decimal point is not active
        put the text of field "display" * 10 into the text of field "display"
        increment the text of field "display" by the caption of target
    end if
    put false into sEquals
end buttonup
```

By using the caption of the button pressed within a group and a group script, only one script is needed for the nine numeric buttons, captioned "1" through "9."

4. The "0" and "00" buttons operate in a similar manner. Enter the following handler in the script of the button labeled "0" .

```
to handle buttonup
    system decimalFlag,sEquals
    if the text of field "display" = "ERROR" then
        put 0 into text of field "display"
    end if
    if sEquals = true then
        put false into sEquals
        put 0 into text of field "display"
    end if
    if decimalFlag > 0 then
        put decimalFlag * 10 into decimalFlag
        if "." is not in text of field display then
            put ".0" after the text of field "display"
        else
            put "0" after text of field "display"
        end if
    else
        put the text of field "display" * 10 into the text of field "display"
    end if
end
```

Enter the following script for the button labeled "00".

```
to handle buttonup
    system decimalFlag,sEquals
    if the text of field "display" = "ERROR" then
        put 0 into text of field "display"
    end if
```

```
        if sEquals = true then
            put false into sEquals
            put 0 into text of field "display"
        end if
        if decimalFlag > 0 then
            put decimalFlag * 100 into decimalFlag
            if "." is not in text of field display then
                put ".00" after the text of field "display"
            else
                put "00" after text of field "display"
            end if
        else
            put the text of field "display" * 100 into the text of field "display"
        end if
    end
```

5. Place the following handler in the script of the "." button.

```
    to handle buttonup
        system decimalFlag,sEquals
        if sEquals = true then
            put 0 into text of field display
            put false into sEquals
        end if
        if decimalFlag = 0 then
            put 10 into decimalFlag
            put "." after text of field "display"
        end if
    end
```

6. Place the following handler in the script of the button representing the multiplication sign:

```
    to handle buttonup
        system memory,decimalFlag,calcOperation
        put the text of field "display" into memory
        put "0" into text of field display
        put "mult" into calcOperation
        put 0 into decimalFlag
    end
```

The memory system variable is used to store a value for calculation purposes. The calcOperation system variable is used to store the operation that will be performed when the "=" button is pressed.

7. Place the following handler in the script of the "/" button.

```
    to handle buttonup
        system memory,decimalFlag,calcOperation
        put the text of field "display" into memory
        put "0" into text of field display
        put "div" into calcOperation
        put 0 into decimalFlag
    end
```

8. Place the following handler in the script of the button representing subtraction.

```
to handle buttonup
    system memory,decimalFlag,calcOperation
    put the text of field "display" into memory
    put "0" into text of field display
    put "sub" into calcOperation
    put 0 into decimalFlag
end
```

9. Place the following handler in the script of the button representing addition.

```
to handle buttonup
    system memory,decimalFlag,calcOperation
    put the text of field "display" into memory
    put "0" into text of field display
    put "add" into calcOperation
    put 0 into decimalFlag
end
```

10. Place the following handler in the script of the button representing operations to calculate percentage.

```
to handle buttonup
    put the text of field "display" / 100 into the text of field "display"
end
```

11. Place the following handler in the script of the button that clears the display; the button's caption is "C."

```
to handle buttonup
    system decimalFlag
    put "0" into text of field "display"
    put "0" into decimalFlag
end
```

12. Place the following handlers in the script of the button representing the equals sign.

```
to handle buttonup
    system memory,calcOperation,decimalFlag,sEqua's
    conditions
        when calcOperation = "add"
            put addition(memory) into text of field "display"
        when calcOperation = "sub"
            put subtraction(memory) into text of field "display"
        when calcOperation = "mult"
            put multiplication(memory) into text of field "display"
        when calcOperation = "div"
            put division(memory) into text of field "display"
        else
    end conditions
    put  0 into decimalFlag
    put "" into calcOperation
    put "true" into sEquals
```

```
end

to get addition x
    return (x + the text of field "display")
end addition

to get subtraction x
    return (x − the text of field "display")
end subtraction

to get multiplication x
    return (x * the text of field "display")
end multiplication

to handle division x
    if the text of field "display" = 0 then
        return "ERROR"
    else
        return (memory / the text of field "display")
    end if
end division
```

13. To allow the user to exit the book, place the following handler in the script for the "power switch."

```
to handle buttonup
    send exit
end buttonup
```

14. Go to the Reader mode and test the application. Make corrections as necessary until the calculator works as intended.

Setting the Table for the User

Working with Menus and the User-Interface Design

An important part of programming is designing the user interface. A powerful and useful program can be ineffective and unprofitable if the user finds it too difficult to use. The user's productivity is greatly affected by the understandability, organization, and explanation of the interface.

Menus are a popular interface element of today's graphical user interface (GUI) applications, and ToolBook provides a set of default menus in the Reader mode. These default menus or the items they contain may be customized, disabled, or removed. New menus and new menu items may be added. The routines handling the menu events may be defined or altered. ToolBook includes a utility for easing menu design, a utility called the menu editor.

Other interface elements include combo boxes and pop-up menus. Combo boxes and pop-up menus allow the user to select an item from a predefined list. Fields and recordfields may also be set as single- or multiple-line select fields in which the user may choose one or more items from a list.

Providing help to a user is also an important consideration in the design process. Help may be provided in the form of a separate "read-me" file, a pop-up field, or instructions on the screen or in the statusbar.

Disabling and Removing Menu Items and Menus

Both the Reader mode and Author mode of ToolBook have default menus, as Chapters 5 and 6 explained. Using the default menus, the user can save the application under a new name, print a page or a range of pages, and search for text. In some instances, a developer may not wish the user to have these default capabilities. The menubar may be hidden, using the hide command, by issuing the statement

```
hide menubar
```

If the statement is issued in an enterBook handler, the menubar will be hidden when the book is opened. For example:

```
to handle enterBook
    hide menubar
end enterBook
```

The menubar remains hidden until a show menubar statement is executed. This might be when the book is left:

```
to handle leaveBook
    show menubar
end leaveBook
```

Even though the menubar might be hidden, the commands of its menus remain active and can be accessed if the user knows the keyboard shortcuts for the commands. For instance, while the menubar is hidden, the user might press Ctrl-O. This is the keyboard shortcut for opening another application or book. The "File Open" dialog box would appear.

OpenScript includes commands for retaining the visibility of the menubar, while disabling specific menu items or full menus. To disable a specific menu item, the disable menuItem command is utilized as explained in Figure 20.1. Disabled menu items are grayed-out when the menu is dropped down. (ToolBook temporarily disables menu items according to the state of the program. For instance, the copy command is invalid if no object is selected. The "Copy" option on the Edit menu will be grayed-out unless an item is selected that can be copied.) To disable the "Open" option in the Reader-mode File menu, either of the following statements would do the trick:

        disable menuItem "Open" at reader

        disable menuItem "Open" in menu "File" at reader

The reference to the menu in which the command is found is optional in most cases. If the menubar had two menus with "Open" options, it would disable the one in the leftmost menu, unless the menu was specified as in the second disable statement in the preceding lines of code. In most cases, disabling the menu item in Reader mode is sufficient, since a developer would normally not want to give the user access to the Author mode while in his or her application. And unless the user has a full version of ToolBook or Multimedia ToolBook, he or she cannot access the Author mode

Figure 20.1
The disable menuItem *command is used to gray-out a menu item on the menubar.*

The disable menuItem command

Syntax: **disable menuItem** *name* **[in menu** *menu***] [at** *level***]**

Purpose: Disables a menu item on a menu so that it appears dimmed at the specified level and may not be selected.

Parameters: If the specified item is located in more than one menu, the menu name, *menu*, should be specified to ensure that the correct item is disabled. An assigned alias may be specified instead of *name*; *level* may be specified as author, reader, or both.

Examples: disable menuItem "Character" at reader

            disable menuItem "Paragraph" in menu "Text" at both

---

Figure 20.2
The disable menu *command is used to inactivate a menu at a specified level.*

The disable menu command

Syntax: **disable menu** *name* **[at** *level***]**

Purpose: Disables a menu so that it appears dimmed at the specified level and may not be selected.

Parameters: An assigned alias may be specified instead of *name*; *level* may be specified as author, reader, or both.

Example: disable menu "Text" at reader

---

anyway. Secondly, you as the author would likely want to have access to all the menu items while developing the application in Author mode. By disabling a menu item in the Reader mode only, you do not have to enable it in Author mode before being able to select the menu item and execute its routine. The keyboard shortcut for a disabled menu item is also disabled. When the "Open" option is disabled, the user can no longer press Ctrl-O to access the "Open File" dialog box.

In the same manner, entire menus may be disabled by issuing a disable menu command as described in Figure 20.2. The command

```
disable menu "File" at reader
```

grays-out the "File" option and does not allow the File menu to drop down. Disabling the menu, however, does not disable the keyboard shortcuts for the items on the menu. Even though the File menu might be disabled and the "Open..." option cannot be chosen, the keyboard shortcut for the "Open" command, Ctrl-O, is still enabled and may be activated by the user.

Menus and specific menu items may also be removed from the menubar. This is accomplished by using the remove menuItem or remove menu command as described in Figures 20.3 and 20.4. The handler

```
to handle enterBook
    remove menuItem "Save As" in menu "File" at reader
end enterBook
```

completely removes the "Save As" item from the Reader-mode File menu. The "Save As" command will still be on the Author-mode File menu. To remove it from both the Author- and Reader-mode menus, the handler should be changed to

---

The remove menuItem command

Syntax: **remove menuItem *name* [in menu *menu*] [at *level*]**

Purpose: Removes a menu item so that it does not appear when the specified menu is selected.

Parameters: An assigned alias may be specified instead of *name*. A menu may be referenced by *menu* if the menu item name appears in more than one menu; *level* may be specified as author, reader, or both.

Examples: remove menuItem "Character" in menu "Text" at reader

remove menuItem "Transparent" at author

Figure 20.3
The remove menuItem *command is used to remove an item from a menu.*

The remove menu command

Syntax: **remove menu *name* [at *level*]**

Purpose: Removes, from the menubar, a menu at the specified level.

Parameters: An assigned alias may be specified instead of *name*; *level* may be specified as author, reader, or both.

Example: remove menu "Text" at reader

Figure 20.4
The remove menu *command is used to remove a menu from the menubar.*

```
to handle enterBook
    remove menuItem "Save As" in menu "File" at both
end enterBook
```

The following handler completely removes the File menu in the Reader mode:

```
to handle enterBook
    remove menu "File" at reader
end enterBook
```

When a menu item is removed, its keyboard shortcut is also disabled. When a menu is removed, the keyboard shortcuts for all of its items are disabled as well.

Restoring Menus

The default menu may be restored by issuing the restore menubar command as described in Figure 20.5. By issuing the statement

```
restore menubar
```

any disabled or removed menus or menu items are enabled and made fully functional. Individual menu items may be restored using the enable menuItem command (see Figure 20.6). Executing the handler

```
to handle enterPage
    enable menuItem "Open" in menu "File" at reader
end enterPage
```

restores the "Open" option in the "File" menu in Reader mode. It may then be selected by the user and executed. Specific menus may also be restored using the similar

Figure 20.5
The restore menubar *command restores the menubar to the default menus and menu items.*

The restore menubar command
Syntax: **restore menubar**
Purpose: Restores any removed menus and/or menu items and activates any disabled menus and/or menu items. It also removes any added menus and/or menu items.
Example: restore menubar

Figure 20.6
The enable menuItem *command is used to restore a previously disabled menu item.*

The enable menuItem command
Syntax: **enable menuItem *name* [in menu *menu*] [at *level*]**
Purpose: Enables a disabled menu item so that it may be selected.
Parameters: An assigned alias may be specified instead of *name*. A menu may be referenced by *menu* if the menu item name appears in more than one menu. The parameter *level* may be specified as author, reader, or both.
Examples: enable menuItem "Character" in menu "Text" at reader
enable menuItem "Transparent" at author

enable menu command as described in Figure 20.7. The following handler restores a previously disabled or removed File menu.

```
to handle buttonClick
    enable menu "File" at reader
end buttonClick
```

Any specific items in the restored menu that were previously disabled or removed with the disable menuItem or remove menuItem commands will not be enabled or restored. To be available, the items must be restored with the enable menuItem or restore menubar commands.

The enable menu command
Syntax: **enable menu *name* [at *level*]**
Purpose: Enables a disabled menu at the specified level so that it may be selected.
Parameters: An assigned alias may be specified instead of *name*; *level* may be specified as author, reader, or both.
Example: enable menu "Text" at reader

Figure 20.7
The enable menu *command is used to restore a previously disabled menu.*

Adding New Menus and Menu Items

Besides removing default menus and menu items, new menus and menu items may be added to the menubar. Adding a functional menu item requires two steps. First, the item is added to the menu by using the add menuItem command as described in Figure 20.8. Secondly, the routine to be executed when the menu item is selected must be defined in a handler. The message handled is the same as the menu item name defined in the add menuItem statement. In most cases, menu handlers are best placed in the book script or a system book script. The following two handlers add an "Inventory" menu item in both Reader- and Author-mode File menus, in the third position of the menu (as shown in Figure 20.9). When the "Inventory" option is selected, a book in a file named INVNTORY.TBK is accessed.

```
to handle enterBook
    add menuItem "Inventory" to menu "File" position 3 at both
end enterBook
```

The add menuItem command
Syntax: **add menuItem *name* to menu *menu* [position *number*][at *level*]**
Purpose: Adds a menu item to the referenced menu at the specified level.
Parameters: A position of the menu item on the menu may be specified. If no position is specified, the item is added to the bottom of the menu. The parameter *level* may be specified as author, reader, or both.
Examples: add menuItem "Main Menu Page" to menu "Navigate" position 5 at reader
add menuItem "Blue" to menu "Color" at both

Figure 20.8
The add menuItem *command allows a new menu item to be created in a specified menu.*

Figure 20.9
By using the add
menuItem *command, the*
"Inventory" option may be
added to the File menu. The
new option allows access to
an inventory file .

```
to handle inventory
    go to book "INVNTORY.TBK"
end inventory
```

If the menu item name contains spaces or ellipses (...), the spaces and punctuation marks are removed in the handler name. (By convention, ellipses in a menu item name mean that a dialog box is displayed when the item is selected.) For instance, if the menu item in the preceding script is changed to "Access Inventory", the handler name would be accessInventory, as the following code shows.

```
to handle enterBook
    add menuItem "Access Inventory" to menu "File" position 3 at both
end enterBook

to handle accessInventory
    go to book "INVNTORY.TBK"
end accessInventory
```

A new menu is added to the menubar in a similar manner. The add menu command is used to define the menu name and its position on the menubar, as described in Figure 20.10. Specific items on the menu are added to the menubar as described in the preceding code. The following book script includes an enterBook handler to define a Colors menu with several menu items, and handlers for each menu-item routine.

```
to handle enterBook
    add menu "Colors" position 2 at reader
    add menuItem "Red" to menu "Colors" at reader
    add menuItem "Blue" to menu "Colors" at reader
    add menuItem "Yellow" to menu "Colors" at reader
    add menuItem "Green" to menu "Colors" at reader
end enterBook

to handle red
    set the fillColor of rectangle id 0 to red
end red

to handle blue
    set the fillColor of rectangle id 0 to blue
end blue
```

Figure 20.10
The add menu *command*
adds a new menu to the
menubar.

The add menu command

Syntax: **add menu *name* [position *position*][at *level*]**

Purpose: Creates a new menu at the specified level on the menubar..

Parameters: An assigned alias may be specified instead of *name*; *level* may be specified as author, reader, or both. The *position* dictates where the menu name will appear on the menubar (if not specified, the new menu will be placed after the current menus).

Example: add menu "Sections" position 5 at reader

```
to handle yellow
    set the fillColor of rectangle id 0 to yellow
end yellow

to handle green
    set the fillColor of rectangle id 0 to green
end green
```

Figure 20.11 shows the Colors menu the preceding script creates.

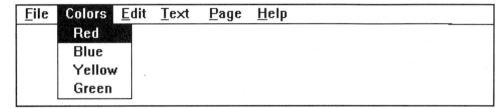

Figure 20.11
A menu is created using the add menu *command. The items under the new menu are created with the* add menuItem *command.*

Using the Menu Editor Utility

Accompanying ToolBook is a separate executable utility for creating menubars. Using the menu editor, the menus and the items they contain are easily laid out. The menu editor is a dialog box in which the names of menus and menu items are specified and a preview of the created menubar may be seen (see Figure 20.12). The menu editor is accessible from the Windows' Program Manager by clicking the Menu Editor icon in the ToolBook or Multimedia ToolBook group. It is also accessible through the Resource Manager in ToolBook's Author mode by selecting the resource of "Menu" and then choosing "New."

To add a menu or menu item, the menu name or menu item name is entered in the name field and the Enter key pressed. Menu items are indented under the menu name in the "Menu Bar Items" list field. An alias may be assigned by entering the alias name in the field provided. The alias allows another message name to be handled instead of the menu item name when the item is selected. This is useful if the same name is used on multiple menus but each executes a unique routine. In Figure 20.12 a menubar has been created that lists the menu names Rectangle, Circle, and Triangle. Under each is the menu item "Red." The "Red" item on the Rectangle menu is given an alias of "RedR", the "Red" item on the Circle menu is given an alias of "RedC", and the "Red" item on the Triangle menu is assigned an alias of "RedT". The "Red" menu item in the Rectangle menu would be handled with the to handle redR handler; to handle RedC and to handle RedT handlers are written to handle the "Red" option chosen from the Circle and Triangle menus, respectively.

The "Insert" button allows a new menu or menu item to be inserted in the list. The up and down arrow buttons are used to move an item up or down in the list. The right and left arrow buttons are used to indent (demote) or promote an item on the list. A separator may be inserted between menu items by placing a menu item with no name or clicking the "Separator" button. Accelerator keys may be assigned to a menu item by specifying the keystroke combination in the "Accelerator" group. The "Help Text" field contains text to be displayed in the statusbar when the menu item is highlighted. The menubar is previewed in a separate window, and the menus may be viewed by clicking them in the preview.

When the menubar looks like it should, it may be saved as a resource in the current book; as a resource in a different book, or as an external .MNU file, which may be later imported into a book.

Figure 20.12
*ToolBook comes with a
handy utility for creating
menubar resources. The
menu editor even allows
you to preview the menubar
(right) while laying out the
menus and menu items.*

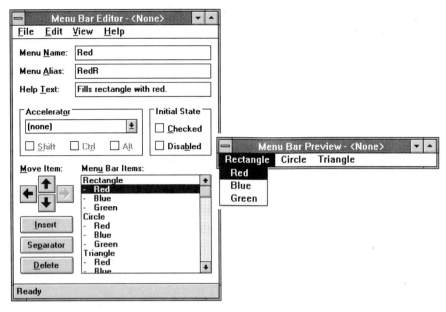

To use the created menubar in a book, it must first be loaded as a resource in the book. This can be done either by saving it, from the menu editor, as a resource in the book or by importing it into the Resource Manager as an .MNU file. The menubar resource is chosen in the Resource Manager to become the active menubar (see Figure 20.13). A menubar resource may also be assigned to a viewer through the "Viewer Properties" dialog box. In the "Viewer Properties" dialog, the menubar is assigned through the "Menubar" button.

Handlers for the various menu items must be written as described in the preceding sections. The best place for these handlers is usually the book script or the system book's script.

Figure 20.13
*Menubar resources may be
assigned to a book through
the Resources Manager in
Author mode.*

Specifying Mnemonic Characters for Menus or Menu Items

Mnemonic characters are characters used in conjunction with the Alt key (instead of the mouse) to select a menu or menu item. A mnemonic character appears underscored in the name of a menu or menu item name. A mnemonic character is created in the add menu or add menuItem command by placing an ampersand (&) before the character in the name. In the statement

   add menu "&Colors" at reader

the "C" in the menu name Colors would be underscored and serve as a mnemonic character. The Colors menu would be opened when the user presses Alt-C. Mnemonic characters of menu items are designated in the same manner. The statement

   add menuItem "Re&d" to menu "Colors" at reader

adds the "Red" option to the Colors menu; the "d" is underscored. Mnemonic menu items are selected by pressing the appropriate key only (without the Alt key) once the menu has been opened. Using the preceding two examples, the user would press Alt-C to open the Colors menu and then type "d" (upper- or lowercase) to select and execute the "Red" option. Figure 20.14 illustrates the underscored mnemonic characters of the menu created with the preceding two statements.

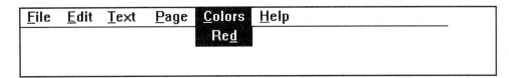

Figure 20.14
The Colors menu can be opened by pressing Alt-C. The "Red" option can then be accessed by typing "d".

   OpenScript sends a keyMnemonic message when the Alt key is pressed. Handling the message in a book or background script allows mnemonic characters to be utilized without having to define menu and menu items. An author who wishes to allow the user to enter comments at any time by pressing the Alt-+ might use the following handler in a book script to open an ask dialog box. The box would allow the user to enter comments and record them along with the page ID, to a hidden field on the first page.

```
to handle keyMnemonic keyCode
    conditions
        when keyCode = 61  -- 61 is the keyCode for the "+" key
            ask "Enter comment:"
            put crlf & the id of this page && it after text of field id 5 of page id 0
        else
            forward
    end conditions
end keyMnemonic
```

A conditions...when structure is used in the preceding handler to make it easily editable. If the author wishes to specify additional mnemonic characters, he or she may simply add additional when clauses to the conditions structure.

Using Single-Select List Boxes and Combo Boxes

Menus can also be simulated with fields (or less commonly, recordfields) by using the single-select list box type or with combo box objects. Such devices allow a user to select an item from a list of choices. Figure 20.15 shows a list box and two views of a combo box, one with the drop-down list undisplayed and the other with it displayed. List and combo boxes are frequently used to specify items in a data-entry form, make choices in a dialog box, or select configuration options in an application.

Figure 20.15
A single-select list box (left)
allows the user to highlight
one line of its text. A
combo box performs the
same function but hides the
choices (middle) until the
down arrow at its right is
clicked (right).

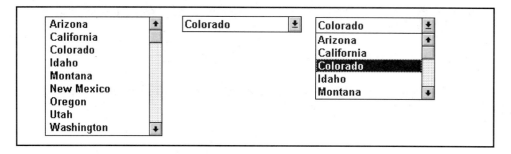

List boxes are created by first generating a field (or recordfield) and then selecting the field type by choosing "Single-Select List Box" as the field type in the "Field Properties" dialog box. In a single-select list box, the user can highlight one item at a time in the list by clicking the desired line of text or by using the up and down arrows if the field has the focus. The selectedTextlines property of a field may be retrieved in a handler to determine which line is selected by the user. The value of the selectedTextlines property is the line number of the selected line.

```
to handle buttonClick
    put the selectedTextlines of field id 1 into x
    put textline x of text of field id 1 into menuChoice
    conditions
        when menuChoice is "red"
            set the fillColor of ellipse id 0 to red
        when menuChoice is "blue"
            set the fillColor of ellipse id 0 to blue
        when menuChoice is "yellow"
            set the fillColor of ellipse id 0 to yellow
        when menuChoice is "green"
            set the fillColor of ellipse id 0 to green
    end conditions
end buttonClick
```

Combo boxes function in the same manner as single-select list boxes. The current selection is revealed in the combo box. It contains a push button for displaying the drop-down list from which the user makes his or her selection. The advantage of the combo box over a single-select box is that the combo box takes up less display space in the layout of the page. A disadvantage is that the user cannot see the available choices unless the drop-down list is displayed.

Combo boxes are created with the Combo Box tool. Five items are displayed at a time in the drop-down list. If the combo box contains more than five items, the scrollable property of the combo box should be set to true (checked in the "Combo Box Properties" dialog).

ToolBook sends a selectChange message when the user selects an item from the drop-down list. This message may be handled in the combo box's script to perform an action based on the user's selection. The selectChange message includes an itemString parameter, which contains the text of the selected item. This parameter might be used in a conditions...when structure:

```
to handle selectChange itemString
    conditions
        when itemString = red
            set the fillColor of ellipse id 0 to red
        when itemString = blue
```

```
            set the fillColor of ellipse id 0 to blue
        when itemString = yellow
            set the fillColor of ellipse id 0 to yellow
        when itemString = green
            set the fillColor of ellipse id 0 to green
    end conditions
end selectChange
```

ToolBook also sends an enterDropDown message when the user clicks the combo box's push button to display the drop-down list and a **leaveDropDown** message when the drop-down list is closed. The text displayed in the combo box's edit box (the portion of the combo box that displays the current selection) may be gotten (or set) in a script by referring to the text property of the combo box:

```
to handle buttonClick
    put the text of comboBox id 12 into menuChoice
    . . .
end buttonClick
```

The text of the combo box's edit box is uneditable from the keyboard unless the edit-able property of the combo box has been set to true (that is, the "Editable" checkbox in the "Combo Box Properties" dialog is checked [see Figure 20.16]).

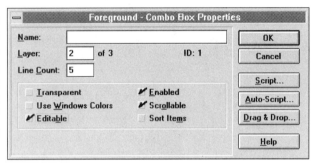

Figure 20.16
Combo boxes text may be made editable by the user if the "editable" option is checked in the "Combo Box Properties" dialog box.

Providing Help to the User

Providing instructions and assistance to the user is a key element of a well-designed user interface. This is paramount if your design is not easily understood, if your audience is computer illiterate, or if the readers are novices. Help may be provided in several ways. Instructions might be printed on the screen in a field that is always displayed on the page. A "Help" button might link to a separate page on which help and instructions are provided. In such cases, a "Return" button is usually provided on the page; the associated handler returns control to the previously viewed page.

```
to handle buttonClick
    send back
end buttonClick
```

A "Help" button on a page might toggle the visibility of a field containing help text. Its handler might be

```
to handle buttonClick
    if the visible of field "helpText" is false then
        show field "helpText"
    else
        hide field "helpText"
    end if
end buttonClick
```

When using a hidden help field, it is generally wise to make sure the field is hidden upon exiting the page. This ensures that the user will not see it next time unless he or she requests to view it by clicking the "Help" button. This can be accomplished with a leavePage handler.

```
to handle leavePage
    hide field "helpText"
end leavePage
```

The next section includes instructions on using the statusbar to display help information.

Providing Information Through the Statusbar

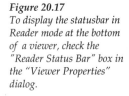

Figure 20.17
To display the statusbar in Reader mode at the bottom of a viewer, check the "Reader Status Bar" box in the "Viewer Properties" dialog.

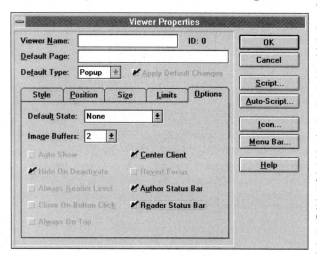

The statusbar at the bottom of a viewer may be used to display help text and captions, as well as navigation controls and information about the position of the mouse. By default, the statusbar is visible in Author mode only in the main window viewer. However, it is easily turned on in the Reader mode for any viewer, by setting the readerStatusBar property of the viewer to true. On the "Options" screen of the "Viewer Properties" dialog box, the author may check the "Reader Status Bar" box to display the statusbar in Reader mode (see Figure 20.17). A statusbar whose readerStatusBar property is set to true may be hidden or shown using the hide statusBar and show statusBar statements or setting the visible property of statusBar to true or false. The statusbar then could also be set in a handler subroutine by setting the readerStatusBar and visible properties:

```
to handle revealStatusBar
    set the readerStatusBar of viewer id 0 to true
    set the visible of statusBar to true
end revealStatusBar
```

There are several objects associated with the statusbar for displaying information to the user. When the statusControls object is shown, navigational buttons are displayed at the far right of the statusbar. These allow the user to navigate backwards or forwards through a book. Figure 20.18 shows a statusbar with the statusControls set to true. This may be accomplished with the command:

```
show statusControls
```

Figure 20.18
When statusControls is set to true, the statusbar displays buttons for navigating to the previous and next pages.

When the statusBox object is visible, the status bar displays the current page number out of the total number of pages on its right side. If the user clicks the status box, he or she is prompted for a page number to navigate to. Figure 20.19 shows a statusbar with the statusBox object visible. As with the status controls, the status box is displayed with the command

```
show statusBox
```

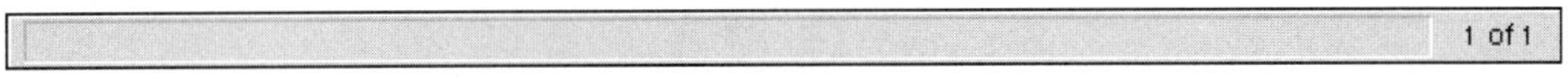

Figure 20.19
When the statusBox is shown, the page number of the current page and the total number of pages in the book are displayed in the statusbar.

The caption shown in the statusbar is specified in a couple ways. The caption property of the statusbar may be set to a specific string in a handler. For instance, to display information about a button when the mouse pointer enters its boundaries, the caption property can be set in a mouseEnter handler and a mouseLeave handler:

```
to handle mouseEnter
    set the caption of statusBar to "This button navigates to the book's main menu."
end mouseEnter

to handle mouseLeave
    set the caption of the statusBar to ""
end mouseLeave
```

When the mouse pointer is moved to within the button's boundaries, the "This button navigates to the book's main menu." caption is displayed in the statusbar. When the mouse pointer is moved out of the button's boundaries, the caption is reset to a null string. Figure 20.20 shows a statusbar after the mouseEnter handler has been executed.

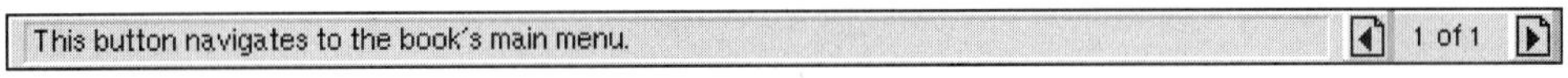

Figure 20.20
Captions may be displayed in the statusbar to provide help to the user.

Caption text may be assigned to menus and menu items to be displayed when the menu or menu item is highlighted. A with helpText *string* parameter may be added to the add menu or add menuItem commands.

```
add menu "Circle" at reader with helpText "Changes fill color of the circle."

add menuItem "Blue" to menu "Circle" at reader with helpText "Fills circle with blue."
```

Help text can also be assigned in the menu editor utility by entering the string in the "Help Text" field for a chosen menu or menu item (refer to Figure 20.12).

Summary Questions
Complete the following statements by filling in the blanks.
1. The _____ _____ command is used for creating new menus.
2. The _____ _____ command is used to gray-out menu items so that the user cannot select them.
3. A _____ object allows the user to select from a list of items in a drop-down box.
4. The _____ _____ command is used to erase a menu from the menubar.
5. The _____ _____ command is used to create a new menu item in a specified menu.

6. Fields of type _____ _____ _____ allow a user to highlight or select one line of text.
7. The _____ _____ command is used to restore the default menus and menu items.
8. The _____ _____ is a utility that accompanies ToolBook and creates menubar resources.
9. The _____ _____ command is used to remove a menu item from a menu so it does not appear when the menu is selected.
10. The _____ _____ command is used to restore a disabled menu item.

Identify the syntax error in the following statements.
11. restore menu bar
12. disable menuItem "Open" under menu "File" at reader
13. add menu "Colors" at both position 4
14. restore menuItem "Open" at reader
15. disable menu "Text" in author mode
16. show status controls
17. set readerStatusBar to 0
18. enable menuItem "Inventory" in menu "File" position 3 at reader
19. set the caption of status bar to "Exit the book."
20. add menuItem "Show Graphics" to menu "Page" at reader and author

Hands-On Projects

A. Examine the software that accompanies this chapter. Open the "Table of Contents" book by double-clicking its icon in the "Developing with ToolBook" group window in the Windows Program Manager. Inside the "Table of Contents," click the book representing Chapter 20. The tutorial provides exposure to the effect of the various menu commands.

B. Use the menu editor to create the menubar and menu items shown in Figure 20.21. Save the menubar as a resource file named MYMENU.MNU.

Figure 20.21
In Hands-On Project B, the menu editor is used to create this menubar with the pictured menu items.

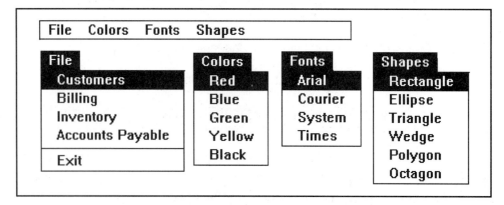

C. Open the book created in Hands-On Project C of Chapter 15 (in which you calculated the area and volume of solid geometric shapes). Write a handler to create a Shapes menu when the book is opened. The menu should include four items ("Box," "Cylinder," "Cone," "Sphere") on the menu. Write a handler to navigate to the appropriate page when each menu item is selected (for example, when the user selects the "Sphere" option, a handler navigates to the page for calculating the area and volume of a sphere).

D. Edit the customer database form created in Hands-On Project E of Chapter 19 so that the "City" field is an editable combo box of cities in your area and the "State" field is a combo box with your state and surrounding states.

E. Create a database of information about various animals. The book should consist of several pages with one animal discussed on each page. Graphics of the animals can be drawn in ToolBook or imported from clipart or from scanned photographs. The menubar should include an "Animals" menu for navigating to the different pages. (Don't forget to write the handlers!) Upon entering each page, display in the statusbar a caption about the animal, perhaps an interesting fact. A sample page is shown in Figure 20.22, but a different design may be used. The book may focus on a particular type of animal such as different breeds of dogs or different types of dinosaurs.

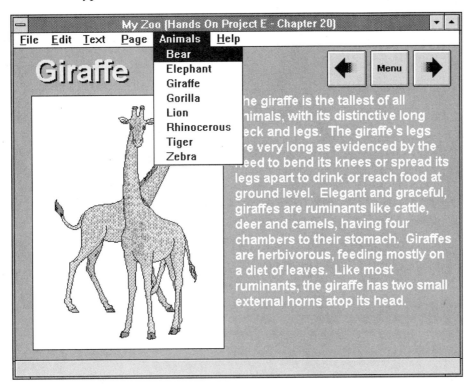

Figure 20.22
Menus can be used to navigate to the different pages of a book.

Chapter 21

How to Stuff a Variable with Values
Working with Arrays

Thus far we have worked with variables that hold one value. Most programming languages allow variables to contain more than one value. These are called **arrays** and OpenScript makes use of these powerful variables. Arrays are similar to a list or table in which each item of the list or each cell of the table contains one unique value. The values are assigned to the array by specifying which position (item or cell) is to hold the specified value. Values are retrieved in the same manner—that is, by specifying which position of the array the value should be retrieved from.

The use of arrays enhances and simplifies working with large amounts of related data. Array values are more easily sorted than a collection of individual variables. Array data is easily summed and portions of it may be subtotaled. Statistical analysis is more easily performed with array data than a group of individual variables.

Like system variables, arrays must be declared before they can be used. Like standard variables, arrays may be declared as having either a local scope or a global (system) scope. Arrays can be one dimensional, like a list of items; two dimensional, like a table; or three dimensional, like a file cabinet (where data is located within a file drawer, inside a folder, and on a document within the folder). In fact, an array may have up to 16 dimensions!

Declaring Arrays

Arrays must be declared in a handler before they can be referenced. The declaration statement for an array indicates whether the array is local or system (global), the name of the array variable, the number of dimensions, and the number of elements for each dimension. The keyword local or system precedes the array name in the declaration statement. The dimensions and the quantity of elements in each is shown through the use of bracket pairs following the array name. A one-dimensional array of global (system) scope named players and containing 12 data items would be declared this way:

    system players[12]

The players variable can contain 12 items, as pictured in Figure 21.1. A data type (see Figure 13.2) may also be specified in the declaration statement. Assigning data types to arrays generally allows them to be processed faster. For instance, assuming the players array contains only string data (the names of players on a team), it can be declared in this way:

    system STRING players[12]

The array and the values it contains may be thought of as a list of 12 compartments, or items, each holding one value, as

Figure 21.1
An array is a variable that can contain multiple values. The number of elements in the array is declared in the code, and that number of data locations is set aside in RAM to be filled with data.

Figure 21.2
Data may be assigned to
each element of an array in
memory. A one-
dimensional array is similar
to a list.

[1]	MacCrate
[2]	Watson
[3]	Herrington
[4]	Konomos
[5]	Fidler
[6]	Mullins
[7]	Emerson
[8]	Kelly
[9]	Brand
[10]	Ahn
[11]	Chesney
[12]	Swanson

depicted in Figure 21.2. Perhaps it is desired that a second data item be kept with each player name in the array, to contain the position each player on the team plays. The array can be declared as a matrix of 12 rows with two columns in each row. The first column contains the names of the players, the second column the position played. This results in the table shown in Figure 21.3. The array would be declared using the statement

system STRING players[12] [2]

The matrix created in RAM to hold the values would have 12 rows (the first dimension) and two columns (the second dimension). If it were desired to have a matrix to hold values of the player's name, position, points scored, rebounds, and assists (a total of five columns), the array would be declared this way:

system players[12] [5]

Since the data contained in the first two columns would be of type **STRING** and the data stored in columns 3 through 5 would be numeric (type **INT** or **WORD**), a type is not declared for the array. All items of the array must be of the same type for the type to be declared. Figure 21.4 depicts what the array might look like once values have been assigned to each element (cell).

If a team plays 20 games in a season, the author may wish to use the same array to track all 20 games for each player. A three-dimensional array could be declared, with the third dimension used for each game. The array could be declared like this:

system players[12] [5] [20]

The format of this array is pictured in Figure 21.5.

Arrays that need only retain their value for the duration of the handler in which they are referenced may be declared as local arrays, as in the declarations that follow.

Figure 21.3
A two-dimensional array
may be compared to a table
in which the first dimension
is the number of rows and
the second dimension is the
number of columns. This
array would be declared as
[12][2].

	[1] Name	[2] Pos.
[1]	MacCrate	C
[2]	Watson	C
[3]	Herrington	F/C
[4]	Konomos	F
[5]	Fidler	F
[6]	Mullins	F
[7]	Emerson	F
[8]	Kelly	G
[9]	Brand	G
[10]	Ahn	G
[11]	Chesney	G
[12]	Swanson	G

Figure 21.4
A two-dimensional array
allows associated data to be
easily grouped.

	[1] Name	[2] Pos.	[3] Pts.	[4] Reb.	[5] Ast.
[1]	MacCrate	C	18	15	2
[2]	Watson	C	10	10	3
[3]	Herrington	F/C	5	5	0
[4]	Konomos	F	4	9	5
[5]	Fidler	F	8	1	2
[6]	Mullins	F	6	3	4
[7]	Emerson	F	6	0	3
[8]	Kelly	G	16	1	7
[9]	Brand	G	9	2	3
[10]	Ahn	G	12	1	3
[11]	Chesney	G	8	2	2
[12]	Swanson	G	6	2	4

local productionCosts[100]

local chessBoard[8] [8]

If the number of elements in the array are unknown, the array may be declared as a **dynamic array** by using a null value for the number of elements. The following

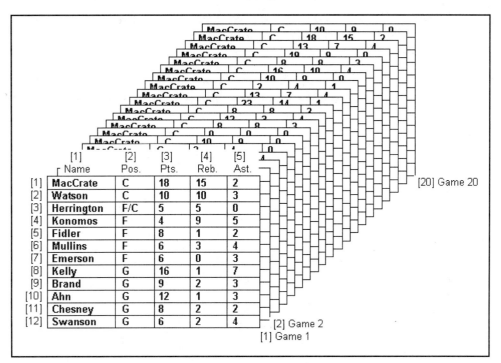

Figure 21.5
Three-dimensional arrays
are often used to store
time-based data.

statement declares a one-dimensional system array named customers whose number of elements is unknown or changes from time to time.

```
system customers[ ]
```

One dimension may be dynamic while another dimension might be static (that is, the number of rows may be undetermined, but it is known that there will be 10 columns needed for each row). For example:

```
system customers[ ] [10]
```

The preceding declaration sets up an array with 10 columns but with a dynamic number of rows. This text will focus on using **static arrays** (in which the number of elements in each dimension is declared). The following list cites a few rules to keep in mind when declaring arrays in OpenScript.

- An array cannot have more than 16 dimensions.
- Any one dimension cannot have more than 65,536 elements.
- The total number of elements (all dimensions combined) in an array may be limited by memory.

Referencing Values of an Array's Elements

Values are assigned to elements of an array by using the same methods used to assign values to individual variables. That is, values can be assigned through the use of a put statement or an assignment operator. The only difference is that the element must be specified. For instance, the following handler assigns the name Kelly to the eighth element of the players array:

```
to handle buttonClick
    system STRING players[12]
    put "Kelly" into players[8]
end buttonClick
```

Figure 21.6
*Data may be assigned to
specific elements of an array
by using the* put *statement
or the assignment operator
(=).*

[1]	
[2]	
[3]	
[4]	
[5]	
[6]	
[7]	
[8]	**Kelly**
[9]	
[10]	
[11]	
[12]	

Assuming all values of the array to have previously been null, after executing the preceding handler, the array might be depicted as in Figure 21.6. To assign a value to a multidimensional array, the element of each dimension must be specified. For instance, in a two-dimensional array like that depicted in Figure 21.4, the name Kelly would be assigned to the eighth row and first column by using the statement:

```
put "Kelly" into players[8][1]
```

To assign the 18 points to MacCrate, as depicted in Figure 21.4, either of the following statements could be utilized.

```
put 18 into players[1][3]
```

```
players[1][3] = 18
```

Both of these statements place a value of 18 into the element located at the first row and third column of the players array. (Tip: Before writing code to describe an array, it is often helpful to draw a table on a piece of paper to keep track of what data is placed in which rows and columns.) Refer to the three-dimensional array shown in Figure 21.5. If Watson pulled down nine rebounds in the 15th game of the season, the value 9 would be assigned to the array by using either of the following statements:

```
put 9 into players[2][4][15]
```

```
players[2][4][15] = 9
```

These statements assign the value 9 to the second row, fourth column of the 15th table.

Likewise values are retrieved from an array by specifying the element location of each dimension. To retrieve the number of points scored by the player named Konomos in the array depicted in Figure 21.4, the value in the fourth row and third column would be specified. The get command could be used to place the value in variable it.

```
get player[4][3]
```

Or the put statement might be used to place the value in another variable.

```
put player[4][3] into konomosPoints
```

Array elements might also be used in conjunction with other statements, such as a request or ask statement. Using the player array pictured in Figure 21.4, the following request statement produces the request dialog pictured in Figure 21.7. The statement retrieves two elements from the array and uses the values in the prompt string.

Figure 21.7
*Data may be retrieved from
an array and used in a
prompt string in a request
or ask dialog box.*

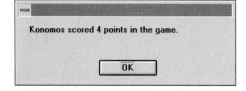

request player[4][1] && "scored" && player[4][3] && "points in the game."

Arrays are generally used in conjunction with loop structures. The following handler prompts the user to enter the 12 players' names and the corresponding positions. The handler also assigns the values to the first and second elements of the second dimension for all 12 elements of the first dimension.

```
to handle enterPlayerNames
    system player[12][5]
    step i from 1 to 12
        ask "Enter last name of player " & i & ":"
        put it into player[i][1]
        ask "Enter position played by" && player[i][1] & ":"
        put it into player[i][2]
    end step
end enterPlayerNames
```

In the three-dimensional array depicted in Figure 21.5, the game statistics might be input using the following subroutine:

```
to handle inputGameStats
    ask "Which game number are you entering (1-20):"
    put it into gameNum
    step i from 1 to 12
        ask "How many points for" && player[i][1][1] & "?"
        put it into player[i][3][gameNum]
        ask "How many rebounds for" && player[i][1][1] & "?"
        put it into player[i][4][gameNum]
        ask "How many assists for" && player[i][1][1] & "?"
        put it into player[i][5][gameNum]
    end step
end inputGameStats
```

Assuming the players would be listed in the same order for all 20 games, the players' names need only be stored on the first table (element 1 of the third dimension). Thus they are pulled from the array and inserted in the **ask** statements. The input values are assigned to the appropriate table (in the third dimension) by using the **gameNum** variable. The step counter, i, ensures that the values are assigned to the correct rows. A constant of value 3, 4, or 5 is used to specify the column (second dimension) for each **put** statement.

Filling an Array with One Value

All elements of an array may be set to one value with the fill command. The syntax of the fill command is described in Figure 21.8. The fill command is useful for resetting or erasing the values contained in an array. For example, the following subroutine sets all values of the **players** array to null strings.

```
to handle resetArray
    system players[12][5]
    fill players with ""
end resetArray
```

The following handler assigns a value of 0 to all the elements of an array.

The fill command

Syntax: **fill *arrayName* with *value***

Purpose: Assigns the specified value to all elements of an array.

Examples: fill myArray with 0

fill players with ""

fill areaCodes with "602"

```
to handle buttonClick
    system accountBalances[500]
    fill accountBalances with 0
end buttonClick
```

Finding the Size of an Array

In working with dynamic arrays (where the number of elements in one or more dimensions is undeclared), there may be occasions where knowing the number of elements is needed. OpenScript includes a function for finding the number of elements. The dimensions( ) function returns the number of elements for each dimension in a comma-delimited list. If a one-dimensional array named costs has 20 elements, the statement

```
put dimensions(costs) into x
```

would assign the value 20 to the variable x. The three-dimensional players array discussed previously (the array for 12 players with five categories for 20 games), when referenced in a dimensions( ) function, would return the value 12,5,20. The following statement assigns the value 12,5,20 to z.

```
put dimensions(players) into z
```

The dimensions( ) function is particularly useful in referencing the elements of an array in a loop structure. The next handler sums the elements of a dynamic array by first finding the number of elements with the dimensions( ) function and using that value in a loop structure to step through the individual elements, adding them to a variable.

```
to handle buttonClick
    system array1[ ], arraySum
    x = dimensions(array1)
    arraySum = 0
    step y from 1 to x
        increment arraySum by array1(y)
    end step
end buttonClick
```

Using Arrays in Parameters

Arrays may be passed as parameters when calling subroutines or user-defined functions, just as an individual variable would be passed. The handler for the called subroutine or function must be written to accept the array as its argument. The dimensions of the array are declared in the handler of the routine or function.

Consider an array containing the names of items bought by a customer, the quantity of each, and their cost (see Figure 21.9). The following script sends the array as a parameter to a user-defined function to find the total cost of the items bought.

	[1] Item	[2] Quantity	[3] Item Cost
[1]	Kitchen Table	1	249.88
[2]	Kitchen Chairs	4	57.98
[3]	Sofa	1	480.00
[4]	End tables	2	50.00
[5]	Lamps	2	79.67

Figure 21.9
An array might be used to store data about items purchased by a customer.

```
to handle buttonClick
    system sale[ ][3]
    put totalCost(sale) into text of field id 7
end buttonClick

to get totalCost myArray[ ][3]
    put item 1 of dimensions(myArray) into i
    put 0 into total
    step k from 1 to i
        increment total by myArray[k][2] * myArray[k][3]
    end step
    return total
end totalCost
```

In the preceding handler, the array named sale is passed to the totalCost( ) function. Since the number of items bought by a customer would vary, the first dimension of the sale array is dynamic (it has an unfixed number of elements). The second dimension is declared as having three elements: the item name, quantity bought, and item cost. In the totalCost( ) function, the array is assigned to the argument array named myArray, which is also declared as having a dynamic first dimension and a second dimension of three items. Since the number of elements in the first dimension is unknown (it will vary with each invoice being processed), the dimensions( ) function is used to find the number of elements in each dimension of the array. Only the number of elements in the first dimension is needed, and this value (the first item returned by the dimensions command) is placed in variable i. This value is used as the upper limit in a step loop. A total variable is incremented in each step by the product of the second and third items (quantity * item cost) of each row of the array. The summed total is returned to the calling handler and displayed.

Subtotaling Elements

One of the major advantages of using arrays rather than individual variables for large amounts of data is the ease with which the data may be subgrouped and analyzed. In a two-dimensional matrix, columns and rows may be easily subtotaled. Consider the players array shown in Figure 21.4. The total number of points, rebounds, and assists made by the entire team can be calculated by adding the elements of the third, fourth, and fifth columns. The following handler uses a loop to calculate the statistical totals for the team.

```
to handle buttonClick
    system players[12][5]
    put 0 into teamPoints
    put 0 into teamRebounds
    put 0 into teamAssists
    step i from 1 to 12
        increment teamPoints by player[i][3]
        increment teamRebounds by player[i][4]
        increment teamAssists by player[i][5]
    end step
    put teamPoints into text of field "team points"
    put teamRebounds into text of field "team rebounds"
    put teamAssists into text of field "team assists"
end buttonClick
```

Figure 21.10
Arrays are useful for analyzing large amounts of data, including calculating subtotals of data in rows and columns of a table.

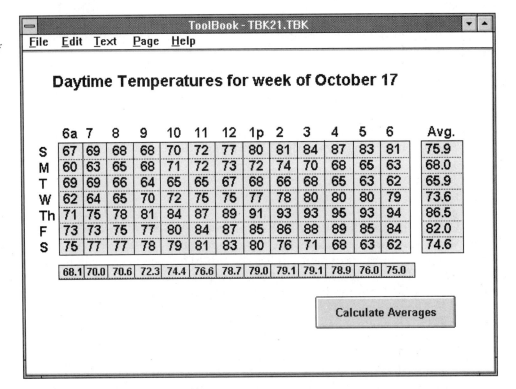

Figure 21.10 shows a page with a table consisting of temperature readings taken at each hour between 6 A.M. and 6 P.M. for a period of one week. The table was created as a field with seven lines of text and each hour reading separated by a tab character on the text line. (Thus there are 13 words on each text line, each word consisting of a temperature reading.) Twelve vertical lines were drawn over the top of the field, to create an image of a table. The table field is named "hourly temps". Another field, named "daily averages", is drawn to the right of the table; it also consists of seven text lines and will contain the average temperature for each day. A third field, named "hourly averages", is located below the table and contains the average temperature for each hour taken over the seven-day period. (Two other fields are used to label the table field.) A button is provided to calculate and display the daily and hourly averages by using the following script:

```
to handle buttonClick
    send fieldTextToArray
```

```
        send calcDailyAvgs
        send calcHourlyAvgs
end buttonClick

to handle fieldTextToArray
    system tempArray[7][13]
    step i from 1 to 7
        step j from 1 to 13
            put word j of textline i of text of field "hourly temps" into tempArray[i][j]
        end step
    end step
end fieldTextToArray

to handle calcDailyAvgs
    system tempArray[7][13]
    step i from 1 to 7
        put 0 into dailyTemp
        step j from 1 to 13
            increment dailyTemp by tempArray[i][j]
        end step
        put dailyTemp / 13 into y
        format y as "00.0"
        put y into textline i of text of field "daily averages"
    end step
end calcDailyAvgs

to handle calcHourlyAvgs
    system tempArray[7][13]
    - -clear out previous hourly averages from field:
    put 0 into text of field "hourly averages"
    step x from 1 to 12
        put tab & "0" after text of field "hourly averages"
    end step
    - -calculate the hourly averages:
    step j from 1 to 13
        put 0 into hourlyTemp
        step i from 1 to 7
            increment hourlyTemp by tempArray[i][j]
        end step
        put hourlyTemp/7 into y
        format y as "00.0"
        put y into word j of text of field "hourly Averages"
    end step
end calcHourlyAvgs
```

The calculation task is divided between three subroutines called from the **buttonClick** handler. The first subroutine, **fieldTextToArray**, reads the text from the field and places it in a 7 by 13 two-dimensional array. This array is used in the other two subroutines to calculate the daily and hourly averages. The **calcHourlyAvgs** handler uses two embedded loops to sum the 13 temperature readings for each day. Each of the seven totals is divided by 13 and displayed in the field to the right of the table, on the appropriate text line. The third subroutine, **calcDailyAvgs**, also uses two embedded fixed loops to sum the seven temperature readings for each hour. This is done for all 13 hours, with each total divided by 7 to arrive at an average.

Common Errors in Working with Arrays

There are two common errors made by programmers in writing code that uses arrays. One is to declare an array that has been previously declared with different dimensions. For instance, the statement

system myArray[10][10]

would result in an error if the array had previously been declared as an 8 by 8 matrix in this statement:

system myArray[8][8]

Such attempts to redefine an array result in an "Execution Suspended" dialog box. Forethought must be given in declaring arrays so that they are large enough to hold any necessary data. If the needed size of the array is unknown, then the array is best declared dynamically, in this way:

system myArray[][]

Another common error is to try to put or get a value into an element that is outside the array dimensions. The following statement declares an array of 30 elements:

system grades[30]

The following statement would result in an error.

put 98 into grades[31]

The error occurs because 31 is outside the dimension range of 1 to 30.

Summary Questions

Complete the following statements by filling in the blanks.
1. Arrays may have up to _____ dimensions.
2. Arrays must be _____ in the handler before values can be assigned to the array's elements.
3. The _____ command is used to assign one value to all the elements of an array.
4. A common error in working with arrays is to refer to an element outside the array's declared _____ .
5. Values are assigned to an array element by using the assignment operator or the _____ command.
6. The _____ function is used to find out the size of an array.
7. An array whose size is undeclared and can change is referred to as _____.
8. An array that has been previously declared may not be redeclared with a new _____ .
9. Arrays are often manipulated within _____ structures.
10. The total number of elements an array may have is limited by _____ .

Assuming the values in the matrix in Figure 21.11 represent an array named cities, answer questions 11 through 15.
11. Write a statement to declare cities as an array with a global scope.

12. How many dimensions would the cities array need?
13. How many elements would the cities array need?
14. What is the value of cities[5]?
15. What is the value of cities[8]?

| Anchorage |
| Denver |
| Los Angeles |
| Phoenix |
| Portland |
| Sacramento |
| San Diego |
| San Francisco |
| Seattle |
| Tucson |

Figure 21.11
This representation of the cities *array is used to answer questions 11 through 15.*

Assuming the values in the matrix in Figure 21.12 represent an array named myArray, answer questions 16 through 20.
16. Write a statement to declare myArray as a local array of type INT.
17. What is the value of myArray[3][2]?
18. What is the value of myArray[5][1]?
19. What is the value of myArray[1][4]?
20. What is the value of myArray[2][6]?

15	7	12	25	18	19
32	19	30	26	10	5
18	20	16	9	12	0
35	29	19	24	38	31
27	4	14	27	33	36

Figure 21.12
This representation of the array called **myArray** *is used to answer questions 16 through 20.*

Hands-On Projects

A. Examine the software that accompanies this chapter. Open the "Table of Contents" book by double-clicking its icon in the "Developing with ToolBook" group window in the Windows Program Manager. Inside the "Table of Contents," click the book representing Chapter 21.

B. Create a book in which the user is prompted to enter a sentence or phrase when he or she clicks a button. The input sentence is displayed in a field and its words are written in reverse order in another field (see Figure 21.13). To write the sentence in reverse order, store each word of the sentence in a dynamic array and

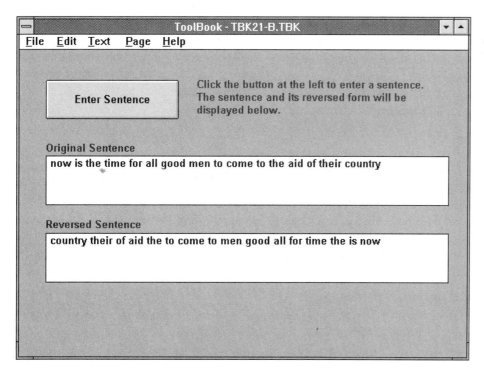

Figure 21.13
An array is used to rewrite a sentence's words in reverse order.

then retrieve the words, beginning with the highest element and working backwards to the first element.

C. The windchill factor is the "felt" temperature based on the actual temperature and the wind velocity. Study the table in Figure 21.14. Create an application like that shown in Figure 21.15, in which the user selects a temperature and wind velocity from grouped radio buttons and the corresponding windchill temperature is displayed. Store the table in Figure 21.14 as an array. The radio buttons should determine the *x* and *y* elements of the array. The value of this element is displayed in the field for the windchill temperature.

Figure 21.14
Windchill temperature is based on the air temperature and the wind velocity. In Hands-On Project C, this table is translated into an array and used to display the windchill temperature for a specified temperature and wind velocity.

		\<5>	\<10>	\<15>	\<20>	\<25>	\<30>
T	**20**	17	3	- 4	- 10	- 15	- 17
E	**15**	12	- 3	- 11	- 17	- 22	- 25
M	**10**	7	- 9	- 18	- 24	- 29	- 33
P	**5**	0	- 15	- 25	- 31	- 36	- 41
E							
R	**0**	- 5	- 22	- 31	- 39	- 44	- 49
A	**-5**	- 10	- 27	- 38	- 46	- 51	- 56
T	**-10**	- 15	- 34	- 45	- 53	- 59	- 64
U							
R	**-15**	- 21	- 40	- 51	- 60	- 66	- 71
E	**-20**	- 26	- 46	- 58	- 67	- 74	- 79

(Table heading: **Wind Velocity in MPH**)

Figure 21.15
The windchill temperature is displayed when the user selects a new temperature or wind velocity by using the grouped radio buttons.

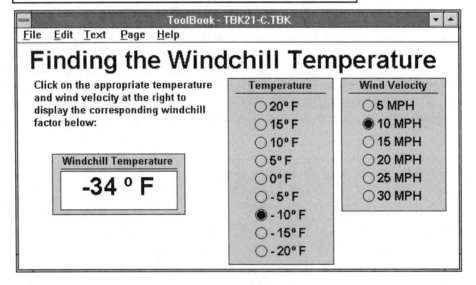

D. The Arizona Widget Company has stores in several cities. Create an application like that in Figure 21.16, which calculates the annual sales for each store (given each store's quarterly sales) as well as the total sales for all stores combined for each quarter. Use the values in Figure 21.16 to test your handler. The handler should read the field text into an array and use the array values to calculate the totals. Include a "Reset" button to clear all values from the array and the display.

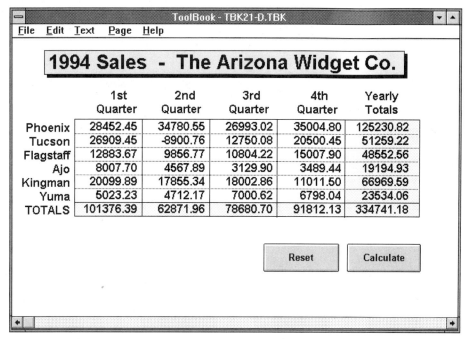

Figure 21.16
An array is used to calculate and display the subtotals of quarterly sales figures. Note that both the rows and columns are totaled.

	1st Quarter	2nd Quarter	3rd Quarter	4th Quarter	Yearly Totals
Phoenix	28452.45	34780.55	26993.02	35004.80	125230.82
Tucson	26909.45	-8900.76	12750.08	20500.45	51259.22
Flagstaff	12883.67	9856.77	10804.22	15007.90	48552.56
Ajo	8007.70	4567.89	3129.90	3489.44	19194.93
Kingman	20099.89	17855.34	18002.86	11011.50	66969.59
Yuma	5023.23	4712.17	7000.62	6798.04	23534.06
TOTALS	101376.39	62871.96	78680.70	91812.13	334741.18

Accessing the File Cabinet
File Input/Output

There is much emphasis in today's computing environment on applications sharing data. Popular applications import and export data in a variety of formats. **Importing** refers to reading external files on a disk into an application; **exporting** is the process of writing data in an application to an external storage file. Data in ToolBook may be exported as text files and thus made available to other programs. Text files may also be imported into ToolBook. For applications distributed on CD-ROM, the use of external files allows data to be stored on other writable media, such as a floppy disk or hard drive, and retrieved from these media and sent into the book.

External files also allow large amounts of data to be stored as one unit. A maximum of 32,000 characters can be stored in a single ToolBook field, but the size of an external text field is limited only by the available storage space.

File Formats

There are two primary types of data files used with OpenScript. A **document file** is a simple word-processed file organized in paragraphs as a letter or article would be. Document files are generally saved as ASCII text files, meaning all formatting and font information has been removed. The file consists of only the text characters. Format strings that create boldface, italics, margins, and the like have been stripped away. Figure 22.1 shows the format of a document file.

Data files are also ASCII text-based, but they consist of items separated by a delimiter. The delimiter is any character whose specified role is to mark the end of a data item. Common delimiters include the carriage return (CR), linefeed (LF), tab, and comma. Carriage return and linefeed characters follow each line of text in an

```
     The text contained in a document file is usually
formatted as paragraphs.  Usually, in reading text from a
document file, the data is read until a carriage return is
encountered, which would mark the end of a paragraph.
     This chapter will focus on the other type of external
file, the data file.  It is more common to read and write
information to a data file than a document file.
```

Figure 22.1
Document files are typically organized in paragraphs.

```
MacCrate,C,18,15,2
Watson, C,10,10,3
Herrington,F/C,5,5,0
Konomos,F,4,9,5
Fidler,F,8,1,2
Mullins,F,6,3,4
Emerson,F,6,0,3
```

Figure 22.2
Data files may consist of data records delimited by carriage return-linefeed characters, with the fields of each record delimited by commas.

ASCII file. Figure 22.2 shows a comma-delimited data file. Both documents and data files end with an **end-of-file (EOF) marker**.

Reading Data from a File

Reading data from a file involves several steps. First, the file must be opened before it can be read from. When the file is opened, it is loaded into the random-access memory (RAM) of the computer. (A maximum of 10 files may be open at any one moment.) A file is opened using the openFile command as described in Figure 22.3.

Figure 22.3
The openFile *command loads an external file into memory so that its contents may be accessed by the ToolBook application.*

The openFile command

Syntax: **openFile *filename***

Purpose: Opens a file so that its contents may be read or data may be written to it.

Examples: openFile "myfile.txt"

`   openFile "D:\TOOLBOOK\DATA\MYFILE.TXT"

                 system dataFile
                 openFile dataFile

Once the file is open, its contents may be read. Data may be read for a fixed number of characters at a time or until a specified delimiter is reached. The reading process is usually performed within a loop structure. As a data file is being read, ToolBook keeps track of what portion of the file has already been read, placing a marker (also referred to as a "pointer") where it left off. With each iteration of the loop, ToolBook starts at the end of the section read in the previous loop iteration and reads for a specified number of characters or until the specified delimiter is encountered. Data is read using the readFile command. The two formats of the readFile command are discussed in Figure 22.4. One format is used for reading a specified number of characters. The other format is used to read data until a specified delimiter is reached. In both cases, the read data is placed in the variable it. If the entire file has been read (an EOF marker was encountered), a null value is assigned to it, the sysError property is set to end of file, and the sysErrorNumber property is set to 565.

When finished with the file, it should be closed. This causes its data to be saved

Figure 22.4
The readFile *command is used to read data from an external file into the ToolBook environment so that ToolBook may utilize the data (assign it to a container, for example)*

The readFile command

Syntax: **readFile *filename* to *character***
                 or
                 readFile *filename* for *numberOfCharacters*

Purpose: Reads data from a file. Reading starts at the current pointer location and continues until a specified character is encountered or until a specified number of characters has been read.

Examples: readFile "myfile.txt" to LF

`   readFile "D:\TOOLBOOK\DATA\MYFILE.TXT" to "*"

                 readFile "c:\autoexec.bat" for 2000

                 system dataFile
                 readFile dataFile for 500

The closeFile command

Syntax: **closeFile** *filename*

Purpose: Closes an open file so that its memory allocation in RAM is freed.

Examples: closeFile "myfile.txt"

`   closeFile "D:\TOOLBOOK\DATA\MYFILE.TXT"

                 . . . .
             system dataFile
             closeFile dataFile

Figure 22.5
The closeFile command should be executed when access to the file is no longer needed, so that the memory allocated to the file is freed for other uses.

to disk. (This is not necessary when reading from a file, but vital when writing data to a file.) Also it frees up memory space and various system resources. Files are closed with the closeFile command (see Figure 22.5).

The three steps of opening the file, reading from the file, and closing the file are commonly performed within the same handler. The following handler opens a data file named SCORES.TXT which is located in the \MYDATA directory of the hard drive (C). This is the data file shown in Figure 22.2. Using a loop, the handler reads one line of text in each iteration and places the items of each text line in an array. The loop continues until the entire file has been read, which is determined by checking the value of the sysError property after each read. If sysError equals end of file the loop is terminated. The file is then closed.

```
to handle importData
    system players[][]
    openFile "C:\windows\scores.txt"
    put "" into sysError
    put 1 into i
    while sysError = ""
        readFile "c:\windows\scores.txt" to LF
        if sysError = "end of file" then
            break while
        end if
        while char 1 of it is CR or char 1 of it is LF
            clear char 1 of it
        end while
        step j from 1 to 5
            put item j of it into players[i][j]
        end step
        increment i by 1
    end while
    closeFile "c:\windows\scores.txt"
end importData
```

The players array is declared with unknown dimensions, since the number of text lines in the data file might vary. Text lines in an ASCII data file are separated by CR and LF characters. These are stripped out by the while char 1 of it is CR or char 1 of it is LF loop. Variable i is used as a counter to keep track of which row a data item should be written to in the array; the variable j is used to track which column the data item belongs in.

If the data file is known to contain 12 lines of text with five items on each line, the preceding handler could be rewritten as

```
to handle importData
    system players[12][5]
    openFile "C:\windows\scores.txt"
    put "" into sysError
    step i form 1 to 12
        readFile "c:\windows\scores.txt" to CR
        while char 1 of it is CR or char 1 of it is LF
            clear char 1 of it
        end while
        step j from 1 to 5
            put item j of it into players[i][j]
        end step
    end step
    closeFile "c:\windows\scores.txt"
end importData
```

A data file might also be read for a specific number of characters. Consider a data file containing automobile identification numbers. Each identification number consists of 20 characters. In the data file, each line consist of one identification number (see Figure 22.6). The following handler reads 22 characters at a time (the 20-character identification number and the CR and LF characters at the end of each line). As each number is read, it is written to the text of a recordfield in a database book. (A new page is created for each number.)

```
to handle buttonClick
    openFile "c:\mydata\autos.txt"
    put 0 into sysErrorNumber
    while sysErrorNumber =0
        readFile "c:\mydata\autos.txt" for 22
        if sysErrorNumber = 565 then
            break while
        end if
        send newPage
        put chars 1 to 20 of it into text of recordField id 0
    end while
    closeFile "c:\mydata\autos.txt"
end buttonClick
```

Figure 22.6
Carriage return and linefeed characters generally separate records in a data file.

```
AHJ98276F61T000PL7K98<CR><LF>
YFG08725F83K972PG1D77<CR><LF>
BHT92010S99I900HL7J89<CR><LF>
AHD60287T02K911HZ7Q82<CR><LF>
DQZ82900F64T821VV8N94<CR><LF>
YTW33211R82X512JM9A92<CR><LF>
AEI62489G63B777CE1U93<CR><LF>
RHY32010W79J902VL7J92<CR><LF>
AYQ65180V02K951HT6Q94<EOF>
```

The filename in the **openFile**, **readFile**, and **closeFile** commands may be a variable. This allows the user to specify which file he or she would like to open and read. The following handler prompts the user to specify a file to import. The text of the chosen file, up to 1000 characters at a time, is opened and read. The read characters are then placed after the text of a field.

```
to handle buttonClick
    ask "Enter path and file name of file to be read:"
    put it into fileName
    openFile fileName
    put 0 into sysErrorNumber
    do
        readFile fileName for 1000
        put it after text of field id 5
    until sysErrorNumber <> 0
    closeFile fileName
end buttonClick
```

In asking the user to enter a filename and path, it is wise to check that the file exists. If it doesn't, the user can be notified and the handler aborted. The preceding handler might be rewritten as

```
to handle buttonClick
    set sysSuspend to false
    put "" into sysError
    ask "Enter path and file name of file to be read:"
    put it into fileName
    openFile fileName
    if sysError is not "" then
        request sysError
        break buttonClick
    end if
    put 0 into sysErrorNumber
    do
        readFile fileName for 1000
        put it after text of field id 5
    until sysErrorNumber <> 0
    closeFile fileName
end buttonClick
```

If the sysSuspend property is set to false, ToolBook does not display an "Execution Suspended" dialog when an error is encountered. If an error is encountered, the sysError is set to a value reflecting the problem. If the file is not found, sysError is set to no such file, which is then displayed in a request dialog. Further execution of the handler is aborted by the break statement.

Writing Data to a File

OpenScript also includes a command for writing data to a file. This process is very similar to reading data from a file. First the file must be opened. Then the data is written to the file; frequently performed in a loop structure; and finally the file is closed. To open and close the file, the code contains openFile and closeFile commands, just as it did when reading data from the file. The writeFile command is utilized to export the information to the external file, as described in Figure 22.7. The writeFile command appends the information to the end of the file. For instance, if the file named RHYME.TXT contains

```
Mary had a little lamb,
Its fleece was white as snow
And everywhere that Mary went,
```

Figure 22.7
The writeFile *command*
appends data to an open
external data file. (It is also
used to overwrite existing
contents of the file if the
seekFile *command has*
been used to set the pointer
to a point other than the
end of the file.)

The writeFile command

Syntax: **writeFile *data* to *filename***

Purpose: Writes data to a file, starting at the current pointer location of the file. By default
this is the end of the file (so the data is appended to the file) unless the seekFile
command (see Figure 22.16) has been used to position the pointer elsewhere in
the file.

Example: writeFile "Donald Duck" to "myfile.txt"

`   writeFile x to "D:\TOOLBOOK\DATA\MYFILE.TXT"

                 system x1,y1,z1,dataFile
                 writeFile x1 & "," & y1 & "," & z1 & CRLF to dataFile

---

and the command

```
    writeFile CRLF & "the lamb was sure to go." to "rhyme.txt"
```

is executed, the RHYME.TXT file would then contain

```
    Mary had a little lamb,
    Its fleece was white as snow
    And everywhere that Mary went,
    the lamb was sure to go.
```

The following handler uses an ask dialog box to ask for a name. The input data is
written to a file named INPUT.DAT.

```
    to handle buttonClick
        openFile "input.dat"
        ask "Enter a name:"
        writeFile CRLF & it to "input.dat"
        closeFile "input.dat"
    end buttonClick
```

If it is desired to input several names, a loop may be used to accept multiple inputs,
writing each one to the external data file with a carriage return-linefeed (CRLF)
separating the inputs. The user is asked to enter additional names until he or she
clicks the "Cancel" button in the ask dialog (which results in a null string ("") being
placed into the variable it).

```
    to handle buttonClick
        openFile "input.dat"
        put "X" into it
        do
            ask "Enter a name (Click cancel to end):"
            if it <> "" then
                writeFile CRLF & it to "input.dat"
            end if
        until it = ""
        closeFile "input.dat"
    end buttonClick
```

Creating a New File

The createFile command allows a new file to be created to accept exported data (see Figure 22.8). The createFile command automatically opens the file when it is created. If the file already exists, its current contents are deleted. (If the read-only attribute of an existent file is active, attempting to create the file results in an error—the message **read only** is assigned to the sysError property and sysErrorNumber is set to 560—and the file is not altered.) If the file is already open, execution of the handler is suspended because of an error.

Figure 22.9 shows a database application. It contains six recordfields named **name, address, city, state, zip,** and **phone.** The following handler (from the "Export Data" button's script) creates a file named CUSTOMER.DAT and then writes the data from each page of the book to it. The handler uses a loop structure, which is repeated for each page of the book.

```
to handle buttonClick
    createFile "customer.dat"
    step i from 1 to pageCount of this book
        writeFile text of recordfield "name" of page i & TAB to "customer.dat"
```

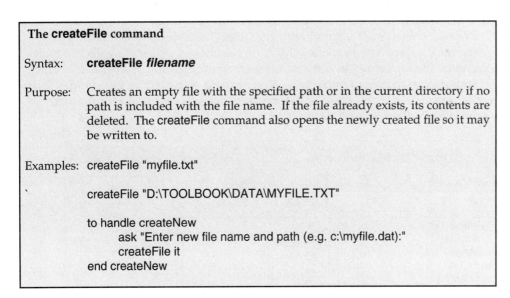

The createFile command

Syntax: **createFile *filename***

Purpose: Creates an empty file with the specified path or in the current directory if no path is included with the file name. If the file already exists, its contents are deleted. The createFile command also opens the newly created file so it may be written to.

Examples: createFile "myfile.txt"

            createFile "D:\TOOLBOOK\DATA\MYFILE.TXT"

            to handle createNew
                ask "Enter new file name and path (e.g. c:\myfile.dat):"
                createFile it
            end createNew

Figure 22.8
The createFile *command is used to create and open a new external file.*

Figure 22.9
A database might include an "Export Data" button to export the text of the recordfields to an external ASCII file.

```
            writeFile text of recordfield "address" of page i & TAB to "customer.dat"
            writeFile text of recordfield "city" of page i & TAB to "customer.dat"
            writeFile text of recordfield "state" of page i & TAB to "customer.dat"
            writeFile text of recordfield "zip" of page i & TAB to "customer.dat"
            writeFile text of recordfield "phone" of page i & TAB to "customer.dat"
        end step
        closeFile "customer.dat"
    end buttonClick
```

Using the "Import..." Option

The "Import..." option in the File menu can be used to import text from an external file into recordfields. When the "Import..." option is chosen, the dialog box pictured in Figure 22.10 is displayed. From this dialog the user can choose a type of file to import. In this case the user chooses "*.txt" in the bottom left combo box. Text may be imported as delimited text or fixed-length by clicking the "Format" button in the dialog box. Because the user chose "*.txt" to indicate text format, the dialog shown in Figure 22.11 is displayed. In this dialog, the file may be specified as either delimited text with a specified delimiter, such as a comma or a tab (the user would type "^t" into the delimiter field to define a tab as the delimiter), or fixed-length text with the author or user specifying the number of characters in the provided field.

After the file is specified and the "OK" button is clicked, a page is created for each record in the file (delimited by CR and LF characters), creating recordfields on the background for each field of the record. A recordfield is created for each field of the record and each field is delimited by the specified character or number of characters. For example, if a file having the contents:

Figure 22.10
ToolBook includes an "Import" screen for importing data in an external file into recordfields.

Figure 22.11
Text files to be imported may be either delimited by a specified character or have fields of specified lengths in terms of the number of characters.

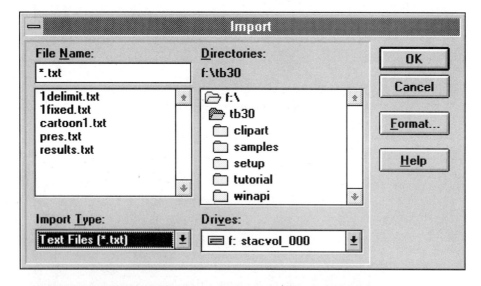

```
George Washington,1732,1799,John Adams<CR><LF>
John Adams,1735,1826,Thomas Jefferson<CR><LF>
Thomas Jefferson,1743,1826,Aaron Burr<CR><LF>
James Madison,1751,1836,George Clinton<CR><LF>
James Monroe,1758,1831,Daniel Tompkins<EOF>
```

is imported into a blank book, four recordfields are created on the background and four pages are added to the book. The text of each field of each record is placed in the appropriate recordfields of each page. For instance, page 2 is pictured in Figure 22.12.

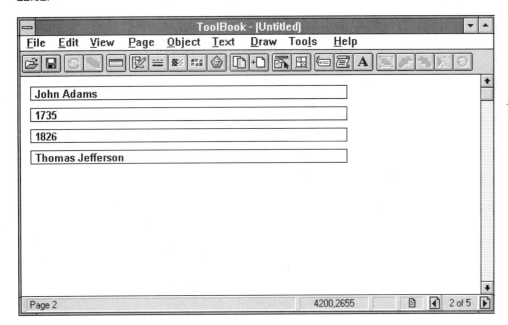

Figure 22.12
When importing data with the "Import..." menu option, ToolBook creates the necessary recordfields and pages to contain all the fields and records of the data file.

Using the "Export..." Option

ToolBook also includes an "Export..." option in the File menu in both Author and Reader modes. The "Export..." option allows a file to be specified. The text of recordfields of the current background can be exported in either a delimited format or a fixed-length format. The user specifies which format and either the delimiter to use or the length of each field in the record. The exported data is truncated as necessary to fit the field length. If the amount of data is insufficient to fill the field, spaces are added. Figure 22.13 shows the pages of a three-page book. The background of the pages contains three recordfields with the name of an invention, the inventor's name, and the year of the invention. If the data is exported as a comma-delimited file, the contents of the file would be

```
"Cotton Gin","Eli Whitney","1794"<CR><LF>
"Dynamite","Alfred Nobel","1867"<CR><LF>
"Alkaline Battery","Thomas Alva Edison","1900"<EOF>
```

Note that each field is surrounded by quotation marks. The fields are separated by commas and the records are separated by CR and LF characters. If the data is exported into fixed-length fields of 20 characters each for the invention and inventor fields and 4 characters for the year field (Figure 22.14), the external file would contain

Figure 22.13
The data contained in the recordfields of a book may be exported to an external ASCII file by using the "Export..." option in the File menu.

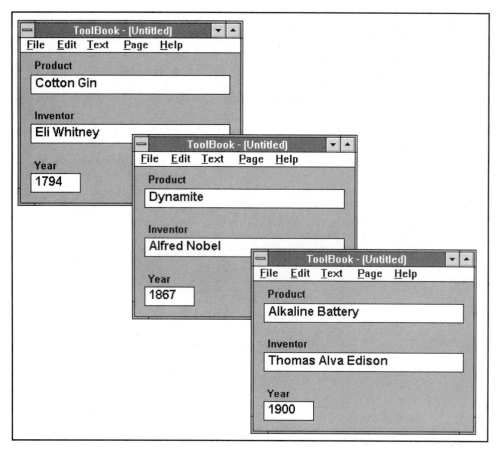

```
Cotton Gin          Eli Whitney         1794
Dynamite            Alfred Nobel        1867
Alkaline Battery    Thomas Alva Edison  1900
```

Note that spaces are inserted to fill each field if the data fills fewer than the specified number of characters.

Figure 22.14
The "Export..." option in the File menu allows data in a background's recordfields to be exported in either a delimited format or a fixed-field format.

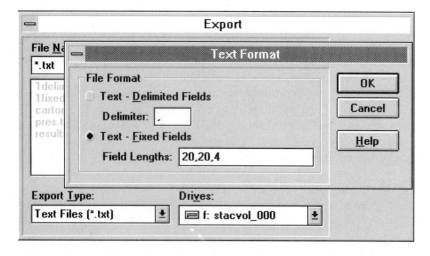

Sequential Files Versus Random-Access Files

Data files are managed in one of two ways. Records in **sequential files** can only be processed in the order in which they are placed in the file. For example, to access the third record of the data file, the first and second records must first be read. New records may only be added to the end of a sequentially managed file. So far this chapter has focused on sequential files. Because of the necessity of reading through all the records preceding a desired record, sequential files are less than ideal for storing and managing large amounts of data.

Random-access files permit any record to be accessed directly by accessing a certain location in the file's data. The number of characters for each record in a random-access file is consistent. (In a sequential file, fields of a record are usually delimited by a character, such as a comma or tab, rather than being a specific number of characters.) If each record consists of 50 characters, the data of the third record would occupy characters 101 through 150. The third record can be read, without having to read the first two records, by specifying that only characters 101 through 150 be read. Data in a random-access file may be sorted and then searched. Some programmers prefer to use a secondary **index file** that is sorted and points to the records in the **master file**. Figure 22.15 shows an unsorted master data file and a secondary index file, which is sorted. (The next chapter will explore how to sort and search data, as well as how to create an index file for an unsorted random-access data file.)

Portland	129.45	237.50	Anchorage	08
Seattle	149.80	250.00	Chicago (Midway)	04
New York (LaGuardia)	345.20	580.00	Chicago (O'Hare)	05
Honolulu	595.00	980.00	Denver (Stapleton)	09
Chicago (O'Hare)	218.50	340.75	Honolulu	04
Chicago (Midway)	203.25	320.00	New York (LaGuardia)	03
Wash. D.C. (Dulles)	310.40	495.50	Orange County (LA)	10
Anchorage	289.40	487.35	Portland	01
Denver (Stapleton)	165.00	210.00	San Diego	11
Orange County (LA)	98.40	135.00	Seattle	02
San Diego	102.45	147.50	Wash. D.C. (Dulles)	07

Master Data File   **Index File (sorted by cities)**

Figure 22.15
In random access files, the data often resides unsorted in a master data file while secondary files serve as index to the sorted file. In this example, the index file contains a list of cities in alphabetical order, with a reference to the record location in the master file. (For instance, the data for Honolulu is located in the fourth record of the master file (04).)

The data of a sequential file might be compared to songs on a cassette tape. The tape must be fast-forwarded past the first two songs to listen to the third song. A random-access file is like a CD disk. On a CD player the listener may access any song with the push of a button, without having to "read" any previous songs. The laser is pointed directly to the location of the disk where the third song resides.

Reading and Writing to Random-Access Files

OpenScript has a seekFile command to move the read-write pointer within an open file, as explained in Figure 22.16. The following handler reads the third record of a data file in which each record consists of 44 characters (the first field is 4 characters, the second and third fields each contain 20 characters). Note that, since the number of characters is fixed for each record, there is no need for the records to be delimited by a specific character.

Figure 22.16
The seekFile *command positions the pointer in a data file to read from or write to the file, beginning with the pointer location.*

The seekFile command

Syntax:　　**seekFile *fileName* for *position* from *location***

Purpose:　Moves the read-write pointer in an external file to the specified location. This is specified as a certain number of characters from the beginning, current location, or end of the file.

Examples:　seekFile "mydata.tx" for 1000 from beginning

　　　　　　seekFile "mydata.txt" for -100 from end

　　　　　　seekFile "students.dat" for -42 from current

```
to handle buttonClick
    system record3
    openFile "mydata.txt"
    seekFile "mydata.txt" for 89 from beginning
    readFile "mydata.txt" for 44
    put it into record3
end buttonClick
```

The handler moves the pointer in the file to the 89th character from the beginning, which is the first character of the third record. Forty-four characters are read from this point in the data file. The characters read are assigned to the system variable, record3.

　　The seekFile command is also used to point to a record. The command is used to overwrite or to point to the end of the file when the goal is to add a new record. The handler that follows replaces the third record of the same file.

```
to handle buttonClick
    ask "Enter year (format: yyyy):"
    put it into year
    ask "Enter invention:"
    put it into invention
    conditions   -- ensure that invention variable is 20 character
        when charcount(invention) < 20
            step i from charcount(invention)+1 to 20
                put " " after invention
            end step
        when charcount(invention) > 20
            clear chars 12 to charcount(invention) of invention
        when charcount(invention) = 20
    end conditions
    ask "Enter inventor:"
    put it into inventor
    conditions   -- ensure that invention variable is 20 character
        when charcount(inventor) < 20
            step i from charcount(inventor)+1 to 20
                put " " after invention
            end step
        when charcount(inventor) > 20
            clear chars 12 to charcount(inventor) of invention
        when charcount(inventor) = 20
    end conditions
```

```
        openFile "mydata.txt"
        seekFile "mydata.txt" for 89 from beginning
        writeFile year & invention & inventor to "mydata.txt"
        closeFile "mydata.txt"
end buttonClick
```

In the preceding handler, the user inputs data for the year, the name of the invention, and the inventory. Conditional structures are used to make sure that there are 20 characters in both the invention and inventor variables. The preceding script does not verify that there are four characters in the year variable; it would be wise to add code that would allow it to do so.

Both of the two preceding handlers are coded to work with the third record of the file. Generally, these handlers would incorporate a variable record number specified by the user or a parameter with the handler written as a subroutine. For example, the handler to read a record from the file might prompt the user for the record to display:

```
to handle buttonClick
        ask "Enter the number of the record to display (e.g. 3):"
        put it into recNum
        openFile "mydata.txt"
        seekFile "mydata.txt" for (((recNum-1)*44)+1) from beginning
        readFile "mydata.txt" for 4
        put it into year
        readFile "mydata.txt" for 20
        put it into invention
        readFile "mydata.txt" for 20
        put it into inventor
        request "Record: "& recNum & CRLF & year & CRLF & invention & CRLF & inventor
end buttonClick
```

If, when the preceding handler is executed, the user enters 2 as the record to display, the file pointer is set to the 45th character by the seekFile command, since the recNum variable would contain a 2 and, therefore, the formula (((recNum-1)*44)+1) would equal 45. First, four characters are read. These are assigned to the year variable. Then the next 20 characters are read from the data file and assigned to the invention variable. In the same manner, the inventor variable is assigned the next 20 characters read from the data file. The request statement displays the record in the dialog box shown in Figure 22.17, concatenating the variables with CR and LF characters.

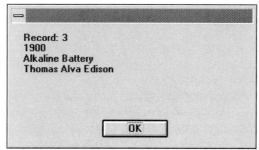

Figure 22.17
A specific record may be pointed to in a random-access file by using the seekFile *command, read into variables, and then displayed in a dialog box.*

Printing from OpenScript

ToolBook offers menu commands for printing pages and printing the text of recordfields in a report. Printing pages and reports may also be initiated by OpenScript handlers. OpenScript's print command (Figure 22.18) prints a specified number of pages, starting with the current page, and can only be used within a start spooler...end spooler control structure (see Figure 22.19). The following handler prints the current page.

Figure 22.18
The print *command is used*
to print page images or
reports for a specified
number of pages.

The **print** command	
Syntax:	**print *number* [pages]**
Purpose:	Prints the specified number of pages of the book or a report of the recordfield data for a specified number of pages of the book The word **all** may be used instead of a number of pages.
Examples:	print 5
	print all

Figure 22.19
Print jobs are specified
within a start spooler...end
spooler *structure.*

The **start spooler...end spooler** structure	
Syntax:	**start spooler**
	. . .
	end spooler
Purpose:	Performs a print job as specified in the statements contained within the **start spooler** and **end spooler** statements
Example:	start spooler
	print 1
	end spooler

```
to handle buttonClick
    start spooler
        print
    end spooler
end buttonClick
```

To print three pages of a book (the current page plus the two following), the **print** command would be

```
print 3
```

The following subroutine prints all the pages of a book.

```
to handle printBook
    start spooler
        print all
    end spooler
end printBook
```

ToolBook has various properties that may be set to define the format of the printed page. The printerArrangement property, for instance, specifies the number of pages to be printed per page. The table in Figure 22.20 lists the various printer system properties and their possible values. The following handler prints the first six pages of the book on one page with two columns of three pages each (that is, a 2 by 3 format). Figure 22.21 shows the result of printing.

```
to handle buttonClick
        put the id of this page into y  --store current page location
```

The Printer System Properties

Property	Purpose	Values
printerArrangement	Specifies how pages are arranged on the printed sheet.	Two integers representing number of pages to print across and down, e.g. 2,4
printerBorders	Prints a border around pages if value is true.	true or false
printerBottomMargin	Specifies width of bottom margin.	Number in page units
printerClipText	Clips text in report if true. Wraps text in report if false.	true or false
printerConditions	Specifies which pages to print.	Boolean expression (in quotation marks)
printerFieldNames	Prints recordfield names in report if true (default is false).	true or false
printerFields	Specifies which recordfields to include in a report.	List of recordfield names
printerFieldWidths	Specifies column widths for each field in a column report. (Declare printerFields first.)	List of numbers (in page units)
printerGroupsAcross	Specifies number of groups to print across the sheet.	Integer from 1 to 4
printerGutterHeight	Defines vertical distance between pages printed on a sheet.	Number in page units
printerGutters	Specifies amount of space between pages on a printed sheet.	Two numbers in page units (vert,horiz)
printerGutterWidth	Defines horizontal distance between pages printed on a sheet.	Number in page units
printerLeftMargin	Specifies width of left margin.	Number in page units
printerMargins	Specifies values for all four margins.	Numbers in page units (left,right,top,bottom)
printerPageBitmap	Prints pages as bitmap images if true (default is false).	true or false
printerRightMargin	Specifies width of right margin.	Number in page units
printerScaling	Specifies size and scale of print margins.	actual, printer, or custom (custom is default)
printerSize	Specifies width and height of groups in a group report.	List of two integers in page units
printerStyle	Specifies the type of report to print.	pages, columns, or groups (Default is pages)
printerTopMargin	Specifies width of top margin	Number in page units

Figure 22.20
There are numerous system properties that may be set to customize the format and information in a printed report.

Figure 22.21
Setting the printerArrangement *property to 2,3*
results in six pages printed
per sheet and placed in a 2
by 3 format.

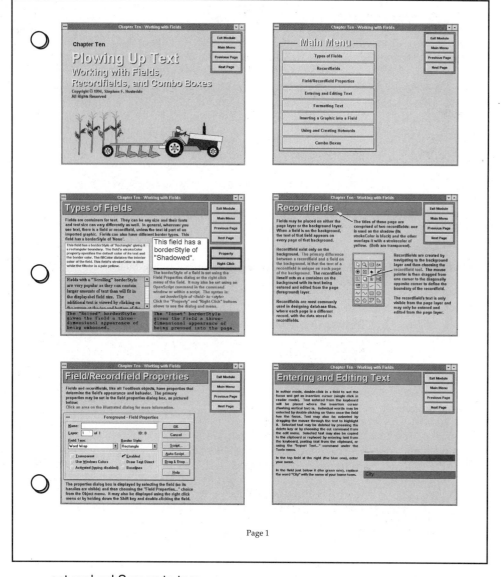

Page 1

```
    set sysLockScreen to true
    set sysCursor to 4  --set cursor to hourglass
    go to page 1
    printerArrangement = 2,3
    printerBorders = true
    start spooler
        print 6 pages
    end spooler
    go to y  -- return to current page
    set sysCursor to 1  --restore cursor to arrow
end buttonClick
```

To print the text of recordfields in a report, the recordfields are identified by setting the printerFields property to a list of their names. Other printer properties (such as printerMargins, printerGroupsAcross, printerStyle, and printerFieldWidths) may be set to specify the margins, the number of groups across the page, whether to print groups or columns, and the width of the columns in a column report. For instance, to print a report of the book pictured in Figure 22.13, the following handler may be deployed.

```
to handle buttonClick
    printerStyle = columns
    printerMargins = 720,720,720,720
    printerFields = "year,invention,inventor"
    printerFieldWidths="1440,3600,3600"
    start spooler
        print
    end spooler
end buttonClick
```

The preceding handler specifies a column report with 0.5 inch margins (720 page units) all the way around (left, right, top, and bottom). The first column will contain the data in the year recordfield and will be 1 inch wide (1440 page units). The second column contains the text of the invention recordfield; the third column contains the data from the inventor recordfield. Both the second and third columns are 2.5 inches wide (3600 page units). The resulting printout is pictured in Figure 22.22.

year	invention	inventor
1974	Cotton Gin	Eli Whitney
1867	Dynamite	Alfred Nobel
1900	Alkaline Battery	Thomas Alva Edison

Figure 22.22
The width of the columns in a column report may specified with the printerColumnWidths *property.*

The text of the report is formatted as the text of the recordfields. The following handler stores the font, style, and size of the recordfields; sets them to new values; prints the report; and then restores the font, style, and size of the recordfields.

```
to handle buttonClick
    put "invention,inventor,year" into y
    set sysLockScreen to true
    step i from 1 to 3   --store face, style and size of recordfield text and set new value
        set the xFace of recordfield (item i of y) to fontFace of recordfield (item i of y)
        set the fontFace of recordfield (item i of y) to Courier
        set the xStyle of recordfield (item i of y) to fontStyle of recordfield (item i of y)
        set the fontStyle of recordfield (item i of y) to 10
        set the xSize of recordfield (item i of y) to fontSize of recordfield (item i of y)
        set the fontSize of recordfield (item i of y) to null
    end step
    printerStyle = columns
    printerMargins = 720,720,720,720
    printerFields = "year,invention,inventor"
    printerFieldWidths = "1440,3600,3600"
    start spooler
        print all
    end spooler
    step i from 1 to 3
        set the fontFace of recordfield (item i of y) to xFace of recordfield (item i of y)
        set the fontStyle of recordfield (item i of y) to xStyle of recordfield (item i of y)
        set the fontSize of recordfield (item i of y) to xSize of recordfield (item i of y)
    end step
end buttonClick
```

Trick: How to Print the Text of a Field

Since the text of a recordfield may be printed in a report, the following subroutine prints the text of a recordfield on the current page.

```
to handle printMyText
    printerStyle = groups
    printerFields = (the name of self)
    printerMargins = "1440,1440,1440,1440"
    printerFieldNames = false
    start spooler
        print 1
    end spooler
end printMyText
```

ToolBook provides neither a menu option nor an OpenScript command for printing the text of a field, however. One way around this omission is to have a hidden recordfield. The handler would copy the text of the field to the text of the recordfield and then print the recordfield. For example:

```
to handle printMyText
    put the text of self into the text of recordfield "to print"
    printerStyle = groups
    printerFields = "to print"
    printerMargins = "1440,1440,1440,1440"
    printerFieldNames = false
    start spooler
        print 1
    end spooler
    put "" into text of recordfield "to print"
end printMyText
```

Summary Questions

Complete the following statements by filling in the blanks.

1. Document files are typically organized in _____ .
2. Files must first be _____ before they can be read from or written to.
3. Files are opened using the _____ command.
4. The three steps of reading data from a file are opening the file, reading the file, and _____ the file.
5. Carriage return and _____ characters generally separate records in a data file.
6. A specific character used to separate records or fields in a data file is referred to as a _____ .
7. The records of a _____ file must be accessed in order (that is, the second record cannot be read until the first record has been read).
8. The records of a _____ file may be accessed in any order.
9. The _____ command is used to position the pointer in a random-access file.
10. To print four pages of a book, the command _____ _____ would be issued.

Write an OpenScript statement to perform the following tasks.

11. Open a data file named CII.DAT.
12. Read the next 100 characters from a data file named CII.DAT.
13. Place the pointer at the 2000th character in a random-access file named ABC.TXT.
14. Place the pointer at the beginning of the 11th record of the random-access file named ABC.TXT. (There are 40 characters in each record.)
15. Append a carriage return, linefeed, and the string My dog has fleas. to the end of an open data file named PETS.TXT.
16. Close the file named PETS.TXT.
17. Print all the pages of a book.
18. Choose the text of recordfields name, idNumber and phone to be printed in a report.
19. Set a 2-inch top margin for a report.
20. Prepare to print eight pages of a book on one sheet of paper. The pages should be in two columns of four pages each.

Hands-On Projects

A. Examine the software that accompanies this chapter. Open the "Table of Contents" book by double-clicking its icon in the "Developing with ToolBook" group window in the Windows Program Manager. Inside the "Table of Contents," click the book representing Chapter 22.

B. Use a word processor such as Windows Write or NotePad to create the sequential data file shown in Figure 22.23. (Note: The *<CR><LF>* symbols denote pressing the Enter key, not typing the string "<CR><LF>".) Save the file as an ASCII text file named CORPORAT.DAT. Create an address book application like that pictured in Figure 22.24; include recordfields for name, title, company, and phone data. Write a script to open the CORPORAT.DAT file. Read each record in a loop, creating a new page (use a send new statement) for each record and placing the data in the correct recordfields. Close the file after all records have been read.

```
Goldie Locks,Trainer,Big Bear Circus,(123) 555-4567<CR><LF>

Hansel & Gretl Smith,Owners,Breadcrumb Bakery,(602) 555-2222<CR><LF>

Ralph Rumplestiltskin,Researcher,"Sleep Disorder Center, The",(123)
555-1234<CR><LF>

Dorothy Tinman,President,Toto Oil,(345) 555-9999<CR><LF>

Louise Cinderella,Designer,Royal Ball Fashions,(602) 555-9876<CR><LF>

Shirley Rapunzel,Stylist,Tower Hair Salon,(602) 555-0011<CR><LF>

Riding Hood,,Grandma's Cookies,(789) 555-5555<CR><LF>

Snow White,Interior Designer,Mirror Creations,(602) 555-8181
```

Figure 22.23
The data for Hands-On Project B may be entered in a word processor and saved as an ASCII text file.

C. Create an application to read in the data from CORPORAT.DAT (see Figure 22.23). In one page field, place all the names followed by the appropriate phone numbers. (Exclude the title and corporation fields.) Figure 22.25 illustrates the finished product.

D. Add a button to the background of the application created in Project E of Chapter 20 (the database about different animals). The button should print all pages of the book. Each printed sheet should have two pages in a 1,2 arrangement.

Figure 22.24
A background with recordfields may be created for placing the data read from an external file.

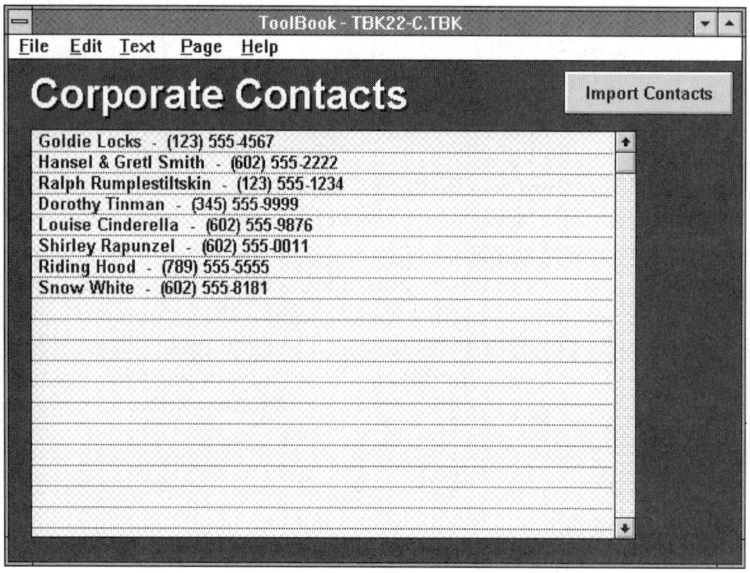

Figure 22.25
In Hands-On Project C, only certain fields of records read in from an external data file are displayed.

E. Add a "Report" button to the background of the application created in Project B of this chapter. The button should allow a user to print a column report of the data after it has been imported. Make each field 1.75 inches wide (2520 page units), and show the names of the fields at the top of each column. Figure 22.26 illustrates the desired appearance of the report.

Figure 22.26
A script to print this column report is the task of Hands-On Project E.

Name	Title	Corporation	Phone
Goldie Locks	Trainer	Big Bear Circus	(123) 555-4567
Hansel 7 Gretl Smith	Owners	Breadcrumb Bakery	(602) 555-2222
Ralph Rumplestiltskin	Researcher	Sleep Disorder Center, The	(123) 555-1234
Dorothy Tinman	President	Toto Oil	(345) 555-9999
Louise Cinderella	Designer	Royal Ball Fashions	(602) 555-9876
Shirley Rapunzel	Stylist	Tower Hair Salon	(602) 555-0011
Riding Hood		Grandma's Cookies	(789) 555-5555
Snow White	Interior Designer	Mirror Creations	(602) 555-8181

F. Add a "Print" button to the bingo-card generator created in Hands-On Project D of Chapter 18. The button should allow the user to print the page containing the generated card.

Chapter 23

Data Manipulation
Sorting and Searching

Working with large amounts of data, such as in a database management application, requires the abilities to both sort through the data, organizing it as desired, and search for specific items within the data. Without these capabilities, the data is likely to be of little use. ToolBook has the ability to sort the pages of a book by the values contained in its recordfields, the names of it pages, or the value of some property. Pages can be sorted by choosing the "Sort..." option or using an OpenScript handler that includes the **sort** statement. There are numerous algorithms designed to sort large amounts of data, and these may be translated into OpenScript commands. Two popular algorithms are the bubble sort and the Shell sort, both of which are discussed in this chapter.

ToolBook and OpenScript have commands for searching the text of a book or field for a specified string. The occurrence of the found string is highlighted in the book. Subsequent occurrences may be found by using the **search again** command. The "Replace" menu option may be used to replace one string with another whenever the first string appears.

For random-access files, indexes may be developed for finding data quickly. An index consists of the data of a selected field of the records in a master file along with the record number for each item. The list is then sorted and may be searched to locate the record number containing the desired information.

The "Sort..." Option

The pages of a database application book may be sorted by choosing the "Sort..." option on the Page menu. This brings up the "Sort" dialog box as pictured in Figure 23.1. The user may select a recordfield or recordfields by which to sort the pages. Recordfields to be sorted are designated by choosing them in the "Available Record Fields" field so that they appear in the "Sort on Record Field(s)" field. The first designated recordfield is the primary sort key, the second one is the secondary sort key, and so on. The recordfields may be sorted in either ascending (A to Z) or descending (Z to A) order. The contents of these recordfields may be specified as text,

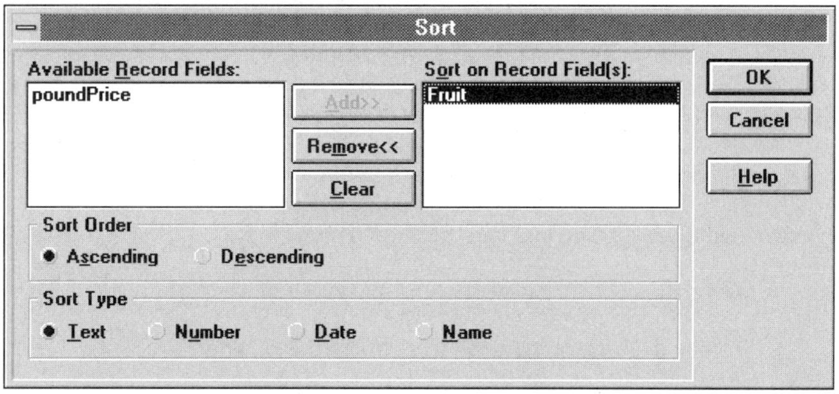

Figure 23.1
The "Sort..." menu option in the Page menu brings up a dialog box from which the recordfields to sort may be specified, as well as the sort method (ascending or descending) and the type of data being sorted (text, numbers, dates, or names).

numeric, date, or name data. (Name fields are sorted by the last word of the field. So, if sorting by ascending order, Zelda Apple would be placed before Amos Watermelon.) Only the pages of the current background are sorted, since the sort is based on the contents of a recordfield on the background.

Sorting with OpenScript

The "Sort" dialog box may be provided to the user through a "Sort" button with the following handler:

```
to handle buttonClick
    send sort
end buttonClick
```

The user may then use the dialog box to specify which recordfields to sort and how.

OpenScript has a sort command for sorting the pages of a book. Figure 23.2 discusses the syntax and use of the sort command. Figure 23.3 shows several unsorted pages of a book about different fruit and their price per pound. The handler of the "Sort by Fruit name" button is

```
to handle buttonClick
    sort by ascending text the text of recordfield "Fruit"
    go to page 1
end buttonClick
```

All the pages of the book are sorted by the text of the recordfield containing the name of the fruit, so the "Apples" page is first and the "Watermelon" page is last. Likewise, the "Sort by Price/lb" button has the following script and sorts the pages so that the cheapest fruit is on the first page and the most expensive fruit is on the last page.

```
to handle buttonClick
    sort by ascending number the text of recordfield "poundPrice"
    go to page 1
end buttonClick
```

The remaining button (labeled "Unsorted") sorts the pages by the idNumber of the page. This is the order in which the pages were created and appears to the user to be unsorted. The script for sorting the book by the page ID numbers is

Figure 23.2
The sort *command is used to sort the pages of a book by the value of a page expression.*

The **sort** command	
Syntax:	**sort [pages *number* to *number*] by [*order*] [*type*] *sortExpression***
Purpose:	Sorts the pages of a book by a specified expression. An order (ascending or descending may be specified, as well as the type of data contained in the sort expression (text, number, date, or name). The *sortExpression* may be any expression associated with a page, such as the text contained in a recordfield, the name of the page, the ID number of the page, etc.
Examples:	sort by ascending text the text of recordfield id 5
	sort pages 5 to 10 by number the idNumber of this page
	sort by descending date the text of recordfield "when"

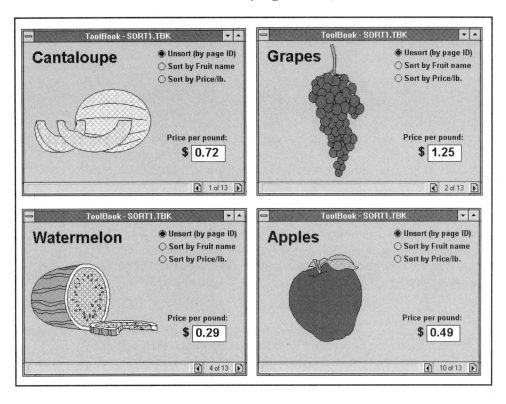

Figure 23.3
The pages of a database can
be sorted by the text of a
recordfield or the ID
number of the pages.

```
to handle buttonClick
    sort by ascending number the idNumber of this page
    go to page 1
end buttonClick
```

In the preceding script, it is critical that the sort is performed numerically if the book is more than nine pages long. If number is not specified, the pages are sorted by the textual values of the ID numbers (text is the default). This would result in the page whose idNumber property is 12 being placed after page whose idNumber is 11 but before the page whose idNumber is 5, since the textual sort starts by comparing the first characters of the data items. The "1" of the number 12 is, of course, less than the "5." If a sort command does not perform as expected, an incorrect sort type is most often the culprit. Another culprit, but a bit more obvious, is an instruction to sort in descending order when ascending is desired, or vice versa.

Sorting the Text of a Container

Neither ToolBook nor OpenScript has commands for sorting the text within a container, such as a field or recordfield. For instance the text lines of the field shown in Figure 23.4 are unsorted. To sort the text lines of the field's text, an algorithm must be developed and written in OpenScript. There are several standard sort algorithms. The bubble sort and the Shell sort are two of the most common. (A dynamic link library (DLL) that accompanies ToolBook contains two functions for sorting items of a list or text lines of a container. These functions, sortItems( ) and sortTextlines( ), will be discussed in Chapter 26, when using DLLs is discussed.)

cantaloupe
watermelon
grapes
pears
grapefruit
cherries
kiwi
apples
tangerines
strawberries
raspberries
oranges
honeydews
mangos

Figure 23.4
The OpenScript sort
command does not work in
sorting the text lines of a
field or recordfield. A sort
algorithm must be written
to handle this task.

The Bubble Sort

In the **bubble sort**, a list of items is sorted by comparing consecutive items in a fixed loop. For instance, suppose the list contains these numbers:

```
20, 4, 23, 1, 17
```

The list may be sorted by taking the number in the first item and comparing it with the number in each of the other items, working down the list and swapping the numbers if the latter is less than the first. In this case, 20 is first compared to 4. Since 4 is less than 20, these two numbers are swapped and the list is now

```
4, 20, 23, 1, 17
```

The first number (which is now 4) is compared to the next item in the list, which is the third number. Because 23 is not less than 4, no swap occurs. Comparison continues with the next item. Because 1 is less than 4, these two items are swapped and the list is now

```
1, 20, 23, 4, 17
```

The first item is then compared to the fifth item. Since 17 is not less than 1, nothing happens. This completes the first pass or loop. (There will be four such passes—always one less than the number of items being sorted.) After the first pass, the smallest item is always positioned as the first item and need not be compared any longer. In the second pass, the second item is compared with each subsequent item, just as items were compared in the first pass. The second item, 20, is compared with 23. Nothing happens. But after 20 is compared with 4, the two numbers are swapped. The list now reads

```
1, 4, 23, 20, 17
```

Now 4 is compared with the next item, 17, and no swap occurs. The second pass is now complete. In the third pass, the 23 and the 20 are swapped:

```
1, 4, 20, 23, 17
```

Now 20 is compared to 17, and the two values are swapped:

```
1, 4, 17, 23, 20
```

This completes the third pass. In the fourth and final pass, the fourth item is compared to the fifth item and the 20 and 23 are swapped, resulting in the list being sorted in ascending order:

```
1, 4, 17, 20, 23
```

This process is illustrated by the flowchart shown in Figure 23.5. The process is driven by two embedded fixed loops. The outer loop is repeated for 1 to the number of items minus 1, and this value is tracked by the counter variable, i. The inner loop is repeated for one less than the counter value of the outer loop (that is, i - 1) to the number of items in the loop. This value is tracked by the counter variable, j. Within the inner loop, the values of the ith item is compared to the jth item and these two values are swapped if item j < item i (or, if sorting in descending order, the values are swapped if item i < item j).

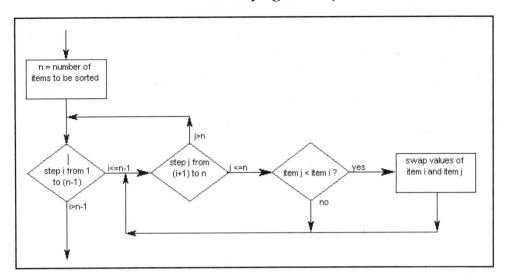

Figure 23.5
The flowchart of a generic bubble sort of n *items.*

The bubble sort algorithm may be translated into the following OpenScript handler, which sorts the text of the field pictured in Figure 23.4.

```
to handle buttonClick
    put the textlineCount(text of field "fruit") into n
    step i from 1 to (n-1)
        step j from (i-1) to n
            if textline j of text of field "fruit" < textline i of \
            text of field "fruit" as text then
                put textline j of text of field "fruit" into temp
                put textline i of text of field "fruit" into \
                textline j of text of field "fruit"
                put temp into textline i of text of field "fruit"
            end if
        end step
    end step
end buttonClick
```

In this handler the number of items to be sorted is determined with the **textlineCount** function. This value of **textlineCount** is then used in the two loops. The upper limit of the outer loop is one less than the number of items being sorted, and this number is used as the upper limit of the inner loop. Within the inner loop the two values of text line i (the counter of the outer loop) and text line j (the counter of the inner loop) are compared. Note that this is specified to be a textual comparison (**as text**)—the default action is to treat the comparison numerically. When comparing text data, if the phrase **as text** is not included, an error results because the value is not a number. If the value of the later text line is less than the value of text line i, the two values are swapped. The swap is done by first placing the value of the greater text in a variable named **temp**, then replacing the value of the greater text with the value of the lesser text. Finally, the value of the lesser text is replaced with the value contained in the **temp** variable (the original value of the greater text). The handler may be changed to perform a descending sort by changing the less than operator in the **if...then** statement to a greater than operator.

```
to handle buttonClick
    put the textlineCount(text of field "fruit") into n
    step i from 1 to (n-1)
```

```
            step j from (i-1) to n
                if textline j of text of field "fruit" > \
                textline i of text of field "fruit" as text then
                    put textline j of text of field "fruit" into temp
                    put textline i of text of field "fruit" into \
                    textline j of text of field "fruit"
                    put temp into textline i of text of field "fruit"
                end if
            end step
        end step
    end buttonClick
```

Just as the Boolean expression in the if...then statement in the preceding handler contains as text, the Boolean expression should be specified as date, when date values are being compared. For example:

```
    if textline j of text of field "birthdates" > \
    textline i of text of field "birthdates" as date then
```

The bubble sort algorithm is suitable for sorting arrays. Instead of referring to text lines of a container, the handler references the elements of the array. The following handler sorts an array named **myArray**, which contains fifty elements of text string values.

```
    to handle sortArray
        system myArray(50)
        put 50 into n
        step i from 1 to 49
            step j from (i-1) to 50
                if myArray(j) < myArray(i) as text then
                    put myArray(j) into temp
                    put myArray(i) into myArray(j)
                    put temp into myArray(j)
                end if
            end step
        end step
    end sortArray
```

Sorting Multiple Fields

The application shown in Figure 23.6 contains several fields that are related. The text of the first text line of the **year** field ("1972") is related to the text of the first text line of the **invention** field ("Video Game") and to the text of the first text line of the **inventor** field ("Noland Bushnell"). If the data contained in the fields were to be sorted by one of the fields, such as by **year**, the data of the other fields must also be swapped. The following handler swaps the data of each of the three fields so that the data is sorted in descending order by date and the related text is sorted with the year:

```
    to handle buttonClick
        put the textlineCount(text of field "year") into n
        step i from 1 to (n-1)
            step j from (i-1) to n
                if textline j of text of field "year" > textline i \
```

```
        of text of field "year" then
              put textline j of text of field "year" into temp
              put textline i of text of field "year" into \
              textline j of text of field "year"
              put temp into textline i of text of field "year"

              put textline j of text of field "invention" into temp
              put textline i of text of field "invention" \
               into textline j of text of field "invention"
              put temp into textline i of text of field "invention"

              put textline j of text of field "inventor" into temp
              put textline i of text of field "inventor"\
               into textline j of text of field "inventor"
              put temp into textline i of text of field "inventor"
        end if
      end step
    end step
  end buttonClick
```

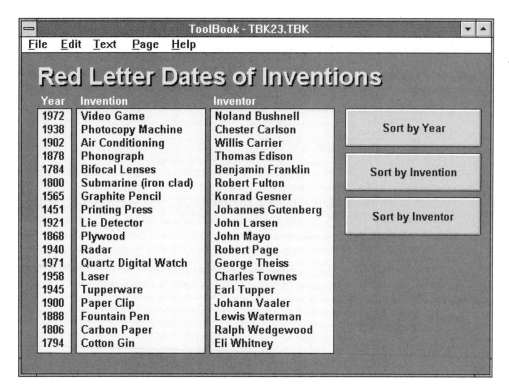

Figure 23.6
A sort handler may be written so that multiple fields are sorted according to the contents of one field, keeping associated information grouped.

The Shell Sort Algorithm

The **Shell sort**, named after its author, Donald Shell, is a revision of the bubble sort that is more efficient for sorting large amounts of data. The greater the number of items to be sorted, the faster a Shell sort is over a bubble sort. Whereas the bubble sort compares and swaps adjacent items in the list, the Shell sort compares and swaps nonadjacent items separated by a distance that diminishes as the sort progresses. The distance starts out being half the number of items to be sorted and is halved whenever there are no swaps performed in the loop. The loop continues executing until the distance between elements is 1 number position and there are no more items being

Figure 23.7
In the Shell sort algorithm,
nonadjacent elements of a
list are compared and
swapped.

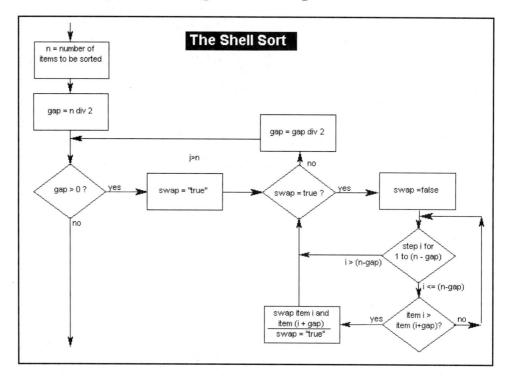

swapped. At this point the list is fully sorted. Figure 23.7 shows a flowchart of the generic Shell sort.

Consider a list of eight numbers to be sorted:

```
12   9   20   1   27   16   5   14
```

The distance between elements to be compared begins at 4 number positions, half the number of items to be sorted. (If the number of items is odd, the starting offset is half of one less than the number of elements—the beginning distance for an array of 201 elements would be 100.) Using the offset of 4, the first item is compared to the fifth item. If the first is larger, the two values are swapped. The number 12 is not larger than 27 and no swap occurs. The second item is compared to the sixth. The number 9 is not larger than 16, so no swap occurs. The third item, 20, is compared to the seventh, 5. These two values are swapped. The fourth item, 1, is not swapped with the eighth, 14. The list at this point would be

```
12   9   5   1   27   16   20   14
```

As long as a swap occurred, the loop is repeated with the same offset. So the first item is again compared with the fourth, the second with the fifth, and so forth. No values are swapped, and the distance between items being compared is then halved. The gap between elements is now 2 (half of 4). The first item is compared with the third and, in this example, the 12 and 5 are swapped. The second item, 9, is compared with the fourth, 1, and these two values are swapped. The list at this point looks like this:

```
5   1   12   9   27   16   20   14
```

The third item, which is now 12, is compared to the fifth item, 27, and no switch occurs. The fourth item, 9, is compared with the sixth, 16. The fifth value, 27, is larger than the value of 20 in the seventh item and these two values are swapped. Finally, the sixth element, 16, is compared with the eighth, 14, and these two values are switched. The list is now

```
5   1   12   9   20   14   27   16
```

Since a swap occurred in this pass of the loop, again the items at a distance of 2 are compared. No values are switched in the next pass and the offset distance is then halved again, becoming 1. Thus, the first value, 5, is compared to the second, 1, and the two values are switched. The second value, now being 5, is compared with the third, 12, and no swap occurs. This comparison of adjacent items continues until the seventh and eighth items are compared. The list after this pass is

```
1   5   9   12   14   20   16   27
```

The loop is reiterated again, since a swap occurred on the last pass. After the next pass, the list is

```
1   5   9   12   14   16   20   27
```

Since a swap occurred on this pass, the loop is reiterated. No swap occurs on the next pass, and the distance is halved. Half of 1 is 0 (the halving is done with integer division: 1 div 2 = 0) and the list is then deemed sorted!

How is this algorithm translated into OpenScript code? The following handler sorts the text lines of field id 1 using the Shell sort algorithm.

```
to handle buttonClick
    put the textlineCount(text of field id 1) into n
    put n div 2 into dist
    while dist > 0
        put "true" into swap
        while swap = "true"
            put "false" into swap
            step x from 1 to (n - dist)
                if textline x of text of field id 1 > \
                textline (x+dist) of text of field id 1 as text then
                    put textline x of text of field id 1 into temp
                    put textline (x+dist) of text of field id 1 into \
                    textline x of text of field id 1
                    put temp into textline (x+dist) of text of field id 1
                    put "true" into swap
                end if
            end step
        end while
        dist = dist div 2
    end while
end buttonClick
```

The algorithm can also be used to sort arrays. The following handler sorts an array named students, which consists of 2000 elements containing text strings.

```
to handle sortArray
    system students(2000)
    put 1000 into dist  --1000 is half of 2000
    while dist > 0
```

```
            put "true" into swap
            while swap = "true"
                put "false" into swap
                step x from 1 to (n - dist)
                    if students(x) > students(x+dist) as text then
                        put students(x) into temp
                        put students(x+dist) into students(x)
                        put temp into students(x+dist)
                        put "true" into swap
                    end if
                end step
            end while
            dist = dist div 2
        end while
    end sortArray
```

The "Find..." Menu Option

The "Find..." option in the Edit menu displays a dialog box in which the user enters a string to search for (see Figure 23.8). The user may specify to search only for occurrences of exact, complete words (for example, if the "Match exact word" checkbox is checked, searching for "blue" would not find the "blue" in "blueberries"). It is also possible to search for only those occurrences where the case (uppercase or lowercase) matches. The user may choose to exclude all background

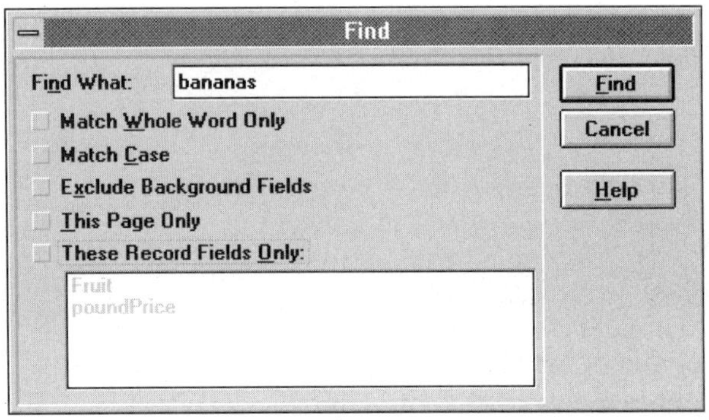

Figure 23.8
The "Find..." option brings up a dialog box from which the user (or author) can search for a specific string. Various options restrict the search to whole words, exact case, or certain recordfields.

fields and search only specific recordfields, or search only the current page. As with the "Sort..." menu item, the "Find..." dialog box can be opened from an OpenScript handler by sending the find message:

```
            to handle buttonClick
                send find
            end buttonClick
```

OpenScript's **search** Command

Like the "Find..." option, a search command in an OpenScript handler can find data. The syntax and use of the search command is discussed in Figure 23.9. This command may be used in a handler that asks the user what string he or she would like to find. Then the command locates that string. For example:

```
    to handle buttonClick
        ask "What would you like to search for?"
        put "" into sysError
        put it into searchString
        search for searchString
        if sysError = "not found" then
            request quote & searchString & quote && "was not found." with "OK"
        end if
    end buttonClick
```

The search command

Syntax: **search [page] for** *string* **[by case] [as word] [locateOnly]**
            or
            search [page] records for *string* **[by case] [as word] [locateOnly]**
            or
            search [page] excluding background for *string* **[by case] [as word] [locateOnly]**
            or
            search [page] in *recordField* **[,***recordField* **. . .] for** *string* **[by case] [as word]**
            [locateOnly]
            or
            search again

Purpose: Searches for a specified string, *string*. The restriction **by case** causes the search
            to find only strings matching the exact case (upper-/lowercase) specified in
            string. The **as word** restriction instructs the computer to find matching whole
            words only—that is, specifying **cat** would not find **catch**. The **locateOnly**
            restriction causes the computer not to highlight or navigate to a match; instead,
            the variable **it** is set to a list containing the field or recordfield name, the starting
            character position, and the ending character position in the field or recordfield's
            text. The **page** restriction limits the search to the current page. If **records**
            appears in the command structure, the search finds *string* in the text of
            recordfields only. If **excluding background** appears, the search is limited to
            page fields only. If **in** *recordField* appears, the search is limited to a list of
            specified recordfields. The instruction **search again** repeats the last search and
            finds the next occurrence of *string*.

Examples: search for "bananas"

            search page for "cat" as word locateOnly

            search in "client","contact1", "contact2" for "Elizabeth Myers" as word

            search page excluding background for "HELLO" by case

            search again

---

*Figure 23.9
OpenScript's* search
*command is used to find a
specific string in the text of
a field or recordfield.
Various options permit the
search to be restricted to the
current page, specific
backgrounds, or the exact
case to be matched.*

When the string is found, it is highlighted in the field or recordfield. The **search again**
format of the **search** command may be used to find additional occurrences of the
same search string. The following might be the handler of a button captioned "Find
Next."

```
to handle buttonClick
     search again
end buttonClick
```

Each time the preceding handler is executed, the next occurrence of the search string
is identified. If all occurrences have been located, nothing happens and the value of
sysError is set to **not found**.

The "Replace..." Menu Option

The "Replace..." option in the Edit menu is similar to the "Find..." option. In the
"Replace" dialog box, the user enters a string to search for as well as a string to replace
it with if found (see Figure 23.10). The same restrictions available in the "Find" dialog
box are available in the "Replace" dialog box. When the search string is located, it

Figure 23.10
The "Replace..." menu
option brings up a dialog in
which a string to be
searched for is specified
along with a string to
replace the found string.

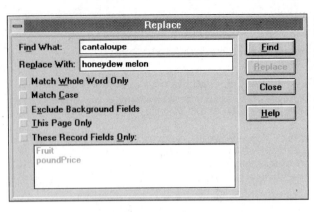

is highlighted and may then be replaced with the replacement string by clicking the "Replace" button. Like the "Find..." option, the "Replace..." option may be simulated by sending the replace message from a handler:

> send replace

Using OpenScript to Replace Text

OpenScript does not have a "replace" command, but such functionality may be scripted by searching for a string and then putting a replacement string into selectedText, since found strings are selected (highlighted). If the string is not found, the value of sysErrorNumber is set to 641. The following script searches for an occurrence of the word bananas and replaces it with the word peaches.

```
to handle buttonClick
    put 0 into sysErrorNumber
    search for "bananas"
    if sysErrorNumber <> 641 then   -- matching string was found
        put "peaches" into selectedText
    end if
end buttonClick
```

To replace all the occurrences of bananas with peaches, the following handler uses the search and search again commands:

```
to handle buttonClick
    put 0 into sysErrorNumber
    search for "bananas"
    while sysErrorNumber <> 641 then   -- matching string was found
        put "peaches" into selectedText
        search again
    end while
end buttonClick
```

The while loop is executed repeatedly until all occurrences of the string bananas have been found and replaced with peaches.

A generic subroutine to perform a search-and-replace function would be

```
to handle replaceAll searchString replacementString
    put 0 into sysErrorNumber
    search for searchString
    while sysErrorNumber <> 641 then   -- matching string was found
        put replacementString into selectedText
    search again
        end while
end replaceAll
```

To use the preceding subroutine to replace all of the occurrences of **oranges** with **cherries**, the following statement would be issued:

    send replaceAll "oranges","cherries"

Creating and Using Indexes for Random-Access Data Files

Figure 23.11 shows an unsorted random-access data file used by a travel agency. The data consists of three fields. The first field contains a destination city and occupies 20 characters. The second field is seven characters long and contains data relating to the price of a one-way ticket. The third field is also seven characters and contains the price of a round-trip ticket. Note that, for display purposes only, the records are separated into separate text lines. In reality, the data would likely exist in a format without carriage returns and linefeeds, like this:

```
Portland              129.45  237.50
Seattle               149.80  250.00
New York (LaGuardia)  345.20  580.00
Honolulu              595.00  980.00
Chicago (O'Hare)      218.50  340.75
Chicago (Midway)      203.25  320.00
Wash. D.C. (Dulles)   310.40  495.50
Anchorage             289.40  487.35
Denver (Stapleton)    165.00  210.00
Orange County (LA)     98.40  135.00
San Diego             102.45  147.50
```

Figure 23.11
The records of a random-access data file are not sorted. Rather, a separate index is created to store the sorted information. With each sorted data item is the record number of its location in the master data file.

```
Portland             129.45 237.50Seattle                 149.80
250.00New York (LaGuardia) 345.20 580.00Honolulu         595.00
980.00Chicago (O'Hare)       218.50 340.75Chicago (Midway)
203.25 320.00Wash. D.C. (Dulles)   310.40 495.50Anchorage
289.40 487.35Denver (Stapleton)    165.00 210.00Orange County
(LA)       98.40 135.00San Diego            102.45 147.50
```

The following handler opens the data file and then reads each record, placing the city name and the record number into a two-dimensional array.

```
to handle readData
    openFile "travel.dat"
    system indexCity[ ][ ], recs
    put 0 into sysErrorNumber
    put 0 into recs
    while sysErrorNumber = 0
        increment recs by 1
        readFile "travel.dat" for 34  --there are 34 chars in each record
        if sysErrorNumber <> 0 then
            break while
        end if
        put chars 1 to 20 of it into indexCity[recs][1]
        put recs into indexCity[recs][2]
    end while
    decrement recs by 1  --recs is the number of records
    closeFile "travel.dat"
end readData
```

After this handler is executed, the **indexCity** array contains the values displayed in Figure 23.12. The following handler takes the **indexCity** array and sorts it according to city name by using a bubble sort.

```
to handle sortByCity
    system indexCity[ ][ ], recs
    set sysCursor to 4
    step i from 1 to (recs - 1)
        step j from (i+1) to recs
            if indexCity[j][1] < indexCity[i][1] as text then
                put indexCity[j][1] into temp1
                put indexCity[j][2] into temp2
                put indexCity[i][1] into indexCity[j][1]
                put indexCity[i][2] into indexCity[j][2]
                put temp1 into indexCity[i][1]
                put temp2 into indexCity[i][2]
            end if
        end step
    end step
    set sysCursor to 1
end sortByCity
```

The indexCity array is sorted alphabetically by city name as shown in Figure 23.13. The second element of the array—the record number in the master data file (see Figure 23.11)—is sorted with the city names, so that the appropriate record number remain attached with each city name.

With the index, the information can more easily be searched: The record number indicated in the index file can be used to look up the information in the master data file and display it. The index could be dumped into a scrolling field and searched using the OpenScript search command.

```
to handle dumpIndexToField
    system indexCity[ ][ ],recs
    put "" into text of field "cities"
    step i from 1 to recs  -- this loop dumps indexCity array to field "cities"
        put CRLF & indexCity[i][1] after text of field "cities"
```

Figure 23.12
The indexCity *array after the data is read from the random-access master data file but before it is sorted.*

	[1] City	[2] Record
[1]	Portland	1
[2]	Seattle	2
[3]	New York (LaGuardia)	3
[4]	Honolulu	4
[5]	Chicago (O'Hare)	5
[6]	Chicago (Midway)	6
[7]	Wash. D.C. (Dulles)	7
[8]	Anchorage	8
[9]	Denver (Stapleton)	9
[10]	Orange COunty (LA)	10
[11]	San Diego	11

Figure 23.13
The indexCity *array after being sorted with the bubble sort alogorithm.*

	[1] City	[2] Record
[1]	Anchorage	8
[2]	Chicago (Midway)	6
[3]	Chicago (O'Hare)	5
[4]	Denver (Stapleton)	9
[5]	Honolulu	4
[6]	New York (LaGuardia)	3
[7]	Orange COunty (LA)	10
[8]	Portland	1
[9]	San Diego	11
[10]	Seattle	2
[11]	Wash. D.C. (Dulles)	7

```
        end step
        while textline 1 of text of field "cities" = ""   —remove any blank lines at beginning
            clear textline 1 of text of field cities
        end while
    end dumpIndexToField
```

The field is then activated and the following handler in the field's script is executed when the field is clicked. It determines which text line was clicked, and looks up the record number in the indexCity array (the second element) of the "row" whose number is the same as the clicked text line number. The record number then is used to retrieve the data from the master file and display it.

```
    to handle buttonClick location
        system indexCity[ ][ ],recs
        put item 1 of textFromPoint(location) into rowNum
        --above statement determines which textline clicked
        put indexCity[rowNum][2] into recNum
        --above statement gets the record number for the master file
        openFile "travel.dat"
        seekFile "travel.dat" for ((recNum-1)*34) from beginning
        --above statement positions pointer at record
        readFile "travel.dat" for 34  --read record
        put chars 1 to 20 of it into city
        put chars 21 to 27 of it into x
        put chars 28 to 34 of it into y
        closeFile "travel.dat"
        request "Airfare to "&city & CRLF & "One way: $" & x & \
        CRLF & "Round Trip: $" & y
    end buttonClick
```

Figure 23.14 is an illustration of this application. The script of the "Update Index" button follows. It calls several of the above routines to read the data, create the index, sort the index by city, and place the sorted cities in the destinations field.

```
    to handle buttonClick
        send readData
        send sortByCity
        send dumpIndexToField
    end buttonClick
```

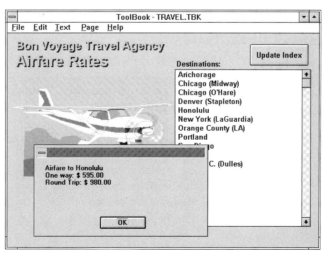

Figure 23.14
An application can be created to read data from a random-access file, sort it, and then call the information of specific records from the data file as needed.

Summary Questions
Complete the following statements by filling in the blanks.
1. The _____ OpenScript command can be used to reorder the pages of a book.
2. Adjacent items in a list are compared and swapped within a fixed loop in the _____ sort algorithm.
3. Nonadjacent items in a list separated by a gap that decreases as the algorithm progresses are compared and swapped in the _____ sort algorithm.
4. The _____ command is used in an OpenScript handler to find a specific string in the text of fields and/or recordfields.
5. The statement _____ _____ locates the next occurrence of a string previously searched for.

Write an OpenScript statement to perform the following tasks.
6. Find the string my dog has fleas in the text of the fields or recordfields on the current page only.
7. Find an occurrence of the word "vision" in a recordfield only. If "vision" is part of a word such as "visionary" or "television," such occurrence should not be located.
8. Repeat the last search performed (finding the next occurrence).
9. Find any occurrence of the phrase "MiRF" but only as a complete word and with the same uppercase and lowercase letters.
10. Put the name of the field or recordfield containing the word "watermelon" into the variable it, along with the starting and ending character numbers.
11. Display the "Replace" dialog box.
12. Sort the first 10 pages of the book alphabetically from Z to A by the string contents of the recordfield "lastname".
13. Sort, in ascending order, all the pages of the book by the ID number of the pages.
14. Sort, in ascending order by the dates in the recordfield named "when", pages 20 through 40 of the book.
15. Sort a book by the numeric data in the "zipcode" recordfield.

Identify the error in each of the following OpenScript statements.
16. sort pages 0 to 10 by descending text text of recordfield id 3
17. send "Find..."
18. search pages 1 to 5 for "bananas"
19. search by case for "AbCdEf"
20. sort the text of recordfield id 1 by ascending text

Hands-On Projects
A. Examine the software that accompanies this chapter. Open the "Table of Contents" book by double-clicking its icon in the "Developing with ToolBook" group window in the Windows Program Manager. Inside the "Table of Contents," click the book representing Chapter 23.

B. Reconsider the application created in Hands-On Project E of Chapter 19. To the application, add background buttons to:
   a. Sort the pages of the book by the last name of the client
   b. Sort the pages of the book by the company name
   c. Sort the pages of the book by values of the "New Balance" recordfield
   d. Search for a given name, city, and so on

C. To the book created in Hands-On Project C of Chapter 22, add a button to sort the text of the field by the contact's last name.

D. Create an address book with recordfields for last name, first name, address, city, state, zip code, phone number, and a person's birth date. Add background buttons to sort the book by name, zip code, or birth date.

E. Create a database of audio CD information, including performer, CD title, a list of songs on the CD, and the recording company. Add buttons to sort the database by performer or CD title. Add a button to search for a performer, or song title, or part of a song title. Also add a button to repeat the search to find the next occurrence. An example solution is pictured in Figure 23.15.

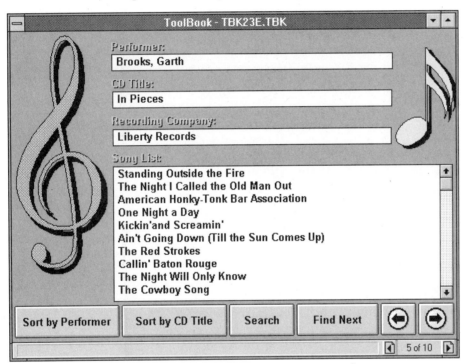

Figure 23.15
A database for audio CDs is developed in Hands-On Project E, with buttons for searching and sorting.

Chapter 24

Advanced Interface Features

Drag and Drop, and Input Sliders

A popular interface design today is known as drag and drop. Objects may be dragged by the user and dropped onto other objects, causing some event to happen. For example, dragging an object and dropping it on top of a trash can icon might result in the object being deleted. Text in fields may be dragged and dropped within itself to reorder a list, or dropped onto another field to choose certain items from the list. Objects to be moved must be defined as draggable; objects that receive a dragged object must be defined as drop-recipients. Dragged objects may only be dropped onto objects that have been defined as drop-recipients. This chapter looks at setting up both draggable and drop-recipient objects, scripting the drag and drop process, and enhancing the process with system cursors.

Uses for Drag and Drop

There are numerous uses for **drag and drop interfaces**. Dragging objects to a trash can icon to delete them has already been mentioned. The File Manager of Windows uses drag and drop to move files between directories. Although the jigsaw puzzle application featured in Chapter 2 was developed with an early version of ToolBook that did not support drag and drop, it would be an obvious candidate for such technology. Drag and drop might be utilized in developing a quiz that asks students to reorder a list of historical events in the correct chronology. The student would grab an item in the list and move it either up or down in the field to the correct slot, or drag the items to another list in the appropriate order. A graphics applications might be developed with drag and drop in which symbols are dragged from a template and dropped on the working drawing. Such an interface would be ideal for a flowcharting application.

Setting Up a Draggable Object

There are two methods of defining an object as being draggable. The simplest is to access the "Drag & Drop" dialog box from the object's "Properties" dialog. The "Drag & Drop" dialog is shown in Figure 24.1. The object may be defined as draggable by checking the "Allow Drag" checkbox. This sets the defaultAllowDrag property of the object to true. This could also be done with the OpenScript command

    set defaultAllowDrag of <object reference> to true

from within either a handler or the "Command" window.

The second method is to write a handler that reports whether an object may be dragged. When a drag operation is initiated by the user, ToolBook checks whether the object is defined as draggable. ToolBook first sends a query to the object by checking for a to get allowDrag handler. This handler returns either a true or false, if it exists. If the value returned by the to get allowDrag function is true, the drag and

Figure 24.1
The allowDrag *property of*
an object may be set to true
by checking the "Allow
Drag" box in the "Drag &
Drop" dialog box.

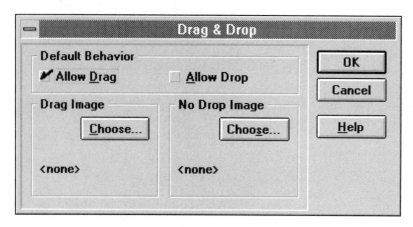

drop process continues. If it is false, nothing happens when the user tries to drag the object. If there is no to get allowDrag handler, ToolBook then checks the defaultAllowDrag property (as set through the "Drag & Drop" dialog). If the defaultAllowDrag property is true, then the drag process continues; otherwise nothing happens. The following handler in an object defines the object as draggable.

```
to get allowDrag
    return true
end allowDrag
```

Obviously, checking the checkbox in the "Drag & Drop" dialog is easier, but this second method is useful if one wishes to allow dragging of an object under certain conditions only. For example, to drag an object with the following handler, the Shift key must be held down. (This helps eliminate accidental dragging by the user.)

```
to handle allowDrag
    if keystate(ShiftKey) is "down" then
        return true
    else
        return false
    end if
end allowDrag
```

The following handler permits an object to be dragged only if the current time is between noon and midnight. (You think of a practical use for this!)

```
to handle allowDrag
    put the sysTime into currentTime
    format time currentTime as "AMPM"
    if currentTime = "PM" then
        return true
    else
        return false
    end if
end allowDrag
```

Setting Up a Drop-Recipient

For a dragged object to be of any use, it must have a destination where it may be dropped. ToolBook allows the developer to restrict where an object may be dropped

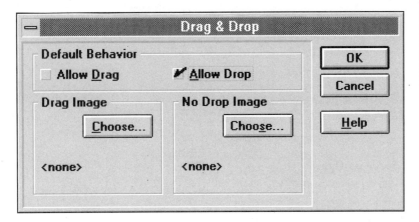

Figure 24.2
The allowDrop *property of an object may be set to* true *by checking the "Allow Drop" box in the "Drag & Drop" dialog box.*

by checking the object's allowDrop and defaultAllowDrop properties when a dragged object is released over its boundaries. As with setting up a draggable object, a drop-recipient may be defined by accessing the "Drag & Drop" dialog from the object's "Properties" dialog. Checking the "Allow Drop" checkbox, assigns a true value to the object's defaultAllowDrop property (see Figure 24.2).

A to get allowDrop handler is checked first by ToolBook when determining if the object allows objects to be dropped. This occurs before checking the object's defaultAllowDrop property, overriding its value. As with the to get allowDrag handler, the to get AllowDrop handler returns either true or false.

```
to get allowDrop
    return true
end allowDrop
```

The handler may be set up to allow objects to be dropped only if certain conditions are met. The following to get allowDrop handler only allows an object of type ellipse to be dropped on it. The allowDrop message has a built-in argument of the name of the source object. The object type of the source name is examined and the appropriate value is returned.

```
to get allowDrop source
    if the object of source is "ellipse" then
        return true
    else
        return false
    end if
end allowDrop
```

Enhancing the Drag and Drop Process with System Cursors

Resources such as cursors, icons, or bitmaps may be displayed to visually tell the user of the status of the drag and drop. The resources are assigned to the dragImage and noDropImage properties of an object either through the "Drag & Drop" dialog box or through OpenScript code. The resource assigned to the dragImage property of an object is displayed when that object is dragged over an object that will accept a drop; the resource assigned to the noDropImage property of an object is displayed when that object is dragged over an object that will not allow a drop. Figure 24.3 shows how resources may be assigned to the dragImage and noDropImage properties of an object through the "Drag & Drop" dialog. For instance, the cursor of an eye-dropper image in the left of Figure 24.3 would be displayed when over an object that will allow a

Figure 24.3
Use the "Drag & Drop"
dialog to choose a cursor to
be displayed when the
dragged object is over a
droppable object, and
another when it is not over
a droppable object.

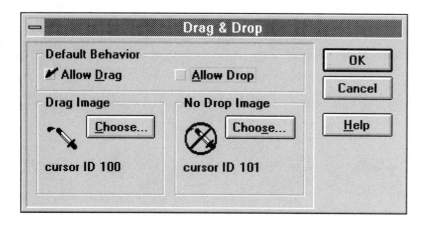

drop; while the "no drop" cursor to its right is displayed when over an object that will not allow a drop. These assignments may also be made in a handler, providing the referenced resources have been imported into the book (via the Resources Manager). For example:

```
dragImage of self = cursor ID 102
noDropImage of self =  cursor ID 103
```

Figure 24.4
During a drag and drop
procedure, several
messages are sent to the
source and destination
objects. These messages
may be handled by
OpenScript scripts to
control the action during
the drag and drop
procedure as well as control
the end result.

The Messages Sent in a Drag and Drop Procedure

beginDrag
> Sent to the source object at the start of being dragged.

enterDrop [*sourceObject*]
> Sent to a destination object when the mouse pointer enters its boundaries during a drag and drop operation. The *sourceObject* parameter is the unique name of the object being dragged.

stillOverDrop [*sourceObject*],[*location*]
> Sent repeatedly to a destination object while the mouse pointer is within its boundaries during a drag and drop procedure. The *sourceObject* parameter is the unique name of the object being dragged, and the *location* is the x,y position of the mouse pointer in page units from the upper left corner of the page.

leaveDrop [*sourceObject*]
> Sent to a destination object when the mouse pointer exits its boundaries during a drag and drop procedure, before the mouse button has been released. The *sourceObject* parameter is the unique name of the object being dragged.

endDrag [*destinationObject*],[*location*]
> Sent to the source object being dragged when the mouse button is released at the end of a drag and drop procedure. The *destinationObject* parameter is the unique name of the recipient object, and the *location* is the x,y position of the mouse pointer in page units from the upper left corner of the page.

objectDropped [*sourceObject*],[*location*]
> Sent to the destination (recipient) object after the mouse button has been released at the end of a drag and drop procedure. The *sourceObject* parameter is the unique name of the object being dragged, and the *location* is the x,y position of the mouse pointer in page units from the upper left corner of the page.

Scripting the Drag and Drop Process

Thus far we have defined objects as draggable and droppable and looked at providing visual clues to the user about where an dragged object may be dropped. The event that occurs, however, when a dragged object is dropped must still be coded through OpenScript handlers for a drag and drop operation to be of any use.

There are six basic messages sent during a drag and drop operation, in addition to the allowDrag and allowDrop messages already discussed. These are summarized in Figure 24.4 in the order in which they generally occur. Scripting either an endDrag handler in the source object or an objectDropped handler in the destination object is the only scripting critical to achieving a successful drag and drop. The other handlers are used primarily for enhancing the process and, of those, beginDrag is the only one commonly used.

The application shown in Figure 24.5 is a coloring book in which different-colored crayons are dragged and dropped over objects to color them. (This application is included with the software tutorial for this chapter.) Each of the 21 crayons at the bottom left of Figure 24.5 is defined as draggable in the "Drag & Drop" dialog (see Figure 24.6). Icons are also assigned to the dragImage and noDropImage

Figure 24.5
This coloring book application uses drag and drop to allow the user to select a color, drag it to the picture, and color an area with the chosen shade.

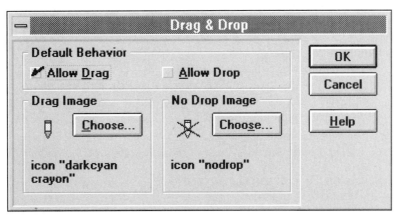

Figure 24.6
Icons are assigned to the drag procedure to indicate what areas may be colored and not colored.

properties through this dialog. (The icons were created with the icon editor utility that accompanies ToolBook.) The objects in the drawing at the right side of the page in Figure 24.5 are all defined as drop-recipients. These are the only objects defined as droppable. Each of the crayons is assigned the following handler:

```
to handle endDrag destination
     set the fillColor of destination to the fillColor of irregularPolygon "tip" of self
end endDrag
```

Each crayon is composed of two parts, an irregular polygon named tip and a rectangle to represent the paper covering of the crayon. Each of these is grouped together (there are 21 separate groups), and it is in the group scripts that the preceding handler resides. This handler defines the event that occurs when the drag and drop process is completed (that is, when the mouse button is released).

The sysSuspend property is set to false in an enterBook handler of the book's script. Dropping a dragged crayon on an object other than a droppable object results in an error. By setting the sysSuspend property to false, the "Execution Suspended" dialog is not displayed and the user is unaware that an error occurred. The sysSuspend property is reset to true in a leaveBook handler.

Figure 24.7
Drag and drop can be used to allow students to rearrange a list of items within a field or recordfield in a computer–aided instruction (CAI) application.

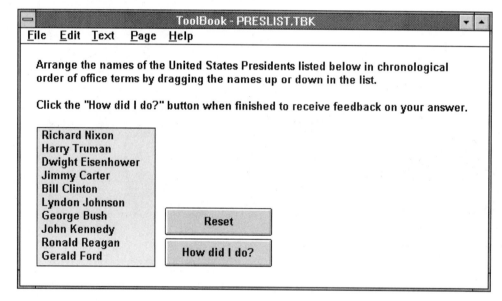

Figure 24.7 shows a book with the names of several United States Presidents listed in a field. The text of the field may be rearranged by dragging the text. The field itself is defined as both draggable and droppable by using the "Drag & Drop" dialog box. The following handlers in the field's script define what happens when the text is dragged and dropped in the field.

```
to handle beginDrag
     system gLine, gText
     put item 1 of the textFromPoint(sysMousePosition) into gLine
     put textline gLine of text of self into gText
     select textline gLine of my text
end beginDrag


to handle endDrag destinationObject, loc
     system gText, gLine
```

```
        put item 1 of textFromPoint(loc) into y
        conditions
            when y < gLine  --move dragged text up
                put gText & CRLF before textline y of my text
                clear textline (gLine + 1) of text of self
            when y > gLine  --move dragged text down
                put gText & crlf before textline y of my text
                clear textline gLine of text of self
            else
        end conditions
    end enddrag
```

The **beginDrag** handler is executed when the user presses the mouse button when the pointer is on a line of text in the field and begins to move the mouse. The **textFromPoint** function is used to return the location of the mouse pointer. Since this function returns a list of two integers (the text line number followed by the character number within the text line), the first item (the text line number) is placed in a system variable named **gLine**. The text of the clicked text line is also placed in a system variable named **gText**. Finally, the text is highlighted.

The **endDrag** handler is executed when the user releases the mouse button. The location of the mouse is examined, with the text line number placed in the local variable, **y**. If **y** is less than **gLine**, the value in the **gText** system variable and a carriage return-linefeed is placed in front of text line **y**, and the original dragged text line (which is now one text line farther down) is deleted. If **y** is greater than **gLine**, (that is, the text was dragged down in the list), the value of system variable **gText** and a carriage return-linefeed is placed in front of text line **y** and the original occurrence of the dragged text line is deleted.

Moving Objects on the Screen

One use of drag and drop might be to allow the user to position objects on the screen. Consider a rectangle that has been drawn on a page (see Figure 24.8). A user might want to drag the rectangle to a new location on the page. Using drag and drop, the rectangle may be defined as draggable via the "Drag & Drop" dialog and assigned the following handler:

```
    to handle endDrag destination, location
        move self to location
    end endDrag
```

The page is then set up to allow a default drop via the "Page Properties" dialog (see Figure 24.9). This allows the rectangle to be moved, but the user does not see the rectangle move until the drag and drop operation is ended (in other words, when the mouse button is released). A **stillOverDrop** message is generated continuously while a dragged object is over a drop target during a drag and drop

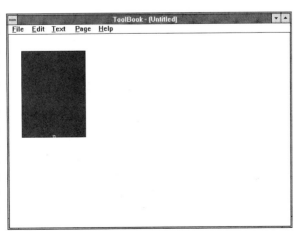

Figure 24.8
The stillOverDrop *message can be handled in a page script to allow a dragged object to move with the mouse pointer during a drag and drop operation.*

Figure 24.9
The "Page Properties"
dialog contains a checkbox
("Default Allow Drop") to
make the page itself a drop–
recipient object.

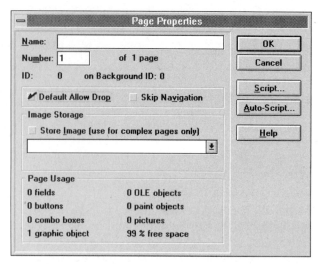

procedure. This message might be handled by a stillOverDrop handler in the script of the droppable object (in this case, the page). The stillOverDrop message includes two parameters: the unique name of the object being dragged (the source), and the location of the mouse pointer. The source object may simply be moved to the location of the mouse pointer:

```
to handle stillOverDrop sourceObject, location
    move sourceObject to location
end stillOverDrop
```

One problem with this approach is that if the rectangle is dropped over an object that does not allow a drop, an error results and the "Execution Suspended" dialog box is displayed (unless the sysSuspend property has been set to false). Nor does the dragged object move to the mouse pointer location when the pointer is over a nondroppable object or a droppable object whose script does not contain the preceding stillOverDrop handler. The author must consider then whether each object should be set up as a drop destination, placing the preceding handler into each object's script.

Using the **move** Command as an Alternative to Drag and Drop

In allowing the user to drag an object on screen to a new location, the use of the move command might be a better solution. The move command is used to move an object to a specified location. Its use and syntax are explained in Figure 24.10. The move command can be used in conjunction with a buttonStillDown handler in an object's script to simulate a drag and drop operation. The following handler placed in the rectangle's script would allow the rectangle to be "dragged" by the user to a new position on the page without setting the rectangle up as a draggable object nor defining the page or any other object as a droppable object.

```
to handle buttonStillDown location
    move self to location
end buttonStillDown
```

The rectangle may now be moved to any location on the page. If it is desired that the object be on top of another object (keeping it from becoming hidden behind an object),

```
The move command

Syntax:        move object to location
               or
               move obejct by offsetAmount

Purpose:       Moves the specified object to the specified location (an x,y coordinate measured
               in page units from the upper left corner of the page) or by a specified offset (also
               a two–integer list of page units in the x and y directions).

Examples:      move ellipse id 3 to 3000,3000

               move self to a,b

               move self by 100,100

               system theObject, xval, yval
               move theObject by xval,yval
```

Figure 24.10
The move *command is*
used to reposition an object
on the page.

a buttonDown handler could be added to the script to bring the dragged object to the front:

```
to handle buttonDown
    select self
    send bringToFront
end buttonDown

to handle buttonStillDown location
    move self to location
end buttonStillDown
```

One problem seen with the method just outlined is that the dragged object first appears to jump to the mouse pointer, since the position of an object is its upper left boundary point. Since the object's position is moved to the mouse pointer location, the upper left corner of the object is moved to the pointer location. A smoother move is achieved by determining the position of the mouse pointer in relation to the position of the dragged object when the button is pressed and then adjusting the movement of the object by the offset value. For example:

```
to handle buttonDown loc
    system x1, y1
    put the position of self into originalPosition
    put item 1 of loc into x
    put item 2 of loc into y
    put x - item 1 of originalPosition into x1
    put y - item 2 of originalPosition into y1
end buttonDown

to handle buttonStillDown loc
    system x1, y1
    put item 1 of loc into x
    put item 2 of loc into y
    move self to x-x1, y-y1
end buttonStillDown
```

In the buttonDown handler, the distance in terms of x page units and y page units between the position of the object and the mouse pointer location is calculated and these values are stored in system variables x1 and y1. The values of these system variables are then used in the buttonStillDown handler to adjust the movement of the object. The result is a smoother movement of the object as it is dragged by the user.

Creating Sliders and Ratchets

A **slider** is a graphical input device in which the user slides an object along a path to set a value between minimum and maximum values. The preceding handlers might be tweaked to produce a slider for accepting input from a user (see Figure 24.11). In this example the slider is used to receive a value between 0 and 100 as the user slides the rectangle on the slider. The slider is created by first drawing the thin horizontal rectangle and the 11 vertical lines used as position markers at the values 10, 20, 30, and so on. It is best to create these by using the "Command" window, since accuracy is important. The slider can be drawn at the bottom of a 6- by 4-inch page, using the command:

draw rectangle from 2100,5025 to 7100,5085

to draw the thin rectangle that the slider knob slides on. The values for the x coordinates were chosen because it was desired to have a measurement that was a multiple of 100. Here, the distance between 2100 and 7100 is 5000 page units. The vertical lines were also drawn using the "Command" window, entering commands such as

draw line from 2100,4855 to 2100,5355

draw line from 2600,4855 to 2600,5355

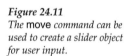

Figure 24.11
The move *command can be used to create a slider object for user input.*

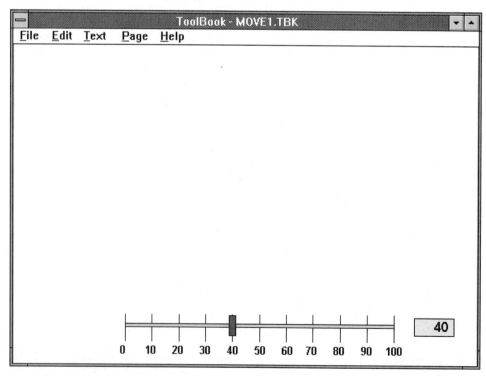

```
draw line from 3100,4855 to 3100,5355
```

and so forth, increasing the x coordinate values by 500 each time until the 11th line is created with the command

```
draw line from 7100,4855 to 7100,5355
```

The vertical lines were selected and sent behind the thin, horizontal rectangle. The lines and the rectangle were then grouped together. A field was added below the vertical lines with "10 20 30 40 ..." to mark the values of the vertical lines. A field is drawn to the right and named sliderValue and it is given a right alignment via the "Paragraph" dialog. Finally a rectangle is drawn at the 0 mark for the slider knob. This is done with the command

```
draw rectangle from 2040,4875 to 2160,5235
```

The value of the slider is the location of its horizontal center. The following script was assigned to the slider knob (rectangle):

```
to handle buttonDown loc
    system x1
    put the position of self into originalPosition
    put item 1 of loc into x
    put x - item 1 of originalPosition into x1
end buttonDown

to handle buttonStillDown loc
    system x1
    put item 1 of loc into x
    conditions
        when x < 2100
            move self to 2040,4875
        when x > 7100
            move self to 7040,4875
        else
            move self to (x-x1-60),4875
    end conditions
    put ((item 1 of position of self) - 2040) div 50 into text of field "sliderValue"
end buttonStillDown
```

The buttonDown handler calculates the horizontal distance of the mouse pointer from the rectangle's left boundary, and stores this value in a system variable for use in the buttonStillDown handler.

In the buttonStillDown handler the horizontal location of the mouse pointer is determined and used in the conditions structure to determine where to move the location of the slider knob. The first condition restricts its movement past the left end of the slider (the 0 mark); the second condition restricts its movement past the right end (the 100 mark). If the rectangle is moved anywhere between the 0 and 100 mark, the else portion of the conditions structure is executed and the position of the slider knob is adjusted accordingly—the x1 value (the distance between the left edge of the knob and the mouse pointer) and the distance between the left edge of the knob and its center are subtracted; the value of the knob is calculated as its position minus the leftmost possible position, with this value divided by 50 (5000 page units divided by 100 desired positions). This final value is placed in the text of the sliderValue field.

To constrain the slider knob so that it may only be moved to the incremental values of the slider (that is, only to the positions corresponding to the hash marks), the buttonStillDown handler of the knob can be changed to

```
to handle buttonStillDown loc
    put item 1 of loc into x
    conditions
        when x < 2350  --move to the 0 position
            move self to 2040,4875
        when x >= 2350 and x < 2850  --move to the 10 position
            move self to 2540,4875
        when x >= 2850 and x < 3350  -- move to the 20 position
            move self to 3040,4875
        when x >= 3350 and x < 3850  -- move to the 30 position
            move self to 3540,4875
        when x >= 3850 and x < 4350  -- move to the 40 position
            move self to 4040,4875
        when x >= 4350 and x < 4850  -- move to the 50 position
            move self to 4540,4875
        when x >= 4850 and x < 5350  -- move to the 60 position
            move self to 5040,4875
        when x >= 5350 and x < 5850  -- move to the 70 position
            move self to 5540,4875
        when x >= 5850 and x < 6350  -- move to the 80 position
            move self to 6040,4875
        when x >= 6350 and x < 6850  -- move to the 90 position
            move self to 6540,4875
        when x >= 6850            -- move to the 100 position
            move self to 7040,4875
    end conditions
    put ((item 1 of position of self) - 2040) div 50 into text of field "sliderValue"
end buttonStillDown
```

This creates a specialized slider, known as a **ratchet**. The knob of a ratchet can only be moved to certain intervals on the slider. Sliders and ratchets are also demonstrated in the Widgets book that accompanies ToolBook and Multimedia ToolBook (see Figure 24.12).

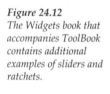
Figure 24.12
The Widgets book that accompanies ToolBook contains additional examples of sliders and ratchets.

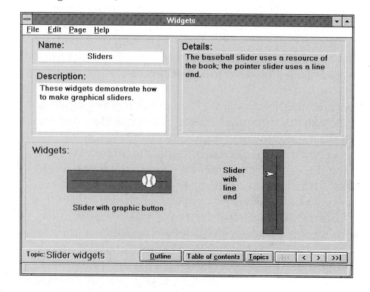

Summary Questions
Complete the following statements by filling in the blanks.

1. An object's _____ property may be set in the "Drag & Drop" dialog to define it as a draggable object.

2. When an object is initially dragged, a to get _____ handler is searched for in the source object.

3. A to get _____ handler is searched for in an object's script to determine whether the object is a drop-recipient.

4. A _____ message is sent to the source object when a drag operation is started.

5. An _____ message is sent to the source object when the mouse button is released at the end of a drag and drop procedure.

6. An _____ message is sent to the drop-recipient after the mouse button is released at the end of a drag and drop procedure.

7. A _____ message is sent continuously to the recipient object while the mouse pointer is within its boundaries during a drag and drop procedure.

8. The _____ command is used to reposition an object on the screen at a specific location.

9. A _____ is a popular input device in which an object is slid along a path to a specific value.

10. A _____ is a specialized slider in which the slider knob can only be moved to certain intervals along the slider's path.

Identify the following statements as being either true or false.

11. An object can only be defined as draggable by checking the "Default Allow Drag" box in its "Drag & Drop" dialog.

12. Icons and cursors can visually identify objects on which an object may be dropped while it is being dragged.

13. An object can only be defined as a drop-recipient by having in its script, a to get allowDrop handler that returns true.

14. Dragged objects automatically move with the mouse pointer while being dragged.

15. The endDrag command is sent to the destination (recipient) object.

Identify the error in the following scripts.

16.
```
to get allowDrag
        put true into defaultAllowDrag
    end allowDrag
```

17.
```
to handle enterPage
        set sysSuspend to 1
    end enterPage
```

18.
```
to handle endDrag location
        system draggedObject
        set the position of the draggedObject to location
    end endDrag
```

19.
```
to handle buttonStillDown location
        move the position of self to location
    end buttonStillDown
```

20.
```
to handle buttonStillDown
        move self to x,y
    end buttonStillDown
```

Hands-On Projects

A. Examine the software that accompanies this chapter. Open the "Table of Contents" book by double-clicking its icon in the "Developing with ToolBook" group window in the Windows Program Manager. Inside the "Table of Contents," click the book representing Chapter 24.

B. Create an application in which items to purchase at the market are copied from a master list to another list by dragging (see Figure 24.13). Using drag and drop to achieve this, include a **beginDrag** handler in the master list to place the value of the clicked text into a system variable and an **objectDropped** handler in the "This Week's List" field to place text after any text in the field. Include a "Clear" button to erase the list. (Hint: To get the scrollbar to work properly on the master list, a "to get allowDrag" handler must be used to return either **true** or **false**, depending on whether the user is trying to drag text or scroll the field. Check the **sysMousePosition** system property. As an added feature, you might include a handler to sort the list alphabetically when right-clicked.

Figure 24.13
An application in which the user copies selected items from one list to another is created in Hands-On Project B.

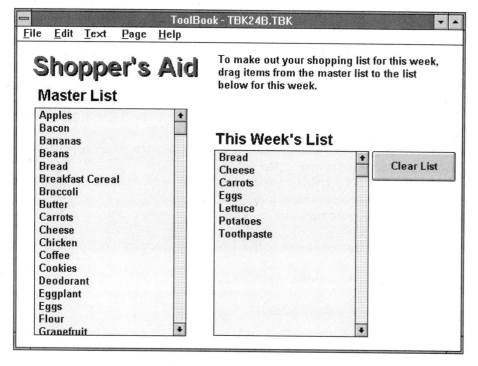

C. Create an application for beginning readers to drag names of objects to spaces provided next to pictures of the objects. Use drag and drop to accomplish this function. A sample application is pictured in Figure 24.14.

D. Design a vertical (not horizontal!) slider to be used to set a value between 0 and 50.

E. Redesign the color swatch application created in Chapter 17 Hands-On Project B to use sliders instead of fields for setting the values of red, green, and blue. Set the fill color of a rectangle to the defined color (created by the chosen RGB values). For best results, set the book's **solidColorsEnabled** property to **true**.

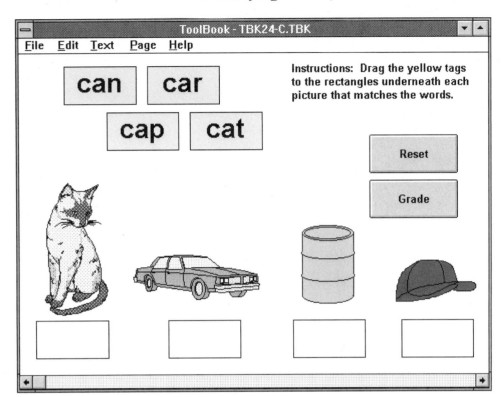

Figure 24.14
In Hands-On Project C, a
quiz is created for
beginning readers to match
words to pictures by
dragging them.

Chapter 25

Move It!
Animation Techniques

There are numerous uses of animation in software. Animation can be used to illustrate a process, such as how a bill is made into law or how a product is assembled. Animation might also be used to provide a visual clue to the user that the computer is processing or to direct the reader's attention to a particular feature. Many developers use animation to entertain the user and keep the reader's attention, especially in writing programs for children. Numerous interactive stories have been written in which animation is used to help the story progress. Animation and multimedia appear in a large percentage of today's popular entertainment software for both children and adults.

The object-oriented nature of ToolBook lends itself well to animation. There are several techniques of animation. Moving an object or multiple objects to a specified point or along a particular path is a quick and easy method of animation. Another easy method is to alter the properties of an object or objects, such as fillColor, position (which creates the same effect as moving the object), or bounds (causing the object to grow or shrink). Layering objects and changing their level is one animation technique; frame animation (hiding and showing a sequence of objects or scenes) is another. Objects may be created by executing a handler with the draw command.

Moving Objects

In the previous chapter, the move command (see Figure 24.10) was introduced as a method for allowing the user to drag objects on the screen. The move command can also be used to perform an animation by moving one or multiple objects to specific points or along a particular path. Figure 25.1 shows a page with an illustration of a jet flying over a landscape. The picture of the jet was imported as clipart from a graphics software package and was named jet. The "Fly by" button animates the jet, making it streak across the top of the page. The following handler is associated with the button.

```
to handle buttonClick
     set position of picture "jet" to -3000,300
     --jet is unseen, positioned off left edge of paper
     move picture "jet" to -2500,300
     move picture "jet" to -2000,300
     move picture "jet" to -1500,300
     move picture "jet" to -1000,300
     move picture "jet" to -500,300
     move picture "jet" to 0,300
     move picture "jet" to 500,300
     move picture "jet" to 1000,300
     move picture "jet" to 1500,300
     move picture "jet" to 2000,300
     move picture "jet" to 2500,300
```

```
move picture "jet" to 3000,300
move picture "jet" to 3500,300
move picture "jet" to 4000,300
move picture "jet" to 4500,300
move picture "jet" to 5000,300
move picture "jet" to 5500,300
move picture "jet" to 6000,300
move picture "jet" to 6500,300
move picture "jet" to 7000,300
move picture "jet" to 7500,300
move picture "jet" to 8000,300
move picture "jet" to 8500,300
move picture "jet" to 9000,300
    --jet is now unseen, positioned off right edge of page
end buttonClick
```

Figure 25.1
The jet on this page can be animated with the move *command.*

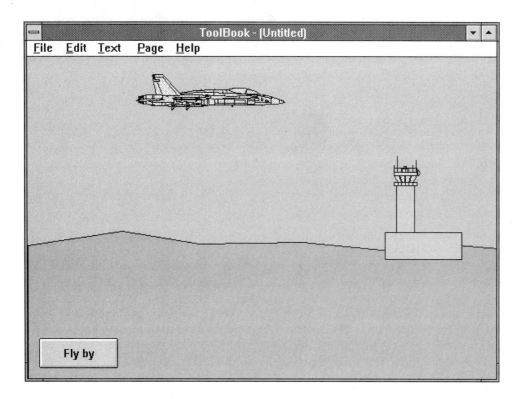

The handler positions the jet off the left side of the screen and then moves it across the page to the right in increments of 500 page units until it disappears past the right-hand edge of the page. The same effect could be achieved by moving the jet by an offset amount in a fixed loop.

```
to handle buttonClick
    set position of picture "jet" to -3000,300
    step i from 1 to 24
        move picture "jet" by 500,0
    end step
end buttonClick
```

The code that uses the offset is shorter and more efficient than the first method. Of course either of these two handlers could be used to move the jet vertically. The programmer would just have to specify a different *y* coordinate or vertical offset.

Adjusting the Speed of an Animation

The pause command (see Figure 17.3) can be used to adjust the speed of an animation by pausing the animation a certain number of seconds or ticks. If the preceding handler moves the jet too fast, inserting a pause command in the loop will slow it down.

```
to handle buttonClick
    set position of picture "jet" to -3000,300
    step i from 1 to 24
        move picture "jet" by 500,0
        pause 10 ticks  --one-tenth of a second
    end step
end buttonClick
```

Another alternative, and one that produces smoother animation, is to increase the iterations of the loop while decreasing the movement offset.

```
to handle buttonClick
    set position of picture "jet" to -3000,300
    step i from 1 to 48
        move picture "jet" by 250,0
    end step
end buttonClick
```

A final alternative, is to allow the user to adjust the speed of the animation. An input device—such as a slider, ratchet, or a group of radio buttons—allows the user to select the speed. In Figure 25.2, a group of radio buttons is provided by which the

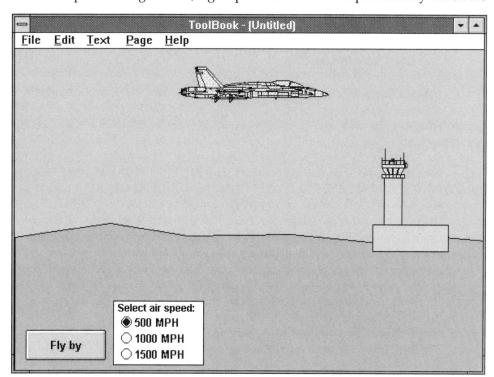

Figure 25.2
Buttons might be added to allow the user to adjust the speed of the animation.

user chooses the speed of the aircraft. A conditions structure is used in the script of the "Fly by" button to execute different iteration and offset values in the animation.

```
to handle buttonClick
    conditions
        when the checked of button "500 MPH" is true
            put 48 into iterations
            put 250 into xValue
        when the checked of button "1000 MPH" is true
            put 24 into iterations
            put 500 into xValue
        when the checked of button "1500 MPH" is true
            put 16 into iterations
            put 750 into xValue
    end conditions
    set position of picture "jet" to -3000,300
    step i from 1 to iterations
        move picture "jet" by xValue,0
    end step
end buttonClick
```

An advantage of allowing the user to select a speed is that it allows the animation to be adjusted according to the speed of the computer on which the application is used.

Moving an Object Along a Path

Consider how an object can be moved along a path. An angled line may be used as the path, with the object moved to each vertex on it. Figure 25.3 shows a page with an angled line between two baseball players and a circle representing the baseball. The code that follows animates the baseball by moving it to the vertices of the angled line. (The angled line may be hidden so that the user does not see it.)

```
to handle buttonClick
    put the vertices of angledLine "ballpath" into coordinates
    put itemcount(coordinates) into x
    step i from 1 to x by 2
        move ellipse "baseball" to item i of coordinates,item (i+1) of coordinates
        pause 5 ticks
    end step
end buttonClick
```

The vertices of the angled line named ballpath are 480,2115,1110,1605,1650,1200, 2520,960,3660,930,4710,990,5730,1200,6660,1515,7515,1965,7800,2145, and this list is placed in the variable named coordinates in the first line of the handler. The number of items in the list is calculated, and this value is used in the loop. The loop is reiterated for the number of items, but by steps of 2, since each vertex consists of a pair of coordinates. In the loop, the counter value and its subsequent number are used to move the ball to the appropriate pair of coordinates. The preceding handler moves the ball in one direction only, but the procedure may be easily adapted to throw the ball in either direction, depending on which "person" has the ball (that is, what its beginning coordinates are). The next handler moves the ball in the appropriate direction based on its starting position.

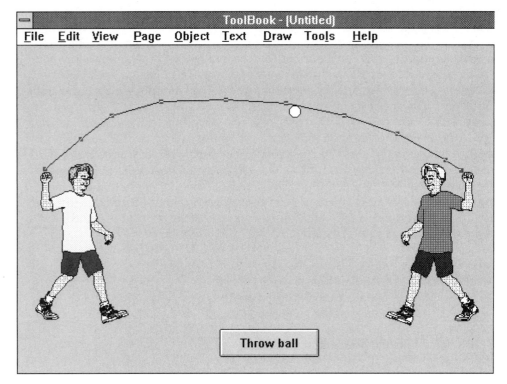

Figure 25.3
An object may be moved
along a path by setting its
position in relation to the
vertices established by an
angled line.

```
to handle buttonClick
    put the vertices of angledLine "ballpath" into coordinates
    put itemcount(coordinates) into x
    if the position of ellipse "baseball" = "480,2115" then  --throw ball from left \
    to right
        step i from 1 to x by 2
            move ellipse "baseball" to item i \
            of coordinates,item (i+1) of coordinates
            pause 5 ticks
        end step
    else   -- throw ball from right to left
        step i from x to 1 by -2
            move ellipse "baseball" to item (i-1) of coordinates,item i of coordinates
            pause 5 ticks
        end step
    end if
end buttonClick
```

Using the Script Recorder

The script recorder is a useful tool for setting up movement applications. The recorder is activated and an object or objects selected and moved to each position during a desired animation. When dragging objects during a recording session, the mouse button must be released at each point you wish the object to be moved to. The recorder is turned off and the resulting handler may be pasted into a script and edited as needed (for instance, any desired pause commands can be added).

Layering

Layering involves several overlapping images. Generally, each image is the same size, opaque, and has the same boundaries. The images create an animation when viewed in a sequence. The sequence of images is shown by adjusting the layering of the various images. The images are brought to the front in the appropriate order and for an appropriate amount of time.

Figure 25.4 shows a page with an image of two people watching television. The image on the television is an animation of a horse running past a tree. There are eight individual images of the horse and tree in various positions (see Figure 25.5); when viewed sequentially, they produce an animation sequence. The animation is performed with an idle handler, that brings one of the eight images to the front by changing its layer. A user-defined property of the page is called and updated to track which image to view next. The eight groups are named screen1, screen2, and so on, with the eighth image named screen8.

```
to handle idle
    get the nextscreen of this page
    if it is 8 then  --update the nextscreen property
        put 1 into the nextscreen of this page
    else
        increment the nextscreen of this page by 1
    end if
    increment the layer of group ("screen" & it) by 7
end idle
```

The handler executes when nothing else is happening while in Reader mode (in other words, the book is idling). It first gets the value of the user-defined nextscreen property, which contains a value between 1 and 8, and is assigned to the it variable. The if then...else...end if structure is used to update the nextscreen property for the next execution of the handler. If the value was 8, nextscreen is changed to 1;

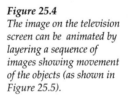

Figure 25.4

The image on the television screen can be animated by layering a sequence of images showing movement of the objects (as shown in Figure 25.5).

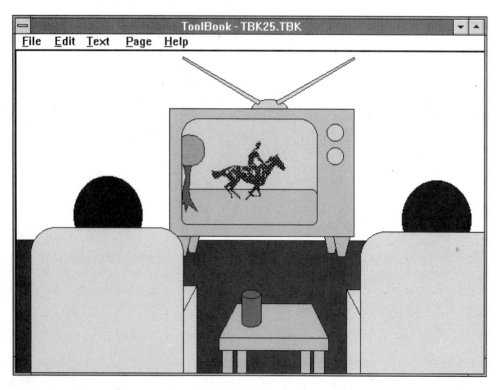

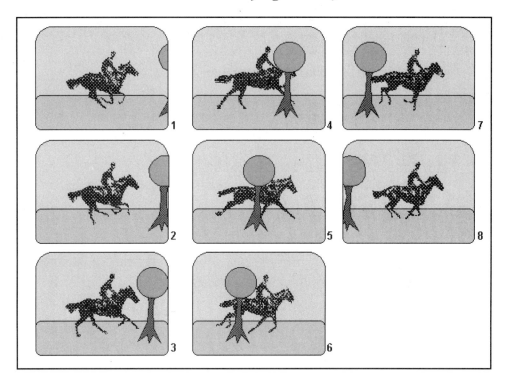

otherwise, its current value is increased by 1 (for example, if nextscreen was 3 it now becomes 4). Finally, the appropriate group is brought forward by seven layers (if nextscreen was 3, then group screen3 is moved seven layers forward). The code that follows provides an alternative to adjusting the layer, assuming the television screen is the frontmost layer of the page.

```
select group ("screen" & it)
send bringToFront
```

Frame Animation

Frame animation is very similar to layering. In **frame animation**, objects are shown and hidden in a sequence. The television screen animation done with layering in the preceding section could be presented through frame animation. In developing the application, all eight screen groups except for the first one would be hidden, and the nextscreen property would be set to 2. The idle handler would then be changed to

```
to handle idle
    conditions
        when the visible of group "screen1" is true
            show group "screen2"
            hide group "screen1"
        when the visible of group "screen2" is true
            show group "screen3"
            hide group "screen2"
        when the visible of group "screen3" is true
            show group "screen4"
            hide group "screen3"
        when the visible of group "screen4" is true
            show group "screen5"
            hide group "screen4"
```

```
        when the visible of group "screen5" is true
            show group "screen6"
            hide group "screen7"
        when the visible of group "screen6" is true
            show group "screen7"
            hide group "screen6"
        when the visible of group "screen7" is true
            show group "screen8"
            hide group "screen7"
        when the visible of group "screen8" is true
            show group "screen1"
            hide group "screen8"
    end conditions
end idle
```

The nextscreen user-defined property could also be used in this frame animation, replacing the preceding handler with a shorter version:

```
to handle idle
    get the nextscreen of this page
    conditions
        when it is 8 then  --update the nextscreen property
            put 1 into the nextscreen of this page
            put 7 into currentScreen
        when it is 1 then
            put 2 into the nextscreen of this page
            put 8 into currentScreen
        else
            increment the nextscreen of this page by 1
            put it - 1 into currentScreen
    end conditions
    show group ("screen" & it)
    hide group ("screen" & currentScreen)
end idle
```

Is it best to use layer or frame animation? In the examples so far, layering and frame animation appear to occur at roughly the same speed, so it is largely an issue of which method the author prefers. One major advantage to frame animation over layering is that, in a frame animation, the objects need not all be at the same position. Consider an animation in which a circle moves across the screen and changes colors as it does so. The moving circle might be produced with a sequence of 26 circles, all shown in Figure 25.6. The following handler, which is attached to the "Animate" button, shows the circles one at a time, from the left to the right.

```
to handle buttonClick
    show ellipse id 1
    pause 10 ticks
    step i from 1 to 24
        show ellipse id (i+1)
        hide ellipse id i
        pause 10 ticks
    end step
    pause 10 ticks
    hide ellipse id 25
end buttonClick
```

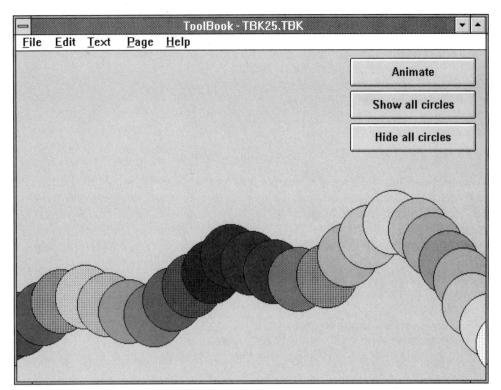

Figure 25.6
One advantage to using
frame animation over
layering techniques is that
the objects need not all be in
the same location on the
screen. In this example,
each of the 26 circles are
shown sequentially to make
the circle appear that it is
traveling across the screen.

Animating by Altering Objects

Changing the properties of an object is another simple method of achieving movement and capturing the reader's attention. For example, the handler that follows alters the RGBstroke color of a field on a title page of a book.

```
to handle idle
     put random(255) into r
     put random(255) into g
     put random(255) into b
     set the RGBstroke of field id 0 to r,g,b
     pause 50 ticks
end idle
```

The following handler changes the bounds of an ellipse so that it appears to breathe, growing and shrinking repeatedly.

```
notifyBefore idle
     step i from 1 to 3  --enlarge ball in three movements
         set sysLockScreen to true
         decrement item 1 of my bounds by 100
         decrement item 2 of my bounds by 100
         increment item 3 of my bounds by 100
         increment item 4 of my bounds by 100
         set sysLockScreen to false
         pause 10 ticks
     end step
     step i from 1 to 3  --shrink ball back to starting size in three movements
         set sysLockScreen to true
```

```
            increment item 1 of my bounds by 100
            increment item 2 of my bounds by 100
            decrement item 3 of my bounds by 100
            decrement item 4 of my bounds by 100
            set sysLockScreen to false
            pause 10 ticks
        end step
        pause 50 ticks
    end idle
```

The "Animate" button in Figure 25.7 moves the plane diagonally toward the bottom of the screen and enlarges the image as it moves, giving the appearance that the plane is flying toward the user. The plane is moved by incrementing the first two items of its bounds. Items 3 and 4 of the plane's bounds are incremented by the same amount as items 1 and 2, plus an additional amount in each direction so that the plane is enlarged.

```
    to handle buttonClick
        step i from 1 to 10
            set sysLockScreen to true
            increment item 1 of bounds of picture id 0 by 300
            increment item 2 of bounds of picture id 0 by 500
            increment item 3 of bounds of picture id 0 by 800
            increment item 4 of bounds of picture id 0 by 1000
            set sysLockScreen to false
            pause 10 ticks
        end step
        set the bounds of picture id 0 to 90,90,1114,1066  --reset plane to original position
    end buttonClick
```

Figure 25.8 shows how the various stages of the animation look on the screen.

Figure 25.7
The airplane in this example can appear to fly toward the user by changing its bounds so that it moves towards the bottom of the page and enlarges simultaneously. (Figure 25.8 shows the various stages of the plane's position and size.)

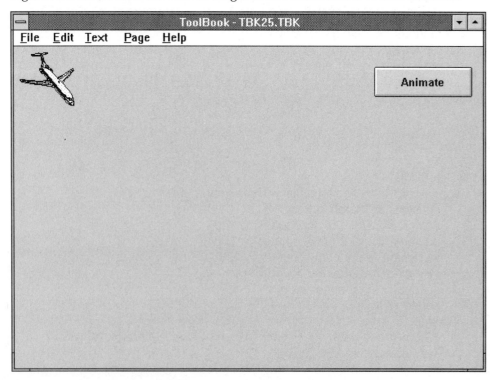

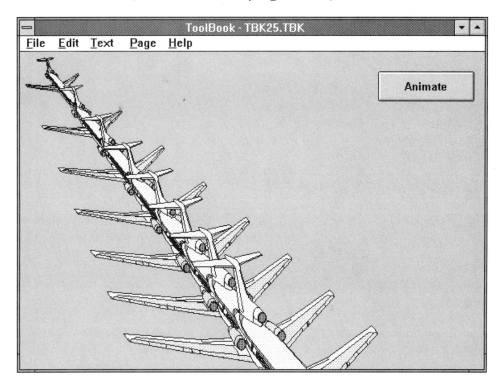

Figure 25.8
The various stages of the
plane animation described
in Figure 25.7. These are
not separate images, but
rather the various positions
of the same image as seen
through time.

The **draw** Command

The draw command can be used to create objects from within a handler. Its syntax and use is explained in Figure 25.9. A square may be drawn with the statement

    draw rectangle from 1000,1000 to 3000,3000

An angled line with several vertices results from the statement:

    draw angledLine from 500,500 to 1000,1000 to 2000,1000 to \
    1500,2000 to 3000,3000

A drawn item is automatically selected, and the newly created object's properties

The **draw** command	
Syntax:	**draw** *objectType* **from** *location* **to** *location* [**to** *location* . . . **to** *location*]
Purpose:	Draws an object of the specified type from one set of coordinates to the diagonally opposite set of coordinates (or for an irregular polygon, curve, or angled line, from one vertex coordinate to another vertex coordinate to another vertex, etc.) *ObjectType* may be angledLine, arc, button, comboBox, curve, ellipse, field, irregularPolygon, line, pie, polygon, rectangle, recordField, or roundedRectangle.
Examples:	draw field from 1000,1000 to 3000,5000
	draw rectangle from 2500,3000 to 3500,4500
	draw irregularPolygon from 1000,1000 to 3000,3000 to 2000,2500 to 1200,500
	draw ellipse from x,y to a,b

Figure 25.9
The draw *command is used*
to create an object with the
specified bounds.

may be altered by referring to the selection in the handler. For instance, the code that follows creates a yellow field in which text will appear in 16-point Arial.

```
to handle buttonClick
    draw field from 1000,1000 to 3000,4500
    set the fontFace of selection to "Arial"
    set the fontSize of selection to 16
    set the fillColor of selection to yellow
end buttonClick
```

Figure 25.10
A complex graphic can be drawn from a handler by issuing several draw *commands.*

Multiple objects may be created in the same handler. The following handler creates the picture of a person shown in Figure 25.10.

```
to handle buttonClick
    set syscursor to 4
    draw irregularPolygon from 705,5745 to 885,4890 to 1335,4350 to \
        2550,4245  to 4575,4260 to 5550,4410 to 6075,4905 to 6285,5745
    set fillColor of selection to blue
    pause 1 seconds
    draw irregularPolygon from 2535,3885 to 4575,3885 to 4605,5025 to \
        3495,5655 to 2580,4800
    set fillColor of selection to 60,87.4375,100
    pause 1 seconds
    draw ellipse from 1890,600 to 5190,4485
    set fillColor of selection to 60,87.4375,100
    pause 1 seconds
    draw ellipse from 2580,1920 to 3360,2325
    pause 1 seconds
    draw ellipse from 3705,1920 to 4485,2325
    pause 1 seconds
```

```
    draw ellipse from 2805,1950 to 3135,2280
    set fillColor of selection to green
    pause 1 seconds
    draw ellipse from 3930,1950 to 4260,2280
    set fillColor of selection to green
    pause 1 seconds
    draw ellipse from 2925,2025 to 3075,2190
    set fillColor of selection to black
    pause 1 seconds
    draw ellipse from 4005,2025 to 4155,2190
    set fillColor of selection to black
    pause 1 seconds
    draw angledLine from 3510,1980 to 3735,2385 to 3840,2685 to 3795,2805 \
        to 3585,2865 to 3360,2790
    pause 1 seconds
    draw irregularPolygon from 2700,3300 to 3330,3225 to 3585,3270 to \
        3810,3210 to 4425,3300 to 4125,3480 to 3810,3585 to 3405,3585 \
        to 2940,3510
    set the fillColor of selection to 0,25.125,100
    pause 1 seconds
    draw angledLine from 2760,3315 to 3165,3405 to 3645,3450 to 4140,3345 \
        to 4395,3300
    pause 1 seconds
    draw irregularPolygon from 4740,1965 to 4815,2310 to 4965,2325 to \
        4965,1920 to 5055,1845 to 5145,2010 to 5175,2355 to 5190,2775 \
        to 5250,2100 to 5190,1605 to 4755,1035 to 4170,615 to 3465,510 \
        to 2880,660 to 2370,1035 to 2055,1575 to 1890,2040 to 1830,2535 \
        to 1980,3165 to 1935,2550 to 1995,2100 to 2160,1860 to 2265,2010 \
        to 2190,2505 to 2370,2430 to 2475,1605 to 2745,1200 to 3180,1005 \
        to 3585,1395 to 4620,1545
    set fillColor of selection to black
    set syscursor to 1
    get flushMessageQueue()
end buttonClick
```

Note that the preceding handler produces a 1-second pause after each object is created. Since the execution of this handler lasts several seconds, the cursor is first set to the hourglass image to visually tell the user to wait. After all the objects have been drawn, the cursor is set back to 1, the default arrow. The flushMessageQueue eliminates any messages that the user may have accidentally (or intentionally) sent while the script was executing.

In writing such scripts it is easiest to use the script recorder while drawing the object in Author mode, or to draw the object and use the "Command" window to discover the bounds or vertices of the objects by selecting an object and issuing the command

```
    put the bounds of selection
```

or

```
    put the vertices of selection
```

Summary Questions

Complete the following statements by filling in the blanks.

1. The _____ command is used to reposition an object at a specified position.
2. The execution speed of an animation can be slowed by using the _____ command to halt it for a specified number of seconds or ticks.
3. An object can be moved along the path of an angled line by defining, in a loop structure, its position in terms of the _____ of the angled line.
4. The_____ animation technique involves bringing overlapped images to the front in a sequence to produce the appearance of movement.
5. In _____ animation, individual objects are shown and hidden in sequence to produce movement.
6. The _____ _____ is useful in designing animation because it captures the necessary movements in sequence. Then they can be pasted into a handler.
7. Objects may be animated by changing their _____ in a handler—their fillColor, bounds, or position, for example.
8. The_____ command is used to create new objects with specific bounds or vertices.
9. The properties of a new object created with the draw command may be altered by referring to the object as the _____ .
10. The_____ function is used to eliminate any messages generated by the user while a time-consuming handler (such as one producing a long animation) was executed.

Write an OpenScript statement to perform the following tasks.

11. Move the ellipse named "red ball" to the coordinate 2000,2000.
12. Move the ellipse named "red ball" to the right by 1000 page units.
13. Move the group named elevator down 2 inches.
14. Show the group named elevator.
15. Draw a rectangle with the bounds 1000,1000,3000,3000.
16. Fill with red the rectangle created in question 15.
17. Draw a circle with the bounds 4000,4000,5000,5000.
18. Draw a field that is 2 inches wide and 3 inches high, with its upper left corner at the coordinate 1000,1000.
19. Set the font of the field created in question 18 to Times.
20. Change the color of the text in field id 5 to red.

Hands-On Projects

A. Examine the software that accompanies this chapter. Open the "Table of Contents" book by double-clicking its icon in the "Developing with ToolBook" group window in the Windows Program Manager. Inside the "Table of Contents," click the book representing Chapter 25.

B. The ToolBook and Multimedia ToolBook packages include a sample application (ANIMATE.TBK) that discusses various animation techniques (see Figure 25.11). The icon shown at the right, which is installed in the ToolBook or Multimedia ToolBook group, allows you to access the application. Open this book and examine its contents to learn more about methods of animation.

C. Design an animation in which an illustrated person shoots a basketball through

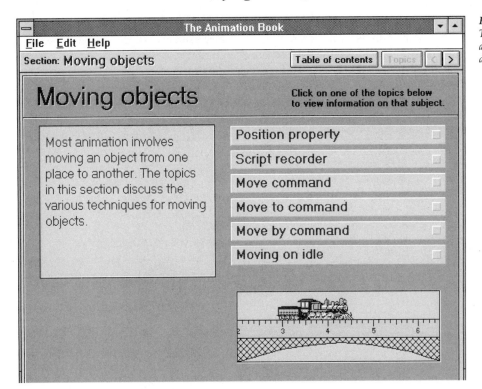

Figure 25.11
ToolBook is accompanied by a sample application that discusses animating objects.

Figure 25.12
Hands-On Project C calls for an animation of a basketball player shooting a basketball through a hoop. Path animation or the script recorder could be used in developing the solution.

a basket when the user clicks a button. An example is illustrated in Figure 25.12 (all graphics were created with ToolBook, but clipart may be used if available).

D. Design a page that looks like Figure 25.13, in which a circle moves randomly in one direction when idling until it encounters the edge of the page. Then the circle changes direction, continuing in a straight line until an edge is encountered, and so forth. (Hint: Use a page property to keep track of which direction the circle is moving [an offset value] and change this value when the edge of the page is encountered.)

E. Create an animation of a bird that flaps its wings when the book is idling. Figure 25.14 shows an example page with the various stages of the wings. Use frame animation to achieve the movement.

F. Write a buttonClick handler to draw a train or locomotive. An example drawing is shown in Figure 25.15.

Figure 25.13
In Hands-On Project D, an animation of a ball randomly moving about a page is created. The ball changes direction when it encounters the edge of the page.

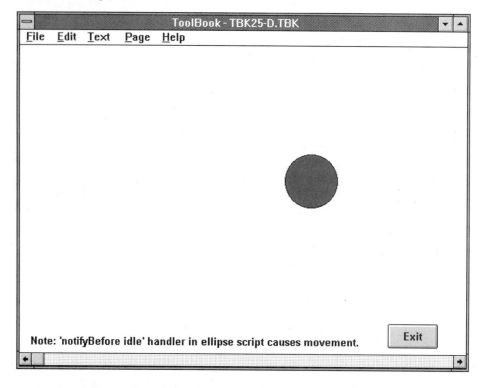

Figure 25.14
In Hands-On Project E, an animation of a bird flapping its wings is created (left) using frame animation to display the five sets of wings shown on the right.

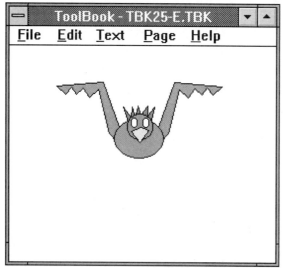

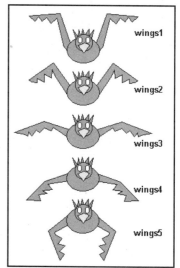

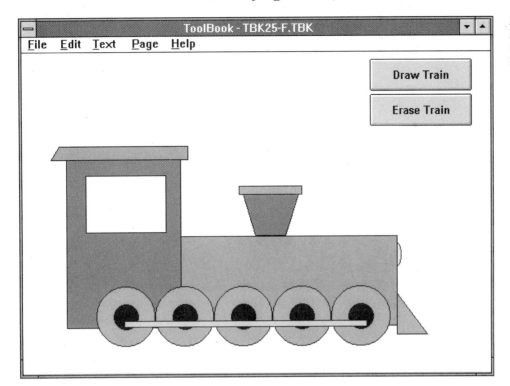

Figure 25.15
In Hands-On Project F, a
train is drawn when the
user clicks a button.

Beyond ToolBook

DDE, OLE, and DLLs

Microsoft Windows dynamic data exchange (DDE) allows client-server applications to be built with ToolBook. DDE permits the retrieval of data from other applications as well as the ability to execute commands remotely in other applications. Windows object linking and embedding (OLE, pronounced "oh-lay") is an expansion of the DDE concept, permitting the inclusion of data from another application and the ability to automatically update the linked reference in ToolBook as the source document is edited. When information is embedded, a copy of the data is placed in the ToolBook book and stored with it. When information is linked, only a reference to the filename is stored in the document. ToolBook examines the source file to see if the file has changed and then changes the book accordingly.

A dynamic link library (DLL) is an external file that defines routines or functions that Windows applications, including ToolBook, can access. These routines, usually written in C or C++, may be called from an OpenScript handler and thus expand the OpenScript language. The ToolBook package includes several DLL files for working with files (that is, for copying, deleting, changing drives and directories, and so on), working with databases, accessing the serial communications ports, and retrieving Windows information. In addition, DLLs are available from other packages, including the DLLs of the Windows API (Application Programming Interface). Customized DLLs may also be written by a C/C++ programmer, and then accessed from ToolBook.

DDE

DDE stands for **dynamic data exchange**. It is a protocol for communicating between Windows applications in a client-server environment. In a **client-server environment**, one application (the client) sends commands to another application (the server). DDE provides a method of controlling another application, such as Microsoft Excel or WordPerfect for Windows, by remotely executing the commands of the other application. Dynamic data exchange also allows the exchange of data between the two applications. Using DDE, a front end to another Windows application may be created with ToolBook.

Not all Windows applications support DDE protocols. ToolBook does support DDE and, though a Toolbook application generally serves as a client, ToolBook may also take on the role of the server. Therefore, the server application for a client book may be another instance of ToolBook. In other words, dynamic data exchange provides a method for linking two separate ToolBook books.

There are several DDE commands that may be executed from an OpenScript handler. The executeRemote command is used to execute commands within the server application. For instance, using DDE, a ToolBook application may tell Microsoft Excel to open a spreadsheet and print it, or to export its data as a comma-delimited ASCII text file. The getRemote command is used to request information from the server application, such as the value located in cell C5 of the Excel

Figure 26.1
DDE server applications
are referred to by specific
names. The reference
names of popular
applications are shown in
this chart.

DDE Names of Common Windows Applications	
Application	**DDE name reference**
Lotus 1-2-3 for Windows	123w
Lotus Ami Pro	Amipro
Microsoft Excel for Windows	Excel
Microsoft Word for Windows	Winword
Microsoft Visual Basic	Filename of executable application without .EXE extension
CrossTalk	xtalk
SPC Superbase4	sb4w
ToolBook/Multimedia ToolBook	Toolbook

spreadsheet. Likewise, the setRemote command could be used to change the value in cell C5 in the Excel spreadsheet.

For dynamic data exchange to function properly, the server application must first be open. An application that supports DDE has a DDE name by which it must be referred to in a DDE command. Microsoft Excel's DDE name is Excel, Microsoft Word for Windows' DDE name is Winword, and ToolBook's is ToolBook. The DDE name for an application can be found in the application's manual. Figure 26.1 shows the DDE name for some popular Windows applications.

Data may be gotten from the server or sent to the server application, or a command may be executed in the server application by using DDE commands. The server responds and errors may be checked by examining the sysError property. The communication link between the client and the server remains open until the handler finishes executing. (The link may be forced to remain open after the handler is done executing by using the keepRemote command. The closeRemote command is then used to close the link that has been kept open.)

Getting Data Remotely with DDE

The getRemote command (see Figure 26.2) is used to get data from another Windows application or another instance of ToolBook. The return value is placed into the variable it. Only certain types of data may be retrieved from the server. In Excel, the value of a cell or range of cells may be retrieved. The cell may be referred to by name or by a row-column reference such as R5C3, which would be cell C5. The following handler retrieves the value of cell A10 (row 10, column 1) from Lotus 1-2-3 spreadsheet named SCORES.WK3. The DDE name for Lotus 1-2-3 is 123w.

Figure 26.2
The getRemote *command*
is used to retrieve data from
another Windows
application.

> **The getRemote command**
>
> Syntax: **getRemote *item* application *application* [topic *serverTopic*]**
>
> Purpose: Returns value of *item* from the server application. The *item* varies from application to application (for example, it might be a cell or range of cells in a spreadsheet or the text of a field in another ToolBook book). The *application* must be cited as a DDE reference name (see Figure 26.1) and support DDE. The *serverTopic* is usually the filename of the file containing the desired data.
>
> Examples: getRemote "R5C5" application "Excel" topic "payroll.wks"
>
> getRemote "text of field id 3 of page id 1" application "ToolBook" topic "data.tbk"
>
> getRemote "SpongeCake" application "Winword" topic "recipes.txt"

```
to handle buttonClick
    getRemote "R10C1" application "123w" topic "scores.wk3"
    put it into the text of recordfield id 3
end buttonClick
```

The run command can be used to open an application and a document in the application. The following handler opens the SCORES.WK3 spreadsheet along with Lotus 1-2-3 and then reads the data of columns A, B, and C of rows 1 through 10, placing the values in an array named grades[ ].

```
to handle buttonClick
    system grades[10][3]
    run "123.exe scores.wk3"
    step i from 1 to 10
        getRemote ("R"&i&"C1") application "123w" topic "scores.wk3"
        put it into grades[i][1]
        getRemote ("R"&i&"C2") application "123w" topic "scores.wk3"
        put it into grades[i][2]
        getRemote ("R"&i&"C3") application "123w" topic "scores.wk3"
        put it into grades[i][3]
    end step
end buttonClick
```

In another instance of ToolBook, any property may be retrieved, including the text of a field or recordfield. The following handler retrieves the text of a recordfield named response located on page ID 4 of another open ToolBook file named QUIZ1.TBK. The value is placed in a system variable of the current book as well as in the text of a field. Figure 26.3 illustrates this process.

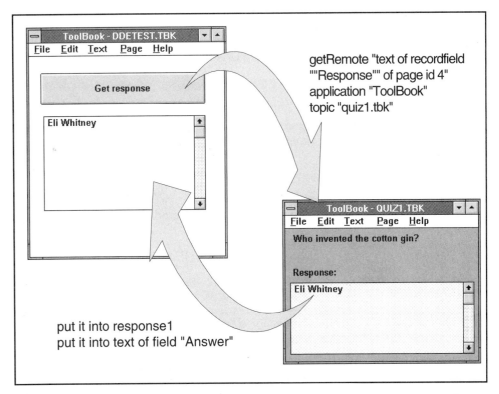

Figure 26.3
The getRemote command polls another application (server) for specific data. The requested information is returned to the calling handler of the book (client). This data may be assigned to a variable or other container, such as the text of a field.

```
to handle getResponse
    system response1
    getRemote "text of recordfield ""Response"" of page id 4" \
    application "ToolBook" topic "quiz1.tbk"
    put it into response1
    put it into text of field "Answer"
end getResponse
```

Evaluating the Success of a DDE Communication

After a DDE command has been executed, it is wise to verify that the command was successfully executed. This is done by checking the value of the sysError property. If the command was successful, the value of the first item of sysError will be OK. Any other value in the first item indicates that the DDE command failed. Figure 26.4 lists the other possible values, following a DDE attempt, of sysError's first item.

A subroutine might be used to check the success of a DDE command:

```
to handle checkDDESuccess
    conditions
    when item 1 of sysError = "OK"
        --successful - do nothing
    when item 1 of sysError = "Failed: Busy"
        request "DDE Command FAILED.  Server responded but was busy."
    when item 1 of sysError = "Failed: Denied"
        request "DDE command FAILED.  Server denied request."
    when item 1 of sysError = "Failed: Memory Error"
        request "DDE command FAILED.  Not enough memory."
    when item 1 of sysError = "Failed: Interrupted"
        request "DDE command FAILED. Connection with server interrupted."
    when item 1 of sysError = "Failed: No Server"
        request "DDE command FAILED. Server didn't respond. " & \
        "Verify application is open."
    else
        request "DDE command FAILED.  Unknown Problem."
    end conditions
end checkDDESuccess
```

Figure 26.4
The success of a DDE command can be determined by checking the value of the first item of sysError.

Possible Values of First Item of **sysError** After an Executed DDE Command	
1st Item of sysError	**Explanation**
OK	Command was successfully executed
Failed: Busy	Application received the command but was too busy to execute the request
Failed: Denied	Application received request but did not execute it
Failed: Memory Error	Not enough memory available for Toolbook to send command or receive the returned value
Failed: Interrupted	Application received request but the connection was broken before it could be fully executed
Failed: No Server	Server not open or did not repond (doesn't support DDE or not correctly referenced)

This handler could be called following each DDE command. For instance, adding send checkDDESuccess to the previous DDE handler would cause a request dialog box to appear with an error message if the DDE command were not successfully executed.

```
to handle getResponse
    system response1
    getRemote "text of recordfield ""Response"" of page id 4" \
    application "ToolBook" topic "quiz1.tbk"
    send checkDDESuccess
    put it into response1
    put it into text of field "answer"
end getResponse
```

Setting Data Values Remotely

Data values may also be set in the server application by using the **setRemote** command (see Figure 26.5). The same items that are gettable in a server application are settable. In Excel or Lotus, data may be placed in the cells of a spreadsheet. If using another ToolBook book as the server, any property may be set from the client book by using the **setRemote** command. The following script places the value of variable sysX into cell B3 of a Lotus 1-2-3 spreadsheet named COSTS.WK3:

```
to handle buttonClick
    system sysX
    setRemote "R3C2" to sysX application "123w" topic "costs.wk3"
    send checkDDESuccess
end buttonClick
```

The preceding handler requires that the checkDDESuccess handler be contained within the script hierarchy of the client book.

The following handler sets the text of a field in the server instance of ToolBook, a book saved as QUIZ1.TBK.

```
to handle buttonClick
    setRemote "text of field id 3 of page id 0" to "Hello." \
    application "ToolBook" topic "quiz1.tbk"
```

Figure 26.5
The setRemote *command is used to set the value of an item in a server application.*

The setRemote command

Syntax: **setRemote** *item* **to** *value* **application** *application* **[topic** *serverTopic***]**

Purpose: Sets value of *item* in the server application. The *item* varies from application to application (for example, it might be a cell or range of cells in a spreadsheet or the text of a field in another ToolBook book). The *application* must be cited as a DDE reference name (see Figure 26.1) and support DDE. The *serverTopic* is usually the filename of the file containing the desired data.

Examples: setRemote "R5C5" to "345.00" application "Excel" topic "payroll.wks"

setRemote "text of field id 3 of page id 1" to "John Doe" application "ToolBook" topic "data.tbk"

setRemote "fillColor of ellipse id 3" to "red" application "Toolbook" topic "test.tbk"

```
      if item 1 of sysError <> "OK" then
           request "An error occurred." with "OK"
      end if
  end buttonClick
```

Any errors encountered in executing the setRemote command are checked for in the if...then statement. If the execution was successful, the word "Hello." is placed in the text of field id 3 on page id 0 in the server instance (in QUIZ1.TBK).

Executing Commands Remotely

From the client book, commands may be executed remotely, in the server application, by using the executeRemote command. The syntax and use of the executeRemote command are discussed in Figure 26.6. The following handler prints the SCORES.XLS spreadsheet from Microsoft Excel.

```
  to handle buttonClick
      executeRemote "[PRINT( )]" application "excel" topic "scores.xls"
      send checkDDESuccess  --requires handler be in client book
  end buttonClick
```

In Microsoft Excel, any macro command can be executed. Excel's DDE support requires that macro commands be enclosed in square brackets. The format and types of commands that can be received differ according to the application. The manual for the server application should be consulted.

With ToolBook as the server application, any OpenScript command can be executed remotely. The following handler navigates the server book (SERVER.TBK) to the first page and then shows a hidden group (ID 72).

```
  to handle buttonClick
      executeRemote "go to page 1" application "toolbook" topic "server.tbk"
      send checkDDESuccess  --requires handler be available in client book
      executeRemote "show group id 72" application "toolbook" topic "server.tbk"
      send checkDDESuccess
  end buttonClick
```

Figure 26.6
The executeRemote *command is used to send a command to another open application (the server).*

The executeRemote command

Syntax: **executeRemote** *command* **application** *application* **[topic** *serverTopic***]**

Purpose: Remotely executes a command in the server application. Supported commands vary from application to application. Multiple commands can be sent in the same executeRemote statement. The *application* must be referred to by its DDE reference name (see Figure 26.1). The topic is usually a filename.

Examples: executeRemote "Print" application "Excel" topic "payroll.wks"

            executeRemote "show rectangle id 5" application "ToolBook" topic "data.tbk"

            executeRemote "draw field from 100,100 to 2000,2000; set fontface or selection to Times; set fontsize of selection to 12; set fillColor of selection to yellow" application "Toolbook" topic "quiz1.tbk"

            executeRemote "[FileOpen ""MEMO1.TXT"", 0]" application winword topic system

---

More than one command can be sent to a ToolBook server in a single executeRemote command. The individual commands must be separated by semicolons. Therefore, the preceding handler could be rewritten as:

```
to handle buttonClick
    executeRemote "go to page 1;show group id 72" application "toolbook" \
    topic "server.tbk"
    send checkDDESuccess  --requires handler to be in client book
end buttonClick
```

OLE

OLE is an acronym for **object linking and embedding**. It is an expansion of the DDE concept. OLE allows objects created in other Windows applications (servers) to be incorporated into a ToolBook application (client). An OLE object may be either linked or embedded, hence the name object linking and embedding. Only objects created with Windows applications that support OLE can be embedded or linked.

When an object is linked, a reference to the original file is stored in the ToolBook book. This reference includes information about the type of object (if it is an Excel chart or Paintbrush graphic, for example), the filename, and its location (for instance, c:\excel\mychart.cht). When the user navigates to the page or background containing the OLE object, ToolBook finds the file and displays it in the appropriate place on the page or background. If the file has been changed (that is, if the chart has been updated in Excel), the latest version is displayed in the ToolBook application. The ToolBook author need not update the book—the OLE object is imported each time. Thus it is essential that the location or name of the file not be altered without altering the reference information in ToolBook; otherwise, the object will not be found.

When an OLE object is embedded, a copy of the object is actually stored in the book. The object in this case is not automatically updated if a newer version of the file exists, and the author must be concerned about the external file being available. A reference of the source application used to create the object is maintained, but not the filename and location.

In both instances, whether the object is linked or embedded, the user can double-click the OLE object in ToolBook to open the server application and edit the document. If the object is linked, the external source file is edited. If the object is embedded, the embedded copy is edited.

Linking Data with OLE

A linked object is created by placing an OLE container object on the page or background and then referencing the file to be linked by setting the properties of the container. The OLE container object is created by choosing the OLE tool from the Tool palette and dragging it diagonally from one corner to the opposite corner (like drawing a rectangle). Until the links are specified, the OLE container will appear as a rectangle. To specify the links, select the container and choose "OLE properties..." from the Objects menu to display the "OLE Properties" dialog box (see Figure 26.7). Use the "Type" combo box to specify a linked type, then click the "Browse" button. Choose a file to be linked in the resulting "Change Source" dialog box (see Figure 26.8). The file name and path will be placed in the "Source" field of the "OLE Properties" dialog box. The application and type of object will be determined and inserted in the "Class" combo box. (A class may be selected first using the "Class" combo box. Then only files of that type will be shown in the "Change Source" dialog box when the "Browse" button is clicked.)

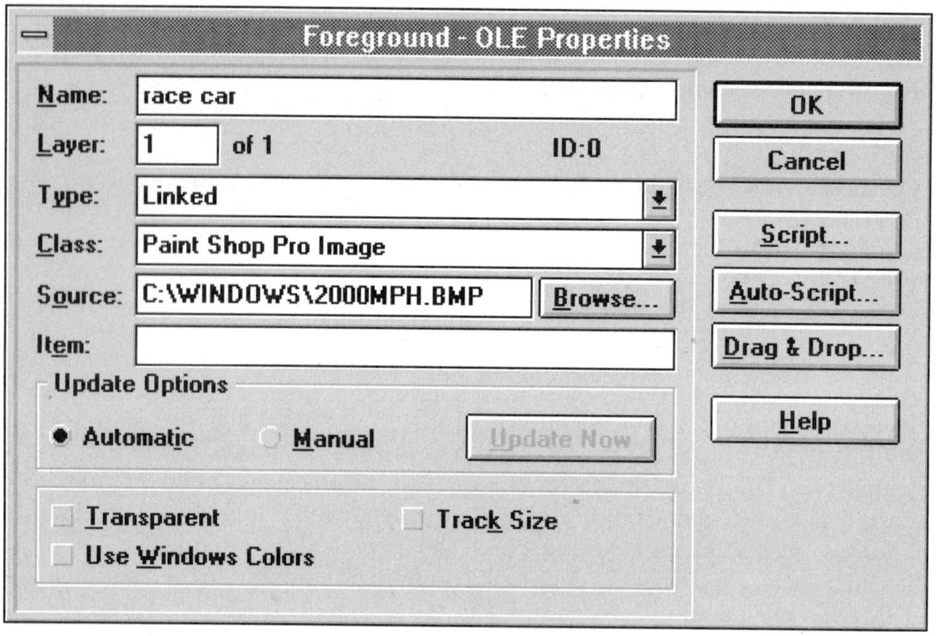

Figure 26.7
In the "OLE Properties" dialog box, the link is established with the external file.

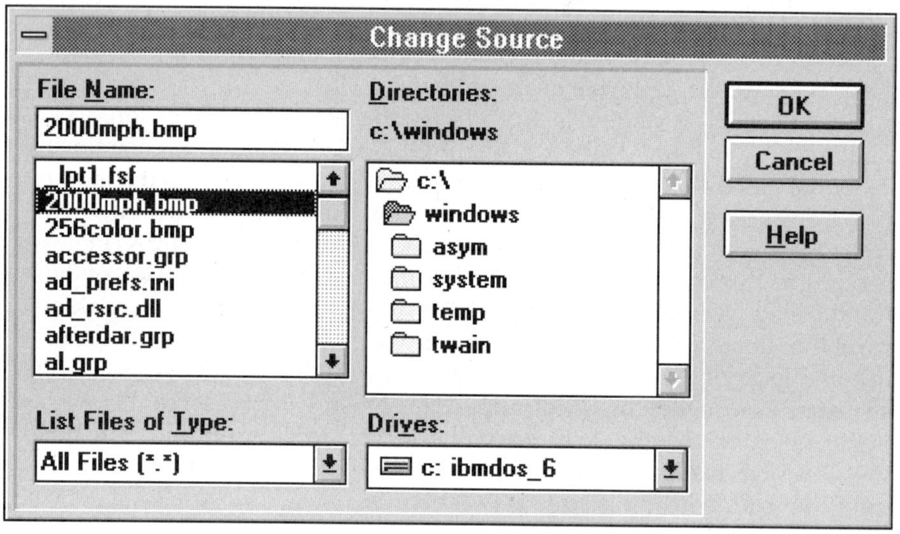

Figure 26.8
Clicking the "Browse" button in the "OLE Properties" dialog box brings up the "Change Source" dialog from which the file to be linked or embedded is chosen.

A name may be assigned to the container through the "OLE Properties" dialog as well. A linked object may be set up to always be updated automatically by checking "Automatic" under "Update Options." If this is done, the object is always refreshed when the user navigates to the page or background. Choosing "Manual" requires that the "Update Now" button be clicked to refresh the displayed object with the latest version of the linked file. A manual link can also be updated from within an OpenScript handler (or the "Command" window) by executing this statement:

```
set upToDate of ole id 1 to true
```

Note that the ID must be changed to reflect the ID number of the OLE container to be updated.

The linked file may also be specified using an OpenScript handler. The reference property of an OLE container has a value of four items. The items specify the type (whether linked or embedded), the class (server application and document type), the source (filename and path), and item (particular item or range of items of the source file to display, such as a set of rows and columns of an Excel spreadsheet). The following statement sets up a linked reference between an OLE container and a Paintbrush picture named BALLOONS.BMP.

```
set reference of ole id 5 to "linked,Paintbrush Picture,c:\windows\balloons.bmp"
```

The following statement sets up a linked reference to the cells ranging from A1 to E5 of a Microsoft Excel worksheet named PAYROLL.XLS.

```
set reference of ole id 7 to \
"linked,Microsoft Excel Worksheet,c:\excel\payroll.xls,R1C1:R5C5"
```

An OLE container could also be created from a handler by using the draw command. The following handler creates an OLE container and imports the BALLOONS.BMP file as a linked object:

```
to handle importBMP
    draw ole from 1000,1000 to 5000,4000
    set reference of selection to \
    "linked,Paintbrush Picture,c:\windows\balloons.bmp"
end importBMP
```

If the file is moved to a different directory or the name of the file is changed, the source reference will need to be re-established from the "OLE Properties" dialog box or from within an OpenScript command (to revise the OLE container's reference property).

Embedding Data with OLE

OLE objects are embedded into the book in the same manner as they are linked. The OLE container is created with the OLE tool. In the "OLE Properties" dialog, the type is set to embedded instead of linked and the class and source chosen as for a linked object.

As with a linked object, an embedded object could be set up from within an OpenScript handler. The following handler uses the draw command to create the OLE container and then sets the reference to an external file, specifying the type as an embedded object.

```
to handle importBMP
    draw ole from 1000,1000 to 5000,4000
    set reference of selection to \
    "embedded,Paintbrush Picture,c:\windows\balloons.bmp"
end importBMP
```

Creating a New Object to Be Embedded

The server application can be opened with a new document from within Tool-Book. Selecting "Insert OLE Object..." from ToolBook's Edit menu displays the dialog box shown in Figure 26.9. A server application may be selected and is opened when the "OK" button is clicked. The document to be linked or embedded may then be created from

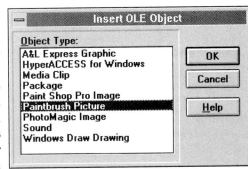

Figure 26.9
The "Insert OLE Object..." menu option displays a dialog box from which a server application may be opened with the document then embedded into the ToolBook book.

within the server application. Choose "Update" from the server application's File menu before closing the new file. ToolBook will automatically create an OLE container and embed the newly created document. As long as the file is open in the server application, a link exists between it and the ToolBook OLE container. The embedded object may be updated until the file is closed in the server application or the ToolBook book is closed.

DLL

Chapter 19 examined the concept of calling subroutines and user-defined functions. A **dynamic link library (DLL)** is an external file containing functions available to ToolBook. A DLL is used in much the same way that a user-defined function or subroutine is used. Dynamic link libraries are usually composed of procedures written in C or C++ and compiled as a DLL file with the extension .DLL. ToolBook includes several DLL files. TB30DLG.DLL has routines for creating and displaying Windows-style dialog boxes. The TB30DOS.DLL file contains routines for managing files and directories; TB30WIN.DLL has functions for determining display resolution, finding out what fonts are available, changing the values in any initialization (.INI) file, and converting an HLS color value to an RGB color value.

Before a DLL function may be called, the DLL file must first be linked (which is similar to opening a data file, as explained in Chapter 22) and the needed function declared. The function may then be called and its returning value used within OpenScript code. Once the function is no longer needed, the DLL file should be closed (unlinked).

Since dynamic link libraries are external to a book using them, they should be distributed with the book, provided such distribution is permitted by their owners and is not a violation of copyright law. Distribution policies can generally be found in the documentation for the DLL.

Linking to a DLL and Declaring a DLL Function

A DLL file is accessed by a handler using the linkDLL control structure. The syntax and use of the linkDLL structure are explained in Figure 26.10. Within this structure the name (and path, if different from the path of the current directory) of the DLL file is specified. The function to be used is also declared within the linkDLL structure. A dynamic link library generally contains many different routines, and multiple functions may be declared within the one linkDLL structure, provided each is a procedure of the linked file. In declaring a function, the type of the value returned is specified along with the function name and the types of any parameters passed to the function from the calling statement. Acceptable data types include BYTE, INT, FLOAT, DOUBLE, LONG, DWORD, WORD, POINTER and STRING. The data types for the declared function must match those specified in the DLL's code, so the author must look these up in the documentation accompanying the DLL file. This information may be in a "read-me" file, printed documentation, or the like. The documentation for each of the functions in the DLL files shipped with ToolBook may be found in Section 3 of the *OpenScript Reference Manual*.

TB30DOS.DLL, for instance, contains a function for getting the current drive. The getCurrentDrive( ) function is declared this way:

```
STRING getCurrentDrive( )
```

You can find this declaration in the *OpenScript Reference Manual* (page 3-38). To link to the DLL file and declare the function, a linkDLL structure would be used within the handler:

Figure 26.10
The linkDLL structure
enables a link to be
established between
ToolBook and an external
dynamic link library file.
Functions within the DLL
file are also declared within
this structure.

The linkDLL structure

Syntax: **linkDLL *DLLFilename***
                returnType functionName(parameterTypes)
            end linkDLL

Purpose: Links to the specified DLL file and declares a function with return a type and
           parameter types. The declared function may then be called from within the
           handler. Valid return type and parameter types are BYTE, INT, FLOAT,
           DOUBLE, DWORD, LONG, POINTER, STRING, and WORD. The correct type
           must be specified (look up in documentation for particular DLL file). Multiple
           functions within the same DLL file may be declared in the same linkDLL
           structure as the second example shows.

Examples: ```
           linkDLL "TB30DLG.DLL"
                INT addComboBoxItem(WORD,STRING,STRING,INT,INT)
           end linkDLL

           linkDLL "TB30WIN.DLL"
                STRING displayFonts(STRING)
                STRING getModuleList( )
                INT horizontalDisplaySize( )
                INT popMenu(WORD,STRING,INT,STRING,STRING,STRING)
                INT verticalDisplaySize( )
           end linkDLL
           ```

```
to handle buttonClick
    linkDLL "TB30DOS.DLL"
        STRING getCurrentDrive( )
    end linkDLL
    . . .
    . . .
    . . .
end buttonClick
```

In the remainder of the handler the getCurrentDrive( ) function would be called, the
return value handled, and the link to TB30DOS.DLL closed. These processes are
described in the sections that follow.

Multiple functions of a DLL may be declared within the linkDLL structure. For
instance, TB30DOS.DLL also contains a function for returning the current directory
path of a specified drive. Both the getCurrentDrive( ) and getCurrentDirectory( )
functions may be declared in the linkDLL structure, since both of these routines are
part of the same DLL file.

```
to handle buttonClick
    linkDLL "TB30DOS.DLL"
        STRING getCurrentDrive( )
        STRING getCurrentDirectory(STRING)
    end linkDLL
    . . .
    . . .
    . . .
end buttonClick
```
```

Calling a DLL Function and Handling the Returned Values

DLL routines are called in the same way that a user-defined function is called. The DLL file must already be linked. DLL functions may be called as part of a get or put statement, as well as used with an assignment operator. Arguments to be passed to a DLL function are included in parentheses after the function name. The getCurrentDrive( ) function has no parameters, but the getCurrentDirectory( ) function has a parameter consisting of the drive letter whose current directory is being sought. The following handler places the current path (drive and directory) into currentPath, a user-defined property of the book.

```
to handle buttonClick
    linkDLL "TB30DOS.DLL"
        STRING getCurrentDrive( )
        STRING getCurrentDirectory(STRING)
    end linkDLL
    put getCurrentDrive( ) into drive
    put drive & ":" & getCurrentDirectory(drive) into the currentPath of this book
    . . .
end buttonClick
```

In the preceding handler, the DLL file is linked and the functions declared as shown earlier. The getCurrentDrive( ) function is called and the value returned is placed into the local variable, drive. This value is simply the letter of the current drive, for example, A or C. The next line concatenates this value (that of the variable drive), a literal string of a colon, and the value returned by the getCurrentDirectory( ) function. The value of the current drive is passed as a parameter in the getCurrentDirectory( ) function. (The ellipses indicate the place where a statement to unlink the DLL file would be inserted. This statement is discussed in the next section.)

Unlinking a DLL

After a linked DLL is no longer needed, it should be unlinked. This is done by the unlinkDLL command, which is discussed in Figure 26.11. Unlinking the DLL frees up allocated memory. After the DLL has been unlinked, its functions may no longer be accessed. The unlinkDLL statement is added to the preceding handler to close the link with TB30DOS.DLL.

```
to handle buttonClick
    linkDLL "TB30DOS.DLL"
        STRING getCurrentDrive( )
        STRING getCurrentDirectory(STRING)
    end linkDLL
    put getCurrentDrive( ) into drive
```

Figure 26.11
The unlinkDLL *command is used to unlink a dynamic link library file that is no longer needed.*

The unlinkDLL command

Syntax: **unlinkDLL *DLLFilename***

Purpose: Breaks the link between ToolBook and the specified dynamic link library, freeing system resources.

Examples: unlinkDLL "TB30DLG.DLL"

            unlinkDLL "TB30WIN.DLL"

```
      put drive & ":" & getCurrentDirectory(drive) into the currentPath of this book
      unlinkDLL "TB30DOS.DLL"
end buttonClick
```

Example: Sorting Containers with DLL Functions

Two very useful functions for sorting the items or text lines of a container are included in the TB30DLG.DLL file but were omitted in the *OpenScript Reference Manual* that accompanied ToolBook 3.0 and Multimedia ToolBook 3.0. The functions sortList( ) and sortTextlines( ) are discussed in the on-line help (search for either function).

The sortList( ) function is passed a comma-delimited list of items (or a reference to a variable or other container consisting of a list of comma-delimited items) and returns the list in sorted order. The list can contain a maximum of 5000 items. The declaration statement for the sortList( ) function is

```
STRING sortList(STRING)
```

If system variable spices contains the value

```
oregano,thyme,salt,pepper,basil,dill,cinnamon,garlic,cayenne,nutmeg
```

the value of spices would be

```
basil,cayenne,cinnamon,dill,garlic,nutmeg,oregano,pepper,salt,thyme
```

after the following handler is executed.

```
to handle buttonClick
    system spices
    linkDLL "tb30dlg.dll"
        STRING sortList(STRING)
    end linkDLL
    put sortList(spices) into spices
end buttonClick
```

The items are sorted by the ASCII value of the characters. Thus an uppercase *Z* would come before a lowercase *a*. If, in the preceding example, the original value of spices were

```
oregano,Thyme,salt,Pepper,basil,Dill,cinnamon,Garlic,cayenne,Nutmeg
```

the sorted list returned by the sortList( ) function would be

```
Dill,Garlic,Nutmeg,Pepper,Thyme,basil,cayenne,cinnamon,oregano,salt
```

A reference to the contents of a field or recordfield may also be sent, with the returned value being the sorted text of the container:

```
to handle buttonClick
    linkDLL "tb30dlg.dll"
        STRING sortList(STRING)
    end linkDLL
    put sortList(text of field id 4) into text of field id 4
end buttonClick
```

The sortTextlines( ) function operates in the same manner, sorting the text lines of a container instead of comma-delimited items. Text lines are delimited by CRLF characters. The declaration statement for the sortTextlines( ) function is

```
STRING sortTextlines(STRING)
```

As with the sortList( ) function, the parameter passed to the sortTextlines( ) function may be a variable or reference to the text of a container. Figure 26.12 shows a page with a field whose text consists of several unsorted text lines. The script of the "Sort with DLL" button contains the following handler to sort the text:

```
buttonClick
    linkDLL "tb30dlg.dll"
        STRING sortList(STRING)
    end linkDLL
    put sortTextlines(text of field id 0) into text of field id 0
end buttonClick
```

Obtaining and Writing Additional DLL files

Besides the DLLs that accompany ToolBook, several DLLs accompany Microsoft Windows, and their routines may be accessed from OpenScript. The Windows Application Programming Interface (API) is the most commonly used. Read the "Windows API Help" file that accompanies ToolBook and Multimedia ToolBook, or the "Windows Multimedia API Help" that accompanies Multimedia ToolBook, for more information. Programmers' reference books discussing the various functions of the API are available from Microsoft as well as third-party publishers. Several titles may be found in the bibliography of this book (Appendix H).

Other third-party DLLs may be obtained from bulletin boards and on-line archives available through CompuServ or the Internet. In downloading a DLL file,

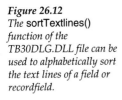

Figure 26.12
The sortTextlines() *function of the TB30DLG.DLL file can be used to alphabetically sort the text lines of a field or recordfield.*

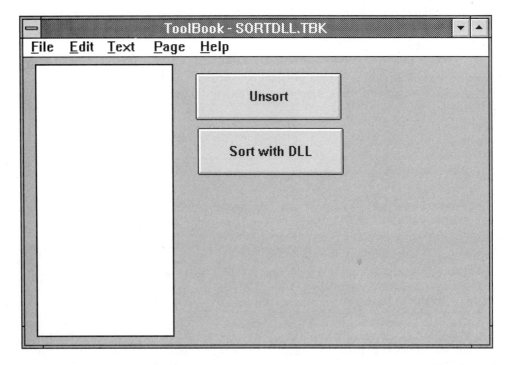

be sure to download any documentation if such is provided separately. A DLL without documentation about its functions, including their return types and parameter types, is of little use.

Dynamic link libraries may also be written in a C or C++ editor and compiled as a .DLL file. Microsoft's Visual C++ for Windows or Borland's TurboC or C++ compiler are popular environments for creating DLL files. The *ToolBook User's Manual* contains additional information on writing DLLs.

Summary Questions

Answer the following true/false questions.
1. Any Windows application may be controlled remotely by using DDE commands.
2. The server is the application receiving commands from a client application.
3. ToolBook books may be used as DDE clients, but not as DDE servers.
4. The "topic" in a DDE command is usually a filename.
5. A server application must be referred to in a DDE command by its DDE name.
6. An object from any Windows application may be linked to a ToolBook book by using OLE.
7. A DLL is an external file containing functions that may be called from an OpenScript handler.
8. Only DLL files shipped with ToolBook may be called from an OpenScript handler.
9. More than one function may be declared in a linkDLL structure.
10. A DLL function may be called in a put statement or with an assignment operator.

Complete the following statements by filling in the blanks.
11. Data may be retrieved from a DDE server by using the _____ command.
12. Errors in executing a DDE command are determined by examining the first item of the _____ property.
13. The _____ command is used to change a value in the server application.
14. The _____ command is used to control the actions of a DDE server.
15. OLE objects are _____ when only the reference to the external object is saved with the ToolBook book.
16. A manually linked OLE object may be updated in ToolBook by setting the _____ property of the OLE container to true.
17. A _____ structure is used to establish the link with a dynamic link library file and declare a function of the DLL file.
18. An open link with a DLL file is closed with the _____ statement.
19. The _____ type and parameter types of a DLL function must be declared.
20. When an OLE object is _____ , a copy of the object itself is stored in the book.

Hands-On Projects

A. Examine the software that accompanies this chapter. Open the "Table of Contents" book by double-clicking its icon in the "Developing with ToolBook" group window in the Windows Program Manager. Inside the "Table of Contents," click the book representing Chapter 26.

B. Using the CD database created in Chapter 23 (Hands-On Project E) as a server application, create as a client to the CD database the one-page book pictured in

Figure 26.13. The client should contain a scrolling field that displays all the performers and CDs in the server database. (This information should be imported from the server by clicking an "Update list" button and should be in the format *performer;CD title* with [one CD to each line] and sorted by performer name. See Figure 26.13). The user should be able to click a text line of the field and see a list of the songs on the CD for that performer or CD title.

Hints: Use **executeRemote** to first sort the pages of the server by the performer's name. Then use **getRemote** to determine the number of pages in the server book and use this value as the upper limit in a fixed loop. In the loop use **getRemote** to return the values of the performer and CD title recordfields for each page. Place this information in the top field of the client. Write a handler for the field to determine which text line has been clicked, and then read the song list from the appropriate page of the server using the **getRemote** command. (Since the pages of the server are sorted, the text line number should correspond to the page number.) Place the returned list in the bottom field.

Figure 26.13
In Hands-On Project B, a DDE client application is created for accessing the data in an database created earlier in Project E of Chapter 23.

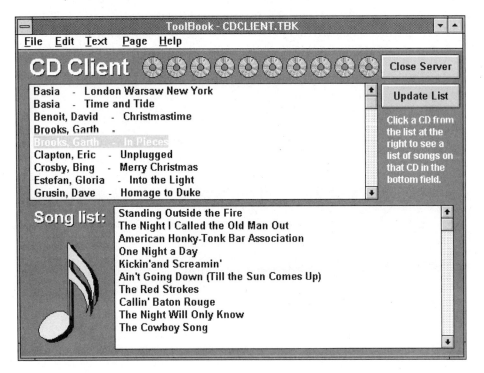

C. Create a server application consisting of a page with a text field. Create a client application consisting of buttons that allow the user to change the fontFace property of the field in the server application by using DDE commands. For instance, clicking a button labeled "Set server field to Arial" in the client sets the font of the server's field to Arial.

D. Create a logo in Windows Paintbrush, saving it as a .BMP file. Create a ToolBook application with two OLE containers. Link the .BMP file to one OLE container and embed the file in the other. Edit the Paintbrush file and watch how the appearance of the logo changes in ToolBook.

E. The TB30WIN.DLL file contains a function for converting a specified RGB (red, green, blue) color value into an HLS (hue, light, saturation) color value. Create a one-page book in which the user enters an RGB value and is told what the HLS equivalent is. The declaration statement for the RGBtoHLS function is

STRING RGBtoHLS(WORD,WORD,WORD)

The syntax for calling the function is

RGBtoHLS(*red,green,blue*)

where *red* is the numeric value of the red component; *green,* the numeric value of the green component; and *blue,* the numeric value of the blue component. Each of these is an integer between 0 and 255. The value returned is a string consisting of three items separated by commas. These items are the equivalent HLS components. (A sample application is shown in Figure 26.14.)

Figure 26.14
In Hands-On Project E, a DLL function is used to convert a specified RGB color value to its equivalent HLS color value.

Chapter 27

A Little Song and Dance
Adding Sound and Video

One of the hottest topics in today's computing world is multimedia. With the increasing availability of large-capacity hard drives and CD-ROM readers, the multimedia market has exploded in recent years. More and more entertainment software titles utilize digitized video, sound, and MIDI music. Multimedia is used in educational courseware to demonstrate procedures, provide interactive role playing, and enhance the interface. Video and sound enhance business presentations, kiosks, and other applications. The multimedia version of ToolBook is specifically designed to easily integrate digitized sound, video, MIDI music, and computer animations into created applications.

An entire book could be written on the subject of incorporating multimedia into applications created with Multimedia ToolBook. This chapter is intended merely to point the reader in the right direction by discussing some basic concepts. It is important to note that, with the exception of playing digitized sound, multimedia cannot be integrated into books created with the "regular" version of ToolBook.

The Multimedia ToolBook package includes two books that provide additional information about incorporating multimedia. The *Multimedia ToolBook User Manual and OpenScript Reference* provides information on the unique features and commands not found in the "regular" ToolBook version. The *Concise Guide to Multimedia* discusses planning a multimedia title and includes information and tips for preparing sound, video, and animation files for inclusion with ToolBook.

The Elements of Multimedia

There are several different types of multimedia information that can be included in a Multimedia ToolBook application. **Digitized sound** is recorded with a microphone and a sound card in the computer. Narrative voice, music, or sound effects can be digitized. Both ToolBook and Multimedia ToolBook can play digitized sounds saved in a **wave (.WAV) format**. **MIDI files (.MID)** contain data that a MIDI processor (synthesizer) on a sound card decodes to play a musical score. MIDI stands for musical instrument digital interface. **Digitized video** (including the video's soundtrack) are created with a video capture board. The **audio/video interleaved (.AVI) format** is the most common format used by Multimedia ToolBook authors, but Apple's QuickTime for Windows and the Motion Pictures Experts Group (MPEG) formats are also supported. Computer **animation files** are created with animation software such as Autodesk Animator or 3D-Studio, also manufactured by Autodesk. Multimedia ToolBook can play animations saved in either the .FLI or .FLC formats.

Hardware Considerations

In adding multimedia to a book, an author must consider several hardware issues. Multimedia files generally require large amounts of storage space. A minute-long digitized sound (.WAV) file can require up to 6 megabytes of storage space, depending on the sampling rate and bit depth used in capturing the sound. Likewise, a minute-long video clip digitized at 15 frames per second at a size of 160 by 120 pixels would require approximately 51 megabytes to store uncompressed at a depth of 24 bits. The sound may be digitized at a lower-quality sampling frequency and the video compressed and reduced to a depth of 8 bits, reducing the files to 1 and 2 megabytes, respectively. But even at these smaller sizes, it is obvious that storage space becomes an important issue.

The author must also consider how the application will be distributed. Distributing a multimedia presentation on diskettes is usually not practical. A larger medium, such as CD-ROM, is usually required. This might reduce the potential audience for the product, since not all computer owners have access to a CD-ROM drive.

To acceptably play back a .WAV sound file, the end-user must have a sound card. A sound digitized at 16 bits will not play on a cheaper 8-bit sound card. It may be necessary, then, to reduce the quality of the digitized sound and save it as 8-bit sound. Although MIDI files require relatively small storage space, not all sound cards have MIDI processors.

Computers with slower processors, such as the 80386 processors, will have trouble displaying digitized video. It will appear very choppy, perhaps displaying only 1 or 2 frames per second. Likewise, computers with less than Super VGA (SVGA) video cards will have trouble displaying 8- and 24-bit video clips and computer animation files.

Source Material and Legal Considerations

There are two ways of obtaining multimedia source materials. One is to create them. Sounds are digitized with a sound card and a microphone. Video clips are digitized with a videocassette recorder or camera connected to a video capture board in the computer. Animations are created with animation software, such as Animator Pro or 3D-Studio. MIDI files can be generated from an electronic keyboard or other MIDI instrument connected to a sound card. MIDI files can also be generated with MIDI composition software.

Precaptured sounds, video, animation, and MIDI files are available from various sources. Multimedia vendors sell collections of these files on disk or CD. Bulletin boards, user's groups, or archives (such as those on the Internet) are also sources of multimedia files.

Whether creating or obtaining multimedia files, one must be careful not to violate copyright laws. Digitizing a song off the radio or CD is illegal without the copyright owner's permission, as is capturing a video clip from a Hollywood movie or television show. Creating a MIDI file of a copyrighted song, such as a top-40 hit, would also be a violation. The best advice is to create original works. Digitize your own voice, shoot your own video footage, and compose your own MIDI music. Hire someone else to perform, or get permission from copyright owners to use available works. If featuring someone in a video clip or using their voice, it is wise to have them sign a release form. In purchasing multimedia works, make sure they are royalty-free or may be distributed as part of an application. Consulting a lawyer before distributing your file can save much money in legal fees, settlements, and court costs.

Playing Digitized Sound (.WAV) Files

Wave sound files have the extension .WAV and can be played in both ToolBook and Multimedia ToolBook. The **playSound( )** function is used to play an external wave

---

The playSound( ) function

Syntax: **playSound(*fileName* [,*wait*])**

Purpose: Plays the specified wave (.WAV format) audio file. A value of true is returned
            if the file was successfully played and false if it was not. The function is usually
            used with a get statement. The optional *wait* parameter may have a value of
            true or false. If true, execution of subsequent statements in the handler is
            paused until the audio file is finished playing.

Examples: get playSound(beep.wav)

            get playSound(c:\windows\sounds\beep.wav)

            get playSound(beep.wav, true)

            system activeWave
            get playSound(activeWave,true)

Figure 27.1
The playSound( ) *function*
is available in both
ToolBook and Multimedia
ToolBook to play .WAV
audio files.

sound file and works best with a file whose size is smaller than 100 kilobytes. Figure
27.1 explains the syntax of the playSound( ) function. The MMSYSTEM.DLL file must
be accessible as well as a sound driver for the installed sound card. MMSYSTEM.DLL
is installed with Windows 3.1 and should be found in the \WINDOWS\SYSTEM
subdirectory.

The following handler plays the CHIMES.WAV sound file, located in the
WINDOWS directory.

```
to handle buttonClick
    get playsound("c:\windows\chimes.wav")
end buttonClick
```

A sound can be played while the subsequent statements of the handler are executing
by including a true parameter after the filename parameter. The following handler
moves a group named cylinder to the right while the EXPLAIN1.WAV file is being
played.

```
to handle buttonClick
    get playsound("explain1.wav",true)
    step i from 1 to 20
        move group "cylinder" by 200,0
    end step
end buttonClick
```

In the following handler, the group cylinder would not be moved until after the sound
file has finished playing. This is because of the lack of a true parameter following the
filename parameter in the playsound statement.

```
to handle buttonClick
    get playsound("explain1.wav")
    step i from 1 to 20
        move group "cylinder" by 200,0
    end step
end buttonClick
```

Recording Sounds

Wave files may be created with a sound card and microphone, using the Sound Recorder software that comes with Windows (see Figure 27.2). To record a sound, click the "Microphone" button at the bottom right. Speak into the microphone and click the "stop" button (labeled with the square) when finished. A digital wave representation of the sound will appear in the window at the center of the screen. The recorded sound may be played or edited. To edit the file, a portion of the wave may be selected by dragging the mouse on the wave. The selected portion may be deleted. An effect may also be applied to the selection. Examples of effects are increasing or decreasing the volume or speed, applying an echo, or reversing the wave. These effects are all available in the Effects menu. The file is named and saved using the "Save..." or "Save As..." options in the File menu. Additional information about using the Windows Sound Recorder may be found in its on-line help.

Figure 27.2
Windows includes a sound recorder application for using a microphone to digitize sounds, voices, and music. Existing sound files may also be edited with the Sound Recorder.

Creating Clips

Other types of multimedia are played by first creating a **clip**. Clips are a reference to a segment of a multimedia file, whether it be a wave sound, an .AVI video file, a MIDI composition, or an .FLI or .FLC animation. Clips are created with the clip manager in Multimedia ToolBook. The clip manager is accessed by clicking its icon

Figure 27.3
The clip manager keeps track of available clips, allowing the author to import, export, create, and edit multimedia clips.

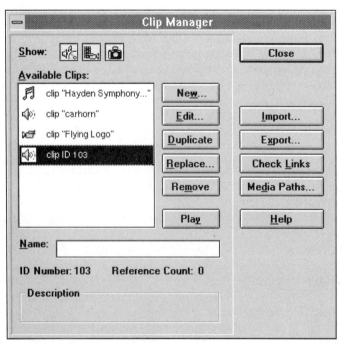

on the toolbar, choosing "Clips..." from the Objects menu, or using the keyboard equivalent of Ctrl-F9. The clip manager (see Figure 27.3) shows a reference to any clip already created or imported into the current book.

To create a clip, click the "New" button in the clip manager. The "Choose Source Type" dialog box will appear in which the format of the multimedia file is specified (see Figure 27.4). The table in Figure 27.5 discusses the meaning of the various source options. Highlight the desired type and click the "OK" button to display the "Choose Source File" dialog (see Figure 27.6). The "Choose Source File" dialog is a standard "file open" dialog in which the drive, path, and filename of a multimedia file are specified. Once the file is chosen, the clip editor is displayed with a reference to the file (see Figure 27.7). In the clip editor, beginning and ending points for the clip segment may be selected. By default, the starting point is the very beginning of the clip and the ending point is the very end of the clip. These may be changed by entering new values in the fields provided (see Figure 27.8) or by using the control buttons to play the clip

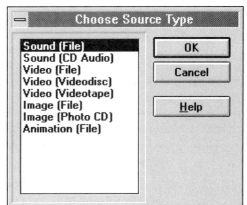

Figure 27.4
Clicking the "New" button in the clip manager brings up a dialog box for choosing the media type of the new clip.

Figure 27.5
Clips support a wide variety of multimedia formats. External devices such as CD-ROM and laser disc players may also be accessed using clips.

Source Types

Clip media type	Description	Formats
Sound (file)	Wave audio, MIDI	.WAV, .MID, .RMI
Sound (CD audio)	Access to audio CD from CD-ROM	
Video (file)	Digitized video	.AVI, .MOV, .PIC, .JPG, .MPG
Video (videodisc)	Access to attached laser disc	
Video (videotape)	Access to attached VCR	
Image (file)	High-resolution graphic	.BMP, .DIB, .RLE, .WMF, .GIF, .TIF, .PCX
Animation (file)	Computer animation file	.FLI, .FLC, .MMM

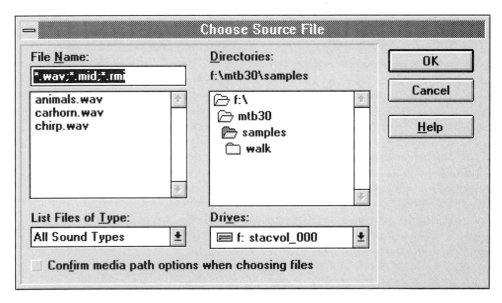

Figure 27.6
Once a source type has been selected, a file of that type may be chosen to create a clip referencing it.

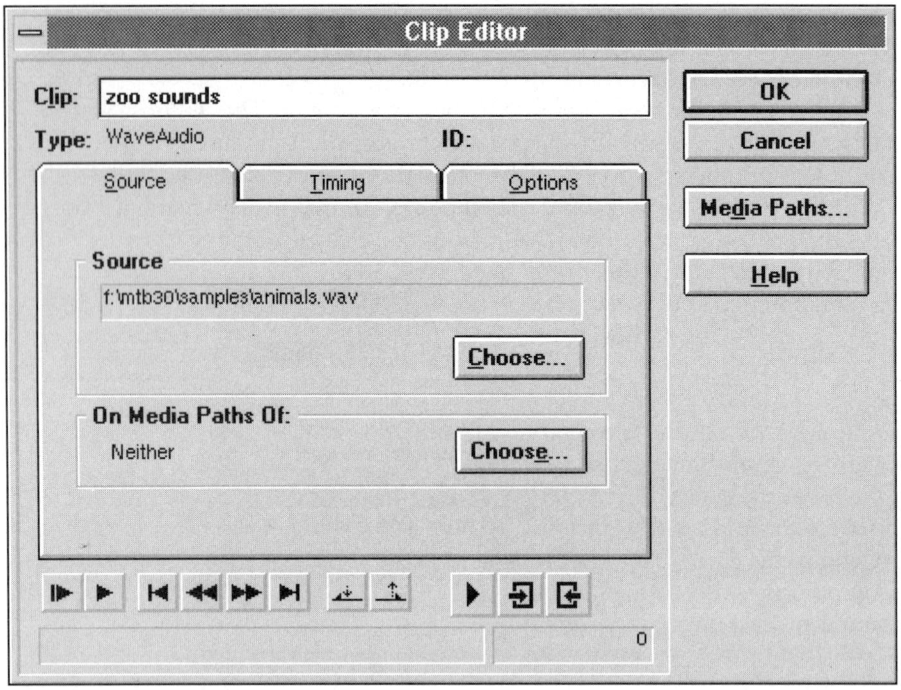

Figure 27.7
The clip editor is displayed
after a source file is chosen.
A name may be assigned to
the clip.

Figure 27.8
By using the "Timing" tab
of the clip editor, starting
and ending points may be
specified, thus allowing the
option of using only a
portion of the media file.

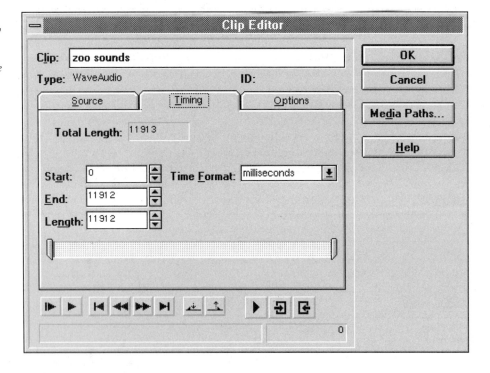

and clicking the "set start" and "set end" buttons to set these points to the current position while the clip is playing. The length of the clip segment is automatically determined from the starting and ending points and displayed. The starting point, ending point, and duration length values may be displayed in a format as specified in the "Time Format" combo box. By using the "Options" tab of the clip editor (see Figure 27.9), the volume may be specified as Mute (ignore any audio of the clip), Normal (use the current volume setting), Full (set the volume to maximum), or Custom (specify a volume level in a rating between 0 and 1000).

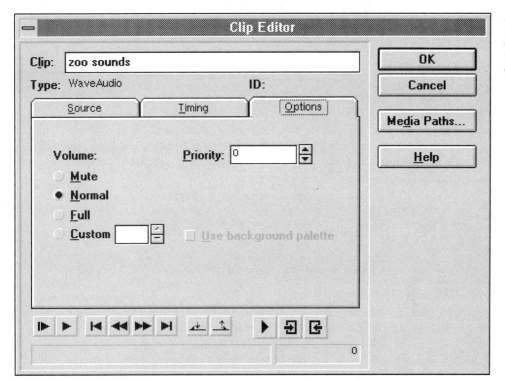

Figure 27.9
By using the "Options" tab of the clip editor, the volume may be set for the audio portion of a clip.

Playing Electronic (MIDI) Music

To play MIDI music, a clip of a MIDI file must first be created. Open the clip manager, choose "New," and select "Sound (File)" as the source type. Select a file with a .MID extension in the "Choose Source File" dialog. In the clip editor, a portion of the MIDI song may be selected by changing the starting and ending points. Enter a name for the clip on the "Source" tab screen of the clip editor and save the clip by clicking the "OK" button. The clip should now appear in the "Clip Manager" dialog. Close the clip manager.

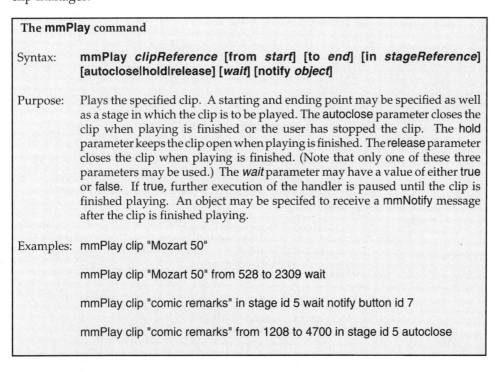

Figure 27.10
The mmPlay *command plays a mulitmedia clip. Starting and ending points may be specified as well as a stage reference for where the clip should be shown.*

The mmPlay command

Syntax: **mmPlay *clipReference* [from *start*] [to *end*] [in *stageReference*] [autoclose|hold|release] [*wait*] [notify *object*]**

Purpose: Plays the specified clip. A starting and ending point may be specified as well as a stage in which the clip is to be played. The autoclose parameter closes the clip when playing is finished or the user has stopped the clip. The hold parameter keeps the clip open when playing is finished. The release parameter closes the clip when playing is finished. (Note that only one of these three parameters may be used.) The *wait* parameter may have a value of either true or false. If true, further execution of the handler is paused until the clip is finished playing. An object may be specifed to receive a mmNotify message after the clip is finished playing.

Examples: mmPlay clip "Mozart 50"

mmPlay clip "Mozart 50" from 528 to 2309 wait

mmPlay clip "comic remarks" in stage id 5 wait notify button id 7

mmPlay clip "comic remarks" from 1208 to 4700 in stage id 5 autoclose

A clip is played using the mmPlay command (see Figure 27.10). Assuming that a MIDI file is selected in a clip named "Beethoven's Fifth", the following handler plays the clip:

```
to handle buttonClick
    mmPlay clip "Beethoven's Fifth"
end buttonClick
```

To play only a portion of a clip, the starting and ending points may also be specified in the mmPlay command. The handler that follows plays the first 10 seconds of the "Beethoven's Fifth" clip:

```
to handle buttonClick
    mmPlay clip "Beethoven's Fifth" from "00:00" to "00:10"
end buttonClick
```

Creating a Stage

Figure 27.11

A stage object is created with the stage tool (circled). A stage is created in the same manner that a rectangle is drawn, by dragging the mouse pointer diagonally from one corner to the opposite corner.

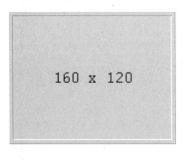

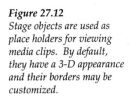

Figure 27.12

Stage objects are used as place holders for viewing media clips. By default, they have a 3-D appearance and their borders may be customized.

Multimedia ToolBook includes a stage object not found in the regular version of ToolBook. A **stage** is created by selecting the Stage tool (see Figure 27.11) and dragging the mouse diagonally from one corner to the opposite corner, in the same manner as one draws a rectangle. The stage object appears as a gray-filled rectangle with a beveled frame (see Figure 27.12). The size of the staging area in pixels is shown when in the Author mode. In the "Stage Properties" dialog (see Figure 27.13), the bevel and frame widths may be altered and a visual effect applied to the start of any graphic, video, or animation clip played in the stage.

The size of the stage may not always match the size of the clip. The stageSizing property of a stage determines how to handle this situation. When the stageSizing property is set to clipMedia, the clip is cropped to conform to the stage dimensions. How it is cropped depends on the value of the stage's stageAnchor property. If the stageAnchor property is center, the clip is centered in the stage and the outside edges cropped as necessary. If the stageAnchor is bottomRight, the bottom right corner of the clip is placed in the bottom right corner of the stage and the top and left edges are cropped as necessary. Other values of the stageAnchor property include bottomLeft, topLeft, and topRight. A stageSizing property of centerMedia centers the clip in the stage and crops the outside edges as necessary to fit the stage dimensions, regardless of the stageAnchor value. A stageSizing property of stretchMedia resizes the clip so that it corresponds to the stage's dimension; a stageSizing property of stretchStage resizes the stage so that it corresponds to the clip's dimensions. Both the stageSizing and stageAnchor properties may be set by using the "Display" tab of the "Stage Properties" dialog (see Figure 27.14) or with OpenScript commands:

```
set the stageSizing of stage id 0 to "centerMedia"
```

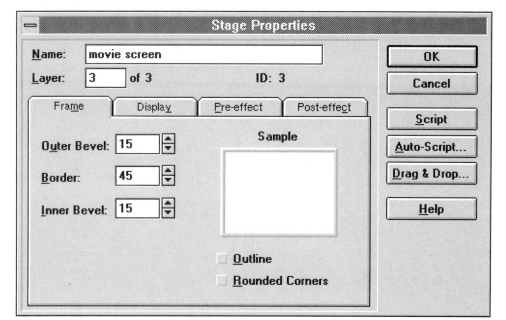

Figure 27.13
The appearance of a stage object may be altered in its "Stage Properties" dialog box by changing the width of its border and bevels. A name may be assigned to the stage, by which it may be referenced in an OpenScript command.

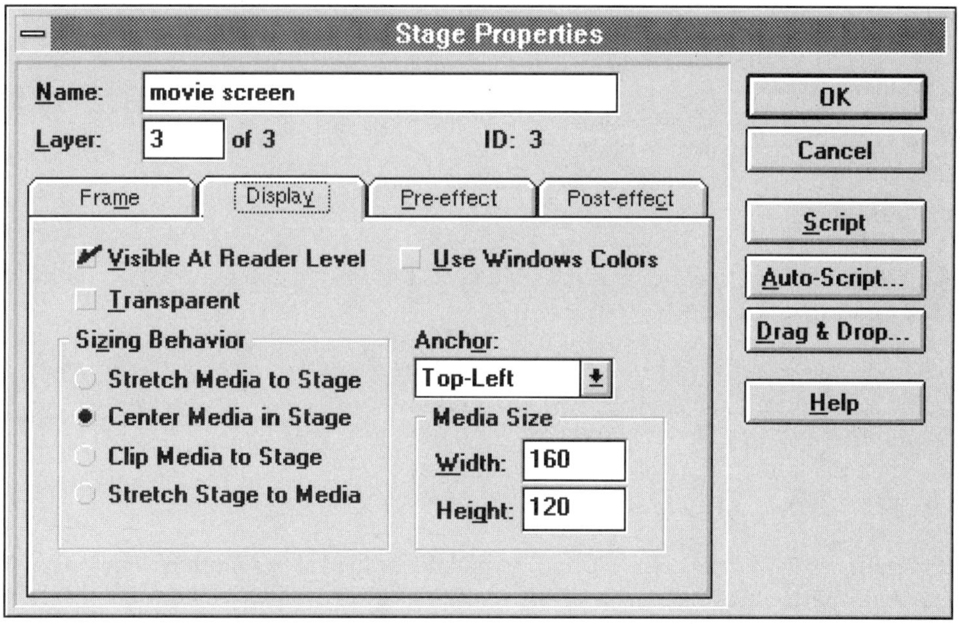

Figure 27.14
How media is displayed in a stage may be set in the "Stage Properties" dialog for the stage object. Media may be clipped to fit the stage or stretched to fit the stage, or the stage may be stretched to fit the media. Clipped media may be anchored in the center or any corner.

```
stageSizing of stage "tv" = "stretchMedia"
```

```
put "topLeft" into the stageAnchor of stage "tv"
```

```
stageAnchor of stage id 9 = "center"
```

In the same manner, the preEffect property of the stage may be set through OpenScript commands. The same effects available in the transition command may be used in the preEffect property.

```
set the preEffect of stage id 12 to "puzzle normal"
```

```
preEffect of stage "tv" = "dissolve slow"
```

```
preEffect of stage id 5 = "spiral out fast"
```

To remove a visual effect from the stage, set the preEffect property to null:

```
put "" into the preEffect of stage id 0
```

Playing a Video or Animation File

To play a video file (.AVI, .MOV, .PIC, .JPG, or .MPG format), you must create a clip of the file. Do this by choosing "Video (file)" as the source type in the "Choose Source Type" dialog accessed from the clip manager. Starting and ending points may be adjusted as desired in the clip editor. The mmPlay command is used in the same manner as playing a MIDI clip. The following handler plays the clip named my film:

```
to handle buttonClick
    mmPlay clip "my film" in stage id 5
end buttonClick
```

Since a large clip may take several seconds to load, it is advisable to set the cursor to an hourglass to visually indicate to the user that the computer is processing.

```
to handle buttonClick
    set sysCursor to 4  --set cursor to hourglass
    mmPlay clip "my film" in stage id 5
    set sysCursor to 1  --set cursor to default arrow
end buttonClick
```

As with the MIDI clip, starting and ending points for a video clip may be specified in the mmPlay command:

```
to handle buttonClick
    set sysCursor to 4  --set cursor to hourglass
    mmPlay clip "my film" from "00:05" to "01:15" in stage id 5
    set sysCursor to 1  --set cursor to default arrow
end buttonClick
```

An animation file (.FLI or .FLC format) is played in the same manner. The only difference is that a clip is made from an .FLI or .FLC file. The following handler plays an animation clip named cartoon1.

```
to handle buttonClick
    set sysCursor to 4
    mmPlay clip "cartoon1"
    set sysCursor to 1
end buttonClick
```

Other Multimedia Commands

There are several commands available for displaying and controlling media clips. Figure 27.15 discusses the syntax and use of these commands.

A clip must first be opened before the other commands may be used to reference the clip. (The mmPlay command is an exception, since it automatically opens the

Multimedia commands

mmClose clipReference [*wait*] [notify *object*]

> Closes the specified clip.
> mmClose clip "Mozart 50"

mmCue clipReference [*wait*] [notify *object*]

> Cues the specified clip to rewind to its starting position.
> mmClose cue "Mozart 50"

mmHide clipReference [*wait*] [notify *object*]

> Hides the specified clip. (Only visual clips may be hidden.)
> mmHide clip "Mozart 50"

mmIsOpen

> A property of the clip that is either true or false. If the clip is open, the value of mmIsOpen is true.
> put mmIsOpen of clip "Mozart 50" into x

mmOpen clipReference [*wait*] [notify *object*]

> Opens the specified clip. The clip must first be opened before other commands may be executed. The mmPlay command automatically opens the file.
> mmOpen clip "Mozart 50" wait

mmPause clipReference [*wait*] [notify *object*]

> Pauses the specified open clip. The clip remains open and play may be resumed with the mmPlay command.
> mmPause clip "Mozart 50" notify this page

mmSeek clipReference to position [from end] [*wait*] [notify *object*]

> Cues the clip to the specified position.
> mmSeek clip "Mozart 50" to 10000 from end

mmShow clipReference [in stageReference] [*wait*] [notify *object*]

> Shows the specified hidden clip (must already be open). A stage may be specified as well.
> mmShow clip "Mozart 50" in stage id 12

mmStatus

> A property of a clip that specifies its current status. Possible values are closed, paused, playing, seeking, stopped.
> put mmStatus of clip "Mozart 50" into clipStatus

mmStep clipReference [back] by *distance* [*wait*] [notify *object*]

> Cues the clip backwards or forwards by a specified distance from the current position. Distance value should correspond to the mmTimeFormat value.
> mmStep clip "Mozart 50" back by 1 -- step backwards by 1 frame
> mmStep clip "Mozart 50" by "00:01:00:00" --move forward by 1 minute

mmStop clipReference [*wait*] [notify *object*]

> Stops the specified clip. The clip remains open.
> mmStop clip "Mozart 50"

mmTimeFormat

> A property of the clip that determines what time format is being used. Values include milliseconds, frames, HMS (hour:minutes:seconds), TMSF (tracks:minutes: seconds:frames), HMSF (hours:minutes:seconds:frames), MS (minutes:seconds), and MSms (minutes:seconds:milliseconds).
> set mmTimeFormat of clip "Mozart 50" to "HMSF"

Figure 27.15
There are several commands and clip properties available in Multimedia ToolBook for manipulating clips from OpenScript handlers.

clip.) The following handler placed in a page script opens a clip upon entering the page:

```
to handle enterPage
    mmOpen clip "my film"
end enterPage
```

A clip name may be assigned to a variable or user-defined property. This allows the clip name to be changed in only one location, but still be available to other handlers by referencing the variable or property.

```
to handle enterPage
    system currentClip
    put "my film" into currentClip
    mmOpen clip currentClip
end enterPage

to handle playClip
    system currentClip
    mmPlay clip currentClip in stage id 0 hold
    -- the hold parameter keeps the clip open when finished playing
end playClip

to handle rewindClip
    system currentClip
    mmRewind clip currentClip
end rewindClip

to handle pauseClip
    system currentClip
    mmPause clip currentClip
end pauseClip
```

The following handler changes the time format of a clip to the HMSF format (hours:minutes:seconds:frames) and then plays a 2-minute segment from the clip, starting at the 1-minute mark:

```
to handle buttonClick
    set mmTimeFormat of clip "my film" to "HMSF"
    mmPlay clip "HMSF" from "00:01:00:00" to "00:03:00:00"
end buttonClick
```

Figure 27.16 shows a page with a stage and several buttons underneath the stage serving as controls for the video clip. The buttons, from left to right, will rewind the clip to the beginning, step the clip backward by 1 frame, play the whole clip, play the clip from the current position, pause the clip, and step the clip forward by 1 frame.

The caption of the button that controls clip opening and closing changes according to whether a clip is currently open or not. If a clip is open, the caption is "Close Clip." If a clip is not open, the button's caption is "Close Clip." The button contains the following script:

```
to handle buttonClick
    system activeClip
    if my caption = "Open Clip" then
```

Developing with Asymetrix ToolBook

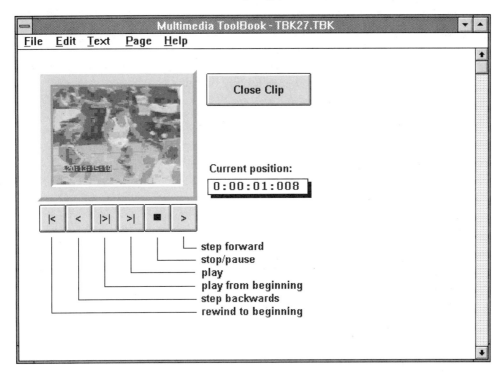

Figure 27.16
Buttons may be created to
control the playing of a clip.

```
        set syscursor to 4
        put "" into text of field clips
        put resourceList(clip,this book) into x
        put itemCount(x) into y
        step i from 1 to y
            if (item 3 of resourceInfo of (item i of x)) contains "video" \
            or (item 3 of resourceInfo of (item i of x)) contains "animation"
                put (item 2 of resourceInfo of (item i of x)) & \
                crlf after text of field clips
            end if
        end step
        clear last textline of text of field "clips"
        if text of field "clips" = "" then
            request "There are no video or animation clips in this book."
        else
            show group chooseClip
        end if
        set sysCursor to 1
        set my caption to "Close Clip"
    else
        mmclose activeClip
        set my caption to "Open Clip"
        put "" into activeClip
        put "no file" into text of field "clip position"
    end if
end buttonClick
```

When no clip is open, this script retrieves the names of all clips associated with the book. It displays the names of those clips whose source is either a video or animation. The user chooses one to open. The field in which these clip names are displayed is initially hidden, and the preceding script shows the field (as part of a group). The caption of the button is changed to "Close Clip." If a clip is open, the script closes the clip (based on the clip name contained in the system variable, activeClip) and puts a null string into activeClip.

The field containing the video or animation clip names is part of the chooseClip group. It is activated and contains the following handler:

```
to handle buttonClick loc
    system activeClip
    put textline (item 1 of textfrompoint(loc)) of my text into activeClip
    mmOpen activeClip
    mmShow activeClip in stage "movie screen"
    hide group chooseClip
    set mmTimeFormat of activeClip to "HMSF"
    put the mmPosition of activeClip into text of field "clip position"
end buttonClick
```

The preceding script determines which line of text the user clicked, placing the text (the name of the clip) into the activeClip variable and then opens the appropriate clip and displays it in the stage. The chooseClip group is hidden, and the cue position of the clip displayed in an hours:minutes:seconds:frames format.

The button for rewinding the clip to the beginning contains the following script:

```
to handle buttonClick
    system activeClip
    if activeClip <> "" then
        mmCue activeClip
        set mmTimeFormat of activeClip to "HMSF"
        put the mmPosition of activeClip into text of field "clip position"
    end if
end buttonClick
```

The end...if causes the command to not execute (and therefore not to generate an error) if no clip is currently open and assigned to the activeClip variable. The time format of the clip is set to the HMSF format and the cue position of the clip is placed in the text of the "Clip Position" field.

The button for stepping the clip backward by 1 frame contains the following script:

```
to handle buttonDown
    system activeClip
    if activeClip <> "" then
        set mmTimeFormat of activeClip to "frames"
        if mmPosition of activeClip > 1 then
            mmStep activeClip back by "1"
            set mmTimeFormat of activeClip to "HMSF"
            put the mmPosition of activeClip into text of field "clip position"
        end if
    end if
end buttonDown

to handle buttonStillDown
    system activeClip
    if activeClip <> "" then
        set mmTimeFormat of activeClip to "frames"
```

```
          if mmPosition of activeClip > 1 then
              mmStep activeClip back by "1"
              set mmTimeFormat of activeClip to "HMSF"
              put the mmPosition of activeClip into text of field "clip position"
          end if
      end if
  end buttonStillDown
```

By having both a buttonDown and buttonStillDown handler, the user can step backward 1 frame by clicking the button. He or she can step backward multiple frames by holding down the left mouse button. This is much more desirable than having to press the mouse button 100 times to move backwards by 100 frames! The mmStep command is used to change the cue position of the clip backward by 1 frame. The current position of the clip is displayed in the "Clip Position" field in an HMSF format.

The script of the button to play the entire clip is

```
  to handle buttonClick
      system activeClip
      if activeClip <> "" then
          mmPlay activeClip from start in stage "movie screen" hold
          --the hold parameter keeps the clip open when finished playing
          set the mmTimeFormat of activeClip to "HMSF"
          put the mmPosition of activeClip into text of field "clip position"
      end if
  end buttonClick
```

The words start and end may be used in lieu of time code. If no starting point is provided in the mmPlay command, the clip begins playing at its current cue position. The "Play" button then has a script identical to the button for playing the entire clip, except that it does not specify the starting point.

```
  to handle buttonClick
      system activeClip
      if activeClip <> "" then
          mmPlay activeClip in stage "movie screen" hold
          --the hold parameter keeps the clip open when finished playing
          set the mmTimeFormat of activeClip to "HMSF"
          put the mmPosition of activeClip into text of field "clip position"
      end if
  end buttonClick
```

The script for the button to pause the clip is

```
  to handle buttonClick
      system activeClip
      if activeClip <> "" then
          mmPause activeClip
          set the mmTimeFormat of activeClip to "HMSF"
          put the mmPosition of activeClip into text of field "clip position"
      end if
  end buttonClick
```

The script for the button to step the clip forward is similar to the script for stepping it backward. The mmLength property of the clip is used as a comparison point to ensure that an attempt is not made to step the clip's position past its ending point. The back parameter is removed from the mmStep command so that the clip is stepped forward and not backward:

```
to handle buttonDown
    system activeClip
    if activeClip <> "" then
        set mmTimeFormat of activeClip to "frames"
        if mmPosition of activeClip < mmLength of activeClip then
            mmStep activeClip by "1"
            set mmTimeFormat of activeClip to "HMSF"
            put the mmPosition of activeClip into text of field "clip position"
        end if
    end if
end buttonDown

to handle buttonStillDown
    system activeClip
    if activeClip <> "" then
        set mmTimeFormat of activeClip to "frames"
        if mmPosition of activeClip < mmLength of activeClip then
            mmStep activeClip by "1"
            set mmTimeFormat of activeClip to "HMSF"
            put the mmPosition of activeClip into text of field "clip position"
        end if
    end if
end buttonStillDown
```

The page script might contain enterPage and leavePage handlers to initially declare the activeClip variable and automatically close a clip if one is open.

```
to handle enterPage
    system activeClip
    put "" into activeClip
end enterPage

to handle leavePage
    system activeClip
    if activeClip <> "" then
        mmClose clip activeClip
        put "" into activeClip
    end if
end leavePage
```

Displaying a Graphic in a Stage

A clip may also be made of a graphic file and displayed in a stage by using the mmPlay command. In developing the clip, an image (file) is chosen as the source type. The following handler is used to toggle the display of a graphic in a stage.

```
to handle buttonClick
    set sysCursor to 0
    if the caption of self is "Show jet bmp" then
        mmPlay clip "jet bmp" in stage id 0
        set caption of self to "Hide jet bmp"
    else
        mmClose clip "jet bmp"
        set caption of self to "Show jet bmp"
    end if
    set sysCursor to 1
end buttonClick
```

The Digital Video Producer

Multimedia ToolBook includes a utility for mixing video and audio files. Digital Video Producer (Figure 27.17) is an A/B editor, which means two separate video sources may be mixed simultaneously and various transition effects applied. Titles may be overlayed on the video, and up to two different audio files may be mixed in. The final production may be saved as an .AVI file, which may then be chosen as a clip source in ToolBook's clip manager. For information on how to use Digital Video Producer, consult its on-line help. (Note: Although Digital Video Producer is shipped with Multimedia ToolBook, it is not automatically installed when ToolBook is installed. It is installed separately as an option through the Multimedia ToolBook Installer.)

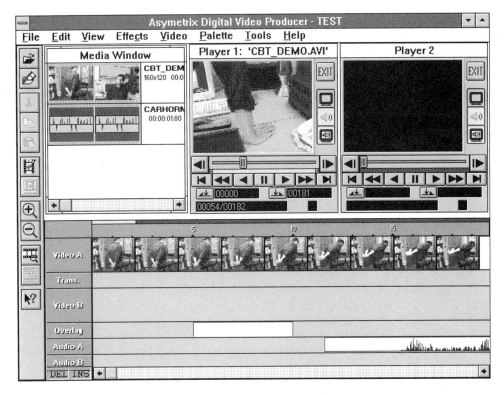

Figure 27.17
Multimedia ToolBook includes Digital Video Producer, an application for mixing multiple video, animation, and audio files into one video file.

Summary Questions
Answer the following true/false questions.
1. Only Multimedia ToolBook (not regular ToolBook) can play a wave (.WAV) audio file.
2. Regular ToolBook cannot play an .AVI movie file.
3. A song digitized from the radio can be legally included in a multimedia presentation as long as credit is given to the composer and performer.
4. Sounds may be digitized using a sound card and a microphone.
5. A file with the extension .FLI is most likely a computer animation file.
6. The mmPlay command is used to play a multimedia clip.
7. An mmTimeFormat setting of HMSF produces an hours:minutes:seconds:fields format.
8. MIDI files may be generated with an electronic keyboard connected to a computer via a MIDI-compatible sound card.
9. Only computers equipped with a sound card having a MIDI processor can play MIDI files.
10. Stage objects are always 160 by 120 pixels in size.

Complete the following statements by filling in the blanks.
11. Musical files containing data that a synthesizer processor on a sound card decodes to play a musical score are referred to as _____ files.
12. _____ are references to a segment or a multimedia file.
13. Wave audio files have the extension _____ .
14. The _____ function is used to play a wave audio file.
15. The _____ property of a stage determines how a clip is cropped in the stage.
16. The _____ property of a stage determines whether the stage is resized to fit the clip, the clip is resized to fit the stage, or the clip is centered in the stage or anchored elsewhere in the stage and cropped to fit.
17. The _____ command is used to cue a clip to a specified position.
18. Stage objects are created with the _____ tool.
19. The most popular digitized video format used by ToolBook authors is _____ .
20. The starting and ending points of a clip are set in the _____ _____ .

Hands-On Projects
A. Examine the software that accompanies this chapter. Open the "Table of Contents" book by double-clicking its icon in the "Developing with ToolBook" group window in the Windows Program Manager. Inside the "Table of Contents," click the book representing Chapter 27. Work your way through the tutorial as a means of reinforcing and demonstrating the information presented in this chapter.

B. Record your voice by using a sound card and microphone. Save the file as wave audio. Create a ToolBook book with a button on the first page that plays your recording when clicked.

C. Multimedia ToolBook ships with several sample multimedia files, such as:
/MTB30/SAMPLES/ASYM01.AVI
/MTB30/SAMPLES/CBT_DEMO.AVI
/MTB30/SAMPLES/WALK/FOUL.AVI
Create a book with a stage and a button that plays one of these files in the stage when clicked. (Remember a clip of the file must first be created.)

D. If you have a MIDI-compatible sound card, locate an .MID file (several probably accompanied the sound card) and create a book with a button that plays the MIDI file when clicked. (Remember to create a clip.)

E. Embellish the animal database created in Chapter 20 in Hands-On Project E by adding buttons that play a digitized reading of the text about each animal and/or sounds made by that animal.

F. Create an application that helps beginning readers recognize letters and/or words. The application should use digitized sound to pronounce words or sound out letters when prompted to do so by the user. Use your creativity!

Appendices

Appendix A

OpenScript Commands, Keywords, and Structures

This appendix contains an alphabetical list of the OpenScript commands and structures available in ToolBook 3.0 and Multimedia ToolBook 3.0. They are listed in the following format:

command   syntax   Page
    Brief description of purpose and use.

Italicized words in the syntax listing indicate references to be specified by author. Phrases in brackets, [ ], indicate optional parts of the statement. Not all the commands listed are discussed in this book. Those not discussed are cited with N/A (not applicable) as a page reference. The on-line help should be consulted for more information on these commands. Commands with a film icon in the margin (as at the right) indicate a command that is only available in Multimedia ToolBook. All other commands are available in both ToolBook and Multimedia ToolBook.

---

activate   activate *viewerReference*   N/A
    Activates a viewer and brings it up to the front.

add menu   add menu *name* [position *number*] [at *level*]   310
    Adds a menu to the menubar.

add menultem add menultem *name* to *menu* [position *number*] [at *level*]   309
    Adds a menu item to the specified menu.

align   align *type*   N/A
    Aligns selected objects according to *type* parameter, for example, left or bottom.

ask   ask *promptString* [with *defaultResponse*]   200
    Generates a dialog box in which the user may input a string.

beep   beep *number*   160
    Plays the system beep sound the specified number of times.

break   break [step|while|do|conditions|*handlerMessage*]   274
    Used to prematurely exit a control structure or handler.

check menultem   check menultem *name* [in *menu*][at *level*]   N/A
    Places a check mark next to the specified menu item.

clear   clear *object*   N/A
    Deletes the object or the contents of the object, such as the text of a field.

close   close *viewerReference*   N/A
          Closes the specified viewer.

closeFile   closeFile *filename*   337
          Closes the specified open file.

closeRemote   closeRemote application *server* topic *topicName*   408
          Closes a DDE channel kept open with the keepRemote command.

conditions...when   conditions   236
                    when *BooleanExpression1*
                         statements to be executed if BooleanExpression1 is true
                    when *BooleanExpression2*
                         statements to be executed if BooleanExpression2 is true
                    . . .
                    when *BooleanExpressionN*
                         statements to be executed if BooleanExpressionN is true
               end conditions
          A decision branch structure that executes the branch statement(s) of the first
          Boolean expression that is true.

continue   continue [do|step [*value*]|while]   274
          Skips the remaining statements within a loop and repeats the loop from the top
          of the structure.

copy resource   copy resource *resource* to *book*   N/A
          Copies a resource from the current book to another book.

createFile   createFile *filename*   341
          Creates and opens an empty file with the specified path and filename.

decrement   decrement *container* [by *value*]   216
          Decreases the numeric value of a container by the specified amount.

disable menu   disable menu *name* [at *level*]   306
          Disables a menu so it appears dimmed and may not be selected.

disable menuItem   disable menuItem *name* [in *menu*] [at *level*]   306
          Disables a menu item on a menu so that it appears dimmed and may not be
          selected.

do...until   do   270
                    statement(s) to be executed with each iteration
               until *BooleanExpression*
          A conditional loop structure that executes repeatedly until the specified
          expression is true.

drag   drag *source* [within *bounds*] [silently]   N/A
          Begins a drag and drop operation.

draw   draw *objectType* from *location* to *location* [to location...]   399
          Creates an object of the specified type, using the specified coordinates.

edit script   edit [the] script of *object*   N/A
          Brings up the script editor with the specified object's script.

enable menu   enable menu *name* [at *level*]   309
    Enables a previously disabled menu so that it may be selected.

enable menuItem   enable menuItem *name* [in *menu*] [at *level*]   308
    Enables a menu item previously disabled so that it may be selected.

end   end [*message*]   158
    Marks the termination point of a handler.

execute   execute *source*   N/A
    Executes the source as an OpenScript statement. (The source might be a concatenated string, the text of a field, etc.)

executeRemote   executeRemote *command* application *application* \
                  [topic *serverTopic*]   412
    Remotely executes a command in the DDE server application.

export   export *fileName* as *type* using *integers\separator*   N/A
    Exports text from all recordfields of current background to ASCII text file.

export resource   export resource *resource* as *fileName*   N/A
    Exports a resource as an external file.

extend select   extend select *object(s)*   N/A
    Extends the current selection to include the specified object or objects.

fill   fill *array* with *expression* [in [*parseOrder* [*parseOrder*] ...]order] 326
    Fills an array with the specified value(s).

flip   flip [all*number*] [pages]   N/A
    Displays the pages of a book in order, as if turning the pages.

format   format [number] *container* as *newFormat* [from *oldFormat*] **or**   219
              format date *container* as *newFormat* [from *oldFormat*] **or**
              format time *container* as *newFormat* [from *oldFormat*]
    Used to convert the format of data contained in a variable or other container.

forward   forward [*message*] [*parameters*]   160
    Sends a message to the next-highest object in the object hierarchy.

fxDissolve   fxDissolve [*speed*] [to *destination*]   N/A
    Provides a visual effect in which the current page seems to dissolve into another page or into solid black, white, or gray. (Compare the transition command.)

fxWipe   fxWipe *direction* [*speed*] [to *destination*]   N/A
    Provides a visual effect that wipes the current page off the screen to reveal another page, or solid black, white, or gray. (Compare the transition command.)

fxZoom   fxZoom *speed* [to *destination*] [at *location*]   N/A
    Provides a visual effect of zooming in from the current page to reveal another page or solid balck, gray, or white. (Compare the transition command.)

get   get *expression*   244
    Evaluates the specified expression, assigning the value to variable it.

getRemote   getRemote *item* application *application* [topic *serverTopic*]   408
Returns the value of the specified item from the server application.

go   go [to] *page*   157
Navigates to the specified page.

hide   hide *object*   183
Sets the visible property of an object to false, making it invisible.

if...then   if *BooleanExpression* then   232
                     statements to execute if true
          [else
                     statements to execute if false]
          end if
Decision branch structure used to execute statements based on whether a specified condition is true or not.

import   import *fileName* as *type* using *integer/separator*   N/A
Imports a file into the current book.

import book   import book fileName   N/A
Imports the pages from the specified book, placing them after the current page.

import pages   import pages *startingPage* to *endingPage* of book *fileName*   N/A
Imports a range of pages from a book, placing them after the current page.

import resource   import *type* resource *fileName* [as *name*]   N/A
Imports a resource file into a book.

importGraphic   importGraphic *fileName*   N/A
Imports an object-oriented graphic file as a picture or a bitmap graphic file as a paint object.

increment   increment *container* [by *value*]   216
Increases the numeric value of a container by the specified amount.

insert graphic   insert graphic *resource placement container*   N/A
Inserts a graphic as a character in a text container.

installFontResource   installFontResource *resourceReference*   N/A
Installs a TrueType font resource, stored in the book, into Windows.

keepRemote   keepRemote application *server* topic *topicName*   408
Keeps the DDE communication channel between ToolBook and the specified server application open.

linkDLL   linkDLL *DLLFilename*   417
                     returnType functionName(parameterTypes)
          end linkDLL
Links a DLL file and declares a function or functions of the DLL file.

local   local [*type*] *variable(s)*   176
Used to declare a variable or list of variables as having a local scope and/or to declare the type (for example, INT) of data contained by a variable.

magnify   magnify *power* [at *location*]   N/A
    Magnifies view of current page at specified location.

mmClose   mmClose *clipReference* [*wait*][notify *object*]   435
    Closes an open multimedia clip.

mmCue   mmCue *clipReference* [*wait*][notify *object*]   435
    Rewinds the clip to its starting point.

mmHide   mmHide *clipReference* [*wait*][notify *object*]   435
    Hides a visual clip.

mmOpen   mmOpen *clipReference* [*wait*][notify *object*]   435
    Opens a multimedia clip.

mmPause   mmPause *clipReference* [*wait*][notify *object*]   435
    Pauses a clip being played. (Play may be resumed with the mmPlay command.)

mmPlay   mmPlay *clipReference* [from *start*][to *end*] \   431
                     [in *stageReference*][autoclose|hold|release][*wait*][notify *object*]
    Opens and plays the specified audio/video clip.

mmRewind   mmRewind *clipReference* [*wait*][notify *object*]   N/A
    Stops a clip if it is playing and cues it to the beginning position.

mmSeek   mmSeek *clipReference* to *position* [from end][*wait*]\   435
                     [notify *object*]
    Cues the clip to the specified position.

mmShow   mmShow *clipReference* [in *stageReference*][*wait*][notify *object*]435
    Shows the hidden clip (which must already be open).

mmStep   mmStep *clipReference* [back] by *distance* [*wait*][notify *object*] 435
    Cues, by the specified distance, the clip backwards or forwards from the current
    position.

mmStop   mmStop *clipReference* [*wait*][notify *object*]   435
    Stops the clip while playing.

move   move *object* to *location* **or**   381
                     move *object* by *offsetAmount*
    Moves an object to a specified location or by a specified distance.

new clip   new clip from *mediaSource*   N/A
    Creates a new clip.

new viewer   new viewer   N/A
    Creates a new viewer and assigns the reference of itself to the varaible it.

notifyAfter   notifyAfter   197
    Begins a handler that allows an object to receive a message targeted for the page
    after the message is handled by the page script.

notifyBefore   notifyBefore *message*   197
Begins a handler that allows an object to receive a message targeted for the page before the message is sent to the page.

open   open *viewer*   N/A
Opens a viewer without showing it.

openFile   openFile *filename*   336
Opens a file for the purpose of reading from it or writing to it.

pause   pause *duration*   247
Pauses the execution of a handler for the specified length of time.

pop   pop *stack* into|after|before *container*   275
Places first item of stack into, after, or before the value of the specified container.

print   print *number* [pages]   348
Prints the specified number of pages of the book, or a report of recordfield data.

print eject   print eject   N/A
Advances printer to the top of the next sheet (that is, sends a form feed to the printer).

push   push *value* onto *stack*   275
Places a value as the first item in a comma-delimited list (stack).

put   put *value* into *container*   180
Assigns a value to a variable or property, such as the text of a field.

readFile   readFile *filename* to *character* **or**   336
                    readFile *filename* for *numberOfCharacters*
Reads data from the specified open file.

remove backgroundImage   remove backgroundImage   N/A
Removes all stored images of the current background.

remove menu   remove menu *name* [at *level*]   .   307
Removes menu and its menu items from the menubar.

remove menuItem   remove menuItem *name* [in *menu*] [at *level*]   307
Removes a menu item so that it does not appear.

remove pageImage   remove pageImage   N/A
Removes all stored images of the current page.

remove separator   remove separator *number* in menu *name* [at *level*] N/A
Removes the separator bar between menu items on a menu.

replace resource   replace resource *resourceReference* with *fileName*   N/A
Replaces a resource in the current book with a resource file.

request   request *prompt* [with *response1* [or *response2* [or *response3*]]] 198
Displays an input dialog box consisting of a prompt string and up to three response buttons.

respondRemote respondRemote *response* N/A
    Sends, from the server application to the client application, a message regarding the success of a command sent from the client.

restore menubar restore menubar 308
    Restores menubar to default menus and menu items.

restore system restore system N/A
    Destroys all system variables, restores system properties to their defaults, and unlinks all DLLs.

return return value 288
    Returns a value to the calling statement from a user-defined function.

run run application *fileName* minimized N/A
    Launches an application and opens the specified file.

save as save as *fileName, overwrite* N/A
    Saves the current book under the specified file and path.

save as EXE save as EXE *fileName, overwrite* N/A
    Saves the current book as an executable (.EXE) file under the specified name.

save changes save changes to *bookReference* N/A
    Saves the changes made to a book (which does not have to be the current book).

search search [page] for *string* [by case][as word][locateOnly] **or** 365
    search [page] records for string [by case][as word][locateOnly] **or**
    search [page] excluding background for string [by case]\
        [as word][locateOnly]
    or
    search [page] in *recordfield* [,*recordField*...] for *string* [by case]\
        [as word][locateOnly]
    or
    search again
    Searches for a specified string.

seed seed *number* 220
    Provides a number for use by the algorithm used in generating a random number.

seekFile seekFile *filename* for *position* from *location* 346
    Moves, to the specified location, the read-write pointer in an external open file.

select select *object* **or** N/A
    select *string* **or**
    select all **or**
    select all from *location* to *location*
    Changes current selection to that specified.

send send *message* [to *targetObject*] 282
    Sends a message to the specified object (or to itself if no target is given).

sendNotifyAfter sendNotifyAfter *message* [*parameters*] [to *object*] N/A
    Executes a notifyAfter handler for the specified message of the target object.

sendNotifyBefore   sendNotifyBefore *message* [*parameters*] [to *object*]   N/A
Executes a notifyBefore handler for the specified message of the target object.

set   set *container* to *value*   246
Assigns a value to a container, most often a property.

setRemote   setRemote *item* to *value* application *application* \   411
                   [topic *serverTopic*]
Sets value of specified item in the server application.

show   show object   183
Sets the visible property of an object to true, making it visible.

sort   sort [pages *start* to *end*] by [*order*] [*type*] *sortExpression*   356
Sorts the pages of a book by the specified expression.

start spooler start spooler   348
                        print statements go here
                   end spooler
Structure for performing a print job.

step...end step step *counter* from *beginning* to *ending* [by *stepValue*]   267
                        statements to be executed with each iteration of the loop
                   end [step]
A fixed-iteration loop structure that executes its contained statement(s) a certain
number of times.

store backgroundImage   store backgroundImage   N/A
Stores a compressed device-dependent version of the current background.

store pageImage   store pageImage   N/A
Stores a compressed device-dependent version of the current page.

system   system [*type*] *variable(s)*   177
Used to declare a variable or list of variables as having a global (system) scope.
The type of data contained by the system variable may also be specified.

to get   to get *functionName* [*parameters*]   288
Defines the beginning of a user-defined function handler.

to handle   to handle *message* [*parameters*]   157
Defines the beginning of a handler for responding to a specified message.

to set   to set *property* [*parameters*] to *value*   286
A handler structure used for setting the value of a user-defined property.

transition   transition *effect* [at *coordinate*] to *destination*   N/A
Performs a visual transition effect from the current page to another page or solid
color.

translateWindowMessage   translateWindowMessage [for *winHandle*]\ N/A
                                on *winMsg* send *tbkMsg* [to *tbkObj*]
Control structure for establishing Windows-to-OpenScript message
translation.

uncheck menuItem   uncheck menuItem *name* [in *menu*] [at *level*]   N/A
  Removes a check mark from before the specified menu item.

unlinkDLL   unlinkDLL *DLLFilename*   418
  Closes the link between ToolBook and the specified DLL file.

unselect   unselect *objects*   N/A
  Unselects any selected object(s).

untranslateAllWindowMessages untranslateAllWindowMessages \   N/A
          [for *winHandle*]
  Removes all Windows-to-Openscript translation for the specified window.

untranslateWindowMessage   untranslateWindowMessage *winMsg* \   N/A
          [for *winHandle*]
  Stops translating to OpenScript the specified Windows message.

while...end while   while BooleanExpression   268
        statements to be executed while BooleanExpression is true
        end [while]
  A conditional loop structure that executes its contained statements repeatedly as
  long as the specified condition is met.

writeFile   writeFile *data* to *filename*   340
  Writes data to an open file.

Appendix

B

Object Properties

This appendix lists the default properties of various objects. They are organized alphabetically by object and a brief description of the property accompanies each in this format:

Object
property   A brief description of the property.

Italicized property names are available in Multimedia ToolBook only. All others are available in both ToolBook and Multimedia ToolBook. Properties whose descriptions are followed by an asterisk, *, indicate a property that may not be set by the author or user, but which are gettable.

Background Properties

fillColor   Specifies, in HLS format, the fill color of the background.
idNumber   Specifies the ID number of the background assigned by ToolBook.*
imageInvalid   Indicates whether the image has been changed since last stored.
name   Identifies name of up to 32 characters.
notifyObjects   Lists background objects containing notifyBefore or notifyAfter handlers.*
object   Specifies the type of object (i.e., background).*
objects   Lists the unique name of each background object.*
pageCount   Contains the number of pages that share the background.*
parent   Specifies the next-highest object in the object hierarchy.*
pattern   Contains the current fill pattern of the background.
percentFreeSpace   Approximates free memory available to the background.*
rgbFill   Specifies, in RGB format, the fill color of the background.
rgbStroke   Specifies, in RGB format, the stroke color of the background.
script   Contains the handlers associated with the background.
size   Cites, in page units, the width and height of a background.
storedImages   Provides information about stored images of the background.*
storeImage   Defines if the off-screen image of the background is stored automatically or not.
strokeColor   Cites, in HLS format, the stroke color of the background.
uniqueName   Specifies, the unique name of the background.*
userProperties   Provides a list of user-defined background properties.*
useWindowsColors   Specifies whether background is drawn with default Windows colors as determined in the Windows control panel.

Book Properties

activeCacheFile	Specifies whether a cache file is used by the book and if so, what type it is. (Used in optimizing book for CD-ROM.)*
backgroundCount	Cites the number of backgrounds contained in the book.*
buildCacheFile	Specifies whether a CD-ROM application uses a cache file.
cacheFileType	Defines the amount of data saved to a cache file.
CDMediaPath	Specifies CD-ROM directories searched for multimedia files.
customColors	Specifies the 64 different colors contained in the Color palette.
ftsIndexname	Defines the filename of the index settings file for full-text searching.
ftsSetFile	Specifies the path of the index settings file for full-text searching.
footer	Defines the contents of the footer printed on each page of a report.
HDMediaPath	Defines the hard drive directories searched for multimedia files.
header	Defines the contents of the header printed on each page of a report.
hotwordStyle	Defines the default style for hotwords in the book.
keepMenuBar	Defines how the menubar is managed when navigating from book to book.
name	Cites the filename of the book.
object	Specifies the type of object (i.e., book).*
pageCount	Cites the number of pages contained in the book.*
palette	Specifies the Color palette associated with the book.
saveOnClose	Defines when and how a book is automatically saved.
script	Contains the handlers associated with the book.
size	Cites in page units, the width and height of a default page.
solidColorsEnabled	Specifies whether book uses solid colors or dithered colors.
uniqueName	Defines the unique name of the book (including path name and filename).*
userProperties	Cites a list of user-defined book properties.*
windows	Cites a list of viewers contained in the book.*

Button Properties

borderStyle	Defines the visual style of button (e.g., pushButton).
bounds	Cites, in page units, the upper left and lower right coordinates.
caption	Defines the text (up to 255 characters) that appears on the button.
captionPosition	Defines location of caption on the button.
checked	Defines the checked state of the button.
checkedGraphic	Cites the graphic shown when button is in the checked state.
defaultAllowDrag	Defines whether button may be dragged by default.
defaultAllowDrop	Defines whether button accepts a drop by default.
disabledGraphic	Cites the graphic shown when button is in disabled state.
dragImage	Cites graphic shown as cursor when button is being dragged.
drawDirect	Defines whether button is drawn directly or off screen.
enabled	Defines whether the button is active and can receive the focus.
excludeTab	Defines whether button can receive focus by tabbing, etc.
fillColor	Cites, in HLS format, the fill color of the button.

fontFace	Defines the font used for the button's caption.
fontSize	Defines, in points, the text size of the button's caption.
fontStyle	Defines the font style (e.g., **bold** or *italic*) used for the caption.
ftsExclude	Specifies whether button is excluded or not from full-text searching.
ftsSection	Specifies section assigned to button for full-text searching.
highlight	Specifies whether a button flashes briefly when clicked.
idNumber	Cites the ID number of the button assigned by ToolBook.*
invert	Specifies whether a button appears in reverse video.
invertGraphic	Specifies the graphic displayed when the button is in an inverted state.
layer	Specifies the button's layer number on the page or background.
name	Establishes name of up to 32 characters, given by author.
noDropImage	Specifies graphic used as cursor when dragged object is over button and button does not allow a drop.
normalGraphic	Cites the graphic displayed when button is in normal state.
object	Specifies the type of object (i.e., button).*
parent	Refers to the next-highest object in the object hierarchy.*
position	Cites the upper left coordinates of the button.
rgbFill	Specifies, in RGB format, the fill color of the button.
rgbStroke	Specifies, in RGB format, the stroke color of the button.
size	Cites, in page units, the width and height of the button.
script	Contains the handlers associated with the button.
stretchGraphic	Specifies whether a bitmap is stretched to fill the whole graphic area of a button.
strokeColor	Specifies, in HLS format, the stroke color of the button.
textOverFlow	Cites the number of characters clipped in the button's caption at the right or bottom edges.*
textUnderFlow	Cites the number of characters clipped in the button's caption at the left or top edges.*
transparent	Specifies whether a button is transparent or opaque.
uniqueName	Provides the unique name of the button.
userProperties	Provides a list of user-defined button properties.
useWindowsColors	Specifies whether a button is drawn with default Windows colors as determined in the Windows control panel.
vertices	Defines, in page units, the coordinates of the four corners of the button's boundary.
visible	Specifies whether the button is in a hidden or shown state.

Clip Properties

idNumber	Cites the ID number of the clip assigned by ToolBook.*
mmBackgroundPalette	Defines whether book's palette or clip's palette has higher priority.
mmBeginPoint	Specifies beginning of clip in relation to beginning of source.
mmClipHandle	Cites handle reference of MMTB window owning the clip's play window (as created by the device driver).*
mmDeviceAlias	Cites alias used for the clip (assigned by MMTB).*
mmDeviceHandle	Specifies handle reference of the clip's play window.*
mmEndPoint	Specifies ending of clip in relation to beginning of source.
mmIsOpen	Defines whether a clip is open or not.*
mmLength	Cites the length of the clip in the time format as specified by the clip's mmTimeFormat property.*

mmMediaType	Specifies the type of media that the clip consists of.*
mmPlayable	Defines whether the clip can be played on the current system or not.*
mmPosition	Defines the current position of the clip in relation to mmBeginpath.*
mmPriority	Specifies the clip's priority relative to other clips using the same device channel.
mmSearchCD	Cites whether MMTB searches directories specified in the book's **CDMediaPath** property for media files.
mmSearchHD	Defines whether MMTB searches directories specified in the book's **HDMediaPath** property for media files.
mmSource	References media source file or device.
mmSourceLength	Defines length of clip's source file.*
mmSourcePosition	Cites current position of clip relative to source file beginning.*
mmSourceTrackCount	Specifies the number of tracks in the clip's source file.*
mmSourceTrackInfo	Cites beginning and length of track in the clip's source file.*
mmStatus	Defines the current status of the clip.*
mmTimeFormat	Specifies the time format used by the clip.
mmTrackCount	Specifies the number of tracks in the clip.*
mmVisible	Defines whether the clip is visible or not.
mmVisualSize	Defines the default size of the visual media of a clip.
mmVolume	Specifies the volume level of the clip.
name	Identifies name of up to 32 characters given by author.

Combo Box Properties

bounds	Specifies, in page units, the upper left and lower right coordinates.
defaultAllowDrag	Defines whether combo box items may be dragged by default.
defaultAllowDrop	Defines whether combo box accepts a drop by default.
dragImage	Defines graphic shown as cursor when combo box item is being dragged.
drawDirect	Defines whether object is drawn directly or off-screen.
dropDownItems	Defines the contents of the drop-down list box.
editable	Specifies whether user can edit the choice or not.
enabled	Defines whether the combo box can receive the focus.
fillColor	Defines, in HLS format, the fill color of the combo box.
fontFace	Specifies the default font used for the text of the combo box.
fontSize	Defines, in points, the default text size of the combo box's text.
fontStyle	Specifies the font style (e.g., **bold** or *italic*) used for the text.
ftsExclude	Specifies whether object's text is excluded or not from full-text searching.
ftsSection	Specifies section assigned to combo box for full-text searching.
idNumber	Cites the ID number of the combo box assigned by ToolBook.*
layer	Specifies the combo box's layer number on the page or background.
lineCount	Specifies the number of text lines displayed in the drop-down list.
name	Identifies name of up to 32 characters given by author.
noDropImage	Cites graphic used as cursor when dragged object is over combo box and combo box does not allow a drop.

notifyAfterMessages	Cites list of messages handled by notifyAfter handlers in script.*
notifyBeforeMessages	Cites list of messages handled by notifyBefore handlers in script.*
object	Specifies the type of object (i.e., comboBox).*
parent	References the next-highest object in the object hierarchy.*
position	Defines the upper left coordinates of the combo box.
rgbFill	Defines, in RGB format, the fill color of the combo box.
rgbStroke	Defines, in RGB format, the stroke color of the combo box.
richText	Specifies whether text is in a rich-text format (RTF).
script	Contains the handlers associated with the combo box.
scrollable	Specifies whether list box items are scrollable or not.
selectedItem	Specifies which item is selected in the drop-down list box.
size	Cites, in page units, the width and height of the combo box.
sortItems	Specifies whether drop-down box items are automatically alphabetized.
strokeColor	Defines, in HLS format, the stroke color of the combo box.
text	Specifies the text located in the edit box of the combo box.
textOverFlow	Cites the number of characters clipped in the combo box's text at the right or bottom edges.*
textUnderFlow	Defines the number of characters clipped in the combo box's text at the left or top edges.*
transparent	Specifies whether a combo box is transparent or opaque.
uniqueName	Cites the unique name of the combo box.*
userProperties	Cites a list of user-defined combo box properties.
useWindowsColors	Specifies whether object is drawn with default Windows colors as determined in the Windows control panel.
vertices	Specifies, in page units, coordinates of the four corners of the combo box's boundary.
visible	Defines whether the combo box is in a hidden or shown state.

Field or Recordfield Properties

activated	Specifies whether text is editable and object can receive mouse messages.
baseline	Specifies whether baselines are shown or not.
borderStyle	Defines the visual style of field or recordfield (e.g., scrolling or shadowed).
bounds	Defines, in page units, the upper left and lower right coordinates.
defaultAllowDrag	Defines whether object may be dragged by default.
defaultAllowDrop	Defines whether object accepts a drop by default.
dragImage	Specifies graphic shown as cursor when object is being dragged.
drawDirect	Defines whether object is drawn directly or off screen.
drawTextDirect	Specifies method for drawing text in the field.
enabled	Specifies whether object can receive the focus and mouse event messages.
fieldType	Specifies word wrap and selection behaviors.
fillColor	Defines, in HLS format, the fill color of the field.
fontFace	Cites the default font used for the field's text.
fontSize	Defines, in points, the default text size of the field's text.
fontStyle	Specifies the default font style (e.g., bold or italic) used for the text.

ftsExclude	Specifies whether object's text is excluded or not from full-text searching.
ftsSection	Specifies section assigned to button for full-text searching.
idNumber	Defines the ID number ToolBook assigns to the field or recordfield.*
indents	Cites the width of first-line, left-margin, and right-margin indents.
layer	Cites the page or background layer number of the field.
name	Identifies name of up to 32 characters given by author.
noDropImage	Specifies graphic used as cursor when dragged object is over field and field does not allow a drop.
notifyAfterMessages	Cites list of messages handled by notifyAfter handlers in script.*
notifyBeforeMessages	Cites list of messages handled by notifyBefore handlers in script.*
object	Specifies the type of object (i.e., Field or RecordField).*
objects	Specifies the unique name of each hotword within field's text.
parent	References the next-highest object in the object hierarchy.*
position	Specifies the upper left coordinates of the field.
rgbFill	Defines, in RGB format, the fillColor of the field.
rgbStroke	Defines, in RGB format, the stroke color of the field.
richText	Specifies whether text is in a rich-text format (RTF).
script	Contains the handlers associated with the field.
scroll	Specifies the number of text lines that are hidden above the visible text.
selectedTextlines	Specifies which lines of text are currently selected.
size	Defines, in page units, the width and height of the field.
spacing	Specifies the spacing between lines of text.
strokeColor	Defines, in HLS format, the stroke color of the field.
tabSpacing	Defines the tab stop settings for the text of the field.
tabType	Specifies whether left or decimal tabs are being used for the tab stops.
text	Defines the text contained in the field.
textAlignment	Cites the alignment of the text (left, right, center or justify).
textOverFlow	Specifies the number of characters clipped at the right or bottom edges in the field's text.*
textUnderFlow	Cites the number of characters clipped at the left or top edges in the field's text.*
transparent	Specifies whether a field is transparent or opaque.
uniqueName	Defines the unique name of the field.
userProperties	Cites a list of user-defined field or recordfield properties.
useWindowsColors	Specifies whether object is drawn with default Windows colors as determined in the Windows control panel.
vertices	Defines, in page units, coordinates of the four corners of the field's boundary.
visible	Specifies whether the field is hidden or shown.

Graphic Object Properties

bounds	Defines, in page units, the upper left and lower right coordinates.
defaultAllowDrag	Defines whether object may be dragged by default.
defaultAllowDrop	Defines whether object accepts a drop by default.

dragImage	Specifies graphic shown as cursor when object is being dragged.
drawDirect	Defines whether object is drawn directly or off screen.
fillColor	Defines, in HLS format, the fill color of a graphic.
idNumber	Specifies the ID number of the graphic assigned by ToolBook.*
layer	Cites the page or background layer number of the field.
lineEndSize	Defines the size of line ends (e.g. arrows) in an open-shape graphic.
lineEndStyle	Defines the style of the line ends (e.g. arrows) in a line graphic.
lineStyle	Specifies the line width or style (e.g., **dotted**).
name	Identifies name of up to 32 characters given by author.
noDropImage	Specifies graphic used as cursor when dragged object is over graphic and the graphic does not allow a drop.
notifyAfterMessages	Cites a list of messages handled by **notifyAfter** handlers in script.*
notifyBeforeMessages	Cites a list of messages handled by **notifyBefore** handlers in script.*
object	Specifies the type of object (i.e. **Arc, Ellipse, Rectangle**).*
parent	References the next-highest object in the object hierarchy.*
pattern	Defines the pattern style used in filling the graphic.
position	Specifies the upper left coordinates of the graphic.
rgbFill	Defines, in RGB format, the fill color of the graphic.
rgbStroke	Defines, in RGB format, the stroke color of the graphic.
script	Contains the handlers associated with the graphic.
size	Defines, in page units, the width and height of the graphic.
strokeColor	Defines, in HLS format, the stroke color of the graphic.
transparent	Specifies whether the graphic is transparent or opaque.
uniqueName	Defines the unique name of the object.
userProperties	Cites a list of user-defined properties associated with the graphic.
useWindowsColors	Specifies whether object is drawn with default Windows colors as determined in the Windows control panel.
vertices	Defines, in page units, coordinates of the four corners of the graphic's boundary.
visible	Defines whether the graphic is hidden or shown.

Group Properties

autoRadioButtons	Specifies selection behavior for grouped radio buttons.
bounds	Defines, in page units, the upper left and lower right coordinates.
defaultAllowDrag	Defines whether object may be dragged by default.
defaultAllowDrop	Defines whether object accepts a drop by default.
dragImage	Specifies graphic shown as cursor when object is being dragged.
drawDirect	Defines whether object is drawn directly or off screen.
idNumber	Cites the ID number of the group assigned by ToolBook.*
layer	Cites the page or background layer number of the field.
name	Identifies name of up to 32 characters given by author.
noDropImage	Defines graphic used as cursor when dragged object is over group and the group does not allow a drop.
notifyAfterMessages	Cites list of messages handled by **notifyAfter** handlers in script.*
notifyBeforeMessages	Cites list of messages handled by **notifyBefore** handlers in script.*

object	Specifies the type of object (i.e., group).*
objects	Cites a list of the unique names of the objects forming the group.
parent	References the next-highest object in the object hierarchy.*
position	Defines the upper left coordinates of the group.
script	Contains the handlers associated with the group.
size	Defines, in page units, the width and height of the graphic.
uniqueName	Specifies the unique name of the group.
userProperties	Cites a list of user-defined properties associated with groups.
vertices	Defines, in page units, coordinates of the four corners of the group's boundary.
visible	Defines whether the group is hidden or shown.

Hotword Properties

bounds	Defines, in page units, the upper left and lower right coordinates.
defaultAllowDrag	Defines whether object may be dragged by default.
defaultAllowDrop	Defines whether object accepts a drop by default.
dragImage	Specifies graphic shown as cursor when object is being dragged.
ftsTag	Specifies name of hotword's tag for full-text searching.
ftsTagValue	Specifies overriding value of hotword's tag for full-text searching.
highlight	Controls whether hotword flashes briefly when clicked.
hotwordStyle	Controls the appearance of the hotword.
idNumber	Specifies the ID number of the hotword assigned by ToolBook.*
invert	Specifies whether stroke color of the hotword is reversed.
name	Identifies name of up to 32 characters given by author.
noDropImage	Defines graphic used as cursor when dragged object is over hotword and the hotword does not allow a drop.
notifyAfterMessages	Cites list of messages handled by notifyAfter handlers in script.*
notifyBeforeMessages	Cites list of messages handled by notifyBefore handlers in script.*
object	Specifies the type of object (i.e., Hotword).*
parent	References the next-highest object in the object hierarchy.*
script	Contains the handlers associated with the hotword.
text	Defines the text of the hotword.
textOffset	Specifies the position of the hotword's first character in the field's text.
uniqueName	Defines the unique name of the hotword.
userProperties	Cites a list of user-defined properties associated with hot words.

OLE Object Properties

action	Specifies current command acting on OLE object.
bounds	Defines, in page units, the upper left and lower right coordinates.
defaultAllowDrag	Defines whether object may be dragged by default.
defaultAllowDrop	Defines whether object accepts a drop by default.

dragImage	Specifies graphic shown as cursor when object is being dragged.
drawDirect	Defines whether object is drawn directly or off screen.
fillColor	Defines, in HLS format, the fill color of the OLE object.
idNumber	Specifies, the ID number of the OLE object assigned by ToolBook.*
layer	Defines the page or background layer number of the OLE object.
lineStyle	Specifies the line width or style (e.g., dotted).
name	Identifies name of up to 32 characters given by author.
noDropImage	Specifies graphic used as cursor when dragged object is over OLE object and the OLE object does not allow a drop.
notifyAfterMessages	Cites list of messages handled by notifyAfter handlers in script.*
notifyBeforeMessages	Cites list of messages handled by notifyBefore handlers in script.*
object	Specifies the type of object (i.e., OLE).*
parent	References the next-highest object in the object hierarchy.*
position	Specifies the upper left coordinates of the OLE object.
reference	Specifies data type, source, class, or item range for server application.
rgbFill	Defines, in RGB format, the fill color of the OLE object.
rgbStroke	Defines, in RGB format, the stroke color of the OLE object.
script	Contains the handlers associated with the OLE object.
size	Defines, in page units, the width and height of the OLE object.
strokeColor	Defines, in HLS format, the stroke color of the OLE object.
trackSize	Specifies whether OLE object must be same size as server source object.
transparent	Defines whether the OLE object is transparent or opaque.
uniqueName	Cites the unique name of the OLE object.
updateType	Defines whether ToolBook automatically updates the OLE object from the source file.
upToDate	Specifies whether OLE object data is up-to-date with the source file data.
userProperties	Cites a list of user-defined properties associated with OLE objects.
useWindowsColors	Specifies whether object is drawn with default Windows colors as determined in the Windows control panel.
vertices	Defines, in page units, coordinates of the four corners of the object's boundary.
visible	Defines whether the OLE object is hidden or shown.

Page Properties

defaultAllowDrop	Defines whether object accepts a drop by default.
ftsAdditionalText	Specifies that values for user-defined properties and variables be included in the index for full-text searching.
ftsContext	Specifies the context of a page for full-text searching.
ftsIgnore	Specifies whether page is excluded from full-text searching.
ftsKeywords	Cites list of keywords used in finding page in a full-text search.
ftsTitle	Specifies title displayed as page's identification in a full-text search.

ftsTitleOverride	Specifies whether ftsTitle value should be used instead of the default value of title property.
idNumber	Cites the ID number of the page assigned by ToolBook.*
imageInvalid	Indicates whether image has changed since last stored.*
name	Identifies name of up to 32 characters given by author.
notifyObjects	Cites list of page objects with notifyBefore or notifyAfter handlers.*
object	Specifies the type of object (i.e., Page).*
objects	Cites, by their unique names, a list of objects located on the page.*
pageNumber	Specifies the page number of the page within the book.
parent	References the next-highest object in the object hierarchy.*
percentFreeSpace	Approximates free memory available to the page.*
script	Contains the handlers associated with the page.
uniqueName	Cites the unique name of the page.
userProperties	Cites a list of user-defined properties associated with page.

Stage Properties

borderWidth	Defines the width of the stage frame in page units (default is 45).
bounds	Defines, in page units, the upper left and lower right coordinates.
defaultAllowDrag	Defines whether object may be dragged by default.
defaultAllowDrop	Defines whether object accepts a drop by default.
dragImage	Specifies graphic shown as cursor when object is being dragged.
drawDirect	Defines whether object is drawn directly or off screen.
fillColor	Defines, in HLS format, the fill color of stage.
idNumber	Cites the ID number of the stage object assigned by ToolBook.*
innerBevelWidth	Defines, in page units, the width of the inner 3-D bevel.
innerBounds	Specifies the coordinates for the display area of the stage.
layer	Specifies the page or background layer number of the stage.
mediaBounds	Defines in pixels relative to upper left of stage display area, the coordinates of media being played in the stage.*
mediaOpen	References clip or bitmap being displayed in stage.*
mediaSize	Specifies default width and height of stage's media display.
name	Identifies name of up to 32 characters given by author.
noDropImage	Specifies graphic used as cursor when dragged object is over stage and the stage does not allow a drop.
notifyAfterMessages	Cites list of messages handled by notifyAfter handlers in script.*
notifyBeforeMessages	Cites list of messages handled by notifyBefore handlers in script.*
object	Specifies the type of object (i.e., Stage).*
outerBevelWidth	Defines, in page units, the width of the outer 3-D frame bevel.
outline	Specifies whether stage frame is outlined with a thin line.
overlayOpen	Specifies whether stage can display image from live video source.
parent	References the next-highest object in the object hierarchy.*
position	Specifies the upper left coordinates of the graphic.
postEffect	Specifies the visual effect used after the media has finished playing.

preEffect	Defines the visual effect used before the media has started playing.
readerVisible	Specifies if stage can be seen at reader level.
rgbFill	Defines, in RGB format, the fill color of the stage.
rgbStroke	Defines, in RGB format, the stroke color of the stage.
roundedCorners	Specifies if the stage outline has rounded corners or not.
script	Contains the handlers associated with the stage.
size	Defines, in page units, the width and height of the stage.
stageAnchor	Specifies the anchor position of media displayed in the stage or how the media is positioned in the stage.
stageSizing	Specifies how media should be displayed in a stage when the two are of different sizes.
strokeColor	Defines, in HLS format, the stroke color of the stage.
transparent	Specifies whether the stage object is transparent or opaque.
uniqueName	Defines the unique name of the stage.
userProperties	Cites a list of user-defined properties associated with stages.
useWindowsColors	Specifies whether object is drawn with default Windows colors as determined in the Windows control panel.
vertices	Defines, in page units, coordinates of the four corners of the stage's boundary.
visible	Specifies whether the stage object is in a hidden or shown state.

System Properties

activeWindowHandle	Cites the number assigned by Windows as the window handle of the currently active window.*
caretLocation	Defines the location of the insertion point in a field or recordfield.
focusWindow	Refers to the viewer that has the focus.
mainWindow	Refers to the viewer used as ToolBook's main window.*
self	Refers to the object containing the script that is being executed.*
sys3DInterface	Specifies whether ToolBook dialog boxes have 3-D controls.
sysAlignment	Specifies the default alignment for field or recordfield text.
sysAutoScriptFile	Specifies the current autoscript file.
sysBooks	Cites a list of the current system books in the object hierarchy.
sysCentered	Specifies whether new objects are drawn from center-out or corner to corner.
sysChangesDB	Specifies whether "Save changes?" dialog box is displayed when the book is closed and changes have been made to it.
sysClientHandle	Defines the window handle of the main window's client.*
sysCursor	Defines the shape (design) of the mouse pointer (cursor).
sysDate	Specifies, according to the computer's CMOS, the current date.
sysDateFormat	Defines the format used in referring to dates, including the value of the sysDate property.
sysDrawDirect	Defines whether new objects are created with their drawDirect property set to true or false.
sysError	Cites a string reference to the last encountered error.
sysErrorNumber	Cites a numeric reference to the last encountered error.
sysFillColor	Defines, in HLS format, the default fill color used for new objects.

sysFontFace	Specifies the default font face for field or recordfield text.
sysFontSize	Defines, in points, the default size of field or recordfield text.
sysFontStyle	The default text style (e.g., **bold**) of field or recordfield text.
sysGrid	Specifies whether grid is being shown or not.
sysGridSnap	Specifies whether objects are snapped to the grid as they are created or moved.
sysGridSpacing	Specifies the spacing between points of the grid.
sysHistory	Cites a list of the last 100 pages displayed during the current session.
sysHistoryRecord	Specifies whether pages are added to the sysHistory.
sysHotwordsShown	Specifies whether a hotword is shown on the current page.
sysIndents	Defines the default value of left and right margins and first line indent for field or recordfield text.
sysLevel	Specifies system working level.
sysLineEndSize	Defines the default line end size used for linear graphic objects.
sysLineEndStyle	Specifies the default line end style used for linear graphic objects.
sysLineSpacing	Defines the default line spacing for text of new fields or recordfields.
sysLineStyle	Specifies the default line style for new graphics.
sysLinkedDLLs	Cites list of currently linked dynamic link libraries.
sysLockScreen	Specifies whether screen is updated while current handler is executing.
sysMediaBreakKey	Specifies a key that may be used to stop playing media.
sysMediaSuspend	Defines whether the "Execution Suspended" dialog is displayed when a media-related error is encountered.
sysMMEngineVersion	Cites the version number of the Multimedia ToolBook play engine.*
sysNumberFormat	Defines the default format used when numeric data is formatted.
sysOpenMedia	Cites list of all currently open media.*
sysOpenWindows	Cites list of all open viewers in current instance of ToolBook.*
sysOperatingSystem	References current operating system and version.*
sysOptimizedSave	Specifies if the current book is optimized for CD-ROM.
sysPageScroll	Defines the position of the page in relation to the upper left corner of the main window.
SysPageUnitsPerPixel	Specifies number of page units per pixel for current monitor.*
sysPasswords	Cites list of encrypted passwords checked before requesting a password from the user.
sysPattern	Defines the default **pattern** used in creating new objects.
sysPolygonShape	Defines the number of sides used in creating new regular polygons.
sysReaderRightClick	Specifies whether Right-Click menus may be viewed at reader level.
sysRGBfill	Defines, in RGB format, default fill color used for new objects.
sysRGBStroke	Defines, in RGB format, default stroke color used for new objects.
sysRuntime	Specifies whether user is using the runtime version of ToolBook or Multimedia ToolBook.*
sysShowMRUFiles	Specifies whether most recently used files are displayed at the bottom of the File menu.

sysStrokeColor	Defines, in HLS format, default stroke color used for new objects.
sysSupportedMedia	Specifies media devices supported by current computer.
sysSuspend	Specifies whether the "Execution Suspended" dialog is displayed when an error is encountered.
sysSuspendMessages	Specifies whether enter, leave, and menu event messages are generated automatically.
sysSystemVariables	Cites list of system (global) variables in current instance of ToolBook for which memory is allocated.*
sysTabSpacing	Sets default tab spacing for field or recordfield text.
sysTabType	Sets default tab type for field or recordfield text.
sysTime	Defines, according to the computer's CMOS, the current time.*
sysTimeFormat	Defines the format used in referring to temporal data, including the value of the sysTime property.
sysTool	Specifies the currently selected tool (e.g., Rectangle).
sysToolBookDirectory	Cites the path of the ToolBook executable file.
sysTransparent	Cites the default value of the transparent property for new objects.
sysUnits	Defines the unit of measure used in rulers, grids, indents, etc.
sysUseWindowColors	Specifies the default value of the useWindowsColors property for new objects.
sysVersion	Cites the version number of ToolBook currently running (e.g. 3.0).*
sysWindowsHandle	Cites the window handle of the ToolBook main window as assigned by Windows.*
target	References the object that originally received the current message (for example, the object that was clicked on.)*
targetWindow	References the viewer in which commands are executed and objects searched for.*

(Note: There are additional system properties that relate to international use that are not discussed here. They include sysCountry, sysCurrency, sysDecimal, sysEvening, sysICountry, sysICurrDigits, sysICurrency, sysIDate, sysIDigits, sysIZero, sysIMeasure, sysINegCurr, sysITime, sysITLZero, sysLanguage, sysList, sysLongDate, sysMorning, sysShortDate, sysThousand, sysTimeChar. For more information, consult the *OpenScript Reference Manual* or the on-line help.)

Viewer Properties

alwaysOnTop	Specifies whether viewer is always displayed on top of other viewers.
alwaysReader	Specifies whether viewer may only be viewed in Reader level.
authorStatusBar	Specifies whether statusbar is visible in viewer in Author mode.
autoClose	Specifies if viewer may be closed with a single click.
autoShow	Specifies whether viewer is opened automatically when book is opened.
autoSize	Specifies whether viewer is resized whenever page size of current page changes.
borderStyle	Defines the visual style of viewer.
bounds	Defines, in page units, the upper left and lower right coordinates.

caption   Defines text (up to 255 characters) that appears on the title bar.

captionBar   Specifies style of the caption bar (title bar).

centerClient   Specifies if the page is centered in the viewer if the viewer is larger than the page size.

clientHandle   Defines the number assigned by Windows as the viewer handle.*

clientSize   Defines, in page units, the width and height of the viewer's client window.

currentPage   References the current page being displayed in the viewer.

defaultClientSize   Defines, in page units, the default width and height of the viewer's client windows.

defaultPage   References the page displaycd in the viewer when opened.

defaultPosition   Defines, in terms of the upper left coordinates, the default position of the viewer when opened.

defaultState   Specifies initial state of viewer (e.g., minimized, maximized, normal, etc.) when the viewer is first opened.

defaultType   Specifies default type of viewer when opened.

enabled   Defines whether the viewer can receive the focus.

focus   Specifies which object has the focus.

hideOnDeactivate   Specifies whether viewer is hidden when book is deactivated.

icon   Specifies icon seen when viewer window is minimized.

idNumber   Cites the ID number of the viewer assigned by ToolBook.*

imageBuffers   Specifies how many image buffers are allocated to viewer.

isOpen   Specifies whether the viewer is open.*

lockScreen   Specifies whether changes made to the screen are visible while handler is executing.

magnification   Defines the magnification level at which the viewer is displayed.

matColor   Specifies, in HLS format, the color of the mat (area surrounding the page) when page is smaller than viewer.

maximumSize   Defines, in pixels, maximum size allowed for the viewer in pixels.

menuBar   Specifies menubar resource assigned to the viewer.

minimumSize   Defines, in pixels, minimum size allowed for the viewer in pixels.

mousePosition   Defines the coordinates of the mouse pointer (cursor).

name   Identifies name of up to 32 characters given by author.

object   Specifies the type of object (i.e., Viewer).*

onBackground   Specifies whether page or background is being displayed.

parent   References the next-highest object in the object hierarchy*.

parentHandle   References Windows-assigned handle of parent window.

parentWindow   References name of parent window.

position   Defines the upper left coordinates of the viewer window.

readerStatusBar   Specifies whether statusbar is visible in viewer in Reader mode.

revertFocus   Specifies whether viewer keeps focus.

rulers   Specifies whether rulers are displayed in viewer.

script   Contains the handlers associated with the viewer.

selectedHotwords   Cites list of hotwords in the currently selected text.*

selectedText   Defines the string value of the currently selected text.

selectedTextState   Cites information about currently selected text.*

selection   Cites list of currently selected objects in the viewer.

size	Specifies, in page units, the width and height of the viewer.
state	Specifies the display state of the viewer (e.g., normal or minimized).
style	Cites list of elements comprising the viewer frame.
tile	Specifies position of a palette or child window.
tileOrder	Specifies titling order for child windows and/or palettes.
type	Defines the type of viewer, (e.g., child or popup).
uniqueName	Defines the unique name of the viewer.
userProperties	Cites a list of user-defined properties associated with the viewer.
useWindowsColors	Specifies whether object is drawn with default Windows colors as determined in the Windows control panel.
vertices	Defines, in page units, coordinates of the four corners of the viewer's boundary.
visible	Specifies whether the viewer is hidden or shown.
windowHandle	Defines the number assigned by Windows as the window handle.*

Appendix C

OpenScript Functions

Functions are used for returning a value to the calling routine. Functions are identifiable in that they always have parentheses following the function name. Arguments are enclosed in the parentheses. Functions are used in OpenScript to return arithmetic, financial, logarithmic, statistical, string, and trigonometric values. The use of functions is discussed in Chapter 15 (string functions are discussed in Chapter 17). In this appendix, functions are grouped into types by operation (e.g., arithmetic) and listed alphabetically within the group. A brief description of the type of value returned by the function appears. Argument types are listed within parentheses, in italics. The following sample shows the format used in this appendix.

Operation Type
function(*argument*)   Description of returned value.

Arithmetic Functions
abs(*number*)   Returns the absolute value of a number.
ceiling(*number*) Returns smallest integer greater than or equal to number specified.
floor(*number*)   Returns the largest integer less than or equal to the number specified.
random( )   Returns an integer from 1 through the number specified (inclusive).
round(*number*) Returns the number rounded to the nearest integer.
sqrt(*number*)   Returns the square root of a number.
truncate(*number*) Returns the integer value of a number, truncating any decimal portion.

Financial Functions
annuityFactor(*rate, periods*)
    Returns factor of present value of an ordinary annuity to the payment.
compoundFactor(*rate, periods*)
    Returns future value of interest-bearing account
ddb(*cost, salvage, life, period, rate*)
    Returns depreciation of an asset for a specified period of time.
fv(*rate, periods, payment, currentValue, beginningOrEnd?*)
    Returns the future value of an investment.
ipmt(*rate, period, totalPeriods, presValue, futureValue, type*)
    Returns amount of interest on an investment or loan.
irr(*valueList, expectedRate*)
    Returns the interest rate or return for a series of cash-flow amounts.
nper(*rate, payment, presentValue, futureValue, type*)
    Returns number of periods required for an investment or loan to reach a value.
npv(*rate, cashFlowValues, type*)
    Returns present value of investment based on cash-flow values.

pmt(*rate, totalPeriods, principal, futureValue, type*)
     Returns the periodic payment of an annuity.
ppmt(*rate, period, totalPeriods, principal, futureValue, type*)
     Returns the payment on the principal for an investment or loan.
pv(*rate, totalPeriods, payment, futureValue, type*)
     Returns the present value of an investment or loan.
rate(*totalPeriods, payment, presVal, futVal, type, expectRate*)
     Returns the interest rate per period for an investment or loan.
syd(*cost, salvage, life, period*)
     Returns the depreciation of an asset, using an accelerated depreciation method.

Full-Text Searching Functions

The following functions are for performing full-text searches. This feature is only available in Multimedia Toolbook. Full-text searches are not discussed in this text. For more information, consult the *Multimedia ToolBook User Manual and OpenScript Reference* or see the on-line help.

ftsAddContext(*indexHandle, contextTitle*)
ftsAddPage(*indexHandle, pageRef, pageTitle, keywords, contextNumber*)
ftsAddSectionsToPage(*indexHandle*)
ftsAddTextToSection(*indexHandle, text, section*)
ftsAllContextTitles(*indexHandle, maximumCharacters*)
ftsAllMatchingRefs(*indexHandle, maximumCharacters*)
ftsAllMatchingTitles(*indexHandle, maximumCharacters*)
ftsBuildIndex(*indexHandle*)
ftsCloseIndex(*indexHandle*)
ftsContextCount(*indexHandle*)
ftsContextTitle(*indexHandle, contextNumber, maximumCharacters*)
ftsGetErrorNotify( )
ftsGetErrorNumber( )
ftsGetErrorString( )
ftsGetOffsets(*indexHandle, sourceText*)
ftsInitIndex(*indexName, initFile, windowHandle*)
ftsMatchRef(*indexHandle, matchNumber, maximumCharacters*)
ftsMatchTitle(*indexHandle, matchNumber, maximumCharacters*)
ftsNamedSections(*indexHandle, maximumCharacters*)
ftsOpenIndex(*indexName*)
ftsQuery(*indexHandle, queryString, maximumHits*)
ftsRemoveIndex(*indexName*)
ftsReQuery(*indexHandle, queryString, maximumHits*)
ftsSetContextScope(*indexHandle, contextList*)
ftsSetErrorNotify(*errorMode*)
ftsTagEntries(*indexHandle, tag, maximumCharacters*)
ftsTags(*indexHandle, maximumCharacters*)

Logarithmic Functions

exp(*power*)   Returns value of *e* (2.7182818) raised to a specified power.
ln(*number*)   Returns the natural logarithm (base *e* log) of a number.
log(*number, base*)   Returns the logarithm of a value in a specified base.

Miscellaneous Functions

clientToPageUnits(*coordinates*)
   Converts pixel coordinates to page units.
clientToScreen(*coordinates, viewerReference*)
   Converts pixel coordinates of window to pixel coordinates of screen.
clipboardFormats( )   Returns list of clipboard formats supported by ToolBook.
copyObject(*object, destination*)
   Copies object from one location to another.
dimensions(*array*)   Returns list of dimensions for the specified array.
flushMessageQueue( ) Removes all messages waiting to be handled.
frameToPageUnits(*coordinates, viewerReference*)
   Converts pixel coordinates to page units.
frameToScreen(*coordinates, viewerReference*)
   Converts pixel coordinates of frame to pixel coordinates of screen.
isObject(*container*)   Determines validity of object reference.
isType(*type, container, formatList*)
   Returns whether container contains values of specifed format(s).
keyState(*key*)   Returns up/down status of a keyboard key.
objectFromPoint(*location, viewerReference*)
   Returns the object at the specified location.
oleActionList(*class*)   Returns list of commands supported by specific OLE object.
oleClassList( )
   Returns list of supported OLE applications installed on current system.
pageUnitsToClient(*coordinates*)
   Converts page unit coordinates to pixels.
pageUnitsToFrame(*coordinates, viewerReference*)
   Converts page unit coordinates of window frame to those relative to screen.
pageUnitsToScreen(*coordinates, viewerReference*)
   Converts page unit coordinates of window to those relative to screen.
playSound(*soundFile, wait*)   Plays the specified sound file.
screenToClient(*coordinates, viewerReference*)
   Converts screen pixel coordinates to those relative to client window.
screenToFrame(*coordinates, viewerReference*)
   Converts screen pixel coordinates to those relative to window frame.
screenToPageUnits(*coordinates, viewerReference*)
   Converts screen pixel coordinates to those relative to client area.
windowFromPoint(*coordinates*) Returns topmost viewer located at specified point.

Multimedia Functions

(Note: Functions in this group are only available in Multimedia Toolbook.)
callMCI("*command device arguments wait*", *notifyObject*)
   Controls an MCI device. Returns information about success or failure of
   command.
imageCommand("*command device arguments*", *notifyObject*)
   Controls external graphic files. Returns information about success or failure of
   command.
importPhoto(*CDDrive, photoNumber, size, rotation, mirror, colorDepth*)
   Imports photo from Kodak Photo CD. Returns information about success or
   failure.
mixerCommand("*command device arguments*")
   Controls volume level of device. Returns information about success or failure
   of command.

timerCapability( )
>   Returns information about the timer.

timerStart(*singleOrPerodic, delay, resolution, notifyObject*)
>   Starts Windows timer services. Returns ID of timer.

timerStop(*timerID*)
>   Stops Windows timer services. Returns 0 or null depending on success or failure.

Resource Functions

chooseResource(*type, bookReference*)
>   Accesses the Resource Manager.

GDIHandle(*resourceReference*)
>   Returns handle to a block of memory.

menuEnabled(*namelalias* in *menuReference* at *level, viewerReference*)
>   Returns whether a particular menu is enabled or disabled.

menuItemChecked(*namelalias* in *menuReference* at *level, viewerReference*)
>   Returns whether or not a particular menu item is checked.

menuItemEnabled(*namelalias* in *menuReference* at *level, viewerReference*)
>   Returns whether a particular menu item is enabled or disabled.

popupMenu(*location, resourceReference, menuName*)
>   Displays a pop-up menu at the given location.

resourceCount(*type, bookReference*)
>   Returns the number of resources embedded in the book of the specified type.

resourceHandle(*resourceReference*)
>   Returns handle for the memory block containing the specified reference.

resourceList(*type, bookReference*)
>   Returns a list of the resources of the specified type embedded in the book.

setMenuHelpText(*namelalias, newHelpText, viewerReference*)
>   Assigns the help text displayed for a menu in the statusbar.

setMenuItemHelpText(*namelalias, newHelpText, viewerReference*)
>   Assigns the help text displayed for a menu item in the statusbar.

setMenuItemName(*namelalias, newName, viewerReference*)
>   Assigns a new name to a menu item.

setMenuName(*namelalias, newName, viewerReference*)
>   Assigns a new name to a menu.

Statistical Functions

average(*list*)	Returns the average value of a list of numbers.
max(*list*)	Returns the largest value in a list of numbers.
min(*list*)	Returns the smallest value in a list of numbers.
sum(*list*)	Returns the sum of a list of numbers.

String Functions

ansiToChar(*integer*)	Returns character equivalent of ANSI integer.
charCount(*string*)	Returns number of characters in string.
charToAnsi(*character*)	Returns ANSI equivalent of character.
itemCount(*string*)	Returns number of items in a string.
lowercase(*string*)	Returns string in all lowercase characters.
offset(*subString,source*)	Returns character position number of substring in source.
textLineCount(*string*)	Returns number of text lines in a string.
uppercase(*string*)	Returns string in all uppercase characters.
wordCount(*string*)	Returns the number of words in a string.

Trigonometric Functions

acos(*number*)

  Returns the arccosine of number from -1 through 1 (inclusive) in radians.

asin(*number*)

  Returns the arcsine of a number from –1 and 1 (inclusive) in radians.

atan(*number*)   Returns the arctangent of a number in radians.

cos(angle)   Returns the cosine of an angle measured in radians.

cosh(*angle*)   Returns the hyperbolic cosine of an angle measured in radians.

hypotenuse(*side1, side2*)

  Returns the hypotenuse of right triangle given length of the sides.

sin(*angle*)   Returns the sine of an angle measured in radians.

sinh(*angle*)   Returns the hyperbolic sine of an angle measured in radians.

tan(*angle*)   Returns the tangent of an angle measured in radians.

tanh(*angle*)   Returns the hyperbolic tangent of an angle measured in radians.

Appendix D

ToolBook Event Messages

ToolBook generates numerous event messages as the user interacts with the program. Messages are generated, for example, when the mouse pointer enters or leaves the boundaries of an object, when the user navigates to a different page, clicks an object, or enters data from the keyboard. This appendix lists the various messages in alphabetical order, indicates their recipients, and explains the events that generate them. The format this appendix uses follows.

message   Description of recipient and event.

Some of the messages also generate parameters, which are not listed in this appendix. For more information about any of the messages, consult the *OpenScript Reference Manual* or the on-line help of ToolBook or Multimedia ToolBook.

---

activateInstance	Sent to current page when an instance of ToolBook becomes active.
allowDrag	Sent to an object to query whether it can be dragged when a drag and drop procedure is being initiated.
allowDrop	Sent to an object to query whether it can receive a drop in a drag and drop procedure.
beginDrag	Sent to the dragged object when a drag and drop procedure begins.
buttonClick	Sent to an object when the user clicks it by pressing the left mouse button.
buttonDoubleClick	Sent to an object when the user double clicks it by pressing the left mouse button.
buttonDown	Sent to an object when the reader uses the left mouse button to click it.
buttonStillDown	Sent repeatedly to an object when the user holds down either mouse button when the pointer is on it.
buttonUp	Sent to an object when the user releases the left mouse button when the pointer is on it.
closeWindow	Sent to a viewer when it is being closed.
destroy	Sent to an object just before it is cut or cleared.
endDrag	Sent to a dragged object when the mouse button is released in a drag and drop operation.
enterApplication	Sent to the book when the ToolBook main window is opened.
enterBackgournd	Sent to the background when the user navigates to a page that has a different background.
enterBook	Sent to the book when it is opened.
enterButton	Sent to a button when it receives the focus (i.e., the user tabs to it, sets the **focus** property to the button, or clicks it).

enterComboBox	Sent to a combo box when it receives the focus.
enterDrop	Sent to an object that can receive a drop in a drag and drop process when the mouse pointer enters its bounds.
enterDropDown	Sent to a combo box when the user clicks the arrow at its right to view the drop-down list.
enterField	Sent to a field when it receives the focus (i.e., the user tabs to it, sets the focus property to the field, or clicks it).
enterMenu	Sent to the viewer when a menu is selected.
enterPage	Sent to the page when the user navigates to it.
enterRecordField	Sent to a recordfield when it receives the focus (i.e., the user tabs to it, sets the focus property to the recordfield, or clicks it).
enterSystem	Sent when a new instance of ToolBook is opened.
enterWindow	Sent to a viewer when it is activated.
hidden	Sent to a viewer when it is being hidden.
idle	Sent repeatedly to the page when no other events are being generated.
imageNotify	Sent to the object referenced in an imageCommand command after it has executed. (*This message is available in Multimedia Toolbook only.*)
keyChar	Sent to the object having the focus when a key is pressed. If no object has the focus, the message is sent to the page.
keyDown	Sent to the object having the focus when a key is pressed. If no object has the focus, the message is sent to the page.
keyMnemonic	Sent to the page when the user presses a mnemonic access character (i.e., the Alt key in combination with another key) that is not currently defined for a button or menu.
keyUp	Sent to the object having the focus when a pressed key is released. If no object has the focus, the message is sent to the page.
leaveApplication	Sent to the book when the ToolBook main window is closed.
leaveBackgournd	Sent to the current background when the user navigates to a page that has a different background or closes the book.
leaveBook	Sent to the book when it is closed.
leaveButton	Sent to a button just before it loses the focus.
leaveComboBox	Sent to a combo box just before it loses the focus.
leaveDrop	Sent to an object that can receive a drop in a drag and drop process when the mouse pointer exits its bounds.
leaveDropDown	Sent to a combo box when its drop-down list closes (e.g., the user has made a selection).
leaveField	Sent to a field just before it loses the focus.
leavePage	Sent to the current page when the user navigates to a different page.
leaveRecordField	Sent to a recordfield just before it loses the focus.
leaveSystem	Sent when the current instance of ToolBook is closed.
leaveWindow	Sent to a viewer when it is deactivated (e.g., it is closed).
linkSysBook	Sent to a system book when it is linked to the current book.
make	Sent to an object just after it is created.
MCINotify	Sent to the object referenced in a callMCI command after it has executed. (*Available in Multimedia Toolbook only.*)
menuItemSelected	Sent to the viewer when a menu item is selected.
mmNotify	Sent to the object referenced in a notify command after it has executed. (*Available in Multimedia Toolbook only.*)
mouseEnter	Sent to an object when the mouse pointer enters its boundaries.

mouseLeave	Sent to an object when the mouse pointer leaves its boundaries.
moved	Sent to an object when the object is repositioned at the author level.
objectDropped	Sent to an object when an object is dropped onto it during a drag and drop operation.
openWindow	Sent to a viewer when the viewer is opened.
pageScrolled	Sent to the viewer when the page scroll is changed.
remoteCommand	Sent to the viewer of a DDE server instance of ToolBook when a DDE client instance sends it a command.
remoteGet	Sent to the viewer of a DDE server instance of ToolBook when a DDE client instance requests a value from it.
remoteSet	Sent to the viewer of a DDE server instance of ToolBook when a DDE client instance tries to set a value of a container in the server.
rightButtonDoubleClick	Sent to an object when the user double-clicks it with the right mouse button.
rightButtonDown	Sent to an object when the user clicks it by using the right mouse button.
rightButtonUp	Sent to an object when, with the pointer on it, the user releases the right mouse button.
selectChange	Sent to a combo box when an item is selected from its drop-down list.
selectionChanged	Sent to the page whenever a different object is selected.
shown	Sent to a viewer when the viewer is shown.
sized	Sent to an object when the object is resized at author level.
stillOverDrop	Sent to an object that can receive a drop in a drag and drop process when the mouse pointer is within its bounds.
textScrolled	Sent to a field or recordfield whenever its scroll property changes.
timerNotify	Sent to the object referenced in the timerStart function at time intervals specified in the timerStart function. (*Available in Multimedia Toolbook only.*)
unlinkSysBook	Sent to the system book when it is unlinked from the current book.

In addition to the preceding event messages, a message is generated whenever a menu option is chosen. The message name corresponds to the menu item name (without any spaces). These messages may be used by a handler and, therefore, their functionality altered. For example, a flipHorizontal message is generated when the "Flip Horizontal" menu option is chosen. The following handler in the page script sets to red the fill color of any page object that is flipped horizontally:

```
to handle flipHorizontal
     set the fillColor of selection to red
     forward  --send message to system to flip the selected object horizontally
end flipHorizontal
```

ANSI Chart

The following chart lists the ANSI decimal codes and the corresponding characters. The characters displayed differ according to font, particularly for the extended characters (ANSI numbers 128 through 255). The chart shows the character sets for the Arial, Courier, Symbol, System, and Times fonts for characters whose ANSI number is greater than 32. (Note that some ANSI numbers have no displayable characters. An ANSI 9 for example, is the tab character.) A character may be entered from the keyboard using its ANSI number. To type a character, hold down the Alt key and type "0" (zero) followed by the three-digit ANSI number on the numeric keypad (using the numbers above the alpha keys will not work). For instance, Alt–0169 enters the copyright symbol, ©.

		Ansi #	Arial	Courier	Symbol	System	Times
000		033	!	!	!	!	!
001		034	"	"		"	"
002		035	#	#	#	#	#
003		036	$	$	∃	$	$
004		037	%	%	%	%	%
005		038	&	&	&	&	&
006		039	'	'	∋	`	'
007		040	(	(	(	(	(
008	Backspace	041	)	)	)	)	)
009	Tab	042	*	*	*	*	*
010	Linefeed	043	+	+	+	+	+
011	Home	044	,	,	,	,	,
012	Form feed	045	-	–	−	-	-
013	Carriage return	046	.	.	.	.	.
014		047	/	/	/	/	/
015		048	0	0	0	0	0
016		049	1	1	1	1	1
017		050	2	2	2	2	2
018		051	3	3	3	3	3
019		052	4	4	4	4	4
020		053	5	5	5	5	5
021		054	6	6	6	6	6
022		055	7	7	7	7	7
023		056	8	8	8	8	8
024		057	9	9	9	9	9
025		058	:	:	:	:	:
026		059	;	;	;	;	;
027		060	<	<	<	<	<
028	Cursor right	061	=	=	=	=	=
029	Cursor left	062	>	>	>	>	>
030	Cursor up	063	?	?	?	?	?
031	Cursor down	064	@	@	≅	@	@
032	Space						

Ansi #	Arial	Courier	Symbol	System	Times	Ansi #	Arial	Courier	Symbol	System	Times
065	A	A	A	A	A	118	v	v	ϖ	V	v
066	B	B	B	B	B	119	w	w	ω	W	w
067	C	C	X	C	C	120	x	x	ξ	X	x
068	D	D	Δ	D	D	121	y	y	ψ	Y	y
069	E	E	E	E	E	122	z	z	ζ	Z	z
070	F	F	Φ	F	F	123	{	{	{	{	{
071	G	G	Γ	G	G	124	|	|	|	|	|
072	H	H	H	H	H	125	}	}	}	}	}
073	I	I	I	I	I	126	~	~	~	~	~
074	J	J	ϑ	J	J	127					
075	K	K	K	K	K	128					
076	L	L	Λ	L	L	129					
077	M	M	M	M	M	130	‚				‚
078	N	N	N	N	N	131	*f*				*f*
079	O	O	O	O	O	132	„				„
080	P	P	Π	P	P	133	…				…
081	Q	Q	Θ	Q	Q	134	†				†
082	R	R	P	R	R	135	‡				‡
083	S	S	Σ	S	S	136	ˆ				ˆ
084	T	T	T	T	T	137	‰				‰
085	U	U	Y	U	U	138	Š				Š
086	V	V	ς	V	V	139	‹				‹
087	W	W	Ω	W	W	140	Œ				Œ
088	X	X	Ξ	X	X	141					
089	Y	Y	Ψ	Y	Y	142					
090	Z	Z	Z	Z	Z	143					
091	[	[	[	(	[	144					
092	\	\	∴	\	\	145	'	'	`		'
093	]	]	]	)	]	146	'	'	´		'
094	^	^	⊥	^	^	147	"				"
095	_	_	_	_	_	148	"				"
096	`	´	‾	`	`	149	•				•
097	a	a	α	a	a	150	–				–
098	b	b	β	b	b	151	—				—
099	c	c	χ	c	c	152	˜				˜
100	d	d	δ	d	d	153	™				™
101	e	e	ε	e	e	154	š				š
102	f	f	φ	f	f	155	›				›
103	g	g	γ	g	g	156	œ				œ
104	h	h	η	h	h	157					
105	i	i	ι	i	i	158					
106	j	j	φ	j	j	159	Ÿ				Ÿ
107	k	k	κ	k	k	160					
108	l	l	λ	l	l	161	¡	¡	ϒ	¡	¡
109	m	m	μ	m	m	162	¢	¢	′	¢	¢
110	n	n	ν	n	n	163	£	£	≤	£	£
111	o	o	o	o	o	164	¤	¤	/	¤	¤
112	p	p	π	p	p	165	¥	¥	∞	¥	¥
113	q	q	θ	q	q	166	¦	¦	*f*	¦	¦
114	r	r	ρ	r	r	167	§	§	♣	§	§
115	s	s	σ	s	s	168	¨	¨	♦	¨	¨
116	t	t	τ	t	t	169	©	©	♥	©	©
117	u	u	υ	u	u	170	ª	ª	♠	ª	ª

Ansi #	Arial	Courier	Symbol	System	Times	Ansi #	Arial	Courier	Symbol	System	Times
171	«	«	↔	«	«	224	à	à	◊	à	à
172	¬	¬	←	¬	¬	225	á	á	〈	á	á
173	-	-	↑	-	-	226	â	â	®	â	â
174	®	®	→	®	®	227	ã	ã	©	ã	ã
175	‾	‾	↓	‾	‾	228	ä	ä	™	ä	ä
176	°	°	°	°	°	229	å	å	Σ	å	å
177	±	±	±	±	±	230	æ	æ	⌠	Œ	æ
178	²	²	″	²	²	231	ç	ç	⎮	ç	ç
179	³	³	≥	³	³	232	è	è	⌡	è	è
180	´	´	×	´	´	233	é	é	⎧	é	é
181	µ	µ	∝	µ	µ	234	ê	ê	⎨	ê	ê
182	¶	¶	∂	¶	¶	235	ë	ë	⎩	ë	ë
183	·	·	•	·	·	236	ì	ì	⎰	ì	ì
184	¸	¸	÷	¸	¸	237	í	í	⎱	í	í
185	¹	¹	≠	¹	¹	238	î	î	⎪	î	î
186	º	º	≡	º	º	239	ï	ï		ï	ï
187	»	»	≈	»	»	240	ð	ð		ð	ð
188	¼	¼	…	¼	¼	241	ñ	ñ	〉	ñ	ñ
189	½	½	│	½	½	242	ò	ò	∫	ò	ò
190	¾	¾	─	¾	¾	243	ó	ó	⌠	ó	ó
191	¿	¿	↵	¿	¿	244	ô	ô	⎮	ô	ô
192	À	À	ℵ	À	À	245	õ	õ	⌡	õ	õ
193	Á	Á	ℑ	Á	Á	246	ö	ö	⎞	ö	ö
194	Â	Â	ℜ	Â	Â	247	÷	÷	⎟	÷	÷
195	Ã	Ã	℘	Ã	Ã	248	ø	ø	⎟	ø	ø
196	Ä	Ä	⊗	Ä	Ä	249	ù	ù	⎟	ù	ù
197	Å	Å	⊕	Å	Å	250	ú	ú	⎟	ú	ú
198	Æ	Æ	∅	Æ	Æ	251	û	û	⎠	û	û
199	Ç	Ç	∩	Ç	Ç	252	ü	ü	⎞	ü	ü
200	È	È	∪	È	È	253	ý	ý	}	ý	ý
201	É	É	⊃	É	É	254	þ	þ	⎠	þ	þ
202	Ê	Ê	⊇	Ê	Ê	255	ÿ	ÿ		ÿ	ÿ
203	Ë	Ë	⊄	Ë	Ë						
204	Ì	Ì	⊂	Ì	Ì						
205	Í	Í	⊆	Í	Í						
206	Î	Î	∈	Î	Î						
207	Ï	Ï	∉	Ï	Ï						
208	Ð	Ð	∠	Ð	Ð						
209	Ñ	Ñ	∇	Ñ	Ñ						
210	Ò	Ò	®	Ò	Ò						
211	Ó	Ó	©	Ó	Ó						
212	Ô	Ô	™	Ô	Ô						
213	Õ	Õ	∏	Õ	Õ						
214	Ö	Ö	√	Ö	Ö						
215	×	×	·	×	×						
216	Ø	Ø	¬	Ø	Ø						
217	Ù	Ù	∧	Ù	Ù						
218	Ú	Ú	∨	Ú	Ú						
219	Û	Û	⇔	Û	Û						
220	Ü	Ü	⇐	Ü	Ü						
221	Ý	Ý	⇑	Ý	Ý						
222	Þ	Þ	⇒	Þ	Þ						
223	ß	ß	⇓	ß	ß						

The HyperCard Developer's Guide to ToolBook

This author started out as a HyperCard developer and switched to developing ToolBook applications. The similarities between the two environments make this an easy transition. Both products offer object-oriented development, having objects such as buttons and fields. Although the terminology relating to both products may be slightly different, HyperCard and ToolBook take the same approach to application development. Where ToolBook has books formed by pages, HyperCard has stacks consisting of cards. As multiple cards in a HyperCard stack may share a common background, so multiple pages in a ToolBook book share a background. Both products allow external resources—such as icons, fonts, and bitmaps—to be imported into created applications and distributed with them. Both have their own proprietary scripting language. These two languages, ToolBook's OpenScript and HyperCard's HyperTalk, are very similar in functionality and syntax. In both cases, the scripts are driven by similar event messages.

There are some differences between the two products, however. The most obvious is that HyperCard uses paint graphics while ToolBook utilizes vectored, or draw, graphics. This is to ToolBook's advantage because scripts may be attached to the graphic objects. Those unfamiliar with drawing software may find the transition from painting to drawing difficult at first, but they will soon realize the advantages that drawing offers in terms of resizing, reshaping, and grouping. Another striking difference is ToolBook's full support of color.

In scripting, the HyperCard author will quickly notice that an OpenScript command may be slightly different but that it will usually perform the same task as its HyperTalk counterpart. The on *message* handlers of HyperTalk, for example, are replaced with to handle *message* handlers in OpenScript. The HyperTalk script

```
on mouseUp
    global ageGroup
    answer "What is your age range?" with "18-29" or "30-45" or "over 45"
    if it = "18-29" then
        put 1 into ageGroup
    else if it = "30-45" then
        put 2 into ageGroup
    else
        put 3 into ageGroup
    end if
end mouseUp
```

written as an OpenScript script, would be

```
to handle buttonUp
    system ageGroup
    request "What is your age range?" with "18-29" or "30-45" or "Over 45"
    conditions
```

```
          when it = "18-29"
               put 1 into ageGroup
          when it = "30-45"
               put 2 into ageGroup
          else
               put 3 into ageGroup
          end if
     end conditions
end buttonUp
```

This author finds ToolBook to be more powerful than HyperCard. Drag and drop procedures, for example, are easily accomplished in ToolBook. Developing client-server applications via Windows DDE capabilities is easy with ToolBook. User-defined properties and arrays offer additional flexibility and power in handling data. Multimedia ToolBook also offers built-in spell-checking and full-text searching capabilities, not discussed in this text.

To assist the experienced HyperCard developer writing OpenScript handlers, this author has developed a reference utility included with the software accompanying this text. The reference lists the commands, functions, properties, and messages of HyperCard and HyperTalk and provides the ToolBook and OpenScript equivalent (see Figure F.1). To access the reference, click the "HyperTalk to OpenScript" icon in the "Developing with ToolBook" group (assuming the software has been installed on the computer), or access it through the "Appendices" volume of the "Developing with ToolBook" front-end application.

Figure F.1
A reference utility is included with the software accompanying this text. It shows the OpenScript equivalents of HyperTalk commands, functions, keywords, and so on.

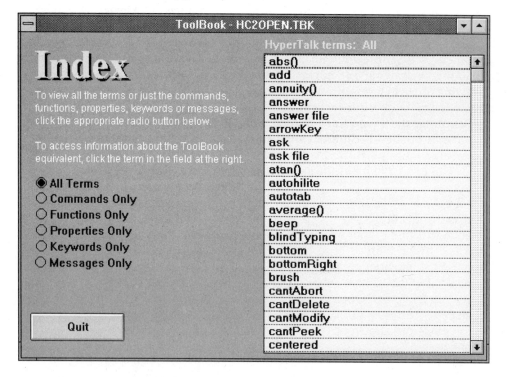

Appendix G

Debugging Techniques

It is not uncommon, even for the most experienced of programmers, to have errors in program code. Debugging, the process of finding and correcting errors, is generally a necessary procedure in developing an application. Errors may be the result of typographical errors, missing statements, incorrect or inaccurate logic, referencing a system variable as a local variable, trying to open a file that doesn't exist, or many other causes. There are numerous ways of finding and correcting these bugs.

Preventive "medicine" is perhaps the most time-saving. Careful planning of the algorithms, checking your syntax, keeping track of what variables contain what values, and considering all the possible scenarios of data input can go a long way in preventing errors. But, for when those inevitable errors do pop up, there are several tools and methods available to help find them.

Dealing with Compiler Errors

Compiler errors occur when exiting and saving a syntactically incorrect script or when the syntax checker is run on a script. When a compiler error occurs, ToolBook will warn the author of an error. A dialog, like that pictured in Figure G.1, may pop up to verify that you want to exit the script editor, even though an error has occurred and the script has not been compiled. If you respond by clicking the "Cancel" button, the editor will highlight where the offense occurred (which sometimes is due to a logic problem higher up in the code). The script is edited to combat the error, and then another attempt is made to compile the script by exiting and saving it. This process is repeated until the script successfully compiles. However, just because a script has successfully compiled does not mean it is error-free. It simply means there appear to be no syntactical errors (all the statements are valid statements). A typographical error (such as misspelling a variable name) or logic error (such as adding when you really should have subtracted) can also result in erroneous answers. The syntax of a handler may be checked by choosing the "Check Syntax" option in the script editor's File menu.

Using the "Command Window" or a Dialog Box

The "Command" window is a great place for displaying data from a script. An author may check the value of a container by putting it in the "Command" window. The

Figure G.1
When exiting a script, the compiler examines the syntax and warns of any errors found. Clicking "Cancel" will return you to the script editor where the offending statement will be highlighted.

following script multiplies two numbers together and then subtracts the two numbers from the product.

```
to handle buttonClick
    ask "Enter a number:"
    put it into x
    ask "Enter another number:"
    put it into y
    put x * y into z
    put z − (x − y) into z
    request "The answer is " & z & "." with "OK"
end buttonClick
```

If, for instance a wrong answer was appeared as you tested the program with sample data, you could add the command put z into commandWindow.

```
to handle buttonClick
    ask "Enter a number:"
    put it into x
    ask "Enter another number:"
    put it into y
    put x * y into z
    put z into commandWindow
    put z − (x − y) into z
    request "The answer is " & z & "." with "OK"
end buttonClick
```

The preceding code would display the product of the multiplication operation inside the command window. Such a procedure would only be used for testing purposes, and the line would be eliminated after the problem was solved or was no longer needed. In the preceding example, the author would examine the output in the "Command" window and quickly realize that the multiplication of the two numbers is being carried out correctly. The problem, therefore, must occur after this statement, when the two numbers are subtracted from the product. By using the "Command" window to check for variable values, the logic or typographical error may be isolated. Looking at the statement where the two numbers are subtracted reveals that the second number is subtracted from the first and the sum is then subtracted from the product. This results in an erroneous answer, with the second variable, y, being added to z by virtue of subtracting its negative value.

Suppose you want to pause the script until the mouse button is pressed, so the value can be examined (for instance, if performing this operation inside a loop or where this procedure is carried out at more than one point in the script.) In this case you can insert a loop after the put command. The loop will reiterate until the left mouse button is pressed.

```
to handle buttonClick
    ask "Enter a number:"
    put it into x
    ask "Enter another number:"
    put it into y
    put x * y into z
    put z into the commandWindow
    do
    until the keystate(keyLeftButton) is "down"
```

```
    put z − (x − y) into z
    request "The answer is " & z & "." with "OK"
end buttonClick
```

In the same manner, a dialog box (such as a request dialog) might be used to display a value and pause until the user (in this case, the author) clicks the "OK" button in the dialog. For instance:

```
to handle buttonClick
    ask "Enter a number:"
    put it into x
    ask "Enter another number:"
    put it into y
    put x * y into z
    request "The value of the two numbers multiplied is: " & z & "." with "OK"
    put z − (x − y) into z
    request "The answer is " & z & "." with "OK"
end buttonClick
```

Using the Debugger

ToolBook comes with its own debugger, a utility for finding errors in a script. When a handler encounters an error, the debugger (see Figure G.2) may be accessed by clicking the "Debug" button in the "Execution Suspended" dialog (see Figure G.3). An executing script may also be halted and the debugger accessed by pressing both Shift keys on the keyboard simultaneously. (This is particularly useful when testing a script that contains an infinite loop, causing the handler never to terminate.)

The debugger contains the script to be debugged, and above it, in the "Debugger" window, the trace box. The trace box shows a reference to the handler name and its location (e.g., "buttonClick of button id 5"). The location in the statement that was executing when the handler was suspended is highlighted.

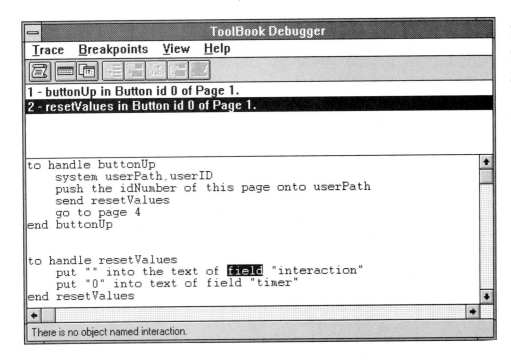

Figure G.2
The debugger shows the script with the offending term highlighted in the lower part of the screen. The upper part, referred to as the trace box, shows the handler name and parent object.

Figure G.3
When a syntax or runtime
error occurs, ToolBook
displays the "Execution
Suspended" dialog. The
debugger may be accessed
by clicking the "Debug"
button in this dialog.

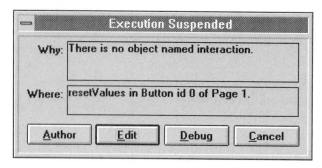

Within the debugger, the values of variables may be examined by choosing the "Variables" selection from the View menu. The "Variables" window is displayed, showing the names and corresponding values of all local and global variables. Arguments are referenced in the handler, as are system variables sysError, target, and targetWindow (see Figure G.4). By examining the values of variables and comparing them to what they should be for a given set of test data, logic errors can often be found. The value of a variable may be changed by clicking the variable name, entering a new value, and then clicking the check-mark button in the upper left.

In the same manner, all of the system variables may be viewed by choosing "System Variables" from the View menu. This includes all the system variables thus declared in an instance of ToolBook, regardless of whether they are referenced in the

Figure G.4
The "Variables" window
may be displayed from the
debugger. The window
shows all the system and
local variables referenced by
the script being debugged,
along with their values.

1 - buttonUp in Button id 0 of Page 1.

sysError	No menu item named "tbk_sysInfo".
Target	Button id 0 of Page id 0
TargetWindow	Viewer id 0 of Book ""
L x	25
L y	This is a test
S userID	555-55-5555
S userPath	2345,1987

Figure G.5
Breakpoints, locations
where the script's execution
is paused, are set by
clicking a term in the script
displayed in the debugger.
Breakpoints are displayed
as slashes through the term.

ToolBook Debugger

Trace   Breakpoints   View   Help

1 - buttonUp in Button id 0 of Page 1.
2 - resetValues in Button id 0 of Page 1.

```
to handle buttonUp
    system userPath,userID
    push the idNumber of this page onto userPath
    send resetValues
    go to page 4
end buttonUp


to handle resetValues
    put "" into the text of field "interaction"
    put "0" into text of field "timer"
end resetValues
```

There is no object named interaction.

current handler or not. Their values may be edited in the same way as are those in the "Variables" window. Likewise, all the user-defined properties in the current book and their values may be displayed by choosing "User Properties" from the View menu.

Breakpoints may be set within the debugger to assist in examining where errors are occurring. A breakpoint is a position in the script where executing should be halted. Breakpoints may be set by simply clicking a word in the script. The word is overstruck with slashes (see Figure G.5). When the script runs, the execution stops when the breakpoint is encountered and the debugger is then displayed, allowing the author to examine variable values or trace the script's execution (tracing will be explained in a moment). Clicking a breakpoint in the debugger will remove the breakpoint from the script. Multiple breakpoints may be specified if desired. Choosing "Clear All Breakpoints" from the Breakpoints menu will remove all breakpoints from the current script.

Tracing a script means to execute it one statement at a time. By observing the script's execution in slow motion, the programmer can visualize the order in which statements are executed and/or monitor how the values of variables change. Tracing a script requires that a breakpoint be set. When the execution of the script is halted and the debugger displayed, the programmer chooses "Trace Statement" from the Trace menu. The next line will be executed. The process of choosing "Trace Statement" is repeated for each statement to be executed. Choosing the "Continue Execution" option from the Trace menu closes the debugger and continues execution of the script until its end is reached, another breakpoint is encountered, or an error is encountered. The "Trace Call" option continues execution of the current handler and pauses when another handler (subroutine or user-defined function) is called. The "Trace Expression" option can be used to incrementally execute a single statement, allowing the programmer to verify the evaluation order of an expression in the statement. The "Trace Return" option is used to execute the remainder of a called handler and then pause at the next statement in the handler that called the current handler.

Appendix
H

Answers to
Summary Questions

Chapter 1: What Is ToolBook?
1. True; 2. True; 3. False; 4. True; 5. False; 6. True; 7. False; 8. True; 9. True; 10. True; 11. authoring; 12. OpenScript; 13. HyperCard; 14. books; 15. browsing (or reading); 16. Asymetrix; 17. User's Guide; 18. event; 19. setup; 20. Microsoft

Chapter 2: What Can I Do with ToolBook?
1. False; 2. False; 3. True; 4. True; 5. True; 6. True; 7. False; 8. False; 9. True; 10. False; 11. presentation; 12. graphical user interface; 13. prototype; 14. Drill-and-practice; 15. Simulations; 16. Information; 17. role playing; 18. script; 19. Utilities; 20. Interpreted

Chapter 3: Planning and Developing a Program
1. False; 2. True; 3. False; 4. True; 5. True; 6. True; 7. False; 8. True; 9. True; 10. True; 11. algorithm; 12. flowchart; 13. process; 14. decision; 15. storyboard; 16. debugging; 17. input/output; 18. start, end; 19. Comments; 20. psuedocode

Chapter 4: The Parts of a ToolBook Book
1. False; 2. True; 3. False; 4. True; 5. True; 6. False; 7. True; 8. False; 9. True; 10. True; 11. .TBK; 12. viewers; 13. background; 14. button; 15. recordfields; 16. hotwords; 17. script; 18. field; 19. handler; 20. OpenScript

Chapter 5: How To Read a ToolBook Book
1. True; 2. True; 3. False; 4. False; 5. False; 6. True; 7. False; 8. False; 9. True; 10. True; 11. pointing; 12. "Next"; 13. double click; 14. focus; 15. Edit; 16. Request; 17. column; 18. group; 19. Author; 20. F3

Chapter 6: The ToolBook Authoring Environment
1. False; 2. True; 3. True; 4.True; 5. False; 6. True; 7. False; 8. True; 9. False; 10. True; 11. Author; 12. F4; 13. Object; 14. toolbar; 15. Ctrl; 16. fill, stroke; 17. statusbar; 18. "Command" window; 19. Line Ends; 20. Right-Click

Chapter 7: Working with a New Book
1. True; 2. False; 3. False; 4. True; 5. False; 6. False; 7. False; 8. True; 9. False; 10. False; 11. Properties; 12. 640, 480; 13. Yes; 14. landscape; 15. Shift; 16. script editor; 17. PAL; 18. "Command"; 19. main window; 20. "Save As"

Chapter 8: Working with Pages and Backgrounds
1. False; 2. True; 3. True; 4. False; 5. True; 6. True; 7. True; 8. True; 9. False; 10. True; 11. background; 12. "New Page"; 13. F4; 14. selected; 15. fillColor; 16. Control Panel; 17. 64; 18. pageNumber; 19. background; 20. Ctrl

Chapter 9: Working with Buttons
1. True; 2. False; 3. False; 4. True; 5. True; 6. True; 7. True; 8. False; 9. True; 10.

False; 11. radioButton; 12. label; 13. handles; 14. &; 15. transparent; 16. focus; 17. layer; 18. group; 19. "Enabled"; 20. hyperlink

Chapter 10: Working with Fields and Recordfields
1. False; 2. True; 3. True; 4. True; 5. False; 6. False; 7. True; 8. True; 9. False; 10. False; 11. Recordfields; 12. borderStyle; 13. Multi-select; 14. activated; 15. "Character"; 16. "Paragraph"; 17. "Insert Graphic..."; 18. hotwords; 19. Combo boxes; 20. none

Chapter 11: Drawing in ToolBook
1. False; 2. False; 3. True; 4. True; 5. False; 6. True; 7. False; 8. True; 9. True; 10. True; 11. drawing; 12. Ctrl; 13. Ellipse; 14. "Draw Centered"; 15. transparent; 16. picture; 17. vertex; 18. Pie; 19. Shift; 20. 99

Chapter 12: Working with Scripts
1. True; 2. True; 3. False; 4. True; 5. True; 6. False; 7. False; 8. False; 9. True; 10. False; 11. Events; 12. target; 13. handlers; 14. parent; 15. forward; 16. book; 17. compiled; 18. autoscripts; 19. script recorder; 20. debugger

Chapter 13: Variables and Other Containers
1. containers; 2. type; 3. STRING; 4. WORD; 5. put; 6. system; 7. local; 8. hide; 9. property; 10. quotation marks; 11. valid; 12. invalid (can't use $); 13. valid; 14. valid; 15. valid; 16. invalid (put is an OpenScript command); 17. invalid (can't use %); 18. valid; 19. invalid (can't begin with a number); 20. valid

Chapter 14: Handling Events and Input/Output
1. rightButtonDown; 2. byte; 3. 85; 4. parameters; 5. charToAnsi; 6. idle; 7. notifyBefore; 8. ask; 9. request; 10. it; 11. c; 12. d; 13. b; 14. d; 15. b; 16. Commas must separate the parameters (put one after loc and another after shiftState); 17. The word to is not used with the notifyBefore structure; 18. The request command cannot have more than three response captions; 19. The prompt string should be surrounded with quotation marks rather than apostrophes; 20. The word and must be replaced with the word or between the response captions

Chapters 15: Performing Mathematical Calculations
1. 47; 2. 32; 3. 28; 4. 2; 5. 6; 6. 0; 7. 6; 8. 40; 9. 3; 10. -11; 11. 12345.68; 12. 12345.67890; 13. $12,345.68; 14. 12346; 15. 1.23457E+4; 16. December 06, 1961; 17. 12/6/61; 18. 6 December 1961; 19. 1:30; 20. 5400

Chapter 16: Decision Branching
1. false; 2. true; 3. true; 4. true; 5. true; 6. false; 7. false; 8. true; 9. false; 10. false; 11. 9; 12. 4; 13. 21; 14. 10; 15. 12; 16. 9; 17. 3; 18. 4; 19. 1; 20. 5

Chapter 17: Changing Properties and Manipulating Text Strings
1. 31; 2. 7; 3. brown; 4. bear; 5. 1; 6. 8; 7. 1; 8. A big brown bear; 9. gate; 10. team; 11. strokeColor (or RGBStroke); 12. sysCursor; 13. text; 14. sysDate; 15. sysTime; 16. banana; 17. DOLL; 18. 5; 19. TOUCHdown; 20. My dog has a leash.

Chapter 18: Loop Structures
1. fixed-iteration; 2. conditional; 3. break; 4. step...end step; 5. continue; 6. do...until; 7. pause; 8. endless; 9. Shift; 10. true; 11. 17; 12. 1; 13. 30; 14. 16; 15. 4; 16. 190; 17. 40; 18. 5; 19. 2; 20. 25

Chapter 19: Substrings and User-Defined Functions
1. subroutines; 2. user-defined functions; 3. send; 4. arguments; 5. parameters; 6. to set; 7. to get; 8. return; 9. recursion; 10. System; 11. 6; 12. 2; 13. 13; 14. 5; 15. 43; 16. 7; 17. 10; 18. A user-defined function must include a return statement.; 19. This user-defined function calls itself, resulting in excessive recursion; 20. The function yeeHaw calls the yippee subroutine, which in turn calls the yeeHaw function and so forth in a never-ending loop. This is called excessive recursion.

Chapter 20: Working with Menus and the User-Interface Design
1. add menu; 2. disable menuItem; 3. combo box; 4. remove menu; 5. add menuItem; 6. single-select list box; 7. restore menubar; 8. menu editor; 9. remove menuItem; 10. enable menuItem; 11. menubar should be one word; 12. under needs to be replaced with in; 13. position 4 should come before at reader; 14. enable menuitem is the command to restore a disabled menu item, not restore menuitem; 15. in author mode needs to be replaced with at author; 16. statusControls is one word; 17. the readerStatusBar property can only be set to true or false, not 0; 18. the enable menuItem command does not take a position parameter; 19. statusBar is one word; 20. reader and author needs to be changed to both

Chapter 21: Working with Arrays
1. 16; 2. declared; 3. fill; 4. range; 5. put; 6. dimensions( ); 7. dynamic; 8. size; 9. loop; 10. memory; 11. system cities[10]; 12. one; 13. 10; 14. Portland; 15. San Francisco; 16. local INT myArray[5][6]; 17. 20; 18. 35; 19. 25; 20. 5

Chapter 22: File Input/Output
1. paragraphs; 2. opened; 3. openFile; 4. closing; 5. linefeed; 6. delimiter; 7. sequential; 8. random-access; 9. seekFile; 10. print 4; 11. openFile "CII.DAT"; 12. readFile "CII.DAT" for 100; 13. seekFile "ABC.TXT" to 2000 from beginning; 14. seekFile "ABC.TXT" to 401 from beginning; 15. writeFile CRLF & "My dog has fleas."; 16. closeFile "PETS.TXT"; 17. print all; 18. printerFields = "name,IDNumber,phone"; 19. printerTopMargin = "2880"; 20. printerArrangement = 2,4

Chapter 23: Sorting and Searching
1. sort; 2. bubble; 3. Shell; 4. search; 5. search again; 6. search page for "my dog has fleas"; 7. search records for "vision" as word; 8. search again; 9. search for "MiRF" by case as word; 10. search for "watermelon" locateOnly; 11. send replace; 12. sort pages 1 to 10 by descending text text of recordfield "lastname"; 13. sort by ascending number the idNumber of this page; 14. sort pages 20 to 40 by ascending date text of recordfield "when"; 15. sort by ascending number text of recordfield "zipcode"; 16. There is no page 0, the command should read sort pages 1 to 10 by descending text text of recordfield id 3; 17. The message should not be in quotation marks and the ellipses should be left off; 18. Page range cannot be specified in the search command; 19.) by case should be after the search string; 20. The sort command does not sort the text of a container

Chapter 24: Drag and Drop, and Input Sliders
1. defaultAllowDrag; 2. allowDrag; 3. allowDrop; 4. beginDrag; 5. endDrag; 6. objectDropped; 7. stillOverDrop; 8. move; 9. slider; 10. ratchet; 11. false; 12. true; 13. false; 14. false; 15. false; 16. Must return a value of either true or false; 17. sysSuspend must be set to either true or false; 18. location must be the second argument of the endDrag handler; 19. Should be move self to location; 20. x and y are undefined

Chapter 25: Animation Techniques
1. move; 2. pause; 3. vertices; 4. layering; 5. frame; 6. script recorder; 7. properties;

8. draw; 9. selection; 10. flushMessageQueue(); 11. move ellipse "red ball" to 2000,2000; 12. move ellipse "red ball" by 1000,0; 13. move group elevator by 0,2880; 14. show group elevator; 15. draw rectangle from 1000,1000 to 3000,3000; 16. set fillColor of selection to red; 17. draw ellipse from 4000,4000 to 5000,5000; 18. draw field from 1000,1000 to 3880,6760; 19. set the fontFace of selection to "Times"; 20. set fillColor of field id 5 to red

Chapter 26: DDE, OLE, and DLLs
1. false; 2. true; 3. false; 4. true; 5. true; 6. false; 7. true; 8. false; 9. true; 10. true; 11. getRemote; 12. sysError; 13. setRemote; 14. executeRemote; 15. linked; 16. upToDate; 17. linkDLL; 18. unlinkDLL; 19. return; 20. embedded

Chapter 27: Adding Sound and Video
1. False; 2. True; 3. False; 4. True; 5. True; 6. True; 7. False; 8. True; 9. True; 10. False; 11. MIDI; 12. Clips; 13. .WAV; 14. playSound(); 15. stageAnchor; 16. stageSizing; 17. mmSeek; 18. Stage; 19. .AVI; 20. clip editor

Glossary

Algorithm The set of steps prescribed to solve a problem.

Alphanumeric string Text of data type STRING.

Animation file A file created with animation software. ToolBook supports .FLI and .FLC formats.

ANSI value The numeric value of a character as assigned in the American National Standards Institute character set. ANSI values are 0 through 255. (Values 0-127 are the same as those in the ASCII character set.) For example, an *A* has an ANSI value of 65.

Application A program written to satisfy a specific need. An application developed with ToolBook may consist of one or several interrelated books.

Argument A value, passed to a handler or function, on which the handler or function operates.

Arithmetic function A function that returns the absolute value of a number, the ceiling of a number, or the floor of a number; picks a random number; returns the square root of a value; or truncates the decimal portion of a floating-point value.

Array A special type of variable that can hold multiple values.

ASCII value The numeric value of a character as assigned in the American Standard Code for Information Interchange character set. ASCII values are 0 through 255. (Values 0-127 are the same as those in the ANSI character set.) For example, an *A* has an ASCII value of 65.

Ask dialog A dialog that requires the user to enter an alphanumeric string. An ask dialog is used to receive input for a script, verify passwords, or edit existing text. *See also* Request dialog.

Audio/video interleaved (.AVI) format The most common video file format used by Multimedia ToolBook authors.

Author mode The mode of ToolBook in which a book is developed. *See also* Reader mode.

Background A "layer" behind a page; may contain objects shared by multiple pages. Every book has at least one background.

Binary digit A 1 or 0 that refers to the presence or absence of electricity in circuit.

Bit Contraction of *binary digit*; a bit is the basic building block of data and has a value of either 0 or 1.

Bitmap image A graphic created of pixels (dots) by using a paint software. Also called a bitmapped image or paint image.

Bitmapped image *See* Bitmap image.

Book A file, created with ToolBook, that contains one or more pages. Choosing "New" from the File menu results in the creation of a book, initially with one blank page.

Boolean expression A comparative expression that evaluates to either **true** or **false**. For example, the Boolean expression 3 + 2 = 5 is **true** while the expression 3 + 2 > 6 is **false**. Also called a logical expression.

Branching Processing that takes one of two or more paths, depending on a specified condition.

Brainstorming A problem-solving technique that involves the spontaneous contributions of ideas from members of a group.

Browsing Using a ToolBook book as an end-user. Also known as reading.

Bubble sort A sort algorithm in which a list of items is sorted by comparing consecutive items in a fixed loop.

Bug An error.

Button A basic object of ToolBook, usually part of the user interface, which initiates some action when acted upon (when clicked, for example). A button may appear in one of several styles.

Byte A combination of 8 bits, having a value from 0 through 255.

CD-ROM Stands for *Compact Disk-Read Only Memory*. A compact disk, used as a storage and distribution medium, can hold up to 650 megabytes of information and is more economical to produce than several floppy diskettes.

Checkbox style The button style that includes a checkbox in front of a caption.

Clicking Choosing an object by positioning the mouse pointer over it and then pressing and releasing a mouse button.

Client An application that requests information from a server application.

Client-server environment An environment in which one application (the client) sends commands to another application (the server).

Clip A reference to an external multimedia file or source (such as a laserdisc player) in Multimedia ToolBook.

Code A collection of instructions written in a computer language, such as OpenScript, that expresses an algorithm.

Combo box An object that contains a drop-down list of items accessed via a push button. The user may select an item from the list, with the item being displayed in an edit box.

Command A statement of code that carries out a specific instruction.

"Command" window A window that can be used to execute commands and display information. The display of the "Command" window may be toggled on and off by pressing Shift-F3 in Author mode.

Comment A line of code preceded by two preceding hyphens. The computer ignores comments when accompanying code is executed.

Compile To translate a higher-level language (such as OpenScript) into machine language so that it runs faster.

Compiled program A program in a format the computer can read and understand quickly. *See also* Interpreted program.

Concatenation operator An operator that joins two or more string values into one string value. Concatenating the strings Hello and world produces the string Hello world. Concatenation operators in OpenScript are & and &&.

Conditional loop A loop that reiterates while a certain condition is true or until a specified condition is met. Conditional loop structures include while...end while and do...until. *See also* Fixed-iteration loop.

Connector symbol In a flowchart, a circle that represents an exit from or entry to another part of a flowchart.

Container A variable, field, recordfield, container, or object property used to hold a value.

Control structure A block of code that is executed under specified circumstances. Control structures include blocks that perform decision branching and loops.

Copy To transfer a copy of a selected item or text onto the Windows clipboard.

Cut To delete a selected item or text, placing it onto the Windows clipboard.

Data file An ASCII text-based file that consists of items separated by a delimiter.

Data type A genre of data, such as integer (INT) or alphanumeric (STRING).

DDE *See* Dynamic data exchange.

Debugging Finding and correcting errors (bugs) in a program.

Decision symbol In a flowchart, a diamond shape that indicates branches in program flow.

Declare To specify the scope of a variable and/or the type of data it will contain.

Dialog box A pop-up window that solicits or displays information. A dialog box requires the user to respond before anything else can happen.

Digitized sound Audio that has been converted to a digital representation so that it may be stored as a file and played back using a sound card.

Digitized video Video that has been converted to a digital representation so that it may be stored as a file and played back on the computer monitor.

Disabled button A button whose enabled property is set to false. Consider a button whose script is set to run when the button is clicked. If the button is disabled, the computer will ignore the click.

Dithered color A color made up of a pattern of two or more colors. Orange, for instance, might be made up of a pattern of red and yellow pixels.

DLL *See* Dynamic link library.

Document file A word-processed file organized in paragraphs.

Drag and drop Using the mouse pointer to move an object to another object.

Dragging Moving an object by pointing to it and then holding the mouse button down while moving the mouse or trackball.

Draw image An image defined by mathematical formulas. Also known as a vectored image, draw-type image, or object-oriented image.

Draw-type image An image defined by mathematical formulas. Also known as a vectored image, draw-type image, or object-oriented image.

Drill-and-practice software A program that teaches students by testing them interactively. This type of software usually contains an element of information publishing.

Dynamic Values that do not remain constant. *See also* Static.

Dynamic array An array whose number of elements is unknown or variable. *See also* Local array.

Dynamic data exchange (DDE) A communications protocol used by various Microsoft Windows applications for sharing information and sending commands remotely, from one application to another.

Dynamic link library (DLL) An external file containing functions that may be accessed and used in an OpenScript handler. DLL functions are usually written in C or C++.

Endless loop Code in which control never exits a conditional loop.

EOF marker A pointer that signals the end of a data or document file.

Event An action that results in ToolBook sending one or more messages. For example, the user pressing a key on the keyboard is an event that generates keyDown, keyChar, and keyUp messages.

Equation statement A statement that includes an equals sign.

Exporting Writing data from ToolBook to an external file.

Field A object used to hold and display textual information.

File A named collection of information that resides on a disk or other storage medium.

Fill color The interior shade of enclosed objects. *See also* Stroke color.

Financial function In OpenScript, a function that calculates annuity payment or value, interest rate or amount, or depreciation.

Fixed-iteration loop A loop that executes a prescribed number of times. The step...end step control structure is used to define fixed-iteration loops. *See also* Conditional loop.

Floating-point value A number that contains a decimal point.

Flowchart A graphical representation of a process or algorithm.

Font The style and size of type.

Format The way information is structured and displayed.

Frame animation A method of animation in which objects are shown and hidden in a sequence.

Function A handler or operation that returns a value.

Function keys The keys at the top of the keyboard, labeled F1, F2, F3, and so forth.

Global variable *See* System variable.

Graphical object A shape (such as a rectangle, ellipse, or line) created by a ToolBook tool. In ToolBook, graphical objects are draw-type (also called vector- or object-oriented).

Group An object consisting of two or more objects that have been "tied" together as a single object.

Grouped Treated, after selection, as a single object.

Handler A named group of OpenScript statements that defines the process to be performed in response to a specified message.

Hotword A word or phrase, in the text of a field or recordfield, that has been defined to respond to a click.

Hyperlink The process of automatically generating a handler or handlers for navigating from page to page in a book.

Hypertext A document containing navigational links between pieces of information within a document or collection of documents. Users can click on a designated word or phrase to navigate to another related area.

Icon A small graphic resource of up to 32 pixels square.

Importing Reading information from an external file and saving it in a ToolBook book.

Index file A secondary file that is sorted and points to the records in a master file.

Information publishing The dissemination of textbooks in electronic form.

Input (1) To enter data into a computer, or (2) data entered into a computer.

Input/output symbol In a flowchart, a parallelogram that represents data entering the computer.

Insertion point The location where text, when entered, will be placed in a field or recordfield. Its location is marked by a flashing vertical bar.

Integer A whole number (that is, a number without a decimal portion).

Interpreted program A program that, while it runs, must be translated into a format the computer can understand. *See also* Compiled program.

it A local variable in which the value returned by **ask**, **request**, and **get** statements is automatically placed.

Keyword A reserved word directly interpreted by OpenScript.

Label-style button A button without a border. The caption is the emphasis of a label-style button.

Landscape orientation A page format in which the width is greater than the height. *See also* Portrait orientation.

Last in, first out (LIFO) A process in which data items stored in a list are retrieved in the order that is the reverse of that in which they were entered.

Layer The plane of a page or background on which an object resides. Layers may be changed with the "Bring to Front," "Bring Closer," "Send to Back," and "Send Farther" options.

Layering Overlapping images so that, when viewed in sequence, they produce the illusion of movement.

LIFO *See* Last in, first out.

Listserv A topic-specific discussion group administered via electronic mail.

Local array An array that only retains its value for the duration of the handler in which it is referenced. *See also* Dynamic array.

Local variable A variable that ceases existing when the handler in which it is referenced is finished executing.

Logarithmic function In OpenScript, a function that returns the value of *e*, the natural logarithm, or the logarithm of a value in a specified base.

Logical expression *See* Boolean Expression.

Loop A block of statements that may be executed multiple times. *See also* Conditional loop and Fixed-iteration loop.

Marker A variable that keeps track of the portion of a file that has already been read. Also known as a pointer.

Master file An unsorted file whose records are pointed to by an index file, which is sorted.

Menu A list of options from which the user may select.

Menu item A specific option in a menu.

Message A communication sent by ToolBook in response to an event.

MIDI (1) Musical instrument digital interface. (2) Electronic synthesized music saved in a digital format and played back using a MIDI-compatible sound card.

MIDI (.MID) file A file that contains data that a MIDI processor (synthesizer) on a sound card decodes to play music. Also, the format of such a file.

Mnemonic character A character used in conjunction with the Alt key to choose a menu or menu item.

Modular programming environment A programming environment in which the programmer breaks a large algorithm into smaller routines.

Modulo A mathematical operation that returns the remainder of an integer division. For example, 10 mod 3 returns 1.

Mouse pointer The arrow-shaped cursor that mirrors the movement of the mouse.

Multimedia An application involving the integration of audio and/or video.

Mutually exclusive radio button A button in a group set up so that when the user selects it, all other buttons in the group are de-selected. Checkbox-style buttons can also be mutually exclusive.

Nested control structure A control structure within another control structure.

Nested if...then...else structure One if...then...else structure within another.

Nested loop A loop within another loop.

None-style button A button that looks like a captionless label-style button. A none-style button is usually used as a transparent overlay.

Null string An empty string.

Object An element of the ToolBook environment—such as a button, field, record-field, or graphic—that can have a script attached to it. Along with scripts, objects determine the usefulness, aesthetics, and functionality of a ToolBook program.

Object linking and embedding A Microsoft Windows protocol for applications to exchange data. Data may be linked (one application retrieves updated data from the originating application) or embedded (the data is stored in the secondary application).

Object-oriented image An image defined by mathematical formulas. Also known as vectored image, draw-type image, or draw image.

Object-oriented programming Program development environment in which code is associated with individual objects rather than a single linear program.

Off-page connector symbol In a flowchart, the home base-shaped object that connects processes across pages.

OLE *See* Object linking and embedding.

OpenScript ToolBook's proprietary programming language.

Operand In an expression, a value on which an operation is performed. In the expression, 3 + 5, both 3 and 5 are operands.

Operator A symbol or word that combines two operands to produce a single result. Operators include +, -, *, /, mod, div, &, &&, and so forth.

Output (1) To display of information produced by the computer. (2) Information produced by a computer.

Page The basic building block of a book; an object that represents a screen and may contain text information, graphics, buttons, and so on.

Page area The screen area that reveals the pages and backgrounds as they would be viewed in Reader mode; the area in which objects are drawn and edited.

Page units A measure used for specifying the bounds or position of an object. There are 1440 page units in 1 inch.

Paint image *See* Bitmap image.

Paint-type image An image created of pixels (dots) by using paint software. Also known as a bitmap image, bitmapped image, or paint image.

Palette (1) In a floating window, a graphical menu from which various tools or options may be selected. There are six standard palettes in ToolBook: the Tool, Color, Line Width, Line Ends, Polygon, and Pattern palettes. (2) A resource consisting of a specific color scheme.

Parameter A value passed to a handler or function.

Parent The next-highest object in the hierarchical chain.

Pass To transfer a value from one handler to another.

Paste To place a copy of what is on the Windows clipboard onto a page or into a selected field.

Pixel A single dot of a computer monitor.

Pointer (1) The arrow-shaped on-screen cursor that mirrors the movement of the mouse. (2) A variable that keeps track of the portion of a file that has already been read. Also known as a marker.

Pointing Positioning the mouse pointer or cursor on an on-screen object by moving a mouse or trackball.

Portrait orientation A page format in which the height is greater than the width. *See also* Landscape orientation.

Precedence The order in which the parts of an expression are evaluated.

Process symbol A rectangle that represents an internal operation performed by the computer.

Program A set of instructions that tells a computer how to perform a task or set of tasks.

Programming The process of translating an algorithm into computer language.

Property An attribute of an object that specifies its appearance or behavior. Examples include name, fillColor, and position.

Prototype A fully functional program usually used for personal purposes rather than mass distribution. A prototype can be used to achieve financing, build interest, and show programmers how the finished product will work.

Pseudocode The steps of an algorithm, written in everyday English.

Push-button style A style that makes a button look like a three-dimensional rectangle.

Radio button A button with an appearance of a circle and a caption. The circle may be filled when clicked.

Random access file A group of records, stored in a file, in which each record is the same length and specific records may be accessed directly.

Ratchet An input device similar to a slider, but in which the value knob may only be moved to specific points.

Reader mode The mode of ToolBook in which a book is navigated and run by the end-user. *See also* Author mode.

Reading Using a ToolBook book as an end-user. Also known as browsing.

Read-only file A file that may be read from a disk or other storage medium, but to which changes cannot be made.

Recordfield A specialized field, on the background, in which text may be entered on the different pages sharing the background.

Rectangle button A button with a rectangle border.

Relational operator An operator that compares two values.

Request dialog A box that presents a prompt statement along with one to three buttons. A request dialog is used to present output and allow the user to make a choice. *See also* Ask dialog.

Resource An external interface object imported into a book. Examples include bitmaps, icons, fonts, cursors, and palettes.

Right-click menu A pop-up menu for accessing the properties of an object when the author (or user) right-clicks the object.

Role playing In educational software, a technique in which students answer questions from the point of view of someone the software specifies.

Rounded button Rectangle buttons with rounded corners.

Script OpenScript code attached to an object. Scripts define ToolBook's behavior and consist of one or more handlers.

Script editor The editor that allows an author to construct or modify OpenScript scripts.

Script recorder A ToolBook utility that an author uses to create scripts that mirror menu options.

Scrollbar A bar that appears on the right and/or bottom of a field, recordfield, combo box, or page. Clicking a scrollbar allows the user to see items that are not otherwise visible.

Seed The number used as the basis for random-number generation.

Sequential file An external data file in which the records may be of different length and a record may only be accessed after the preceding record has been accessed.

Select To choose an object by placing the Selection tool on it and then pressing the left mouse button. Selected objects are displayed with handles.

Server An application that receives commands remotely from a client application and/or sends information to a client.

Shadowed button A button that looks like a rectangle with a shadow behind it.

Shell sort A sort that compares and swaps nonadjacent items separated by a distance that diminishes as the sort progresses.

Simulation A program that places students in a specific scenario and asks them to respond.

Slider A graphical input device in which the user slides a knob along a path to set a value between minimum and maximum values.

Stack A list of data items.

Stage An object in Multimedia ToolBook in which a media clip is played.

Static Constant; not changing. *See also* Dynamic.

Static array An array in which the number of elements in each dimension is declared.

Statistical function In OpenScript, a function that returns the average, the maximum of minimum value, or the sum of a list of numbers.

Statusbar A graphical interface object, at the bottom of a window, in which information (page number or mouse location, for example) is provided to the user or author.

Storyboard A design tool utilized in planning a program. Storyboards consist of sketches of screen design and information about the objects.

String A data item consisting of alphanumeric characters.

Stroke color The color of the text and borders of objects. *See also* Fill color.

Subroutine A handler called by another handler.

Syntax The rules surrounding the use and writing of OpenScript statements.

System book A ToolBook file containing handlers that can be placed in other books and accessed as part of the object hierarchy.

System variable A variable that retains its value until ToolBook is closed. System variables must be declared in each handler in which they are referenced. Also called a global variable.

Target The object to which a specific message is sent first.

Terminal symbol In a flowchart, the cigar-shaped object that indicates the start or end of a procedure. A terminal symbol contains the word "Start" or "End".

3-D checkbox button A checkbox button with a three-dimensional appearance.

3-D radio button A radio button with a three-dimensional appearance.

Tick A unit of time; approximately 1/100 second.

Toolbar A palette of buttons that allows quick access to popular menu options.

Trigonometric function In OpenScript, a function that calculates the sine, cosine, or tangent of an angle; the arccosine, arcsine, or arctangent of a number between −1 and 1; the hyperbolic cosine, sine, or tangent of an angle; or the hypotenuse of a right triangle.

TrueType font A font defined by a particular type of definition, TrueType fonts are scalable to any height and print exactly as they appear on screen. TrueType fonts may be embedded as resources in a Multimedia ToolBook book.

User-defined function A function that performs an operation and returns a value or values to the calling handler.

User's group A gathering of developers or users of a particular product or who are interested in a particular topic.

Utility A program usually used for multiple purposes, often in conjunction with an application. A calculator is an example of a utility.

Variable An invisible named container in memory; used for storing a value.

Vectored image An image defined by a mathematical formula. Also known as draw image, draw-type image, or object-oriented image.

Viewer A window in which pages are displayed.

Wave (.WAV) format A format for files that store digitized sound.

Appendix

J

Annotated Bibliography

Other Books About ToolBook

Asymetrix Corporation. *Multimedia ToolBook User Manual and OpenScript Reference*. Bellevue, WA: Asymetrix, 1994 (Part No. 026230).

A reference that addresses the additional features of Multimedia ToolBook, it is included with the Multimedia ToolBook package in addition to *OpenScript Reference Manual* and *ToolBook User's Guide.* Includes general discussions of incorporating multimedia, using full-text searching, using the spell-checker, and so on, as well as a syntax and usage reference of OpenScript commands, properties, and functions unique to the Multimedia version of ToolBook 3.0.

Asymetrix Corporation. *OpenScript Reference Manual*. Bellevue, WA: Asymetrix, 1994 (Part No. 020829).

A reference manual that presents the syntax and use of all OpenScript commands, messages, properties, and functions common to both ToolBook 3.0 and Multimedia ToolBook 3.0. An invaluable resource, the same information is included in the on-line help of ToolBook and Multimedia ToolBook. The manual is included with the ToolBook and Multimedia ToolBook packages.

Asymetrix Corporation. *ToolBook User Manual*. Bellevue, WA: Asymetrix, 1994 (Part No. 020828).

Included with the ToolBook and Multimedia ToolBook products, this manual discusses basic concepts common to both versions. Covers some topics not discussed in detail in this text, such as viewers.

Hall, Tom. *Utilizing Multimedia ToolBook 3.0*. Boyd & Fraser, 1996 (ISBN 0–7895–0030–2).

Not released at the time this text was written, the preliminary table of contents indicates that the book will present a simplified approach to Multimedia ToolBook. It does not appear to cover OpenScript programming in any depth.

Hall, Tom. *Utilizing ToolBook 3.0*. Boyd & Fraser, 1996 (ISBN 0–7895–0031–0).

Not released at the time this text was written, the preliminary table of contents indicates that the book will present a simplified approach to ToolBook. It does not appear to cover OpenScript programming in any depth.

Holtz, Matthew. *The Multimedia Workshop: Multimedia ToolBook 3.0*. Belmont, CA: Wadsworth Publishing Company, 1995 (ISBN 0–534–31059–1).

Designed for the novice, this text covers the basic tools and techniques of authoring a ToolBook book, but does not cover programming with OpenScript.

Pierce, Joseph R. *The ToolBook Companion*. Redmond, WA: Microsoft Press, 1990 (ISBN 0–936767–16–2).

Out of print. Although dealing with version 1.0, this text does focus on OpenScript programming.

Smith, Gina, and John Pallatto. *Building Applications with ToolBook.* **New York: Brady Publishing, 1991 (ISBN 0–13–092420–2).**

A very basic text that discusses how to develop visual applications. Contains many "screen dump" graphics as well as exercises and hands–on suggestions. It is written for the nonprogrammer and only introduces scripting. This text addresses version 1.5 of ToolBook. I am unaware of an updated version for Toolbook 3.0.

Tway, Linda. *Welcome to . . . Multimedia.* **New York: MIS Press, 1992 (ISBN 1–55828–229–7).**

This text deals extensively with building multimedia applications using Tool-Book. The book includes a CD–ROM containing an evaluation copy of Multimedia ToolBook 1.5, which is full featured, but limits development of a book to 6 hours authoring time. It does not explore aspects of programming with OpenScript. To my knowledge, it has not been updated for version 3.0.

Books About Programming, Algorithms, API, Etc.

Appleman, Daniel. *How Computer Programming Works.* **Emeryville, CA: Ziff–Davis, 1994 (ISBN 1–56276–195–1).**

An illustrated guide to the basic concepts of computer programming, this book covers the phases of development, common algorithms (such as the bubble sort), how data is stored and retrieved, and a look at various computer languages.

Conger, Jim. *Windows API New Testament.* **Corte Madera, CA: Waite Group Press, 1993 (ISBN 1–878739–37–9).**

Programmer's reference to the Application Programming Interface (API) functions of Microsoft Windows, including function names, syntax, descriptions, uses, and return values.

Maguire, Steve. *Debugging the Development Process.* **Redmond, WA: Microsoft Press, 1994 (ISBN 1–55615–650–2).**

Written by a former Microsoft developer, this book focuses on strategies for developing effective software, including team organization and management, scheduling, debugging, and writing effective and efficient code.

Maguire, Steve. *Writing Solid Code.* **Redmond, WA: Microsoft Press, 1993 (ISBN 1–55615–551–4).**

For the experienced programmer, this text examines methods for detecting and avoiding bugs in code, including developing good programming habits.

Microsoft Corporation. *Microsoft ODBC 2.0 Programmer's Reference and SDK Guide.* **Redmond, CA: Microsoft Press, 1994 (ISBN 1–55615–658–8).**

Too heavy and beyond the scope of ToolBook development, this text does include a reference of API calls that the advanced programmer may find useful.

McConnell, Steve. *Code Complete.* **Redmond, WA: Microsoft Press, 1994 (ISBN 1–55615–484–4).**

Topics include planning software, making effective use of data, using control structures, writing self–documenting code, and managing the software production process. Not language specific, but focuses on programming techniques for the experienced programmer.

Books About Interface Design

Apple Computer. *HyperCard Stack Design Guidelines*. **Reading, MA: Addison–Wesley, 1989 (ISBN 0–201–51784–1).**

Though written specifically for HyperCard developers, the contents of this text are fully applicable to ToolBook authors. Covers navigation principles; design principles regarding specific elements such as buttons, graphics, and fields; and the use of sound. Appendix B, a design checklist, is well worth the price of the book. The text also includes an extensive annotated bibliography of design books (both computer– and otherwise).

Heckel, Paul. *The Elements of Friendly Software Design*. **San Francisco: Sybex, 1991 (ISBN 0–7821–1538–1).**

Focuses on addressing user's needs. This text examines 30 principles of good, friendly software design. (Heckel's work at Xerox PARC was influential in the creation of Apple's HyperCard product, a predecessor of ToolBook.)

Wolfgram, Douglas E. *Creating Multimedia Presentations*. **Indianapolis: Que Corporation, 1994 (ISBN 1–56529–667–2).**

Focuses on the planning and design of multimedia presentations, including issues of readability, layout, object position, navigation, style and theme, target audience, flowcharting, and storyboarding.

Books About Multimedia

Asymetrix Corporation. *The Concise Guide to Multimedia*. **Bellevue, WA: Asymetrix, 1994 (ISBN 0–9641915–0–4).**

Included with the Multimedia ToolBook product, this short booklet covers general concepts about multimedia types and how to design with multimedia. Color illustrations help explain processes and design elements.

Holsinger, Erik. *How Multimedia Works*. **Emeryville, CA: Ziff–Davis, 1994 (ISBN 1–56276–208–7).**

An illustrated text about how multimedia technology works and how multimedia files are produced—how audio is digitized and played back, for example.

Lindstrom, Robert L. *Business Week Guide to Multimedia Presentations*. **Berkeley, CA: Osborne McGraw–Hill, 1994 (ISBN 0–07–882057–X).**

Contains an overview of multimedia, including hardware and software, planning and design, authoring tools, aesthetic issues, and distribution.

Smedinghoff, Thomas J. *The Software Publishers Association Legal Guide to Multimedia*. **Reading, MA: Addison–Wesley, 1994 (ISBN 0–201–40931–3).**

Addresses legal issues relating to multimedia technology and content. Includes useful information on copyright, trademarks, patents, privacy, trade secrets, defamation, infringement, consent, licensing, and marketing legalities.

Vaughn, Tay. *Multimedia: Making It Work*. **Berkeley, CA: Osborne McGraw–Hill, 1994 (ISBN 0–07–882035–9).**

Discusses hardware and software basics, the skills needed to produce multimedia, authoring tools, acquisition and creation of source material, planning, design, and production. Also includes helpful information on estimating costs and budgeting, locating talent, and packaging and distribution.

Index

This index does not reference OpenScript commands, functions, object properties, or events and messages. For more information on OpenScript commands, keywords, and structures, including page references, see Appendix A. For more information about object properties, see Appendix B. Appendix C contains syntax information about OpenScript functions, while Appendix D contains reference information about messages, the events that trigger them, and their target objects.

282446

This book is to be returned on or before
the last date stamped below.

13 MAY 1998	03 OCT 2003	
27 APR 1999		
-1 OCT 1999		
5 MAY 2000		
28 MAR 2000		
-5 MAY 2000		
31 MAY 2000		
29 SEP 2000		
-4 MAY 2001	LIBREX	

HUSTEDDE   282446

0151 - 291 - 2000

LIVERPOOL HOPE   OLLEGE